Integrated Science

Volume 27

Editor-in-Chief

Nima Rezaei, Tehran University of Medical Sciences, Tehran, Iran

The **Integrated Science** Series aims to publish the most relevant and novel research in all areas of Formal Sciences, Physical and Chemical Sciences, Biological Sciences, Medical Sciences, and Social Sciences. We are especially focused on the research involving the integration of two of more academic fields offering an innovative view, which is one of the main focuses of Universal Scientific Education and Research Network (USERN), science without borders.

Integrated Science is committed to upholding the integrity of the scientific record and will follow the Committee on Publication Ethics (COPE) guidelines on how to deal with potential acts of misconduct and correcting the literature.

Fouad Jawab
Editor

Hospital Supply Chain

Challenges and Opportunities for Improving Healthcare

Springer

Editor
Fouad Jawab
Sidi Mohamed Ben Abdellah University
Fes, Morocco

ISSN 2662-9461 ISSN 2662-947X (electronic)
Integrated Science
ISBN 978-3-031-70291-4 ISBN 978-3-031-70292-1 (eBook)
https://doi.org/10.1007/978-3-031-70292-1

This Springer imprint is published by the registered company Springer Nature Switzerland AG
The registered company address is: Gewerbestrasse 11, 6330 Cham, Switzerland

Preface

In a world marked by the multiplication and complexity of health crises, the rise of digitalization, the rise of artificial intelligence, growing constraints in terms of resources, Supply Hospital chains are facing unprecedented challenges. These challenges are not limited to simple inventory management and delivery of medical products. They require a strategic and proactive approach that embraces technological innovations, cross-sector collaboration and critical reflection on traditional management paradigms.

This collective work aims to be rich and exhaustive. It is structured around thirty chapters written by specialists from more than fifteen countries and seeks to position itself as an essential reference for navigating this complex landscape. It brings together the contributions of researchers and international experts from academic, hospital and industrial environments, in order to offer a global and multidisciplinary vision of current issues and future prospects for Supply Hospital chains.

Recent health crises, such as the COVID-19 pandemic, have highlighted the vulnerabilities of Supply Hospital chains. Shortages of critical medical supplies, supply disruptions International chains and the urgency to respond to ever-changing needs have jeopardized the ability of health systems to meet the needs of patients across the planet.

In this collective work, we sought to explore resilience strategies to strengthen Supply Hospital chains facing future health crises. The book examines resilience assessment tools, healthcare inventory management approaches and cross-sector collaboration strategies to ensure continuity of patient care.

Growing resource constraints, both financial and human, constitute a major challenge for Supply Hospital chains. This work aims to decipher resource optimization strategies and examines issues of equity in access to health care and the allocation of medical resources, particularly in developing countries.

Digitization is profoundly transforming the methods of communication, collaboration and information sharing in the healthcare sector. Artificial intelligence (AI) is revolutionizing every aspect of our society, and Supply Hospital chains are no exception.

This book explores digital platforms that facilitate collaboration between different actors in the Supply Chain, such as suppliers, hospitals and government agencies. It explores the potential of AI to optimize supply chain processes, from demand forecasting to inventory management to optimizing delivery routes. It also examines the use of blockchain to ensure the traceability of medical products and combating counterfeiting, while taking into account the ethical and regulatory considerations linked to the adoption of AI in the healthcare field.

This book is intended for a broad audience, including healthcare professionals, supply chain management researchers, health policymakers, and anyone interested in improving healthcare delivery and health. It provides valuable knowledge and practical insights to address challenges and opportunities for hospital supply chain optimization to improve the quality of patient care and the health of populations around the world.

Alongside several other laudable initiatives on a global scale, this collective work is intended to be an essential contribution to reflection on the future of Supply Hospital chains. It offers a solid conceptual framework and concrete examples to guide health sector stakeholders in their quest for more effective, efficient and equitable management of medical resources, thereby contributing to a better future for humanity.

Fes, Morocco Fouad Jawab

Acknowledgements

This book is the culmination of an intellectually stimulating enterprise that took place over several months. It would not have been possible without the collaboration and unconditional commitment of an exceptional community of researchers and international experts from academic, hospital and industrial environments in more than sixteen countries.

I would like to express my deepest gratitude to each of you for the trust you have placed in this project and for your unwavering dedication throughout its completion. Your expertise and involvement were key elements in the richness and quality of the content offered.

I am deeply grateful to you for your exemplary collaboration and your team spirit, which made it possible to create remarkable synergy and overcome the challenges encountered.

This project is part of the research work on the "hospital supply chain" carried out by the research team in industrial and logistics management at the Higher School of Technology of Fez. It is part of the continuity of research carried out in this area for more than fifteen years. I could not have produced this book without the unwavering support of the members of this team. I express my gratitude to them for their exemplary collaboration and their constant commitment to the advancement of our research.

I would also like to warmly thank the Springer staff, especially Gonzalo Cordova and Arumugam Deivasigamani, for their invaluable assistance and unwavering support throughout the publication process. Their professionalism and responsiveness contributed to the final quality of this work.

Contents

Part I Design, Optimization and Collaboration in the Hospital Supply Chain

1 Organizational Configuration of Logistics Activities in Healthcare Institutions 3
Martin Beaulieu, Omar Bentahar, and Smail Benzidia

2 Care Unit Implementation Strategies to Optimise the Design for Healthcare Facilities 23
Lamia Triqui

3 Healthcare Facility Design 47
Amina Ouhoud and Amine Hakim Guezzen

4 Supply Chain Strengthening in Developing Countries: Challenges and Barriers 75
Felicia Setiawan, Valencia Hadinata, Grace Alvina, Claudia Alexandra, Gerry Dwi Putro, and Fritzie A. Rexana

5 Understanding the Barriers to Logistics Collaboration in the Healthcare Supply Chain: A Canadian Case Study 99
Jacques Roy, Martin Beaulieu, Frederik G. S. Vos, and Carolina Belotti Pedroso

6 Emergency Medical Supply Chain Optimization Readiness in Developing Countries 117
Felicia Setiawan, Valencia Hadinata, Grace Alvina, Gerry Dwi Putro, Claudia Alexandra, and Fritzie A. Rexana

7 Halal and Health: Applying Theory of Constraints to Optimise Halal Healthcare Supply Chain 141
Mohamed Syazwan Ab Talib and Siti Norida Wahab

8 A Dyadic Perspective on Cooperation in the Pharmaceutical Supply Chain in the Light of Current and Future Trends in the Pharmaceutical Market in Poland 161
Mariusz Jedliński

Part II Integrated Management of Health Products: Supply, Storage and Waste

9 Challenges of Purchasing Physician Preference Items (PPIs) in the Healthcare Sector 185
Carolina Belotti Pedroso, Martin Beaulieu, and Claudia Rebolledo

10 Organ Donation Supply Chain: A Bibliometric Analysis of Risk Initiatives 205
Maria Eduarda Alves da Silva, Ingrid Teixeira do Nascimento, Fernanda Pinto Torres, Pedro Senna, Ana Carla de Souza Gomes dos Santos, Lino G. Marujo, and Leonardo Mangia Rodrigues

11 The Blood Product Supply Chain and Transfusion Network 225
Lamia Triqui

12 Medical Waste Management: From a Literature Review to a Conceptual and Multidimensional Framework 245
Ahmed Chtioui, Imane Bouhaddou, and Asmaa Benghabrit

13 Inventory Management Performance of Medical Analysis Laboratory in a Public Hospital 267
Imen Mejri, Safa Bhar Layeb, Najla Aissaoui, and Mohamed Yassine Kaabar

14 Medicines Strategic Sourcing in Moroccan Public Hospital: Development of Purchasing Portfolio and Strategies 285
Imane Ibn El Farouk, Fatima Zahra Majidi, and Fouad Jawab

15 Logistics of Local Produced Food for Increased Health 313
Andrej Lisec and Jabir Arif

Part III Patient Flow Optimization and Transport Logistics for Healthcare Services

16 A Multi-objective Programming Model for Physician Scheduling: A Case Study 337
Khadija Werghi, Jihene Jlassi, Ines Rekik, and Abderrahman El Mhamedi

17 Use of Participatory Ergonomics to Ensure the Safety of Patients and Healthcare Workers in Cancer Care Settings; PECS Framework 359
Safa Elkefi and Roa Sabra

18 Critical Analysis of the Evolution of Methods for Calculating Costs of Patient-Centered Health Services 379
Abdelaziz Zerka and Fouad Jawab

19 Optimization of a Meal Distribution Circuit in a Hospital: Vehicle Routing Problem 395
Jihene Jlassi, Ines Rekik, and Habib Chabchoub

20 Simulation Optimization Models for Reducing Inequities in Ambulance Coverage 413
Youness Frichi and Fouad Jawab

Part IV Major Health Crises; Maturity and Resilience of Hospital Supply Chains

21 Healthcare Supply Chain: Resilience Qualitative Evaluation 439
Naima Rahiel, Abderrahman El Mhamedi, and Khalid Hachemi

22 Hospital Medicines Supply Chain Maturity Assessment Tool Based on Processes Modeling: Case Study of a Public Hospital in Morocco 461
Imane Ibn El Farouk, Amine El Asri, and Fouad Jawab

23 Hospital Supply Chain Resilience: An Experimental Case Study from the Covid-19 Crisis 485
Ahmed Chtioui, Imane Bouhaddou, and Asmaa Benghabrit

24 Calibrating Resilience Strategies for PPE: Lessons from the COVID-19 Pandemic 511
Reza Shahin, Martin Beaulieu, Valérie Bélanger, and Martin Cousineau

Part V Revolution of the Hospital Supply Chain: Information Systems; Artificial Intelligence; Digital Transition and Innovative Technologies

25 The Future of Healthcare Supply Chains: Integrating Industry 4.0 Technologies for Improved Resilience and Sustainability 533
Thomas K. Dasaklis and Giannis T. Tsoulfas

26 Navigating the Future: AI-Driven Healthcare Supply Chains 553
Ivan Kudrenko

27 Role of Digital Twins, Generative AI, and Extended Reality in Cancer Care; CanConTech, a Human Factors Framework for Technology Connectedness 571
Safa Elkefi

28 Leveraging the Role of Blockchain Technology in the Hospital Supply Chain: A Systematic Literature Review and Future Trends 587
Asmae El Jaouhari, Jabir Arif, Fouad Jawab, Ashutosh Samadhiya, and Anil Kumar

29 Supporting Doctor-Patient Communication and the Therapeutic Alliance in Pediatric Care Through Extended Reality: A Systematic Review 619
Safa Elkefi and Noureddine Lourimi

30 Digital Transformation in Public Healthcare Organizations: A Case Study 643
Bilel Ben Arbia and Safa Bhar Layeb

Author Index 663

Subject Index 665

Editor and Contributors

About the Editor

Fouad Jawab is a Professor of Supply Chain at the Higher School of Technology of the Sidi Mohamed Ben Abdellah University of Fez, Morocco.

He has held several scientific and administrative responsibilities. He founded the International Conference on Logistics and Supply Chain Management (LOGISTI-QUA), which he continues to develop with the support of several research teams in Morocco and abroad.

He is the author and co-author of more than 180 publications in national and international journals and proceedings. His research focuses on modeling, simulation and optimization of the supply chain, hospital supply chains and urban logistics. He is also an expert with several renowned organizations and a reviewer for prestigious journals.

Contributors

Najla Aissaoui LR-OASIS, National Engineering School of Tunis, University of Tunis El Manar, Tunis, Tunisia;
National Engineering School of Carthage, University of Carthage, Ariana, Tunisia

Claudia Alexandra Department of Hospital Administration, Universitas Pelita Harapan, Tangerang, Indonesia

Grace Alvina Prostacia Clinic, Tangerang, Jakarta, Indonesia

Bilel Ben Arbia Tunis Business School, Tunis, Tunisia

Jabir Arif Laboratory of Technologies and Industrial Services, Higher School of Technology, Sidi Mohamed Ben Abdellah University, Fez, Morocco

Valérie Bélanger HEC Montréal, Montréal, QC, Canada

Martin Beaulieu CHAINE Research Group, HEC Montreal, Montreal, QC, Canada

Asmaa Benghabrit LMAID Laboratory, L2M3S Laboratory, ENSMR, Rabat, Morocco

Omar Bentahar IAE Metz School of Management, University of Lorraine, Metz, France

Smail Benzidia IAE Metz School of Management, Metz, France

Imane Bouhaddou L2M3S Laboratory ENSAM, Moulay Ismail University, Meknes, Morocco

Habib Chabchoub College of Business, Al Ain University, Abu Dhabi, United Arab Emirates

Ahmed Chtioui L2M3S Laboratory ENSAM, Moulay Ismail University, Meknes, Morocco

Martin Cousineau HEC Montréal, Montréal, QC, Canada

Maria Eduarda Alves da Silva Department Postgraduate Program in Production Engineering and Systems (PPPRO), Federal Centre for Technological Education Celso Suckow da Fonseca (CEFET/RJ), Rio de Janeiro, Brazil

Thomas K. Dasaklis School of Social Sciences, Hellenic Open University, Patras, Greece

Ana Carla de Souza Gomes dos Santos Department Industrial Engineering, University/Institution: IFRJ—Niterói/RJ, Niterói, Brazil

Ingrid Teixeira do Nascimento Department Postgraduate Program in Production Engineering and Systems (PPPRO), Federal Centre for Technological Education Celso Suckow da Fonseca (CEFET/RJ), Rio de Janeiro, Brazil

Amine El Asri Laboratory for Studies and Research in Economics and Management Sciences, LERSEM. ENCGJ, Chouaib Doukalli El Jadida University, El Jadida, Morocco

Safa Elkefi School of Nursing, Columbia University, New York, USA; Hphactors Lab, New York, USA

Abderrahman El Mhamedi QUARTZ Laboratory, IUT Montreuil University Paris 8, Paris, France;
QUARTZ, Paris 8 Vincennes-Saint-Denis University, Saint-Denis, France

Youness Frichi Technologies and Industrial Services, High School of Technology, Sidi Mohamed Ben Abdellah University, Fez, Morocco

Amine Hakim Guezzen Manufacturing Engineering Laboratory of Tlemcen, Tlemcen University, Tlemcen, Algeria

Khalid Hachemi LGPMI, Oran 2 University, Oran, Algeria

Valencia Hadinata Department of Hospital Administration, Universitas Pelita Harapan, Tangerang, Indonesia

Imane Ibn El Farouk Laboratory for Studies and Research in Economics and Management Sciences, LERSEM, ENCGJ, Chouaib Doukkali University, El Jadida, Morocco

Asmae El Jaouhari Laboratory of Technologies and Industrial Services, Higher School of Technology, Sidi Mohamed Ben Abdellah University, Fez, Morocco

Fouad Jawab Laboratory of Technologies and Industrial Services, Higher School of Technology, Sidi Mohamed Ben Abdellah University, Fez, Morocco

Mariusz Jedliński Faculty of Economics and Engineering of Transport, Maritime University of Szczecin, Szczecin, Poland

Jihene Jlassi OLID Laboratory, Higher Institute of Management Industrial of Sfax (ISGIS), University of Sfax, Sfax, Tunisia

Mohamed Yassine Kaabar Medical Analysis Laboratory of the Tahar Maamouri Hospital, Nabeul, Tunisia

Ivan Kudrenko The Boeing Company, Charleston, USA

Anil Kumar Guildhall School of Business and Law, London Metropolitan University, London, UK

Safa Bhar Layeb LR-OASIS, National Engineering School of Tunis, University of Tunis El Manar, Tunis, Tunisia

Andrej Lisec Landscape Governance College GRM Novo mesto, Novo mesto, Slovenia

Noureddine Lourimi Hphactors Lab, New York, USA;
Industrial Engineering Department, National Engineering School of Tunis, Tunis, Tunisia

Fatima Zahra Majidi Laboratory for Studies and Research in Economics and Management Sciences, LERSEM, ENCGJ, Chouaib Doukkali University, El Jadida, Morocco

Lino G. Marujo Department Production Engineering Program, Universidade Cândido Mendes/PEP/COPPE-UFRJ, Rio de Janeiro, Brazil

Imen Mejri LR-OASIS, National Engineering School of Tunis, University of Tunis El Manar, Tunis, Tunisia;
National Higher Engineering School of Tunis (ENSIT), University of Tunis, Tunis, Tunisia

Amina Ouhoud École Supérieure en Sciences Appliquées Tlemcen (ESSA-Tlemcen), Tlemcen, Algeria

Carolina Belotti Pedroso University of Twente, Enschede, Netherlands

Gerry Dwi Putro Department of Orthopedic and Traumatology, Jakarta Hospital, Jakarta, Indonesia

Naima Rahiel QUARTZ, Paris 8 Vincennes-Saint-Denis University, Saint-Denis, France

Claudia Rebolledo HEC Montreal, Montreal, Canada

Ines Rekik OLID Laboratory, Higher Institute of Management Industrial of Sfax (ISGIS), University of Sfax, Sfax, Tunisia

Fritzie A. Rexana Department of Business Management, Universitas Tarumanegara, Tarumanegara, Jakarta, Indonesia

Leonardo Mangia Rodrigues Department Production Engineering Program, Universidade Cândido Mendes/PEP/COPPE-UFRJ, Rio de Janeiro, Brazil

Jacques Roy HEC Montreal, Montreal, Canada

Roa Sabra Faculty of Health Sciences, University of Ottawa, Ottawa, ON, Canada

Ashutosh Samadhiya Jindal Global Business School, OP Jindal Global University, Sonipat, India

Pedro Senna Department Postgraduate Program in Production Engineering and Systems (PPPRO), Federal Centre for Technological Education Celso Suckow da Fonseca (CEFET/RJ), Rio de Janeiro, Brazil

Felicia Setiawan Department of Hospital Administration, Universitas Pelita Harapan, Tangerang, Indonesia

Reza Shahin COSYS-ESTAS, Université Gustave Eiffel, Villeneuve d'Ascq, France

Mohamed Syazwan Ab Talib School of Business and Economics, UBD, Universiti Brunei Darussalam, Gadong, Brunei Darussalam

Fernanda Pinto Torres Department Postgraduate Program in Production Engineering and Systems (PPPRO), Federal Centre for Technological Education Celso Suckow da Fonseca (CEFET/RJ), Rio de Janeiro, Brazil

Lamia Triqui Manufacturing Engineering Laboratory of Tlemcen (MELT), Abou Bekr Belkaid University of Tlemcen, Tlemcen, Algeria

Giannis T. Tsoulfas Department of Agribusiness and Supply Chain Management, Agricultural University of Athens, Thiva, Greece

Frederik G. S. Vos Portland State University—School of Business, Portland, USA

Siti Norida Wahab Faculty of Business and Management, Universiti Teknologi MARA, Puncak Alam, Selangor, Malaysia

Khadija Werghi OLID Laboratory, Higher Institute of Management Industrial of Sfax (ISGIS), University of Sfax, Sfax, Tunisia

Abdelaziz Zerka Faculty of Sciences Dhar El Mahraz, Industrial Technologies and Services Laboratory, Sidi Mohamed Ben Abdelah University, Fez, Morocco

Part I

Design, Optimization and Collaboration in the Hospital Supply Chain

Organizational Configuration of Logistics Activities in Healthcare Institutions

1

Martin Beaulieu, Omar Bentahar, and Smail Benzidia

Abstract

Within hospitals, supply chain activities support the clinical mission of these organizations. As a result, the departments in charge of supply chain activities often lack the attention of top hospital management. This situation hinders the implementation of best practices that can enhance healthcare supply chain performance. This chapter offers an integrated understanding of the dynamics of supply chain activity configurations in hospitals. The research adopts a qualitative approach "based on" the case study of the public health system of a Canadian province and the systematic observation of six units of analysis to understand the evolution of their supply chain activity configurations. The results of the study show that the knowledge acquired in the logistics function, the experience of the supply chain manager and his team, and political maneuvers influence the configuration of logistics activities. The study also underlines that the new configurations provided a foundation for improving organizational performance.

Keywords

Healthcare • Logistics • Structure • Evolution

M. Beaulieu (✉)
CHAINE Research Group, HEC Montreal, Montreal, Canada
e-mail: martin.beaulieu@hec.ca

O. Bentahar · S. Benzidia
IAE Metz School of Management, University of Lorraine, Metz, France
e-mail: omar.bentahar@univ-lorraine.fr

S. Benzidia
e-mail: smail.benzidia@univ-lorraine.fr

F. Jawab (ed.), *Hospital Supply Chain*, Integrated Science 27,
https://doi.org/10.1007/978-3-031-70292-1_1

Abbreviations

CEO	Chief executive officer
L&SC	Logistics and supply chain

1 Introduction

The COVID-19 pandemic highlighted the historical shortcomings of supply chain management in the healthcare sector [37]. Raising the performance of this supply chain will require an improvement in logistics practices within healthcare institutions, which constitute the first point of uncertainty for upstream partners [4]. Since the mid-1980s, interest in logistics issues has grown, and organizations have begun to configure their activities in this area [29].

In this context, two interrelated research questions can be formulated: first, how do healthcare institutions configure their logistics and supply chain activities, and second, what are the factors that influence the adoption of these organizational configurations? This research question is not only relevant to the healthcare sector, but for the field of logistics and supply chain (L&SC). Turkulainen et al. [42] point out that we must not only seek to demonstrate the link between structure and logistics performance, but also understand the context in which these same configurations are developed. Picking up on previous work, Kim [23] presents the five main structures framing L&SC activities. Taking up this nomenclature, Nakano and Matsuyama [33] demonstrate that corporate reality is more nuanced, and that there is an interest in better understanding these underlined the interest of grasping the spectrum of activities supervised by a logistics and supply chain manager regardless of the sector of activity [12]. In fact, Esper et al. [16] concede that there is a great deal of ambiguity when it comes to the responsibilities associated with logistics and the supply chain.

To answer these questions, we will study the organizational configurations of healthcare logistics and supply chain activities in the province of Quebec (Canada) resulting from the reform of the public health system in 2015. Beeler et al. [10] indicated that "critical events can be influential enough to produce change or variation over time in regards to subsequent events, ultimately driving structural organizational change" (p. 67). At the same time, Klüppel et al. [24] asserted that researchers do not give sufficient attention to historical events that have generated profound organizational impacts. For example, this reform led to a revision of organizational structures resulting, in several cases, in the creation of a separate department for L&SC activities.

In this context, the first part of this chapter will be devoted to a review of the literature to position the historical evolution of logistics and supply chain activities in hospitals. The experience of the American healthcare sector will serve as a background to this literature review, since it contains a greater number of articles that allow us to reconstruct a historical evolution. The next section will specify the methodology. The chosen strategy is case study, as it allows to reconstruct the historical context of the integrated changes while targeting specific situations in hospitals [45]. The presentation of the results will offer a general context while using six units of analysis to nuance the events. The discussion will provide sufficiently broad observations to guide decision-makers, but will also offer new avenues of research for researchers interested in developments in the organizational structures of logistics and supply chain activities.

Readers will note that we used the expression logistics and supply chain (L&SC) applied by Wilson and Barbat [44]. We are aware that the concept of supply chain is different from that of logistics [11], but at this stage of our work, we do not wish to open a semantic discussion on these two terms.

2 Literature Review

Srivastava et al. [37] identified various barriers to healthcare supply chain performance. Table 1 identifies barriers originating within the hospital, which contribute to supply chain underperformance. To overcome these barriers, it is imperative to cultivate logistics and supply chain leadership within the hospital. Such leadership could be manifested through the organizational configuration of L&SC activities.

Gloch and Hochrein [20] use the concept of configuration to address the structure supporting supply management in an organization. According to these authors, configuration refers to the authority structure and includes dimensions such as the vertical and lateral extent of tasks, the criteria for segmenting these same tasks and the number of positions in the different segments. Richter [36] adds that organizational configuration characterizes the orchestration of internal resources. Consequently, the configuration of L&SC activities in healthcare institutions will be analyzed from two angles: (1) hierarchical position and (2) spectrum of L&SC activities.

Table 1 Barriers to healthcare supply chain performance

Ineffective practices	Consequences	References
Lack of product standardization in the medical supplies field	Fragmentation of purchasing power, leading to additional ordering and storage costs	[46]
Underutilization of product database	Reactive management of inventory parameters	Beaulieu et Bentahar (2021)
Underutilization of collaborative strategies with suppliers	Hospitals assume significant risks of supply chain failure	

2.1 The Hierarchical Position of the Head of L&SC

The distribution of decision-making power is often formulated in terms of the degree of centralization by which "the power to make supply chain management decisions is concentrated in an organization" ([23], p. 325). Centralization translates into a concentration of decision-making power at higher levels. Precisely, over a 25 year period, various surveys of multiple sectors show that the purchasing/logistics function integrates more responsibilities, increasing its direct control over the organization's purchasing expenditures, and occupying an increasingly strategic position in the organization [22, 44].

The American healthcare sector is inspired by the private sector. Surveys show that 35–50% of healthcare institutions have the title of senior or executive vice president for materials or supply chain management [26]. A senior position in the organization would imply an equal recognition of L&SC to that of other senior management positions [25]. However, studies show that the chief procurement officer or the vice-president of the supply chain are ultimately little involved in the strategic decisions of the organization [30]. As Trent [41] pointed out, a hierarchical position alone cannot explain superior performance for its incumbent. The manager becomes part of the fabric of his organization and his colleagues' perception of his contribution [43]. In fact, studies tend to show that the lack of support from hospital senior management for L&SC activities is a hindrance to the organization's performance [17]. In this sense, beyond formal recognition, the organizational perception of a function's role is crucial to its value [35]. Tchokogué et al. [39] emphasized the legitimacy of a function beyond mere formal recognition through an organization chart.

This assertion justifies the findings of Kwon et al. [26], who see stagnation in the performance of the US healthcare supply chain. In fact, the hierarchical position provides levers, but it remains for the manager in place, the executive champion [41], to articulate them. It should also be noted that the contribution of an L&SC management to an institution's performance is not a linear relationship [1], and there would be a tipping point where the management no longer has to demonstrate its relevance. In this context, there is a political dimension that the L&SC manager cannot neglect if he wants to acquire legitimacy [39].

2.2 Sprectrum of Healthcare Logistics Activities

Studies evoking the distribution of different logistical responsibilities may overlap with the concept of integration at the heart of supply chain management [13]. This integration would reduce conflicts and ensure more coherent actions [18]. Synergies could also be developed between a set of activities [38]. This integration would not have to be embodied under a single authority, but through internal cross-functional mecanisms [13, 42]. The difficulties of integration also stem from the fact that the boundaries of L&SC responsibilities are ambiguous [16].

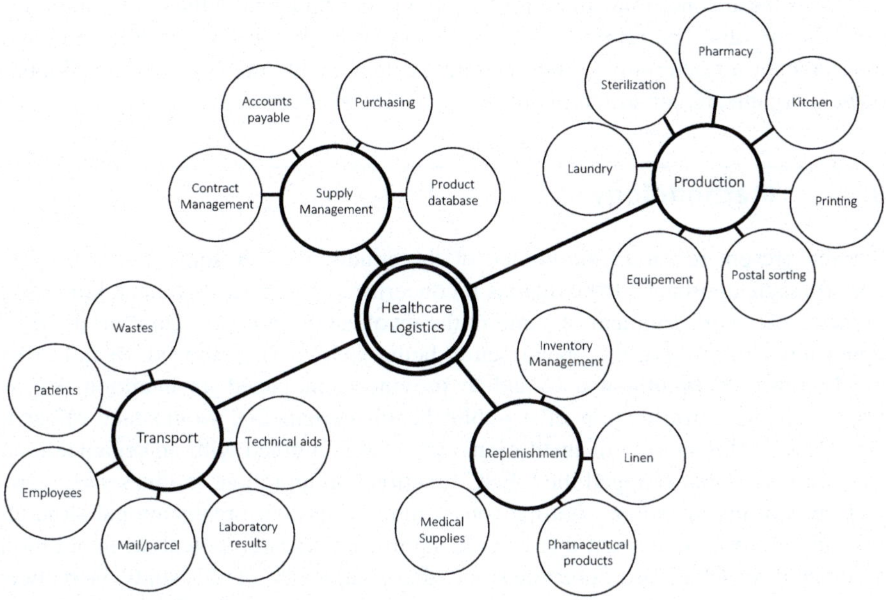

Fig. 1 The ramifications of healthcare logistics

To this end, Landry and Beaulieu [27] trace the evolution of responsibilities that can be found in a healthcare L&SC department. Such a department developed around two poles: supply management and inventory management. These responsibilities have expanded to include the replenishment of care units with various products, mainly medical supplies. More recently, transport activities have been added as a fourth pole [5]. Also, in the French model, the L&SC department will take charge of many internal production activities, such as food production or laundry.

In this dynamic evolution of healthcare logistics, Beaulieu et al. [6] proposed four major areas of activity: supply management, replenishment, transport, and production (see Fig. 1). Figure 1 shows these four poles and the 21 activities that can be historically linked to them.

2.3 Conclusion De La Section

Aubry and Lavoie-Tremblay [2] trace the evolution of the theories associated with the design of organizational structure. Contingency theory postulates that structure must adapt to variables in the external environment. This early work evolved into more political and social considerations, with the internal context of the organization shaping its structure. This perspective is in line with Turkulainen et al. [42], who argue for a better understanding of organizational context to understand L&SC structures.

Under these conditions, there is a need to better understand the configuration of L&SC activities. The reform of Quebec's public health system provides a unique environment for determining the institutional factors that may explain the adoption of new organizational structures in these healthcare institutions.

3 Methodology

For the present research, the choice of the situation under study stems from an opportunistic approach [19], whereas it concerns contemporary events taking place in the research environment of some of the involved researchers. This was a unique opportunity to observe the phenomenon being studied [14]. Indeed, in fall 2014, the Ministry of Health of a Canadian province announced its intention to proceed with the consolidation of a public health system that would take effect in April 2015. This merger of institutions was also combined with an organizational transformation that changed the L&SC function configuration. In this sense, a critical mass of organizations simultaneously modifying their organizational structure was an almost unique event that offered significant research potential. In addition, contextual variables are controlled and the complexity of the study is reduced because it concerns the same sector of activity (health sector), the same environment (public sector), the same region (the province of Quebec, Canada), and the same temporality, with a four-year period between spring 2015 and fall 2019.

From this perspective, we retain a Type II case study [45]. The public health system in the province of Quebec will be treated as a single case, but we will use six units of analysis in the form of L&SC function (or their equivalent) in hospitals to diversify perspectives on the configuration choices and identify the factors influencing their adoption.

3.1 Data Collection

The case study can combine different data sources [45], contributing to its flexibility. Thus, data collection was structured into three phases. The first phase was to understand the value of the L&SC function in the new healthcare institutions in the spring of 2015. To do so, artefacts were consulted (organization charts of the institutions and documents recommending the constitution of L&SC departments).

The second phase involved analyzing the results of a survey conducted by the Ministry of Health. The data were collected in spring 2018. The objective of this survey was to identify the different activities undertaken by the L&SC departments. Before administering the questionnaire to the institutions, the Ministry of Health had previously contacted the same institutions to identify the activities within the L&SC departments. For the purpose of this study, we targeted only 21 activities included in the theoretical design (Fig. 1).

All 34 healthcare institutions in the province completed the Ministry of Health questionnaire, which equated to a 100% response rate. This was due to the mandatory nature of the application. However, these health care organizations are not of the same size, and the spectrum of their service offerings may be disparate. Additionally, they may serve a small population spread over a very large territory or, conversely, they may have a large and localized supply of services. Therefore, to reduce these variances, which can bias the analysis, all respondents with an operating budget of less than 300 million Canadian dollars for the 2017–2018 fiscal year were removed from the sample. Under these circumstances, 25 out of the 34 establishments in Quebec were retained, representing 73.4% of the total population.

Secondary data allow for more objectivity because it averts the interviewees' perceptions. However, they do not allow us to apprehend representations that reveal organizational paradoxes. Thus, with the objective of triangulation and complementarity of methods, a third phase was carried out and consisted of interviews with L&SC managers from a group of institutions in the Quebec health system. These interviews aimed to understand the factors that influence organizational choices. Given this objective, semi-structured interviews were chosen as the data collection strategy.

As noted in the literature review, the interviews were intended to cover the following themes: (1) The respondent as a potential "champion" to leverage available resources and/or counterbalance a lack of formal authority [30]; this dimension would be studied from the perspective of the respondent's career path. (2) The arguments put forward to justify the choices made in terms of the configuration of L&SC activities. (3) The respondent's participation in the institution's executive committee and the perception of its perceived influence on strategic orientations [30]. (4) Using the strategy of McCue and Pitzer [31], we asked our respondents to estimate their perception of the impact of the new L&SC configuration on the organization's performance. This section of the interview was completed by asking the respondents for their contributions as well as the limitations of the new L&SC configurations. Unlike other surveys on the subject [3], the interview grid did not contain questions on external factors. According to what was mentioned earlier, we assumed that these external factors are the same and concern institutional reform. Appendix provides the interview grid used. To counterbalance the perception of L&SC managers, interviews were conducted with a dozen managers working in clinical areas. The interviews were shorter and focused on answering the question: has the new configuration of L&SC activities generated additional benefits for your department?

3.2 Choice of Analytical Units

To have a diversity of perspectives, we decided to study six units of analysis. These units were chosen according to the scope of the activities carried out by the L&SC

department, the presence or absence of the L&SC function on the executive committee, and the presence or absence of a two-headed department (to the extent that purchasing activities were left to a finance department). These criteria allowed to study units that are representative of the diversity of configurations found in the public health system in the province of Quebec. These choices also enable more extreme experiences instead of selecting those that are more in line with the average. In this sense, we followed the case study approach recommended by Eisenhardt and Graebner [14]. In addition to the diversity of configurations mentioned above, another criterion taken into consideration when choosing the L&SC managers to be interviewed was having been in position for the entire period covered by the case study, i.e., from spring 2015 to fall 2019. Table 2 provides an overview of the main characteristics of these units of analysis and their diversity.

3.3 Data Analysis

The case study was conducted in two stages: first of all, a description of the context, understanding the critical events [10] mentioned in the introduction, which create a rupture in the old order. Then, this context will lead to the representation of the choices of new configurations of L&SC activities in Quebec healthcare institutions. This section will also be analyzed in two parts: the nature of the activities making up the scope of this department and the hierarchical position in the organizational structure.

From the interviews, the arguments that militated in favor of one or the other configuration will be coded according to the procedure suggested by [32]. The selected codes reflect the major themes and sub-themes that constitute the interview grid. A separate matrix was constructed for the different dimensions of the performance studied. This methodology allowed us to capture the key elements of our interviews while reducing the mass of data. We cross-referenced our results across the units of analysis studied. In this way, we will be able to discern whether certain phenomena are specific to an organization or whether they tend to be replicated in more than one healthcare institution.

4 Presentation of Results

This section is structured into three parts. The first presents the general context of the public health system in the province of Quebec and the place occupied by L&SC's activities prior to the spring 2015 reform. The second part specifies the activities being taken over by these new L&SC departments. Finally, the last section specifies perception of new configurations for internal customers. For the last two parts, we will include the comments of the L&SC managers of the six units analyzed to consolidate our understanding of the organizational choices.

Table 2 Characteristics of the units studied

	Institutions					
	A	B	C	D	E	F
Revenue (millions)	1340	931	930	1087	950	1400
No. of employees	17,700	12,850	12,100	12,500	13,500	19,000
Characteristics of the respondent	Master's degree 20 years in the health system	Master's degree in Organizational Development 15 years in the health system	Master's degree in Health Administration 24 years in the health system	Bachelor's degree in Engineering and 23 years in the health system	Bachelor's degree in Accounting and Master's degree in Health Law and Policy	Bachelor's degree in Computer Science
Number of activities under the control of an L&SC branch in spring 2018	16	11	13	12	10	10
Year of implementation of the new L&SC structure	2015	2012	2015	2015	2015	2015
Distinctive characteristics of the structure	Cover production activities including sterilization activities	Involvement of a continuous improvement team	Initially, the logistics function was under the financial department	The purchasing function is integrated with the finance department	The purchasing function is integrated with the finance department	Initially, the logistics function was under the financial department

4.1 General Context of Logistics Activities Before the Reform

The province of Quebec has a population of more than eight million people, representing just under a quarter of the entire Canadian population. In Canada, health falls under the jurisdiction of the provinces, which can define for themselves the organization of healthcare that respects broad national guidelines. Thus, a very large part of the supply of care is provided by public healthcare institutions under the responsibility of the Ministry of Health [5].

It was only in the early 2010s' that the term logistics was used in a few services to describe the administrative unit in the institutions that took over the activities of L&SC. Generally, this administrative unit was known as the purchasing department. It was managed by a coordinator, usually reporting to a director of finance [7]. Despite its name, this service had two main areas of activity: purchasing and replenishment of medical supplies to care units (see Fig. 1). The activities of the production were generally split between clinical departments (e.g., sterilization) and/or technical departments (laundry, kitchen etc.) [7]. The transport activities were often highly decentralized among different departments [34]. Surveys have shown that the performance of these services varied considerably from one institution to another [9]. Historically, several managers in the L&SC department consider it difficult to improve logistics performance when logistics investment projects are in competition with clinical projects, which are often a organizational priority [28].

The reform of the Quebec public health system in spring 2015 consolidated the number of institutions, which went from 182 to 34. The reform was also accompanied by a review of organizational structures through the creation of the position of the chief executive officer (CEO). In addition to this change, the reform suggested the creation of an L&SC department under the leadership of one of the senior officials who steered the reform within the Ministry of Health. This civil servant had previously headed one of the first Quebec institutions to create the position of the L&SC director, who was integrated into the steering committee. However, at the time of the reform, the Ministry of Health did not want to impose a structure on the new institutions, so he suggested six organizational charts that could serve as a basis for the new directions. All the suggested organizational charts proposed an L&SC department on the steering committee. These organizational charts did not specify the activities that the new department could directly manage.

The structures proposed by the Ministry of Health have not been fully adopted by new CEOs. The interviews highlighted a two-phase approach: the executive management, human resources, and finance departments were the first components to be set up in the new institutions; in the second phase, the other departments, including L&SC, shared the organization's various remaining activities.

4.2 Scope of the Logistics Activities of the New L&SC Departments

Table 3 shows the number of institutions that account for each of the 21 major logistics activities, as represented in Fig. 1. Thus, out of a possible 21 activities, the L&SC departments handle an average of 11 activities, while the department with the most control manages 16 and the department with the least control manages 8.

Since the finance department was one of the first to be established, this explains why D and E decided to integrate purchasing under their control (see Table 2). Respondent E mentions several reasons for this configuration: "This formula had demonstrated its effectiveness in the healthcare institutions prior to the reform. It provided a means of securing financial control during a critical transition period. Also, from the point of view of sound control practices, it made it possible to separate the activities of launching orders from those of receiving goods. Finally, I already had the expertise to take charge of supply chain activities, having done so before."

Table 3 Degree of support for healthcarelogistics activities

Logistics activities	Number of facilities
Inventory management	25
Replenishment of medical supplies	25
Transportation (supplies, small parcels, furniture) and courier services	25
Postal sorting	24
Contract management	23
Purchasing	23
Product database	23
Printing	20
Transportation of users	19
Transport of laboratory tests	15
Supplier accounts	13
Lingerie replenishment	13
Technical aids	12
Stretcher room	12
Laundry	10
Food services	5
Equipment	2
Waste	2
Sterilization	1
Replenishment of drugs	1
Pharmacy	0

When the new Director of L&SC at Institution A was hired, he articulated his vision. At that time, he adhered to the framework shown in Fig. 1, which explains why it is the institution with the largest number of activities being handled by the L&SC department (Table 2). At the same time, beyond the theoretical positioning, the director wanted to find a linking element between all these activities: all of them required transportation to receive an input and/or to deliver an output. For this manager, although the production activities (sterilization, food production, and laundry) seemed disparate, they all required the same skills. It should be pointed out that this institution offers mainly long-term care, with a marginal operating room activity.

In contrast, Institution B chose a more focused structure with 12 activities. "We didn't want to be involved in production activities and we didn't want to 'touch' the patient. On the other hand, we wanted to relieve the clinical staff of logistical tasks, so for the activities that were being taken care of, we wanted to be present in the user services." Also, the L&SC manager of institution B has accounts payable activities under his control, seeing it as a way to identify problems upstream when formulating the contract, placing an order, or receiving goods.

Although respondents A and B tend to present a deliberate approach in choosing which activities would be included in the L&SC departments, there was often a bargaining effect. For example, in the second phase of implementation of the new institutions, the remaining activities were shared among the other directors who were subsequently appointed. According to respondents C and F, the choice of activities was made based on L&SC knowledge of the Quebec public health system at the time. This may explain why many of these new L&SC structures are simply extensions of the previous ones. A major difference is the addition of the transportation hub and, more rarely, production activities. In the latter case, the skills mastered by managers in place may justify organizational choices. For example, in facility D, the new L&SC manager had already managed food production activities, whereas the new technical manager did not have the same experience.

The configuration of respondents C, E, and F continued to evolve beyond the 2015 reform. For the C and F institutions, the L&SC department integrated new activities and appointed its holder to the steering committee. Respondent F explained, "In 2018, a new CEO took office and he wanted to review our role. We took the time to formulate a 5 to 10 year vision that would guide our development and role in the institution. With respect to Institution E, the departure of the Director of L&SC highlighted the difficulty in recruiting a candidate with the expertise for this type of responsibility. For equivalent positions, private sector salaries are more attractive than those in the public sector," says respondent E.

Respondent C could observe the negative effect of the lack of its involvement in strategic decisions. The recent reorganization of facility C in fall 2019 adjusted the situation by appointing him (respondent C) in the steering committee. "Previously, there was a disconnect between the lines of information, so we became more in reaction than in action." That's why respondent A says, "Our relevance is now understood." Furthermore, respondent B comments, "When L&SC reports to a CEO, he has his own reading grid, he won't see the priorities the same way or consider the same constraints. Thus, we can capture directly what the CEO wants. From there, we can influence other projects." Respondent F emphasizes that this gain in influence is not only the result of a better hierarchical position. Internally, "the Ministry of Health has made representations to the CEOs of all the institutions to better explain the role of logistics in the organization."

For institutions where the purchasing function is in a financial department, respondents agree that there must be concerted efforts before presenting a position to the executive committee. "We held a strategic meeting between my department and the finance department to clarify our respective roles. Also, we have statutory meetings a few times a year to take action of common issues," comments respondent D. Respondent E explains that he had an excellent personal relationship with the first incumbent of the purchasing management team, "but there will always be conflicts between purchasing and inventory management, which are two distinct logics."

4.3 Impact on Internal Customers

Regarding the impact of the configuration of L&SC activities, some respondents mentioned that their new structures have or will make it possible to generate savings through projects (A, C, D, and E), to improve service (A and F), or internal customer satisfaction (F). Clinical managers confirm this finding. One such respondent explains, "Several departments could use the same supplies, but ordered according to their needs. Since 2015, orders have been centralized and allow for volume ordering, resulting in savings on delivery costs as well as better prices thanks to single orders." There is also a standardization of working practices.

However, clinical respondents note that these new, larger organizations have created a sense of distance as far as the L&SC department is concerned. One respondent explains: "Before the merger, everything was managed in-house; we had our own storeroom in our hospital. Now, lead times for obtaining materials have increased considerably, from a few minutes to sometimes several weeks."

It should also be noted that clinical managers offering mental health services, for example, can hardly judge the impact of the reorganization since their material needs were very limited.

Almost everyone agreed that L&SC management still lacks performance indicators to track the day-to-day improvement of operations. "We do projects, but we lack day-to-day monitoring of our operations," comments respondent C. Respondent A adds, "The L&SC processes of our former organizations are standardized, but they are not yet optimized."

Furthermore, Respondent B doubts that the organizational structure is the only element that explains the increase in logistics performance. “It’s multifactorial. For example, there has been a new generation of clinical managers who are willing to entrust logistics tasks historically performed by nurses. This has helped improve our performance.”

5 Discussion

Our research question was twofold: the nature of the configurations of L&SC activities in healthcare institutions in the province of Quebec following the reorganization of the public health system in 2015 and the factors that influenced these configurations.

The willingness of the Ministry of Health to provide L&SC management to health care institutions in the province of Quebec mainly followed a trend that was visible in the American healthcare sector [26]. However, this global orientation was translated into several logistical configurations in the field. Figure 2 shows the six analysis units on the two axes that characterize our configurations. The first binary axis specifies whether the L&SC manager is a member of the steering committee in 2015 (yes vs. no). The second axis is nominal and specifies the number of activities supported by L&SC management. The position of the six analysis units on the matrix is intended to provide a clear view of the different institutions and not to provide an absolute position.

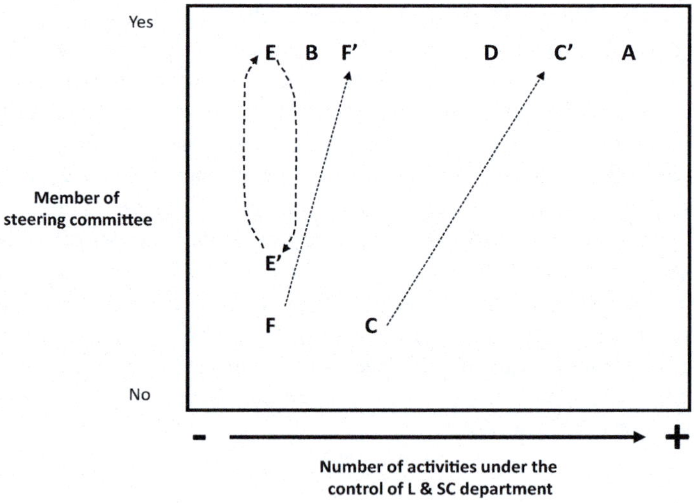

Fig. 2 Position and evolution of analysis units

We identified two main logics in the studied configurations. The logic of material management centered on the flow of materials, as in cases B and C, and the logic of a support service center for cases A and D (and the advanced version of case C) where production activities are supported. We do not point out that one logic is superior to the other, but it has a lot to do with the manager's ability to identify synergies between a collection of activities. For example, by holding the accounts payable activity, Institution B, can identify and correct problems in the purchasing cycle.

Institutions C and F show that there can be changes in the C' and F' positions. These two directions have made lateral shifts by becoming members of senior management and taking over other activities. The effect of time on the evolution of the structure cannot be neglected. For example, the time needed to articulate a thought on the outlines that the holder wishes for his department (B and F when reorganizing their department) or the time needed for new conditions to emerge, favoring a new configuration: arrival or departure of certain executives from the steering committee.

The experience of Institution E is more unusual as it questions the position in the L&SC department in the organization structure, creating a back-and-forth effect between its initial position (E) and a new desired position (E') to finally return to the initial position. Tchokogué et al. [40] also highlighted this pendulum effect in the search for an ideal organizational structure. This "back-and-forth" movement had already been noted for a L&SC structure in healthcare institutions [1]. More recently, F's organizational configuration was dismantled following quality issues in the food production department. L&SC activities were returned to a Finance department [8]. These events show that the position of L&SC activities remains fragile within healthcare institutions.

With regard to the factors that have influenced these configurations, there are naturally external forces that tend to be triggers for a revision of organizational structures [40], as was the reform of spring 2015, or the arrival of a new CEO in the Institution F.

The vision of the department top manager naturally influences the nature of the activities that are integrated into these configurations. For example, A and B have a different vision of the poles of activities to be mastered, even if the purpose remains similar. The study also shows that these configurations are also the result of political forces within the organization [21]. For example, the ambition or the negotiation of some finance directors to retain purchasing activities in several institutions influenced the nature of these new L&SC departments.

As mentioned earlier, it is difficult to identify a superior configuration at this stage of our work. First, respondents agree that the reorganization of L&SC activities in 2015 has created an environment that has allowed the development of projects that have generated positive impacts for the organization. At the same time, several respondents pointed out that there has been a change in the attitude of the rest of the organization regarding their contribution to the organization's performance. L&SC managers no longer have to sell their role and contribution to the organization. To echo Pearson and Gritzmacher [35], the organizational perception of management's role is much better understood. In the sense that, beyond the formal recognition associated with the title, there is a legitimacy that has now been developed [39]: presence on the steering committee can help create this tipping point where a function moves from obscurity to established recognition and from operational contribution to a more strategic contribution within the organization [1]. However, this contribution remains theoretical, and several respondents pointed out the absence of performance indicators, a historical shortcoming in the Quebec health system [9]. Trent [41] reminds us that improving performance does not only result from the organizational structure, which is a tool available to the "executive champion."

6 Conclusion

The study of organizational configuration is a recurrent research theme in the field of supply management [20] and more recently, in logistics [44]. It may overlap with questions about the hierarchical position of this function in the organization [21] or the scope of activities that are handled by the same function [11]. Such work interacts with discussions surrounding the integration or differentiation of the terms supply management, logistics, and supply chain management [15]. This study decided to address these issues more holistically, hence, the use of the term L&SC configurations in healthcare sector. The transformation of the public health system in the province of Quebec provided a unique opportunity to study them. It became a receptacle where different forces converged, such as previous knowledge on logistical issues, political games to position one's organizational territory, the vision of managers, time to reflect on the outlines of this structure, or the search for synergies.

This study has some limitations which may become relevant research opportunities. This research was conducted in a single setting, which may limit the generalizability of the results. There is a need to diversify the environments in which such a study could be replicated. From there, it would be interesting to validate whether the potential of L&SC activities unfolds mainly according to internal variables, as our study suggests, or whether certain variables in the external environment have a major impact? If the latter question is answered in the affirmative, would it be possible to reproduce such external variables?

Also, the data collected was prior to the COVID-19 pandemic. They may offer some insight into the personal protective equipment management challenges that many health systems experienced in early 2020. How did the pandemic affect the organizational configurations of L&SC activities within healthcare institutions? If critical events profoundly influence organizational structure [10], it would be interesting to study the impact of the COVID-19 pandemic on the configuration of L&SC activities in hospitals. Tchokogué et al. [39] discussed the legitimacy of the holder of an L&SC position: Were they able to use this crisis to position themselves differently in the eyes of the other directors of their hospital? Can these events serve as a catalyst for becoming this executive champion [41]?

Although our study identifies two broad categories of configuration, it is not possible to conclude that one is superior to the other. At the same time, our respondents agree that there is a lack of performance indicators, the presence of which could enhance the demonstration of the relevance of better-structured L&SC activities within healthcare institutions. The next step would be to conduct new case studies, but using quantifiable performance indicators (customer service, economies of scale, price reduction, etc.) to partially overcome this limitation. As can be seen, this study is therefore far from being the final piece of work on the organizational configurations of logistics activities in healthcare institutions.

Conflict of Interest The authors declare no conflicts of interest.

Appendix: Interview Protocol

Characteristics of the respondent

1. Describe your career path, experience, and basic training
2. What challenges attracted you to the position associated with hospital management?

The configuration of the organizational structure

3. How did you influence the contours of the L&SC organizational structure at its conception? Who are the key stakeholders influencing its configuration? On what basis were the activities that would be integrated into this L&SC division decided?
4. Since the first configuration, have new activities been added to the L&SC management structure? Why were these activities added? What are the reasons for these organizational changes?

Presence on the steering committee

5. If you are on the steering committee, what are the benefits that you get? Do you feel that you have an influence on your institution's strategic direction?
6. If you are not on the steering committee, what are the disadvantages of not being on the steering committee? How can you change this situation?

The performance of L&SC management

7. How do you feel the organizational structure of management has impacted the following dimensions of performance? Provide examples to illustrate your points.

- Efficiency: reduction in the price of purchases
- Efficiency: reduction of the operating costs of logistics activities
- Economies of scale: increasing the service offer with equivalent resources
- User satisfaction?
- Legal disputes with suppliers?

8. In general, what are the benefits and limitations of the organizational structure of your L&SC department?

References

1. Amaya C, Beaulieu M, Landry S, Rebolledo C, Velasco N (2010) Potenciando la contribución de la logística hospitalaria: tres casos, tres trayectorias. Int Manag 14(4):85–98
2. Aubry M, Lavoie-Tremblay M (2018) Rethinking organizational design for managing multiple project. Int J Project Manag 36(1):12–26
3. Bals L, Laine J, Mugurusi G (2018) Evolving purchasing and supply organizations: a contingency model for structural alternatives. J Purch Supply Manag 24(1):41–58
4. Beaulieu M, Bentaha O (2021) Digitalization of the healthcare supply chain: a roadmap to generate benefits and effectively support healthcare delivery. Technol Forecast Soc Chang 167, 120717
5. Beaulieu M, Bentahar O, Benzidia S (2020) The evolution of healthcare logistics: the Canadian experience. J Appl Bus Econ 22(14):196–202
6. Beaulieu M, Roy J, Landry S, Michaud M, Roy C (2014) La logistique hospitalière au Québec: passé, présent et futur. Gestion 39(3):56–62
7. Beaulieu M, Landry S (2002) Comment gérer la logistique hospitalière? Deux pays, deux réalités. Gestion 27(3):91–98
8. Beaulieu M, Roy J (2022) Le développement d'une stratégie logistique dans un établissement de santé: étude exploratoire et avenues de recherche. Manag Avenir Santé 9(1):13–35
9. Beaulieu M, Roy J (2015) Benchmarking de la gestion des achats et des stocks en milieu hospitalier: une démarche canadienne. Logist Manag 23(3):17–27
10. Beeler L, Zablah A, Johnston WJ (2017) How critical events shape the evolution of sales organizations: a case study of a business-to-business services firm. J Bus Res 74:66–76
11. Cooper MC, Lambert DM, Pagh JD (1997) Supply chain management: more than a new name for logistics. Int J Logist Manag 8(1):1–14
12. Derwik P, Hellströ D, Karlsson S (2016) Manager competences in logistics and supply chain practice. J Bus Res 69(11):482–4825
13. Ebrahimi SM, Koh SCL, Genovese A, Kumar N (2018) Structure-integration relationships in oil and gas supply chains. Int J Oper Prod Manag 38(2):424–445
14. Eisenhardt KM, Graebner ME (2007) Theory building from cases: opportunities and challenges. Acad Manag J 50(1):25–32
15. Ellram LM, Harland CM, van Weele A, Essig M, Johnsen T, Nassimbeni G, Pagell M, van Raaij E, Rozemeijer F, Tate W, Wynstra F (2020) Purchasing and supply management's identity: crisis? What crisis? J Purchas Supply Manag 26(1):100583
16. Esper TL, Defee CC, Mentzer JT (2010) A framework of supply chain orientation. Int J Logist Manag 21:161–179
17. Fibuch E, Ahmed A (2015) Health care's supply chain: issues to consider. Phys Leadersh J 2(6):26–30
18. Germain R, Dröge C, Daugherty PJ (1994) The effect of just-in-time selling on organizational structure: an empirical investigation. J Mark Res 31(4):471–483

19. Girin J (1989) "L'opportunisme méthodique dans les recherches sur la gestion des organisations, La recherche-action en action et en question, AFCET, Collège de systémique, École Centrale de Paris, 10 mars
20. Glock CH, Hochrein S (2011) Purchasing organization and design: a literature review. Bus Res 4(2):149–191
21. Hall RH (1999) Organizations, structures, processes and outcomes, 7th edn. Prentice Hall, Upper Saddle River
22. Johnson PF, Shafiq A, Awaysheh A, Leenders MR (2014) Supply organization in North America: a 24 year perspective on roles and responsibilities 1987–2011. J Purch Supply Manag 20(2):130–141
23. Kim SW (2007) Organizational structures and the performance of supply chain management. Int J Prod Econ 106(2):323–345
24. Klüppel LM, Pierce L, Snyder JA (2018) The deep historical roots of organization and strategy: traumatic shocks, culture, and institutions. Organ Sci 29(4):702–721
25. Knoppen D, Sáenz MJ (2015) Purchasing: can we bridge the gap between strategy and daily reality? Bus Horiz 58(1):123–133
26. Kwon IWG, Kim SH, Martin DG (2016) Healthcare supply chain management; strategic areas for quality and financial improvement. Technol Forecast Soc Change 113:422–428
27. Landry S, Beaulieu M (2018) Formulation et mise en œuvre d'une stratégie logistique hospitalière: un exemple d'industrialisation. Manag Avenir Santé 3(1):31–48
28. Landry S, Beaulieu M (1999) L'approvisionnement face aux bouleversements du secteur de la santé. Revue Int de l'Achat 19(3/4):17–25
29. Liao S, Widowati R (2021) A supply chain management study: a review of theoretical models from 2014 to 2019. Oper Supply Chain Manag: Int J 14(2):173–188
30. Luzzini D, Ronchi S (2006) Cinderella purchasing transformation: linking purchasing status to purchasing practices and business performance. Prod Plann Control 27(10):787–796
31. McCue CP, Pitzer JT (2000) Centralized vs. decentralized purchasing: current trends in governmental procurement practices. J Public Budg Account Financ Manag 12(3):400–420
32. Miles MB, Hubermann AM, Saldana J (2013) Qualitative data analysis: a methods sourcebook. SAGE Publications, Thousand Oaks, CA
33. Nakano M, Matsuyama K (2021) Internal supply chain structure design: a multiple case study of Japanese manufacturers. Int J Logist 24(1):79–101
34. Paquette J, Roy J, Beaulieu M (2015) Gestion du transport intersites: le secteur des services peut apprendre de celui de la santé. Gestion 39(4):36–43
35. Pearson JN, Gritzmacher KJ (1990) Integrating purchasing into strategic management. Long Range Plan 23(3):91–99
36. Richter P (2021) Shared services: configurations, dynamics and performance. Balt J Manag 16(4):501–518
37. Srivastava S, Garg D, Agarwal A (2021) A step towards responsive healthcare supply chain management: an overview. In: Singari RM, Mathiyazhagan K, Kumar H, (eds). Advances in manufacturing and industrial engineering. Lecture Notes in Mechanical Engineering, Springer
38. Strikwerda J, Stoelhorst JW (2009) The emergence and evolution of the multidimensional organization. Calif Manag Rev 51(4):11–31
39. Tchokogué A, Paché G, Nollet J, Stoleru RM (2017) Intra-organizational legitimization strategies used by purchasing managers. J Purch Supply Manag 23(3):163–175
40. Tchokogué A, Nollet J, Gobeil K (2011) Supply structure: the pendulum in action. J Purch Supply Manag 17(3):148–157
41. Trent RJ (2004) The use of organizational design features in purchasing and supply management. J Supply Chain Manag 40(3):4–18
42. Turkulainen V, Roh J, Whipple JM, Swink M (2017) Managing internal supply chain integration: integration mechanisms and requirements. J Bus Logist 38(4):290–309
43. Wagner SM, Kemmerling R (2014) Supply chain management executives in corporate upper echelons. J Purch Supply Manag 20(3):156–166

44. Wilson K, Barbat V (2015) The supply chain manager as political-entrepreneur? Ind Mark Manag 49:67–79
45. Yin RK (2009) Case study research: design and methods, 4th edn. SAGE Publications, Thousand Oaks, CA
46. Yokl RT (2011) The future of supply chain expense management. Healthc Financ Manag 65(3):38–40

Martin Beaulieu (M.Sc.) is a Research Associate at HEC Montréal's Supply Chain Research Group. His research focuses on supply chain integration dynamics. He is a noted researcher on supply chain management and healthcare operations management with numerous articles and case studies published in the last two decades as well as government commissioned studies. Amongst other outlets, he has published in journals such as the International Journal of Operations and Production Management, Supply Chain Management: An International Journal, Journal of Purchasing and Supply Management, International Journal of Logistics Management or IEEE Transactions on Engineering Management.

Omar Bentahar Received the Ph.D. degree in management sciences from the University of Caen Normandie, Caen, France, in 2011. He is currently a Full Professor of project and supply chain management with the IAE Metz/Université de Lorraine, Metz, France, and a Member of the European Centre CEREFIGE. He has authored or coauthored papers published in journals, including IEEE Transactions on Engineering Management, Technological Forecasting and Social Change, or Annals of Operations Research. His research interests include management of complex projects and supply chain digitalization. Dr. Bentahar is the Co-Founder of the International Conference PROLOG: "Project & Logistics."

Smail Benzidia Received the Ph.D. degree in management sciences from Aix Marseille University, Marseille, France, in 2010. He is currently a Full Professor of supply chain management with the University of Lorraine/IAE Metz, Metz, France, and a Member of the European Centre CEREFIGE. He is a Co-Founder of the International Conference PROLOG: "Project Logistic." He has authored or coauthored several papers published in academic journals and conference proceedings. His research interests include interorganizational information systems, development of E-business, especially the business model of electronic marketplaces, and collaborative supply chain management.

Care Unit Implementation Strategies to Optimise the Design for Healthcare Facilities

2

Lamia Triqui

Healthy citizens are the greatest asset any country can have.

Winston Churchill

Abstract

Health coverage is one of the most discussed topics and the major priorities for public authorities and individuals in communities and countries around the world. The distribution of healthcare resources has posed enormous challenges to the efficiency and equity of healthcare services at the inter-regional level. Decisions related to the location of healthcare services are very important and have become quite critical for policymakers as they affect the direct and social costs of the well-being of the inhabitants of the region. In this chapter, we have sought to optimize the location of different healthcare units in a healthcare network: hospitals, secondary health centres, laboratories, pharmacies, distribution platforms for paramedical equipment, and waste disposal centers for hospital waste. The aim of this area is to serve the population through health services and to ensure equitable access between different places of residence, based on allocation location models and their variants. Then, the authors present the new trends that accompany the configuration of health networks such as cloud computing, blockchain, and cooperation. The authors present the impact of these technologies and approaches and their major role in the continuous

L. Triqui (✉)
Manufacturing Engineering Laboratory of Tlemcen (MELT), Abou Bekr Belkaid University of Tlemcen, Tlemcen, Algeria
e-mail: Lamia.triqui@univ-tlemcen.dz

F. Jawab (ed.), *Hospital Supply Chain*, Integrated Science 27,
https://doi.org/10.1007/978-3-031-70292-1_2

improvement of care units by providing the networks with more communication, traceability, and efficiency through information exchange and the exchange of resources. These considerably improve and increase this sector to allow optimal decision-making and optimal location decisions.

Keywords

Healthcare facility location • Healthcare resources • Healthcare unit management • Decision-making • New trends of care units

Abbreviations

CPLP	Capacitated plant location problem
FCFLP	Fixed charge facility location problem
UCFLP	Uncapacitated fixed charge facility location problem
CCCP	Capacitated centered clustering problem
AI	Artificial intelligence
IT	Information technology

1 Introduction

Hospital logistics is a cross-functional function and a performance driver within the hospital. It aims for continuous improvement in overall performance, where activities are organized and structured around the patient. In other words, hospital logistics ensure that all services operate efficiently, guaranteeing quality and safety at the lowest possible cost [14, 22]. Logistics activities in healthcare facilities are evolving day by day, widening their range through the variation and diversification of the activities. According to Rivard-Royer and Beaulieu [34], logistics in healthcare establishments can take a variety of forms and there are no clear limits to its activities; the objective is to provide the best possible care for patients in all internal and external care units. Optimizing the supply chain for care units is essential to ensure efficient operation and maximum quality of care. Health systems, therefore, adopt strategies for implementing care units that aim to improve the quality of care, operational efficiency, and patient satisfaction.

It is often impossible to offer healthcare services in every area of a country or region, due to various constraints and limitations such as the unavailability of material and human resources, including the lack of qualified medical staff, medical equipment, and medicines, which are often limited. Additionally, low population density in rural or isolated areas exacerbates these challenges. Another point concerns geographical accessibility, especially in mountainous regions, which requires significant investment in terms of construction, equipment, and staff to run healthcare installations. Security and stability issues in areas affected by natural disasters or humanitarian crises further compound the problem, compromising the safety

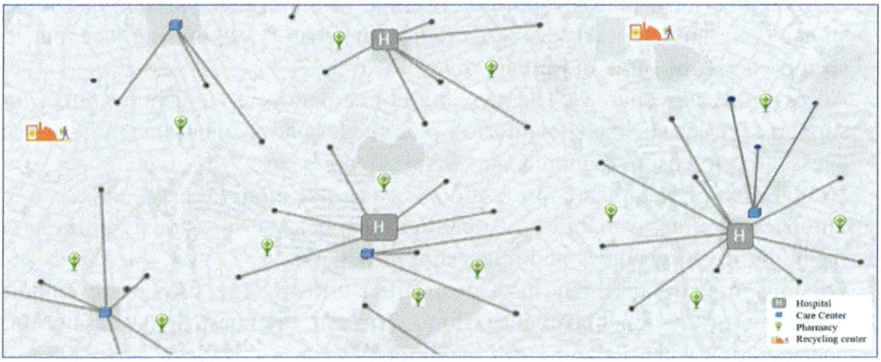

Fig. 1 Spatial allocation of healthcare resources

of healthcare staff and the protection of medical facilities, making it impossible to provide healthcare services. Therefore, it is difficult to distribute them evenly throughout an area, especially in isolated or underdeveloped regions. Overall, providing healthcare services everywhere can be a challenge for healthcare supply chains due to these factors. However, efforts are often made to extend access to healthcare.

The question of healthcare coverage is one of persistent problems facing countries around the world. The inappropriate allocation of healthcare resources has become quite critical for policymakers. To address this concern, one of the strategic challenges for configuring healthcare chains concerns the choice of locations for healthcare sites, drug distribution platforms, or medical equipment supply warehouses. In this context, several optimization approaches are studied in the literature concerning the spatial allocation of healthcare resources such as hospitals, care units, and pharmaceutical platforms (Fig. 1) in order to maximize population coverage of healthcare services.

The location of care units depends on several factors, including the population served, accessibility, the health needs of the community, available resources, and public health policies. Decisions about where to locate care units are very important and highly strategic, as they condition decisions about how to ensure efficient and equitable provision of healthcare services. Some factors are necessary when making decisions about future locations:

a. Population density: the location of care units is generally linked to the concentration of the population in a geographical area. The choice of site takes into account the area with the highest population density to offer a service to the greatest number of people while reducing travel times for patients.
b. Accessibility of means of transport: one of the conditions that has a considerable influence on the choice of locations is the availability of roads, public transport infrastructure, and parking facilities.

c. Geographical distribution: optimal coverage of care units must be distributed strategically and equitably across a region or territory, taking into account the specific needs of rural and urban areas.
d. Accessibility to resources: The proximity of care units to medical resources and support services such as laboratories, pharmacies and medical imaging services is essential to ensure comprehensive and effective care.
e. Availability of healthcare professionals: The location of care units can be influenced by the availability of qualified healthcare professionals in the area, including doctors, nurses and other care providers.
f. Existing infrastructure: The use of existing infrastructure such as community health centres, regional hospitals or long-term care facilities can be an important consideration when locating new care units.
g. Community involvement: Involving the community in the siting process can help ensure that care units respond to local needs and concerns, which can promote acceptance and use of healthcare services.
h. In summary, the location of care units should be based on a thorough assessment of the population's needs, accessibility, available resources and community involvement to ensure effective and equitable delivery of healthcare services.

2 Implementation of Care Units Localisation-Allocation

Location is often perceived as the crucial element in the success of an organisation, regardless of its size, maturity or managerial positioning. The challenge of choosing sites for the completion and establishment of an organisation lies in determining the site's strategic position within a region. These decisions are planned at a strategic level in the decision-making hierarchy of a healthcare organization, which is why the latter is concerned with optimizing it to ensure efficiency at the tactical and operational levels. The term localization refers to the determination of the location of sites, which may be sites for the provision of healthcare services or sites for the distribution of pharmaceutical products or pharmacies that ensure the availability of medicines in an area (see Fig. 2). The term allocation refers to the assignment of individuals or customers to treatment sites (hospitals, health centers) or to annex pharmacy, radiology, and other platforms (see Fig. 3).

Location and allocation are problems that can be addressed in two different ways: the first is to find the optimal allocation of new health resources [9]. The second is to reallocate existing health resources according to dynamic criteria and constraints [5, 30, 43] that could significantly improve efficiency and equity. The main questions to ask in order to minimize the resulting costs are:

- How many sites should be opened?
- Where should they be located?
- How should customers be allocated?

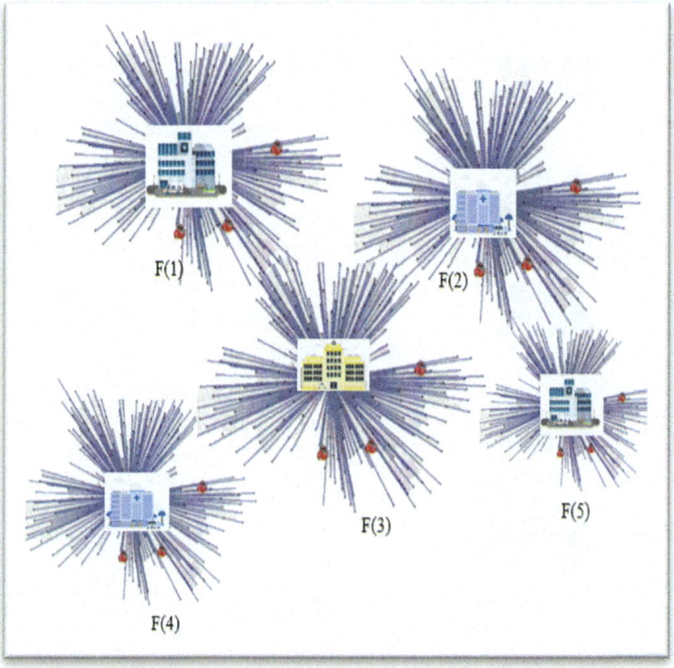

Fig. 2 The location of sites

The main objectives of location-allocation models are to determine the number of sites to be located while optimizing the distance between these sites (supply points) and a set of customers (patients), and then to optimize the allocation of customers to these sites in order to determine the supply capacity of the sites. The installation and opening of a site require a rigorous study because of the colossal investment and costs involved in building and commissioning the care site. Each site requires highly specialized logistics and management, including equipping the site with qualified staff and ensuring that all means of transport to the site are available. Each site will have a shop containing all the equipment needed for care, blood banks, and warehouses for parpharmaceutical products with high levels of security, including extensive sterilization stations and additional equipment such as gowns, gloves, and disinfectants to ensure very high standards of hygiene. In addition, each site installed is accompanied by a fair and sufficient location of pharmacies in the region for better care and continuous improvement of the quality of life of citizens. Location-allocation models are generally based on five basic components:

- The objective function: which incorporates the distance separating customers from potential site locations, transport costs, transport times, etc.
- Demand points: these generally correspond to densely populated areas.

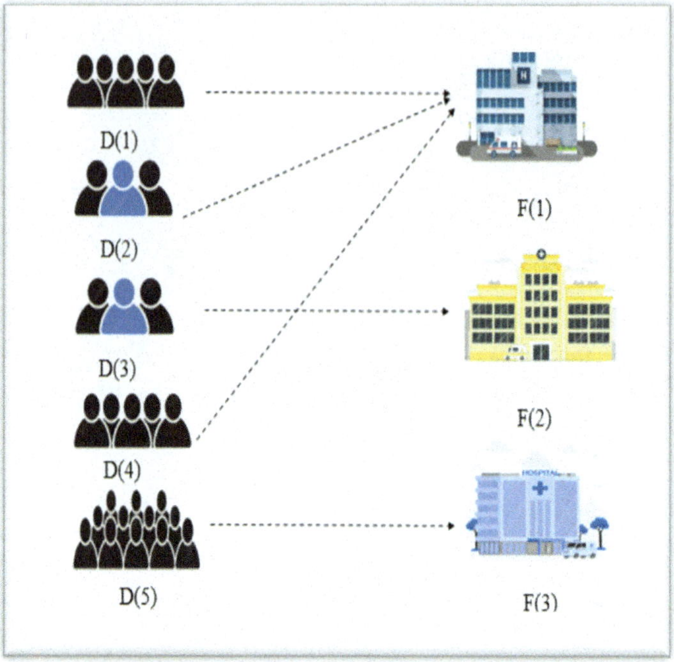

Fig. 3 The assignment of individuals to sites

- Potential locations: these are the possible distances between sites in terms of land availability, cost, accessibility, etc.
- Distance or time matrix: this matrix shows the geographical or temporal distance separating potential locations from points of demand.
- Allocation rule: this rule shows the way in which potential locations are allocated to points of demand (for example, the allocation rule may be based on geographical proximity, in which case each customer will use the point of supply closest to their home).

The origins of location-allocation models go back to [44], he was one of the founders of the localisation problem. His first works were dedicated to describing the optimal location of each warehouse in order to minimise the costs between warehouses and different customers. Subsequently, several researchers interested in this type of problem developed a whole line of research. One of the best-known works is that proposed by [19, 20]. Is the researcher, who developed a mathematical model of the P-median problem aimed to locate P facilities in order to minimise the sum of the total distances between each point of demand and the nearest installation. Based on this principle, several researchers have introduced the P-median location allocation model into the hospital chain [1]. Among the work carried out in this direction, we can cite [35], Several mathematical formulations have been provided to address location and allocation decisions within a hospital supply chain established in Turkey. Other studies have been carried out by Güneş and Nickel [18], who collected existing work in this area, and [23], who determined the optimal location of facilities to ensure equitable allocation to each facility. Marić et al. [27] studied the problem of locating long-term healthcare facilities by focusing on the minimax of the number of patients in each facility. Ndiaye and Alfares [29] presented a model for the location of facilities with seasonal operation. Brancolini et al. [6] compare different strategies and their effects on strategic, tactical and operational location decisions. Chou et al. [10] tested the impact of strategic tactical decision making in a multi-criteria context. [8] analysed the strategic location of existing facilities on a network in order to determine the position and quantity of new facilities that both ensure medical coverage while minimising the different costs. Sonmez and Lim [37], proposing future extensions for new facilities, taking into account the initial facilities based on demographic estimation in a region with the objective of minimizing weighted customer travel distances over the entire planning horizon. Multi-objective and multi-criteria optimization approaches have been adopted by [16] and [45]. Syam and Cote [39] proposed a model that maximizes both efficiency and coverage of facilities. The authors have provided a model for locating health services, Syam and Côté [40] taking into consideration levels of activity and acuity. Zhang et al. [46] mentioned the inequality of access to quality care that differs from one site to another in the allocation. Jay Pan et al. [32] studied the location and allocation of newly added sites that preserve the best quality of health.

The p-median problem, developed by Hakimi in 1964, was the first localisation and allocation model [19]. It serves as a reference and a basic model for the various extensions developed subsequently. Obviously, from this p-median model, several variants have been determined according to the different constraints to be considered and the additional parameters to be taken into account. This has resulted in a wide variety of models in the literature that can be used in practice. In what follows, the authors list some of the most relevant to the medical field: starting with the basic P-median problem, followed by a presentation of the P-centre problem, then the set covering problem, another type of problem that deals with the location of the two-level site, and ending with the centred clustering with capacity problem (CCCP). For each problem, we will reference its usefulness in the health service network.

2.1 The P-Median/P-Center Problem

2.1.1 P-Median

The P-median is one of the basic models for location problems, which consists of locating P hospitals on P candidate sites in order to optimise the travel routes and the time taken between the location of one hospital and the surrounding customers (demand zones) [15] by selecting P locations for the facilities. The main objective is to ensure the coverage of health services in a region that maximises customer satisfaction while minimising costs and total travel distances for the population [7, 11]. The P-median has the advantage of being easily adaptable to the specific requirements of the user and of being solved by efficient, fast, and flexible methods [21]. The model not only makes it possible to consider the shape of zones and optimal locations but also to suggest the ideal number of services and to simulate solutions under various constraints and hypotheses. The problem is therefore to choose the geographical configuration of the supply units in order to minimise the sum of the distances travelled. P-median model is designed to guarantee efficient coverage of the environment. (mathematical model in appendix I.a).

2.1.2 P-Center

The p-centre is a variant of the p-median problem, where the objective function aims to optimise and minimise the longest route between clients and predetermined care units or hospitals from a set of P pre-selected establishments. (mathematical model in appendix I.b).

The two models, p-median and p-center, are used to solve location problems; they differ in their objectives and in their flexibility approach. The P-median selects a set of new sites from among several possibilities, to carry out the installations, while the p-center model attempts to determine the best location within a group of existing installations to minimise the distance between customers and installations. Both the p-median and p-center models are highly suitable for locating hospitals in a region. Knowing that the installation of hospitals must respond to a massive grouping and a very important investment, to determine the most suitable location, we use the two variants of the problem, p-median and p-centre, to find the best location in relation to all the districts and towns in a region or city.

2.2 Set Covering Problem

One of the extensions of P median is the "set covering problem", which was developed to ensure coverage of all zones of demand. (mathematical model in appendix I.c) which consists of covering all customers. Guan et al. [17] minimizing location costs. The maximum coverage problem aims to maximize all demand areas that can be served by as many facilities as possible. The central "minimax problem" aims to minimize the distances between care units and customers as much as possible.

The "set covering problem" was first formulated by [41]. Several authors have used this model in the literature. The objective is to determine a minimum-cost covering. An example of application is the opening of a number of secondary health and care centers. These centres are relay unit care that provide a range of basic services such as care, radiology examinations, dentists, ophthalmologists, and pediatric emergencies. But they do not carry out surgical procedures or advanced emergency care, which are tasks that fall to higher-priority organizations such as hospitals and clinics equipped with operating theaters and suitable equipment and qualifications for this type of intervention. Decision-makers are trying to increase population satisfaction in a region made up of several demand zones. It aims to determine the minimum resources required to serve all customers with the same quality of service. In contrast to the classical coverage problem, the "maximum coverage problem" aims to serve as many customers as possible from the chosen locations, as described by [36] who applied the principle using an approach based on genetic algorithms in the healthcare facility. The maximal covering problem model has been widely applied to the installation of mobile centers with mental health platforms, especially in disasters or in regions of war, or the installation of hospitals and mobile care units, which are highly desired. The problems of overlap, P-median, and center, presented above, form a solid basis for the deterministic models encountered in the theory of location problems. (mathematical model in appendix I.c).

2.3 Two-Level Location Problem

The two-level location problem generally encountered is the ≪ Fixed Charge Facility Location Problem ≫ (mathematical model in appendix I.d). This is another category of extensions to location problems. Its principle is to identify the best possible combination of locations for fixed sites, taking transport into account, and then to distribute the different areas of demand in order to minimise location and transport costs. For this problem, all the data is known deterministically. The objective is to find the best locations for the sites (hospital/pharmacy, hospital/supply system, etc.) and the modes of transport to be used to serve the different areas of demand while minimising the fixed location and transport costs under the constraint that all the demands are satisfied.

The objective is to locate sites with limited capacity while respecting the storage requirements, which can generate significant costs. This problem is widely used when it comes to setting up pharmacies, for example, taking into account the installation of a health centre or hospital, or even the installation of mobile collection sites containing the fixed location of the blood bank. This problem can also be applied to the installation of hospital waste treatment areas, which requires joint optimisation between the installed care site and ancillary sites such as pharmacies, hospital and medical equipment platforms, etc. in terms of distance and capacity of the centres.

Other variants exist depending on the nature of the added constraint, such as the Capacitated Plant Location Problem (CPLP), (mathematical model in appendix I.f) which is one of the versions of the FCFLP problem, under different stochastic scenarios with random demands. For the (CPLP) problem classes, a restrictive assumption imposes that care units and distribution centres have finite capacities. This problem forms the basis of many location problems in supply chain design. Sridharan [38] carried out a comprehensive literature search of the different methods used and algorithms developed to solve the (CPLP). Banthao and Jittamai [2] determined the location of blood banks and the allocation of hospitals to these blood banks [12]. The authors addressed a continuous location allocation problem involving multiple facilities, where they considered demand zones with the single allocation constraint. Berman et al. [4] formulated a model to find the optimal allocation between a set of patients and a healthcare institution. Li et al. [25] provide an innovative two-stage approach to optimize decisions about both the location and capacity of healthcare facilities. There are other types of problems such as the problem where site capacity is unlimited, known as the "uncapacitated fixed charge facility location problem (UCFLP)", or the problem formulation does not take the constraint related to site capacity into account. In most works, researchers assume that each client is served by one and only one care center (hospital).

2.4 Capacitated Centred Clustering Problem (CCCP)

The Capacity Centred Clustering Problem (CCCP) consists of distributing and fractioning a set of locations (n points) into clusters (p groups). which minimise the total distance between each location and the chosen centre and respect the capacity of each centre [33]. The objective of the CCCP (mathematical model in appendix I.g) is to determine the optimal displacement within each group (cluster), without exceeding the tolerated capacity of a cluster (Fig. 4).

This problem is often used to determine the pharmaceutical network of a city. Where all pharmacies closest in distance are grouped together in a customer cluster with the condition that the sum of orders from different pharmacies is less than the capacity of the cluster centre (Fig. 4). This type of problem can be referred to as a multi-level allocation location problem. The first level involves choosing a set of pharmaceutical wholesalers from several candidate wholesalers and assigning them to a cluster [31]. The second level involves allocating the different customers (all retailers) in a cluster to the localized wholesalers while respecting cost and time.

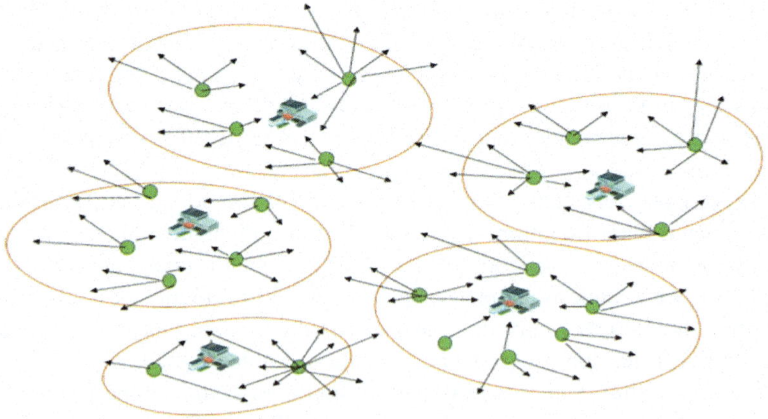

Fig. 4 Representing a cluster of customers

2.5 Synthesis of Localisation-Allocation Problem

In reality, medical facilities are limited by their capacity. Increased demand due to population growth and urbanization will create operational capacity constraints over time. New facilities must therefore be added to maintain satisfactory service levels. If this does not take into account future increases in demand and decisions about additional equipment are only made when new demand arises, previously optimal decisions will remain suboptimal in the long term. Patients may be transferred to a newly built remote facility from that location when existing nearby facilities are at capacity, in which case future needs must be taken into account for facility location and long-term optimal patient allocation decisions.

3 New Trends in the Strategic Management of the Implementation and Location of Care Units

Care unit implementation strategies aim to improve the quality of care, operational efficiency, and patient satisfaction. Of course, to ensure the efficient operation of care units, certain basic strategies must be respected. These include analyzing needs and planning to ensure the supply of equipment and various medicines, taking into account the number of patients, the most common treatments, medical conditions, etc. The second point concerns stock management, which ensures that various products are obtained efficiently and in real-time, in accordance with appropriate restocking and ordering policies to avoid shortages and stockpiling. It is necessary to ensure and rely on well-trained staff, be they nurses, doctors, or any other person involved in a care unit, where everyone has to do their job rigorously. Another key strategy in care units is quality monitoring and continuous improvement, which can be implemented based on the results of quality assessments and safety actions to minimize the risks and dysfunctions that can occur and affect the functioning of these units.

New areas of strategic improvement have been introduced as a result of current developments in technological equipment, where several technologies have been adopted to facilitate the management of different units, accompanied by an improvement in the quality of life of patients and individuals by relieving administrative bodies such as health insurance and the cnas. These new technologies rely heavily on the technical and IT optimisation of the interconnections between the various care units: hospitals, health centres, pharmacies and waste disposal centres (the technical interconnections can be resolved by the allocation localisation problems cited previously). However, the technological interconnections are mainly due to the IT tools that have contributed greatly to this development by adopting Cloud computing technology, the blockchain or even the use of cooperative approaches through inter-professional and inter-organisational collaboration. In what follows, we will provide an overview of the impact of these three new trends on healthcare networks.

3.1 Cloud Computing in Medical Services

- The current competition between organisations is trying to adopt the most elaborate and revolutionary new technologies within their departments and organisations with a view to continuously improving customer service quality.This has given rise to the fourth industrial revolution, which has enabled billions of devices to be connected between doctors, pharmacists and National Social Security Funds services. This interconnection has been established through the use of Cloud Computing to ensure better interconnection between the different links in the medical supply chain to achieve total patient satisfaction.
- Cloud computing is an infrastructure that connects a set of clients and users to storage spaces hosted on remote servers, which are managed by remote servers. Access to these spaces is made via a secure internet link using desktop computers, laptops, mobile phones, touch-screen tablets, etc. These clouds are equipped with large storage capacity and a great computing power [24, 26, 28].

Cloud computing enables files to be stored and data to be shared within an organization, with separate locations. It offers a range of related services, including allocated storage space, a messaging service, collaborative tools, agility, availability, production, and customer relations. Cloud hosting is a service model designed to enable different users to register for access to databases and applications on servers via the Internet, using central software where processes are filtered and redirected to the appropriate hardware, which can be accessed according to demand and usage. Cloud hosting eliminates the need for a direct link to the physical infrastructure. In the context of healthcare network management, it would be necessary to link the doctor and patient to the pharmacist (Fig. 5) on an IT basis, in able to direct patients in a more appropriate way between hospital pharmacy, between radiology, respecting the load of the different points and limiting the risk of error. This model offers greater flexibility, guaranteed scalability and high availability for users, making it a popular option for many organizations, particularly in the healthcare sector, where all individuals are closely involved with this vital service.

All this work will be carried out over a network and could even be operated by a third-party application on a smartphone or other communication device, in order to provide the patient with the information they need to feel better and to generally satisfy them.

3.2 Blockchain Technology and Medical Services

Today's hospitals and medical services are faced with a gigantic task: managing billions of pieces of medical data, much of it confidential. This data is essential for medical research and the creation of innovations in healthcare. A concrete example of this is the creation of a shared hospital medical file, which enables patient health information to be transferred effortlessly and securely across a given territory.

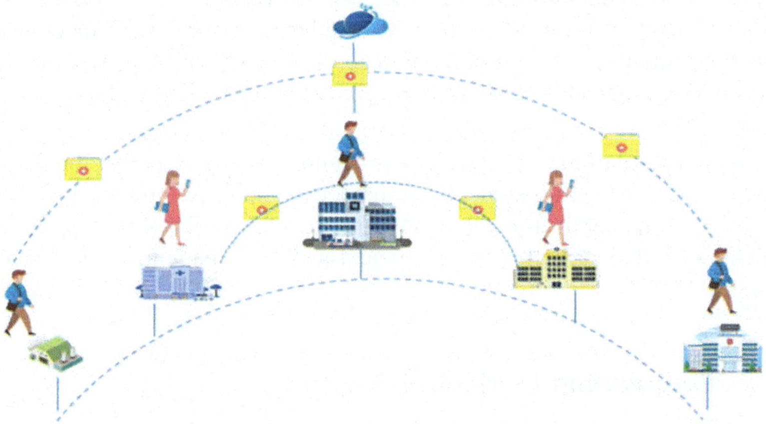

Fig. 5 Linked to physical servers

Blockchain is an innovative technology that enables value to be redistributed between different players with maximum transparency. Blockchain is a database distributed over a network of blocks, where each block is a "smart contract", defined as a type of digital contract manifested by codes inscribed in a blockchain, enabling the automated transfer of assets from one entity to another according to predefined management rules. This network is often likened to a register in which all the data or transactions exchanged/pass within an organization and its external environment are recorded [13].

One of the thorniest issues in healthcare is striking a balance between the confidentiality of medical data and the ease of access to electronic medical records. The rules on privacy and medical confidentiality vary from one jurisdiction to another. In addition, records are currently spread across many different IT solutions. The aim is to use blockchain to establish a completely transparent and secure link between the various parties involved—patients, hospitals, researchers and, of course, healthcare practitioners—with the aim of enhancing the value of healthcare data with the consent of all concerned.

Example 1 Blockchain could be used to ensure the traceability of medicines. Laboratories could register drugs manufactured on blockchain before they are marketed. Pharmaceutical companies could then check that batches of drugs have been manufactured by an authorised laboratory. Lastly, consumers buying the drugs could check how the product was distributed, and pharmacists would be able to find it easily in the event of a batch being recalled.

Example 2 Blockchain would encourage the interoperability of patient medical records between the various players in the healthcare sector. Health insurance companies and mutual societies could automate the repayment of healthcare costs as soon as eligible medical procedures are recorded in the patient's file.

The digital revolution in healthcare has begun, and it is changing the way health authorities, medical establishments, insurance companies, and patients interact. Blockchain and its applications in healthcare are a fundamental part of this revolution, helping to deliver better, more efficient and more patient-focused healthcare system.

3.3 Cooperation in Medical Services

Cooperation in a network is a collective approach directed towards a common goal, where sharing information and resources helps decision-making. Cooperation in the care service is intended to present all the cooperation mechanisms used by hospitals to share and make available to each other the resources available. These resources take several forms, which are expressed by the sharing of material resources (such as laboratories, emergency medicines, ambulances, or mobile blood) or human resources (nurses) with a high degree of competence and practical skills.

Cooperation projects between hospital establishments result from local initiatives, motivated in particular by the proximity of the structures, as well as by the potential for complementarity identified. Their aim is to bring real added value to hospital technical platforms and care teams improving patient care, by adopting a quality of care approach to services and facilities.

Cooperation between healthcare professionals provides an innovative response to the expectations of patients and professionals alike, and helps to broaden the range of care provided, reduce the time taken to access care, and therefore improve healthcare pathways. This enables the delegating professional (usually a doctor) to refocus on situations requiring greater expertise, and the delegated healthcare professional to develop new skills. Cooperation also makes it possible to delegate certain activities to paramedical staff that were previously carried out solely by doctors. This enables the delegating professional (usually a doctor) to refocus on situations requiring greater expertise, and the delegated healthcare professional to develop new skills. Cooperation also makes it possible to delegate to paramedical staff certain activities that were previously carried out solely by doctors.

The implementation of one or more cooperation protocols can be described by contracts and profit allocations expressing a remuneration for the team to be distributed between the team members according to the methods of their choice to ensure profitability and encourage the participants to collaborate and generate a "win–win" situation which can be selected at the end of a negotiation process between the parties [3, 42].

4 Conclusion

Many countries around the world have recognized that optimizing the accessibility of healthcare services and promoting equity are persistent challenges. The choice to establish a health center has social and economic implications for the local community over the long term. The location of hospitals and their ability to deliver health care are crucial to extending the population's coverage of health services. One of the preoccupations of decision-makers and politicians in order to guarantee a better quality of life for citizens. The choice of geographical location of sites is very important, as we need to take into account the costs of setting up the facilities, while at the same time ensuring greater profitability in the future. In addition, decisions concerning the location of healthcare facilities for patients have a relevant consequence on people's lives and health.

In this chapter, we have addressed the different problems of locating the most frequently used allocations in healthcare networks: hospitals, health centers, pharmacies, laboratories, distribution platforms for para-medical products, etc. We have highlighted effective optimization approaches to maximize population coverage of health services and improve equity of spatial access. These models need to be applied in the field by political decision-makers, particularly in the health sector, in order to establish an equitable and rational allocation of healthcare resources. These decisions need to be taken within the framework of a strategic and dynamic planning approach, in order to guarantee an equitable distribution of healthcare services in a region where urbanization and demographic growth are increasing daily.

The author have highlighted the new technologies and new trends within its networks that greatly facilitate and improve the management and strategies developed by the medical sector. More specifically, we introduced the impact of Cloud Computing, blockchain and cooperation, which improves the quality of service, the quality of care and helps to promote sectors while minimising costs and increasing the satisfaction and quality of care of individuals.

Appendix

I.a—**P median**

i:	Set of demand zones (customers)
j:	Set of the possible locations for factories
P:	Number of factories to be located
Dem_i:	Total demand of the customer i
CT_{ij}	The total cost of transport from unit j to customer i (which may be the distance between customer i and unit j)
$X_j =$	$\begin{cases} 1 & \text{if unit j is located} \\ 0 & \text{else} \end{cases}$
$Y_{ij} =$	$\begin{cases} 1 & \text{if customer i is served by unit j} \\ 0 & \text{else} \end{cases}$

Objective function

$$Min\ F1 = \sum_{i \in I} \sum_{j \in J} D_i * CT_{ij} * Y_{ij} \tag{1}$$

Under the constraints

$$\sum_{j \in J} Y_{ij} = 1 \quad \forall\, i \in I \tag{1.1}$$

$$\sum_{j \in J} X_j = P \tag{1.2}$$

$$Y_{ij} \le X_j \quad \forall\, i \in I \quad \forall j \in J \tag{1.3}$$

$$X_j \in \{0, 1\} \quad Y_{ij} \in \{0, 1\} \quad \forall\, i \in I \quad \forall j \in J \tag{1.4}$$

I.b P—Center problem
Objective function

$$Min\ D \tag{2}$$

Under the constraints

$$\sum_{j \in J} X_j = P \tag{2.1}$$

$$\sum_{j \in J} Y_{ij} = 1 \quad \forall i \in I \tag{2.2}$$

$$Y_{ij} \le X_j \quad \forall i \in I \quad \forall j \in J \tag{2.3}$$

$$D \ge \sum_{j \in J} CT_{ij} * Y_{ij} \quad \forall i \in I \tag{2.4}$$

$$X_j \in \{0, 1\} \quad Y_{ij} \in \{0, 1\} \quad \forall i \in I \quad \forall j \in J \tag{2.5}$$

Constraints (2.1), (2.2) and (2.3) are identical to constraints (1.1), (1.2) and (1.3) of the median problem, while constraint (2.4) defines the maximum distance between demand zone i and the nearest unit j.

I.c The problem of covering all demand zones:

N_i:	The set of factories j that can serve customer i, i.e. $N_i = \{j \in J / CT_{ij} \le Dmx\}$
Dmx:	Maximum distance for acceptable service time
CL_j	The cost of locating a unit in region j

Objective function

$$Min\ F2 = \sum_{j \in J} CL_j * X_j \tag{3}$$

Under the constraints

$$\sum_{j \in N_i} X_j \ge 1 \quad \forall i \in I \tag{3.1}$$

$$X_j \in \{0, 1\} \quad \forall j \in J \tag{3.2}$$

Constraint (3.1) ensures that each customer i is served by at least one unit j with an acceptable service distance.

I.d The problem of maximizing the rate of coverage demand

N_i:	The set of factories j that can serve customer i,
Dem_i:	Total demand of the customer i
$\mathbf{X_j}$ =	$\begin{cases} 1 & \text{if factory j is located} \\ 0 & \text{else} \end{cases}$
Z_i =	$\begin{cases} 1 & \text{if demand zone i is covered} \\ 0 & \text{else} \end{cases}$

Objective function

$$Max\ F3 = \sum_{i \in I} Dem_i * Z_i \tag{4}$$

Under the constraints

$$Z_i \leq \sum_{j \in N_i} X_j \qquad \forall\, i \in I \tag{4.1}$$

$$\sum_{j \in J} X_j \leq P \tag{4.2}$$

$$X_j \in \{0, 1\} \quad Z_i \in \{0, 1\} \qquad \forall\, i \in I \qquad \forall j \in J \tag{4.3}$$

The aim is to maximize demand coverage, and constraint (4.1) dictates that a demand area i can only be covered (Yi = 1) if there is at least one unit j open at a service distance less than Dmx (i.e. $\forall\, j \in J/X_j = 1$ and $j \in N_i$). If no unit is open, then no demand zone will be covered. Constraint (4.2) limits the number of factories to be opened.

I.e Fixed Charge Facility Location Problem "UCFLP"

$$Min\ F5 = \sum_{j \in J} CL_j * X_j + a * \sum_{i \in I} \sum_{j \in J} Dem_i * CT_{ij} * Y_{ij} \tag{5}$$

Under the constraints

$$\sum_{j \in J} Y_{ij} = 1 \qquad \forall\, i \in I \tag{5.1}$$

$$Y_{ij} \leq X_j \qquad \forall\, i \in I \qquad \forall j \in J \tag{5.2}$$

$$X_j \in \{0, 1\} \quad Y_{ij} \in \{0, 1\} \qquad \forall\, i \in I \qquad \forall j \in J \tag{5.3}$$

where, the unit demand cost per unit distance. It is clear that the (UCFLP) problem is formulated by adding the total fixed cost of locating sites to the objective function of the median problem and removing the constraint limiting the number of sites to be located. Constraints (1.1), (1.2) and (1.3) are identical to those of the median problem.

I.f The Problem CPLP

Cmx_j:	The maximum capacity of the unit j

$$Min\ F6 = \sum_{j \in J} CL_j * X_j + a * \sum_{i \in I} \sum_{j \in J} Dem_i * CT_{ij} * Y_{ij} \tag{6}$$

Under the constraints

$$\sum_{j \in J} Y_{ij} = 1 \qquad \forall\, i \in I \tag{6.1}$$

$$Y_{ij} \leq X_j \qquad \forall\, i \in I \qquad \forall j \in J \tag{6.2}$$

$$a * \sum_{i \in I} Dem_i * Y_{ij} \leq Cmx_j * X_j \quad \forall j \in J \tag{6.3}$$

$$X_j \in \{0, 1\} \quad Y_{ij} \in \{0, 1\} \qquad \forall\, i \in I \qquad \forall j \in J \tag{6.4}$$

where Constraint (1.3) ensures that the sum of demands covered by unit j does not exceed the maximum capacity of that unit.

I.g Capacitated Centred Clustering Problem (CCCP)

m:	Set of clients, m ε M
k:	Set of customers clusters indexed by k, k ε K
l:	Set d products, l ε L
x_m et y_m	Geometric position of customers m
x'_k et y'_k	Geometric position of customer cluster k
Q_k	Capacity of customer cluster k
$DC_{m,l}$	Demand of customer m for the product l
Y_{mk} =	$\begin{cases} 1 \text{ if} \\ 0 \text{ else} \end{cases}$
NC_k	Number of customers assigned to the customers cluster k

$$F7 = \sum_{m \in M} \sum_{k \in K} \left[\left(x_m - x'_k\right)^2 + \left(y_m - y'_k\right)^2 \right] * Y_{m\,k} \tag{7}$$

Under the constraints

$$\sum_{k \in K} Y_{m\,k} = 1 \quad \forall\, m \in M \tag{7.1}$$

$$\sum_{m \in M} Y_{m\,k} = NC_k \quad \forall\, k \in K \tag{7.2}$$

$$\sum_{m \in M} x_m * Y_{m\,k} = NC_k * x'_k \quad \forall\, k \in K \tag{7.3}$$

$$\sum_{m \in M} y_m * Y_{m\,k} \le NC_k * y'_k \quad \forall\, k \in K \tag{7.4}$$

$$\sum_{m \in M} DC_{m\,l} * Y_{m\,k} \le Q_k \quad \forall\, l \in L \quad \forall k \in K \tag{7.5}$$

$$(x_m, y_m) \in R \quad \left(x'_k, y'_k\right) \in R \quad \forall\, m \in M \quad \forall k \in K \tag{7.6}$$

$$Y_{m\,k} \in \{0, 1\} NC_k \in N \quad \forall\, m \in M \quad \forall k \in K \tag{7.7}$$

Equation (7) presents the objective function of the problem, Constraint (7.1) requires each customer to be assigned to a single customer cluster. Constraint (7.2) gives the number of customers in a customer cluster. Constraints (7.3) and (7.4) give the location of the centres of gravity of the customer clusters. Constraint (7.5) imposes that customer demand does not exceed the capacity of the cluster centre allocated to it, and constraints (7.6) and (7.7) define the bounds of the decision variables.

References

1. Ahmadi-Javid A, Seyedi P, Syam SS (2017) A survey of healthcare facility location. Comput Oper Res 79:223–263
2. Banthao J, Jittamai P (2012) An analysis of alternative blood bank locations with emergency referral. In: Proceedings of the world congress on engineering and computer science. vol 2, pp 24–26
3. Benfriha AI, Lamia ST, Bougloula AE, Bennekrouf M (2023) A new green cooperative approach for a multi-levels distribution network: real application. Acad J Manuf Eng 21(3):13
4. Berman O, Drezner Z, Tamir A, Wesolowsky GO (2009) Optimal location with equitable loads. Ann Oper Res 167(1):307–325
5. Bevan G, Hood C (2006) What's measured is what matters: targets and gaming in the English public health care system. Public Adm 84(3):517–538
6. Brancolini A, Buttazzo G, Santambrogio F, Stepanov E (2009) Long-term planning versus short-term planning in the asymptotical location problem. ESAIM: Control Optim Calc Var 15(3):509–524
7. Burkey ML, Bhadury J, Eiselt HA (2012) A location-based comparison of health care services in four U.S. states with efficiency and equity. Soc. Econ. Plann. Sci. 46:157–163
8. Carlo HJ, Aldarondo F, Saavedra PM, Torres SN (2012) Capacitated continuous facility location problem with unknown number of facilities. Eng Manag J 24(3):24–31
9. Chen LT, Zeng HT, Wu LQ, Tian QN, Zhang N, He RX et al (2023) Spatial accessibility evaluation and location optimization of primary healthcare in China: a case study of Shenzhen. GeoHealth 7:e2022GH000753
10. Chou CC (2009) Integrated short-term and long-term MCDM model for solving location selection problems. J Transp Eng 135(11):880–893
11. Deng YF, Zhang YM, Pan J (2021) Optimization for locating emergency medical service facilities: a case study for health planning from China. Risk Manag Healthc Pol 14:1791–1802
12. Dinler D, Tural MK, Iyigun C (2015) Heuristics for a continuous multi-facility location problem with demand regions. Comput Oper Res 62:237–256
13. El Amine BM, Lamia ST (2023) Blockchain adoption for a sustainable agricultural supply chain: opportunities and challenges for the dairy industry. In: 2023 international conference on decision aid sciences and applications (DASA). IEEE, pp 331–336
14. Eskandari-Khanghahi M, Tavakkoli-Moghaddam R, Taleizadeh AA, Amin SH (2018) Designing and optimizing a sustainable supply chain network for a blood platelet bank under uncertainty. Eng Appl Artif Intell 71:236–250
15. Garey MR, Johnson DS (1979) Computers and intractability (Vol. 174). San Francisco: Freeman
16. Gu W, Wang X, McGregor SE (2010) Optimization of preventive health care facility locations. Int J Health Geogr 9(1):1–16
17. Guan X, Bi F, Liu M, Chen H, Zhou L (2018) Study on location allocation of earthquake emergency service depots based on hybrid multi-attribute decision making. Nat Hazards 90:337–348
18. Güneş ED, Nickel S (2015) Location problems in healthcare. In: Laporteo G, Nickel S, Saldanha da Gama F (eds): Location Science. Springer InternationalPublishing, Berlin, pp 555–579
19. Hakimi SL (1964) Optimal location of switching centers and the absolute centers and medians of a graph. Oper Res 12:450–459

20. Hakimi SL (1965) Optimum distribution of switching centers in a communication network and some related graph theoretic problems. Oper Res 13:462–475
21. Hanjoul P, Peeters D (1985) A comparison of two dual-based procedures for solving the p-median problem. Eur J Oper Res 20(3):387–396
22. Heidari-Fathian H, Pasandideh SHR (2018) Green-blood supply chain network design: Robust optimization, bounded objective function and Lagrangian relaxation. Comput Ind Eng 122:95–105
23. Kim DG, Kim YD (2010) A branch and bound algorithm for determining locations of long-term care facilities. Eur J Oper Res 206(1):168–177
24. Kumar S, Goudar RH (2012) Cloud computing-research issues, challenges, architecture, platforms and applications: a survey. Int J Future Comput Commun 1(4):356
25. Li X, Wang FH, Yi H (2017) A two-step approach to planning new facilities towards equal accessibility. Environ Plan B Urban Anal City Sci 44:994–1011
26. Malik MI, Wani SH, Rashid A (2018) Cloud computing-technologies. Int J Adv Res Comput Sci 9(2):379
27. Marić M, Stanimirović Z, Božović S (2015) Hybrid metaheuristic method for determining locations for long-term health care facilities. Ann Oper Res 227(1):3–23
28. Namasudra S (2018) Cloud computing: a new era. J Fundam Appl Sci, 10(2)
29. Ndiaye M, Alfares H (2008) Modeling health care facility location for moving population groups. Comput Oper Res 35(7):2154–2161
30. Oliveira MD, Bevan G (2006) Modelling the redistribution of hospital supply to achieve equity taking account of patient's behaviour. Health Care Manag Sci 9:19–30
31. Özceylan E, Uslu A, Erbaş M, Çetinkaya C, İşleyen SK (2017) Optimizing the location-allocation problem of pharmacy warehouses: A case study in Gaziantep. Int J Optim Control: Theor Appl 7(1): 117–129
32. Pan J, Deng Y, Yang Y, Zhang Y (2023) Location-allocation modelling for rational health planning: applying a two-step optimization approach to evaluate the spatial accessibility improvement of newly added tertiary hospitals in a metropolitan city of China. Soc Sci Med 338:116296
33. Pereira MA, Senne EL (2008) A column generation method for the capacitated centred clustering problem. Ann VI ALIO/EURO, 1–6
34. Rivard-Royer H, Beaulieu M (2004) Logistique hospitalière: Franchir les nouvelles frontières. Cahier de recherche, (04-03)
35. Şahin G, Süral H, Meral S (2007) Locational analysis for regionalization of Turkish red crescent blood services. Comput Oper Res 34(3):692–704
36. Shariff SR, Moin NH, Omar M (2012) Location allocation modeling for healthcare facility planning in Malaysia. Comput Ind Eng 62(4):1000–1010
37. Sonmez AD, Lim GJ (2012) A decomposition approach for facility location and relocation problem with uncertain number of future facilities. Eur J Oper Res 218(2):327–338
38. Sridharan R (1995) The capacitated plant location problem. Eur J Oper Res 87(2):203–213
39. Syam SS, Côté MJ (2010) A location-allocation model for service providers with application to not-for-profit health care organizations. Omega 38(3):157–166
40. Syam SS, Côté MJ (2012) A comprehensive location-allocation method for specialized healthcare services. Oper Res Health Care 1:73–83
41. Toregas C, Swain R, ReVelle C, Bergman L (1971) The location of emergency service facilities. Oper Res 19(6):1363–1373
42. Triqui Sari L, Hennet JC (2016) Cooperative inventory planning in a distribution network. Int J Prod Res 54(19):5916–5931
43. Wang XL, Yang HZ, Duan ZQ, Pan J (2018) Spatial accessibility of primary health care in China: a case study in Sichuan province. Soc Sci Med 209:14–24
44. Weber CA (1902) Über die vegetation und entstehung des hochmoors von Augstumal: im memeldelta mit vergleichenden ausblicken auf andere hochmoore der erde; eine formationsbiologisch-historische und geologische studie. Parey

45. Zhang W, Cao K, Liu S, Huang B (2016) A multi-objective optimization approach for healthcare facility location-allocation problems in highly developed cities such as Hong Kong. Comput Environ Urban Syst 59:220–230
46. Zhang YM, Yang HZ, Pan J (2021) Gaining from rational health planning: spatial reallocation of top-tier general hospital beds in China. Comput Ind Eng 157:107344

Lamia Triqui Is currently an Associate Professor in the Faculty of Technology within the Industrial Engineering Department at Aboubekr Belkaïd University of Tlemcen. She obtained her Doctorate degree from the Laboratory for Sciences of Information and Systems (LSIS) in Marseille, France, and another Doctorate in Manufacturing Engineering. Her current degrees include HDR from the University of Tlemcen. Her main research interests lie in the field of supply chain management, Operations Research, and Game Theory. Her research aims to propose new learning management systems integrating cutting-edge technologies such as artificial intelligence (AI), machine learning (ML), blockchain, and mixed reality (MR) to design and implement intelligent industrial systems.

Healthcare Facility Design

3

Amina Ouhoud and Amine Hakim Guezzen

Abstract

Efficient facility layout is crucial, particularly due to its impact on material handling and transportation costs. This chapter focuses on hospital facility layout problems (HLP), aiming to optimize patient and resource movements within predefined facility boundaries. While traditionally limited to manufacturing facilities, there has been a lack of analysis for hospitals. This work presents a two-part approach: first, a model for multi-floor layouts minimizing movement costs, considering parameters like travel frequency, difficulty, baseline cost, and distance. Second, additional parameters and constraints are introduced.

Keywords

Patients • Hospital • Optimization • Department • Flow • Closeness

1 Introduction

The Facility Layout Problem (FLP) is a crucial aspect of industrial management, aiming to allocate facilities efficiently within designated areas of a plant. This optimization process involves considering various constraints such as departmental boundaries, and operational requirements [9]. The fundamentals, tools, and

A. Ouhoud (✉)
École Supérieure en Sciences Appliquées Tlemcen (ESSA-Tlemcen), Tlemcen, Algeria
e-mail: amina.ouhoud@essa-tlemcen.dz

A. H. Guezzen
Manufacturing Engineering Laboratory of Tlemcen, Tlemcen University, Tlemcen, Algeria
e-mail: aminehakim.guezzen@univ-tlemcen.dz

F. Jawab (ed.), *Hospital Supply Chain*, Integrated Science 27,
https://doi.org/10.1007/978-3-031-70292-1_3

procedures for addressing hospital facility layout problems resonate with those utilized in other manufacturing and non-manufacturing contexts. In designing hospital layouts, a structured approach is followed [15].

- Defining or redefining the primary objectives of the hospital layout.
- Identifying primary and secondary activities necessary to achieve these objectives.
- Establishing interdepartmental relationships.
- Assessing spatial requirements for each department.
- Generating alternative facility layouts.
- Evaluating and comparing alternative layouts.
- Selecting the most suitable facility layout.
- Implementing, maintaining, and adapting the chosen layout over time.

These steps, while crucial for effective facility layout planning in hospitals, share commonalities with industrial facility layout planning. Both endeavors ultimately aim to optimize resource utilization, enhance operational efficiency, and minimize operating expenses [15].

Figure 1 Illustrates a typical arrangement of operating units denoted by letters A through G, each characterized by rectangular shapes of varying sizes. These units are intended to be positioned within a rectangular plane, adhering to specific criteria and restrictions dictated by the layout design objectives. This visualization offers a clear representation of the spatial planning involved in the facility layout problem, showcasing how different units can be strategically placed within the designated area to optimize operational efficiency and resource utilization

The Facility Layout Problem (FLP) holds both practical and theoretical significance, being extensively utilized by researchers for designing floor layouts across diverse settings such as buildings, airports, warehouses, and hospitals [12]. This problem has garnered considerable research attention, leading to various method

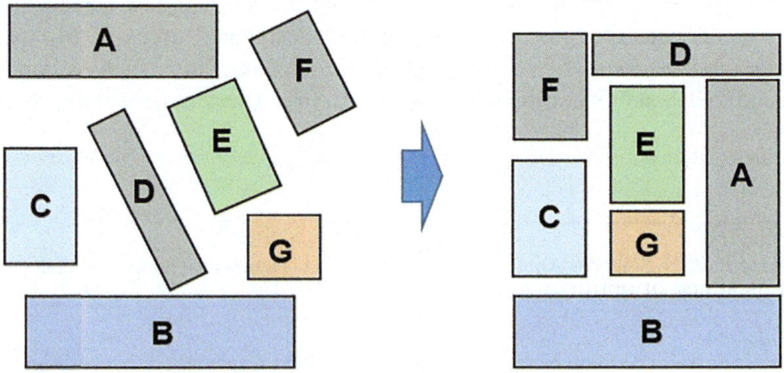

Fig. 1 Visual representation of facility arrangement Chraibi (2015)

classifications that cater to different application domains, including manufacturing systems and service configurations, as well as addressing diverse objective functions, facility shapes, and operating constraints [2].

2 Terminology

Definition. Facility design refers to the process of planning and designing the physical facilities of an organization to optimize their operation, efficiency, and resource utilization. It involves strategically laying out spaces, equipment, and workflows to create a safe, efficient, and productive work environment. Facility design considers various factors such as operational needs, budgetary constraints, safety standards, and ergonomic requirements to create facilities that effectively support the organization's commercial or institutional activities.

Key terms used in understanding the representation of hospital facility layout problems:

- Facility: Refers to a healthcare service or room within a hospital.
- Section: Denoting a specific zone or area within the hospital's layout, typically designated for particular medical activities or services.
- Department: Representing a larger organizational unit within the hospital that encompasses multiple sections and functions.
- Entity: Encompasses the collective personnel involved in the healthcare environment, including doctors, patients, medical staff, and non-medical staff who move between different facilities within the hospital or department.

3 Hospital Facility Layout Problems

The issues about the structure of hospital facilities can generally be classified into four distinct areas. According to [11].

3.1 Adjustments in the Existing Hospital Layout

This category involves making minor adjustments or rearrangements within the existing layout of the hospital facility to improve patient flow, enhance operational efficiency, or accommodate new medical equipment. Characteristics of these projects include minimal planning required, few human resources needed, and solutions aimed at optimizing patient care and staff workflow.

3.2 Rearrangement of Existing Hospital Departments

In this category, the focus is on rearranging existing hospital departments to address evolving healthcare needs or technological advancements. The goal is to streamline patient treatment pathways and adapt to changes in medical practices. Characteristics of this category include the availability of implementation methods and procedures, as well as the consideration of patient safety and the quality of care during the process of departmental reorganization.

3.3 Relocating Hospital Facilities to Existing Buildings

The relocation of hospital facilities to a new building or location is a complex process that requires meticulous planning to ensure uninterrupted patient care and operational continuity. The primary goal is to minimize disruptions to medical services while transitioning to the new facility. This category is characterized by the implementation of strategies to minimize expenses and maintain service levels during the relocation, as well as careful attention to logistical challenges and patient accessibility throughout the transition period.

3.4 Building a New Hospital

The construction of a new hospital facility is a category that involves the comprehensive planning and design of auxiliary areas necessary for efficient healthcare delivery. The primary focus is on creating a functional layout that accommodates various medical departments and services. This category is characterized by detailed planning for specialized areas such as operating theaters, intensive care units, and diagnostic imaging departments. Additionally, the integration of medical facilities into the building design is prioritized to optimize patient care and enhance staff efficiency.

4 Special Considerations in Hospital Layout

When designing a hospital layout, several primary objectives are essential to consider:

1. Reducing the distance travelled by medical staff and patients within the facility to optimize efficiency and ensure prompt care delivery.
2. Allowing flexibility in the layout design to accommodate changes in medical services, technology advancements, or fluctuations in patient volume. This adaptability facilitates seamless adjustments, expansions, or contractions of hospital departments as needed.

3. Creating a safe and conducive environment for healthcare professionals, patients, and visitors. This includes considerations for infection control, ergonomic design, adequate lighting, and clear wayfinding to promote comfort and well-being.
4. Minimizing both initial capital expenditures and ongoing operational costs associated with the hospital facility. This involves careful planning to optimize resource utilization, energy efficiency, and maintenance requirements while ensuring high-quality patient care standards are maintained.

5 Layout Classifications

The Facility Layout Problem (FLP) can be categorized according to various aspects as described by [2]. These aspects include the evolution of layout, representation methods, manufacturing systems, layout configurations, facility shapes, objectives of layout design, layout constraints, and more.

5.1 Layout Evolution

The Facility Layout Problem (FLP) can be classified into two main categories based on material handling flows:

5.1.1 Static Facility Layout Problem (SFLP)

This category assumes that the flows between facilities and product demands remain constant within a single period. In other words, the layout is designed considering a fixed set of material handling flows and product demands.

5.1.2 Dynamic Facility Layout Problem (DFLP)

This category involves the evaluation and modification of layouts multiple times. Unlike SFLP, DFLP considers that material handling flows and product demands can change over time. Therefore, it is necessary to periodically assess these changes in product demands to determine if layout rearrangements are needed to maintain an optimal facility layout.

The DFLP extends the concept of SFLP by addressing the dynamic nature of material handling flows and product demands, requiring continuous evaluation and potential adjustments to ensure an efficient facility layout [2].

5.2 Layout Representation

The classification of the Facility Layout Problem (FLP) can also be determined by the approach employed for representation. According to the findings of [15], there are two main representations.

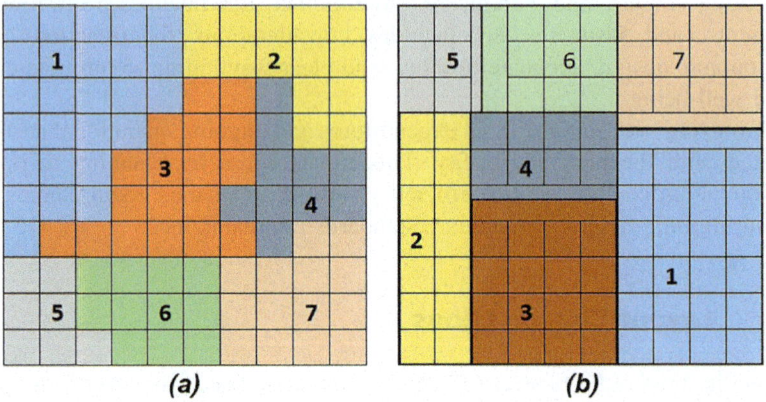

Fig. 2 Comparative layout representations: **a** discrete model and **b** continuous model

5.2.1 Discrete Representation

The proposed approach involves the utilization of a grid structure to represent the layout of the facility, as seen in Fig. 2a. Each department or region inside the facility is rounded off to ensure that it is contained within an integer number of grid cells.

5.2.2 Continuous Representation

Contrary to discrete representation, the dimensions of departments are not constrained to an underlying grid structure. Instead, as illustrated in Fig. 2b, the dimensions of departments can take on non-integer values, offering more flexibility in the layout design process.

It can be argued that continuous representation offers a more precise and representative approach compared to discrete representation in solving the Facility Layout Problem (FLP). Continuous representation allows for greater flexibility by accommodating non-integer values for department dimensions, thereby capturing more nuanced spatial relationships and layout configurations.

However, it is important to note that the increased precision of continuous representation comes at the cost of greater complexity in solving the FLP. The optimization process for continuous representation involves dealing with a larger solution space and more intricate mathematical formulations, which can be computationally demanding and time-consuming.

Despite the challenges associated with increased complexity, continuous representation has the potential to yield a "real optimal" final layout solution that closely reflects the actual spatial requirements and operational needs of the facility. Therefore, while continuous representation may require more computational resources, it offers the advantage of generating layouts that better align with the underlying objectives and constraints of the FLP.

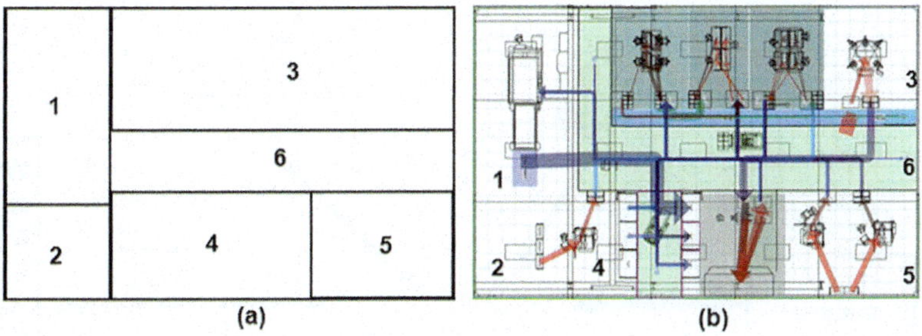

Fig. 3 Comparative layout representations: **a** block layout, **b** detailed layout

5.3 Design Level

The categorization of layout types is determined by the design levels, as described by [15]. These levels include:

5.3.1 Block Layout

This particular design level emphasizes the macro flows occurring within the facility. The block layout illustrates the comprehensive positioning and dimensions of every department or region within the facility. The provided visual representation offers a comprehensive overview of the arrangement of the facility, highlighting the spatial connections among various departments, as depicted in Fig. 3a.

5.3.2 Detailed Layout

At this level, the design delves into micro flows within the facility. The detailed layout provides specific and precise information about the exact locations of each facility, aisle structures, input/output (I/O) point locations, and the layout within each facility. It offers a comprehensive view of the facility layout, including detailed configurations and spatial arrangements, as depicted in Fig. 3b.

These two levels of layout design cater to different aspects of facility planning and design, with the block layout focusing on the broader spatial organization and the detailed layout providing more granular information about the facility's layout and infrastructure.

5.4 Manufacturing System

Facility layout problems, regardless of whether they include a manufacturing unit or a service organization such as a hospital, may generally be categorized into four main categories of layouts. The layouts encompassed in this category consist of process layout, product layout, fixed-position, and cellular layout. Each category presents unique benefits and is appropriate for varying operating needs and limitations.

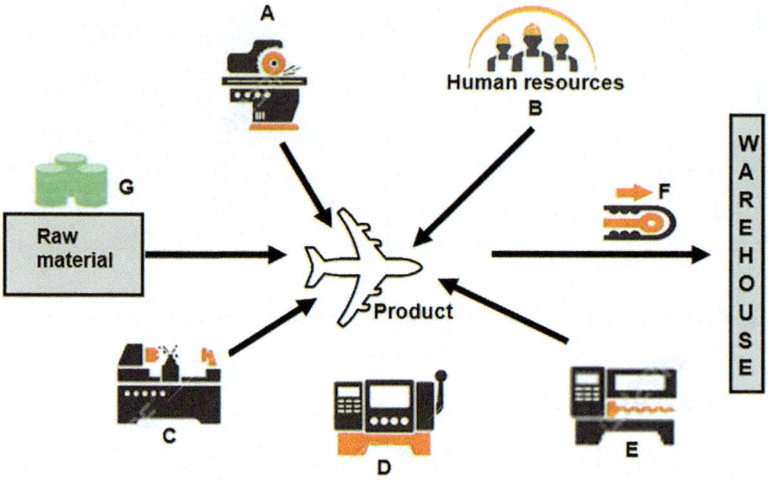

Fig. 4 Fixed location department layout

Layout types are determined by the material flow system, and as stated by [15], there are four universally acknowledged standard forms of layouts.

5.4.1 Fixed Location Department Layout

The permanent location layout is characterized by its concept, setting it apart from other variants. Instead of conveying materials to workstations, this arrangement involves bringing workstations to the department for material processing. The workstations are strategically positioned in proximity to the material or product, facilitating streamlined processing without the need for material displacement. Although frequently employed for sizable and cumbersome items, the utilization of this particular arrangement transcends these constraints. In the domain of computer system assembly, a multitude of materials, subassemblies, housings, peripherals, and components are conveyed to system integration and test workstations, where the ultimate result is constructed and undergoes testing. Figure 4 depicts a department structure that is fixed in position, where workstations are represented by letters A, B, C, D, and E. These workstations are designated for conducting operations on materials or entities. Arrow symbols are used to represent the movement of materials or entities inside a given arrangement.

5.4.2 Product Layout

The product layout is structured around the sequential processing of parts along the production line. Materials move directly from one workstation to the next adjacent workstation, following the predetermined processing sequence. This streamlined flow of materials is conducive to high-volume environments, particularly when flow paths are meticulously planned. Figure 5 illustrates a production line product department layout, with workstations denoted by letters A, B, C, D, E, and F where

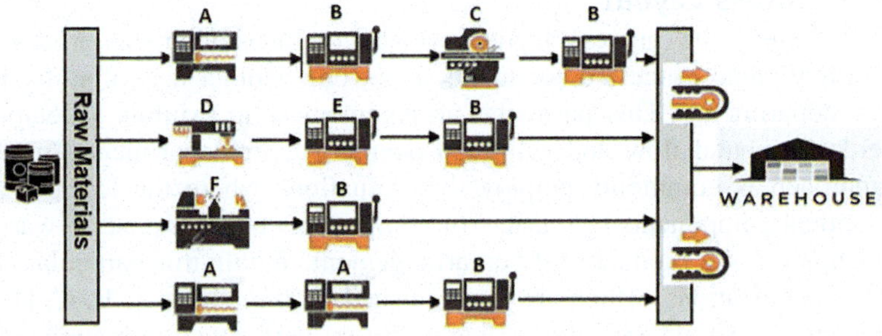

Fig. 5 Product layout

tasks are conducted on materials or entities. Arrows within the figure delineate the flow of materials or entities, displaying the efficient progression along the production line.

5.4.3 Group Layout

The product family department layout also referred to as the cellular layout, is an organized arrangement that organizes parts into product families. Non-identical parts are categorized into families according to several variables, including processing sequences, forms, material composition, tooling requirements, and handling/storage/control necessary. The requisite processing equipment for each product family is consolidated and positioned within a designated cell. As a result, this particular arrangement demonstrates a significant level of intra-departmental flow, while exhibiting negligible interdepartmental flow. Figure 6 depicts a particular arrangement, whereby workstations are represented by the letters A, B, C, D, and E. These workstations are utilized for performing operations on various materials or entities. The arrows depicted in the picture serve to illustrate the movement of materials or entities within the layout of the product family department.

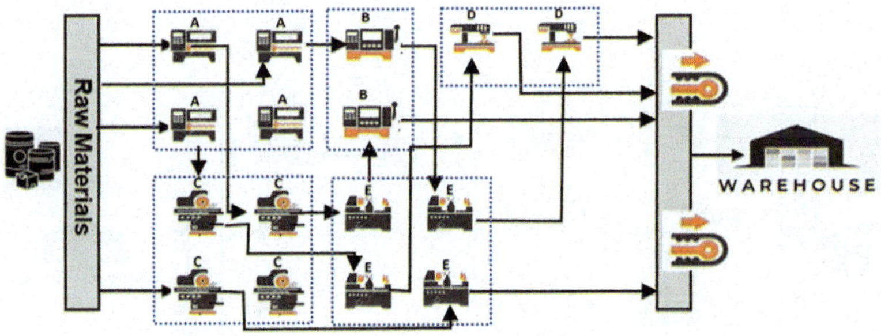

Fig. 6 Group layout

5.4.4 Process Layout

Figure 7 depicts the process layout, which combines identical processes and arranges individual process departments about one another according to the flow between departments. This particular arrangement style exhibits a notable level of interdepartmental flow and a limited degree of intradepartmental movement. This approach is commonly employed in situations where the level of activity for individual components or clusters of components is inadequate to warrant the implementation of a product or group arrangement. Within this particular arrangement, the workstations, which are distinguished by the letters A, B, C, D, E, and F serve as locations where various operations are performed on materials or entities. The arrows depicted in the diagram illustrate the movement of materials or entities across several departments within the conceptual framework of functional or process departments.

6 The Hospital Facility Layout Problem

The objective of the Hospital Facility Layout Problem (HFLP) is to determine an optimal and non-overlapping configuration of n facilities within a designated area. The literature on High-Frequency Localization Problems (HFLP) commonly employs two primary objectives: minimizing the overall trip cost and maximizing the total proximity rating between each pair of departures [10].

6.1 Minimization of Total Traveling Cost Function

The total traveling cost is often minimized by defining a distance-based function. This function calculates the overall distance traveled by individuals or materials between various facilities within the hospital facility layout. The distance-based function is typically formulated as follows:

$$\text{Minimize } \Sigma\Sigma\left(f_{ij} * c_{ij} * d_{ij}\right)$$

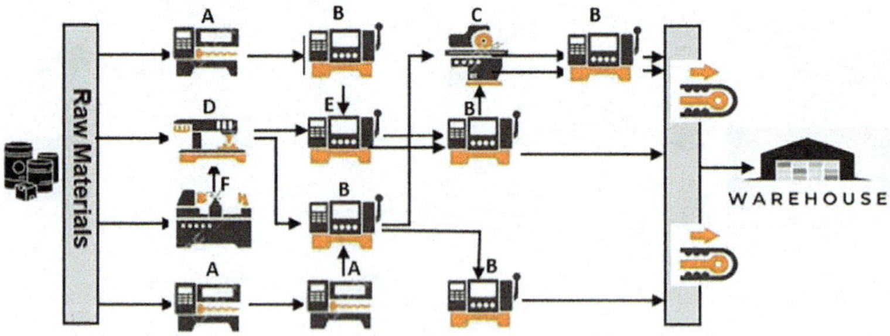

Fig. 7 Process layout

Where:

- f_{ij} represents the material flow from point i to point j,
- c_{ij} is the unit cost (the cost to move one unit of load from point i to point j),
- d_{ij} is the distance between point i and point j.

The rectilinear distance, or the Manhattan distance, ignores diagonal movement and considers only horizontal and vertical movement. To calculate the distance between two facilities (i and j) with centroid coordinates (x_i, y_i) and (x_j, y_j), we can use the following formula with only one floor:

$$d_{ij} = |x_i - x_j| + |y_i - y_j|$$

The equation for the distance between facilities (d_{ij}) in a multi-floor layout considers not only the horizontal and vertical distance between the facility centroids but also the factors related to using the elevator to move between floors. Here's the breakdown:

$$d_{ij} = |x_i - x_e| + |y_i - y_e| + \varepsilon|F_i - F_j| + |x_e - x_j| + |y_e - y_j|$$

where

- (x_i, y_i): Coordinates of the first facility's centroid.
- (x_j, y_j): Coordinates of the second facility's centroid.
- (x_e, y_e): Coordinates of the elevator's centroid relative to (0, 0).
- F_i: Floor on which the first facility is located.
- F_j: Floor on which the second facility is located.
- ε: Factor for vertical direction transport and waiting times.

Let's understand each term:

- $|x_i - x_e| + |y_i - y_e|$: This remains the same as the single-floor case and represents the rectilinear distance between the facility centroid (i) and the elevator centroid.
- $F_i - F_j$: This captures the difference in floors between the two facilities.
- $\varepsilon\ |Fi-Fj|$: This term introduces the weight factor (ε) for the vertical movement and waiting times. It penalizes the distance based on the floor difference and the factor ε.
- The factor ε considers the additional time and cost associated with using the elevator to move between floors. A higher value of ε signifies a greater penalty for moving between floors, making the optimizer prefer facilities on closer floors.

6.2 Maximizing the Closeness Rating Function

Muther (1973) employed a systematic qualitative approach to tackle the facility layout problem. His method revolves around defining adjacency relationships for each department pair, categorized into classes of closeness ratings denoted by specific letter codes: A (Necessary), E (Especially important), I (Important), O (Ordinary), U (Unimportant), and X (Undesirable). These ratings signify the importance of positioning department pairs next to each other, with A indicating utmost importance and X denoting undesirability. For instance, department pairs with an A rating must always be adjacent, while those with an X rating must never be adjacent under any circumstances. Muther emphasized maintaining the number of A relationships within 5% of the total relationships to optimize placement efficiency. The letter codes follow a hierarchy based on importance, with X sharing priority equivalent to A. The closeness rating function is formulated as follows: [7]

$$\text{Maximise} \sum_i \sum_j r_{ij} x_{ij}$$

where r_{ij} represents the numerical value of a closeness rating between facilities i and j

$$x_{ij} = \begin{cases} 1 \text{ if facilities } i \text{ and } j \text{ are adjacent} \\ 0 \qquad\qquad \text{otherwise} \end{cases}$$

6.3 The Weighted Sum Function

Understanding the benefits and drawbacks associated with each objective [9], certain authors have opted to integrate both objectives into a weighted format as follows:

$$Min\alpha \sum_i \sum_j f_{ij} c_{ij} d_{ij} - (1-\alpha) \sum_i \sum_j r_{ij} x_{ij}$$

where α represents the weights assigned to the objective functions, [9] examined the optimal setting of α to optimize the weighted criteria function.

7 Resolution Approaches

Facility Layout Problems (FLPs), regardless of whether they involve Static-Facility Location Problems (SFLP), discrete-Facility layout problems (DFLP), or employ Discrete or Continuous formulations, can be approached using either quantitative, qualitative methods, or a combination of both. Quantitative methods focus on numerical optimization, typically aiming to minimize costs such as material handling costs. In contrast, qualitative methods prioritize subjective factors such as maximizing closeness rating measures. Effective solutions often integrate aspects of both approaches to achieve optimal facility layouts.

7.1 Quantitative Methods

Quantitative methods focus on numerical optimization, typically aiming to minimize costs such as material handling costs.

7.1.1 Exact Method

The utilization of precise algorithms is theoretically employed to acquire a global optimum solution for the FLP, hence ensuring the optimality of the ultimate layout. Regrettably, these methods are excessively laborious and limited to addressing issues of extremely small scales [12], which are significantly far from the actual challenges encountered in industrial difficulties spanning 30–40 departments. The often employed techniques for addressing these categories include the methods utilized for solving quadratic assignment problems, graph-based approaches, and mixed integer programming models.

7.1.2 Quadratic Assignment Problem (QAP)

The Quadratic Assignment Problem is a specific instance of the FLP Problem. The assumption is made that the locations are stable and known, with equal portions allocated to each department, and that there is a one-to-one correspondence between departments and locations. The formulation of a typical QAP is provided as follows, as stated by [8].

$$\min \sum_{i}^{n} \sum_{j}^{n} \sum_{k}^{n} \sum_{l}^{n} c_{ijkl} x_{ik} x_{jl}$$

Subject to

$$\sum_{i}^{n} x_{ik} = 1 k = 1, \ldots, n$$

$$\sum_{i}^{n} x_{jl} = 1 l = 1, \ldots, n$$

$$x_{ik} = \begin{cases} 1 \text{ if facility i id affected to position or location } k \\ 0 \qquad \text{otherwise} \end{cases} \quad i, k = 1, \ldots, n$$

where

- c_{ijkl} is the cost associated with locating facility i to location k and facility j to location l.

The solving of QAP involves the utilization of precise algorithms, which encompass several methodologies such as branch and bound, cutting planes, and dynamic programming. The branch and bound algorithms have demonstrated remarkable progress, although they remain incapable of solving instances of significant size. The authors [5] provided a comprehensive examination of these heuristics.

7.1.3 Mixed-Integer Programming

Mixed-integer programming (MIP) is a novel approach introduced by Montreuil (1990) to solve the FLP, distinguishing it from other methods. This methodology employs a distance-based objective function and operates under the assumption of a continuous representation of a given layout. The MIP may address issues with both equal and unequal areas by precisely determining the position and alignment of departments using binary integer variables to avoid department overlap.

7.1.4 Heuristic and Metaheuristics

Researchers have attempted to address the limitations of QAP, graph theory models, and MIP in achieving optimal solutions for large-scale layout problems. To overcome this, they have employed heuristic approaches to obtain approximate answers. There are two distinct sorts of heuristics: construction heuristics and improvement heuristics. Construction heuristics involve the initial selection and successful location of a new department until the layout is fully completed, resulting in a single solution. On the other hand, improvement heuristics involve enhancing an initial layout using an improvement algorithm until all possible improvements have been exhausted through pairwise and other types of exchanges. Both Adjacency-based and Distance-based techniques are utilized by these groups.

According to Osman et al. [13], the notion of metaheuristics pertains to a process of iterative production that guides a subordinate heuristic by including intelligently unique concepts to explore and exploit the search area. To effectively uncover near-optimal solutions, learning strategies are utilized to organize information. The aforementioned methods represent the most recent category of approximate techniques that facilitate the exploration of classical construction and improvement procedures to overcome local optima. They are extensively employed to address intricate issues in several industrial domains, as stated by Osman et al. Zuo et al. [16] assert that meta-heuristics comprise a range of methodologies, including tabu search (TS), genetic algorithm (GA), ant colony optimization (ACO), simulated annealing (SA), particle swarm optimization (PSO), and hyper-heuristics, among other techniques. Barsegar [1] offers a contemporary evaluation of research about the use of metaheuristics in the context of FLP, whereas Osman et al. [12] brings insights into the historical development of meta-heuristics.6.2 Qualitative Methods.

7.2 Qualitative Approach

Qualitative research approaches place emphasis on subjective elements, specifically aiming to maximize proximity rating measures. SLP and the graph-theoretic technique are mostly qualitative methodologies that focus on optimizing closeness-rating metrics.

7.2.1 Systematic Layout Planning (SLP)

Muther (1973) introduced a systematic qualitative approach to address facility layout problems, focusing on defining adjacency relationships for department pairs categorized into classes denoted by specific letter codes: A (Necessary), E (Especially important), I (Important), O (Ordinary), U (Unimportant), and X (Undesirable). This method prioritizes the importance of positioning department pairs next to each other, with A representing utmost necessity and X indicating undesirability. Sunderesh S. Heragu [6] outlines the enduring popularity of the SLP technique, spanning over three decades, attributed to its straightforward, phased approach to facility design. The method unfolds across four distinct phases:

Phase I—Location Determination: Pinpointing optimal areas for departmental placement, whether within existing structures or adjacent to current manufacturing facilities.

Phase II—General Layout Establishment: Crafting the overarching layout blueprint, mapping material flow, accommodating adjacency requirements, and assessing spatial needs while considering practical constraints like budget and safety.

Phase III—Detailed Layout Planning: Focusing on the precise arrangement of machinery, equipment, and support services within each department, mirroring Phase II methodology with **a** narrower scope.

Phase IV—Implementation of Chosen Layout: Securing stakeholder approval, preparing detailed schematics, allocating resources for relocation, and physically moving machinery and services to designated positions.

7.2.2 Graph-Theoretic

Graph-theoretic techniques operate on the assumption that the inter-facility proximity ratings are known. Subsequently, every facility is depicted as a node in a graph, while the adjacency factors are illustrated as an arc linking two neighboring facilities. In this particular scenario, the primary goal is to optimize the overall closeness rating function.

To construct a layout with graph-theoretic methodologies, the initial step involves the creation of an adjacency graph based on the provided facility relationships. Subsequently, this adjacency network is converted into a dual graph, which is then utilized to generate a block layout. In the context of QAP, it is not possible to ensure optimality for problems of significant magnitude. Consequently, numerous construction methods have been created, drawing upon graph theoretic models. The authors [5] comprehensively examined these heuristics.

8 Modeling the Hospital Layout Problem

Designing efficient hospital layouts is crucial for balancing patient care with cost-effectiveness. While factors like staffing and equipment impact workflow, the physical arrangement of departments significantly influences productivity. The optimal layout considers patient flow, departmental interaction, and travel distances. Demographic trends and service needs are factored in to create a future-proof plan that can adapt to changing demands, even with space limitations. This intricate process involves modeling patient movement, resource allocation, and departmental placement to minimize travel costs and ensure smooth operation.

8.1 Foundational Principles for Hospital Facility Layout Design

The essential factors to be taken into account in the design of healthcare facility layout are outlined as follows:

8.1.1 Movement Costs

One of the primary considerations in hospital facility layout design is understanding movement costs, which can be categorized as follows:

Cost Associated with Movement of Travel Entities

When designing facility layouts for hospitals, movement costs play a crucial role. These costs primarily stem from the movement of travel entities, particularly patients. The complexity and expense of patient movement vary depending on factors such as the severity of the patient's condition, the urgency of required treatments, and the need for immediate surgical interventions. Patients often face challenges in movement, especially after surgeries or intense medical procedures, which can significantly increase costs. Additionally, patients are often accompanied by resources such as medical equipment or personnel, further contributing to movement costs. The level of difficulty in patient movement is a key determinant of these costs, with additional weights assigned to account for accompanying resources. The independence of resource movement also influences costs, with additional weights assigned based on whether resources move autonomously or require assistance. Overall, understanding and optimizing movement costs are essential for designing efficient hospital facility layouts focused on patient-centered care.

Cost Associated with Department Arrangement

In hospital facility layout design, minimizing the Quadratic Assignment Problem (QAP) objective is essential. This involves minimizing the sum of transportation costs multiplied by distance for all pairs of facilities. Departments within the hospital serve as facilities and need to be strategically placed within cells to optimize efficiency. The number of cells typically exceeds the number of departments, sometimes necessitating the addition of dummy departments. Placement decisions consider the interaction intensity between departments, with those having higher interaction placed closer together to minimize distances. Additionally, area constraints and other considerations may influence department placement on different floors. Various methods are employed to solve QAP problems, often generating lower bounds due to the complexity of large-scale problems. By assigning departments to cells in a building, the hospital facility layout problem is addressed as a QAP, aiming to minimize total movement costs [4].

8.1.2 Vertical Transportation in Multi-floor Hospital Layouts

The vertical transportation of personnel and equipment within hospitals is eased by the utilization of lifts. The objective is to achieve efficient transportation between departments while minimizing costs, which depends on elevator selection. Factors such as relative cost, elevator capacity, and proximity to departments influence elevator choice. The number of elevators required is typically determined by hospital size and traffic intensity, with accessibility based on availability. Given the high travel frequency in hospitals, departments with frequent interactions across floors are strategically positioned closer to elevators to reduce costs. In multi-floor layouts, additional costs and constraints are present, with non-linear costs due to waiting times.

- The duration of travel between different floors encompasses multiple elements:
- The duration between the initial department and the designated lift.
- The duration of waiting for the lift.
- The duration of travel between floors is determined by the quantity of intermediate stops.
- the travel time from the lift to the target department is taken into consideration.

It's important to note that, unlike horizontal travel, vertical transportation costs vary, adding complexity to multi-floor layout problems. Additionally, different devices may have varying transportation costs, further complicating the layout design. Considering these factors, vertical distances are given greater weight in calculations compared to horizontal distances [6].

8.1.3 Modeling Entities in Hospital Facility Layouts

Entities within hospitals can be categorized into travel entities and departments, each playing a crucial role in facility layout design.

Travel Entities

These entities encompass individuals physically moving within the hospital. They are further classified into primary and secondary travel entities to aid in modeling hospital facility layouts effectively.

Primary Travel Entities

Patients constitute the primary travel entities in hospitals. Designing hospital facilities revolves around optimizing patient movement to provide the best possible care efficiently. Minimizing patient movements is paramount, as it also reduces the overall movement of other entities. This objective is achieved by strategically placing departments frequently visited by patients closer to patient wards. Additionally, employing portable medical devices within wards can further reduce patient movements. The hospital commonly employs several portable gadgets, such as the phototherapy unit, X-ray unit, anesthesia apparatus, Fluoroscopy unit, and machine of ECG, among other examples. rs.

Secondary Travel Entities

As their movements depend on the requirements of primary travel entities, doctors, medical personnel, and non-medical staff are classified as secondary travel entities. The non-medical staff is made up of employees who work in wards, administration, payment, registration, and nutrition services, among other roles. The medical staff is made up of nurses, laboratory, and clinical personnel. Optimizing primary entity motions is strongly related to minimizing secondary entity movements.

Departments catering to secondary entity movements toward patient rooms are strategically placed nearer to patient wards. The movement cost incurred by secondary entities depends on factors such as the speed of service delivery and whether the entity accompanies a patient or carries equipment items like portable devices. Hospital facility layout models incorporate these considerations by assigning additional weights to reflect the associated costs.

In summary, effective hospital facility layout design involves meticulous modeling of both primary and secondary travel entities, with a focus on optimizing patient care and minimizing movement costs.

9 Practical Example

Illustrating these principles, a hospital layout design may involve the placement of 38 departments, each strategically positioned based on their interaction and travel frequency, ensuring optimal functionality and efficiency in delivering patient care. The list of hospital departments considered in the layout design is crucial for patient care and operational efficiency. The information was acquired from Saint Michael's Medical Centre and is detailed in Table 1, offering a thorough comprehension of the healthcare facility's amenities and services [14]. The total area for all hospital departments listed in Table 1 is 181,000 square feet, resulting in an average of 774 square feet per hospital bed, considering the hospital has 150 beds. This total area allocation for departments includes space for patient rooms, bathrooms, storage, nursing stations, and other necessary areas. The standard specification for area per hospital bed typically falls in the range of 700 to 800 sq. ft.

Table 1 Hospital departments

No	Department	Abbreviation	Area (sq. ft.) 10^2
1	Department of anesthesia	AN	16
2	Birthing center	BC	1 8
3	Blood bank	Blood	3 6
4	Blood test	BT	12
5	Cafeteria	Cafeteria	40
6	Cashier	Cashier	6
7	Catheterization lab	Cath lab	18
8	Cobalt Machine lab	COM/C	22
9	CT scan	CT	21
10	Conference room	CR	27
11	Doctors' lounge	DR	60
12	Examination room	ER	21
13	General care unit	GCW	125
14	Hematology lab	Hematol lab	16.5
15	Inpatient registration	InReg	8
16	Intensive care unit	ICU	65
17	Linear accelerator lab	LINAC	15
18	Mammography lab	Mammo	20
19	Medical records room	MRR	28
20	Nurses' station	Nurses station	40
21	Nutrition services	Nutrition	25
22	Obstetrics & gynecology unit	OB/GYN unit	50
23	Operating room	OR	43
24	Orthovoltage lab	OvolM/C	25
25	Outpatient registration	OutReg	10
26	Pharmacy	Pharmacy	24
27	Planning computer lab	PC Lab	12
28	Recovery room	RR	24
29	Rehabilitation center	Rehab center	41
30	Social services	Social services	16
31	Special unit	SW	87.5
32	Specialty clinic	Specialty clinic	80
33	Surgical equipment room	SterEq room	22
34	Ultrasound lab	US	18
35	Waiting room	WE	39

(continued)

Table 1 (continued)

No	Department	Abbreviation	Area (sq. ft.) 10^2
36	Walk-in clinic	Walk-in clinic	22
37	X-ray lab	X-ray	16
38	X-ray simulation lab	Sim X-ray lab	12

Designing optimal facility layouts for hospitals yields significant long-term advantages, including:

- Optimal Department Locations: By carefully arranging departments within the hospital layout, the most efficient and effective configuration is achieved, enhancing patient care and operational workflow.
- Future Demand Analysis: Capacity modeling enables the anticipation of future demand and capacity requirements, allowing hospitals to proactively plan for expansion or adjustments to meet evolving healthcare needs.
- Interdepartmental Interaction Analysis: Detailed analysis of interactions between departments provides valuable insights for predicting future trends and optimizing workflow efficiency.
- Micro and Macro Layout Optimization: Both micro and macro layouts benefit from optimal workstations and instrument placement within work cells, contributing to overall operational efficiency.
- Resource Optimization: Factors such as equipment clearances, ergonomic considerations, sample handling requirements, and walking distances are meticulously optimized, ensuring resources are utilized effectively and efficiently.

9.1 The Hospital Facility Layout Representation

The task is to design a hospital with 'n' departments in an efficient manner while only using one lift for vertical mobility. For simplicity's sake, the lift's capacity is ignored, and accessibility is determined by availability. The position of the lift, represented by (xe, ye), is fixed in the model and is determined at the point (0, 0) during the layout design.

To determine the mobility cost, the healthcare facility layout design entails putting departments in a rectangular floor plan. Complexities such as room layouts, locations of entry and exit points, and precise movement routes are overlooked in favor of simplicity. Rather, the supposition is that travel entities go in rectilinear pathways across departments.

The departments are initially placed in alphabetical order and assigned to floors according to their respective areas. As many departments as feasible can fit on a single level in each of the subsets that make up the department sequence. At this point, departmental interactions are ignored. Ai represents the ith department's area, and Fi, xi, and yi decide where its placement coordinates are.

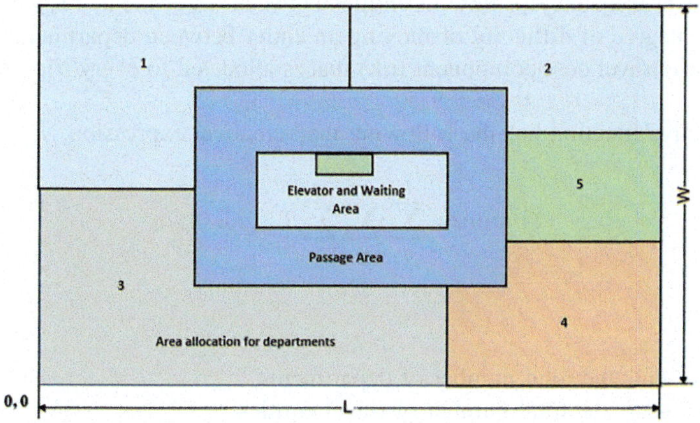

Fig. 8 Hospital building floor dimensions

Where:

Fi: Stands for the floor that the department is situated on.
xi: Indicates the department's X-coordinate from the starting position (0, 0).
yi: Indicates the department's Y-coordinate from the starting position (0, 0).

9.2 Area Analysis

Figure 8 depicts the standard floor layout of the hospital building, showcasing the positioning of the elevator. The layout adopts a rectangular shape for the building, with both length and width designated as 'W'. Departments are arranged along the building's sides, with a consistent passage running through the center. This layout assumption applies uniformly across all floors of the hospital for consistency.

9.3 The Cost Function Generation

The goal of the hospital facility layout problem is to find the best possible departmental arrangement within the available space to minimize the value of the objective function, given a collection of departments and their area over a 2D space (Fig. 8). The development of this objective function takes into account several factors related to the arrangement of departments and the flow of entities within the hospital.

The following affects the movement cost:

- The distance between two departments, determined by their placement coordinates (d_{ij}).

- The travel frequency or flow of entities between departments (T_{ijk}).
- $_{ijk}$ The degree of difficulty of moving an entity between departments (d_{ijk}).
- The base travel cost component (αk) that is allocated to every trip entity.

The objective function has the following mathematical expression:

$$\text{Minimize} \sum_{i}^{n}\sum_{j}^{n}\sum_{k}^{m} \mathrm{T_{ijk}}\ \mathrm{d_{ijk}}\ \xi_{ijk}\alpha_{\mathrm{k}}$$

Where:

- n: represents the total number of departments.
- m: represents the total number of travel entities.

An original matrix, denoted as base-line travel cost x Trip difficulty rating, is generated through the multiplication of the baseline travel cost components utilized for entities with the difficulty rating values present in the trip difficulty-rating matrix. Both the distance matrix and the trip frequency matrix are multiplied by the resulting matrix to shift the cost matrix.

The total movement cost is then obtained by summing the values of the objective function matrix. The primary objective in modeling a hospital facility layout problem is to minimize this total movement cost.

9.4 Experimental Results

The practical use of the suggested formulation is exemplified by an example that acts as a point of reference throughout this chapter. The task at hand entails creating a facility arrangement for a hospital with 150 beds, which includes 38 departments. The entire size of each level in the building is 25,000 square feet. Out of this, 2100 square feet is designated for passage spaces, while 1500 square feet is assigned for lift and waiting areas. This leaves a remaining 21,400 square feet for department placement on each floor. All floors possess equal dimensions.

The initial step in the layout development process involves the generation of a department sequence through the alphabetical arrangement of departments. The placement of these departments on floors is done manually, beginning with the first department and proceeding in a counter-clockwise direction. Every level is designed to handle a maximum number of departments. All departments necessitate a total of 7 stories. To generate floor plans, a 1:10 scale is employed, and the placement coordinates are determined based on the center of gravity of the geometric shape of each floor, commencing at the point (0, 0).

The distance matrix is obtained by subtracting the rectilinear distance measures from the placement coordinates. The travel frequency matrix is subsequently generated using the frequencies of travel between department pairs every week,

Table 2 Experimental results

Entities	Cost function ($)
The patients	1,533,804
The doctors	1,503,259
The medical personal	2,343,224
The non-medical personal	562,571
Total	5,942,860

which were gathered through surveys conducted at Saint Michael's Medical Centre in Newark, NJ. [14]. For example, if Department 1 denotes the General Ward and Department 2 denotes the Operating Theatre, and $T_{121} = 15$, $T_{122} = 5$, $T_{123} = 25$, $T_{124} = 10$, it can be inferred that there are 15 weekly journeys from the General Ward to the Operating Theatre by patients, 5 journeys by doctors, 25 journeys by medical staff, and 10 journeys by other non-medical staff.

The subsequent step involves the generation of a matrix that combines the Trip Difficulty Rating and Baseline Travel Cost. This matrix assigns trip difficulty ratings to each department pair for every type of travel entity. It is assumed that the baseline trip expenses are as follows: $\alpha_{\text{patients}} = 10$, $\alpha_{\text{doctor}} = 20$, $\alpha_{\text{medical personal}} = 15$, $\alpha_{\text{non-medical personal}} = 5$, where $\alpha_{\text{doctor}} > \alpha_{\text{medical personal}} > \alpha_{\text{patients}} > \alpha_{\text{non-medical personal}}$.

Ultimately, the movement cost matrix is obtained from the previously mentioned metrics, and the objective function value, which represents the total movement cost associated with all entities, is calculated, as described in Table 2. According to [14],

The results indicate that the cost of movement for doctors and medical personnel is significantly more in comparison to non-medical personnel. The observed disparity arises from the circumstance that physicians and healthcare professionals frequently follow patients to attend to their requirements and enable their mobility within the hospital environment. Moreover, the data reveals that the total cost of mobility associated with medical personnel exceeds that of physicians. This disparity emerges because nurses, laboratory technicians, and other such personnel are obligated to make multiple journeys to address urgent patient needs, frequently while transporting equipment. On the other hand, the actions of doctors often encompass activities such as surgical procedures, examinations, clinical assessments, and emergency interventions, which generally do not necessitate the use of additional technology.

By reducing the cost of patient transportation, there is a subsequent decrease in the cost of movement associated with secondary resources, leading to an overall reduction in the total cost of movement. Attaining this decrease is achievable by strategically organizing hospital departments.

The floor layouts depicted in Figs. 9, 10, 11, 12, 13 and 14 and 15 showcase the arrangement of departments over all seven floors. The designs are shown at a ratio of 1:10, providing a visual representation of the optimal distribution of departments inside the healthcare establishment.

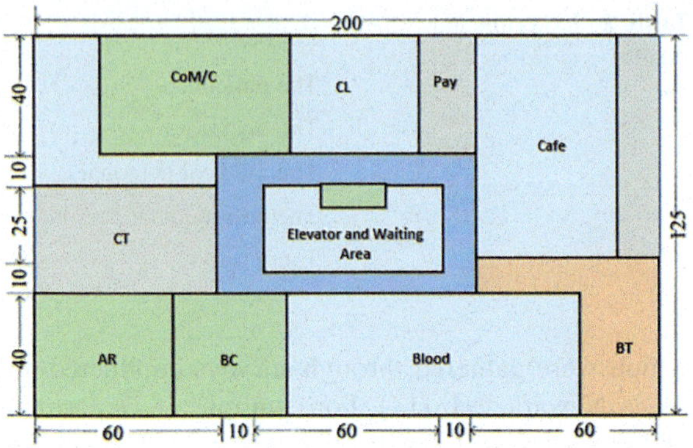

Fig. 9 Sample floor 1 layout

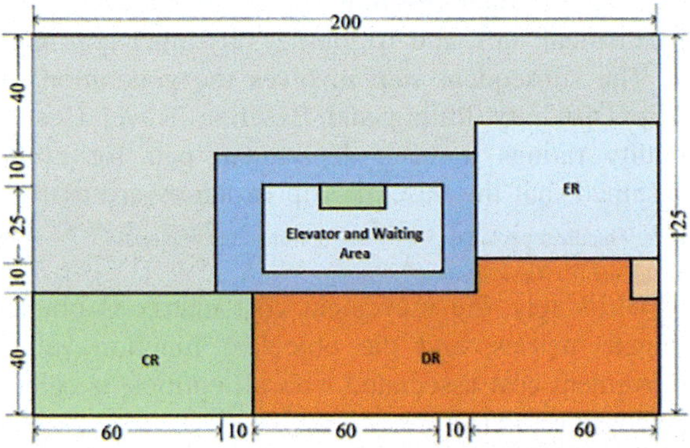

Fig. 10 Sample floor 2 layouts

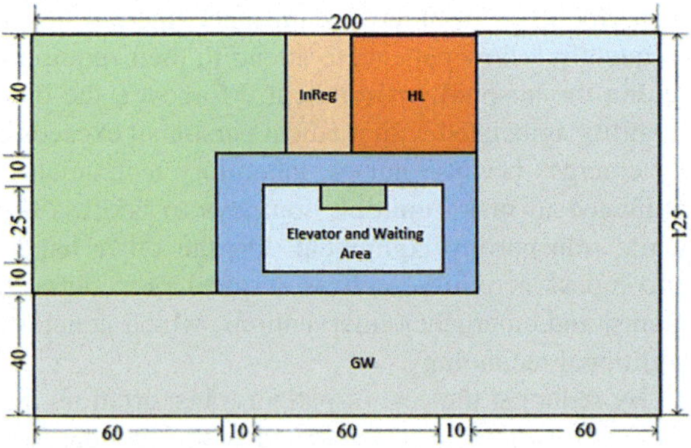

Fig. 11 Sample floor 3 layouts

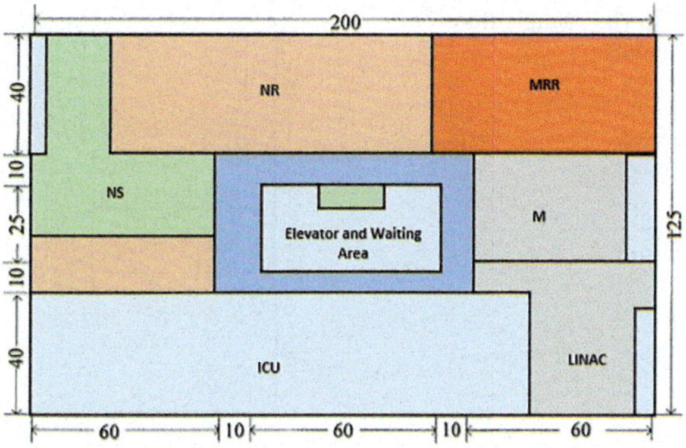

Fig. 12 Sample floor 4 layouts

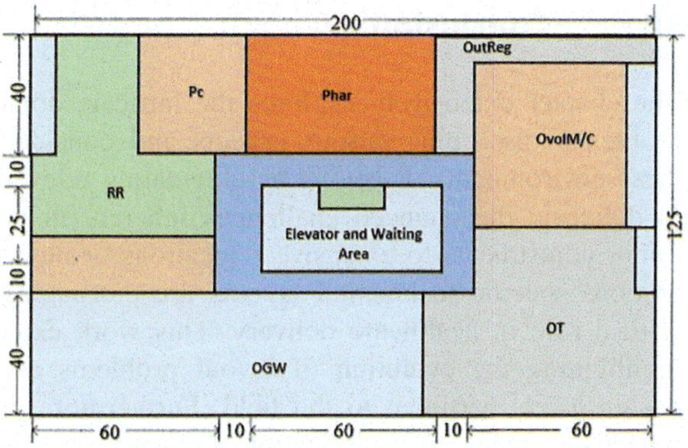

Fig. 13 Sample floor 5 layouts

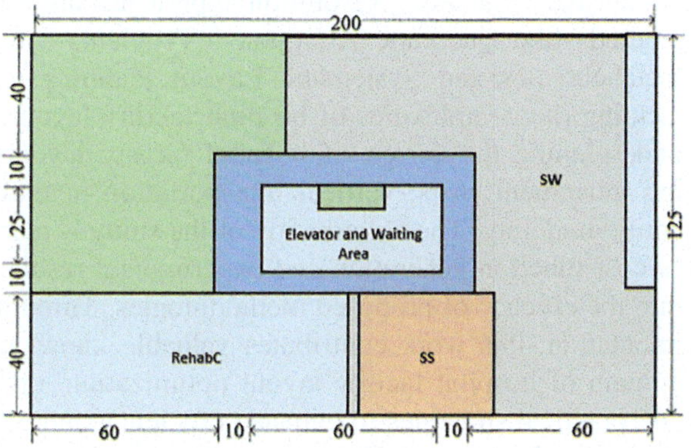

Fig. 14 Sample floor 6 layouts

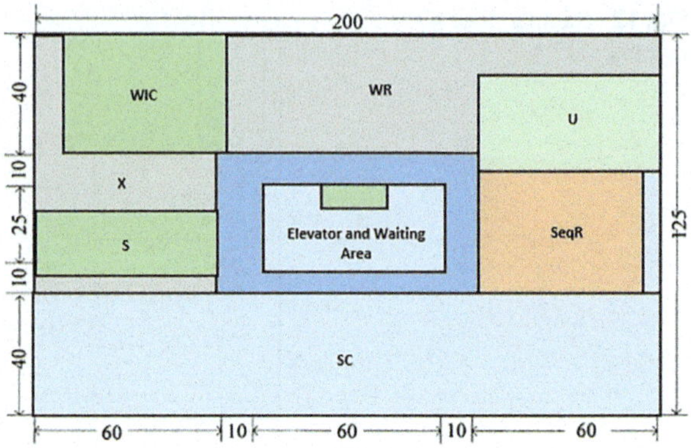

Fig. 15 Sample floor 7 layouts

10 Conclusion

The chapter extensively explores the intricate domain of hospital facility layout problems, dissecting various aspects and considerations crucial for optimizing these environments. It begins by elucidating relevant terminology and progresses to delineate the nuanced challenges inherent in hospital layouts, encompassing minor adjustments to extensive relocations or new constructions. Unique considerations specific to hospital layouts are thoroughly examined, recognizing their critical role in healthcare delivery. This work extends to classification schemes, highlighting the evolution of layout problems and diverse representations and design levels pertinent to the field. Furthermore, the study delves into the core objectives of layout optimization, focusing on minimizing total traveling costs, maximizing closeness ratings, and employing weighted sum functions for comprehensive evaluation. Resolution approaches are scrutinized, encompassing exact methods like Quadratic Assignment Problems and heuristic procedures such as metaheuristics and Systematic Layout Planning, offering diverse strategies for tackling the complexities of hospital facility layouts. Fundamental considerations underpinning the design of hospital facility layouts are underscored, emphasizing movement costs, vertical transportation in multi-floor layouts, and accurate entity modeling. The culmination of the study is marked by a detailed examination of cost function generation and experimental results, providing empirical insights into the efficacy of proposed methodologies. Through rigorous analysis and experimentation, this work contributes valuable knowledge and methodologies to the domain of hospital facility layout optimization, offering both theoretical insights and practical strategies to enhance efficiency and effectiveness in healthcare environments. In essence, this comprehensive exploration serves as a roadmap for navigating the intricate landscape of hospital facility layout problems, providing theoretical insights and practical strategies to enhance efficiency and effectiveness in healthcare environments.

References

1. Barsegar J (2011) A survey of metaheuristics for facility layout problems. University of Rhode Island
2. Drira A, Pierreval H, Hajri-Gabouj S (2007) Facility layout problems: a survey. Annu Rev Control 31(2):255–267
3. Singh SP, Sharma RRK (2006) A review of different approaches to the facility layout problems. Int J Adv Manuf Technol 30:425–433. https://doi.org/10.1007/s00170-005-0087-9
4. Hahn P, Krarup J (2001) A hospital facility layout problem finally solved. Klinikum Regensburg Hospital, Germany
5. Hassan MM, Hogg GL, Smith DR (1986) SHAPE: a construction algorithm for area placement evaluation. Int J Prod Res 24(5):1283–1295
6. Heragu SS (2018) Facilities design. CRC Press
7. Kochhar J, Heragu S (1998) Multi-hope: a tool for multiple floor layout problems. Int J Prod Res 38(12):3421–3435
8. Koopmans TC, Beckman M (1957) Assignment problems and the location of economic activities. Econometric 25:53–76
9. Meller RD, Gau KY (1996) Facility layout objective functions and robust layouts. Int J Prod Res 34(10):2727–2742
10. Meller RD, Gau KY (1996) The facility layout problem: recent and emerging trends and perspectives. J Manuf Syst 15(5):351–366
11. Moore J (1970) Plant layout and design, 4th edn. The Macmillan Company, No. 12, 2567–2593
12. Osman IH, Hasan M, Abdullah A (2002) Linear programming based meta-heuristics for the weighted maximal planar graph. J Oper Res Soc 53(10):1142–1149
13. Osman IH, Al-Ayoubi B, Barake MA (2003) A greedy random adaptive search procedure for the weighted maximal planar graph problem. Comput Ind Eng 45:635–651
14. Padgaonkar AS (2003) Modeling and analysis of hospital facility layout problem. Theses, p 528
15. Tompkins J, White J, Bozer W, Tanchoco J (2010) Facilities planning, 3rd edn. Wiley, New York, USA
16. Zuo X, Li B, Huang X, Zhou M, Cheng C, Zhao X, Liu Z (2019) Optimizing hospital emergency department layout via multiobjective tabu search. IEEE Trans Autom Sci Eng 16(3):1137–1147

Amina Ouhoud is currently serving as an associate Professor at the Higher School of Applied Sciences of Tlemcen (ESSA-Tlemcen). Born in Tlemcen, Algeria on February 14th, 1987, she embarked on her academic journey at Tlemcen University, where she earned her Bachelor of Science degree in 2005. Following her undergraduate studies, she pursued higher education and obtained her Master's degree in 2009. In 2015, she achieved her Ph.D. degree in industrial engineering from the University of Tlemcen.Since 2010, Dr. Ouhoud has been an esteemed member of the manufacturing laboratory of Tlemcen. Her research portfolio encompasses a wide array of interests, including automated storage and retrieval systems, facilities design, machine learning, deep learning, and data analysis. She has contributed significantly to the academic community through her authored and co-authored papers, which have been presented at numerous national and international scientific conferences. For further communication and collaboration opportunities.

Amine Hakim Guezzen serves as an Assistant Professor and Researcher at the University of Tlemcen (UABT), Faculty of Technology, Algeria, where he is an integral member of the Manufacturing Engineering Laboratory of Tlemcen (MELT). He earned his Bachelor's degree in Control Engineering from the University of Tlemcen in 2002, followed by a Master's degree in Manufacturing Engineering from the same institution in 2006. In 2015, he completed his

Ph.D. in Manufacturing Engineering. His primary research interests lie in the realm of industrial maintenance, encompassing the design, modeling, simulation, and control of Automated Storage and Retrieval Systems (AS/RS). Amine GUEZZEN has conducted extensive investigations into various AS/RS configurations, including mobile racks AS/RS systems and multi-aisle AS/RS systems.

4 Supply Chain Strengthening in Developing Countries: Challenges and Barriers

Felicia Setiawan, Valencia Hadinata, Grace Alvina, Claudia Alexandra, Gerry Dwi Putro, and Fritzie A. Rexana

Abstract

Strengthening supply chains in developing nations is a crucial task, fraught with obstacles that greatly affect the delivery of vital healthcare services. Given the intricate nature of healthcare supply chains and their interdependence for timely access to quality resources, the significance of resource reliance amplifies, given the potentially dire outcomes of any breakdown.

Keywords

Policy • Resources allocation • Infrastructure constraints • Supply chain resilience

1 Introduction

Strengthening supply chains in developing nations is a crucial task, fraught with obstacles that greatly affect the delivery of vital healthcare services. Given the intricate nature of healthcare supply chains and their interdependence for timely access to quality resources, the significance of resource reliance amplifies, given

F. Setiawan (✉) · V. Hadinata · C. Alexandra
Department of Hospital Administration, Universitas Pelita Harapan, Tangerang, Indonesia
e-mail: feliciasetiawanmd@gmail.com

G. Alvina
Prostacia Clinic, Tangerang, Jakarta, Indonesia

G. D. Putro
Department of Orthopedic and Traumatology, Jakarta Hospital, Jakarta, Indonesia

F. A. Rexana
Department of Business Management, Universitas Tarumanegara, Jakarta, Indonesia

F. Jawab (ed.), *Hospital Supply Chain*, Integrated Science 27,
https://doi.org/10.1007/978-3-031-70292-1_4

the potentially dire outcomes of any breakdown. Consequently, collaborative planning, execution, and decision-making emerge as pivotal components of effective supply chain management (SCM) [22]. This problem becomes even greater when the economy is in recession, especially for developing countries [6].

The term "developing countries" encompasses a broad spectrum of nations facing socio-economic challenges that impede their overall progress. Developing countries, also known as less developed or underdeveloped nations, are characterized by lower income levels, limited access to healthcare resources, and challenges in infrastructure development. Developing countries, which account for as much as 84% of the world's population and shoulder 93% of the global disease burden, only contribute 18% of the global income and allocate merely 11% of the global health expenditure [35]. These countries frequently contend with challenges such as poverty, insufficient healthcare infrastructure, and limited technological progress. The term broadly encompasses economies undergoing industrialization and confronting diverse developmental obstacles [6]. Within this context, the World Bank classifies countries into Low-Income, Middle-Income, and Low-Middle-Income categories, often referred to as LIC (Low-Income Countries) and LMIC (Low- and Middle-Income Countries). As per July 2023, total 28 countries categorized as LIC and 54 countries categorized as LMIC [32]. These distinctions acknowledge the diversity of economic conditions and underscore the shared challenges these countries encounter in strengthening their healthcare supply chains. LMICs exhibit a diverse range of economic conditions, with economies transitioning from low to moderate income levels. Low-Income Countries (LIC) specifically refer to nations with the lowest gross national income per capita. Both LMICs and LICs share common challenges in strengthening their healthcare systems, particularly in the context of supply chain management, where issues of accessibility, affordability, and availability of essential medical commodities often arise [10, 11].

Healthcare supply chain management is a series of processes which integrate physical and technical resources such as medicines, equipment, food, manufacturers, distributors, and transportation in an effective and efficient way to deliver a good service to patients and achieve total quality management [4]. Accomplishing this requires collaborative and strategic planning from the various stakeholders involved and also demands a strong commitment from all levels of decision-makers. Enhancing the performance of Healthcare SCM is crucial in developing countries to establish a more robust healthcare system. This improvement serves as a foundation to mitigate the risk of disruptions in the medical supply chain caused by future uncertainties, contributing to the overarching goal of ensuring patient safety [16].

The supply chain of the future face challenges among others environmental protection, energy availability and population growth, and also have unprecedented access to technology, which enables real-time connectivity almost anywhere anyone in the world. The challenges and barriers to supply chain strengthening in these nations are multifaceted. Issues such as complex regulatory and policy, inadequate infrastructure, insufficient financial resources, insufficient resources allocation, and inadequate technology contribute to the complexities of managing healthcare supply chains. Understanding and addressing these challenges are crucial for devising effective strategies that can enhance the resilience and efficiency of supply chains in the context of developing countries.

2 Policy and Regulatory Challenges in Supply Chain

Supply chains that extend across numerous countries have become commonplace for businesses of all sizes. However, the regulatory frameworks on a global scale have not kept up with this evolution. Many developing nations still struggle with weak rule of law, leading to considerable uncertainty and enforcement challenges, particularly in cross-border legal proceedings. Certain international protocols, like the Guidelines for Multinational Enterprises and the UN Guiding Principles for Human Rights and Business, have emerged as crucial instruments for addressing these regulatory deficiencies. For instance, the Guidelines set forth an expectation for businesses to act responsibly throughout their supply chains, even in regions with potentially inadequate enforcement of international standards and local laws [26]. There are several policy and regulatory challenges that could weaken health supply chain management which in turn could put patient treatment programs at risk [18, 40].

SCM policies are essential to establish transparent, accountable, and efficient supply chains, especially in contexts where vulnerabilities to corruption may be heightened. By implementing and enforcing SCM policies, developing nations can mitigate the risks of bribery, fraud, and other corrupt practices that could compromise the accessibility and affordability of essential goods, including pharmaceuticals. Such policies contribute to building a foundation of integrity and fairness within the supply chain, fostering trust among stakeholders and ensuring that resources are allocated ethically. In the realm of developing countries, SCM policies not only enhance the reliability of supply chains but also play a pivotal role in promoting sustainable development and equitable access to crucial goods and services [12, 28, 35].

Every medical product must follow a procedure, such as purchasing, information of usage, inventory control, stocking, warehousing, transportation, product delivery, and disposing. Every step must be aimed for quality, including item form, placement, quantity, operational costs, and appropriate usage. These products include goods and services like pharmaceuticals, catering, waste management, home-care products, vehicles, waste management, and general supplies. All supplies have either a time-limited usage, temperature-specified storage, regular maintenance, specific handling; thus making it critical to maintain their sustainability and efficacy [6, 13]. Policies governing procurement, distribution, and inventory management are often outdated or inadequately enforced, leading to inefficiencies, delays, and stockouts. Insufficient alignment between policies and the dynamic healthcare landscape contributes to suboptimal performance in the delivery of essential health commodities [26, 40].

One of the main challenges include ineffective supply chains. In low-and-middle-income countries (LMICs), especially in remote and fragile settings, healthcare product and supply system chains face various challenge in the absence of adequate policies, including:

- Policies related to stock-outs

Inventory holds an important part towards managing supply chain, as failure of its management might lead to effectiveness in procurement, forecasting, and requisitioning. Various bottlenecks within the supply chain, including ineffective inventory management, insufficient supervision and control, the presence of expired goods, improper commodity storage and administration, and a shortage of qualified personnel in the supply chain system, can result in stock-outs [20]. Olutuase et al. conducted a systematic review to delineate the diverse challenges within the supply chain in LMICs like Nigeria. The review identifies procurement, distribution, inventory management, and storage infrastructure as key areas beset by issues leading to frequent stock-outs of essential medicines. These challenges are further exacerbated by financial limitations, inadequate information management, and a shortage of human resources [27].

- Policies related with logistics

In handling logistics, reliability is the most important aspect to carry out, especially in the field of patient transport. This said reliability comes from the flow of patients, information, medical staff, and the material goods to ensure the continuity of healthcare. Logistics challenges come from the differences in every level of healthcare. There is yet a standardized nor coordinated framework system, thus this will create a gap and withhold said flow between facilities. There is a need to improve the regulation and certified practitioners to help develop and enforce globally-used guidelines. The usage of developed information and technology systems were proven to give hospitals fairly well in performance, but LMICs are facing inadequate healthcare systems, with their limited logistics resource needs to support their vulnerable position. Their condition got worsened by the lack of national infrastructure, such as insufficient road networks, limited access towards remote areas, limited transportation choices, and poor connectivity between central and peripheral areas. There is a need to control and regulate national policy to focus on the strategy to build effective and fair healthcare services. Inadequate storage facilities combined with poor transportation cause delays in the delivery of medications. Insufficient storage facilities and unstable power supplies, are frequent issues mentioned in a number of the publications this study analyzed [27].

- Policies related with pharmaceuticals.

Pharmaceuticals, vaccines, and other healthcare products play pivotal roles within health systems, constituting a substantial portion of total health expenditures in low- and middle-income countries (LMICs), ranging from 7.7 to 67.6% of total health spending in 2006. However, access to essential pharmaceuticals, such as essential medicines, remains a challenge in LMICs, with only 61.5% of these crucial medicines being available [31]. The availability of vaccines in LMICs is also a major concern. Despite having easier access to vaccines in today's world, LMICs continue to face challenges to deliver reliable and safe immunizations to health units. Since 2010, the World Health Organization (WHO) initiated the Effective Vaccine Management (EVM) program, however, scores continue to fall below optimal levels, especially at the lowest tiers of the healthcare system. These programs often face challenges due to inadequate staffing, limited resources, insufficient tools, and a lack of equipment needed to manage the intricate supply chain for vaccines, which are sensitive to temperature and perishable [21]. SCM policy establish transparent procurement processes, robust auditing mechanisms, and ethical guidelines, acting as safeguards against corrupt activities within the supply chain. By promoting accountability and fairness, SCM policies not only protect public health but also contribute to building trust among stakeholders. Efforts to combat corruption within pharmaceutical supply chains are essential to ensure that medications reach patients without compromise, fostering a system that prioritizes health outcomes over unethical practices [28]. Pharmaceutical supply chains are a very vulnerable entry point towards corruption, starting from product registration and procurement to the end of the line, which is last mile distribution [12]. For instance, due to the rigorous implementation of Good Distribution Practice standards, the count of pharmaceutical wholesalers in China dropped significantly from 16,000 to 7445. Undoubtedly, implementing such a policy change poses considerable challenges within the political and economic landscape. Smaller wholesalers, who stand to lose from these policies, are inclined to oppose such initiatives [40].

Promoting good governance and creating greater transparency of product flow information in the public sector supply chain is an important pre-requisite for many of the technical solutions described above to work. Stringent licensing, registration, and quality assurance standards, while crucial for patient safety, sometimes create bottlenecks in the supply chain. The bureaucratic processes associated with compliance may result in delays and increased costs, affecting the timely delivery of health commodities to end-users. Fragmented regulatory landscapes can lead to inconsistencies, duplication of efforts, and a lack of standardization. A harmonized approach is essential to streamline processes, reduce redundancy, and enhance overall supply chain efficiency. Insufficient expertise and resources within regulatory agencies may hinder the effective formulation and enforcement of policies. Investing in training programs and leveraging international collaborations can strengthen the regulatory landscape and enhance the overall resilience of the supply chain [29, 34].

Establishing robust governance in the supply chain involves establishing systems wherein elected officials, policymakers, and public servants overseeing supply chain operations are answerable to the populace (or representatives thereof, including healthcare facility managers) for critical supply chain outcomes. Although cultivating transparency and promoting effective governance within the pharmaceutical supply chain poses considerable challenges and requires substantial effort, the implementation of relatively straightforward technologies enabling health clinics to report shortages of vital medications can facilitate the creation of necessary data sets. The division of government oversight and operational management of public hospitals resulted in significant enhancements in healthcare provision, indicating that governmental efforts should prioritize market regulation within the healthcare sector, while allowing hospital operations to function within a free-market framework [29]. Veronica et al. [38] is describing the policies that healthcare management need to focus and develop to ensure the sustainability of the healthcare management of its facilities as described in Fig. 1, focusing on strategic management and leadership, supplier relationship management, patient flow management, and also customer relationship management [38]. Separation of regulatory and operational control can introduce market dynamics and competition within the healthcare sector. With greater autonomy, public hospitals may be incentivized to optimize their supply chains, negotiate better deals with suppliers, and adopt cost-effective practices to remain competitive.

Healthcare supply chain protocols in developing countries are often hindered by resource constraints, fragmented infrastructure, and limited access to technology. This poses challenges in maintaining consistent supply levels, accurate inventory management, and swift response times. These issues can be further compounded by bureaucratic inefficiencies and insufficient training, making routine protocols less agile and adaptive to sudden shifts in demand during emergencies. Developing countries need to establish agile and scalable systems that can rapidly respond to surges in demand, whether caused by natural disasters, disease outbreaks, or other emergencies. The development of contingency plans, stockpiling essential supplies, and establishing communication channels with key stakeholders are crucial elements in ensuring a swift and effective response [16].

Figure 2 describes the Healthcare Supply Chain process encompasses the coordination of resources and supplies, along with the distribution of medical products and services to healthcare providers and patients. The entirety of this process involves the movement of both physical goods and information through diverse stakeholders. These stakeholders within the Healthcare Supply Chain consist of suppliers, manufacturers/importers, hospitals/clinics, healthcare providers, group purchasing organizations, and regulatory agencies. Suppliers in the healthcare supply chain provide raw materials, components, or finished products needed for medical treatments. This can include pharmaceutical companies, medical device manufacturers, and other vendors. They manufacture, produce, or source medical products, ensuring compliance with quality and regulatory standards. Manufacturers or importers take raw materials or components from suppliers and produce finished medical products. Importers may handle the distribution of products from international suppliers. Manufacturers or importers will do assembling/importing and ensuring quality control measures are in place. Sometimes Group Purchasing Organizations (GPOs) can take place for easier importing. GPOs aggregate the purchasing power of multiple healthcare facilities to negotiate bulk deals with

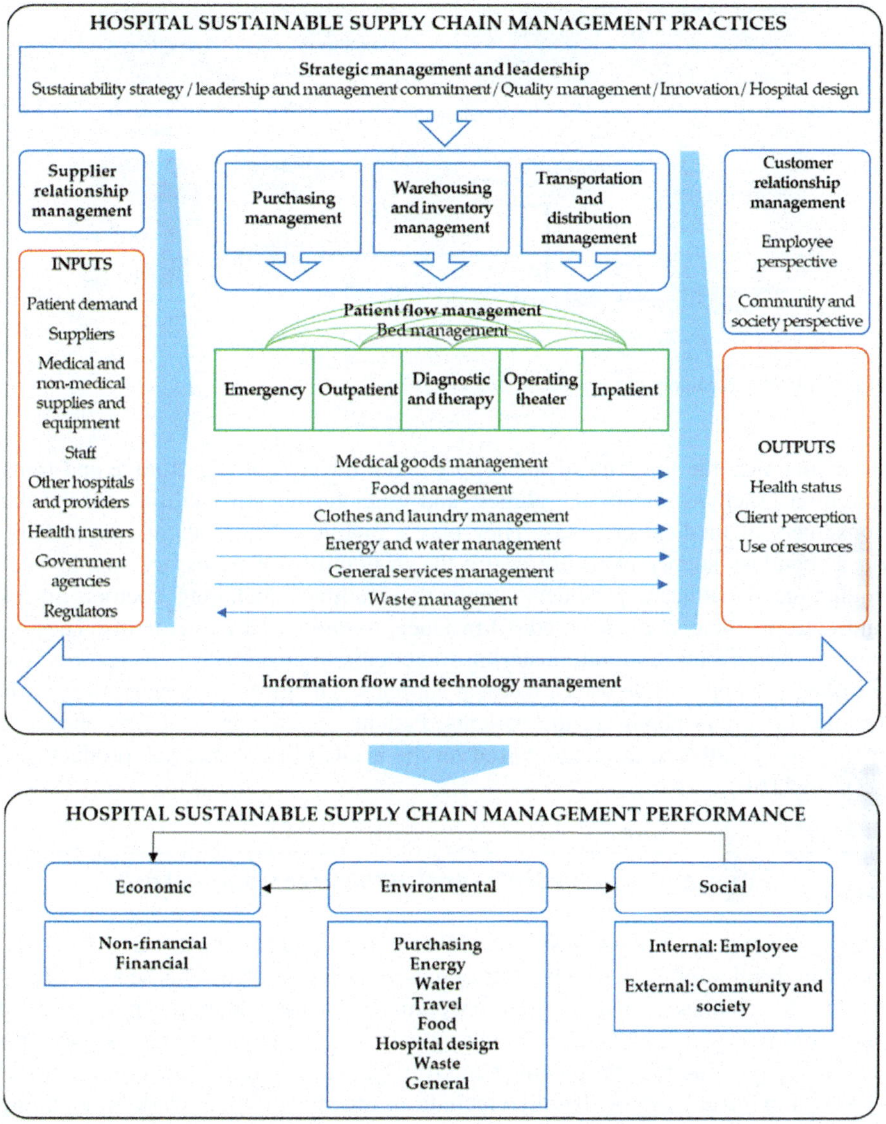

Fig. 1 Sustainable supply chain management practices in healthcare facilit framework. *Source* [38]

suppliers and manufacturers. This helps in achieving cost savings for the participating healthcare organizations. GPOs negotiate contracts, streamline procurement processes, and provide cost-effective purchasing solutions for healthcare providers. Distributors and logistics providers facilitate the transportation and storage of medical products from manufacturers to healthcare facilities. They play a crucial role

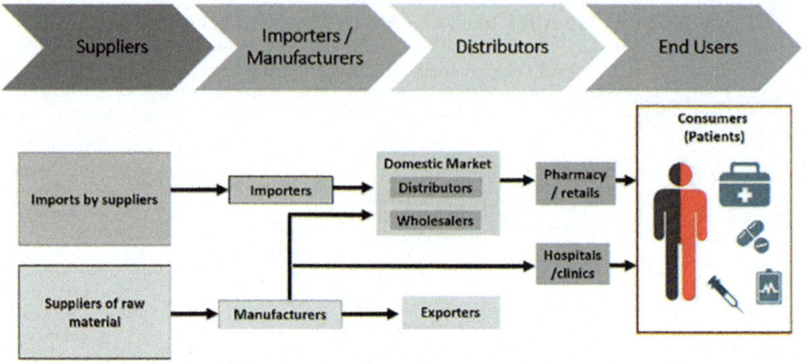

Fig. 2 Healthcare supply chain process, *Source* [16]

in maintaining the integrity of the supply chain through proper storage and transportation practices. Hospitals, clinics, and other healthcare facilities are the end consumers of medical products. They play a pivotal role in patient care and rely on a seamless supply chain to ensure the availability of necessary supplies and equipment. Healthcare providers within the facilities, including doctors, nurses, and other medical staff, use medical products to deliver care to patients. They are the one prescribing and administering treatments, managing patient records, and ensuring the appropriate use of medical supplies. The ultimate beneficiaries of the healthcare supply chain are the patients. Patients receive medical care and treatment from healthcare providers based on the availability of medical products and services [16].

3 Financial Constraints and Resources Allocation

Supply chain management plays a pivotal role in efficient healthcare delivery, especially in developing nations where resources are often limited. This section aims to explore the challenges and obstacles encountered in strengthening supply chains in such contexts, with a particular emphasis on financial constraints and resource allocation in Low- and Middle-Income Countries (LMICs) and Low-Income Countries (LICs). Financial barriers identified include an insufficient framework for planning, coordination, and management, inadequate funding, a shortage of skilled personnel, weak regulatory and governance frameworks at national and sub-national levels, and slow adoption of Electronic Logistics Information Systems to support supply chain operations. Overcoming these challenges requires increased investments to improve policy formulation and implementation, infrastructure, equipment, support systems, and the knowledge and skills of supply chain personnel. It also necessitates enhanced funding, alongside governance and accountability improvements. The system encompasses structures and processes ensuring the sourcing, purchasing, transportation, and distribution of equipment, commodities, and supplies to end-users. The interactions among these elements significantly affect the availability of medical products across all levels of healthcare. Key factors facilitating access to essential medicines and commodities throughout the healthcare system include availability, affordability, geographical accessibility, acceptability (rational selection and use), and quality. Interventions have targeted various aspects of the health supply chain, including human resources, infrastructure, equipment, information systems, medicines management, policy formulation and implementation, efficiency enhancements, transparency improvements, and the promotion of effective stakeholder collaborations [10].

In developing countries, a prolonged cycle of supply chain management (SCM) can be linked to a myriad of interconnected issues, forming a complex network of challenges that impede the smooth flow of goods and services. Figure 3 depicts the extensive array of stakeholders engaged in financing and physically distributing drugs and healthcare commodities in Low-Income Countries (LICs) and Low- and Middle-Income Countries (LMICs). The illustration demonstrates the intricate combination of institutions specializing in funding, manufacturing, importation, wholesaling, retailing, and various other support functions that must collaborate to ensure the availability of drugs to the end-patient [18]. As an instance, within the public sector supply chain of Zambia, it is evident that 12 primary categories of health products were acquired through 19 distinct funding sources, involving 17 procurement organizations and more than six first-tier warehousing providers [7].

The foremost challenge is the limited financial resources available for supply chain improvement initiatives. Financial constraints in developing countries limit firms' access to capital, leading to lower value-added stages in the supply chain and affecting their choice of trade regime and profitability. This financial limitation directly impacts the procurement, storage, and distribution of medical supplies, leading to inefficiencies and disruptions in the healthcare supply chain. Understanding how these financial constraints hinder supply chain strengthening efforts is crucial for formulating effective strategies to navigate these challenges [23]. Funding allocated to the healthcare sector has persistently remained at low levels over multiple years in Low-Income Countries (LICs) and Low- and Middle-Income Countries (LMICs). For instance, in Uganda, the healthcare sector received 5.1% of the national budget for the Fiscal Year 2020/2021, a decrease from 7.9% in the previous fiscal year. More than 70% of public expenditure on medications for HIV/AIDS, malaria, and tuberculosis is provided by development partners. In Uganda, the procurement of x-ray devices is occasionally facilitated through donations, although operational challenges are encountered with the machinery [20].

In Low- and Middle-Income Countries (LMICs) and Low-Income Countries (LICs), resource allocation emerges as a significant obstacle to enhancing supply chains. Health product supply chains in these regions face numerous challenges. Ineffectual supply chains undermine the broader healthcare system's capacity to address the population's healthcare requirements and jeopardize treatment initiatives. The allocation of limited resources necessitates strategic planning to ensure efficient distribution across different facets of the supply chain. Whether it involves optimizing transportation networks, integrating technological solutions,

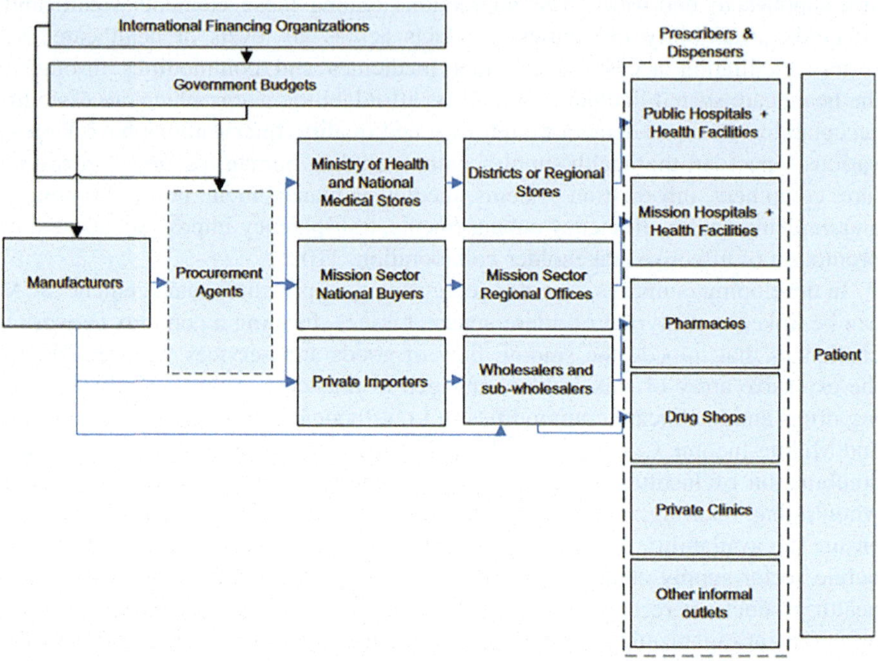

Fig. 3 Physical and financial flows in the supply chain for drugs and health commodities LIC and LMIC, *Source* [18]

or enhancing personnel training, determining resource allocation becomes a pivotal decision-making process [18, 40]. Another case in Eastern Uganda, a regional hospital receives an x-ray machine that initially appears to be in satisfactory condition. However, the machine malfunctions during a procedure shortly after being put into service, leaving the hospital staff in a predicament. Lacking trained biomedical technicians on-site, the machine remains idle for several months. Eventually, a technician from Kampala is located, but upon examination, they are unable to determine the required replacement part without the machine's manual. The hospital discovers that the replacement part is not only more expensive than anticipated but also unavailable locally, necessitating a special order from abroad. Faced with competing financial priorities and limited resources, the hospital administration reluctantly decides against pursuing the costly repair. Despite the pressing need for its diagnostic capabilities, the x-ray machine remains inoperable. [20].

Moreover, the role of international collaborations and partnerships in mitigating these challenges will be explored. Leveraging external support, knowledge transfer, and innovative funding mechanisms can play a pivotal role in overcoming financial constraints. Additionally, we will examine case studies and success stories to extract valuable lessons and best practices that can be adapted and scaled in similar settings. The study by Mandal and Jha (2017) has shown that collaborative planning, execution, and decision-making are important collaborative assets for developing successful hospital-supplier integration [22]. Study in Canada (2008) also showed St. Michael's Hospital and Baxter Canada's partnership has streamlined backorder management, leading to better patient care and a more efficient supply chain process [25].

In conclusion, addressing the challenges and barriers to supply chain strengthening in developing countries requires a nuanced understanding of financial constraints and resource allocation dynamics. By shedding light on these intricacies, this article aims to contribute to the discourse on improving healthcare supply chains in the context of limited resources, fostering resilience and sustainability in healthcare delivery systems worldwide.

4 Infrastructure Constraints and Supply Chain Resilience

In developing countries, infrastructure deficiencies present a major barrier to the effective operation of healthcare supply chains. Insufficient transportation networks, inadequate storage facilities, and unreliable energy sources lead to delays and interruptions in the distribution of medical supplies. Overcoming these infrastructure challenges demands a holistic approach that integrates innovative technological solutions and fosters collaboration among governments, non-profit organizations, and the private sector. Many LMICs and LICs struggle with inadequate information regarding consumption and stock levels, as well as constraints in funding and capacity, compounded by deficient infrastructure, all contributing to inappropriate stock levels [30].

For example, a qualitative research study conducted in Nigeria in 2018, involving interviews with pharmacists, revealed several recurring themes. These encompassed subpar supply chain management practices, inadequate forecasting and data collection, reported obstacles to local drug manufacturing, regulatory concerns, and ineffective policy enforcement. Additionally, there were concerns about insufficient support for in-country medical logisticians. Community pharmacists expressed apprehensions about receiving damaged products from wholesalers and suppliers, ranging from compromised packaging to alterations in dosage forms. Reports surfaced indicating therapeutic failures, particularly with cold chain items such as ophthalmic solutions, suppositories, and injectables. Representatives from pharmaceutical companies suggested that the existence of disparate logistics and distribution channels resulted in disjointed supply chains, increased incidents of theft and leakage, losses during transit, and unauthorized diversion of drugs for personal use. Hospital pharmacists frequently encountered recurring stock-outs of essential medicines due to deficient procurement processes, inadequate forecasting, ineffective data management, inefficient inventory control, and a shortage of personnel. Pharmaceutical manufacturers criticized government initiatives aimed at boosting local drug production, citing high import tariffs on active pharmaceutical ingredients and raw materials compared to finished medicines. Regulatory and administrative pharmacists from agencies like the National Agency for Food and Drug Administration and Control and the Pharmacists Council of Nigeria underscored corruption, insufficient infrastructure, funding, and workforce, deficient policy formulation and implementation, and a lack of cohesive collaboration among stakeholders as primary impediments to the effective supervision and regulation of the medicine supply chain. Insufficient funding for public health initiatives and interventions resulted in limited resources to maintain a resilient medicine supply chain. Studies conducted in Nigeria highlighted delays in the importation of antimalarials and challenges in maintaining delivery vehicles, as well as disruptions in the distribution of medicines for multi-drug resistant tuberculosis due to delayed inventory reports, inaccuracies in reporting, and transportation setbacks like vehicle breakdowns. Challenges such as the inability to maintain optimal vaccine temperatures during transportation, interruptions in the supply of tuberculosis drugs by logistics companies due to distribution inefficiencies, insecurity during vaccine transportation, integrity concerns, and logistical distances between manufacturers and Nigeria have all been identified as vaccine supply chain challenges. Additionally, issues like damaged products and packaging, disorganized supply chains due to multiple distribution channels resulting in high levels of theft and losses during transit, and delays in submitting inventory reports leading to distribution hiccups and inaccuracies have been observed [9].

Infrastructure-related obstacles are a common theme across various studies. For instance, in a survey involving healthcare professionals, 62% of respondents identified inadequate storage facilities for medicines as a primary challenge encountered during the distribution of ivermectin. The disruption of supply chains due to the destruction of storage facilities has also been emphasized. Concerns regarding inadequate and substandard storage facilities for vaccines, particularly in Nigeria's local government areas, have been raised as significant issues. Factors impacting cold chain performance include the inadequacy of both dry and cold chain storage facilities. A study examining vaccine storage practices in a Nigerian state found that only 28.6% of healthcare facilities had functional thermometers in their storage areas. Challenges identified include supply chain disruptions caused by storage facility destruction, limited storage space for ivermectin, insufficient cold storage infrastructure, and a lack of adequate ice packs [9].

Collaborative approaches to infrastructure development involve partnerships with technology companies for the implementation of cutting-edge solutions. For instance, deploying temperature-controlled storage units and utilizing real-time tracking systems can enhance the visibility and efficiency of the supply chain. International collaborations can facilitate the transfer of knowledge and resources to develop and maintain resilient infrastructure, ensuring the consistent flow of medical supplies even in challenging environments. Supply chain resilience is crucial, especially in the face of unforeseen events such as natural disasters, conflicts, or pandemics. Developing countries are often disproportionately affected by such events, underscoring the need for adaptable and robust supply chain systems. Collaborative efforts in this context involve the establishment of contingency plans, training programs for local responders, and the creation of strategic stockpiles to address emergency situations promptly. Furthermore, capacity building at the local level is integral to enhancing supply chain resilience. Collaborations can involve training programs for healthcare personnel, logistics professionals, and community leaders. This knowledge-sharing approach empowers local communities to actively participate in and contribute to the resilience of the healthcare supply chain. In conclusion, the challenges posed by infrastructure constraints in developing countries necessitate collaborative approaches that prioritize resilience. By forging partnerships between various stakeholders, including governments, technology providers, and local communities, sustainable solutions can be devised. This article advocates for the importance of collaborative efforts in overcoming infrastructure challenges, ultimately contributing to the development of resilient and effective healthcare supply chains in developing nations.

5 Technological Innovations and Overcoming Barriers

Over the past two decades, various sectors, including healthcare, have encountered heightened complexity in their supply chains, fueled by increased global operations and technological advancements, particularly in digital innovation. The dynamic nature of the business environment is compelling many sectors, including healthcare, to competitively redesign their supply chains. This dynamic supply chain design is primarily motivated by objectives such as cost reduction, enhanced delivery reliability, and the need for agility. However, barriers to this redesign process include challenges like weak forecasting, supply chain intricacy, and product complexity. Technological or digital innovations within the supply chain realm can yield benefits such as enhanced process automation, expanded distribution capabilities, and improved competitive positioning. Nonetheless, the implementation of such innovations faces hurdles such as cost considerations and the need for relevant competencies. Key technologies identified as best practices for sustainable supply chain management include the Internet of Things (IoT), Big Data and Predictive Analytics, Blockchain, Design for Environment, and Artificial Intelligence. An early application of IoT in supply chain processes involves the utilization of Radio Frequency Identification (RFID) tags for product recognition and Wireless Sensor Network (WSN) for analytical functions like data acquisition and signal recording. Big Data and Predictive Analytics play crucial roles in controlling supply chain operations, leveraging data-intensive systems that can be continuously updated based on product usage. Geographical Information Systems (GIS) are also utilized for forecasting and planning purposes, leveraging big data capabilities. Additionally, considerations for environmental impacts in the manufacturing process underscore the importance of implementing technological innovations that support environmentally sustainable supply chains, such as designs aimed at mitigating negative environmental effects [14].

Heeres et al. [14] have classified the factors influencing the adoption of Internet of Things (IoT) in healthcare supply chains, as depicted in Fig. 4. Drivers for implementation encompass financial, operational, strategic, and supply chain-related factors, while barriers include financial, strategic, supply chain-related, technological, and user-related challenges. Despite potential high initial costs, IoT adoption promises significant cost reductions through various means. For instance, reduced personnel requirements result in lowered labor expenses for hospitals. Additionally, IoT facilitates enhanced inventory management, leading to decreased rush orders and minimized instances of expired inventory. The extensive data collected through IoT holds promise for enhancing overall performance, while automation of certain processes increases operational efficiency and flexibility, while reducing human errors. Real-time inventory insights provided by IoT improve inventory management, tackling issues of excess stock and stock-outs prevalent in many healthcare facilities. Interviewees also emphasized the potential for operational automation, such as automating the ordering process and utilizing robots for intra-hospital logistics. Regulatory pressures drive innovation, encouraging compliance with evolving regulations or capitalizing on relaxed regulations. Organizations are increasingly prioritizing innovation within healthcare supply chains, acknowledging the urgency of change, a sentiment reinforced by the pandemic's spotlight on critical processes like logistics and procurement. Supply chain-related drivers include enhanced collaboration with suppliers, improved traceability, and increased transparency. Effective collaboration often requires IoT adoption to synchronize information systems, enabling seamless information exchange. Moreover, IoT facilitates information sharing along the supply chain, enabling suppliers to anticipate demand irregularities and respond promptly [14].

One of the main hurdles in developing countries relates to the lack of transparency and visibility within supply chains. Technological advancements, such

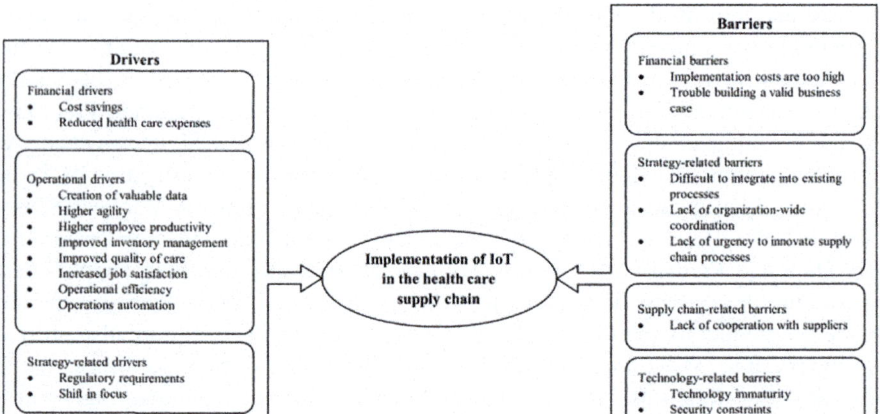

Fig. 4 Drivers and barriers to implementing Internet of Things (IoT) in the health care supply chain. *Source* [14]

as blockchain and Internet of Things (IoT) applications, present solutions to improve traceability and transparency. The implementation of blockchain technology enables secure and transparent recording of transactions, fostering trust and accountability across the supply chain. When combined with IoT devices, real-time monitoring of shipments becomes achievable, reducing the risk of loss, theft, or spoilage. Currently, the literature regarding the use of Artificial Intelligence (AI) and Big Data Analysis (BDA) to bolster supply chain resilience appears somewhat fragmented, focusing predominantly on available computational techniques to support various mitigation strategies. Nevertheless, the rapid advancement of these technologies and the continuous disruption of supply chain systems present an opportunity to delve deeper into their specific benefits and their potential roles in different phases of supply chain resilience efforts. This exploration should consider both observed and anticipated challenges related to their implementation and utilization [14].

Integrating artificial intelligence (AI) into supply chain management further enhances efficiency. AI-powered predictive analytics can forecast demand, optimize inventory levels, and streamline distribution processes. Machine learning algorithms can adapt to evolving circumstances, ensuring a responsive and resilient supply chain. One of the latest applications of AI to logistics is autonomous cars and trucks, which can increase logistics safety by excluding human involvement in transportation. Furthermore, with the application of AI, network management is also improving; many sectors are now able to achieve a higher level of efficiency in the sorting and route management. Resource constraints often impede the implementation of advanced technologies in developing regions. However, overcoming financial barriers can be achieved through innovative models, such as technology-sharing initiatives and public–private partnerships. Collaboration between governments, non-profit organizations, and the private sector can facilitate the adoption of cost-effective technological solutions tailored to the specific needs of each region. Mobile technology, in particular, plays a pivotal role in overcoming communication challenges, enabling real-time data exchange and facilitating more efficient coordination among stakeholders [14].

Technological innovation can improve supply chain resilience, customer service, and efficiency by enhancing communication and information distribution throughout its network. Successful supply chain collaboration is primarily driven by people with technology, information, and measurement systems as major barriers. Addressing the digital divide is crucial in leveraging the benefits of technological innovations. Initiatives to improve digital literacy and provide training for healthcare professionals and supply chain managers are essential. The people's issues, such as culture, trust, aversion to change, and willingness to collaborate, are more intractable. People are the key bridge to successful collaborative innovation in the supply chain. This can impact customer satisfaction and service, which is considered more lasting than cost savings [14, 19].

In conclusion, the challenges and barriers in developing countries' supply chains can be effectively addressed through the strategic application of technological innovations. Embracing blockchain, IoT, and AI technologies, while simultaneously promoting digital literacy and fostering collaboration, paves the way for resilient and efficient supply chains. This article advocates for a technology-centric approach, emphasizing the transformative potential of innovations in strengthening supply chains and improving healthcare outcomes in developing nations [3, 14].

6 Collaborative Approaches for Sustainable Solutions

One of the major challenges lies in the lack of infrastructure and technology. Many developing countries struggle with outdated or insufficient infrastructure for transportation, storage, and distribution of medical supplies. Collaborative approaches can involve partnerships with technology companies or international organizations to implement innovative solutions, such as real-time tracking systems, to enhance visibility and efficiency in the supply chain. Financial constraints are another significant barrier that collaborative efforts can address. By pooling resources through partnerships between governments, non-governmental organizations (NGOs), and private sector entities, a more substantial financial base can be created. This collective investment can be directed towards building robust supply chain systems, including investing in modern storage facilities, improving transportation networks, and implementing training programs for personnel [9, 39, 40].

Efficient supply chains are vital for the effective functioning of healthcare systems, especially in developing countries facing unique challenges. Simplifying the health supply chain, namely by decreasing lead time and uncertainties, increasing order frequency, and also by adjusting order points and safety stocks, are found to result in improved customer service. This is because there are minimal stock shortages and lower expenses are maintained. With these changes, better integration between information and the movement of goods could be made, ultimately reducing bottlenecks in the supply chain [15]. Considering these critical enhancements to healthcare supply chains, exploring the pivotal role of Public–Private Partnerships (PPPs), advocating for multi stakeholder collaboration, and embracing Global Standards and Best Practices become imperative subheadings to further optimize these systems.

1. Public–private partnerships (PPPs)

Public–Private Partnerships (PPPs) are defined as extended agreements between a government entity and a private company, which aims to deliver public services or assets. In these arrangements, the private company commonly assumes considerable risk and managerial duties, and compensation is tied to the company's performance [1]. On a global scale, governments in both developed and developing countries view PPPs as a crucial mechanism to broaden the reach of high-quality healthcare services, improve the healthcare financing system, and tap into the managerial expertise available within the private sector [37].

As stated from a study by Carter and Rogers (2008), the sustainability of the supply chain involves combining environmental, social, and economic standards to enable an organization to attain prolonged economic feasibility. The integration of sustainability principles within Public–Private Partnerships (PPPs) is very important in ensuring the long-term economic, environmental, and social viability of collaborative initiatives. The central idea of PPPs is that added value can be achieved through greater cooperation between public and private sectors (Steijn et al. 2011; Amman et al. 2014; Davis and Friske, 2015). This trend has been growing since the great recession started in 2008 and in infrastructural investments PPP is a key-driver for sustainability [24].

Around the world, governments in both advanced and emerging nations view Public–Private Partnerships (PPPs) as a crucial tool for broadening access to high-quality healthcare services. They see PPPs as a means to improve the health financing system and utilize the managerial expertise of the private sector [5]. A study by [8] shows that Public–Private Partnerships (PPPs) have a significant role in managing the Health Supply Chain in Rwanda. Enhancing PPPs in Health Supply Chain Management (HSCM) involved successful coordination of PPPs (93.3%) and the enhancement of dialogue and formal platforms (90.6%).[8]

In developed countries, PPP has been proven to boost the distribution of healthcare logistics and economics. If a country has the objective of optimizing PPP for healthcare supply chain, there are certain key strategies that might be considered and implemented to further strengthen their relationship [12]:

1. Establish clear governance and regulations. This is necessary to guide the implementation of the medical supply chain. Defining the roles of each sector's partners and also their responsibilities is important to ensure the accountability and transparency of each sector which ultimately prevents corruption.
2. Developing mechanisms of risk sharing and also providing incentives to each sector is important in encouraging private sectors to collaborate with public sectors. This risk and incentive mechanism also mitigates the risk of PPP, and further aligns the interests of both sectors in the supply chain.
3. Promoting the usage of platforms of information sharing and common technology to support the visibility and efficiency of the medical supply chain. Promoting such platforms can enhance the coordination and also collaboration of both sectors, which is beneficial to broaden the distributional regions, and also in turn ensure a more secure healthcare supply chain.
4. Implementing a competent monitoring and evaluation system of both sectors is necessary to track the performance of the PPP, the sectors included, and the medical supply chain itself. A system with good reliability can help identify the areas in need for improvement and also ensure the alignment of the PPP to the intended objectives and benefits.

In developing countries, the collaboration of public and private sectors in enhancing the efficiency of medical supply chain has its own advantages and drawbacks. The advantages of PPP include a leverage of the private sector expertise in logistics, technology, medical innovations; an opportunity to refine the operations of supply chain; an increased access to crucial medical resources, accurate financial funding, IT, human resources; in which all collaborate in enhancing the overall supply chain and medical services needed to shape an effective healthcare system. These collaborations can also enhance the nationwide access to healthcare services and medical supplies, quality and performance of patient care, and patient satisfaction to the healthcare system. Innovations and flexibility, which are key components of private sectors, is important in navigating and addressing the challenges, obstacles, and threats of universal national healthcare in developing countries, especially in times where adaptation is necessary [1, 8].

However, the disadvantages and challenges of PPP as a collaborative model needs to also be examined and addressed accordingly. A risk of healthcare service privatization can significantly diminish vulnerable populations' access to care. This privatization can also increase the treatment cost for patients, thus burdening them. A potential lack of accountability is also possible due to the possibility of private sectors partners prioritizing profits over public health. An unequal power dynamic between the two sectors might also emerge. Private sectors might have the probability to dominate the decision-making process in ensuring the supply chain, and if unfavorable and unprofitable outcomes were to happen to the healthcare system, private sectors might withdraw from the collaborations. Such outcomes were prone to be influenced by the political or economic environment of the country changes. Albeit having both advantages and disadvantages, the collaboration between public and private sectors in improving medical supply chains in developing countries and LMICs is multifaceted, and establishing a clear governance structure, comprehensive policies, promoting accountability, and ensuring that partnerships are sustainable and equitable for a long time is important to providing a safe and effective medical supply chain [12, 24].

2. Multi-stakeholder collaboration

Another collaborative approach necessary to understand to address the problems, challenges, and obstacles of the medical supply chain involves multiple stakeholders coming from the government, non-government, and international organizations. A secure and effective collaborative approach of these stakeholders can lead to the share of medical resources, expertise, and practice across the different sectors of the same country. It is hoped that the presence of the collaboration itself can in turn induce the creation of comprehensive and targeted sets of strategies aimed to ensure better coordination and communication among the medical supply chain aspects within developing countries and LMICs. However, to get to the solution, a unified and common vision and goals of the collaboration needs to be defined at the beginning of the collaboration to then initiate an unified and effective approach to the challenges and obstacles of the supply chain. The shared commitment between those sectors can enhance cooperation, minimize conflicts, and reinforce the collaborative spirit needed of each sector for effective supply chain management. It is essential and fundamental to establish a clear and concise partnership agreement and contract, with the hopes of ensuring an accountable and transparent multiple stakeholder partnership. The existence of this agreement and contract can determine the definition of roles, responsibilities, and expectations of each stakeholders included. This agreement is also hoped to foster a sense of accountability and trust within the collaborative framework. Consistently applying these strategies might optimize the collaborative approach of the multiple stakeholders in improving the medical supply chain management within developing countries and LMICs. This all aims for the final goal of improving healthcare access across the nation, achieving a better health outcome in patients, enhancing the overall efficiency of the healthcare system, and creating multinational networks needed for future collaborations [2, 17].

3. Global standards and best practices

The standards provided and created to be implemented globally can be one of the guiding standards of medical supply chain management in developing countries and LMICs. Standards provided in terms of guidelines of supply chain management might include the usage of standardized procedures, technologies, and measures in achieving a better quality of the medical products and services. If a developing country has a struggle in developing its own standards and guidelines, adhering to the global and international one might prove as an alternative solution in ensuring the availability and quality of the healthcare services, for having a standard for medical procedures and processes is one of the crucial requirements of a developed medical supply chain. The framework used to standardize the performance of healthcare personnels in charge of the medical supply chain can provide a step-to-step guideline for ensuring consistent and efficient task management. These steps included in the guideline need to provide a uniform establishment of procedures regarding the procurement, inventory, and distribution of healthcare supplies and services. Not only does it need specific steps, it also needs consistency to help avoid restrictions, errors, operational problems, which all contribute to an improved overall efficiency. The standard is also used to define each sector and personnels' roles and responsibilities in those procedures and processes, thus making performance tracking and problem identification an easier task for the general manager. All these advantages of the framework can provide a better and more effective supply chain that can make a timely and accurate delivery of medical supplies possible [33, 36].

The implementation of a global standard and guideline in a developing country's healthcare setting can ensure that each step included in the chain adheres to a minimum quality standard, from product procurement to storage and to distribution. The quality of these steps can directly influence the medical supply and service quality, which in turn causes an effect on patient outcomes. Not only is a guideline in general necessary, but the compliance of regulatory requirements is also a key factor in creating the flawless healthcare service flow and environment. The presence of procedural and process standards can ensure each sector and personnels involved in the framework adhere to the relevant regulations and standards. It is hoped that legal issues of the framework will not pose a threat on the medical supply chain, for it aligns with the framework of current national policies. In general, the standard of procedures of the medical supply chain can promote its efficiency, accountability, adaptability, and compliance. It is hoped that these improvements can then affect the better outcome of patients and also the resilience of the nationwide healthcare systems of the developing countries [33, 41].

Collaborations can facilitate the development of standardized regulatory frameworks that streamline processes and ensure compliance. International partnerships can provide technical assistance to help countries align their regulatory practices with global standards, thereby reducing barriers to the efficient movement of medical goods. The engagement of local communities is essential for the success of any supply chain initiative. Collaborative approaches must involve community stakeholders, including healthcare providers, to gain insights into local needs and challenges. This participatory approach ensures that supply chain solutions are culturally sensitive, sustainable, and aligned with the unique dynamics of the communities they serve [10, 39, 40].

7 Conclusion

In conclusion, addressing the multifaceted challenges surrounding supply chain strengthening in developing countries demands a comprehensive and concerted effort from various stakeholders. The intricate web of policy and regulatory challenges requires governments to take proactive measures in streamlining regulations, fostering transparency, and promoting public–private partnerships. By creating an enabling environment that facilitates smoother logistics and enhances competitiveness, policymakers can pave the way for a more resilient supply chain ecosystem.

Moreover, overcoming financial constraints and effectively allocating resources are critical steps in bolstering supply chain resilience. Innovative financing mechanisms, coupled with efforts to promote financial inclusion, can empower businesses, particularly small and medium enterprises, to invest in essential infrastructure and technology. This investment not only improves operational efficiency but also enhances the overall adaptability of supply chains to external shocks and disruptions.

Furthermore, embracing technological innovations and adopting collaborative approaches are paramount for overcoming barriers and fostering sustainable solutions. Leveraging advancements such as digitalization, data analytics, and automation can significantly enhance supply chain efficiency, visibility, and responsiveness. Additionally, fostering collaboration among stakeholders, including governments, businesses, civil society, and international organizations, can lead to the development of holistic solutions that address systemic challenges and promote inclusive growth. By harnessing the collective expertise and resources of these diverse actors, developing countries can unlock the full potential of their supply chains, driving economic development and resilience in the face of evolving global dynamics.

References

1. Abuzaineh N, Brashers E, Foong S, Feachem R, Da Rita P (2018) PPPs in healthcare: models, lessons and trends for the future [WWW document]. Healthcare public–private partnership series. URL https://www.pwc.com/gx/en/healthcare/assets/ppps-in-healthcare.pdf. Accessed 26 Dec 2023
2. Akenroye TO, Abubakre A, Elbaz J, Vishnu CR, BekaBeNguema JN, Rana G, Ihua UB, Kalili H, Falode O (2022) Modeling the barriers to multistakeholder collaboration for COVID-19 pandemic response: evidence from Sub-Saharan Africa. Int Public Manag J 25(2):192–216. https://doi.org/10.1080/10967494.2021.1970061
3. Ananthakrishnan A, Luz ACG, Kc S, Ong L, Oh C, Isaranuwatchai W, Dabak SV, Teerawattananon Y, Turner HC (2022) How can health technology assessment support our response to public health emergencies? Health Res Policy Syst 20(1):124. https://doi.org/10.1186/s12961-022-00925-z
4. Arora M, Yogita G (2018) Importance of supply chain management in healthcare of third world countries. Int J Supply Oper Manag 5(1):101–106
5. Ashby A, Leat M, Hudson-Smith M (2012) Making connections: a review of supply chain management and sustainability literature. Supply Chain Manag: Int J 17:497–516. https://doi.org/10.1108/13598541211258573
6. Baig SA, Abrar M, Batool A, Hashim M, Shabbir R (2020) Barriers to the adoption of sustainable supply chain management practices: moderating role of firm size. Cogent Bus Manag 7:1841525. https://doi.org/10.1080/23311975.2020.1841525
7. Brown A, Syacumpi M (2006) RHCS country case study: Zambia final version commissioned jointly by the department for international development and the Netherlands ministry of foreign affairs. [WWW document]. http://www.heart-resources.org/wp-content/uploads/2012/10/RHCS-Zambia.pdf. Accessed 15 Dec 2023
8. Byomuhangi E, Kayumba PC, Umuhoza SM (2021) The use of public–private partnerships in health supply chain management in Rwanda. Rwanda J Med Health Sci 4:237–256. https://doi.org/10.4314/rjmhs.v4i2.4
9. Chukwu OA, Chukwu U, Lemoha C (2018) Poor performance of medicines logistics and supply chain systems in a developing country context: lessons from Nigeria. J Pharm Health Serv Res 9:289–291. https://doi.org/10.1111/jphs.12274
10. Dowling P (2011) Healthcare supply chains in developing countries, situational analysis
11. Gamessa TW, Abebe ST, Abate LD, Abo MK, Mekonnen AA, Tadesse ZK, Woyesa AF, Obse RB, Ibrahim MA, Simegn GL (2022) Planning and budgeting of medical devices among ethiopian public hospitals. Clinico Econ Outcomes Res 14:405–413. https://doi.org/10.2147/CEOR.S363376
12. Ghafoor L (2023) A conceptual study on corruption in public–private partnerships
13. Gupta U, Ramesh A (2015) Analyzing the barriers of health care supply chain in India: the contribution and interaction of factors. Proc Soc Behav Sci 189:217–228. https://doi.org/10.1016/j.sbspro.2015.03.217

14. Heeres TJ, Tran TM, Noort BAC (2023) Drivers and barriers to implementing the internet of things in the health care supply chain: mixed methods multicase study. J Med Internet Res 25:e48730. https://doi.org/10.2196/48730
15. Jahre M, Dumoulin L, Greenhalgh LB, Hudspeth C, Limlim P, Spindler A (2012) Improving health in developing countries: reducing complexity of drug supply chains. J Hum Logist Supply Chain Manag 2:54–84. https://doi.org/10.1108/20426741211226000
16. Kanokphanvanich C, Rattanawong W, Vongmanee V (2022) A Meta-analysis of health care supply chain performance for patient safety. In: 2022 14th international conference on software, knowledge, information management and applications (SKIMA). IEEE, pp 13–20. https://doi.org/10.1109/SKIMA57145.2022.10029487
17. Kazancoglu Y, Sezer MD, Ozbiltekin-Pala M, Kucukvar M (2022) Investigating the role of stakeholder engagement for more resilient vaccine supply chains during COVID-19. Oper Manag Res 15:428–439. https://doi.org/10.1007/s12063-021-00223-x
18. Kraiselburd S, Yadav P (2013) Supply chains and global health: an imperative for bringing operations management scholarship into action. Prod Oper Manag 22:377–381. https://doi.org/10.1111/j.1937-5956.2011.01315.x
19. Kruse C, Heinemann K (2022) Facilitators and barriers to the adoption of telemedicine during the first year of COVID-19: systematic review. J Med Internet Res. https://doi.org/10.2196/31752
20. Lugada E, Komakech H, Ochola I, Mwebaze S, OlowoOteba M, OkidiLadwar D (2022) Health supply chain system in Uganda: current issues, structure, performance, and implications for systems strengthening. J Pharm Policy Pract 15:14. https://doi.org/10.1186/s40545-022-00412-4
21. Luzze H, Badiane O, MamadouNdiaye EH, Ndiaye AS, Atuhaire B, Atuhebwe P, Guinot P, Fry Sosne E, Gueye A (2017) Understanding the policy environment for immunization supply chains: lessons learned from landscape analyses in Uganda and Senegal. Vaccine 35:2141–2147. https://doi.org/10.1016/j.vaccine.2016.10.089
22. Mandal S, Jha RR (2018) Exploring the importance of collaborative assets to hospital-supplier integration in healthcare supply chains. Int J Prod Res 56:2666–2683. https://doi.org/10.1080/00207543.2017.1381349
23. Manova KB, Yu Z (2012) Firms and credit constraints along the value-added chain: processing trade in China. SSRN Electron J. https://doi.org/10.2139/ssrn.2177073
24. Moro Visconti R (2015) Healthcare public–private partnerships and infrastructural supply chain sustainability. SSRN Electron J. https://doi.org/10.2139/ssrn.2684038
25. Motiwala SS, McLaughlin JE, King J, Hodgson B, Hamilton M (2008) Advancing the health care supply chain and promoting leadership through strategic partnerships with industry. Healthc Manag Forum 21:23–28. https://doi.org/10.1016/S0840-4704(10)60542-X
26. Nieuwenkamp R (2016) Legislation on responsible business conduct must reinforce the wheel, not reinvent it. In: Debate the issues: investment. OECD, pp 29–33. https://doi.org/10.1787/9789264242661-en
27. Olutuase VO, Iwu-Jaja CJ, Akuoko CP, Adewuyi EO, Khanal V (2022) Medicines and vaccines supply chains challenges in Nigeria: a scoping review. BMC Public Health 22:11. https://doi.org/10.1186/s12889-021-12361-9
28. Onwujekwe O, Agwu P, Odii A, Charles O, Divine O, Nwokolo CC, Roy P, Eleanor H, Mckee M, Dina B (2020) Corruption in the procurement of pharmaceuticals in Anglophone sub-Saharan Africa: a scoping literature review
29. Pan J, Liu GG, Gao C (2013) How does separating government regulatory and operational control of public hospitals matter to healthcare supply? China Econ Rev 27:1–14. https://doi.org/10.1016/j.chieco.2013.07.002
30. Schöpperle A (2013) Analysis of challenges of medical supply chains in sub-Saharan Africa regarding inventory management and transport and distribution project thesis [WWW document]. https://iaphl.org/wp-content/uploads/2016/05/Medical-Supply-Chain-Challenges.Masterthesis.ASchoepperle.pdf. Accessed 26 Dec 2023

31. Seidman G, Atun R (2017) Do changes to supply chains and procurement processes yield cost savings and improve availability of pharmaceuticals, vaccines or health products? A systematic review of evidence from low-income and middle-income countries. BMJ Glob Health 2:e000243. https://doi.org/10.1136/bmjgh-2016-000243
32. Sheedy K (n. d) n.d. Annual report 2022–2023 LMIC-CIMT. [WWW document]. https://lmic-cimt.ca/annual-report-2022-2023. Accessed 15 Dec 2023
33. Shukor AAA, Newaz MdS, Rahman MK, Taha AZ (2021) Supply chain integration and its impact on supply chain agility and organizational flexibility in manufacturing firms. Int J Emerg Mark 16:1721–1744. https://doi.org/10.1108/IJOEM-04-2020-0418
34. Thapa R, Yih A, Chauhan A, Poudel S, Singh S, Shrestha S, Tamang S, Shrestha R, Rajbhandari R (2022) Effect of deploying biomedical equipment technician on the functionality of medical equipment in the government hospitals of rural Nepal. Hum Resour Health 20:21. https://doi.org/10.1186/s12960-022-00719-y
35. The World Bank (2006) Health financing revisited a practioner's guide. The World Bank, Washington DC
36. USAID (2020) Best practices in supply chain preparedness for public health emergencies. [WWW document]. US: United States agency for international development (USAID). https://www.ghsupplychain.org/sites/default/files/2021-12/Best-Practices-in-Supply-Chain-Preparedness-for-Public-Health-Emergencies_January-2018_English.pdf. Accessed 17 Jan 2024
37. USAID (2015) USAID African strategies for health. Rwanda health private sector engagement assessment
38. Duque-Uribe V, Sarache W, Gutiérrez EV (2021) Sustainable supply chain management practices and sustainable performance in hospitals: a systematic review and integrative framework. Sustainability 11(21):5949
39. Webber CM, Martínez-Gálvez G, Higuita ML, Ben-Abraham EI, Berry BM, Porras MAG, Aristizabal S, Asp A, Lujan JL, Wilson JW (2020) Developing strategies for sustainable medical equipment maintenance in under-resourced settings. Ann Glob Health. https://doi.org/10.5334/aogh.2584
40. Yadav P (2015) Health product supply chains in developing countries: diagnosis of the root causes of underperformance and an agenda for reform. Health Syst Reform 1:142–154. https://doi.org/10.4161/23288604.2014.968005
41. Yu K, Luo BN, Feng X, Liu J (2018) Supply chain information integration, flexibility, and operational performance. Int J Logist Manag 29:340–364. https://doi.org/10.1108/IJLM-08-2016-0185

Felicia Setiawan Completed her medical education at Atma Jaya University in 2012. She has 3 Master's Degrees; Master of Occupational Health from University of Indonesia in 2017, Master of Healthcare Administration from University of Pelita Harapan in 2023, and Master of Business Administration and Fellowship of Quality Healthcare from University of Michigan in 2023. Her research is related to healthcare and hospital management, as well as marketing, patient safety, human resources, and supply chain.

Valencia Hadinata Is currently pursuing her medical education at University of Indonesia since 2018 and Master's Degree in Healthcare Administration from the University of Pelita Harapan since 2022. Her research focuses on clinical medicine and hospital management including supply chain practices.

Grace Alvina Obtained her medical education at Atma Jaya University in 2012. Currently, she serves as a medical tutor at University of Pelita Harapan with a desire to share her experience and knowledge with medical students. Her research focuses on clinical medicine and hospital management including supply chain practices, particularly in the context of vaccine procurement.

Claudia Alexandra Graduated her medical education in 2017 from Atma Jaya Jakarta University. She is now pursuing a degree in Hospital Management at University of Pelita Harapan since 2022. She is a clinician who is actively serving the community and would like to have the chance to contribute more, particularly in the field of healthcare supply chain management.

Gerry Dwi Putro Graduated as medical doctor from Atma Jaya University Jakarta in 2012 and as Orthopaedic and Traumatology Surgeon from Hasanuddin University Makassar in 2023. Now working as Orthopaedic Traumatology Surgeon at Jakarta Hospital. His research focuses mainly in clinical medicine and healthcare management such as supply chain practices.

Fritzie A. Rexana Is a doctor from Atma Jaya University who graduated in 2012. She completed a Master's Degree in Management at Tarumanagara University in 2021. She is currently active as a doctor in hospitals and has an interest in being more involved in healthcare management. Her research focused mainly in healthcare management such as finance, pharmacy, and supply chain.

Understanding the Barriers to Logistics Collaboration in the Healthcare Supply Chain: A Canadian Case Study

5

Jacques Roy, Martin Beaulieu, Frederik G. S. Vos, and Carolina Belotti Pedroso

Abstract

The effects of the pandemic have left many healthcare logistics managers searching for new models for managing the healthcare supply chain. Studies tend to show a delay in the deployment of collaborative strategies between hospitals and their suppliers. To this end, a research team is involved in implementing and studying the impacts of a pilot project for such a collaborative strategy in the healthcare sector. Using a participant-observer methodology, the researchers were able to detect the challenges of developing trust between supply chain partners when no incentives were put in place to encourage strategic exchanges between the parties. The case also highlights the challenge of obtaining and managing high-quality data and the shift towards proactive management, which requires new business processes.

Keywords

Inventory management • Forecasting • Implementation • Trust • Data quality

J. Roy
HEC Montreal, Montreal, Canada
e-mail: jacques.roy@hec.ca

M. Beaulieu (✉)
CHAINE Research Group, HEC Montreal, Montreal, Canada
e-mail: martin.beaulieu@hec.ca

F. G. S. Vos
Portland State University—School of Business, Portland, USA
e-mail: fvos@pdx.edu

C. B. Pedroso
University of Twente, Enschede, Netherlands
e-mail: c.belottipedroso@utwente.nl

F. Jawab (ed.), *Hospital Supply Chain*, Integrated Science 27,
https://doi.org/10.1007/978-3-031-70292-1_5

1 Introduction

"Our observation is that most hospital supply chain characteristics resemble supply chains of the 1960's & 1970's", this harsh statement was made by Harvey Rickles, then Director of Strategic Planning for UPS, back in… 1999! [42] This statement could still apply today in many cases, as [6] demonstrate that logistics collaboration strategies between healthcare institutions and their suppliers are not widespread. Collaborative strategies emerged in the 1980s and expanded in the following decade to the food and retail sectors [44]. Such strategies aim to move away from purely transactional relationships between suppliers and their buyers towards partnerships. They are developed around the principle of visibility, enabling suppliers to better plan their own operations [20]. Forrester [18] demonstrated that this lack of visibility on demand tends to distort production levels for upstream players, creating a misallocation of resources. Forty years later, [31] came to a similar conclusion. These collaborative strategies are frequently associated with supply chain resilience initiatives [12, 26]. In a post-pandemic environment, these strategies need to be considered. Such strategies could alleviate the shortages of medical supplies that have increased since the COVID-19 pandemic [52]. However, today, to avoid a disruption in their activities, healthcare institutions keep large stocks to cope with the fluctuations in supplier deliveries. Such a strategy is limited by the physical warehousing capacities held by the institution and increases costs for healthcare institutions. At the same time, suppliers often rely on their own forecasts based on past sales, but the addition of new customers, new products or simply a change in clinical practices may disrupt such forecasts, leading the supplier to manage its operations blindly.

Despite its benefits and successes in other industries, the healthcare sector has been hesitant to deploy logistics collaborative practices [47]. However, barriers to the implementation of such strategies have already been identified [39]. In this context, the following question emerges: *what are the barriers to implementing logistics collaborative strategies in the healthcare sector?* To this end, a research team was involved in supporting such an implementation between a healthcare institution in the province of Quebec (Canada) and a medical supplies supplier. Using a participant-observer methodology, the researchers were able to adopt an insider's perspective and gain access to the reflections of the various parties involved. In this way, we hope to present both practical and theoretical insights into the barriers collaborative strategies in the healthcare sector and how to overcome them.

In the following literature review, we will clarify the challenges of the healthcare supply chain and define collaborative strategies and their applications to date in the healthcare sector. Next, the methodology adopted is discussed. Then, the results will be presented in the form a case study and will be followed by a discussion to answer the research question. The conclusion will provide an opportunity to open up new research perspectives.

2 Literature Review

The literature review is divided into two parts. The first part describes the challenge of integrating the external and internal supply chains that characterize the healthcare sector. This is followed by a definition of the concept of of logistics collaboration strategies and the main barriers identified in the literature.

2.1 Two Supply Chains—External and Internal

The healthcare supply chain is characterized by fragmentation, rather than a full integration between the supply chain actors [42]. In the retail sector, suppliers' most important customers can account for 15–20% of their sales. In the healthcare sector, the largest hospitals will represent only a fraction of this percentage in the eyes of suppliers. Medical supplies (e.g., needles, syringes, medical gloves) are a critical input in healthcare delivery [41, 43]. As many have noted, the management of this material is characterized by the presence of two supply chains: an external chain that includes suppliers delivering to the healthcare institution, and an internal chain that takes the form of a distribution network from the hospital's receiving docks to the care unit [30].

In fact, this internal distribution network is more complex, as each care unit is equipped with a medical supply storeroom containing often 150–400 different product codes [7]. These storerooms are generally replenished from a warehouse or distribution center belonging to the healthcare institution [1].

This same warehouse usually becomes the interface between the external and internal supply chains [5]. It is a consolidation point for the various deliveries made by suppliers, in order to simplify internal distribution circuits within the hospital. Regardless of its size and the number of care units being replenished, this storage location will play three roles: (1) decondition products delivered by suppliers from their transport format to packaging that is better suited to consumption on the care unit, (2), assemble the various supplies that need to be replenished in order to replenish the quantities consumed on the care unit; (3) build up a safety stock to meet fluctuating demand in the hospital.

2.2 Collaborative Logistics Strategies

In an environment of increasingly frequent shortages of medical supplies, hospitals alone cannot assume the risk of supply chain failure by overstocking their facilities. Collaborative strategies can be a way of sharing some of the risks with suppliers [12, 26]. These strategies are based on a fundamental principle in supply chain management: offering partners upstream of the user visibility on demand originating from the user [20, 24, 28]. Implementing such a strategy can generate lower costs in the supply chain [22]. Since the supplier can then better plan its own operations, which can lead to an improvement of the service level without increasing the inventory levels [24, 48]. The literature review by [19] confirmed these results two decades ago. Machado Guimarães et.al [33] see a lean logic in these initiatives, as increased collaboration would reveal poor inventory practices or other dysfunctions that would require correction.

Despite these benefits, companies would be reluctant to adopt such strategies. Ma et al. [32], p. 2217 mention: "Most enterprises are reluctant to sacrifice own benefits (resources) to obtain maximum benefits as a whole. They are only willing to collaborate through certain type of coordinating contract to form temporary collaborative relationships with others." This reluctance may be explained by the asymmetry of the benefits thus generated [19]. Fawcett et.al [16] considered that some companies had an important motivation, often in the form of an organizational crisis, to initiate a shift in favor of such strategies.

Several studies have identified the conditions for success or barriers to the implementation of such strategies [10, 23, 34]. Table 1 presents these barriers. This table is based on the work of [39], to which we have added the barriers identified by [15]. It should be pointed out that the latter speak of resistance forces. This concept implies that this force may reflect a success condition that is not fully articulated. Of all these studies, two crucial conditions emerge: trust in the partner and data quality. Interestingly, trust grows as a partner makes investments that solidify the relationship between the parties [29]. As these collaborative strategies are usually based on information sharing [8, 20, 21, 24, 46] sees also a technological challenge, whereas [43], several years later does not see technological investment as a barrier to collaboration anymore. At the same time, Choi and Sethi [9] consider that it is the actors' trust in the data that is neuralgic. In fact, there will even be a learning process, with forecasting models tending to become more accurate over time [53]. Another barrier concerns the support of senior management [10]. In an environment such as a hospital, this barrier can be significant when logistics managers do not always have the support of their institution's senior management [17]. Finally, Sumrit [48] spoke of the convergence of objectives between each party in the implementation of a collaborative strategy. Such goal alignment is an important success factor and, reversely, not being aligned can be a major barrier to successful collaboration.

Although some of the work cited above is based on observations of the healthcare sector, most of these studies are already quite dated and we need to take a fresh look at the research question: *what are the barriers to implementing logistics collaborative strategies in the healthcare sector?* Answering this question would also help us to understand the causes of the healthcare sector's historic delay in implementing practices that have proved their superiority in other industries. As a project evolved from the necessity of investigating how to incentivize the implementation of such collaborative strategy in practice, a study at a pivotal moment can shed a meaningful light on the dynamics of the players involved.

Table 1 List of of barriers to collaborative strategies

Lack of trust among the supply chain partners
Lack of training for new mindset and skills
Lack of collaborative and strategic planning
Lack of top management commitment
Lack of supply chain vision/understanding
Disparity in technological capability among partners
Inadequate information sharing or unwillingness to share information
Unwillingness to share risk and rewards
Inconsistent and inadequate performance metrics
Non-aligned strategic and operating policies

3 Methodology

The chosen methodology can be subsumed under the broad umbrella of collaborative research [3]. However, unlike other works where this strategy involves the partner's participation in the research process aimed at solving his organization's problem, the research process has evolved where one of the researchers has become an active organizational actor in the development of the solution, thus becoming a participant-observer of the process. To capture this evolution, we use formula developed by Parker [37] to describe the researcher's involvement.

One of the researchers in this study, hereinafter referred to as the participant, has been conducting research in the field of healthcare supply chain for over 20 years. His work has led him to collaborate more specifically with the institution that will be the subject of the study from 2016 to 2021. In 2019, the participant had discussions with the institution's logistics director about the difficulties of integrating healthcare supply chain. Analyses produced with two suppliers confirmed deficient service levels. Discussions between the logistics director and the participant continued with a view to piloting a collaborative strategy. In the fall of 2019, the institution obtained funding for this from the Ministry of Health. However, the COVID-19 pandemic redirected the health system's logistical priorities for several months. It wasn't until late autumn 2020 that the research team obtained data to classify more than half of the medical supplies held in the central warehouse of one of the hospitals. The findings identified a critical mass of products that could be the focus of a collaborative strategy between the institution and one of its key suppliers.

In April 2021, a new director took charge of the institution's logistical activities. She was further pursuing this initiative and the researcher's role has evolved into that of participant-observer. He became an active promoter of a collaborative strategy pilot project. In July 2021, he made a presentation to this effect to the new director, followed by another in September to executives responsible for warehousing and purchasing management activities, and finally, in early November of the same year to the supplier. The participant was, therefore, in a privileged position to hear the points of view of the various players and stakeholders.

In this context, the case study research approach was chosen as a means of rendering the information collected during this collaborative research useful [51]. The case offers flexibility in terms of data collection strategies [54], while also having the latitude to present contextual elements that allow us to grasp the environment in which this collaborative logistics initiative is embedded

3.1 Case Selection and Data Collection

It was while carrying out this collaborative research that the research object became clear: to identify the barriers to the implementation of collaborative strategy in the healthcare sector. In this sense, the research object stems from an opportunistic procedure [13]. In these circumstances, it is a unique case study [54]. Ellram [14], p. 100 states that a single-case study "is suitable when the case represents [...] an extreme or unique case, or a case which reveals a previously inaccessible phenomenon." Eisenhardt [13] emphasize that a single case need not be representative of a population, but it must have theoretical representativeness to illustrate the relationships between concepts. Our previous comments confirm this representativeness.

Two data sources were used to gather information. The case context is based on various reports produced over the years on supply chain practices in the healthcare sector. This contextualization will also contain information accumulated by the participant during various private exchanges with decision-makers in this field, or by attending various professional conferences bringing together logistics managers from healthcare institutions or suppliers over the past five years.

Finally, from January 2021 to mid-December 2021, the participant had the opportunity to produce various documents: data analyses, and presentations of the pilot project. These various documents become a sort of logbook of the collaboration with the institution. He was also able to take numerous notes during "Tuesday meetings" with the management team, or during exchanges with the supplier. For example, during these "Tuesday meetings", performance indicators associated database management (duplicate product codes, inactive product codes) were presented, along with actions to be taken and follow-up on actions taken.

3.2 Data Analysis

We have identified a number of observations and comments that we can associate with barriers to a collaborative strategy. Such barriers were not always formulated explicitly by the various players. They were often related to questions addressed to the participant-observer, including questions whose unsatisfactory response would have halted the development of the pilot project.

While the participant-observer strategy has its benefits [50], it does run the risk of the researcher imposing his or her perspective on events without any objective hindsight [2, 27]. To circumvent this weakness, the research team was composed of two researchers. The first researcher, the participant, was in the field and in contact with the various organizations involved in this logistics collaboration pilot project. Other researcher remained in the background. These researchers would, therefore, not be "contaminated" by being too close to the object of study. There was the necessary distance to make a more neutral judgment on the data collected and the analyses produced. This strategy was also used by Radnejad et al [38] in similar circumstances.

4 Case Presentation

The case will be presented in three parts. First, the organizations involved and the general context will be presented. Next, we present the first stages of a pilot project aimed at implementing a logistics collaboration strategy between the partner healthcare institution and a supplier.

4.1 Actors and General Context

Canada is a federal state made up of 10 provinces and three territories. Health administration falls under the jurisdiction of the provinces and territories. The healthcare institution in this study is a component of the public health system in the province of Quebec. This institution was created in 2015 following a system reform that reduced the number of institutions from 182 to 34. The institution in this study is regionally based, with 80 facilities. It has 14,000 employees and manages a budget of over one billion Canadian dollars. The institution covers a territory of over 20,000 km^2 and serves a population of 620,000. It offers the full spectrum of first-, second-, and third-line services.

The healthcare institution has seven warehouses that, among other things, replenish medical supplies for the care units in their respective sub-territories. Like the vast majority of healthcare institution warehouses in the province of Quebec, these storage facilities are located within hospital walls and often suffer from the same architectural constraints found already in several previous studies in hospital settings (relatively low ceilings, divided space, presence of beams, rudimentary storage equipment) [4]. Also, the material management systems used in the Quebec health system were initially developed to meet financial control requirements. It counts with a cycle of care replenishment unit storeroom. In this scenario, when an item leaves the hospital warehouse for a care unit's storeroom the item is immediately charged to the care unit's budget, even if this item remains on the storeroom shelves for weeks. This process is performed taking into consideration an accounting point of view.

As a result, very few hospitals in Quebec have visibility over their care unit inventories. In this way, supply or inventory management practices in the province of Quebec's healthcare system are reactive to events. There are few planning tools and inventory management decision parameters are revised when necessary [4].

The Public Contracts Act governing public-sector purchasing in the province of Quebec is potentially one of the most elaborate in the country. The Act and its regulations provide a great deal of detail in terms of the actions that can be taken by public-sector buyers and suppliers. There are various mechanisms for awarding contracts that provide for the use of qualitative criteria to avoid using only the lowest compliant bidder, but in reality, studies show that price becomes, in almost all the cases, the sole criterion for selecting a supplier [36]. The law on public contracts tends to induce a transactional logic in supplier–buyer relations.

4.2 The First Collaborative Initiatives

In 2019, the institution's supply chain department decided to develop a team of database analysts for their activities. A few months later, when the COVID-19 pandemic broke out, this team developed a personal protective equipment forecasting tool to anticipate the demand and, therefore the accurate quantities of items to be ordered from suppliers. These forecasts were shared with the main PPE suppliers. Their reaction varied across suppliers. The logistics manager at the time commented:

> For two suppliers, when we first shared our forecasts with them, they weren't sure what to make of the information. The third supplier clearly saw the value of this information and was able to suggest substitute products that would then be available almost as soon as our needs arose. It's worth noting that in subsequent meetings, the first two suppliers were then able to suggest solutions to future problems.

4.3 The Contours of the Pilot Project

The aim of the pilot project was to achieve a proof of concept. This last one consisted of developing a project that would see the reactions of the healthcare institution's logistics team and the supplier to working with forecasts. These forecasts would make it possible to anticipate when the supplier should receive an order from the institution. The model is based on the principles of a production planning grid. According to the forecast, the projected inventory level is adjusted according to the inventory level initially on hand. When the anticipated stock level falls below the order threshold, a projected order quantity is suggested by the system in order to reach the maximum stock level again, or according to the supplier's minimum order. Depending on the supplier's lead time, the order would be released to the supplier in the same week as its anticipated receipt, or the week before (for a one-week lead time), or even longer, depending on the supplier's instructions. The research team aimed to develop a forecasting model with an accuracy rate of 80%.

The forecasting model corrected a lack of precision in certain data. For example, it would require knowledge of the supplier's delivery lead time for the product under study. At that time, when a contract was renewed, a lead time of five days was automatically entered into the information system of the healthcare institution's supply chain department, irrespective of the supplier's actual lead time.

For the purposes of this study, the collaborative strategy developed focuses on the needs of a single warehouse, the one associated with the regional hospital center, which accounts for 60% of all medical supply business volume consumed within the entire institution. The project would target 60 products over a period of two to three months. The targeted products would come from the supplier who had been the most receptive to the PPE forecast presentation. This is a very large North American supplier of medical supplies. This supplier delivers 57% of the 1836 medical supplies held in the central warehouse under study. This percentage is representative of the size of this supplier's market share in the province of Quebec.

4.4 Characteristics of the Collaborative Model

To understand the collaborative model, the regular flow of exchanges between healthcare institutions and their suppliers must be explained. The supplier explains the nature of the exchanges:

> When a call for tenders is issued, generally for a three-year period, the institution sends us a global consumption projection for the entire duration of the contract. If it's a contract for a purchasing group involving several health institutions, the same thing will happen: we'll have a global quantity corresponding to the needs of the participating institutions. If we win the tender, we'll have to formulate our own forecasts based on seasonal fluctuations over the year and overall trends over three years.

A purchasing group manager in the province of Quebec confided the complaints of suppliers about this way of operating:

> Suppliers contact us to tell us that their contract has been active for six months and that they have not yet received any orders from the institutions, or conversely, that the contract has been in force for six months and the orders placed to date are equivalent to the total quantities in the resquest for quotation.

4.5 Implementing the Pilot Project

In view of the arrival of a new logistics director at the healthcare institution in June 2021, a meeting was held between the researcher-participant and senior logistics managers. The aim of this meeting was to continue the pilot project. The new logistics director wanted to improve the quality of the material management system database and validate that the pilot project was synergistic with his priorities. The researcher-participant mentioned that a collaborative strategy created an environment in which anomalies within the database could be quickly detected. Senior management agreed on the condition that middle management adopt and lead the project. To this end, a meeting was held with middle management in the the supply chain department in September 2021. At this point, the main issue raised concerned the use of resources for the project. The researcher-participant indicated that the pilot project would be developed to minimize the intervention of logistics personnel. The purchasing coordinator raised the point that the products to be used for the pilot project were not under contract renewal at the time of the study. The researcher-participant clarified that this would not be an issue, as the list of products selected for the pilot project would be shared. As the number of possible products was quite large, it would be possible to choose products that would not have this characteristic. At the end of the meeting, middle management agreed to implement the pilot project.

From there, the logistics department arranged a meeting with the potential supplier for the pilot project. In the meantime, the researcher-participant further developed the collaborative model and recruited a resource to oversee the development of the forecasting algorithms. At the end of October 2021, the researcher-participant presented the middle management team with the document that would be presented to the supplier. At this point, one of the managers asked: "The model projects a quantity that would be ordered, but could we then order a larger quantity?" The researcher-participant then replied that the pilot project was intended to deal with this type of situation and that business rules would be developed to frame different situations. A middle manager commented that he did not want the supplier to have access to the inventory levels of the various items in the pilot project. "With this information, if the supplier has supply challenges for certain products, they may look to deliver their products to other hospitals believing that we could meet our demand with our stock," he explains. The researcher-participant commented:

> In the short term, it may be preferable for the supplier not to know your inventory levels. So during the project, we won't be adjusting inventory levels. If we do, it will be after the pilot project.

The tripartite meeting (healthcare institution, supplier, and the university researcher) took place in early November. The supplier agreed in principle to the pilot project. In a private conversation with the researcher-participant, the supplier commented: "At last, a vision for the healthcare supply chain! At the same meeting, the supplier added: "Such a project would be more valuable for us if it could include, for example, all the institutions associated with the same group contract. Also, the forecasts would be more valuable if the projection horizon were longer, two to three months. We could then share them with some of our suppliers. To these comments, the university partner replied: "This pilot project is a first phase. There's a proof of concept to be achieved. From there, the project can be extended in terms of products, in terms of planning horizons, and in terms of institution." The supplier bounces off the last statement by indicating that it could suggest institution names for the expansion phase.

On December 1, 2021, the supplier provided its response to the offer to participate in the pilot project: "We are open to collaborating [...] in this project. We agree that this is a very interesting project, worth exploring, although to see a real impact on the chain, several institutions would have to join. What's more, the global situation (shortage of raw materials, delays in overseas and overland transport, resumption of activities resulting in major fluctuations in demand, etc.) could skew the results somewhat."

At the beginning of December 2021, another meeting took place between the researcher-participant and middle management. He presented the latest forecast accuracy results for the pilot project products. At this point, the accuracy level was just under 70%. He was confident of reaching the 80% accuracy target to start the pilot project. He requests a more recent data set to validate certain results. Analyses reveal inconsistencies between the new data and the old ones obtained. The healthcare institution's analyses found that the information system had accounted for quantities delivered as quantities issued from the central warehouse to the care units. As a result, product demand for certain weeks had been inflated. This finding tended to invalidate the initial analyses calling into question the choice of products and efforts to develop a forecasting model. As the logistics department had other priorities at the time, the participating researcher and the healthcare institution decided to put the pilot project on ice.

5 Discussion

Although the experiment documented was not conclusive according to its initial objectives, there are benefits to studying a case of failure [5], especially in a post-pandemic environment, where collaboration within the healthcare supply chain can improve resilience. The literature review highlighted the main challenges associated with implementing such collaborative strategies [15, 20, 28, 39, 48]. To discuss the data collected, Table 2 positions the barriers identified in the literature and draws out the observations that can be gleaned from our case study.

Clearly, data quality [9] has become a major obstacle to the continuation of the pilot project. Poor-quality data did not allow the project to target the best candidates for a collaborative strategy, but more importantly, it makes it very difficult to formulate relatively accurate forecasts when the historical data on which they

Table 2 Summary of observations

Barriers	Comments
Data quality	After months of work, some of the data proved to be erroneous, invalidating much of the data
Trust	The healthcare institution is distrustful of its suppliers
Senior management support	Senior logistics managers were not marginally involved in the pilot project
Converging goals	The healthcare institution wanted to achieve benefits with minimal effort

will be based is corrupted. This barrier proved fatal to the pilot project, especially at the stage of early development. This reality is not unique to the province of Quebec, where [45] identified the absence of a standardized product nomenclature as a hindrance to data management in the healthcare sector.

Trust in the partner is a frequently named ingredient in the success of a collaborative strategy [10, 23, 29, 34]. In this sense, the reluctance of logistics managers to share inventory levels creates, according to [8], an asymmetry of information that would weaken this very trust between each of the parties. There is a transition phase where trust can develop as mentioned by the study of [15]. The pilot project could not be brought to a conclusion, as it was not possible to measure the development of this dimension.

The case documented suggests other challenges if the pilot project had continued. It's not just about developing accurate forecasts; it would be necessary to learn how to use them and develop processes to effectively leverage them [53]. For example, if managers receive signals of an increase in consumption of a product, an increase that diverges from the forecast, how do they apply this data as part of a collaborative strategy? The broader implementation of the pilot project would have been an opportunity to design the work processes associated with this new working environment for both the healthcare institution and the supplier. The reactive work environment creates all kinds of dysfunctions that have to be resolved on a daily basis, but without really tackling the root causes of these problems. The proposed logistics collaborative model is not just an opportunity to offer visibility on demand [24], it would have created a much less ambiguous environment. It offers a point of comparison to challenge, for example, extreme variations in demand in relation to the forecast formulated. It will require processes to ensure database integrity. It will require dialogue with suppliers to specify order lots or delivery times for each product. As Machado Guimarães [33] suggest, such situations become an opportunity to adopt a lean logic where the root causes of these stock-outs are sought in other stores. Again, this is not a feature unique to the province of Quebec's healthcare system. Hut [25] argued for a forecasting environment for the U.S. healthcare sector.

However, implementing this new working environment requires an investment in time. There's a challenge in converting resources to a long-term improvement project when there are urgent problems to solve in the short term. And time is resource seems limited, while the supply chain department would have other priorities. This reality is not unique to the internal logistics activities but it can also be generalized to an organization like a hospital, in which the organization's mission creates pressure on the daily tasks, making it difficult to step back and analyze the work processes [49].

Fawcett [16] mention the presence of a trigger element, a crisis that leads managers to consider new practices. The COVID-19 pandemic had created such an environment for developing a forecasting model for personal protective equipment. However, when the pilot project was proposed, that sense of urgency was no longer present, and the willingness to change was not as strong. The supply chain managers at the healthcare institution could be satisfied with the status quo.

This aspect nuances the support of top management. Too often, this barrier is associated with a lack of top management support [17], whereas our case shows that this barrier is present even within logistics management. Thus, middle managers may adhere to the objectives, they just don't want to invest the necessary resources. Senior logistics managers could have prioritized the pilot project, but they remained in the background, leaving middle management to lead the project. The healthcare sector is faced with a paradox: the working environment is so unstable that many emergencies have to be resolved, leaving little time to address the root causes of these instabilities, which means that the unstable environment cannot be corrected.

Logistical activities remain on the periphery of the core mission of a healthcare institutions, which is to care for patients. Under these conditions, logistics managers do not have all the necessary resources to carry out their projects, and these can be postponed to make way for new priorities set by senior executives. This reality may explain the historical delay in the healthcare sector in adopting best practices that have demonstrated their superiority in other industries. This observation is not revolutionary in itself, but what the case highlights is that logistics managers have internalized this logic of subordination, which prevents them from imposing their own agenda.

6 Conclusion

This case study was intended to be the first step in a broader approach aimed at a more fundamental transformation of supply chain management in the healthcare sector, and at bridging some of its historical gap with practices in other industries [40]. In the short term, the aim was to share forecasts and validate how each party-buyers and suppliers-could handle them. However, we are confident that in the medium term, some form of supply chain coordination will be put in place, if only for problem-solving purposes. In this sense, the ultimate aim of this study was to deploy large-scale collaborative strategies, such as those seen in other sectors for many decades [44]. Despite the recognition of the benefits obtained from the adoption of supply chain management practices developed in the industrial setting, the implementation is still very challenging in healthcare organizations

[11]. This context signals the need for a major change. Such a transformation in the healthcare sector cannot be spontaneous. That's why we've taken the time to fully understand the concerns of the organizations involved in this dynamic. In this sense, presenting the contours of the competitive perimeter within which both parties would have to work was one way of providing a framework for channeling these concerns. Although present case study has come to an impasse, the researcher-participant is looking for a second health institution to take over, one that is better suited to carrying out a pilot project.

The case opens up another perspective that would merit a separate analysis. The case suggests a challenge identified by Govindan [20]: collaborative strategies may not generate as many benefits for the supplier as for the retailer. Our discussions with the supplier hinted at this aspect. This is in line with the idea of critical mass evoked by Mathews [35]. This notion tends to differ for each party. For the buyer, there needs to be a sufficient volume of products to be supported by this type of strategy, in order to generate profits that cover the investments in the field. For the supplier, there should also be a critical mass of customers adopting this same strategy in order to have a consolidated view of demand forecasts. When [48] talks about the convergence of objectives between the two parties to ensure the success of such initiatives, according to the critical mass of customers issue, we can see that this is not as simple as it may seem a priori. We, therefore, need to study the conditions that ensure the emergence of this critical mass for both buyer and supplier. We also need to understand the essential conditions that partners must have in order to succeed in a collaborative strategy. Future research should focus on these issues.

Declaration of interest The authors declare no conflicts of interest.

References

1. Abdulsalam Y, Gopalakrishnan M, Maltz A, Schneller E (2015) The emergence of consolidated service centers in health care. J Bus Logist 36(4):321–334
2. Barr PS (2004) Current and potential importance of qualitative methods in strategy research. Res Methodol Strategy Manage 1:165–188
3. Beaulieu M, Rebolledo C, Lissillour R (2024) Collaborative research competencies in supply chain management: the role of boundary spanning and reflexivity. Int J Logist Manag 35(2):305–331
4. Beaulieu M, Roy J (2015) Benchmarking de la gestion des achats et des stocks en milieu hospitalier: une démarche canadienne. Logistique Manage 23(3):17–27
5. Beaulieu M, Roy J, Landry S (2018) Logistics outsourcing in the healthcare sector: lessons from a Canadian experience. Can J Adm Sci 35(4):635–648
6. Beaulieu M, Roy J (2019) La chaîne logistique du secteur de la santé: ses coûts et ses économies potentielles. Center on Productivity and Prosperity, HEC Montréal
7. Bélanger V, Beaulieu M, Landry S, Morales P (2018) Where to locate medical supplies in nursing units: an exploratory study. Supply Chain Forum 19(1):81–89
8. Chakraborty A, Chatterjee AK, Mateen A (2015) A vendor-managed inventory scheme as a supply chain coordination mechanism. Int J Prod Res 53(1):13–24

9. Choi T-M, Sethi S (2010) Innovative quick response programs: a review. Int J Prod Econ 127(1):1–12
10. Daugherty PJ (2011) Review of logistics and supply chain relationship literature and suggested research agenda. Int J Phys Distrib Logist Manag 41(1):16–31
11. De Vries J, Huijsman R (2011) Supply chain management in health services: an overview. Supply chain manag: Int J 16(3):159–165
12. Duong LNK, Chong J (2020) Supply chain collaboration in the presence of disruptions: a literature review. Int J Prod Res 58(11):3488–3507
13. Eisenhardt KM, Graebner ME (2007) Theory building from cases: opportunities and challenges. Acad Manag J 50(1):25–32
14. Ellram LM (1996) The use of case study method in logistics research. J Bus Logist 17(2):93–138
15. Fawcett SE, Magnan GM, Fawcett AM (2010) Mitigating resisting forces to achieve the collaboration-enabled supply chain. Benchmarking 17(2):269–293
16. Fawcett S, Magnan G, McCarter M (2008) A three-stage implementation model for supply chain collaboration. J Bus Logist 29(1):93–112
17. Fibuch E, Ahmed A (2015) Health care's supply chain: issues to consider. Phys Leadersh J 2(6):26–30
18. Forrester JW (1958) Industrial dynamics. Harv Bus Rev 36(4):37–66
19. Fu Y, Piplani R (2004) Supply-side collaboration and its value in supply chains. Eur J Oper Res 152(1):281–288
20. Govindan K (2013) Vendor-managed inventory: a review based on dimensions. Int J Prod Res 51(13):3808–3835
21. Haavik S (2000) Building a demand-driven, vendor-managed supply chain. Healthc Financ Manage 54(2):56–61
22. Ho D, Kumar A, Shiwakoti N (2019) A literature review of supply chain collaboration mechanisms and their impact on performance. Eng Manag J 31(1):47–68
23. Hollmann RL, Scavarda LF, Thome AMT (2015) Collaborative planning, forecasting and replenishment: a literature review. Int J Prod Perform Manag 64(7):971–993
24. Holweg M, Disney SM, Holmström J, Småros J (2005) Supply chain collaboration: making sense of the strategy continuum. Eur Manag J 23(2):170–181
25. Hut N (2020) Reimagining the healthcare supply chain to bolster resilience and efficiency. Healthc Financ Manage 74(9):24–29
26. Jain V, Kumar S, Soni U, Chandra C (2017) Supply chain resilience: model development and empirical analysis. Int J Prod Res 55(22):6779–6800
27. Kitchenham BA, Budgen D, Brereton P (2011) Using mapping studies as the basis for further research—a participant-observer case study. Inf Softw Technol 53(6):638–651
28. Krichanchai S, MacCarthy BL (2017) The adoption of vendor managed inventory for hospital pharmaceutical supply. Int J Logist Manag 28(3):755–780
29. Kwon I-WG, Suh T (2004) Factors affecting the level of trust and commitment in supply chain relationships. J Supply Chain Manag 40(2):4–14
30. Landry S, Beaulieu M (2013) The challenges of hospital supply chain management, from central stores to nursing units. In: Denton BT (ed) Handbook of healthcare operations management. Springer, Ann Arbor
31. Lee HL, Padmanabhan V, Whang S (1997) The bullwhip effect in supply chains. Sloan Manage Rev 38(3):93–102
32. Ma K, Pal R, Gustafsson E (2019) What modelling research on supply chain collaboration informs us? Identifying key themes and future directions through a literature review. Int J Prod Res 57(7):2203–2225
33. Machado Guimarães C, Crespo de Carvalho J, Maia A (2013) Vendor managed inventory (VMI): evidences from lean deployment in healthcare. Strateg Outsourc: Int J 6(1):8–24
34. Marquès G, Thierry C, Lamothe J, Gourc D (2010) A review of vendor managed inventory (VMI): from concept to processes. Prod Plann Control 21(6):547–547
35. Mathews R (1994) How critical is critical mass? Progress Groc 73(10):43–46

36. Montreuil L (2020) *Concurrence dans les marchés publics en technologies médicales au Québec: les implications pour l'innovation*. École Polytechnique, Montréal
37. Parker LD (2008) Boardroom operational and financial control: an insider view. Br J Manag 19(1):65–88
38. Radnejad AB, Osiyevskyy O, Vredenburg H (2020) Barriers to radical process innovation: a case of environmental technology in the oil industry. J Strateg Manag 13(4):453–476
39. Ramesh A, Banwet DK, Shankar R (2010) Modeling the barriers of supply chain collaboration. J Model Manag 5(2):176–193
40. Rickles H (1999) The mysterious case of healthcare logistics. In: AHRMM annual conference, setting the standard. San Francisco
41. Rossetti MD (2008) Inventory management issues in health care supply chains. University of Arkansas
42. Schneller E, Abdulsalam Y (2022) Supply chain management and health services research: aligning strange bedfellows. Health Serv Res 57(2):223–226
43. Småros J (2007) Forecasting collaboration in the European grocery sector: observations from a case study. J Oper Manag 25(3):702–716
44. Sparks L (1999) The retail logistics transformation. In: Fernie J, Sparks L (eds) Logistics and retail management. Kogan Page, London
45. Srivastava S, Garg D, Agarwal A (2021) A step towards responsive healthcare supply chain management: An overview. In: Singari RM, Mathiyazhagan K, Kumar H, (Eds). Advances in manufacturing and industrial engineering. Lecture notes in mechanical engineering, Springer.
46. Stanger SHW (2013) Vendor managed inventory in the blood supply chain in Germany: Evidence from multiple case studies. Strategic Outsourcing: An International J 6(1):25–47
47. Su SII, Gammelgaard B, Yang SL (2011) Logistics innovation process revisited: Insights from hospital case study. Int J Phys Distrib Logist Manag 41(6):577–600
48. Sumrit D (2021) Understanding critical success factors of vendor-managed inventory in healthcare sector: A case study in Thailand. Int J Healthc Manage 14(3):629–640
49. Tucker AL, Edmondson AC (2003) Why hospitals don't learn from failures: organizational and psychological dynamics that inhibit system change. Calif Manage Rev 45(2):55–72
50. Vinten G (1994) Participant observation: a model for organizational investigation? J Manag Psychol 9(2):30–38
51. Westbrook R (1995) Action research: a new paradigm for research in production and operations management. Int J Oper Prod Manag 15(12):6–20
52. Yancopoulous L (2023) Hospitals face mounting shortages of essential medical supplies. *Supply Chain Brain*, November 7
53. Yao Y, Kohli R, Sherer SA, Cederlund J (2013) Learning curves in collaborative planning, forecasting, and replenishment (CPFR) information systems: an empirical analysis from a cell phone manufacturer. J Oper Manag 31(6):285–297
54. Yin RK (2014) Case study research: design and methods, 5th edn. SAGE Publications, Thousand Oaks, CA

Jacques Roy (Ph.D.) is a full professor at the Department of Logistics and Operations Management at HEC Montreal where he is also Director of the Carrefour logistique, a university-industry forum on Supply Chain Management and Director of the research group CHAÎNE that is conducting research activities in the field of Supply Chain Management. Jacques Roy graduated with a B.Sc. from the Royal Military College in Saint-Jean and completed his education with an M.B.A. and a Ph.D. in Business Administration at HEC Montréal. Prior to his teaching career, Dr. Roy was employed as an aerospace engineering officer with the Canadian Armed Forces. He also possesses many years of experience as a management consultant with several large Canadian corporations and governmental organizations. His expertise lies in the areas of logistics and transportation management. Dr. Roy has authored several articles and publications in this subject area and has participated in many conferences at both national and international levels.

Martin Beaulieu (M.Sc.) is a Research Associate at HEC Montréal's Supply Chain Research Group. His research focuses on supply chain integration dynamics. He is a noted researcher on supply chain management and healthcare operations management with numerous articles and case studies published in the last two decades as well as government commissioned studies. Amongst other outlets, he has published in journals such as the International Journal of Operations and Production Management, Supply Chain Management: An International Journal, Journal of Purchasing and Supply Management, International Journal of Logistics Management or IEEE Transactions on Engineering Management.

Frederik G.S. Vos (Ph.D) is Assistant Professor in Logistics and Supply Chain Management at the School of Business of Portland State University. Next to his main work at PSU, he is Executive Committee member of the International Purchasing, Supply Education & Research Association (IPSERA), Associate Editor of the Journal of Purchasing and Supply Management (JPSM), and co-founder of the serious game company suPlay. His areas of expertise include buyer–supplier relationships, resource allocation of suppliers, and digitalization in public, healthcare and industrial procurement. He is regularly awarded for his teaching excellence (best teacher awards) as well as academic accomplishments (best reviewer and outstanding associate editor awards). Dr. Vos is holding a PhD in Supply Management and three Master of Science degrees in Business Administration, Psychology and Communication Science from the University of Twente, The Netherlands.

Carolina Belotti Pedroso Is an assistant professor in Healthcare Procurement & Purchasing at the University of Twente. Previous to that, she was a postdoctoral researcher of the Logistics and Operations Management department at HEC Montreal. She holds a Ph.D. from University of São Paulo (2015–2019), and she was a visiting scholar at University of Tennessee at the Marketing & Supply Chain Department (2017–2018). She has experience in the following topics: Healthcare Procurement, Public Procurement, Value-based Healthcare, Innovation and Sustainability. She has published in journals such as International Journal of Production Economics, Journal of Cleaner Production or International Journal of Procurement Management.

Emergency Medical Supply Chain Optimization Readiness in Developing Countries

6

Felicia Setiawan, Valencia Hadinata, Grace Alvina, Gerry Dwi Putro, Claudia Alexandra, and Fritzie A. Rexana

Abstract

Developing nations often face unique challenges in preparing and responding to health emergencies, and the efficiency of their medical supply chains plays a pivotal role in mitigating the impact of crises. Emergency Medical Supply Chain Optimization Readiness in Developing Countries necessitates a nuanced understanding of the differences between routine and emergency protocols, with a focus on their distinct implementation strategies. Emergency protocols in the medical supply chain of developing countries should first and foremost emphasize a risk-based approach to resource allocation. This involves conducting thorough risk assessments to identify potential scenarios and allocating resources based on the severity and likelihood of different emergencies. Training simulations play a crucial role in preparing for emergency medical supply chain optimization in developing countries to identify gaps and enhance their readiness. In conclusion, an integrated approach encompassing adaptive supply chain models, resource allocation strategies, capacity scaling, and ongoing training and simulation efforts is essential for achieving optimal emergency medical supply chain readiness in developing countries.

F. Setiawan (✉) · V. Hadinata · C. Alexandra
Department of Hospital Administration, Universitas Pelita Harapan, Tangerang, Indonesia
e-mail: feliciasetiawanmd@gmail.com

G. Alvina
Prostacia Clinic, Tangerang, Jakarta, Indonesia

G. D. Putro
Department of Orthopedic and Traumatology, Jakarta Hospital, Jakarta, Indonesia

F. A. Rexana
Department of Business Management, Universitas Tarumanegara, Tarumanegara, Indonesia

F. Jawab (ed.), *Hospital Supply Chain*, Integrated Science 27,
https://doi.org/10.1007/978-3-031-70292-1_6

Keywords

Routine protocols • Emergency protocols • Resource allocation strategies • Capacity scaling • Simulation

1 Introduction

Emergency Medical Supply Chain Optimization Readiness in Developing Countries is a critical aspect of public health infrastructure that demands careful consideration and strategic planning. Developing nations often face unique challenges in preparing and responding to health emergencies, and the efficiency of their medical supply chains plays a pivotal role in mitigating the impact of crises. In many developing countries, the existing medical supply chain infrastructure may lack the robustness required for swift and effective response during emergencies. Supply chain may be disrupted by disaster. The Centre for Research on the Epidemiology of Disasters (CRED) defines disaster as "*a situation or event which overwhelms local capacity, necessitating a request to a national or international level for external assistance: an unforeseen and often sudden event that causes great damage, destruction, and human suffering.*" For example, earthquake in Tehran or floods and landslide in Brazil [2, 5].

Another terminology commonly used is a "crisis", defined to as any event that causes destruction, environmental damage, loss of human life, or even human suffering, threatens health, or health services in away that the areas affected by the event would need relief and response from the surrounding areas, such as earthquake [21, 30].

In the dynamic landscape of emergency response and disaster management, the discovery of gaps in emergency supply chain protocols is a critical undertaking. As organizations strive to enhance their preparedness and resilience, the identification of vulnerabilities within the supply chain becomes paramount for effective response and recovery. The intricate interplay of various stakeholders, logistical challenges, and unforeseen disruptions necessitates a meticulous examination of existing protocols. This exploration not only sheds light on potential weak links but also serves as a catalyst for innovation and improvement, ensuring that emergency supply chains evolve to meet the demands of an ever-changing environment. In the pursuit of discovering these protocol gaps, organizations embark on a journey to fortify their capabilities, safeguard communities, and build a more robust foundation for emergency response efforts [17, 28, 35].

The recent COVID19 pandemic also become big disruption in healthcare supply chain [30]. During the onset of Covid-19, the World Health Organization (WHO) declared that the situation led to a deficiency in worldwide medical resources, including Personal Protective Equipment (PPE), N95 masks, sanitizers, and diagnostic test kits. This shortage was attributed to heightened competition, panic-driven purchasing, and the stockpiling of goods by both individuals and countries. As the world grappled with the pandemic's unprecedented demands, the strain on the supply chain became glaringly evident, further compounded by the compounding impact of a natural disaster. Shortages of critical medical supplies, disrupted transportation routes, and overwhelmed distribution networks underscored the fragility of our emergency response infrastructure. This dual catastrophe highlighted the imperative to reassess and fortify supply chain protocols, emphasizing the need for flexibility, adaptability, and resilience in the face of multifaceted challenges. Analyzing this real-world scenario becomes a crucial step in not only understanding the intricacies of supply chain gaps but also in fostering a more robust and responsive system for future emergencies [3, 29]. In the initial phase of the pandemic in Cambodia, the Ministry of Health implemented various strategies to promptly respond to the virus's spread. With the help of World Health Organization (WHO) and partner countries, Cambodia worked towards fortifying its healthcare system to effectively combat the pandemic. However, the global impact of COVID-19 disrupted the production of essential medications and vaccines crucial in the fight against the virus. The disruption led to a shortage of vital medicines, vaccines, and medical supplies, with notable scarcities, particularly in critical components such as PPE, including N95 masks crucial for protecting healthcare workers. India faced a severe crisis in this regard. In Southeast Asia, Thailand also grappled with shortage of negative pressure rooms and PPE [21].

An example of recent major emergency supply chain disruption is latex shortage in Malaysia on 2016. Latex as a major component of sterile glove production, with Malaysia supplying the majority of it in 2016. Due many countries depended on Malaysia for raw materials, any disruption there might lead to a scarcity of sterile gloves globally. Purchasing resources from several suppliers across the world would reduce the impact of crises that arise in one location. Beyond the challenge of a homogeneous source of raw materials for products like sterile gloves, another issue that emerges later in the supply chain is "phantom demand." This means that when anticipating or experiencing a crisis, warehouses, retail locations, pharmacies, hospitals, and other non-individual consumers place greater orders than necessary, which they subsequently cancel once they are able to meet demand. This causes an artificial demand increase, upsetting the supply chain and requiring the needless reallocation of resources [19]. The supply chain may experience issues later on, just as it does with "phantom demand" and individual customer purchases. But problems that arise early in the supply chain, including those related to manufacturing and material sourcing, prove to be the most troublesome since they have the potential to stop the supply chain entirely rather than just a part of it. The possibility of a crisis-related disruption in the supply chain is reduced by diversifying the geographical distribution of the source materials. This would entail procuring materials internationally and stepping up manufacturing in the USA. The avoidance of loss that would occur in the event of a shortage makes this less expensive than the present supply chain model, even though some material providers may charge higher rates than others. Diverse sourcing could be a means of reducing damages at the national or international levels [28].

A holistic approach to emergency medical supply chain readiness involves community engagement and education. Local communities should be educated on the importance of adhering to emergency protocols, reporting health incidents promptly, and participating in disaster preparedness initiatives. Developing a community-centric approach ensures that emergency response efforts are supported by the active involvement of those directly impacted, creating a more resilient and responsive healthcare system [6]. As each organization and each nation continuously analyze and address the identified gaps, we pave the way for a more agile, interconnected, and robust emergency supply chain. This ongoing process ensures that lessons learned from each discovery contribute to a collective knowledge base, ultimately fortifying our ability to navigate the complexities of unforeseen challenges. By diligently closing these protocol gaps, we not only strengthen the foundation of emergency response but also affirm our commitment to safeguarding communities and mitigating the impact of disasters.

2 Adaptive Supply Chain Models: Routine versus Emergency Protocols

Emergency Medical Supply Chain Optimization Readiness in Developing Countries necessitates a nuanced understanding of the differences between routine and emergency protocols, with a focus on their distinct implementation strategies. Routine protocols are designed to address the day-to-day healthcare needs of the population, encompassing the procurement, storage, and distribution of medical supplies based on predictable demand patterns. In contrast, emergency protocols are activated in response to unexpected and often high-intensity events, such as natural disasters or disease outbreaks, demanding rapid and adaptive supply chain responses [28]. Unstable conditions surrounding emergency supply chain management frequently face many different risks and uncertainties compare to routine one, such as unpredictable demand, uncertain supply, missing or damaged infrastructure, insufficient resources for logistics, unstable political environments, security concerns, and a lack of information [11]. The summary of the difference between routine and emergency protocol in supply chain can be found on Table 1.

On the other hand, emergency protocols require a rapid and agile response to unpredictable surges in demand for medical supplies. The implementation of these protocols involves establishing mechanisms for quick decision-making, prioritizing critical items, and streamlining procurement processes to secure additional supplies swiftly. Inventory management under emergency protocols often involves strategic stockpiling of essential items, dynamic reordering strategies, and real-time tracking to respond effectively to the evolving demands of the crisis. Planning under emergency protocols necessitates a different set of considerations, including rapid response mechanisms, quick procurement strategies, and the establishment of alternative supply chain routes. Budgeting for emergencies requires setting aside funds

Table 1 Difference between routine and emergency protocol in supply chain

Category	Routine protocol	Emergency protocol
Planning horizon	Typically involves long-term planning with a focus on regular and predictable demand	Involves short-term and often rapid planning to respond to unexpected events or crises. Emergency supply chain management requires quick decision-making and adaptability to address immediate needs
Demand predictability	Often more predictable, allowing for smoother production scheduling and inventory management. Historical data and forecasting play a significant role in planning regular supply chain activities	Often unpredictable and can fluctuate rapidly. The focus in emergency supply chain management is on agility and responsiveness to address urgent and unforeseen needs
Inventory levels	Aim to maintain optimal inventory levels to meet expected demand without excess or shortages	May involve the pre-positioning of critical resources, such as medical supplies or disaster relief items, to respond rapidly to post disaster unforeseen events
Supplier relationships	• Often have established, long-term relationships with suppliers. These relationships are built on mutual understanding, contracts, and consistent orders • Using local suppliers who are closer based on geographic location so that it is easier to deliver routine supply needs	• May involve engaging new suppliers or collaborating with existing ones in unconventional ways. The focus is on securing essential supplies as quickly as possible • Usually use global suppliers, due to limited conditions around locations that require supplies of health needs, it is often more difficult to provide the necessary supplies, such as roads damaged due to disasters and others
Flexibility and redundancy	Optimization and cost-effectiveness are central to routine supply chain operations	Prioritize flexibility and redundancy to ensure the ability to quickly adapt to unforeseen disruptions

for stockpiling critical supplies, investing in surge capacity, and developing contingency plans to ensure the immediate availability of medical resources during crises [17, 28, 35, 48]. Medical supply chain systems that occur in emergencies must pay attention to improving the following [48]:

1. Collaborative management of supply chain provision in emergencies, namely by carrying out the following two stages:
   (a) Establishment of a coordination system,
   (b) Building collaboration through a digital platform for medical supply chains in emergencies.
2. Optimize the emergency network chain structure medical supply chain by building a cloud warehouse emergency supply chain model.

3. Build an emergency risk prevention system medical supply chain, by:
   (a) maintain emergency medical supply chain redundancy for improving the supply chain's ability to combat risk,
   (b) implement emergency medical supply chain coordination strategies contract.

Identifying the most important risk factors is a multi-criteria decision-making (MCDM) problem. The analytical hierarchy process (AHP) can be useful with this trouble. AHP is a method for assessing the relative relevance of system variables. Since it can be difficult to focus on all potential danger factors, practitioners and policymakers need to be aware of the specific risk factors that can likely inhibit the emergency system's ability to function effectively. They also need to pay more attention to the most significant risk factors. By classifying risk and choosing only the most relevant supply chain strategies, practitioners and policymakers may effectively change their practices by being aware and immediately identify which part of the chain has been disrupted in emergency supply chains. The management of hazards in emergency supply chains is vital since their consequences may affect the chain's functioning and could result in loss of life [11].

The importance of maturity of a health system's data and digital infrastructure in actively monitoring supply chain capacity as a basis for making decisions on supply disruption risk management. Data and digital infrastructure inform decisions on the distribution of products based on risk to patients, to make sure products are allocated to those who are most in need, or who are at greatest risk. Data adequacy refers to real time tracking of demand for products, utilization rates of product inventory, and supply availability. Sustainable solutions to greater supply chain capacity have now become a significant bottleneck that must be solved, even for the most basic health products like vaccinations, masks, medications, and devices, which are commonly disrupted in global supply chains [5, 44].

3 Resource Allocation Strategies

Emergency protocols in the medical supply chain of developing countries should first and foremost emphasize a risk-based approach to resource allocation. This involves conducting thorough risk assessments to identify potential scenarios and allocating resources based on the severity and likelihood of different emergencies. By prioritizing high-impact, high-probability events, healthcare systems can direct resources where they are most needed during crises, optimizing their response efforts. To enhance resource allocation strategies, developing countries must invest in advanced technologies and data analytics that enable real-time monitoring and forecasting of medical supply needs. Predictive analytics can help identify trends and patterns, allowing for proactive decision-making and the allocation of resources to areas likely to be most affected. This technology-driven approach enhances the efficiency of emergency protocols, ensuring a timely and targeted response. Collaborative partnerships between government agencies, non-governmental organizations, and the private sector are also crucial for effective resource allocation during emergencies. Developing countries can leverage these partnerships to access additional resources, expertise, and support in times of crisis. Such collaborations contribute to a more comprehensive and coordinated approach, preventing duplications in resource allocation and addressing gaps in the medical supply chain [16, 28].

Every emergency that occurs, including disasters, requires synchronization of resources with a short or immediate response time to prevent delays in receiving supplies, including health care. The resources used are categorized into: renewable resources, which include social workers and medical teams, and non-renewable resources, which include medical supplies such as medicine and medical equipment. In this case, the scheduling of these two types of resources must be managed appropriately so that they can overcome disasters that occur. Scheduling the allocation of these resources can use an emergency assistance chain consisting of [17, 28]:

1. Regional distribution centers that are closer to the point of request for assistance and central distribution centers located in surrounding areas that are safe and not affected by disasters with a larger and more strategic capacity.
2. Local and global suppliers, where local (domestic) suppliers may be more hampered in distributing supplies due to post-disaster conditions that make it impossible to send supplies, so it is more possible to schedule distribution of supply deliveries through global suppliers.
3. Operational institutions such as hospitals or social health institutions, places where aid is provided to people in need.

In implementing effective emergency resource allocation through a cross-organizational emergency response process, the following two stages are required. The initial stage, namely the stage where each emergency organization determines its own emergency response process based on emergency needs. Then, each emergency organization submits its emergency response process to the emergency command center, through an integrated system and with further evaluation. After that, the emergency command center integrates all emergency response processes received from its subordinate emergency organizations. The next stage, namely the stage where the emergency command center first carries out an analysis of emergency resource requirements in terms of minimum consumable resource requirements, minimum reusable resource requirements, and reliable reusable resource requirements. Based on the results of the resource requirements analysis, two strategies are obtained, namely the minimum execution time strategy and the minimum resource consumption strategy, to guide resource allocation. This way, stakeholders can determine which strategy is more appropriate based on the number of resources available and the estimated completion time. These two stages are able to provide appropriate decision-making information to support effective emergency resource allocation throughout the organization [16].

In the event of a medical emergency, the supply chain may experience distribution delays up to the service user level, the following are suggestions for overcoming supply chain vulnerability mitigation strategies including medicines and technology, provided to hospitals through the health system [36]:

1. Purchase of medicines and major medical supplies needed in an emergency must be obtained from more than one supplier.
2. Medicines and replacement medical equipment supplies should ideally be similar to those already used by the provider agency previously.
3. Records of the use of medicines and medical devices must be tracked digitally to monitor inventory levels.
4. Consider a higher amount from recording medicines and supplies that are known or estimated to be limited, so that even though the supply of medicines and medical devices is not yet available, the supply is still sufficient.
5. Collaborate with institutions use of alternative protocols when (potential) medical supply chain shortages begin to be identified.
6. Participate in supporting the government and non-governmental organizations in efforts to overcome supply chain vulnerabilities in all aspects, so that all health services continue to receive an adequate medical supply chain.

Capacity building is integral to the success of emergency protocols and resource allocation strategies. Healthcare professionals, logistics personnel, and emergency responders must be trained to implement protocols effectively. Simulation exercises and drills can help refine resource allocation strategies, allowing stakeholders to practice and improve their responses to various emergency scenarios.

1. Governance

An important aspect of the readiness of emergency medical supply chain based on USAID report on Best Practices in Supply Chain Preparedness for Public Health Emergencies is appointing an emergency supply chain (ESC) leader. This leader must possess a blend of technical proficiency in managing supply chain operations along with robust leadership and organizational abilities. This is pivotal to achieve a clear and transparent chain of command. Their responsibilities include assembling a specialized team proficient in predicting demands, sourcing, transporting, and warehousing emergency supplies. It is also very advantageous if the said leader has established connections with various distributors, public health figures, and local community groups, which will facilitate a streamlined collaboration [23, 28, 46].

2. Financing

Recommendation from USAID report on best practices in supply chain preparedness for Public Health Emergencies suggests breaking down the initial ESC budget into two segments, which are a readiness fund and a response reserve fund. The preparedness fund is designed to cover various expenses, including the storage of emergency supplies, inventory management (such as rotating out outdated stock), administrative costs for emergency personnel, and routine preparedness training [38]. On the other hand, the reserve fund is intended to be an additional allocation to the preparedness budget in the event of an emergency. Estimating the required amount for a reserve fund proves to be no small task due to the limited insight and predictive ability into both supply and demand that may fluctuate during a potential crisis. Consequently, this budget should be discussed frequently and adjusted based on the latest forecasting and surveillance data [34].

3. Demand Forecasting

Forecasting assists in identifying the needs for health commodities that have been satisfied or that will have enough purchasing power to result in actual orders. At the facility and end-user levels, effective demand can serve as an indicator of the true need for vital health commodities. The short-and long-term demands must be clearly understood by key stakeholders before deciding which medications and diagnostics will be stocked. Here, forecasting is utilized to determine how much of each product a program will provide to users over a given time frame in the future. Globally, in the healthcare industry, forecasting is done annually or semi-annually to adapt with the current objectives and procurement needs [18, 34]. By using demand forecasting, producers can make capacity investments, guarantee that supply meets demand, and benefit from economies of scale. Moreover, Forecasting assists in identifying gaps in the healthcare market's demand and notifies researchers and producers, enabling them to devote resources to creating fill-ins. This will quicken the pace of product availability and help the healthcare community respond to the requirements of LMICs. This in turn, helps local pharmaceutical manufacturers in low- and middle-income countries (LMICs) meet the challenge of lowering the burden of disease and raising living standards. Forecasts ensure proper prices and sufficient supplies of health commodities, which assists donors and the global community in making efficient financial allocation decisions. Lastly, in order to direct advocacy and policy initiatives, forecasting can pinpoint and emphasize supply-side and demand-side restrictions. This can help shape the future healthcare portfolio and increase access, particularly in low- and middle-income countries [34].

There are a few strategies to forecast demand accurately and adaptively. To name a few:

a. All health supply chain systems need to have a solid understanding of demand forecasting in order to increase their forecasting capabilities, especially while operating under resource constraints. In order to support decisions made based on the projections, all entities involved in health supply chain forecasting should abide by common principles. By doing this, risks will be reduced and market dynamics will be better understood [34].

b. The communities involved in the global health supply chain generally agree that more effective data management and information exchange will result in more accurate projections. The benefits of this come from two sources: diversity of information gives different stakeholders a better understanding of the supply chain's limits and desires, and it may also have a confirmation impact [8]. The unequal allocation of incentives in global health supply chains is a primary factor contributing to the resistance towards knowledge sharing. Risks among many stakeholders are not matched to the supply and demand of health commodities, as the literature and our study have both studied and examined. The two biggest obstacles preventing the exchange of knowledge are politics and information culture. Having an information middleman can be a crucial first step in resolving these problems. The middleman will serve as the main keeper of all forecasting operations. With the help of transparent baselines at the national and regional levels and market research, it will take the lead in the data gathering and analysis phase. This will guarantee that gathering and updating forecasting data is a continuous procedure [34].
c. By implementing changes to contractual procedures, risk allocation throughout the health supply chains can be accomplished. A minimum purchase agreement, buyback agreements, revenue sharing plans, and adjustable quantity contracts are a few examples of this. Remember that not every circumstance calls for a particular style of contracting. For more accurate demand forecasting of health commodities and better risk allocation, a combination method should be investigated [14].
d. The involvement of the private sector is increasingly important for the effective execution of health interventions and increases the accessibility of health resources. Therefore, until the main bottlenecks are eliminated, policy changes in the public sector might not have an effect on the private sector [34].

4. Inventory Management

Inventory control is a process of inventory management that controls the amount of inventory to satisfy customer demands with the least amount of expense and investment. Some academics have suggested using simulation and a numerical technique to attain the best inventory costs. One of the simulation approach is by assessing inventory management expenses item per item depending on healthcare facilities' service level, consumption level, and necessity for important products [40]. According to Brandon-Jones [7], improper inventory management causes significant losses for medical institutions and has a detrimental effect on patient care quality. Poor management has the ability to result in overstocking, which is the retention of excess inventory, which limits cash flow and the organization's ability to grow [7]. On the other hand, understocking causes shortages and compromises the organization's ability to maintain the stability of its services. One of the main reasons for inefficiency in the healthcare industry is poor inventory management, and hospitals can cut expenses and improve operations by implementing effective supply chain management [25].

5. Risk Prioritization and Emergency Protocols

Risk assessment is a fundamental component of emergency medical supply chain optimization. This involves identifying potential risks, evaluating their impact, and developing strategies to mitigate or manage these risks effectively. Risks may include natural disasters, geopolitical instability, transportation disruptions, or sudden outbreaks of diseases. By conducting a thorough risk assessment, supply chain managers can proactively implement measures such as diversifying suppliers, establishing contingency plans, and investing in resilient infrastructure to minimize the impact of potential disruptions on the supply chain. A threshold must be defined by the governing bodies in case ESC is needed to be activated. This is because failure to identify crises and delay in activating an ESC can cause the extent of the harm to spread quickly. To assess the readiness of emergency medical supply chains in developing countries, stakeholders should:

(a) Review the documentation and implementation of risk assessment methods.
(b) Evaluate the integration of identified risks into emergency protocols.
(c) Assess the extent of training programs for personnel involved in emergency responses.
(d) Examine the utilization of technology for real-time tracking and monitoring of medical supplies during emergencies.
(e) Analyze the coordination mechanisms among different stakeholders within the supply chain during emergencies.
(f) Evaluate the existence and effectiveness of contingency plans and stockpile strategies.

Collaboration and information-sharing are critical throughout this process. Engaging with international organizations, governments, and non-governmental entities can provide additional resources and expertise. Implementing technological solutions, such as real-time tracking and data analytics, further enhances the visibility and traceability of medical supplies, facilitating a more responsive and adaptive supply chain [10, 18, 28].

Employing comprehensive risk assessment methodologies, such as Hazard Vulnerability Analysis (HVA) and the Risk Identification and Site Criticality (RISC) Toolkit, is pivotal for informed prioritization. In many industries, including healthcare facilities, regulatory accreditation bodies will require organizations to conduct risk assessments as part of emergency preparedness and compliance measures on annual basis. Compliance with such regulations not only ensures legal adherence but also reinforces the importance of risk management in safeguarding supply chains. HVA allows healthcare organizations to systematically evaluate potential hazards, assess vulnerabilities, and identify critical resources that may be at risk during emergencies. By understanding the specific risks associated with each hazard, healthcare providers can prioritize the allocation of resources based on the likelihood and impact of different events [15]. The Risk Identification and Site Criticality (RISC) Toolkit further enhances prioritization efforts by providing a structured approach to identify critical sites and assess their vulnerability to specific risks. This toolkit allows for a comprehensive analysis of supply chain nodes, helping healthcare organizations identify key dependencies and potential points of failure (Administration for Strategic Preparedness and Response (ASPR), n. d.). Through the integration of these risk assessment tools, emergency supply chain prioritization becomes a strategic process that aligns resources with the highest risks and criticality, ensuring a targeted and effective response during crises.

6. Technology Integration

Health Services IT Preparedness Planning needs to be well prepared and integrated to meet supply needs during emergencies, namely in the form of providing information technology systems (hard disks and servers), planning adequate electricity supplies in times of crisis, as well as providing local area network facilities to provide services. Is important and must still be able to protect patient health information data. It is recommended that the health IT system have a real-time database connection to upload and download the necessary data [36, 45]. SCM integration makes use of IT to enable real-time data sharing between businesses. Better communication and quicker decision-making are two benefits of internal integration, which entails coordinating all internal operations [33]. According to a Taiwanese study, third-party logistics providers that integrate their internal and external customers have much more resilient supply chains, whereas the integration of their logistic collaborators has less of an effect. Building robust supply chain partnerships requires supply chain integration. By utilizing information technology, businesses can integrate their systems and become more responsive, which is a type of resilience for the supply chain. While operational integration between organizations increases supply chain resilience in the face of disruptions, internal integration makes information sharing easier [22]. Information technology is needed to discover the gap in emergency crisis is also known as Essential Medicines and Heath Supplies (EMHS) and Emergency logistics management information system (eELMIS). This system need real time data and availability of reliable commodities and supplies for fastest decision making during the crisis. This system contains stock ordering, receiving issuing and reporting [42, 46].

The eELMIS have four levels, that is district, node, partner and central national modules. These modules support routine transactions, tracking, ordering and distribution of supplies and commodities. This system have real time track transactions of orders, receipts, issues, and reports emergency supplies. This is the example tripartite model of emergency collaboration. This model has collaboration between government, retailer, and the supplier. These three big groups have a big role to achieve optimal mechanism of emergency supply chain. This system is based on the actual situation of China's emergency supply chain development. At the beginning of the crisis, the government acts as emergency supervision, the retailer acts as emergency collaboration, but the supplier don't act as emergency collaboration. Then at the incarceration period of crisis, the government increases penalties, provides emergency subsidies and improve supervision or encourage participation by supplier. In the later recovery period of crisis, the government will withdraw from emergency supervision gradually with the benefits from both retailer and the supplier participation. Psychological factor also has a role in determining effectiveness of the emergency response [41, 42].

7. Flexibility and Resilience

The synchronization of the supply chain flow is largely dependent on the integration of supply chain management (SCM) between businesses and their partners. By providing accurate information and lowering uncertainty about the external environment, collaborative supply chain management (SCM) efforts with suppliers and customers enhance manufacturing flexibility. Quicker and more accurate reactions to changing market conditions are made possible by this increased flexibility. Manufacturing companies can achieve manufacturing flexibility through a combination of external integration with suppliers and customers and internal integration involving cross-functional collaboration [9, 33].

4 Capacity Scaling

Capacity scaling on the track stockpiling commodities can be done by cooperation between countries. International cooperation by forming regional logistics hub or joint external evaluation to reduce the need for cross border imports for emergency commodities and identify current capabilities and gaps. If the national capacity is not sufficient, it can be more cost effective for covering several countries. Effective stockpile management will make the state preparing immediate response in the first phase of a crisis [38].

At the primary healthcare level, often the first point of contact for communities, emergency protocols must emphasize rapid response capabilities. Developing countries should prioritize the establishment of resilient supply chains at primary healthcare facilities, ensuring they are well-equipped with essential medical resources. Capacity scaling in these settings involves maintaining a strategic stockpile, training healthcare workers in emergency response procedures, and establishing communication channels for timely alerts and mobilization. The network chain structure of an emergency supply chain involves a systematic flow chart comprising key stages: raise, delivery, storage, and distribution. The process begins with the "raise" phase, where information about the emergency is gathered, and the need for supplies is assessed. Once the requirements are identified, the "delivery" phase comes into play, involving the transportation of emergency goods to designated storage facilities. The "storage" stage focuses on strategically placing supplies in accessible and secure locations, ensuring their availability when required. Finally, the "distribution" phase entails a well-coordinated effort to deliver the stored goods to the affected areas efficiently. This structured flow chart ensures a streamlined and responsive emergency supply chain, enabling timely and effective support during crises. The detailed flowchart as described in Fig. 2 [48].

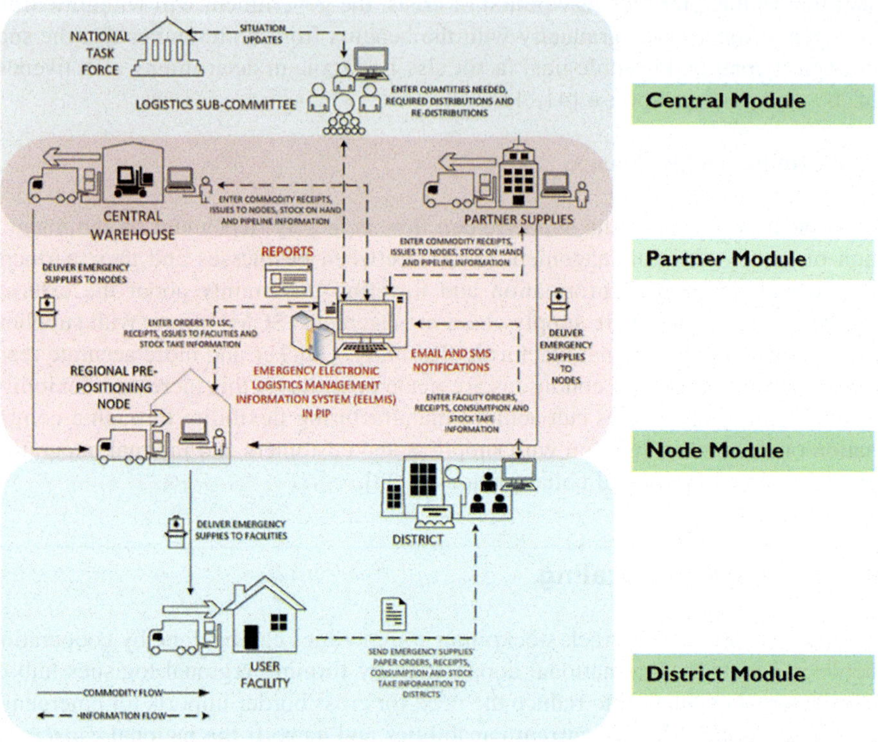

Fig. 1 EELMIS emergency commodity flow. *Source* Wasswa et al. [42]

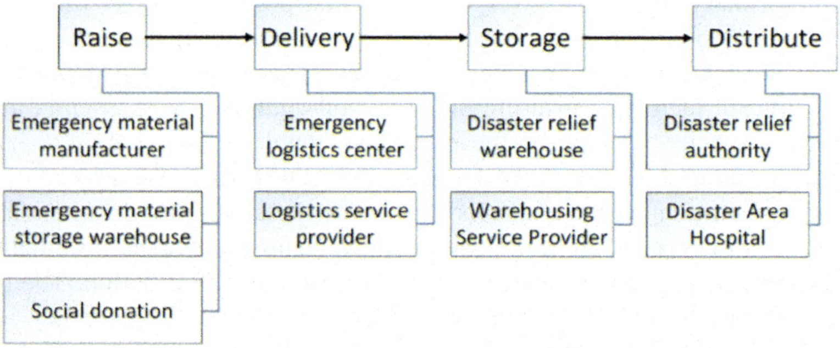

Fig. 2 The flow chart of network chain structure of emergency supply chain *Source* Zeng [48]

Moving to secondary healthcare facilities, which typically serve larger communities or districts, the emergency protocols need to account for increased demand and complexity. These facilities should have the capability to scale up their capacity by maintaining a diverse range of medical supplies, including those needed for more specialized treatments. Collaborative efforts between primary and secondary facilities become crucial in ensuring a seamless flow of supplies and information during emergencies. Tertiary healthcare facilities, often located at the regional or provincial level, play a critical role in handling more severe cases and coordinating resources for a broader geographical area. Emergency protocols at this level require sophisticated planning and coordination mechanisms. The capacity scaling involves not only maintaining adequate medical supplies but also establishing efficient communication networks, transportation systems, and partnerships with relevant stakeholders to facilitate the rapid deployment of resources. At the district, province, and national levels, emergency protocols should be comprehensive and well-integrated into broader disaster management frameworks. These higher-level facilities are responsible for strategic planning, resource allocation, and coordination across regions.

There are two degrees of control that could be done in coordination, one is a centralized structure, and another is a non-centralized structure. If members of the chain management plan and acts individually, the objective of the supply chain may not be achieved. On the other hand, coordinated supply chain planning has been shown to improve some performance metrics, including delivery times, production costs, and customer service perception. Additionally, it has shown to reduce the overall supply chain costs. In order to achieve this kind of coordination, enterprise resource planning systems (ERP) and the links that go with them must be implemented, as well as collaborative planning procedures and synchronized forecast development. In order to effectively coordinate, it is necessary to remove obstacles to communication and overcome information reluctance. It also entails coordinating disparate management styles and interests. Coordination can proceed toward integrated chain management, which eventually takes the place of all other functional process management techniques, thanks to these requirements. When production planning policies and programming operations have been implemented, coordination is demonstrated when members of a supply chain work together to minimize operating costs and share profits [6]. The organizations participating in each supply chain process must coordinate their efforts in a harmonized and coordinated manner. These steps ought to encourage the creation of value and the minimization of losses. High standards of communication and standardization are required to achieve coordination of logistic processes and to build trust among chain members [6, 38, 39].

The coordination deployment strategy starts with a diagnostic stage. This first stage aims to determine the information requirements of the processes that need to be integrated, the attributes of the participants' tangible and intangible components, and the team members who create joint operation plans. During the planning horizon, these members are in charge of carrying out the required logistical coordination as described in Fig. 3. As a result, several other factors must be ascertained, including the organization of the channels for communication, the primary information producers, the decision-making authority levels, the command channels, the response times, and the accountable members who oversee each process along with their replacement members if needed. Once the manuals and instructions have

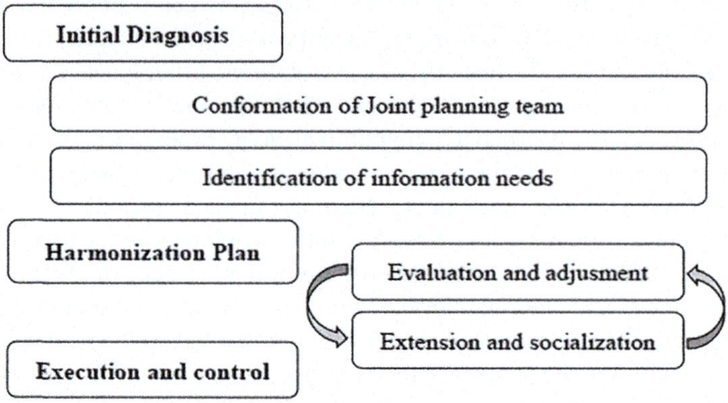

Fig. 3 Deployment strategy for coordination. *Source* Balcázar Camacho et al. [6]

been finalized, this information ought to lessen the impact of both any deviation from the plans and likely contingencies. Operational delays and minor negative effects are caused in part by these actions [6].

Delegates from every organization that takes part in the harmonization and coordination process, as well as experts from all organizational levels who are familiar with every step of the logistic cycle, must make up the SC planning team as describe in Fig. 4. The identification of redundant and harmonious issues in operations and planning across organizations is a key component of supply chain coordination planning. It is essential that operations line up with the strategies of each business unit. Eliminating redundant tasks requires careful consideration of how they affect value creation, in order to prevent delays and non-value-adding endeavors. It is crucial to closely examine every step of the logistic cycle, including labeling, storage, packing, and inspections. The best-case scenario involves thorough coordination planning between all organizations for supply, distribution, and storage in order to identify the best locations for inventory based on factors like production/storage capacity, demand, and resource availability. Whether in production or distribution, a centralized midpoint in the chain acts as a point of reference for information sharing, enabling centralized decision-making and inventory control, which lowers costs worldwide [6].

5 Training Simulation of Emergency Supply Chain Protocol

To discover gaps in emergency protocols, a thorough risk assessment of the existing supply chain infrastructure and protocols is essential, such as using HVA and RISC Toolkit. This involves examining the entire supply chain, from procurement to distribution, and identifying potential weaknesses. Key areas of scrutiny

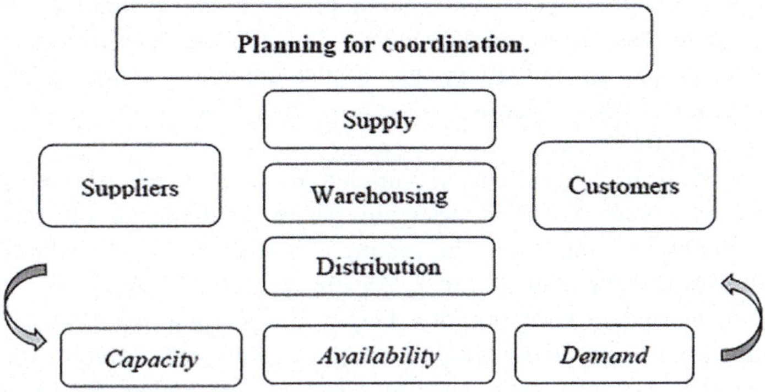

Fig. 4 Planning for coordination. *Source* Balcázar Camacho et al. [6]

include inventory management, transportation logistics, storage capacity, and communication systems. Engaging stakeholders at various levels, including healthcare professionals, logistics personnel, and supply chain managers, can provide valuable insights into real-world challenges and potential vulnerabilities. Simulation exercises play a pivotal role in gauging the effectiveness of emergency protocols. By creating scenarios that mimic crisis situations, stakeholders can practice and refine their responses, ensuring a coordinated and efficient reaction to unforeseen challenges. Simulations help in testing the robustness of communication channels, evaluating the speed of decision-making, and identifying areas that may require improvement. The insights gained from these exercises enable the fine-tuning of emergency protocols and enhance the overall preparedness of the supply chain [28].

Training simulations play a crucial role in preparing for emergency medical supply chain optimization in developing countries. They offer a dynamic platform to identify gaps and enhance readiness. Here's an exploration of how training simulations can uncover gaps in emergency medical supply chain optimization readiness [12, 26]

1. Simulation Scenarios: Designing simulated emergency scenarios allows stakeholders to enact and test supply chain responses in crisis situations. By mimicking real-life emergencies, these simulations reveal potential bottlenecks, delays, or inefficiencies in the supply chain process (Davis and Steven J. Warrington., 2023; [26]).
2. Identifying Weak Links: Through simulations, it becomes evident where breakdowns or weak links occur in the supply chain. This might involve issues related to procurement, transportation, storage, or distribution of medical supplies (Davis and Steven J. Warrington., 2023; [26]).

3. Assessment of Decision-Making: Simulations enable evaluation of decision-making processes during emergencies. It uncovers whether decisions are prompt, appropriate, and effectively implemented or if there are delays or miscommunications hindering the supply chain flow (Davis and Steven J. Warrington., 2023; [26]).
4. Resource Allocation Challenges: Simulations help in recognizing challenges related to resource allocation strategies. These challenges could include inadequate stockpiles, incorrect forecasting, or distribution imbalances among regions (David Davis and Steven J. Warrington., 2023; [26]).
5. Communication and Collaboration Gaps: The simulation exercises highlight communication gaps and coordination issues between different stakeholders involved in the supply chain, such as governmental bodies, NGOs, healthcare providers, and suppliers. There are yet clear mechanisms in place in developing countries or Lower Middle-Income Countries that experience ongoing shortages of medical supplies that facilitate easy access to crucial information about the financing, distribution, and supply of pharmaceuticals. Furthermore, there is a lack of data or inaccurate statistics regarding demand and usage. Increased sector-to-sector contact is necessary to improve access to such vital information. Both developed and developing country hospitals sometimes have little to no communication between the people ordering and prescribing medications. Additionally, this may result in an overabundance or shortage of medications. Insufficient drug supply prevents patients from receiving critical medications and prevents doctors from providing the care that patients need. The fact that pharmaceuticals expire makes it also not advantageous to have too many of them. Such results may result from inadequate information flow (David Davis and Steven J. Warrington., 2023; [26]). Health organizations need to be informed about the availability of pharmaceuticals and medical supplies.
6. Technology Integration Issues: Testing simulations also reveal technological hurdles. This might involve issues with tracking systems, data management, or the integration of new technologies within the supply chain (David Davis and Steven J. Warrington., 2023; [26]).
7. Training Needs Analysis: Observing the performance of participants in simulations aids in identifying training needs. It allows for tailored training programs to address specific skill gaps and improve overall preparedness (David Davis and Steven J. Warrington., 2023; [26]).
8. Policy and Procedure Evaluation: Simulations provide an opportunity to evaluate the effectiveness of existing policies and procedures. This includes examining whether established protocols align with the realities of emergency situations in developing countries (David Davis and Steven J. Warrington., 2023; [26]).

Fig. 5 Preparedness cycle simulation. *Source* World Health Organization [43]

9. Feedback Mechanism: Post-simulation, gathering feedback from participants helps in understanding their experiences, challenges faced, and suggestions for improvement. This information is invaluable for refining and optimizing the emergency supply chain (Davis and Steven J. Warrington., 2023; [26]).

Simulation should be conducted as a part of a well-thought-out exercise program that guarantees a shared strategic objective is met. They shouldn't be isolated activities. One essential part of the emergency preparedness cycle is the fitness regimen. The planning, organizing, training, equipping, exercising, assessing, and corrective action phases make up the preparedness cycle. Activities based on actual occurrences are also incorporated into the cycle following action reviews and lessons learnt, as seen in Fig. 5. In summary, training simulations serve as a proactive tool to discover and address gaps in emergency medical supply chain optimization readiness in developing countries. These simulations provide a safe environment to learn, test strategies, and improve preparedness for real-life emergencies [43].

From this Fig. 6, we delve into a simulation disaster scenario set. There are two stages, first is pre-disaster decisions, prior to the occurrence of a disaster, it is crucial to strategically outline the quantity and designated locations for prepositioned emergency aid. Simultaneously, we need to assess the overall capacity of each vehicle type for effective execution, since securing an appropriate fleet can involve a highly bureaucratic and time-consuming process through public bidding. Next, post-disaster decisions, that depend on the updated information on the quality of the routes, supplies, demands, and donation. These decisions encompass the distribution of emergency aid across different paths, the required quantity and types of vehicles for efficient delivery, procurement issues, as well as inventory and backlogging management [2].

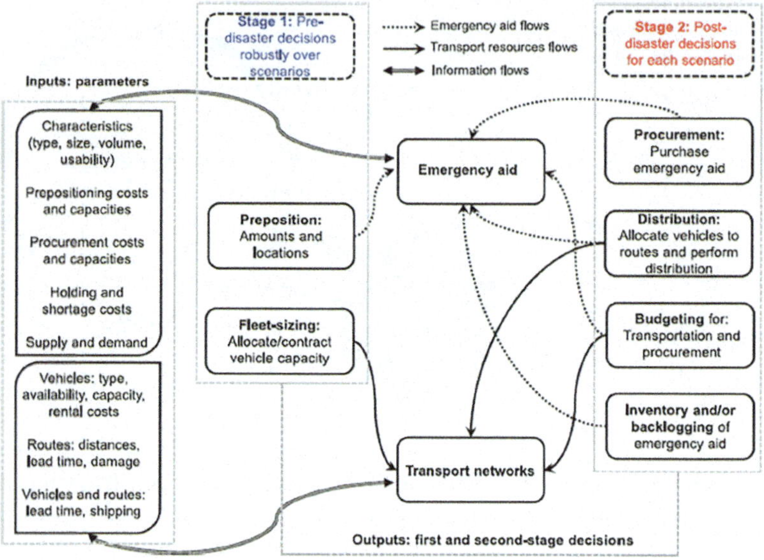

Fig. 6 Overview of disaster humanitarian operation's structure and usage. *Source* Alem et al. [2]

6 Conclusion

In conclusion, optimizing the emergency medical supply chain readiness in developing countries requires a paradigm shift towards adaptive supply chain models that seamlessly integrate routine and emergency protocols. The traditional linear supply chain approach often falls short in addressing the dynamic and unpredictable nature of emergencies. Implementing adaptive models allows for a more responsive and flexible supply chain, ensuring that the distribution of medical resources is swift and effective during crises. This requires the development of protocols that can be seamlessly transitioned from routine to emergency modes, enabling rapid adjustments to changing circumstances. By embracing adaptive supply chain models, developing countries can enhance their preparedness and resilience in the face of unforeseen medical challenges.

Furthermore, effective emergency medical supply chain optimization demands strategic resource allocation, which involves identifying and prioritizing critical areas for maximum impact. Developing countries should invest in robust resource allocation strategies that consider the scarcity of resources during emergencies. This includes establishing clear guidelines for the allocation of medical supplies based on the severity and urgency of cases. Additionally, capacity scaling plays a pivotal role in ensuring the supply chain's ability to meet escalating demands. Developing countries must invest in scalable infrastructure, technology, and human resources to promptly adapt to surges in medical supply requirements. Integrating advanced forecasting methods and data-driven decision-making can further enhance the accuracy of resource allocation, promoting efficient and equitable distribution of medical supplies in times of crisis. Lastly, a comprehensive approach to emergency medical supply chain readiness involves regular training, simulation exercises, and identifying gaps in the existing system. By engaging in realistic scenarios, healthcare professionals can refine their response mechanisms and uncover potential weaknesses in the supply chain. Continuous training and simulation exercises provide an opportunity to evaluate the effectiveness of protocols, improve communication channels, and enhance overall preparedness. Identifying gaps in the system allows for targeted improvements, ensuring that the supply chain is resilient, adaptive, and capable of delivering life-saving resources efficiently in times of emergencies. In conclusion, an integrated approach encompassing adaptive supply chain models, resource allocation strategies, capacity scaling, and ongoing training and simulation efforts is essential for achieving optimal emergency medical supply chain readiness in developing countries.

References

1. Administration for Strategic Preparedness and Response (ASPR) (n.d.) RISC toolkit 2.0 risk identification and site criticality [WWW Document]. Administration for Strategic Preparedness and Response (ASPR). https://aspr.hhs.gov/RISC/Pages/default.aspx. Accessed 13 Jan 2024
2. Alem D, Clark A, Moreno A (2016) Stochastic network models for logistics planning in disaster relief. Eur J Oper Res 255:187–206. https://doi.org/10.1016/j.ejor.2016.04.041
3. Alonso SG, Marques G, Barrachina I, Garcia-Zapirain B, Arambarri J, Salvador JC, de la Torre Díez I (2021) Telemedicine and e-health research solutions in literature for combatting COVID-19: a systematic review. Health Technol (Berl) 11:257–266. https://doi.org/10.1007/s12553-021-00529-7
4. Al-Qatawneh L, Hafeez K (2011 Healthcare logistics cost optimization using a multi-criteria inventory classification. In: International conference on industrial engineering and operations management
5. Arji G, Ahmadi H, Avazpoor P, Hemmat M (2023) Identifying resilience strategies for disruption management in the healthcare supply chain during COVID-19 by digital innovations: a systematic literature review. Inform Med Unlocked 38:101199. https://doi.org/10.1016/j.imu.2023.101199
6. Balcázar Camacho DA, López Bello CA, Adarme Jaimes W (2016) Strategic guidelines for supply chain coordination in healthcare and a mathematical model as a proposed mechanism for the measurement of coordination effects. DYNA (Medellin) 83:203. https://doi.org/10.15446/dyna.v83n197.55596
7. Brandon-Jones E, Squire B, Autry CW, Petersen KJ (2014) A Contingent resource-based perspective of supply chain resilience and robustness. J Supply Chain Manag 50:55–73. https://doi.org/10.1111/jscm.12050
8. Brun A, Karaosman H, Barresi T (2020) Supply chain collaboration for transparency. Sustainability 12:4429. https://doi.org/10.3390/su12114429
9. Chan HK, Wang WYC, Luong LHS, Chan FTS (2009) Flexibility and adaptability in supply chains: a lesson learnt from a practitioner. Supply Chain Manage Int J 14:407–410. https://doi.org/10.1108/13598540910995165
10. Chaudhuri A, Boer H, Taran Y (2018) Supply chain integration, risk management and manufacturing flexibility. Int J Oper Prod Manag 38:690–712. https://doi.org/10.1108/IJOPM-08-2015-0508

11. Chukwu OA, Chukwu U, Lemoha C (2018) Poor performance of medicines logistics and supply chain systems in a developing country context: lessons from Nigeria. J Pharm Health Serv Res 9:289–291. https://doi.org/10.1111/jphs.12274
12. Davis D, Warrington SJ (2023) Simulation training and skill assessment in emergency medicine. StatPearls Publishing
13. Dowling P (2011) Healthcare supply chains in developing countries', situational analysis
14. Duong MH, Moles RJ, Chaar B, Chen TF (2019) Stakeholder roles in facilitating access to essential medicines. Res Soc Adm Pharm 15:260–266. https://doi.org/10.1016/j.sapharm.2018.04.034
15. Fares S, Femino M, Sayah A, Weiner DL, Yim ES, Douthwright S, Molloy MS, Irfan FB, Karkoukli MA, Lipton R, Burstein JL, Mazrouei MA, Ciottone G (2014) Health care system hazard vulnerability analysis: an assessment of all public hospitals in Abu Dhabi. Disasters 38:420–433. https://doi.org/10.1111/disa.12047
16. Gao Y, Liu C, Zeng Q, Duan H (2021) Two effective strategies to support cross-organization emergency resource allocation optimization. Mob Inf Syst 2021:1–15. https://doi.org/10.1155/2021/7965935
17. Ghaffari Z, Nasiri MM, Bozorgi-Amiri A, Rahbari A (2020) Emergency supply chain scheduling problem with multiple resources in disaster relief operations. Transportmetrica A: Transp Sci 16:930–956. https://doi.org/10.1080/23249935.2020.1720858
18. Global Health Forecasting Working Group (2007) A risky business: saving money and improving global health through better demand forecasts
19. ISEAS Yusof Ishak Institute (2021) Malaysia's rubber glove industry—the good, the bad and the ugly. ISEAS Yusof Ishak Institute, 35
20. Kabantiyok D, Ninyio N, Shittu I, Meseko C, Emeto TI, Adegboye OA (2022) Human respiratory infections in Nigeria: Influenza and the emergence of SARS-CoV-2 pandemic. Vaccines (Basel) 10:1551. https://doi.org/10.3390/vaccines10091551
21. Kanokphanvanich C, Rattanawong W, Vongmanee V (2022) A meta-analysis of health care supply chain performance for patient safety. In: 2022 14th International conference on software, knowledge, information management and applications (SKIMA). IEEE, pp 13–20. https://doi.org/10.1109/SKIMA57145.2022.10029487
22. Liu C-L, Shang K-C, Lirn T-C, Lai K-H, Lun YHV (2018) Supply chain resilience, firm performance, and management policies in the liner shipping industry. Transp Res Part A Policy Pract 110:202–219. https://doi.org/10.1016/j.tra.2017.02.004
23. Luo J, Huang M, Bai Y, Li J (2023) Supply chain management during a public health emergency of international concern: a bibliometric and content analysis. Processes 11:713. https://doi.org/10.3390/pr11030713
24. Mandal S, Jha RR (2018) Exploring the importance of collaborative assets to hospital-supplier integration in healthcare supply chains. Int J Prod Res 56:2666–2683. https://doi.org/10.1080/00207543.2017.1381349
25. Moons K, Waeyenbergh G, Pintelon L (2019) Measuring the logistics performance of internal hospital supply chains—a literature study. Omega (Westport) 82:205–217. https://doi.org/10.1016/j.omega.2018.01.007
26. Moslehi S, Masoumi G, Barghi-Shirazi F (2022) Benefits of simulation-based education in hospital emergency departments: a systematic review. J Educ Health Prom 11
27. Motiwala SS, McLaughlin JE, King J, Hodgson B, Hamilton M (2008) Advancing the health care supply chain and promoting leadership through strategic partnerships with industry. Healthc Manage Forum 21:23–28. https://doi.org/10.1016/S0840-4704(10)60542-X
28. Okeagu CN, Reed DS, Sun L, Colontonio MM, Rezayev A, Ghaffar YA, Kaye RJ, Liu H, Cornett EM, Fox CJ, Urman RD, Kaye AD (2021) Principles of supply chain management in the time of crisis. Best Pract Res Clin Anaesthesiol 35:369–376. https://doi.org/10.1016/j.bpa.2020.11.007
29. Schatteman O, Woodhouse D, Terino J (2020) Supply chain lessons from Covid-19: time to refocus on resilience [WWW Document]. https://www.bain.com/insights/supply-chain-lessons-from-covid-19/. Accessed 20 Jan 2024

30. Salehi F, Mahootchi M, Husseini SMM (2019) Developing a robust stochastic model for designing a blood supply chain network in a crisis: a possible earthquake in Tehran. Ann Oper Res 283:679–703. https://doi.org/10.1007/s10479-017-2533-0
31. Sallwa AA (2024) Supply chain gaps analysis during COVID-19 pandemic—the case of medical supplies in Tanzania. J Hum Logist Supply Chain Manage 14:82–89. https://doi.org/10.1108/JHLSCM-05-2022-0057
32. Shukor AAA, Newaz MdS, Rahman MK, Taha AZ (2021) Supply chain integration and its impact on supply chain agility and organizational flexibility in manufacturing firms. Int J Emerg Mark 16:1721–1744. https://doi.org/10.1108/IJOEM-04-2020-0418
33. Siagian H, Tarigan ZJH, Jie F (2021) Supply chain integration enables resilience, flexibility, and innovation to improve business performance in COVID-19 era. Sustainability 13:4669. https://doi.org/10.3390/su13094669
34. Subramanian L (2021) Effective demand forecasting in health supply chains: emerging trend, enablers, and blockers. Logistics 5:12. https://doi.org/10.3390/logistics5010012
35. Syahrir I, Suparno VI (2019) Inventory management in healthcare supply chain under uncertainty and emergency: a literature review. J Adv Res Dyn Control Syst 7:702–709
36. Tosh PK, Feldman H, Christian MD, Devereaux AV, Kissoon N, Dichter JR (2014) Business and continuity of operations. Chest 146:e103S-e117S. https://doi.org/10.1378/chest.14-0739
37. United Nations World Food Program (2017) Innovative supply chain information platform will help prepare for the next pandemic. [WWW Document]. United Nations World Food Program. https://www.wfp.org/news/innovative-supply-chain-information-platform-will-help-prepare-next-pandemic. Accessed 22 Jan 2024
38. USAID (2020) Best practices in supply chain preparedness for public health emergencies. [WWW Document]. United States Agency for International Development (USAID), US. https://www.ghsupplychain.org/sites/default/files/2021-12/Best-Practices-in-Supply-Chain-Preparedness-for-Public-Health-Emergencies_January-2018_English.pdf. Accessed 17 Jan 2024
39. USAID (2015) USAID African strategies for health. Rwanda Health Private Sector Engagement Assessment
40. Uthayakumar R, Priyan S (2013) Pharmaceutical supply chain and inventory management strategies: optimization for a pharmaceutical company and a hospital. Oper Res Health Care 2:52–64. https://doi.org/10.1016/j.orhc.2013.08.001
41. Wang J, Hu Y, Qu W, Ma L (2022) Research on emergency supply chain collaboration based on tripartite evolutionary game. Sustainability 14:11893. https://doi.org/10.3390/su141911893
42. Wasswa JH, Oundo H, Oteba MO, Komakech H, Ochola I, Mwebaze S, Okidi D, Kirunda A, Nakadde S, Oteba NO, Lugada E (2023) Leveraging electronic logistics management information systems to enhance and optimize supply chain response during public health emergencies: lessons from COVID-19 response in Uganda. J Pharm Policy Pract 16:6. https://doi.org/10.1186/s40545-023-00517-4
43. World Health Organization (2017) WHO simulation exercise manual. Geneva
44. Wright AM, Snowdon A, Saunders M, Trampas D (2023) The necessity of healthcare supply chain resilience for crisis preparedness. Healthc Manage Forum. https://doi.org/10.1177/08404704231207386
45. Wu T-C, Ho C-TB (2023) Blockchain revolutionizing in emergency medicine: a scoping review of patient journey through the ED. Healthcare 11:2497. https://doi.org/10.3390/healthcare11182497
46. Xie K, Zhu S, Gui P, Chen Y (2023) Coordinating an emergency medical material supply chain with CVaR under the pandemic considering corporate social responsibility. Comput Ind Eng 176:108989. https://doi.org/10.1016/j.cie.2023.108989

47. Yu K, Luo BN, Feng X, Liu J (2018) Supply chain information integration, flexibility, and operational performance. Int J Logist Manage 29:340–364. https://doi.org/10.1108/IJLM-08-2016-0185
48. Zeng S (2021) Research on problems and countermeasures in the emergency supply chain in case of sudden disasters. In: 2021 2nd International conference on urban engineering and management science (ICUEMS). IEEE, pp 164–167. https://doi.org/10.1109/ICUEMS52408.2021.00041

Felicia Setiawan Completed her medical education at Atma Jaya University in 2012. She has 3 Master's Degrees; Master of Occupational Health from University of Indonesia in 2017, Master of Healthcare Administration from University of Pelita Harapan in 2023, and Master of Business Administration and Fellowship of Quality Healthcare from University of Michigan in 2023. Her research is related to healthcare and hospital management, as well as marketing, patient safety, human resources, and supply chain.

Valencia Hadinata is currently pursuing her medical education at University of Indonesia since 2018 and Master's Degree in Healthcare Administration from the University of Pelita Harapan since 2022. Her research focuses on clinical medicine and hospital management including supply chain practices.

Grace Alvina Obtained her medical education at Atma Jaya University in 2012. Currently, she serves as a medical tutor at University of Pelita Harapan with a desire to share her experience and knowledge with medical students. Her research focuses on clinical medicine and hospital management including supply chain practices, particularly in the context of vaccine procurement.

Gerry Dwi Putro Graduated as medical doctor from Atma Jaya University Jakarta in 2012 and as Orthopaedic and Traumatology Surgeon from Hasanuddin University Makassar in 2023. Now working as Orthopaedic Traumatology Surgeon at Jakarta Hospital. His research focuses mainly in clinical medicine and healthcare management such as supply chain practices.

Claudia Alexandra Graduated her medical education in 2017 from Atma Jaya Jakarta University. She is now pursuing a degree in Hospital Management at University of Pelita Harapan since 2022. She is a clinician who is actively serving the community and would like to have the chance to contribute more, particularly in the field of healthcare supply chain management.

Fritzie A. Rexana is a doctor from Atma Jaya University who graduated in 2012. She completed a Master's Degree in Management at Tarumanagara University in 2021. She is currently active as a doctor in hospitals and has an interest in being more involved in healthcare management. Her research focused mainly in healthcare management such as finance, pharmacy, and supply chain.

7 Halal and Health: Applying Theory of Constraints to Optimise Halal Healthcare Supply Chain

Mohamed Syazwan Ab Talib and Siti Norida Wahab

Abstract

Integrating halal principles into healthcare supply chain management is essential to comply with Islamic laws and lifestyle. With the increasing demand for halal healthcare, it is crucial to address the unique challenges in the sector. Despite its growing popularity, the halal healthcare sector often receives less attention than the food industry. This chapter explores integrating the Theory of Constraints (TOC) into a systemic healthcare supply chain to enhance operational optimisation in healthcare provision that addresses halal compliance requirements. Using a qualitative case study methodology involving a private hospital, the implementation of TOC and halal-centric initiatives from a supply chain perspective are analyzed. The findings indicate tangible improvements in supply chain efficiency, financial prudence, and service quality are imperative. This chapter emphasises the significance of aligning operational processes with operational and religious imperatives in healthcare provision. It calls for further research into the intersection of TOC and explores the impact of religiously compliant healthcare practices on patient satisfaction and health outcomes. This chapter is pertinent as it emphasizes the potential for broader implementation of the TOC process across various industries, particularly in accommodating the rising demand for halal-certified healthcare.

M. S. A. Talib
School of Business and Economics, UBD, Universiti Brunei Darussalam, Gadong, Brunei Darussalam
e-mail: syazwan.talib@ubd.edu.bn

S. N. Wahab (✉)
Faculty of Business and Management, Universiti Teknologi MARA, 42300 Puncak Alam, Selangor, Malaysia
e-mail: sitinorida23@uitm.edu.my

F. Jawab (ed.), *Hospital Supply Chain*, Integrated Science 27,
https://doi.org/10.1007/978-3-031-70292-1_7

Keywords

Halal • Healthcare • Islamic economy • Management constraints • Supply chain management • Theory

1 Introduction

Halal is a fundamental aspect of the Islamic lifestyle. It is traditionally related to food and dietary intake that adheres to Islamic law [36]. However, the concept of halal has expanded to various aspects of the modern business world, such as banking [13], tourism [45], and marketing [40]. Moreover, the halal doctrine has also been applied to the healthcare sector, primarily in the pharmaceutical and cosmetics fields [48]. The wide presence of halal in various industry sectors highlights the growing interest and significance of the Islamic economy. The Islamic economy has seven core sectors: food and beverages, pharmaceuticals and healthcare, cosmetics and personal care, modest fashion and clothing, tourism and hospitality, media and entertainment, and Islamic finance and is estimated to be valued at over $2 trillion globally and is projected to reach $2.8 trillion by 2025 [16].

The immense valuation signifies an excellent potential for the halal industry, with ever-increasing demand for halal products and services by Muslim and non-Muslim consumers [21, 49]. Besides, businesses recognise the importance of catering to the growing halal demand and consumer preferences, leading to the development of halal products and services in various industries. For instance, McDonald's has introduced halal-certified menu items in certain regions with a large Muslim population [49], and major brands and packaged goods companies, such as Unilever, have long offered halal-certified cosmetics and personal care products [8, 24]. Similarly, the healthcare sector within the halal industry has also been expanding rapidly, with a niche in providing halal-certified pharmaceuticals and healthcare services [30].

Despite the growing demand and popularity of the halal healthcare sector, the attention and focus are often overshadowed by the prevalent halal food industry [11, 16, 19]. The uneven attention is understandable, given that the halal food industry contributes US$1.19 trillion to the global Islamic economy compared to halal healthcare, which contributes only US$100 billion [16]. Additionally, the halal food industry has a more extended history and established infrastructure than the relatively untapped halal healthcare sector [30]. Furthermore, in academic research, contemporary halal-centred scholars have primarily focused on the halal food industry [11, 31], leaving a gap in understanding and analysing the unique challenges and opportunities within the halal healthcare sector.

Considering the vast and lucrative global halal economy yet underexplored potential of the halal healthcare sector, it is crucial to understand possible elements that hinder the progress and potential. One possible element that hinders the progress and potential of the halal healthcare sector is the limited optimisation in the supply chains [32, 33]. Nonetheless, the lack of progress in the halal healthcare supply chain (HHSC) offers an enormous potential for research and improvement. One worthy initiative is to optimise the HHSC from a Theory of Constraints (TOC) perspective, which can unearth inhibiting factors that may impede the growth of the halal healthcare sector [4]. Applying the TOC to the HHSC makes it possible to identify bottlenecks and areas of improvement that can enhance the overall performance of the supply chain.

Therefore, this chapter explores optimising HHSC from a TOC lens. It applies the TOC to HHSC by adopting a system thinking approach, which considers the interconnectedness and interdependencies of various elements within the supply chain (Talib, 2021). Moreover, this paper will provide a practical application to demonstrate how the TOC can be implemented in the HHSC. This useful application will include the identification of constraints, developing solutions to overcome these constraints, and adopting a continuous improvement mindset to ensure ongoing optimisation of the HHSC using a case study of a renowned private healthcare provider.

In the next section, this chapter will deliberate on the foundations of halal supply chain management (HSCM) and its incorporation into the healthcare supply chain domain. Subsequently, the chapter will introduce the theoretical foundations of the TOC and its relevance to HHSC from a system thinking angle. Afterwards, the chapter continues by underlining the practical step-by-step application of TOC to HHSC using a case study of a private healthcare provider and the results achieved through the implementation of TOC in their HHSC. Lastly, the chapter will summarise, highlighting the implications and drawing recommendations for future research in HHSC.

2 Halal and Healthcare Supply Chain Management Overview

2.1 Halal Supply Chain Management

HSCM refers to producing, processing, and distributing goods following Islamic principles and guidelines. In Arabic, 'halal' means permissible or lawful according to Islamic law. HSCM is crucial in the food and pharmaceutical industries, where adherence to Islamic dietary laws is vital. The HSCM begins with sourcing raw materials that comply with Islamic principles. This includes ensuring that animals used for meat are slaughtered following halal guidelines, with emphasis on humane treatment and proper Islamic rituals. It then moves to processing and manufacturing, where strict attention is paid to the ingredients used, avoiding prohibited substances such as alcohol and pork derivatives. To ensure the whole process adheres to Islamic principles, the certification plays a pivotal role in the

HSCM [52]. Products must undergo thorough inspections by certified halal authorities to ensure compliance with Islamic standards. This certification extends to all stages of production, packaging, and labelling. Companies involved in the HSCM often seek accreditation from recognised Islamic certification (i.e. JAKIM) bodies to build consumer trust [1, 2].

Moreover, distribution and logistics in the HSCM must also adhere to Islamic principles. Separate storage and transportation facilities are often maintained to prevent contamination with non-halal products. Retailers in the HSCM must ensure proper segregation of halal and non-halal products, and clear labelling is crucial for consumer awareness [44]. The global demand for halal products has spurred the development of a robust and specialised HSCM infrastructure. This includes the establishment of dedicated halal-certified facilities [26], increased awareness among industry stakeholders [51], and the integration of technology for traceability and transparency [6, 43]. Hence, HSCM is a comprehensive system that ensures the production, processing, and distribution of goods, including the healthcare sector, in compliance with Islamic principles [25].

2.2 Healthcare Supply Chain

The healthcare supply chain is a complex and critical process involving efficient planning, sourcing, procurement, storage, and distribution of medical goods and services within the healthcare system. The primary goal is to ensure the timely availability of high-quality healthcare products while minimising costs and maintaining compliance with regulatory standards [50]. The healthcare supply chain encompasses various products, including pharmaceuticals, medical devices, equipment, and consumables. Effective management is essential to meet the demands of healthcare providers, maintain patient safety, and optimise operational efficiency [27].

One key aspect of the healthcare supply chain is demand forecasting. Accurate predictions of the demand for medical products and services help organisations plan their inventory levels, preventing shortages or excess stock [7]. This is crucial for ensuring healthcare providers have access to the necessary supplies to deliver quality patient care. Procurement is another critical element. Healthcare organisations must establish relationships with reliable suppliers to secure a stable and cost-effective supply of medical goods. Negotiating favourable contracts, monitoring supplier performance, and ensuring compliance with quality standards are integral components of this process [10].

Additionally, inventory management is essential for maintaining optimal stock levels. It involves monitoring product expiration dates, minimising waste, and implementing efficient storage systems to enhance accessibility. Likewise, advanced technologies, such as Radio-Frequency Identification (RFID) tracking and inventory management software, are increasingly employed to streamline these processes [17]. Similarly, logistics distribution plays a vital role in the healthcare supply chain. Timely and accurate delivery of medical products to healthcare facilities is essential to avoid disruptions in patient care. Efficient transportation, warehousing, and last-mile delivery are vital components [28]. Besides, regulatory compliance is a constant consideration in the healthcare supply chain. Adherence to local and international regulations, such as Good Distribution Practices (GDP) and Good Manufacturing Practices (GMP), is crucial for ensuring the safety and efficacy of medical products [22].

Therefore, the healthcare supply chain is a multifaceted process that involves forecasting, procurement, inventory management, distribution, and regulatory compliance. A well-organized and efficient supply chain is indispensable for healthcare organisations to deliver quality patient care while managing costs effectively [9]. Hence, advanced technologies continue to play a growing role in enhancing the transparency and efficiency of the healthcare supply chain [39]. Moreover, the demand for halal healthcare is rising as individuals seek healthcare products and services that align with Islamic principles [47]. With a growing awareness of halal practices, there is an increasing preference among Muslim consumers for healthcare options that respect their religious beliefs.

2.3 Halal and Healthcare Supply Chain Management

The integration between halal and SCM is an approach that involves aligning the principles of Islamic dietary laws with the diverse processes of sourcing, producing, and distributing healthcare-related products. This integration is crucial in regions with significant Muslim populations, where adherence to halal standards and healthcare regulations is essential [46]. The integration between these two domains aims to ensure that healthcare products and services comply with Islamic principles and adhere to the rigorous standards set by the healthcare industry. At the core of this integration lies the sourcing and procurement phase. Organisations must ensure that these inputs comply with halal requirements when selecting raw materials for pharmaceuticals, medical devices, and other healthcare products [39]. For instance, in pharmaceuticals, sourcing ingredients should exclude non-halal substances, and the manufacturing process must align with Islamic principles. This includes avoiding alcohol-based solvents and ensuring that raw materials are derived from sources that meet halal standards [38].

Additionally, certification plays a crucial role in this integrated supply chain. Products must undergo dual assessments to meet halal and healthcare standards [37]. Certification bodies specialising in each domain collaborate to provide a comprehensive evaluation, ensuring that the products are safe and effective from a healthcare perspective and halal-compliant. This dual certification enhances consumer confidence and widens the market reach of these products. The integration extends to distribution logistics, where considerations for both healthcare and halal standards come into play [3]. Dedicated storage and transportation facilities are established to prevent contamination between halal and non-halal products.

The segregation also applies to pharmaceuticals, where the supply chain must ensure that halal and non-halal medications are stored and transported separately to prevent cross-contamination [18].

Technology for traceability is critical to enhance the effectiveness of HSCM. This is equally applicable to the integration with halal standards. Technologies such as blockchain can be employed to trace the origin of raw materials, monitor the production process, and track the distribution of healthcare products [43]. This transparency is crucial for demonstrating compliance with healthcare and halal standards [34]. Furthermore, regulatory compliance is a shared concern in this integrated supply chain. Organisations must navigate complex healthcare regulations and halal standards. This involves staying abreast of changes in laws, ensuring that manufacturing processes align with both sets of requirements, and obtaining the necessary certifications and approvals (Talib et al. 2020). The integration demands a meticulous approach to documentation and reporting to demonstrate adherence to all relevant standards [22]. Collectively, the integration between halal and HSCM represents a sophisticated approach to ensuring that healthcare products comply with Islamic principles while meeting the stringent requirements of the healthcare industry [47]. The successful integration of these two domains will satisfy the diverse needs of consumers and open new markets for healthcare products in regions with significant Muslim populations.

3 Theory of Constraints

As described in the previous section, integrating halal principles and practices in healthcare supply chains requires careful consideration and implementation of various logistics and technological aspects. However, as HHSC research is still rudimentary and making gradual progress, there is room for this niche branch of the HSCM to expand. One promising approach to optimising HHSC is applying the theory of constraints (TOC). It is undeniable that theoretical understanding and application are paramount in successfully implementing any SCM strategy [14, 15], and this chapter contends that TOC could well provide a valuable framework for optimising supply chain [29, 41], possibly in HHSC.

The Theory of Constraints is a management philosophy developed by Eliyahu M. Goldratt in the 1980s [35]. In one of his seminal works, The Goal, first published in 1984, he introduced the concept of TOC and its application in improving manufacturing processes. Goldratt illustrated the principles of TOC and its transformative impact on business operations. The TOC tenet derives from the notion that every system, such as a supply chain, manufacturing process, or organisation, has at least one constraint that limits its ability to achieve the much-desired goals. TOC aims to identify and alleviate the constraints to improve the system's performance.

Over the years, TOC has been widely adopted in various industries, including tourism and hospitality [53], automotive [20], and technology [41]. Besides, TOC is often found in various disciplines, including healthcare logistics and SCM management [12, 35, 41, 42]. Similarly, TOC has also appeared in HSCM research to identify hindering factors and evoke change for progress [4]. Regardless of its interdisciplinary application, the TOC core doctrines have benefitted broad production processes addressing micro and macro-operational challenges [23].

According to [35], the TOC has two core components, namely, the logistics paradigm (LP) and the system thinking process (STP). However, Simatupang et.al [42] offer an additional performance management perspective along with LP and STP. Despite the varying views, the present chapter contends that Rahman's two-pronged view encompasses Simatupang and colleagues' standpoint, whereby the performance context is addressed in the LP's five-step focusing process (FFP). Firstly, the FFP emphasises the identification of constraints, the exploitation of existing resources to maximise throughput, and the subordination of all other processes to the needs of the constrained elements. It also advocates for the continuous improvement of the system based on identifying and eliminating constraints as they emerge. Figure 1 illustrates the FFP cycle of the LP. Secondly, the system thinking process strategically analyses the interdependencies and interactions within the system to address constraints. STP emphasises the importance of understanding the impact of decisions on supply chains and fostering the corrective alignment process with the overarching organisational goals.

In the HHSC context, the application of TOC can offer a structured approach to identifying and addressing constraints that affect the integration of halal principles. By utilising TOC's LP and STP components, organisations can systematically analyse their supply chain processes to identify bottlenecks hindering adherence to halal standards and healthcare requirements. This involves assessing the sourcing of raw materials, manufacturing processes, and distribution logistics to pinpoint areas where halal and healthcare standards may conflict or impede each other.

Moreover, the Focused Improvement process within TOC can help organisations prioritise the resolution of constraints in HHSCM. Organisations can effectively align their processes with halal requirements and healthcare standards by identifying and exploiting existing resources to maximise the throughput of halal healthcare products. Additionally, continuous improvement efforts can ensure that any emerging constraints are promptly addressed to maintain the integrity of the HHSCM.

4 TOC Application 'HC Hospital' Case Study

The chapter thus far has explored the integration of halal healthcare and underscored the significance of the Theory of Constraints (TOC). Moving forward, it will explore how TOC can be implemented in a tangible halal-certified healthcare provider, HC Hospital. The abbreviation 'HC' denotes 'Halal-Certified' and is intended to uphold the privacy of the case.

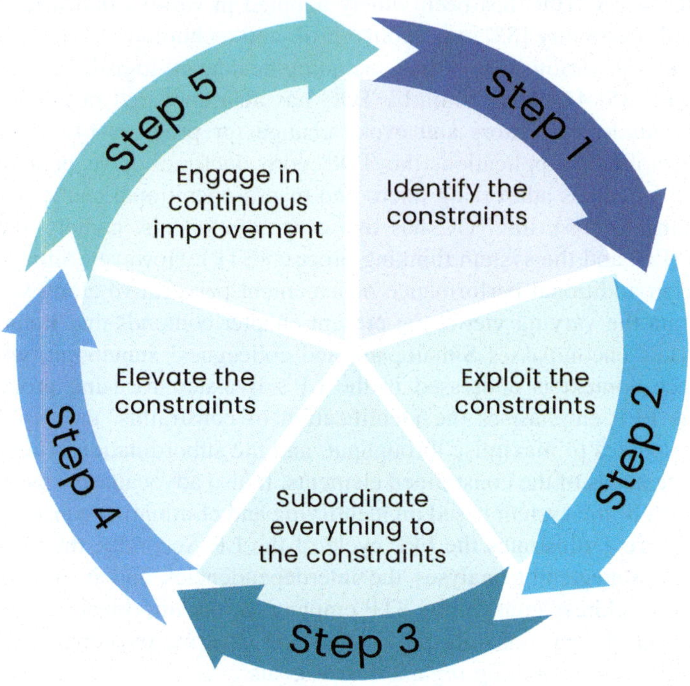

Fig. 1 Five-step focusing process

4.1 Case Background

HC Hospital in Malaysia symbolises progressive healthcare delivery that merges stringent halal principles with cutting-edge medical services. Since its inception as a halal-compliant institution in 2005, HC Hospital has established a niche and diligently transcends the traditional boundaries of private healthcare. It is a leading service provider that harmoniously aligns state-of-the-art operational standards and practices with Islamic law and halal principles. HC is a testament to an unwavering commitment to religious and cultural sensitivity and excellence in patient care. HC Hospital's journey towards integrating halal principles and practices into every patient has been a committed exercise and carefully deliberated strategy that encapsulates the essence of its community's religious and health-conscious values. HC Hospital has attracted those seeking halal-centric treatment and set the benchmark for a healthcare service that respects and upholds patients' beliefs.

HC Hospital has advanced medical facilities with comprehensive diagnostic and therapeutic hubs, reinforced by an impressive array of specialist and sub-specialist expertise. Moreover, the hospital stands proud with its robust 24-h Accident & Emergency Services and hundreds of bed capacity, all housed within facilities that uncompromisingly adhere to halal standards in various locations nationwide. This institution's unwavering dedication to halal compliance has been far from superficial. It has been ingrained into its operations, ensuring that halal principles and practices are respected and reflected from the initial point of service design to the complexities of patient interaction and intricate medical supply chains. The commitment has necessitated a supply chain that is as resilient as it is compliant, ensuring that halal-certified pharmaceuticals and healthcare provisions are perpetually ready, which serves as the backbone of its commendable service delivery model.

The HC Hospital case study is an excellent example of the vast potentialities within the halal healthcare subdiscipline. The narrative underscores the hospital's critical thinking, innovative approaches, and adaptive strategies to remain relevant and set new standards in a competitive industry. As the case progresses, Fig. 2 summarises the intricate details of how HC Hospital, through the adept application of the TOC, has optimised its halal healthcare supply chain to elevate the standards of patient care while staying true to its foundational halal precepts.

4.2 Identifying Constraints

The cross-functional team at HC Hospital had to conduct a thorough analysis to identify the factors hindering the smooth operation of HHSC. The team took an in-depth analysis of the complexities of the supply chain to identify the specific bottlenecks causing issues in the procurement and storage of halal-compliant pharmaceuticals. This was incredibly challenging because the halal pharmaceutical sector is still in its early stages, and sourcing ingredients that meet the strict Islamic principles while satisfying health regulations required precision and ethical adherence. Moreover, the hospital had the challenging task of ensuring strict separation in its logistical operations to maintain halal integrity. However, this requirement often clashes with the fast-paced delivery of medical services. As a result, balancing adherence to halal compliance and meeting healthcare needs became a significant challenge. This constraint could disrupt the balance between ethical adherence and operational efficiency.

The fine line between maintaining uncompromised halal standards and achieving seamless healthcare delivery is always precarious. Hence, this requires a robust and insightful approach to supply chain management. HC Hospital's supply chain was transformed into a dynamic function in pursuit of harmonising the competing priorities. Constraints are also obstacles to be overcome with innovation and strategic insight. Thus, in the following sections, the chapter explains how HC Hospital tackles these challenges and transforms them into operational refinement and competitive advantage catalysts.

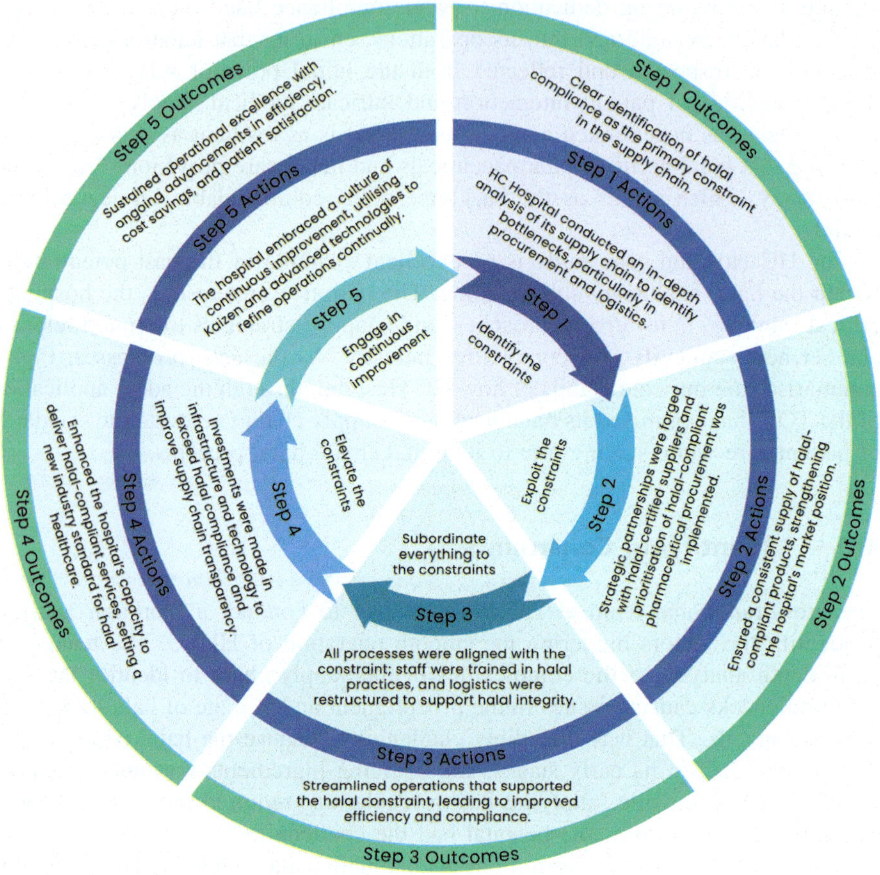

Fig. 2 TOC application actions and outcomes

4.3 Exploiting Constraints

The HC Hospital identified constraints in its HHSC and responded strategically. Rather than just mitigating the issues, they exploited them for competitive and operational gains. The hospital's procurement team was aware of the early stage of the halal pharmaceutical market and pursued an aggressive strategy. Consequently, they formed deep partnerships with a select group of suppliers whose practices were based on halal compliance, with close monitoring and advice from the halal authority. These alliances resulted from collaborative and dedicated efforts in building a network of suppliers whose ethical foundations and quality standards aligned with HC Hospital. However, forming the collaboration was a challenging dual commitment, but the hospital could uphold it by prioritising the halal-certified suppliers. As a result, HC Hospital strengthened its supply chain against rising halal market demand and distinguished itself in the healthcare market by offering a unique service. This focus also allowed the hospital to ensure high-quality, halal-compliant care that aligned with the patient's halal commitment and religious obligations. The hospital's constraints were exploited to address supply issues and to penetrate the once-untapped market segments. This obstacle was cleverly converted into a strategic approach that has enabled a previously limited resource to be transformed into a source of innovation and market differentiation. The upcoming sections will describe how HC Hospital aligned its processes to support this strategic direction and improved its operational framework to emphasise its commitment to halal compliance and healthcare excellence.

4.4 Subordinating Constraints

At HC Hospital, recognising constraints in its HHSC prompted a strategic recalibration of its operational processes. This recalibration involved aligning all processes with the halal standards, ensuring every link in the supply chain supported the objective of halal compliance. The strategy involved several approaches, including enhancing internal competencies and reengineering procurement protocols. Additionally, all ancillary processes were scrutinised and reoriented to support the halal supply chain's operations. For instance, the purchasing department focused exclusively on procuring inputs from suppliers with verified halal certification, which raised halal assurance levels within its medical and support service supply chains.

One of the initiatives taken by HC Hospital was to develop internal competencies. To achieve this, the hospital swiftly instituted training and development programs to ensure that the workforce understood the nuances of halal procurement and logistics. By instilling an internal culture deeply embedded in the principles of Islamic jurisprudence and strict halal requirements, HC Hospital ensured that its employees, from surgeons and medical officers to clerical and supportive roles, became committed to practising and safeguarding the hospital's halal mandate. As a result, the staff's enriched understanding led to a collective effort to prioritise halal compliance across every operational touchpoint, from the receiving docks to patient care delivery.

In addition, logistics, which was once a siloed domain, underwent transformative integration consistent with desired Sharia-compliant operations and distribution. For example, traditional storage practices were meticulously re-evaluated, and dedicated halal-compliant zones were established. These halal-dedicated zones were a physical manifestation of HC Hospital's dedication to upholding halal integrity, where cross-contamination with non-certified halal items was rendered impossible by design. This is because the additional resources utilised for halal operations at HC Hospitals did not signify a reduction in operational efficiency; instead, they improved the hospital's operations and reputation. Collectively, every aspect of the supply chain, from inventory management to behind-the-scenes logistics, was infused with a halal-centric perspective, which unequivocally asserts the hospital's unwavering pledge to its halal commitment.

4.5 Elevating Constraints

HC Hospital's commitment to its halal-centric vision allowed it to transform potential supply chain weaknesses into strengths that propelled it forward. This transformation was a continuous and committed pursuit marked by innovative practices that improved the hospital's capacity to deliver exceptional halal healthcare services.

Therefore, to overcome the challenges inherent in HSCM, HC Hospital implemented a series of forward-thinking investments. Recognising the critical nature of halal compliance, the hospital invested in state-of-the-art facilities that set new industry benchmarks for halal healthcare provision nationally and regionally. These facilities are equipped with cutting-edge technology and staffed by experts in halal and medical practices. It consequently demonstrates the hospital's commitment to excellence and innovation. Furthermore, the investment extended beyond infrastructure. HC Hospital embraced advanced systems for supply chain oversight, implementing sophisticated tracking mechanisms that provided real-time visibility into the halal status of its medical products. By integrating technologies such as radio frequency identification (RFID) and computerised inventory management systems into its operations, the hospital assured transparent and systematic procedures for procuring raw materials to administer healthcare services from various local and overseas suppliers.

Moreover, aside from the technological initiatives, the hospital's focus on continuous quality improvement was a critical factor in its success. The hospital actively seeks and adopts the best practices in healthcare delivery with halal doctrine in mind, often developing new approaches that set industry standards. These combined best practices from conventional medical supply chains and state-of-the-art halal guidelines were adopted, adapted, and refined to fit the hospital's unique operations nationwide. This has resulted in a highly efficient and compliant model. Besides, through innovation and a commitment to quality, HC Hospital was able to turn the constraints of halal compliance into a competitive advantage. This helped solidify the hospital's leadership market position and paved the way for potential improvement through strategic investment and a continuous pursuit of excellence. In the next section, the chapter will explore how HC Hospital's dedication to constant improvement is an integral part of its strategy and how it drives ongoing enhancements throughout its HHSC.

4.6 Continuous Improvement

In HC Hospital's operations, continuous improvement is a vital institutional obligation deeply ingrained in its supply chain management. The hospital's culture is committed to constantly improving its performance and innovation rather than relying on past achievements. As many renowned and successful organisations would do, this philosophy is based on a proactive and iterative approach to identifying and resolving emerging constraints within the hospital's HHSC. The hospital is committed to using advanced data analytics and feedback mechanisms to continuously evaluate and adjust its operations, focusing on emerging AI-powered initiatives. These iterative processes are supported by advanced monitoring systems that track compliance, forecast potential disruptions, intelligent wards, and big data applications that can enable the hospital to adapt its strategies proactively.

Furthermore, HC Hospital has also incorporated a suite of cutting-edge technologies to streamline its operations and strengthen the halal integrity of its supply chain. For instance, implementing RFID technology ensures accurate tracking of halal pharmaceuticals. This effort is integral in reducing errors that could compromise halal standards while improving inventory accuracy. Moreover, using AI in logistics planning optimises the allocation of resources, ensuring that halal products are handled with the utmost care and precision throughout the supply chain.

The commitment to continuous improvement at HC Hospital goes beyond technology and encompasses a holistic approach to developing human capital. Regular training sessions ensure that the workforce, from procurement officers to healthcare practitioners, is well-versed in halal compliance and the latest technology-driven best practices in supply chain management. Besides, the dedication to professional growth fosters a skilled and passionate workforce that advances the hospital's mission. HC Hospital's commitment to improvement is also characterised by a willingness to collaborate and exchange knowledge with external partners. HC Hospital stays at the forefront of emerging trends and innovations by participating in industry forums and engaging with other local and regional halal healthcare providers. These collaborative ventures bring fresh insights that are then transformed into actionable strategies that further enhance the hospital's supply chain processes and halal commitment.

HC Hospital's unwavering pursuit of excellence in its HHSC is a dynamic and never-ending journey that emphasises adaptability, foresight, and an unyielding drive for quality. Through its dedication to continuous improvement, the hospital upholds its halal principles and sets new standards in healthcare service delivery. These efforts reinforced HC Hospital's status as a halal healthcare supply chain management exemplar in the long run.

4.7 Outcomes, Observations, and Replication

Through the discussion of outcomes and observations, along with the potential for replication, HC Hospital's adept application of the TOC and its unwavering commitment to continuous improvement has resulted in a collection of measurable successes and strategic insights. The outcomes of HC Hospital's concentrated efforts on operational optimisation with concentrated halal initiatives are diverse. Financial prudence and improved service levels matched the tangible gains in supply chain efficiency. In addition, there has been a significant decrease in waste and increased logistical velocity. These achievements were evidence of the effectiveness of the TOC methodology in tackling the unique challenges of the HHSC.

The HC Hospital's exploration into halal compliance has provided invaluable insights into the relationship between religious observance and healthcare provision. The hospital's journey underscores the importance of aligning core operational processes with cultural and spiritual imperatives, which many organisations, whether in related or distant industries, must observe to solidify positions in the community and give them the much-desired competitive advantage. Additionally, for hospital operators in Muslim-majority or minority markets, the halal in healthcare alignment has unveiled many market opportunities, often untapped, thus providing a roadmap for ethical business growth that is also commercially viable and astute.

HC Hospital's success can serve as a blueprint for other healthcare institutions, locally or abroad, to harmonise their operations with halal principles. Hence, the potential for replicating HC Hospital's TOC-focusing process, shown in Fig. 2, is substantial. The model's reproducibility lies in its core tenets: steadfast adherence to the TOC, a committed pursuit of continuous improvement, and the willingness to integrate innovative technologies in the halal healthcare supply chain and operations. Furthermore, the transferability of HC Hospital's approach to other contexts within and beyond the healthcare sector signals a promising horizon for expanding HSCM practices. The model's scalability is likely predicated on its flexible yet structured approach to operational excellence, which can be adapted to varying scales and scopes of operation beyond halal or for religious purposes.

HC Hospital's case study collectively exemplifies a comprehensive operational strategy that transcends the mere satisfaction of market demand. The case embodies and exemplifies a forward-thinking ethos that combines practicality with a religious yet contemporary lens. The lessons drawn from HC Hospital's experience possess the potency to inform and inspire a new paradigm in HHSCM, where the principles of TOC serve as a methodological foundation and a catalyst for innovation and growth.

5 Chapter Implications

The case study of HC Hospital's integration of TOC with halal-centric initiatives carries several implications for both academia and industry. Although the results presented in the HC Hospital case cannot guarantee that the outcomes from applying TOC may achieve exact or similar results, the five-step focusing process (as illustrated in Fig. 1) has been proven effective in integrating halal principles and practices in healthcare supply chain context. Hence, healthcare operators and service providers can adopt the TOC methodology to achieve comparable outcomes.

This chapter highlights the need for further research into the intersection of operational methodologies like TOC with cultural and religious imperatives, particularly in diverse settings. Scholars could delve into the specific challenges and opportunities of implementing such strategies in different cultural contexts, providing insights for organisations operating in multicultural environments. Additionally, the chapter emphasises the importance of considering patient preferences and religious observances in healthcare provision. Future research could explore the impact of religiously compliant healthcare practices on patient satisfaction, health outcomes, and overall healthcare delivery models. Understanding these dynamics can enlighten healthcare policies and practices to accommodate diverse patient needs better.

Moreover, the scalability and transferability of HC Hospital's approach present opportunities for broader implementation across various industries beyond healthcare. Researchers could investigate the adaptability of TOC tenets to different sectors and contexts, assessing their effectiveness in promoting operational excellence and cultural integration. Hence, this chapter's discussion prompts further inquiry into integrating operational strategies with cultural and religious considerations, offering valuable insights for academic research and practical application in organisational settings.

6 Limitations and Future Study

While the case study of HC Hospital provides valuable insights, it is essential to acknowledge its limitations and areas for future research. Firstly, the study primarily focuses on applying TOC within a specific cultural and religious context, namely, halal-centric initiatives in healthcare. This narrow focus may limit the generalizability of findings to other industries or cultural settings, warranting further exploration into the applicability of TOC tenets in diverse contexts. Secondly, the study predominantly emphasises HC Hospital's approach's positive outcomes and successes, potentially overlooking challenges or unintended consequences. Future studies could adopt a more balanced perspective by examining potential drawbacks or limitations of integrating TOC with cultural and religious imperatives, such as implementation barriers, resistance to change, or conflicts between operational efficiency and cultural values.

Moreover, while the study touches upon the importance of patient satisfaction metrics, it does not delve into how religiously compliant healthcare practices influence patient experiences and outcomes. Further studies could employ qualitative methods to explore patients' perspectives, values, and preferences regarding culturally sensitive healthcare services, offering a more comprehensive understanding of the impact of such initiatives on patient care. It is hoped that future research will address these limitations by exploring the applicability of TOC tenets, critically examining potential challenges and drawbacks, and deepening our understanding of the relationship between cultural considerations and healthcare outcomes.

7 Conclusion

The expanding significance of halal beyond food into sectors such as banking, tourism, marketing, and healthcare is undeniable. It emphasises the substantial growth and potential of the global halal economy. While halal food dominates attention and revenue, the healthcare sector remains untapped. Challenges such as limited supply chain optimisation hinder its progress. Yet, there's immense potential for improvement through initiatives like applying the Theory of Constraints (TOC) to the halal healthcare supply chain. This approach can identify bottlenecks and drive enhancements, highlighting the need for research and focus on the halal healthcare sector's unique challenges and opportunities amidst the broader Islamic economy's rapid expansion.

Hence, the discourse on applying TOC intertwined with halal-centric initiatives in HC Hospital, which this chapter discusses, provides rich insights applicable across various industries. Findings show that the hospital's success emphasises the significance of aligning operational processes with cultural and spiritual imperatives. This alignment fosters community trust and cultivates a competitive edge, emphasising the importance of understanding and integrating diverse values into organisational strategies. Moreover, HC Hospital's achievements highlight the correlation between operational optimisation and tangible outcomes such as improved supply chain efficiency, financial prudence, and enhanced service levels. These outcomes reflect the efficacy of the TOC tenet and emphasise the value of continuous improvement initiatives in achieving sustainable success.

Additionally, exploring halal compliance lightens the intersection of religious observance and healthcare provision. This highlights the importance of catering to diverse religious and cultural needs within healthcare settings, paving the way for ethical business growth and market opportunities in Muslim-majority and minority markets. Furthermore, the transferability and scalability of HC Hospital's approach demonstrate its potential as a blueprint for other healthcare institutions and beyond. The adaptable nature of the TOC-lens process allows for its replication in various contexts, facilitating operational excellence beyond halal-centric initiatives. Thus, HC Hospital's case study is a comprehensive guide for organisations seeking to harmonise operational strategies with cultural and religious principles. It exemplifies a forward-thinking viewpoint that combines practicality with a contemporary lens, offering valuable lessons in TOC tenet, continuous improvement, and cultural integration for sustainable growth and innovation in healthcare supply chain management.

References

1. Ab Talib MS (2017) Motivations and benefits of Halal food safety certification. J Islamic Mark 8(4):605–624. https://doi.org/10.1108/JIMA-08-2015-0063
2. Ab Talib MS, Ai Chin T, Fischer J (2017) Linking Halal food certification and business performance. Br Food J 119(7):1606–1618. https://doi.org/10.1108/BFJ-01-2017-0019
3. Ab Talib MS, Chin TA, Hamid AA (2018) Halal food certification and business performance in Malaysia. Partridge Publishing, Singapore
4. Ab Talib MS (2021) Identifying halal logistics constraints in Brunei Darussalam. J Islamic Mark 12(6):1145–1158. https://doi.org/10.1108/JIMA-09-2019-0189
5. Ab Talib MS, Pang LL, Ngah AH (2020) The role of government in promoting Halal logistics: a systematic literature review. J Islamic Mark 12(9):1682–1708. https://doi.org/10.1108/JIMA-05-2020-0124
6. Ali MH, Chung L, Kumar A, Zailani S, Tan KH (2021) A sustainable blockchain framework for the halal food supply chain: lessons from Malaysia. Technol Forecast Soc Change 170. https://doi.org/10.1016/j.techfore.2021.120870
7. Al-Zaidi WA, Al-Karawi AJ, Al-Zuhairi AK (2018). Role of demand forecasting and lead time on waste in supply chain: a case study in Diyala Health Sector-Iraq. J Adv Manage Sci 6(3)
8. Aoun I, Tournois L (2015) Building holistic brands: an exploratory study of Halal cosmetics. J Islamic Mark 6(1):109–132. https://doi.org/10.1108/JIMA-05-2014-0035
9. Arji G, Ahmadi H, Avazpoor P, Hemmat M (2023) Identifying resilience strategies for disruption management in the healthcare supply chain during COVID-19 by digital innovations: a systematic literature review. Inf Med Unlocked 38:101199
10. Balkhi B, Alshahrani A, Khan A (2022) Just-in-time approach in healthcare inventory management: does it really work? Saudi Pharm J 30(12):1830–1835
11. Baran T (2021) A literature review and classification of the studies on "Halal" in Islamic business journals (2010–2018). J Islamic Mark 12(5):1012–1024. https://doi.org/10.1108/JIMA-10-2019-0206
12. Bauer JM, Vargas A, Sellitto MA, Souza MC, Vaccaro GL (2019) The thinking process of the theory of constraints applied to public healthcare. Bus Process Manag J 25(7):1543–1563. https://doi.org/10.1108/BPMJ-06-2016-0118
13. Butt MM, Aftab M (2013) Incorporating attitude towards Halal banking in an integrated service quality, satisfaction, trust and loyalty model in online Islamic banking context. Int J Bank Mark 31(1):6–23. https://doi.org/10.1108/02652321311292029
14. Chen IJ, Paulraj A (2004) Understanding supply chain management: critical research and a theoretical framework. Int J Prod Res 42(1):131–163. https://doi.org/10.1080/002075403100 01602865
15. Defee CC, Williams B, Randall WS, Thomas R, Clifford Defee C, Williams B, Randall WS, Thomas R (2010) An inventory of theory in logistics and SCM research. Int J Logist Manage 21(3):404–489. https://doi.org/10.1108/09574091011089817
16. DinarStandard (2022) State of the global islamic economy report 2022: unlocking opportunity. https://www.salaamgateway.com/specialcoverage/SGIE22
17. Dixit A, Routroy S, Dubey SK (2019) A systematic literature review of healthcare supply chain and implications of future research. Int J Pharm Healthc Mark 13(4):405–435
18. Faradina A, Hussein MZ, Husny ZJ, Yazid M, Mazlan Z, Rayner T, Fauziah AR, Zani M, Adnan N (2018). Halal logistics: Halal integrity and legal enforcement challenges. Int J Supply Chain Manag 7(4)

19. Fauzi MA (2022) Consumer purchase of halal certified product: a quantitative systematic literature review. J Islamic Mark. Emerald Group Holdings Ltd. https://doi.org/10.1108/JIMA-09-2021-0299
20. Golmohammadi D (2015) A study of scheduling under the theory of constraints. Int J Prod Econ 165:38–50. https://doi.org/10.1016/j.ijpe.2015.03.015
21. Haleem A, Khan MI, Khan S, Jami AR (2020) Research status in Halal: a review and bibliometric analysis. Modern Supply Chain Res Appl 2(1):23–41. https://doi.org/10.1108/MSCRA-06-2019-0014
22. Hussain M, Ajmal MM, Gunasekaran A, Khan M (2018) Exploration of social sustainability in healthcare supply chain. J Clean Prod 203:977–989
23. Ikeziri LM, de Souza FB, Gupta MC, de Camargo Fiorini P (2019) Theory of constraints: review and bibliometric analysis. Int J Prod Res 57(15–16):5068–5102. Taylor and Francis Ltd. https://doi.org/10.1080/00207543.2018.1518602
24. Izberk-Bilgin E, Nakata CC (2016) A new look at faith-based marketing: the global Halal market. Bus Horiz 59(3):285–292. https://doi.org/10.1016/j.bushor.2016.01.005
25. Kamisah S, Mokhtar A, Hafsah A (2018). Halal practices integrity and halal supply chain trust in Malaysian halal food supply chain. Int Food Res J 25
26. Karia N (2022) Halal logistics: practices, integration and performance of logistics service providers. J Islamic Mark 13(1):100–118. https://doi.org/10.1108/JIMA-08-2018-0132
27. Kritchanchai D, Krichanchai S, Hoeur S, Tan A (2019). Healthcare supply chain management: macro and micro perspectives. Logforum 15(4)
28. Miko NU, Abbas U (2024) Determinants of efficient last-mile delivery: evidence from health facilities and Kaduna Health Supplies Management Agency. J Hum Logist Supply Chain Manag 14(1):4–16
29. Modi K, Lowalekar H, Bhatta NMK (2019) Revolutionizing supply chain management the theory of constraints way: a case study. Int J Prod Res 57(11):3335–3361. https://doi.org/10.1080/00207543.2018.1523579
30. Mohezar S, Zailani S, Tieman M (2017) Tapping into the Halal pharmaceutical market: issues and challenges. In Ab Manan SK, Abd Rahman F, Sahri M (eds) Contemporary issues and development in the global Halal industry. Springer, Singapore. https://doi.org/10.1007/978-981-10-1452-9
31. Mubarrok US, Ulfi I, Sukmana R, Sukoco BM (2020) A bibliometric analysis of Islamic marketing studies in the "Journal of Islamic Marketing." J Islamic Mark. https://doi.org/10.1108/JIMA-05-2020-0158
32. Ngah AH, Ramayah T, Ali MH, Khan MI (2020) Halal transportation adoption among pharmaceuticals and comestics manufacturers. J Islamic Mark 11(6):1619–1639. https://doi.org/10.1108/JIMA-10-2018-0193
33. Norazmi MN, Lim LS (2015) Halal pharmaceutical industry: opportunities and challenges. Trends Pharmacol Sci 36(8):496–497. https://doi.org/10.1016/j.tips.2015.06.006
34. Novianti D, Arkeman Y, Almunawar MN, Haditjaroko L, Ismayana A (2020) Designing a transparent distributed systems for Halal supply chains using blockchain technology. J Bus Econ Anal 3(2):151–170. https://doi.org/10.36924/sbe.2020.3204
35. Rahman S (2002) The theory of constraints' thinking process approach to developing strategies in supply chains. Int J Phys Distrib Logist Manag 32(10):809–828. https://doi.org/10.1108/09600030210455429
36. Regenstein JM (2020) Kosher and Halal: how they affect Muslim and Jewish dietary practices. In Meiselman HL (ed) Handbook of eating and drinking. Springer, pp 593–614. https://doi.org/10.1007/978-3-030-14504-0_158
37. Safira ME, Chotib M, Iriani D, Budiono A (2019) The legal application of consumer and halal product protection in the health sector. Int J Innov Creativity Change 10(5):1–18
38. Sani MSA, Nordin NF, Elgharbawy AAM (2023) Halal detection technologies: analytical method approaches, validation and verification, and multivariate data analysis for halal authentication. In: Innovation of food products in Halal supply chain worldwide, pp 253–271

39. Schneller E, Abdulsalam Y, Conway K, Eckler J (2023) Strategic management of the healthcare supply chain. Wiley
40. Shah SA, Azhar SM, Bhutto NA (2020) Halal marketing: a marketing strategy perspective. J Islamic Mark 11(6):1641–1655. https://doi.org/10.1108/JIMA-11-2018-0211
41. Shashi M (2023) Sustainable digitalization in pharmaceutical supply chains using theory of constraints: a qualitative study. Sustainability 15(11):8752. https://doi.org/10.3390/su15118752
42. Simatupang TM, Wright AC, Sridharan R (2004) Applying the theory of constraints to supply chain collaboration. Supply Chain Manage Int J 9(1):57–70. https://doi.org/10.1108/13598540410517584
43. Tan A, Gligor D, Ngah A (2022) Applying blockchain for Halal food traceability. Int J Log Res Appl 25(6):947–964. https://doi.org/10.1080/13675567.2020.1825653
44. Tieman M, Ruiz-Bejarano B (2020) Halal retailing: closing the last mile in an end-to-end Halal supply chain. ICR J 11(1):147–152
45. Vargas-Sánchez A, Moral-Moral M (2020) Halal tourism: literature review and experts' view. J Islamic Mark 11(3):549–569. https://doi.org/10.1108/JIMA-04-2017-0039
46. Wahab NA, Kamarubahrin AF (2019) Halal industry: are the businesses fully awake? J Fatwa Manage Res 21–35
47. Wahab S, Ahmed N, Uzir MU (2023) Healthcare supply chain system challenges and mitigation measures: a systematic review of qualitative evidence. Oper Supply Chain Manage Int J 16(2):164–176
48. Widyanto HA, Sitohang IAT (2022) Muslim millennial's purchase intention of Halal-certified cosmetics and pharmaceutical products: the mediating effect of attitude. J Islamic Mark 13(6):1373–1394. https://doi.org/10.1108/JIMA-04-2020-0117
49. Wilkins S, Butt MM, Shams F, Pérez A (2019) The acceptance of Halal food in non-Muslim countries: effects of religious identity, national identification, consumer ethnocentrism and consumer cosmopolitanism. J Islamic Mark 10(4):1308–1331. https://doi.org/10.1108/JIMA-11-2017-0132
50. Yanamandra R (2018) Development of an integrated healthcare supply chain model. Supply Chain Forum: Int J 19(2):111–121
51. Zailani S, Iranmanesh M, Aziz AA, Kanapathy K (2017) Halal logistics opportunities and challenges. J Islamic Mark 8(1):127–139. https://doi.org/10.1108/JIMA-04-2015-0028
52. Zainuddin N, Saifudin AM, Deraman N, Mahidin N (2019) Effect of Halal certification and labelling process on Halal supply chain performance. Int J Supply Chain Manage 8(4):1075–1081
53. Zhao X, Hou J (2022) Applying the theory of constraints principles to tourism supply chain management. J Hosp Tourism Res 46(2):400–411. https://doi.org/10.1177/1096348021996791

Mohamed Syazwan Ab Talib is an Assistant Professor of Logistics Management at the UBD School of Business and Economics, Universiti Brunei Darussalam. His research and teaching focus primarily on logistics and supply chain management, with an emphasis on halal principles, sustainable distribution, and halal certification.

Siti Norida Wahab a senior lecturer in the operations management program at the Faculty of Business and Management, UiTM Puncak Alam. She has around 20 years of experience in both the industrial and educational fields. Her previous leadership positions include roles at the managerial level in multinational logistics companies and renowned private universities. Her research interest includes sustainable adoption in logistics and supply chain management. She managed national and international grants and published her research works in high-rated journals, proceedings, book and book chapters. Besides, she supervised a number of MSc and PhD candidates. For excellence, she has won platinum, diamond, gold, and bronze medals in innovation competitions. She also actively serves as a reviewer for journals and academic conferences. Currently, she is a professional technologist of the Malaysia Board of Technologists.

A Dyadic Perspective on Cooperation in the Pharmaceutical Supply Chain in the Light of Current and Future Trends in the Pharmaceutical Market in Poland

8

Mariusz Jedliński

The health of society depends on the health of the pharmaceutical supply chain. The healthier it is, the faster, more complete and cheaper the medicine will be delivered to patients in need.

Mariusz Jedliński

Abstract

The health care system in Poland is a very complex system in which its participants combine their various political, social and economic interests. Often, the diagnosis of the state of this system has a multi-faceted dimension, but always specific social awareness of the quality of its functioning is an expression of the perception of the state's activity in this area. Especially since its basic units (Primary Health Care—(pol. POZ), such as clinics, hospitals or medical, nurse and midwifery practices, could not function properly without an efficient pharmaceutical market. This market can be considered one of the most developed branches of the economy in Poland, but at the same time it is subject to constant changes, both in terms of the ownership structure of entities in this industry, the rules of trading, primarily in medicinal products, and the administrative system of public health care management itself. A special legal and logistical relationship is the "dyatic" connection between the pharmaceutical wholesale market and the pharmacy (retail) market, because the principles of Good Distribution Practice (pol. DPD) are generally applicable in the drug distribution process.

M. Jedliński (✉)
Faculty of Economics and Engineering of Transport, Maritime University of Szczecin, 1-2 Wały Chrobrego Street, 70-500 Szczecin, Poland
e-mail: m.jedlinski@pm.szczecin.pl

F. Jawab (ed.), *Hospital Supply Chain*, Integrated Science 27,
https://doi.org/10.1007/978-3-031-70292-1_8

The main goal of this chapter is to identify and present the characteristics of the basic features and structure of the pharmaceutical market in Poland and the structural and functional key segment of the pharmaceutical supply chain, i.e. the pharmaceutical wholesale and retail pharmacy market. The research process used a methodological approach based primarily on "mixed methods" and "desk research", but also on creative systematics and synthesis. The most important issues were analyzed based on key secondary data and the main legal regulations were analyzed in the context of specific groups of entities (distribution levels) involved in the distribution process on the pharmaceutical market. This allowed for the presentation of the key characteristics and synthetic analysis in terms of logistics of the following key links in the "dyatic" optics, the main intermediaries on the pharmaceutical market, i.e., wholesalers and pharmacies. The most important factors of cooperation in the pharmaceutical supply chain between these links are: punctuality of deliveries, completeness of deliveries and speed of deliveries. However, trade and logistics relations between pharmaceutical wholesale entities and the retail pharmacy market are multi-faceted in terms of complexity and high logistic requirements, and are subject to strong regulation by authorized external entities, and are also shaped by nationwide health care policy.

Keywords

Product • Logistics • Pharmaceutical • Wholesaler • Retailer

Abbreviations

EC	European Commission
EMA	European Medicines Agency
EU	European Union
FMD	Falsifed Medicines Directive
GDP	Good distribution practice
GIF	State Pharmaceutical Inspection
GTIN	Number with the GS1 system
GUS	Central Statistical Office
MZ	Ministry of Health
NFZ	National Health Fund
OTC	Over the counter
PHC	Primary Health Care
PKD	Polish classification of activities
PSC	Pharmaceutical supply chains
PURPL	President of the Office for Registration of Medicinal Products, Medical Devices and Biocidal Products
WIF	Provincial Pharmaceutical Inspector
WHO	World Health Organization

1 Introduction

The pharmaceutical industry is a specific hierarchical market structure. It is a clearly separated and independent part of the country's economic system. Additionally, it is very strongly correlated with the Polish health care system [31]. Based on various criteria and features of the connections between its participants, this market structure can be considered both in the "supply" aspect (from the point of view of related products offered by producers/importers of related products, e.g. medicines) [9] or in the "demand" aspect (from the point of view of products required by recipients, e.g. medicines) [33]. This apparent ambiguity in the perception of this market leads to the conclusion that the "pharmaceutical industry" is a much broader concept than the "pharmaceutical market". It should be emphasized that the pharmaceutical industry is a key economic sector that has a direct impact on people's health and often their lives. Its direct connection with medicine and the broadly understood area of the health care system make it a very important element of the economic life of every society. Therefore, the health care system itself in Poland, which is largely based on universal health insurance [47], is a complex mechanism whose aim is to provide access to programs and technologies that allow each member of society to regain, improve or maintain health [25]. Additionally, the Polish pharmaceutical market has many original features that do not appear in such a combination in other industries. They are associated primarily with strong state regulation, which significantly limits the freedom of operation of the market mechanism. This is due to the fact that the main goal of creating legislation related to the pharmaceutical industry is to ensure permanent protection of life and health of the society that uses the services of entities operating on this market. It is also a common phenomenon that all enterprises that operate within this sector, connecting into advanced networks of logistic connections, are implementing more and more advanced management systems, organizational methods and distribution processes, because the expectations of both customers and patients are constantly growing. It is worth noting that the assessment of the correctness of the perception of the pharmaceutical industry is influenced by the state of development of economic sciences, which assumed that consumers, including patients, in their decisions and market behavior, are guided by premises based on reason, but recent research indicates that it is However, emotions have a decisive influence on the behavior of consumers, including patients, on their choices and market decisions [22]. Hence, the role of the state in the system organized for the health of society increases, which comes down primarily to assuming real and systemic responsibility for the health protection of all its citizens [54]. This special type of state obligation means that the state health care system in its basic dimension is universal and obligatory, although it includes, for example, formal exemptions for certain social groups [55]. Therefore, in addition to it, other well-established subsystems have also been developed, e.g. voluntary private insurance (of a substitute, supplementary or complementary nature). In the most general sense, however, it can be assumed that the health care system in Poland consists of three basic groups, i.e. beneficiaries, healthcare providers and the payer (3rd Party) [20].

The pharmaceutical industry in Poland is an extremely dynamic and complex economic reality because it combines many entities and activities. State-owned and private companies, with Polish and foreign capital, create a unique ecosystem that, in its essence, builds drug safety in Poland. But the specificity of this market may be demonstrated by the fact that due to the need to ensure patient safety, it must be regulated by appropriate institutions. The key market moderators at the European Union level are: the European Commission (EC) and the European Medicines Agency (EMA). The key moderators of the internal market in Poland are: Ministry of Health (pol. MZ), National Health Fund (pol. NFZ), the President of the Office for Registration of Medicinal Products, Medical Devices and Biocidal Products (pol. Prezes URPL, WMiB) and State Pharmaceutical Inspection (pol. GIF). The basic legal act regulating distribution activities on the pharmaceutical market in Poland is the Pharmaceutical Law Act [49].

The starting point for this chapter was a synthetic presentation of the current structure of the Polish health care system and the pharmaceutical market, and then a description of the adopted methodological approach and the methods and techniques used in the research process. Based on the conducted analyses, multi-aspect considerations on the characteristics, structure and ongoing changes on the pharmaceutical market in Poland were presented. The considerations were systematized by distinguishing key links in the pharmaceutical supply chain and separating the logistic "dyad" in the "pharmaceutical wholesale—retail pharmacy market" system. As part of the entity-functional division, key trade and logistics connections were identified at the junction of these two logistics links. The main functions and tasks within the functional duosystem "sales function" and "logistics function" have been enriched with the empirical identification of the dimensions of existing logistics cooperation. The concluding considerations point to the dynamics of change and, therefore, the unchanging research potential of the logistic connections of a separate "dyad" [1].

2 Methods

The main research approach for the description and characterization of the research area and the identification of key interactions between groups of pharmaceutical market entities in Poland was the adoption of a methodology based on "mixed research", which is often referred to as the "third paradigm" [8] or "third methodology" [53]. The use of this type of research method can enrich and provide a better understanding of management problems, especially since these methods are considered the "golden mean" for seeking convergence between qualitative and quantitative research [6]. They allow you to create a general description of the findings, which is usually not possible using a single approach, i.e. quantitative or qualitative [4]. The reason is that they amount to the use of iterative or simultaneous approaches at all or multiple stages of empirical research, including sampling, data collection, data analysis, synthesis of results, and integration and reporting. Additionally, progressive technological development has undoubtedly contributed to increasing the possibility of collecting and archiving huge amounts of research material, which is easily available for the purposes of research, including secondary analyzes [21]. New media (the Internet) allow free access to a lot of quantitative and qualitative data, as well as to formal and informal sources, but also to personal ones [12]. Thanks to this, it was possible to carry out secondary analysis, which allows to generate re-evaluation of the results of primary research. The secondary analysis of existing qualitative data undoubtedly has its own specificity, which can be described as a constructivist-interpretivist paradigm, which clearly distinguishes it from analytical research approaches whose aim is to verify, critically analyze and evaluate theories, methods and results research from existing secondary qualitative data [26]. Most of the sources used in the chapter come from the Internet, so their credibility had to be checked, especially when they were related to several sources relating to the same scope or area, although they were primarily based on the websites of government institutions and professional industry organizations [13]. Attention was also paid to the usefulness of "desk research" because it is one of the research methods of non-reactive research, and E. Babbie distinguishes three types of research, i.e. content analysis, analysis of existing statistical data and historical-comparative analyzes [3]. The adopted "desk research" uses both content analysis (already at the stage of searching for sources), and, to a large extent, existing statistical data, and also allows for cross-sectional analyzes and comparisons of historical data. It is based on the use of existing (secondary) data and is already performed properly during a literature review, but it should not be identified with, for example, a "meta-analysis" or a "scientific review of the literature" [23], because the literature review (state of art) is just one of the types of sources that have been analyzed after careful selection.

The implementation of the adopted research assumptions based on the optics of "mixed research" allowed, first of all, on the basis of literature studies in the field of the pharmaceutical market in Poland and the use of the potential of existing "desk research" data, primarily based on secondary sources, i.e. publications of the Central Statistical Office (pol. GUS), commercial sources [45], magazines and professional publications. The method of "analysis and criticism of literature" and the method of "analysis of legal acts" were also used to identify and discuss operational obstacles and conditions shaping cooperation within a separate "dyad".

3 Results

3.1 Systematics of Subject-Object Characteristics of the Pharmaceutical Market in Poland

The pharmaceutical market in Poland is a unique macroeconomic structure which, in principle, is a regulated and largely closed market (it is not a liberal market). The main participants of the pharmaceutical market in the "subject" approach are primarily: drug manufacturers, importers, responsible entities, distributors, i.e. wholesalers, then pharmacies and finally consumers (patients) and pharmaceutical

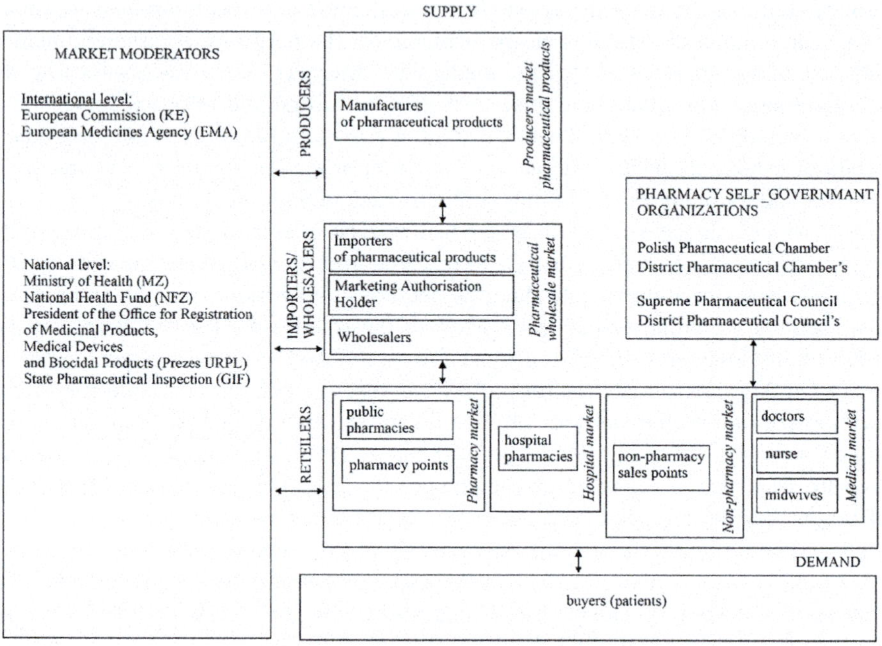

Fig. 1 The "entity" structure of the pharmaceutical market in Poland. *Source* Own study

market moderators who have a significant impact on the conditions in which a purchase and sale transaction takes place, primarily of a medicinal product. However, even an ordinary store can sell certain types of separate, non-reimbursed medical devices (e.g. self-monitoring tests). A simplified "entity" structure of the pharmaceutical market in Poland is presented in Fig. 1.

In turn, as a rule, from the "subject perspective", the pharmaceutical market in Poland offers two types of medicinal products addressed to both doctors and patients, i.e. drugs available only "on prescription" (so-called ethical drugs), which in depending on the category of drug availability, they are divided into groups "Rx" and "Rp" (recipere), i.e. "take it" and drugs available "over the counter" ("OTC"—Over The Counter), whose safety of use is sufficiently well confirmed and correct application is easy for every patient.

In addition, there are also other product groups on this market, e.g. dermo-cosmetics, dietary supplements, dressing and diagnostic materials, etc. In Poland, there are over 160 therapeutic problems (ICD-10) recognized as minor ailments, of which only slightly over 50% are treated as part of the patient's own health care. Undoubtedly, full use of the potential of self-treatment and self-care would translate into a one-quarter reduction in the demand for medical visits under universal health care (this would result in approximately 41 million fewer visits per year). In Europe, there are 1.2 billion cases of minor ailments annually, self-treated with over-the-counter (OTC) drugs, which brings savings of approximately EUR

40 billion to health care systems [24]. In turn, in a Medonet survey on the issue of self-medication in Poland, almost half of the respondents (47%) declared that they take over-the-counter medications every day, 30% rarely do it, and 8% never [16].

3.2 The Size and Dynamics of Changes on the Pharmaceutical Market in Poland

Pharmaceutical market research essentially involves the regular collection, development and analysis of data (information), which in strategic and operational terms is related to the management process [32]. The key commercial principles applicable on this market in the reimbursed medicines segment are that drug manufacturers negotiate drug prices with the Ministry of Health, creating the so-called "list of reimbursed drugs" (every 2 months), the wholesale market adapts to the "official wholesale mark-up" calculated on the official selling price (5%), and the retail market applies the "retail mark-up" which is charged on the wholesale price of the drug constituting the basis for the limit in a given limit group (the same value margin regardless of the price of the drug). For this reason, the size of the Polish pharmaceutical market is extremely difficult to assess, because it can be estimated at three different levels, i.e.: sales from the manufacturer to wholesalers (market value at manufacturer's net prices), sales from wholesalers to pharmacies (market value at wholesale prices) and sales from pharmacies to patients (market value at retail prices). We must also not forget that there is a parallel market for sales to hospital pharmacies, which are supplied by pharmaceutical wholesalers and directly by manufacturers.

The development of the pharmaceutical sector in Poland (according to PKD (Polish Classification of Activities), section C-21) [42, 43] in recent years (2010–2022) has been visible, among others, in the growing number of entities whose activities are related to the production of pharmaceutical products, or the increase in the sales value of these products.

The data presented in Table 1 present the production of basic pharmaceutical substances, medicines and other pharmaceutical products. 76.6% of the production of pharmaceutical sector companies is the production of pharmaceutical products, the remaining 23.4% is secondary production (e.g. production of chemicals and chemical products) [34]. In turn, the production value of pharmaceutical products consists of 85.6% of pharmaceuticals produced in companies belonging to the pharmaceutical sector, the remaining 14.4% is produced in companies belonging to other sections and departments (e.g. veterinary production).

As can be seen, in Poland the value of the pharmaceutical sector has been recording upward trends since 2010, despite the fact that the market dynamics fluctuated to some extent in 2011–2013 and for obvious reasons, i.e. the COVID-19 pandemic in 2020 [48]. This situation resulted in a lower number of infections, limited visits to doctors and travel. Additionally, there has been a reduction in the number of injuries and a general reduction in expenses due to the economic crisis.

Table 1 Number of entities activity during the year and Total Sold Production in Pharmaceutical Industry (in million PLN)

	2010	2011	2012	2013	2014	2015	2016	2017	2018	2019	2020	2021	2022
Number of entities	285	300	310	135	184	342	378	313	378	482	491	129	411
Total Sold Production	12,796	10,857	10,724	11,750	12,336	13,441	13,862	14,236	15,240	14,650	12,763	13,763	16,493

Source Own study—Statistical Yearbook of Industry—Poland (2010–2023) [48]

Table 2 The value of the pharmaceutical market in Poland (in billion PLN)

Years					
2017	2018	2019	2020	2021	2022
32,124	34,058	36.43	37.07	39.8	45.5

Source Own study na podstawie: IQVIA, dane Sell-In (2017–2022) [17, 18]

According to the Report of the Polish Investment and Trade Agency (PFR Group), the global increase in spending on pharmaceuticals will invariably be driven by the sale of original drugs on developed markets, compensating for the impact of patent expiration and discounts, especially on the US market. Without a doubt, the leading global pharmaceutical market is the United States with an expected annual growth of 4–7% over the coming years. At the same time, the Chinese pharmaceutical market is expected to grow dynamically at a rate of 3–6% annually, when the sales value will reach USD 140–170 billion [35]. Currently, the pharmaceutical market in Poland, like in many other countries, is in the maturity phase, which means that the sales growth rate is slowing down. Table 2 presents changes in the years 2017–2022 in the total value of the pharmaceutical market in Poland (excluding the hospital segment). It is created by the value of sales of prescription drugs (RX) and OTC products (including: medicines, dietary supplements, medical supplies and cosmetics, as well as mail order sales of e-pharmacies), calculated at retail prices.

Virtually all major drug manufacturers in the world are present on the Polish pharmaceutical market, but the domestic industry focuses mainly on the production of generic and biosubsequent drugs. According to MarketHub data for 2021, pharmaceutical production in Poland generated part of the gross domestic product worth EUR 7.3 billion (approx. PLN 32 billion), which constitutes 1.33% of GDP, while the value of pharmaceutical distribution of medicines and parapharmaceuticals to patients amounted to PLN 56. billion in gross prices, which meant an increase of 8% per year [3, 45]. Additionally, the pharmaceutical market in Poland is largely supplied by imported drugs, the share of which in terms of value is approximately 74% and is systematically growing [30]. This is confirmed by MarketHub data, because in 2021, Polish imports of pharmaceutical products (including medicines, human blood, cotton wool, bandages, organs) amounted to USD 335 million, which is 17% more than a year earlier [45].

3.3 Logistic Specificity of the "Dyad" in the Pharmaceutical Supply Chain in Poland

According to S. Chopra and P. Meindl, the supply chain consists of all parties involved, directly or indirectly, in meeting customer expectations [5]. At the same time, there is an increasing awareness of the growing interdependence between Pharmaceutical Supply Chains (PSC) [2] and the broader healthcare bundle supply chains [46]. Particular interest is focused on operational strategies for managing a disrupted supply chain in the context of reducing the risk of inventory management (lack of, double coverage, high cost) [27].

For the purposes of achieving the research objectives of the chapter, the pharmaceutical supply chain was segmented into its upper (descending) and lower (ascending) parts. Thus, the pharmaceutical wholesale market and the pharmaceutical pharmacy market adopted a relationship according to neighboring links in the chain in the pharmaceutical wholesale-retail pharmacy market system, considered both in the relational and structural dimensions within the framework of inter-organizational ties created by individual links. The "dyad" approach was used, assuming that three levels of analysis of purchases and supply management in the supply chain [7] and networks [29] can be distinguished, i.e.: dyadic relationships, supply chains and industrial networks [1, 28]. Fine [11] drew attention to a special aspect of supply chain architecture, going beyond the issues of production/purchasing, buyer–supplier relationships or vertical integration. Trade in medicinal products (any form of transfer of ownership of a medicinal product, including under a free title within civil law transactions and pursuant to a legal transaction) may only be carried out on the principles specified in pharmaceutical law and requires obtaining a permit [19]. Additionally, Polish law distinguishes between wholesale and retail trade in medicinal products, and the latter is conducted primarily by generally accessible pharmacies (along with them there are also hospital and company pharmacies) and pharmacy outlets, on the principles set out in the regulation on the criteria for the classification of medicinal products that may be admitted. for sale, as well as non-pharmacy sales outlets (including herbal and medical stores, specialized medical supply stores and generally accessible stores) [40, 41].

The Polish pharmaceutical market in the area of distribution is characterized by a high degree of concentration, because the 10 largest entities concentrate almost 90% of the turnover of the entire pharmaceutical distribution market. Wholesale trade in medicinal products (any activity involving the procurement, storage, delivery or export of medicinal products or veterinary medicinal products owned by the entity performing these activities or another authorized entity, having a marketing authorization, excluding direct supply to the public) in Poland in accordance only pharmaceutical wholesalers can operate under pharmaceutical law. Each entity operating at the level of wholesale trade in the supply chain of medicinal products is obliged to implement the principles of GDP [39]. Proper conduct is required for every entrepreneur dealing with the logistics of wholesale drug trade, which is subject to detailed supervision and control by the pharmaceutical inspection. The purpose of implementing this practice was to create requirements for the pharmaceutical storage and transport environment that guarantee appropriate conditions for the movement, as well as reception, storage and dispensing of drugs (Pharmaceutical Law 2002). The distribution of medicines in Poland is largely focused on the Rx, Rp and OTC pharmacy channels, although some OTC preparations are sold outside pharmacies and are also available on "pro familiae/pro auctore" prescriptions (private medical practices/pharmacists). Pharmaceutical companies, wholesalers and pharmacies require from each other a specific level of service, contract terms, distribution and high quality of the services provided.

Entities authorized to purchase medicinal products in a pharmaceutical wholesaler are the entities listed in Fig. 2 [50–52].

A pharmacy, which is a micro-enterprise, in the light of the Pharmaceutical Act is a public health care facility in which authorized persons provide pharmaceutical services, therefore it plays a special role on the pharmaceutical market, because only authorized persons (pharmacists and pharmaceutical technicians) they can provide pharmaceutical services there. Therefore, the task of pharmacies is not only to supply the population with medicinal products, but also to provide information about drugs (so-called sensitive products) and medical devices, as well as to help patients choose the right medicine (such advice from a pharmacist is particularly important in the process of self-medication of patients) [44]. According to the Central Statistical Office (GUS) [36], the number of generally accessible pharmacies operating in Poland in 2022 was 11,866, i.e. 190 less than a year earlier (a decrease of 1.6%). There were also 24 on-site pharmacies (as in 2020) and

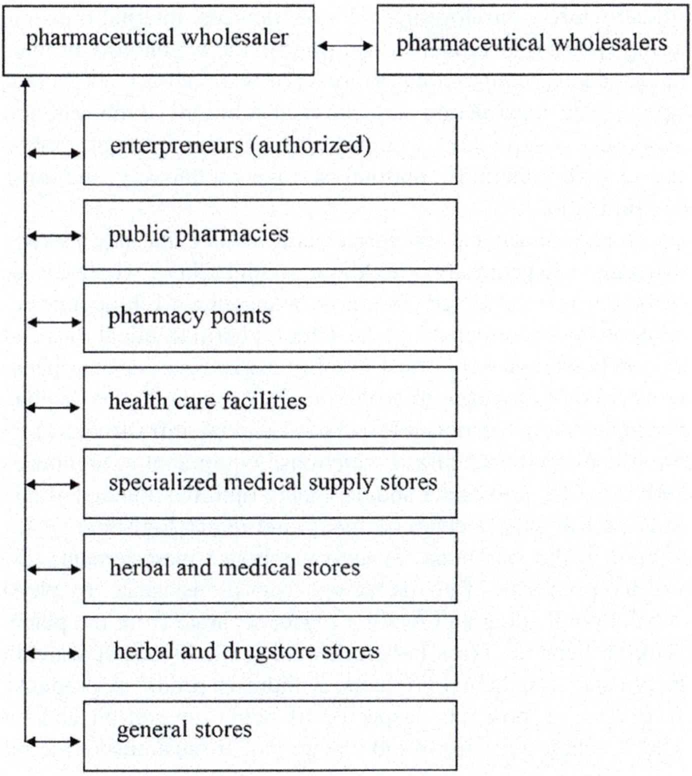

Fig. 2 Entities authorized to purchase medicinal products in a pharmaceutical wholesaler. *Source* Own study

1,147 pharmacy points (0.4% less compared to the previous year). It is worth noting, however, that almost all publicly available pharmacies (11,858) belonged to private owners. In 2021, similarly to the previous year, 2.8% of generally available pharmacies (24-h facilities) had permanent night duties, and over 22.5%—periodic duties [56].

Figure 3 shows the key connections between the pharmaceutical wholesale and retail pharmacy markets in terms of functional subsystems within the "dyad" of the pharmaceutical supply chain in Poland. In this system, both at the level of pharmaceutical wholesale and pharmacy retail sales, typical logistic tasks are carried out within the framework of "material management", i.e. rational trade in medicinal products and packaging, auxiliary materials, consumable materials/parts, etc., in which all activities undertaken and processes carried out concern transport, storage and the rational level of use of available products, as well as the process in the enterprise related to the acquisition, receipt, transfer and issuance of materials necessary to conduct specific commercial activities on the pharmaceutical market. Logistics tasks are also obviously carried out as part of "warehousing management", understood as the organization of the system and management using IT tools (IT system) of the processes of storing utility values, based on dedicated material infrastructure—intralogistics (storage devices, internal transport and auxiliary) ensuring appropriate climatic conditions in the warehouse, proper protection of medicinal products, required qualifications of warehouse workers (social infrastructure), appropriate construction and technical solutions of the warehouse/storage areas (warehouse infrastructure), organization and management corresponding to the required system functions, optimal storage technology and inventory and packaging optimization).

Therefore, a pharmaceutical wholesaler is a facility that has appropriate logistics infrastructure, i.e. primarily warehouse rooms where wholesale activities in medicinal products are conducted (inventory management). It operates on the basis of an appropriate permit issued by the Chief Pharmaceutical Inspector and, in addition to warehouse workers, must employ a manager—a pharmacist who has at least two years of experience in a pharmaceutical wholesaler or pharmacy, and who is referred to as a "responsible person" (social infrastructure). In addition to the location itself and specialized warehouse equipment (warehouse and transport intralogistics), the wholesaler should ensure optimization and efficiency in the entire pharmaceutical supply chain (delivery and return logistics).

It is required in the warehouse space (warehouse management) to ensure the separation of the processes of goods receipt from the issuance, by physically separating a separate unloading and loading place, separate from the place where the goods are stored. Separate areas (when designing the layout of warehouse space) require e.g. cytostatic medicinal products, withdrawn products, products subject to a suspension decision, products suspected of being counterfeit and intended for disposal. The warehouse premises and its equipment must ensure the maintenance of stable temperature and humidity conditions (the warehouse space should be prepared for storing pallets at temperatures from + 15 to + 25 °C, separate cold

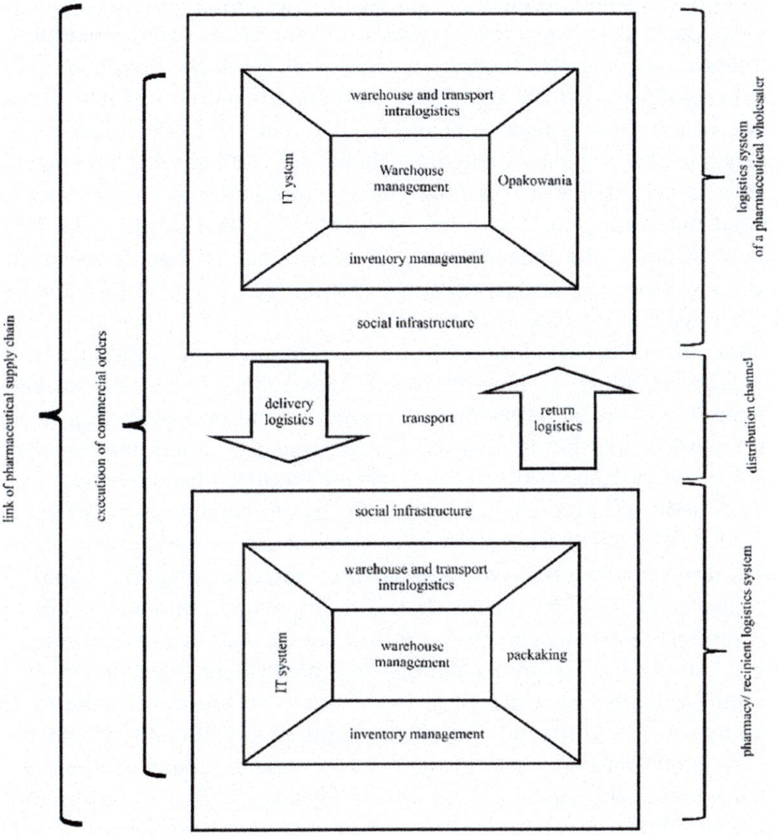

Fig. 3 Functional system within the connections between the pharmaceutical wholesale and retail pharmacy markets in the perspective of a "dyad" in the pharmaceutical supply chain. *Source* Own study

stores and refrigerators) and their monitoring and recording using calibrated sensors/recorders. Additionally, they must ensure protection of pharmaceutical goods against the harmful effects of external factors, damage or access by unauthorized persons, which is why they are covered with electronic access control, an alarm system and CCTV monitoring, and are also protected against insects and rodents (a preventive pest control program has been implemented). The quality of finishing of the facility itself (e.g. quality of wall surfaces and storage areas) also influences compliance with sanitary and hygienic requirements. The entire warehouse infrastructure is subject to the process of qualification and validation of equipment and systems (IT systems), which are to demonstrate in the documented form of protocols and reports that all intralogistics meets the assumptions and has been properly installed and ensures repeated results or conditions that are consistent with expectations (required conditions). It is also required to constantly supervise the person responsible physically in the facility, as well as to have a documented quality system and to supervise activities outsourced to external entities (social infrastructure). During the transport process, all products should be packed in transport packaging, permanently closed and properly marked. Moreover, the loading space of the vehicle must be clean, dry, without mechanical damage, and any exceedance of the boundary conditions should be verified with the manufacturer. Thus, it is expected that the pharmaceutical wholesale link will ensure identification and traceability of stored and transported medical devices, full control of the receipt, storage and transport as well as handling of non-compliant medical devices, as well as a clear procedure for dealing with complaints, claims, returns and withdrawals of medical devices.

In turn, the pharmacy level, which, in addition to the "dispatch room", is increasingly becoming a "pharmaceutical care room" (when e.g. Covid or flu vaccination functions are implemented), is required to be a place (logistics infrastructure) suitable for storing pharmaceutical products, so that their quality is not impaired (in accordance with the Summary of Product Characteristics). Additionally, each medicinal product from a specific group should have its own adapted space and be separated from the others (warehouse management). This mainly concerns drugs for external and internal use, narcotic drugs, psychotropic substances and category 1 precursors, but also suspended, withdrawn, falsified and expired products (inventory management). Regardless of this, it is also required to eliminate excessive exposure to sunlight and medical products should be placed away from walls, floors and heating installations to ensure cleanliness (protection against dust or dirt) and continuous ventilation. Products should be stored (warehouse and transport intralogistics) in appropriate, separate cabinets or drawers, clearly and legibly marked (to eliminate mistakes), and very strong substances (e.g. narcotic drugs, psychotropic substances, category 1 precursors) should additionally be secured with key locks to protect them against theft, substitution and destruction. Equipment is also required for 24-h monitoring of temperature and humidity both in rooms and in refrigeration devices where all medicinal products and medical devices are stored (the system should have a calibration certificate issued by measurement laboratories so that maintaining the appropriate temperature is completely reliable, and each used the instrument met meteorological requirements [38, 39].

Due to the fact that each pharmaceutical wholesaler, in the tactical and operational dimension, carries out its tasks at the sales/logistics interface, the need to separate the main functions and tasks within the functional duosystem of "sales function" and "logistics function" should be considered important. Figure 4 shows the relationship between commercial and logistic functions performed by a pharmaceutical wholesale entity.

Similarly, each pharmacy, in the tactical and operational dimension, carries out its tasks at the interface between sales and logistics, and in this case the main functions and tasks can also be separated within the functional "duosystem" of "sales function" and "logistics function". All the more so because as part of the

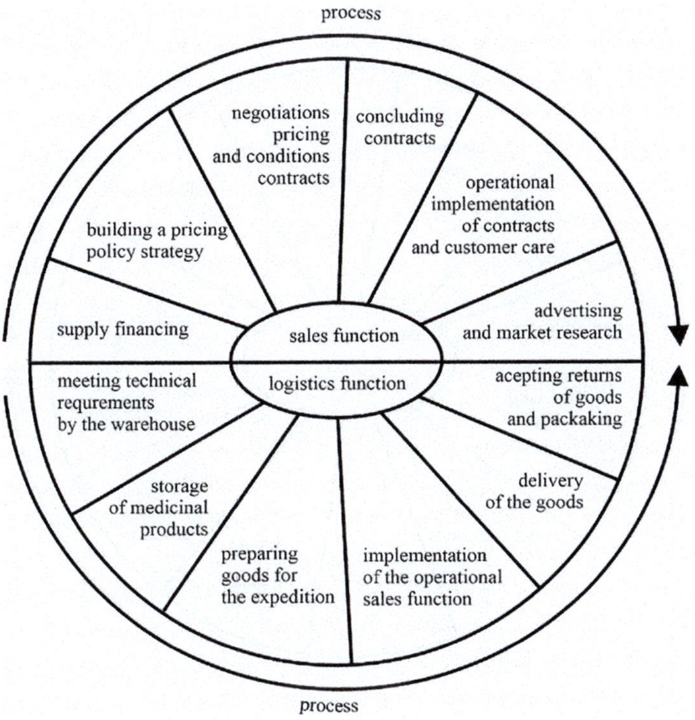

Fig. 4 A typical logistics vs. purchasing functions performed at the warehouse level. *Source* Own study

logistics process, the control of the receipt of medicinal products by the pharmacy is of key importance, which is carried out in two stages. First, it is checked (formal assessment) whether the product delivered by the pharmaceutical wholesaler agrees with the information included in the delivery document (checking the packaging in terms of series, date, compliance of the GTIN number with the GS1 system) and whether the goods contain a current declaration of conformity (CE marking). Then, you should check (visual assessment) whether the required quality of the product is ensured (controlling the conditions in which the goods were delivered to the pharmacy), also based on the UDI-DI/GTIN code, as well as IUDI-PI/IŻ containing the Application identifier (IZ), which informs about the production of the product (according to IZ these are: (17)—expiry date (10)—batch or series number (21)—serial number) and whether there is compliance with the financial document (invoice).

These activities are performed by a pharmaceutical technician or master of pharmacy. Additionally, each pharmacy manager is obliged to provide information to the provincial pharmaceutical inspector on the turnover and stock of specific medicinal products, foodstuffs for particular nutritional uses, pharmaceutical raw

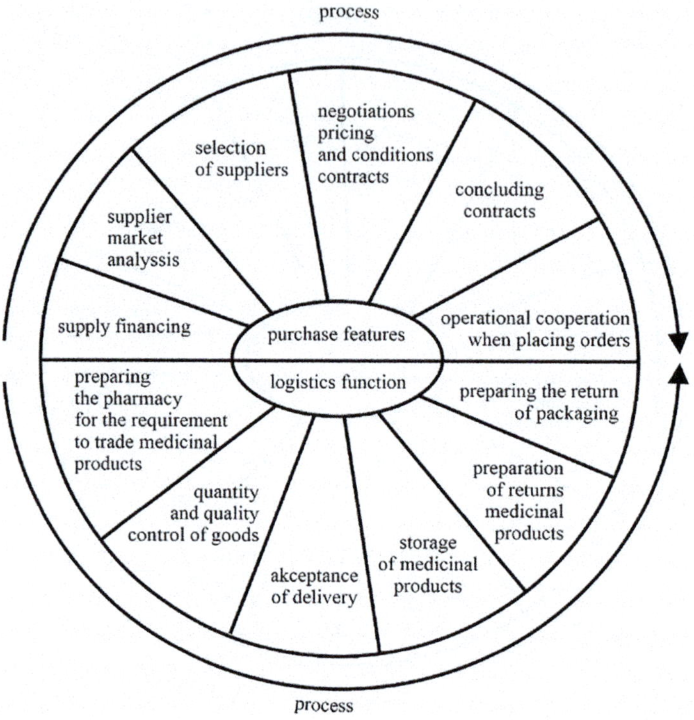

Fig. 5 A typical logistics versus purchasing functions performed at the pharmacy level. *Source* Own study

materials and medical devices. Figure 5 shows the relationship between commercial and logistics functions performed by a retail entity in the pharmaceutical market.

To sum up, the relationships between the "duosystems" indicated in Figs. 4 and 5 within the "dyad" of the pharmaceutical supply chain in Poland largely depend on whether the pharmaceutical wholesale company can become the "supplier of first choice" on the retail pharmacy market. The key factor is the price and availability of the drug, i.e. the system of trade and logistic connections between wholesale market entities and entities creating the pharmacy market.

The quantitative research presented below is included in two time horizons. Firstly, the quantitative and structural aspects of some of the recorded phenomena were re-interpreted on the basis of survey research conducted in December 2003 on a sample of 44 pharmacies out of a total of 35 operating on the Szczecin market at that time [20] and compared with research conducted in March 2024. on a sample of 25 pharmacies out of 179 pharmacies [14]. The research took a dichotomous approach to the problem, i.e. analyzing the current cooperation of the pharmaceutical wholesale and retail pharmacy markets (Table 3).

Table 3 The main demands for service improvement in area of pharmaceuticals' distribution – comparison for 2003 and 2023 year (in percentage of responses)

Postulate	Importance	
	Year 2003	Year 2023
Applying attractive prices	84.1	94.3
Expanding the commercial offer	86.4	89.5
Improving the quality of service	90.1	77.4
Intensification of advertising activities	72.7	84.7
Organizing the regulations governing activities	84.1	91.2
Reduction of service time	81.8	94.5

Source Own study

Analyzing the demands submitted by the pharmacy community in this regard highlights the changes that have taken place over the last 20 years. While in 2003 Respondents considered "Improving the quality of service" to be the most important demand (90.1%), then already in 2024. it was the least important (77.4%). Of course, this change results from achieving a repeatable and high standard of service. The postulate "Applying attractive prices" (94.3%) has become a priority in 2024, compared to 84.1% in 2004, which is primarily due to the desire to increase operational efficiency due to inflation and "frozen" drug reimbursement " Rx", and thus an increase in expectations regarding price reductions, especially for OCT drugs (94.3%).

The postulate to expand the offered assortment ("Expanding the commercial offer" (86.4%) already in 2003 indicated the need to maintain stock levels at an appropriate level (guaranteeing their availability) so that there is no need to additionally replenish the order in other wholesalers, which in 2024 it was maintained (89.5%). In 2003 The speed of delivery was also important for pharmacists (81.8%), compared to which in 2024 this demand became crucial (94.5%), and more daily deliveries were requested (within no longer than 2 h), for products not only based on the CITO formula ("to the rescue").

As part of expert interviews with representatives of pharmacies (25 units) conducted in March 2024. Key problems faced by pharmacies on the Polish pharmaceutical market were also highlighted. The aspect of the constant "Pressure of legal requirements" was raised (a pharmacy as a retail entity of the pharmaceutical market is subject to control by the Provincial Pharmaceutical Inspector (WIF) in three main areas, i.e.: a pharmacy as a premises that must meet certain requirements (pharmacy premises and its equipment, pharmacy signs regarding opening hours, information on the fulfillment of reimbursed prescriptions and a valid contract with the National Health Fund), the pharmacy as the staff employed there (record of masters of pharmacy and pharmaceutical technicians and copies of their diplomas and certificates) and a pharmacy as a place of trade in medicinal products, medical devices, etc. (standard GDP). The unique "product (drug) specificity" was also pointed out, which requires electronic transfer of data on drug trade to the Integrated System for Monitoring Trade in Medicinal Products, which records refusals and summaries of placed orders, as well as archiving all orders and related refusals. There is an obligation to record temperature and humidity measurement in pharmacy rooms, and "anti-false" [50] (Drug Review 2022; Running a Pharmacy 2024) requirements make it necessary to use the NAMS web database (part of the pan-European AMS system) so that the user obtains knowledge about generated "alerts" (often technical) and conduct an investigative procedure in order to verification of the authenticity of the drug.

However, there are problems when scanning 3D codes in the PLMVS system on drug packaging, which means that the authenticity of a given package cannot be verified due to the incorrect structure of the code data in relation to the data entered by the "MAH" into the European EU HUB database. This requires additional activities in the form of manual verification of a given packaging (by entering the product code (PC), batch (Batch), expiry date (EXP) and serial number (SN), and each serialized packaging has its own unique SN code, which must be withdrawn from the NMVO database when the medicine is issued to the patient.

Respondents also drew attention to the problem of "returns" to medicinal products wholesalers, the process of returning to the wholesaler is launched according to established rules, i.e. "concerning the quantitative aspect", e.g. due to "time" (e.g. specifying the time for which from the moment delivery of preparations will be taken into account when returning), "form" (e.g. the return can be reported via the pharmacy modem, by phone, e-mail or the online platform of the wholesaler), or "procedure" for the return (e.g. based on the initiative of the wholesaler to send only an advice note for the driver collecting the return, or the need for the pharmacy to prepare the required return protocol (with the stamp of the responsible person, most often the pharmacy manager, required by wholesalers, confirming the correct storage of returned medicinal products). It is worth remembering that some medicines are not subject to return, just like after dividing the collective packaging (in the case of reimbursed medicines or dressing materials), while full-price medicines do not have such restrictions.

However, full-price medicines have no such restrictions. In the event of a shortage of goods, the pharmaceutical wholesaler may question the shortage after calculating its inventory levels, hence the quantity and value receipt and appropriate annotation on the consignment note are important. However, in cases "concerning the quality aspect", all reports of suspected quality defects and quality complaints (suspicions of failure to meet the quality requirements of a medicinal product) from pharmacies should first be addressed to the Provincial Pharmaceutical Inspectors (in order to immediately secure the reported medicinal product), and only then then to the wholesaler. Finally, the occurrence of the so-called "logistic minimum", which are the amounts for which products must be ordered in order for the wholesaler to fulfill the order.

4 Conclusion

> You can be sure of your exceptional performance perfection, but only the assessment of others can confirm this. A pharmacy is not only a place where you can get medicine. This is a place where we will be provided with professional pharmaceutical care.
>
> Mariusz Jedliński

The pharmaceutical industry in Poland remains one of the most developing industries, although it is constantly undergoing numerous transformations. This is done both on the basis of regulations and internal conditions, as well as global trends (including the share of generic drugs is growing, the area of specialized drugs is developing dynamically, the number of pharmacy chains is increasing, innovative solutions in the field of drug distribution and health monitoring (e-health) are being implemented, as well as strategic agreements are being established and the market consolidation process is progressing. Undoubtedly, as part of a separate entity-process relationship, which is the "dyad" system within the pharmaceutical supply chain, pharmacists want to cooperate with trusted suppliers who offer a wide range of pharmaceutical products.

The unique specificity of the pharmaceutical supply chain, due to the determination of the entire technical and technological chain (intralogistics) by the requirements of Good Distribution Practice, as well as the overriding "service" of providing pharmaceutical products to save health and life, requires conducting multidimensional scientific research. The research potential concerns making logistical considerations of a "systemic" and "functional" nature to indicate opportunities to increase the efficiency and synergy of action between individual links, but also of an economic nature to ensure that the processes taking place within pharmaceutical supply chains are effective and economically efficient. Research confirms that the most important factors of logistics cooperation are the speed and timeliness of deliveries and their completeness. In the commercial aspect, the price becomes crucial (in the case of non-reimbursed drugs), while the least important factor, which has an average impact on cooperation with the wholesaler, is the possibility of delaying payment.

However, taking into account the current political and economic situation, cooperation on the Polish pharmaceutical market is expected to be even closer in order to respond quickly enough to the increased demand for drugs in the event of a crisis, based on the lists of critical drugs and a contingency plan.

References

1. Abdelfattah W, Rebai A (2013) Dyadic supply chains efficiency: a new theoretical framework to consider members power relationship and decision makers preferences. IEEE, p 1, https://doi.org/10.1109/ICMSAO.2013.6552581
2. Azghandi R, Griffin J, Jalali MS (2018) Minimization of drug shortages in pharmaceutical supply chains: a simulation-based analysis of drug recall patterns and inventory policies. Complexity 1–14. https://doi.org/10.1155/2018/6348413

3. Babbie E (2003) Badania społeczne w praktyce. Wyd. Naukowe PWN, Warszawa, p 342. ISBN: 9788301212728
4. Bryman A (2007) Barriers to integrating quantitative and qualitative research. J Mixed Methods Res 1:8–22. https://doi.org/10.1177/2345678906290531
5. Chopra S, Meindl P (2016) Supply chain management. strategy, planning, and operation. Pearson Education Limited, p 13. ISBN: 9781292093574
6. Creswell JW, Plano Clark VL, Guttmann ML, Hanson EE (2003) Advanced mixed methods research design. In: Tashakkori A, Teddlie C (eds) Handbook of mixed methods in social and behavioral research. SAGE, Thousand Oaks, pp 209–240. ISBN: 0761920730
7. Croom S, Romano P, Giannakis M (2000) Supply chain management: an analytical framework for critical literature review. Europ J Purchas Supply Manag 6:67–83. ISSN: 0969-7012
8. Denscombe M (2008) Communities of practice: a research paradigm for the mixed methods approach. J Mixed Methods Res 2(3):270–283. ISSN: 1558-6898
9. Devine J, Jones RM, Lee N, Tyson WJ (1976) An introduction to industrial economics. George Allen and Unwin Ltd., London. ISBN:9781351244633
10. Federchimica Assosalute, Numeri e indici dell'automedicazione, Edizione 2019/2020/2021/ 2022/2023. https://assosalute.federchimica.it/pubblicazioni/numerieindici
11. Fine CH (1998) Clockspeed: winning industry control in the age of temporary advantage. Perseus Books. ISBN: 9780738201535
12. Heaton J (2008) Secondary analysis of qualitative data: an overview. Histor Soc Res 33(3):33–45. ISSN: 0172-6404
13. Hewson C, Yule P, Laurent D, Vogel C (2003) Internet research methods. A practical guide for the social and behavioral sciences. Sage Publications, Newbury Park, pp 12–13. ISBN: 9781446208564
14. https://ktomalek.pl
15. https://rankingi.rp.pl/lista500/2022
16. http://mgr.farm/aktualności/dzieki-lekom-otc-polacy-unikaja-rocznie-ponad-41-mln-wizyt-u-lekarza/
17. https://www.iqvia.com/newsroom/2018/02/iqvia-reports-fourth-quarter-and-full-year-2017-results-issues-first-quarter-and-full-year-2018-guide
18. https://www.iqvia.com/newsroom/2022/10/iqvia-reports-third-quarter-2022-results
19. Jagielska M (2010) Prawo farmaceutyczne. Komentarz, red. L. Ogiegło. C.H.Beck, Warszawa, pp 584–685, ISBN: 9788381289474
20. Jedliński M (2005) Preferencje logistyczne klientów na szczecińskim rynku farmaceutycznym. LogForum 1(1):1–7. ISSN:1734-459X
21. Johnston MP (2014) Secondary data analysis: a method of which the time has come. Qual Quant Methods Libr 3:619–626. ISSN: 2241-1925
22. Kahneman D (2012) Pułapki myślenia. O myśleniu szybkim i wolnym. Media Rodzina, Poznań, pp 1–668. ISBN: 9788372787873
23. Kiecolt KJ, Nathan LE (1985) Secondary analysis of survey data. Sage University Paper Series on Quantiative Applications in the Social Sciences, p 10. https://doi.org/10.4135/9781412985796
24. Kłoda K et al (2024) Rola samoleczenia w systemie opieki zorientowanym na wartość zdrowotną, Instytut Zarządzania w ochronie zdrowia, Wydawnictwo Uczelni Łazarskiego, Warszawa, pp 8, 69. ISBN: 9788360694350
25. Leśniowska-Gontarz M (2019) System ochrony zdrowia w Polsce, CeDeWu, Warszawa. ISBN: 9788381023920
26. Long-Sutehall T, Sque M, Addington-Hall J (2010) Secondary analysis of qualitative data: a valuable method for exploring sensitive issues with an elusive population? J Res Nurs 16(4):335–344. ISSN: 1744-9871
27. Lücker F, Seifert RW (2017) Building up resilience in a pharmaceutical supply chain through inventory, dual sourcing and agility capacity. OMEGA Int J Manage Sci 73:114–124. ISSN: 0305-0483

28. Miemczyk J, Johnsen T, Macquet M (2012) Sustainable purchasing and supply management: a structured literature review of definitions and measures at dyad, chain and network levels. Supply Chain Manage Int J 17(5):478–496. https://doi.org/10.1108/13598541211258564
29. Möller K, Rajala A, Svahn S (2005) Strategic business nets-their type and management. J Bus Res 9(58):1274–1284. ISSN: 1873-7978
30. Obłąkowska K, Bartoszewicz A (2022) Farmaceutyczny wyścig narodów. Instytut Nowa Europa, Warszawa, p 16. ISBN: 9788396435026
31. Paszkowska M (2020) Polski system ochrony zdrowia. Difin, Warszawa. ISBN: 9788380855113
32. Pfaff D (2010) Badania rynku. Jak pozyskiwać najistotniejsze dla firmy informacje marketingowe. Wydawnictwo BC.edu, Warszawa, p 9. ISBN 9788361655886
33. Porter ME (1999) Choix Strategiques et Concurrence. Technique d'analyse des secteurs et de la concurrence dans l'industrie. Economica, Paris. ISBN: 9782717809312
34. Przybyliński M, Świeczewska I, Trębska J, Gorzałczyński A (2020) Makroekonomiczny wpływ sektora farmaceutycznego na polską gospodarkę. Raport przygotowany na zlecenie PZPPF, KPF, Łódź, pp 7–8
35. Raport Bank Pekao (2019) Branża farmaceutyczna. Wzrost znaczenia pozlskich producentów na świecie, Bank Pekao, Departament Strategii i Analiz Międzynarodowych, Warszawa
36. Raport GUS: Polska w liczbach 2023(2023), GUS, Warszawa.
37. Raport PMR (2022) Dystrybucja na rynku farmaceutycznym w Polsce 2022. Analiza rynku i prognozy na lata 2022–2027. PMR Market Expert, Warszawa
38. Rozporządzenie Ministra Zdrowia z dnia 22 lipca 2002 roku w sprawie procedur Dobrej Praktyki Dystrybucyjnej (Dz. U. 2002, poz. 1216
39. Rozporządzenie Ministra Zdrowia z dnia 19 marca 2015r. w sprawie wymagań Dobrej Praktyki Dystrybucyjnej, Dz.U. 2015, poz. 381
40. Rozporządzenie Ministra Zdrowia z dnia 27 października 2022r. w sprawie podstawowych warunków prowadzenia apteki, Dz.U.2022, poz. 381
41. Rozporządzenie Ministra Zdrowia z dnia 2 grudnia 2021 r. w sprawie programu pilotażowego przeglądów lekowych, Dz.U. poz. 2342
42. Rozporządzenie Rady Ministrów z dnia 24 grudnia 2007 r. w sprawie Polskiej Klasyfikacji Działalności (PKD), Dz. U. 2007, poz. 1885
43. Rozporządzenie Rady Ministrów z dnia 16 lipca 2017 r. zmieniające rozporządzenie w sprawie Polskiej Klasyfikacji Działalności (PKD), Dz.U. 2017, poz.1249
44. Rozporządzenie Ministra Zdrowia z dnia 12 grudnia 2002 r. w sprawie podmiotów uprawnionych do zakupu produktów leczniczych w hurtowni farmaceutycznej, Dz.U. 2002, poz.1831
45. Rynek farmaceutyczny w Polsce 2022 (2022) Market Reviews. MarketHub Research & Competitive Intelligence
46. Settani E, Harrington TS, Srai JS (2017) Pharmaceutical supply chain models: a synthesis from a systems view of operations research. Oper Res Perspect 4:74–95. ISSN: 2214-7160
47. Sikorski S (2021) Administracja ochrony zdrowia w Polsce-między świadczeniem a reglamentacją. Wolters Kluwer, Warszawa. ISBN: 978382237955
48. Statistical Yearbook of Industry—Poland (2010–2023). Statistical Publishing Establishment, Warszawa, ISSN: 1231-8957
49. Ustawa z dnia 6 września 2001 r. Prawo farmaceutyczne, Dz.U. 2001, poz. 1381 z późniejszymi zmianami
50. Ustawa z dnia 6 września 2001 r. Prawo farmaceutyczne, Dz. U. 2021, poz. 2301
51. Ustawa z dnia 18 marca 2011 r. o Urzędzie Rejestracji Produktów Leczniczych, Wyrobów Medycznych i Produktów Biobójczych, Dz. U. 2011, poz. 1382
52. Ustawa z dnia 7 kwietnia 2022r. o wyrobach medycznych, Dz.U. 2022, poz. 974
53. Tashakkori A, Teddlie C (2010) Putting the human back in 'human research methodology's: the researcher in mixed methods research. J Mixed Methods Res 4(4):271–277. ISSN: 1558-6898
54. The World Health Report (2000) Health systems: improving performance. WHO, Geneva

55. Woch M (2015) Ochrona zdrowia w Polsce z punktu widzenia filozoficznoprawnego. Marek Woch, Warszawa. ISBN: 9788394010867
56. Zdrowie i ochrona zdrowia w 2021 roku (2023). GUS, Warszawa

Mariusz Jedliński Born November 4, 1961, doctor of economic sciences in the field of logistics. Professor at the Maritime University of Szczecin, Dean's Representative for Contacts with the Socio-Economic Environment (2017–2019) and Member of the University Council (2019-2024). He works at the Department of Management and Logistics of the Faculty of Transport Economics and Engineering.

Professor at several universities, teaches postgraduate, MBA and doctoral courses. He supervised 13 doctorates in economics and sciences. He has published several articles and scientific papers in the field of logistics, logistics systems, supply chain management, sustainable logistics, service business logistics, urban logistics, management warehouses and quality management (TQM).

During the years 2010–2019 he headed the Polish Logistics Association. He is an expert in the field of science and education, member of the team of logistics and transportation processes of the Polish Academy of Sciences (2011-2014), expert of the National Research and Development Center (2012–2016) and evaluator for the Ministry of National Education. He also completed courses and internships: AQIS Expert—Australian Quarantine Inspection Service (since 2008), Fachexperten TÜV Thüringen e.V. (since 2005), course "Auditor/consultant of quality management systems according to ISO series standards 9000"—TÜV Consulting Polska Sp. z o.o. z o. o. (since 1999), "Train for trainers" course—British Know-How Found Certificate (1998), "Effective Consultancy Skills—stage 1" course—International Resource Development U.K. Certificate (1997), English internship and operational management and TQM—Leeds University School of Commerce (1997), French and economic and legal internship—GRETA Rouen Sud (Group of establishments)—(1992). Cooperation with companies includes, among others, logistics projects in logistics services, wood industry, heavy chemicals, industrial, pharmaceutical wholesale.

Part II

Integrated Management of Health Products: Supply, Storage and Waste

Challenges of Purchasing Physician Preference Items (PPIs) in the Healthcare Sector

9

Carolina Belotti Pedroso, Martin Beaulieu, and Claudia Rebolledo

Abstract

The costs of medical supplies have increased considerably in the past few years. Among these diverse sets of medical supplies hospitals purchase, there is a particularly interesting category, characterized by expensive items, in which physicians have strong preferences. These medical items are known as physician preference items (PPIs). They are expensive medical devices generally used in operating rooms, representing an excellent opportunity to achieve cost savings and value improvements in healthcare. Nevertheless, PPIs carry specificities that pose unique challenges to the procurement process. This chapter aims to understand the main challenges faced in PPI purchasing and to bring to light the complexities surrounding it.

Keywords

Purchasing strategies • Supplier relationship • Value-based procurement • Criteria

Abbreviations

GPO Group Purchasing Organizations

C. B. Pedroso (✉)
University of Twente, Enschede, The Netherlands
e-mail: c.belottipedroso@utwente.nl

M. Beaulieu
CHAINE Research Group, HEC Montreal, Montreal, Canada
e-mail: martin.beaulieu@hec.ca

C. Rebolledo
HEC Montreal, Montreal, Canada
e-mail: claudia.rebolledo@hec.ca

F. Jawab (ed.), *Hospital Supply Chain*, Integrated Science 27,
https://doi.org/10.1007/978-3-031-70292-1_9

PPI	Physician preference items
MCDM	Multi-criteria decision-making
SKU	Stock Keeping Unit

1 Introduction

The costs of purchasing medical items, equipment, and pharmaceutical products are equivalent to $240 billion in the United States [47]. Since then, between 2019 and 2021, spending on drugs has risen by almost 37% and on supplies by 20% [5]. In fact, the COVID-19 pandemic has resulted in accelerated cost growth in the healthcare systems of many countries [68]. This amount of expenditure is similar to what is found in other industrialized countries: purchases can represent up to 25% of the overall hospital budget [58]. Factors such as the aging of the population and recent technological developments have contributed to the increase in healthcare costs [64]. As a result, governments have been seeking ways to reduce expenditures in the healthcare sector [67].

Hospitals purchase a wide set of products, such as food, drugs, maintenance products, equipment, and medical supplies. Among the endless types of medical supplies, physician preference items (PPIs) are a particularly important category since they represent up to 60% of the total budget for medical supplies [13]. Physician preference items are high-quality medical supplies such as hip and knee implants, pacemakers, and other high-priced items used in the operating room [22, 35]. PPIs have been increasingly becoming an important source of cost containment in healthcare purchasing [65].

In fact, PPIs purchasing embodies multiple challenges of healthcare purchasing. First, they represent a great part of the sourcing expenditures in hospitals. Second, they can bring many opportunities for cost containment that are underexplored. Third, they can allow for more advanced technology to be incorporated into the hospital. Finally, they cannot be managed as other types of commodities since the physicians' preferences have a significant impact on the procurement process, leading to unique challenges [2].

As evidenced by the COVID-19 pandemic, many healthcare organizations have fragile and unstructured purchasing functions [23]. Understanding the main difficulties encountered in PPIs purchasing is critical to obtain more efficient healthcare supply chains, designing better decision-making, reaching cost containment and adding value. The chapter compares traditional purchasing strategies and their unsuitability for PPIs. This section concludes with a research question. We then present the main parameters of our methodology. From there, the text will focus on two dimensions: the criteria by which physicians select PPIs, and their relationships with suppliers. From there, we will formulate the challenges associated with these two dimensions. Our conclusion will summarize our findings and open up new avenues of research.

2 PPI and Traditional Purchasing Strategies

The significant cost increase in medical supplies occurred during the decade of 2000s, arose awareness towards the search for more effective ways to manage PPIs. This phenomenon accelerated in the wake of the COVID-19 pandemic [68]. Therefore, healthcare organizations have realized the importance of adopting best practices to manage PPIs successfully. Despite of the efforts, healthcare procurement is still lagging behind other sectors, in terms of adoption of best practices, and performance [10]. Two main practices have been traditionally used by hospitals to support PPIs purchasing: standardization and consolidation [32].

Consolidation aims to improve the buyer's bargaining power through volume leverage [56]. It allows to obtain price discount and economies of scale based on the high volume purchased [34]. An effective way to reach consolidation in the healthcare sector is through the use of Group Purchasing Organizations (GPOs). GPOs purchase and negotiate supplies on behalf of its members, leveraging the negotiation power with suppliers [39], offering a more privileged condition than individual organizations would have [55]. Reduced administrative costs are also possible through the use of GPOs. GPOs frequently bring together different types of medical supplies and support building consolidation [59]. Another consolidation practice that shows some similarities is Hospital Purchasing Alliance. In this context, hospitals create a consortium to aggregate their purchases to obtain lower costs and important economies of scale [14]. Almost 30 years ago, Pedersen [44] questioned whether a purchasing group was a good vehicle for generating savings for PPIs. By consolidating the needs of several establishments, it may be difficult to define a consensus standard between hospitals with different vocations.

Standardization provides consistency and establishes purchasing standards [62]. Standardization can provide not only purchasing costs, but also reduced overhead costs [70]. Standardization in hospitals is characterized by establishing predetermined standards and specifications for PPIs purchasing [26]. Standardization considers comprehensive purchasing costs and aligns with the total cost of ownership approach which aims to determine the true costs of the procurement process [61]. Reducing the supply base can also facilitate the standardization of medical supplies [35]. However, physicians tend to resist these standardization exercises that stifle creativity in addressing patients' specific needs [41]. Examples of effective standardization practices applied to PPIs purchasing include the formulary model, and the payment cap model. Whereas, the formulary model restricts supplier choices and the range of products physicians can choose, the payment cap model standardizes costs by setting a maximum price for products, without restricting specific products or suppliers [35]. Considering the challenges brought by the impact of physicians on PPIs purchasing we explore the following research question: *What are the main challenges associated with the purchasing of physician preference items?*

3 Methodological Aspects

This research was conducted through a systematic literature review. The systematic literature was conducted observing the following steps: (i) plan the review; (ii) conduct the review; and (iii) report and dissemination [63]. The first step taken was to formulate the research strings to address the research question. Keywords were derived from the main construct "PPIs," resulting in a set of keywords. Next, the appropriate databases were selected, considering both managerial and healthcare backgrounds. The chosen databases were Medline, Science Direct, ABI Inform, Emerald, and PubMed (see Appendix for more details). The diversification of data bases enables us to deal with the same subject from a clinician's or a manager's point of view. Also, some databases, such as ABI Inform, are integrators covering different publishers, enabling identified articles to be validated and others to be identified. Multiple search strings were tested, and the most promising ones were utilized in the research. The review included the following period of time: 20–30 years [54]. The methodology is described in more detail by Pedroso et al. [46].

4 Physicians and PPI

This section brings into light important topics closely associated with PPIs purchasing: physician's preference criteria, and the complexity of the relationship with suppliers.

4.1 Physician's Preference Criteria

Purchasing PPIs is a complex process because dynamic and interdependent relationships take place between suppliers and the hospital. Procurement professionals may lack knowledge about the medical supplies they purchase. In fact, the physicians are important stakeholders on the procurement process, since they are the internal customers, and the primary users of these medical supplies [8].

Although the procurement department is responsible for conducting the procurement process, they receive important input from physicians who have expertise in defining specifications of medical supplies [13]. However, physicians often have strong preferences over certain suppliers, and they develop strong relationships with the suppliers' salespersons [36]. In some cases, physicians may even bypass the procurement department decisions and negotiate directly with suppliers. This situation can generate conflicts between the procurement department and physicians [7]. This behavior is characterized as maverick buying, as the physicians act as surrogate buyers. Surrogate buyers typically comprise professionals who exhibit varying levels of influence over decisions, based on their training, licensure, certification, and accountability [3].

Hospitals present triadic relationship among the procurement professionals, physicians and suppliers' salespeople. This relationship dynamics becomes an issue because the physicians have closer relationship with the suppliers' salespeople, than with the procurement department [8]. This dynamic leads to SKUs (Stock Keeping Unit) proliferation and the costs of medical supplies can go to the roof [60]. To make the situation worse physicians often do not know the price of the supplies they use [13]. Very often physicians' criteria are not based on costs, but rather on the relationship they have with suppliers [35].

Often, physicians are unaware of the prices of the medical items they use, adding complexity to the situation [22]. Securing engagement from stakeholders, particularly physicians, is crucial to ensure commitment in implementing effective purchasing strategies [12]. The recent surge in the costs of PPIs, attributed to technological advancements, emphasizes the need for well-planned procurement strategies [8]. The challenges outlined in this paragraph are often exacerbated by the lack of a strategic role for the purchasing department. Therefore, empowering the purchasing department becomes essential to centralize decision-making and successfully implement strategies [13]. It means that the procurement department should be empowered to allow effective purchasing decisions and prevent maverick buying. Centralizing purchasing will generate economies of scale in the contracting process, while improving negotiating power to obtain better prices. Centralized procurement would be better suited to commodities. Given the innovative nature of PPI, a decentralized structure would be more appropriate. In this sense, the concept of the category manager can reconcile these two perspectives, as the category manager will have intimate knowledge of the product to be purchased, including the context of use and the characteristics of the supplier market.

Considering the importance of PPIs purchasing, it is critical to understand what are the factors that influence physicians' preferences. Physicians are key players in the procurement process. In the past, physicians were free to choose medical devices according to their own preferences. Nowadays, physicians are required to lower costs in the operating room since they represent an important source of expenditures [17]. Physicians are now aware of the prices paid for medical devices, and they agree that costs should be taken into account when purchasing expensive items [20].

Physicians are key decision-makers regarding purchases of expensive medical devices. Since physicians are directly involved in acquiring and using those items, they have a direct impact on purchasing decisions [13]. Whereas it is widely known that physicians might present preferences for certain suppliers, it is not entirely clear what the main factors are that might affect their decisions toward a supplier, as opposed to another. Some previous research provided some hints about physicians' preference criteria. Burns et al. [13] pointed out that physicians are higly influence by technology and they might have strong preferences for certain suppliers due to the characteristics of the product (such as durability, individual patient necessities, familiarity with the product, resistance to change, consulting arrangements made by suppliers, and relationship with suppliers). A complementary perspective is offered by Burns et al. [12], in which the services provided by the suppliers (as training and post-sales services) play a critical role in physicians' preferences. Nevertheless, costs are rarely part of the criteria considered by physicians [33]. Table 1 summarizes the physicians' preference criteria found in the literature.

The most common physicians' preference criteria identified in the previous studies is the relationship with suppliers. As mentioned previously, in some cases, physicians may develop close relationships with suppliers, jeopardizing the cost-containment efforts implemented by the procurement department (Abdulsalam et al. 2018). It is known that suppliers try to develop a close relationship with physicians by having their sales representatives visit physicians or offering training, for example. Aside from that, some physicians have a weak relationship with the hospital [52]. Accordingly, personal experience is another strong influential criterion for physicians. Physicians prefer to choose suppliers with whom they have previous experience. As physicians are confident with a certain medical device that they had used in the past, they develop familiarity with the supplier [13]. Residency training is another important factor. Suppliers introduce their products to physicians as early as during residency training, and they continue offering training to physicians in exchange for the use of their products. As a result, physicians develop loyalty to these suppliers. Strong preferences for certain items can be enhanced by suppliers' salespersons. Since the physicians are trained with such suppliers' products from early on, the resistance to change is greater [8]. Recent research pointed out that physicians are highly influenced by technology and medical device characteristics and by services provided by suppliers [13]. To summarize, physicians' strong preferences make PPIs management much more challenging [36]. This process can be characterized by power asymmetry and goal misalignment between the supply chain members. Table 2 illustrates the main factors that can affect physicians'preferences over certain suppliers.

4.2 Relationship with Suppliers

The procurement process in healthcare is characterized by the presence of a set of stakeholders with conflicting objectives [25, 66]. Aligning the interests of suppliers, purchasing managers, and physicians are critical to balance buyer–supplier relationship issues that take place in the healthcare arena. Procurement managers should develop social skills, such as conflict resolution, teamwork, and negotiation, to deal with conflicting relationships [14]. On the one hand, suppliers are responsible for manufacturing, supplying, and distributing PPIs. They also provide support staff and training to physicians. In turn, the hospital controls the purchasing process and manages the inventory aiming to provide health services to patients, achieve cost reduction, among other objectives [35].

Some recent studies have focused on the complexities of the buyer–supplier relationship in the healthcare sector (Abdulsalam et al. 2018) [8]. A close relationship between suppliers and physicians can become an undesirable situation for hospitals. It is not uncommon for physicians to have a strong preference for a given

Table 1 Physicians' preference criteria

	Relationship with suppliers	Personal Experience	Residency training	Patient's interests	Clinical outcomes	New technologies available	Suppliers' services	Involvement in Product development
Healy et al [24]	✓			✓			✓	
Montgomery and Schneller [35]	✓	✓	✓	✓			✓	
Burns and Lee [14]	✓	✓	✓	✓	✓	✓		
Robinson [52]	✓		✓					✓
Wilson et al [71]	✓		✓					✓
Burns et al. [12]	✓		✓	✓	✓	✓	✓	
Pennington and DeRienzo [49]	✓	✓	✓	✓				
Rohman et al. [53]	✓							
Plonien and Donovan [50]	✓	✓	✓					
Shbool (2016)	✓	✓	✓		✓		✓	
Gagliardi et al. [19]								
Handfield et al [22]		✓						
Moore et al. [37]		✓		✓				

(continued)

Table 1 (continued)

	Relationship with suppliers	Personal Experience	Residency training	Patient's interests	Clinical outcomes	New technologies available	Suppliers' services	Involvement in Product development
Vertullo et al. [65]				✓	✓	✓		
Wasterlain et al. [69]		✓	✓		✓	✓		
Abdulsalam et al. [3]	✓			✓				
Burns et al. [13]								
Millikan et al. [33]	✓	✓			✓			
Armeni et al. [6]	✓	✓			✓	✓		
Total	13	10	9	8	7	5	4	2

	Cost-effectiveness	Professional expertise	Peers influence	Hospital infrastructure	Literature influence	Financial support	Hospital alignment	Consulting activities
Healy et al [24]								
Montgomery and Schneller [35]								
Burns and Lee [14]							✓	
Robinson [52]								
Wilson et al [71]								
Burns et al. [12]						✓		
Pennington and DeRienzo [49]								

(continued)

Table 1 (continued)

	Cost-effectiveness	Professional expertise	Peers influence	Hospital infrastructure	Literature influence	Financial support	Hospital alignment	Consulting activities
Rohman et al. [53]								
Plonien and Donovan [50]								
Shbool (2016)								
Gagliardi et al. [19]								
Handfield et al [22]								
Moore et al. [37]			✓	✓	✓			
Vertullo et al. [65]								
Wasterlain et al. [69]								✓
Abdulsalam et al. (2018)		✓						
Burns et al. [13]								
Millikan et al. [33]	✓							
Armeni et al. [6]								✓
Total	2	1	1	1	1	1	1	1

Table 2 Main factors affecting Physicians' Preference Criteria

Main factors	Examples
Relationship with suppliers	The suppliers' salesperson can develop a close relationship with physicians, offering them diverse incentives [35]
Personal experience	The physician's familiarity and experience with a product becomes an important criterion for the choice [22]
Residency training	Basic training during residence determines the techniques physicians use, and therefore, their choices [52]
Patients' interests	The patient's condition (age, physical condition, possible comorbidity problems) and the nature of the intervention will influence the product choice. Patient satisfaction becomes an important selection criterion [49]
Clinical outcomes	The clinical results that the products can provide and their reproducibility have a great impact on physicians' choice [12]
New technologies availability	Innovations with superior clinical benefits can lead physicians to switch products [65]
Suppliers' services	Suppliers can offer services, such as post-sales services, influencing the physicians' decisions [12]
Involvement in Product development	Product development involves close relationships between suppliers and physicians. Such an exercise tends to strengthen relations between them [71]
Cost effectiveness	Physicians choose products based on their prices [69]
Professional expertise	Physicians have clinical expertise, which guides their decisions (Abdulsalam et al. 2018)
Peers influence	Recommendations from colleagues, especially those with experience, can influence the choice of physicians [37]
Hospital infrastructure	Both physical (such as facilities) and organizational structures can impact physicians' choices [37]
Literature influence	The physician can obtain information from conferences or scientific journals which present results on the use of certain products [37]
Financial support	Suppliers offer financial support to physicians to maintain their proximity with physicians [12]
Hospital alignment	Physician interests can be aligned with the hospitals' objectives [12]
Consulting activities	Suppliers can offer consulting arrangements to physicians [33]

supplier and develop a close relationship with the supplier's representative [12]. These physicians prefer to work directly with the supplier representative, neglecting the hospital purchasing department's decisions [35]. Some suppliers can even offer both financial and non-financial benefits to physicians in order to motivate them to increase the number of products purchased. Some examples of this practice involve visiting the operating room during surgery and giving physicians financial resources. This practice has caused disruptions in hospitals' supply chains [8].

In some hospitals, there is a missing link between the procurement department that are making decisions regarding purchasing and the physicians that are using the medical supplies. Managing these relationships and providing trust and commitment between the participants of the procurement process is critical to address this problem [21]. It is important to align the hospital's purchasing strategies and physicians' interests; otherwise, purchasing strategies are likely to fail, and the challenges present in this process can not be overcome (Abdulsalam et al. 2018). The success of aligning hospitals' and physicians' interests rests on the ability to create standardization strategies and offer good equivalency to the existing products. Although the hospital cannot control the supplier-physician relationship, it can manage the purchasing decisions that occur inside the hospital [35].

5 Main Challenges

As mentioned on the previous sections of this chapter, PPIs purchasing can bring a set of challenges to healthcare organizations. The results from the literature review show that the influence of physicians in PPIs purchasing is at the core of the complexities. The main challenges surrounding this complex dynamic are discussed in the details in the following paragraphs.

Physicians' preferences—One of the main issues concerning PPIs purchasing is the problem of the strong physicians' preferences for certain suppliers [52]. This attitude can jeopardize purchasing strategies, since the goals elaborated by the procurement department cannot be achieved with full potential [8]. Thus, it is critical to engage the physicians to support the purchasing strategies. This can be done by obtaining physicians' commitment (Abdulsalam et al. 2018). Gaining physicians' commitment is critical to contain costs, but this can be a challenging task when physicians are reluctant to abandon their medical supply preferences. Different mechanisms can be put into practice to improve physicians' commitment (Abdulsalam et al. 2018). For example, it can be noted that a formal engagement of the physician with the hospital can be beneficial, creating a sense of belonging. Another manner to gain physicians' commitment is to involve them in standardization efforts adoption. Key physicians participate actively in the planning process, aiming to reach consensus [42].

Physicians' price awareness—Creating cost consciousness among physicians is critical to PPIs purchasing. In some cases, the physicians do not know the prices of the items they are using. Undoubtedly, it is not an appropriate situation as they cannot judge the prices of these supplies [22]. Thus, it is desirable that physicians be informed about the prices of medical devices [20]. Physicians are key players in PPIs purchasing, so gaining their commitment is critical to reduce the costs associated with the process [47]. It is critical to investigate what criteria guide physicians' preferences in order to understand their choices for certain suppliers and implement more suitable purchasing strategies [13]. Although there are some indicators in the literature about physicians' criteria, what factors influence physicians' choices is not completely clear. As such, this research can shed some light on the physicians' preferences. Physicians are also highly skilled professionals that in general, do not like to have their choices dictated. Offering some room for flexibility could be an appropriate measure [35].

Physicians' close relationship with the suppliers' salesperson—In order to manage the close relationship between the suppliers' salesperson and the physicians, the procurement department can limit the physicians' choices [52]. Montgomery and Schneller [35] suggest two models to limit the choices of physicians: the formulary model and the payment-cap model. The formulary model imposes limitations on the range of suppliers that physicians can consider. In turn, the payment-cap model determines price ceilings for PPIs categories. Both strategies are based on standardization efforts. The payment-cap model might be easier to implement since it still leaves room for physicians to exert some choices. These are practical strategies that can be easily adopted by healthcare organizations aiming to solve the problem of physicians being too close to suppliers. Suppliers also provide services to healthcare organizations. For example, when a supplier provides a new implant, it also offers training sessions to the physicians. Consequently, the physician-supplier dynamic becomes even stronger, imposing further challenges for purchasing strategy implementation (Moore, 2017). Therefore, the procurement department needs to carefully design and implement a strategy that better adapts to the circumstance.

Functional silos—The nature of procurement decision-making involves a wide set of stakeholders, such as the procurement department, suppliers, physicians, clinical staff, and patients. These stakeholders have different goals and interests and can influence the process in distinct ways. The different stakeholders' points of view can lead to a conflicting setting [40]. The distinct differences in procurement decisions can be attributed to professional norms, ethics, and professional autonomy [28]. A great barrier that needs to be overcome is the functional silos. Different functional areas should work together, aiming to reach a common goal [18]. Therefore, the procurement department and the clinical staff should be aligned in order to overcome siloed mindset.

Lack of recognition of the strategic role of the Purchasing department—The purchasing department has been traditionally associated with an operational function. However, in the last decades, its strategic role has been highlighted [15]. An effective way to enhance the strategic purchasing role in the organization is through a centralized purchasing function. A central purchasing unit can be described as an organizational department with its own authority, responsibility, and power to make decisions [27]. One of the main roles of the procurement function is to centralize and coordinate the purchasing of supplies [13]. It is known that the procurement department plays a key role in coordinating the arrival of medical items at the hospital. A centralized purchasing prevents other departments from making decisions on their own without considering the impact of their decisions on the whole organization [4, 51]. If physicians overpass the procurement department's decisions, a serious threat to purchasing strategies is established [11]. A centralized purchasing allows a pre-established pattern approved by the purchasing department, ensuring standardization strategies. For this reason, it is important to empower the purchasing department in healthcare organizations. All medical devices acquired should be on the contract negotiated with selected suppliers [16]. As we mentioned earlier, a category manager position could reconcile the benefits of centralized purchasing management with a decentralized perspective on inventory management.

High costs—The high costs of PPIs can be managed by implement different practices such as consolidation, and standardization. While consolidation practices are based on leveraging the volume of items acquired [57], standardization strategies intend to limit the options and the price paid for PPIs purchasing [22]. Consolidation is more appropriate for commodities acquired in large volumes through the utilization of GPOs, for example [39]. On the other hand, standardization efforts demand more alignment between the departments in the hospital and collaboration of the stakeholders involved in the procurement process [9].

Address patients' specificities—Managing PPIs purchasing effectively may impact the flexibility of the physicians to choose specific medical supplies. Therefore, addressing specific patients' needs can be difficult in this scenario. The decision regarding the purchase of certain PPIs includes selecting the device that best fits the patient's anatomy and pathology [37]. In some cases, the medical device choice is limited to what the hospital had in the inventory at the time of the surgery. There are some other occasions in which only a few suppliers are available in the market. In general, implants don't present a great difference between brands; thus, physicians are willing to switch to a new supplier only if it brings further advantages [19]. Hospitals must adopt effective purchasing strategies and allow some flexibility on their purchasing contracts at the same time for extraordinary situations such as those exposed in this paragraph.

6 Conclusions

Strong physician preferences can jeopardize procurement decisions and impact the costs negatively. PPIs are represented by a wide variety of medical items from diverse categories, such as orthopedic, cardiovascular, and neurological surgical implants. Physicians play a key role in PPIs purchasing, providing important information, since they have clinical expertise. They are also the internal customer, one of the main stakeholders involved in the procurement process for these medical supplies. Healthcare organizations need to make wise decisions to orchestrate the different stakeholders dynamic that take place in the PPIs purchasing scenario.

Although it is known that physicians have strong preferences for certain suppliers, what criteria guide these preferences is still not entirely clear. This critical issue should be investigated in more depth in future research, aiming to explore the mechanisms that can be put in place to attenuate different types of preferences. Even more critical is to understand how to obtain commitment from physicians. Distinct approaches can be used to improve physician's engagement with procurement' s decisions. For example, literature indicates that physicians employed by hospitals are more committed to contribute to procurement decisions, than self-employed ones, since it creates a sense of belonging (Abdulsalam et al. 2018). Another way to obtain physicians' comitment is to involve the key stakeholders very early in the procurement process. This allows room for alignenment of different perspectives and to reach consensus [42]. Creating cost consciousness among physicians is also of utmost importance. In many cases, physicians may not be fully aware of the prices associated with the implants they use. To effectively manage PPIs, it is critical to ensure they are aware of supply costs [47]. Creating awareness and involving physicians in procurement decision-making, enables healthcare organizations to foster commitment towards cost containment and efficiency.

The discussion about determining physicians' preferences and criteria can be further explored with the application of multi-criteria decision-making methods (MCDMs). MCDMs are widely applied to investigate similar issues that involve the evaluation of different criteria, such as supplier selection. They include multi-attribute techniques, artificial intelligence, mathematical programming, among others [31]. An example of an MCDM technique that shows the potential to determine the physician preference criteria is the Fuzzy set theory, which is suitable for addressing decision-making scenarios characterized by imprecision and vagueness in problem information [1]. Within this paradigm, a fuzzy inference system is formulated based on an if–then structure, drawing upon expert judgments to capture human reasoning and subjectivity inherent in decision-making processes [43]. Wherein evaluations heavily rely on the opinions of decision-makers, the application of fuzzy set theory is deemed appropriate to tackle such complexities. In contrast to alternative multi-criteria decision-making techniques, fuzzy set theory offers distinct advantages [45].

PPIs purchasing is the focus of critical issues in the healthcare arena. The interaction between different stakeholders with distinct goals and interests increases the complexity of the procurement process. A particularly confictous interaction can arise between the procurement department and the physicians, in the cases that the later develops close relationships with the suppliers' salesperson [13]. It is known that some suppliers intentionally develop close relationships with physicians aiming to influence their preferences by offering them incentives in exchange for the physicians' loyalty. As a consequence, some physicians can have a very close relationship with the suppliers' sales representatives, affecting the procurement decisions in a negative way, and increasing costs (Abdulsalam et al. 2018).

This dynamic not only has a impact on costs, but also on the strategic role of procurement, as the main decision-maker of the process. Therefore, a turmoiled relationship between the procurement department, physicians, and suppliers can be present. The problem takes place when the physician prefers to work directly with the suppliers, ignoring the hospital's procurement policies. The relationship asymmetry occurs when the supplier-physician relationship is stronger than the physician-hospital relationship, so the hospital cannot control which medical supplies are being purchased [8].

Finally, healthcare organizations have long sought to implement management practices to improve the procurement process. The main practices adopted by healthcare organizations are represented by consolidation and standardization. Whereas these practices can bring benefits in terms of cost reduction, novel ways to improve the procurement process need to be pursue. PPIs are expensive medical products, and represent a considerable burden. These products require a high level of technological innovation. These practices are focused on cost reduction at the short-term, rather than on improving the performance. This brings into light a reactive role of procurement, responding to influences on the process, rather than providing value, improved outcomes and long-term savings. Besides that, PPIs purchasing should be conducted bearing in mind that they are strategic items, and not commodities. Therefore, more sophisticated solutions are needed to deal with PPIs purchasing. As an example of that, opposite to the other price-based purchasing strategies, valued-based procurement considers acquiring supplies that can provide a long-term benefits, and long-term cost-containment [32]. PPIs purchasing has been traditionally conducted taking into account a reactive approach, in which the ultimate goal is to obtain cost reduction. However, these medical supplies carry significant technological features and opportunities to incorporate innovation. Consequently, they should be managed as strategic items rather than as commodities. In this scenario, healthcare organizations should re-think how PPIs purchasing is conducted. Adopting a value-based approach is critical to unlocking the strategic role of procurement [29]. Value-based procurement can lead to improved outcomes for patients and achieve cost containment at the same time [48]. Value-based procurement can be implemented by moving away from the short-term cost-containment mindset and the search for the lowest price - which characterizes how procurement has been traditionally performed in the healthcare sector [32].

To conclude this chapter, we would like to provide some directions for future research. The physician preference criteria should be investigated empirically, with the application of MCDMs, allowing to rank the most important criteria pointed out by the physicians. Another avenue for future research is to understand how to obtain physicians' commitment in order to collaborate closer with the procurement department in hospitals. It is important to align different perspectives to implement the most suitable purchasing strategies for PPIs, and consequently achieve organizational goals. Therefore, a holistic approach is essential to address the misalignment of interests.

Declaration of interest: The authors declare no conflicts of interest.

Appendix: Suitability of the Databases

Nature of the databases	Management	Healthcare
Databases	ScienceDirect, ABI Inform, Emerald	Medline and PubMed
Suitability	Suitable for searching for papers focused on managerial aspects	Suitable to detect papers with a strong healthcare background

References

1. Abdullah S, Aslam M, Khan TA, Naeem M (2013) A new type of fuzzy normal subgroups and fuzzy cosets. J Intell Fuzzy Syst 25(1):37–47
2. Abdulsalam Y, Schneller E (2019) Hospital supply expenses: an important ingredient in health services research. Med Care Res Rev 76(2):240–252
3. Abdulsalam Y, Gopalakrishnan M, Maltz A, Schneller E (2018) The impact of physician-hospital integration on hospital supply management. J Oper Manag 57(January):11–22. https://doi.org/10.1016/j.jom.2018.01.001
4. Altenau J (1987) How do diagnosis related groups affect materiel managers? Hosp Mater Manage Q 9(2):32–40
5. American Hospital Association (2022) Massive growth in expenses and rising inflation fuel continued financial challenges for America's Hospitals and Health Systems. https://www.aha.org/guidesreports/2023-04-20-2022-costs-caring
6. Armeni P, Meregaglia M, Borsoi L, Callea G, Torbica A, Benazzo F, Tarricone R (2023) Collecting physicians' preferences on medical devices: are we doing it right? Evidence from Italian orthopedists using 2 different stated preference methods. Med Decis Making Int J Soc Med Decis Making 43(7–8):886–900
7. Askfors Y, Fornstedt H (2018) The clash of managerial and professional logics in public procurement: Implications for innovation in the health-care sector. Scand J Manag 34(1):78–90. https://doi.org/10.1016/j.scaman.2018.01.001
8. Atilla EA, Steward M, Wu Z, Hartley JL (2018) Triadic relationships in healthcare. Bus Horiz 61(2):221–228
9. Beaulieu M, Roy J, Landry S (2018) Logistics outsourcing in the healthcare sector: lessons from a Canadian experience. Can J Adm Sci 35(4):635–648
10. Beaulieu M, Bentahar O (2021) Digitalization of the healthcare supply chain: a roadmap to generate benefits and effectively support healthcare delivery. Technol Forecast Soc Change 167. https://doi.org/10.1016/j.techfore.2021.120717
11. Beste JT (1989) Materiel management in health care: planning for success. Hosp Mater Manage Q 10(4):37–50
12. Burns LR, Housman MG, Booth RE Jr, Koenig A (2009) Implant vendors and hospitals: competing influences over product choice by orthopedic surgeons. Health Care Manage Rev 34(1):2–18
13. Burns LR, Housman MG, Booth RE, Koenig AM (2018) Physician preference items: what factors matter to surgeons? Does the vendor matter? Medical Devices 11:39–49
14. Burns LR, Lee JA (2008) Hospital purchasing alliances: utilization, services, and performance. Health Care Manage Rev 33(3):203–215
15. Carter JR, Narasimhan R (1996) Purchasing and supply management: future directions and trends. Int J Purch Mater Manag 32(4):2–12
16. Corey ER (1978) Should companies centralize procurement? Harv Bus Rev 56(6):102–102
17. Eiferman D, Bhakta A, Khan S (2015) Implementation of a shared-savings program for surgical supplies decreases inventory cost. Surgery 158(4):996–1002

18. Foerstl K, Hartmann E, Wynstra F, Moser R (2013) Cross-functional integration and functional coordination in purchasing and supply management: antecedents and effects on purchasing and firm performance. Int J Oper Prod Manag 33(6):689–721. https://doi.org/10.1108/IJOPM-09-2011-0349
19. Gagliardi AR, Ducey A, Lehoux P, Turgeon T, Kolbunik J, Ross S, Trbovich P, Easty A, Bell C, Urbach DR (2017) Multiple constraints compromise decision-making about implantable medical devices for individual patients: qualitative interviews with physicians. BMC Med Inform Decis Mak 17(1):178. https://doi.org/10.1186/s12911-017-0577-3
20. Glennie RA, Barry SP, Alant J, Christie S, Oxner WM (2019) Will cost transparency in the operating theatre cause surgeons to change their practice? J Clin Neurosci Off J Neurosurg Soc Austral 60:1–6
21. Gobbi C, Hsuan J (2015) Collaborative purchasing of complex technologies in healthcare: Implications for alignment strategies. Int J Oper Prod Manag 35(3):430–455. https://doi.org/10.1108/IJOPM-08-2013-0362
22. Handfield RB, Venkitaraman J, Murthy S (2019) Do prices vary with purchase volumes in healthcare contracts? J Strateg Contract Negot 3(4):185–214. https://doi.org/10.1177/2055563619837882
23. Harland CM, Knight L, Patrucco AS, Lynch J, Telgen J, Peters E, Tátrai T, Ferk P (2021) Practitioners' learning about healthcare supply chain management in the COVID-19 pandemic: a public procurement perspective. Int J Oper Prod Manag 41(13):178–189
24. Healy WL, Iorio R, Lemos MJ, Patch DA, Pfeifer BA, Smiley PM, Wilk RM (2000) Single price/case price purchasing in orthopaedic surgery: experience at the Lahey Clinic. J Bone Joint Surg 82(5):607–612
25. Hinrichs S, Dickerson T, Clarkson J (2013) Stakeholder challenges in purchasing medical devices for patient safety. J Patient Saf 9(1):36–43
26. Housley CE (1988) Proper leadership and motivation can remove all barriers to group purchasing. Hosp Mater Manage Q 10(1):51–64
27. Karjalainen K (2011) Estimating the cost effects of purchasing centralization-empirical evidence from framework agreements in the public sector. J Purch Supply Manag 17(2):87–97. https://doi.org/10.1016/j.pursup.2010.09.001
28. Kasher A (2005) Professional ethics and collective professional autonomy: a conceptual analysis. Ethical Perspect: J Eur Ethics Netw 11:67–98. https://doi.org/10.2143/EP.12.1.583363
29. Knoppen D, Sáenz MJ (2015) Purchasing: can we bridge the gap between strategy and daily reality? Bus Horiz 58(1):123–133
30. Laczniak GR (1979) An empirical study of hospital buying. Ind Mark Manage 8(1):57–62
31. Lima Junior FR, Osiro L, Carpinetti LCR (2014) A comparison between Fuzzy AHP and Fuzzy TOPSIS methods to supplier selection. Appl Soft Comput 21:194–209. ISSN 1568-4946. https://doi.org/10.1016/j.asoc.2014.03.014
32. Meehan J, Menzies L, Michaelides R (2017) The long shadow of public policy; barriers to a value-based approach in healthcare procurement. J Purch Supply Manag 23(4):229–241
33. Millikan JS, Trachiotis G, Sade RM (2018) Should a surgeon comply with hospital administration's demand to change valve preference ? J Thorac Cardiovasc Surg 156(6):2210–2215. https://doi.org/10.1016/j.jtcvs.2018.07.044
34. Monczka RM, Trent RJ (1995) Purchasing and sourcing strategy: trends and implications. Center for Advanced Purchasing Studies (CAPS report)
35. Montgomery K, Schneller ES (2007) Hospitals' strategies for orchestrating selection of physician preference items. Milbank Q 85(2):307–335
36. Moons K, Waeyenbergh G, Pintelon L (2019) Measuring the logistics performance of internal hospital supply chains—a literature study R. Omega 82:205–217. https://doi.org/10.1016/j.omega.2018.01.007
37. Moore AJ, Blom AW, Whitehouse MR, Gooberman-Hill R (2017) Managing uncertainty—a qualitative study of surgeons' decision-making for one-stage and two-stage revision surgery for prosthetic hip joint infection. BMC Musculoskeletal Disorders 18(1). https://doi.org/10.1186/s12891-017-1499-z

38. Murray AS, Griswold M, Sunesara I, Smith E (2012) Comparison of patient outcomes in academic medical centers with and without value analysis programs. J Healthcare Leadership 4:93–105. https://doi.org/10.2147/JHL.S30421
39. Nollet J, Beaulieu M (2005) Should an organization join a purchasing group? Supply Chain Manag 10(1):11–17
40. Nyaga G, Schneller E (2018) Physician preference items management: challenges, opportunities, and strategies. Research Report sponsored by CAPS Research
41. O'Malley S (1997) Getting physician buy-in to standardization efforts. Qual Lett Healthc Lead 9(4):2–11
42. Olson SA, Obremskey WT, Bozic KJ (2013) Healthcare technology: physician collaboration in reducing the surgical cost. Clin Orthop Relat Res 471(6):1854–1864
43. Osiro L, Lima-Junior FR, Carpinetti LCR (2014) A fuzzy logic approach to supplier evaluation for development. Int J Prod Econ 153:95–112. https://doi.org/10.1016/j.ijpe.2014.02.009
44. Pedersen J (1996) Product standardization playing to win. In Vivo 14(6):15–20
45. Pedroso CB, Calache LDDR, Lima Junior FR, da Silva AL, Carpinetti LCR (2017) Proposal of a model for sales and operations planning (S&OP) maturity evaluation. Production 27:e20170024. https://doi.org/10.1590/0103-6513.20170024
46. Pedroso CB, Beaulieu M, Rebolledo C (2024) Challenges of purchasing physician preference items (PPIs) in the healthcare sector: a buying center perspective. In: 33rd IPSERA conference, Rio de Janeiro
47. Pei KY, Richmond R, Dissanaike S (2020) Surgical instrument standardization—a pilot cost consciousness curriculum for surgery residents. Am J Surg 219(2):295–298. https://doi.org/10.1016/j.amjsurg.2019.10.018
48. Pennestrì F, Lippi G, Banfi G (2019) Pay less and spend more-the real value in healthcare procurement. Ann Transl Med 7(22)
49. Pennington C, Derienzo NR (2010) An effective process for making decisions about major operating room purchases. AORN J 91(3):341–349
50. Plonien C, Donovan L (2015) OR leadership: product evaluation and cost containment. AORN J 102(4):425–433
51. Richardson JC (1989) Group purchasing. Hosp Mater Manage Q 10(4):51–55
52. Robinson JC (2008) Value-based purchasing for medical devices. Health Aff 27(6):1523–1531. https://doi.org/10.1377/hlthaff.27.6.1523
53. Rohman L, Hadi S, Whitwell G (2014) Surgeons' knowledge about the costs of orthopaedic implants. J Orthop Surg 22(2):221–223
54. Rowe F (2014) What literature review is not: diversity, boundaries and recommendations. Eur J Inform Syst 23(3):241–255
55. Rozemeijer F (2000) How to manage corporate purchasing synergy in a decentralised company? Towards design rules for managing and organising purchasing synergy in decentralised companies. Eur J Purchas Suppl Managet 6(1):5–12
56. Rozemeijer F, van Weele A, Weggeman M (2003) Creating corporate advantage through purchasing: toward a contingency model. J Supply Chain Manag 39(1):4–15
57. Schneller ES (2000) The value of group purchasing in the health care supply chain. Arizona State University, Tempe
58. Schneller ES, Burns LR, Smeltzer LR (2006) Strategic management of the health care supply chain. Jossey-Bass, San Francisco
59. Schneller E (2009) The value of group purchasing—2009: meeting the need for strategic savings
60. Shbool MA, Rossetti MD (2020) Decision-making framework for evaluating physicians' preference items using multi-objective decision analysis principles. Sustainability 12(16). https://doi.org/10.3390/su12166415
61. Smith FD (2012) Bone products in surgery: a blueprint for standardization. AORN J 95(2):239–254. https://doi.org/10.1016/j.aorn.2011.06.008
62. Sánchez-Rodríguez C, Hemsworth D, Martínez-Lorente ÁR, Clavel JG (2006) An empirical study on the impact of standardization of materials and purchasing procedures on purchasing

and business performance. Suppl Chain Manage Int J 11(1):56–64. https://doi.org/10.1108/13598540610642475
63. Tranfield D, Denyer D, Smart P (2003) Towards a methodology for developing evidence-informed management knowledge by means of systematic review. Br J Manag 14(3):207–222
64. Uenk N, Taponen S (2020) Risk allocation in service triads: the case of Dutch and Finnish home care procurement. J Purchas Suppl Manage 26(4). https://doi.org/10.1016/j.pursup.2020.100647
65. Vertullo CJ, Grimbeek PM, Graves SE, Lewis PL (2017) Surgeon's preference in total knee replacement: a quantitative examination of attributes, reasons for alteration, and barriers to change. J Arthroplasty 32(10):2980–2989
66. Vincent CJ, Blandford A (2017) How do health service professionals consider human factors when purchasing interactive medical devices? A qualitative interview study. Appl Ergonomics 59(Pt A):114–122
67. Wang P, Vienneau M, Vogeli C, Schiavoni K, Jubelt L, Mendu ML (2023) Reframing value-based care management: beyond cost reduction and toward patient centeredness. JAMA Health Forum 4(6):e231502
68. Wang Y, Bai G, Anderson G (2023) U.S. hospitals' administrative expenses increased sharply during COVID-19. J General Int Med 38(8):1887–1893. https://doi.org/10.1007/s11606-023-08158-8
69. Wasterlain AS, Melamed E, Bello R, Karia R, Capo JT, Science of Variation Group (2017) The effect of price on surgeons' choice of implants: a randomized controlled survey. J Hand Surg 42(8):593–601
70. van Weele AJ, Rozemeijer FA (1996) Revolution in purchasing: building competitive power through pro-active purchasing. Philips Electronics, Eindhoven
71. Wilson NA, Schneller ES, Montgomery K, Bozic KJ (2008) Hip and knee implants: current trends and policy considerations. Health Aff 27(6):1587–1598

Carolina Belotti Pedroso is an assistant professor in Healthcare Procurement & Purchasing at the University of Twente. Previous to that, she was a postdoctoral researcher of the Logistics and Operations Management department at HEC Montreal. She holds a Ph.D. from University of São Paulo (2015–2019), and she was a visiting scholar at University of Tennessee at the Marketing and Supply Chain Department (2017–2018). She has experience in the following topics: Healthcare Procurement, Public Procurement, Value-based Healthcare, Innovation and Sustainability. She has published in journals such as International Journal of Production Economics, Journal of Cleaner Production or International Journal of Procurement Management.

Martin Beaulieu (M.Sc.) is a Research Associate at HEC Montréal's Supply Chain Research Group. His research focuses on supply chain integration dynamics. He is a noted researcher on supply chain management and healthcare operations management with numerous articles and case studies published in the last two decades as well as government commissioned studies. Amongst other outlets, he has published in journals such as the International Journal of Operations and Production Management, Supply Chain Management: An International Journal, Journal of Purchasing and Supply Management, International Journal of Logistics Management or IEEE Transactions on Engineering Management.

Claudia Rebolledo (Ph.D.) is a Full Professor and holder of the Supply Chain Canada Professorship at the Department of Logistics and Operations Management at HEC Montréal, Canada. Her research focuses mainly on inter-firm relationships in supply chains, supplier development, purchasing strategy and sustainable procurement. She uses several empirical research methods, having a deep interest in collaborative research, especially for her projects within the healthcare sector.

Organ Donation Supply Chain: A Bibliometric Analysis of Risk Initiatives

10

Maria Eduarda Alves da Silva, Ingrid Teixeira do Nascimento, Fernanda Pinto Torres, Pedro Senna, Ana Carla de Souza Gomes dos Santos, Lino G. Marujo, and Leonardo Mangia Rodrigues

Abstract

Understanding how SCRM works in the healthcare sector, especially in organ donation, is crucial. However, implementing strategies applicable to SCRM to identify and mitigate risks is a significant challenge across all industries. Nonetheless, the need to identify and mitigate risks in ODS (Organ Donation Supply Chains) is paramount and can bring greater control and efficiency to daily management in healthcare organizations, facilitating organ transplant processes. Mapping the state-of-the-art risk management initiatives for organ donation supply chains is essential. Therefore, this work aims to propose a bibliometric and qualitative analysis of risk management initiatives that cover the entire chain, considering combining factors that involve the supply chain as a whole, and not just logistical factors. As a result, the identification of the main methodologies and tools used for better risk management will be shown,

M. E. A. da Silva · I. T. do Nascimento · F. P. Torres · P. Senna (✉)
Department Postgraduate Program in Production Engineering and Systems (PPPRO), Federal Centre for Technological Education Celso Suckow da Fonseca (CEFET/RJ), Rio de Janeiro RJ, Brazil
e-mail: pedro.senna@cefet-rj.br

A. C. de Souza Gomes dos Santos
Department Industrial Engineering, University/Institution: IFRJ—Niterói/RJ, Niterói RJ, Brazil
e-mail: Ana.carla@ifrj.edu.br

L. G. Marujo · L. M. Rodrigues
Department Production Engineering Program, Universidade Cândido Mendes/PEP/COPPE-UFRJ, Rio de Janeiro RJ, Brazil
e-mail: lgmarujo@ufrj.br

L. M. Rodrigues
e-mail: leonardo.mangia@sage.coppe.ufrj.br

F. Jawab (ed.), *Hospital Supply Chain*, Integrated Science 27,
https://doi.org/10.1007/978-3-031-70292-1_10

along with the main barriers and facilitators, as well as positive and negative outcomes.

Keywords

Organ donation • Bibliometrics • Transplantation • Supply chain management

1 Introduction

The organ donation supply chain, as well as the risks associated with logistical factors, are subjects that lack studies capable of promoting technological and scientific advancements within the context of organ transplantation, encompassing the entire chain. In general, organ transplantation is regularly studied in its medical, legal, or ethical dimensions and few studies have considered the supply chain dimension, even though the organization of organ transport is fundamental to the success of transplants, ensuring the correct state of the organ in such a limited time. According to Goli et al. [14], organizational transplantation is a crucial task in the healthcare supply chain, as it is responsible for organizing the supply and demand of various vital organs.

Supply Chain Risk Management (SCRM) plays an indispensable role in any segment. Without this management, it would not be possible to maintain a functioning supply cycle to identify processes that require improvement. For Fan and Stevenson [11], SCRM aims to develop strategies to identify, evaluate, treat, and monitor risks within supply chains.

The conception of an efficient supply chain for organ transplant networks, closely related to human life, plays a fundamental role in improving network performance [34]. Mantecchini et al. [22] suggested in their study a self-assessment tool for hospitals, which would help hospital managers identify strengths and weaknesses in their donation and transplant processes. In his study on the Supply Chain of Organ Donation (SCOD), Cole [7] seeks to develop systems that facilitate and accelerate the procurement and delivery of organs, creating a logistical network that is standardized, data-driven, and capable of being implemented at any time.

Lewis et al. [19] identified in their study, carried out in the USA and Europe, the main barriers to organ donation that contribute to an imbalance in supply and demand for organs, directly affecting the supply chain. They assert that organ shortages, religion, underrepresented minority groups, difficulties in obtaining consent, lack of understanding, and general ethical concerns become challenging barriers to organ donation, reflecting the complexity of procurement and allocation of organs.

Many factors encompass the organ donation supply chain. It is important to think about possible initiatives that are capable of optimizing them, seeking improvements in the evaluation of the entire organ transplant process, analyzing risks to obtain strategies or tools that can mitigate them, and contributing to the elimination of organ waste. Risks exist in all Supply Chain segments and need to be identified to receive proper treatment, but when it comes to organ transplantation, failure to effectively identify these risks can cost lives.

Although there are some significant studies, as far as we know, none of these studies establish the state of the art considering initiatives to identify and mitigate risks found within the organ donation supply chain. In this regard, this study aims to propose a bibliometric and qualitative analysis of risk management initiatives considering combining factors that involve the supply chain as a whole. Additionally, this study aims to answer four research questions: (RQ1) What is the state of the art on risk management in the organ donation supply chain? (RQ2) What strategies and tools are being used for risk management initiatives in the organ donation supply chain? (RQ3) What are the main barriers and facilitators found in organ transplant logistical processes? and (RQ4) What were the results of risk management in this supply chain?

In addition to this introductory section, Sect. 2 presents the literature review, Sect. 3 presents the methodology, Sect. 4 presents the results of the bibliographic analysis and qualitative findings, as well as the discussion. Section 5 outlines the future agenda, and Sect. 6 concludes the article with conclusions, limitations, and new research opportunities.

2 Literature Review

In recent years, Supply Chain Risk Management (SCRM) has grown increasingly essential across industries, aiming to strengthen resilience and minimize disruptions in complex supply networks. Simultaneously, the healthcare sector, particularly in organ transplantation, faces significant logistical challenges, highlighting the critical importance of Organ Donation Supply Chain (ODSC) management. This review investigates the convergence of SCRM and ODSC, analyzing their interaction, identifying challenges, and proposing strategies to optimize supply chain dynamics in organ donation and transplantation. By examining research, frameworks, and practical applications, it clarifies the complex relationships between risk management and the challenges present in organ procurement, allocation, and distribution.

2.1 Organ Donation Supply Chain

The mission of the ODSC is to develop strategies that refine and hasten the acquisition and distribution of organs, constructing a logistical structure that is not just standardized and data-focused but also flexible enough to operate effectively in

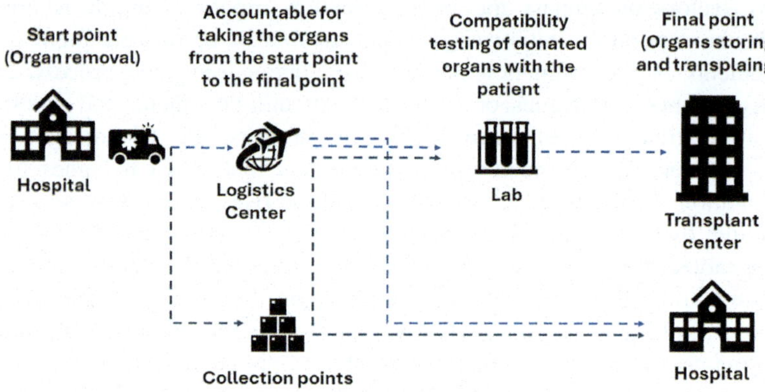

Fig. 1 ODSC diagram. *Source* The authors (2024)

various scenarios. Cole [7] emphasizes the critical importance of such a system in improving the efficiency and accessibility of organ transplantation procedures. Building upon this premise, this essay will delve into the multifaceted dimensions of the ODSC, examining its complex operational methods, technological innovations, and ethical implications within the realm of organ donation. The diagram in Fig. 1 shows the main actors in the organ donation offer. The donated organ makes a journey leaving the hospital where the donor underwent removal surgery (starting point), is collected by the logistics center, or taken to a point of collection where the final journey of the organ takes place will be tracked. Arriving at these locations, the organs can be taken to a laboratory to identify the compatibility of the organs with the patient. Upon passing through the laboratory, the organ is sent to a transplant center. If it does not pass through the laboratory, the organ is sent directly to the hospital. At the hospital or transplant center, the organs are stored and transplanted (full stop).

2.2 Supply Chain Risk Management

The evolution of Supply Chain Risk Management (SCRM) from seminal works by Bowersox et al. [4], Lonsdale [20], Zsidisin et al. [52], and Hallikas et al. [15] laid the groundwork for acknowledging and managing risks in supply chains. Later studies by Juttner [17], Norrman and Jansson [29], Sorensen [41], and Tang [44] contributed to a comprehensive understanding of SCRM, emphasizing the need for proactive risk mitigation measures. SCRM is crucial in organ donation supply chains, as highlighted by studies such as Ahmadvand and Pishvaee [1] and Goli et al. [14], which stress proactive risk identification and mitigation strategies. Colajanni et al. [6] advocate for balancing efficiency with financial sustainability, while Mantecchini et al. [22] emphasize logistical optimization and risk mitigation in the transplant process. Despite individual contributions, a comprehensive review of risk management initiatives in organ donation supply chains is lacking. Conducting a bibliometric and qualitative analysis, as proposed, is crucial for gaining insights into current practices and informing future SCRM initiatives. By addressing these gaps, stakeholders can develop targeted strategies to enhance the efficiency, effectiveness, and resilience of organ transplant networks, leading to improved patient outcomes and a more sustainable organ donation ecosystem.

3 Methodology

This article utilized a systematic review following the Preferred Reporting Items for Systematic Reviews and Meta-Analyses (PRISMA) protocol. The PRISMA protocol was selected for its well-structured steps, inclusion and exclusion criteria, transparency, and assistance in addressing research questions [3, 27, 40] (Prima Flowchart 2020). This protocol consists of 3 stages: Identification, Screaming, and Inclusion. The first stage is Identification, where acceptance criteria are defined, search strategies are devised, and articles are identified. The criteria used were English documents, indexed in Scopus and PubMed, between the years 2005 and 2023. We selected this criterion because English is a universal language (citação lean edu tem), Scopus is a main database and has a large bibliographic [12, 49], PubMed is an important database that focuses on Healthcare [45], and the years 2005–2023 because term Supply Chain with Organ donation started, in Scopus and PubMed with [48]. For the search strategies, the terms "Organ Donation," "Organ transplant," "Supply chain," "Risk," and "Logistic" were used along with Boolean operators (AND and OR) as shown in Table 1.

A total of 1,122 articles were found in both databases, of which 278 duplicates were excluded, leaving one article for each title. The Screaming stage is divided into 2 phases. In the first phase, we read the title review, abstract review, and keywords review of the 844 documents. Of these, 770 were excluded for talk about organ 3D printing, blood/plasma donation, patient mortality by race, treatment for leukemia, cell therapy, cardiovascular risk, Alzheimer's involvement,

Table 1 Search Strings

Strings	Search Strings	Scopus	PubMed
I	"Organ donation" AND "Supply Chain"	7	75
II	"Organ transplant*" AND "supply chain"	30	201
III	"Organ supply chain"	6	1
IV	"Organ donation" AND "logistic"	338	290
V	"Organ donation" AND "supply chain risk"	61	2
VI	"Organ transplant" AND "logistical risk"	57	54
	Total	**499**	**623**

Source The authors (2024)

toxic medicine, books about anesthesia, virus genetic analysis, embryo use, restrictions on children's menus, zoonosis prevention, hospital trash, and implementation and operation of the bus rapid transit system. Leaving 74 documents that were read in full during the second phase. After reading, documents 28 were selected, which addressed the topic. Forty-six articles were excluded, as they dealt with recipient compatibility with the organ, religious interference in donation, legislative creation, animal testing, racial issues, donor glucose levels, non-recovery of donated organs, and the number of surviving transplant patients. Figure 2 shows the PRISMA protocol outcome.

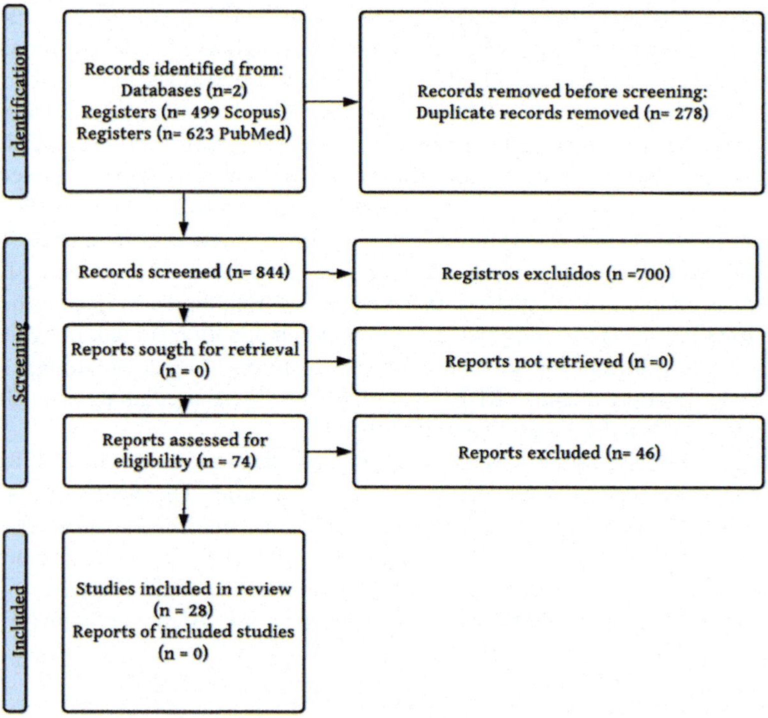

Fig. 2 PRISMA 2020. *Source* The authors (2024)

4 Results and Discussion

In this section, the research questions will be answered.

4.1 (RQ1) What Is the State of the Art Regarding Risk Management in the Organ Donation Supply Chain?

País

The countries with the most publications are located in Asia. Iran and India represent 35% of articles published on SCRM and OD as shown in Fig. 3. Other publications in Asia are China and South Korea. Together they represent 41% of the articles about SCRM and OD identified in this study. Iran's articles mostly focus on case studies prioritizing the reduction of organ movement, and attempting to identify the best transportation methods and routes, but in India, the main objectives were to mitigate the cost of transplant instruments [1, 14, 16, 24, 31, 32, 34, 35, 38, 50, 51]. European countries represent 26% of published articles. Italy came in third place in the number of publications. France and the United Kingdom also published, but less frequently was an article involving the European Union that was about standardizing patient care and assessment criteria [23]. There were also publications from Brazil, Uruguay, the United States, and Australia. Australia has increased its number of publications over the years (1 article in 2019, and 2 in 2023).

Years

About the years of publication, there is an increase in publications from 2013 to 2023, as shown in Fig. 4. This increase indicates the growing relevance of this

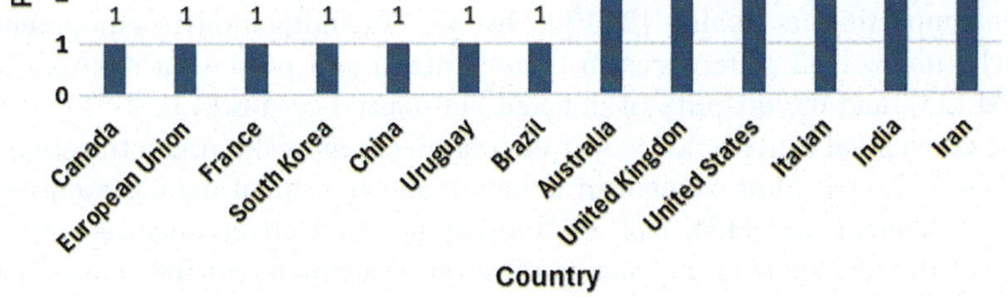

Fig. 3 Country. *Source* The authors (2024)

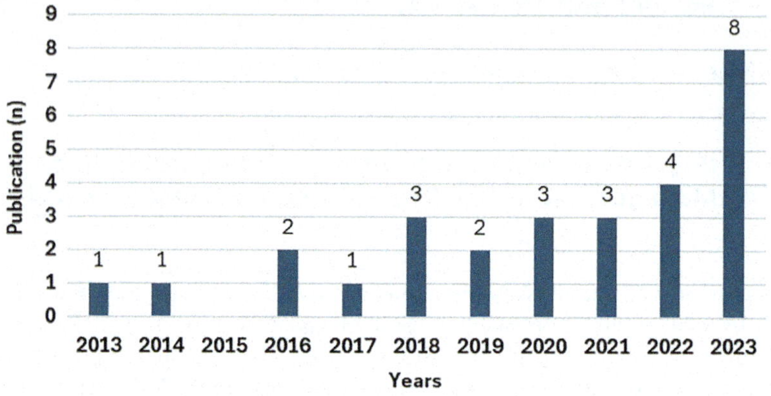

Fig. 4 Years. *Source* The authors (2024)

line of research. Compared to the previous year, 2023 has doubled the number of publications and this shows the latency of the subject. Although a time frame was established from 2005 to 2023, the articles covered in SCRM and OD were only identified in 2013. In other years, the authors addressed logistics in Alzheimer's treatments, and blood and plasma donation, among others as already mentioned in the methodology. In 10 years, the state of the art has been growing, showing that there are possibilities for studies and gaps to be filled.

Analytical versus Conceptual

Analytical articles are those that involve mathematical simulations, interviews, questionnaires, and other means that allow data analysis more practically, and conceptual articles deal with a theoretical approach, elaboration of new techniques or approaches, modeling frameworks, and literature reviews [18, 28, 37, 40]. Most of the studied documents are analytical, as shown in Fig. 5. These articles were motivated to encourage hospitals to use authorized pathways in a non-burdensome manner, with reimbursement from the organization covering transplant costs [24],understand the relationship between productivity and salary [26]; minimize transplant costs [6, 14, 16, 31],comprehend logistical factors for organ ischemia [10], reduce transport time between hospitals and transplant centers [1, 14, 32, 35], develop an efficient supply chain according to organ perishability without impacting its quality [21, 34, 36, 47, 50], mitigation in equipment supply [51], understand differences in donor criteria and propose a risk assessment method [23], and the quantity of donated but unused organs [43].

The conceptual articles addressed the optimization of the organ transplant supply chain [30, 38]; improvement in donation and transplant management through a self-assessment tool [13], lack of transparency and governance and its consequences [5], enhancement and standardization of air transport for organs [22], the

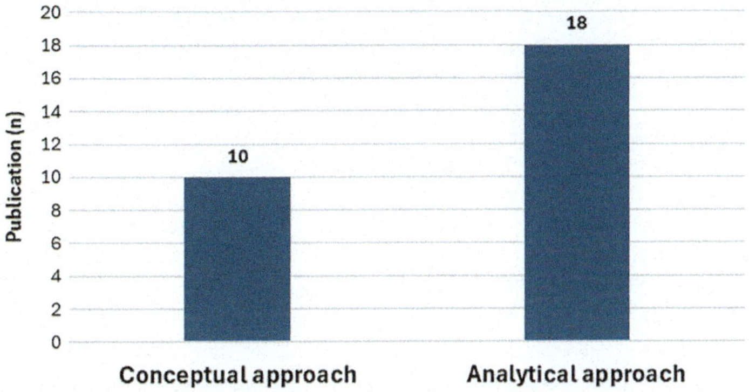

Fig. 5 Analytical and conceptual approach. *Source* The authors (2024)

future of blockchain in organ transportation to overcome inequalities [2], organ preservation process [8], how improvement can affect inequality in access to treatment [6], recycling of donated organs [9], and short- and long-term decisions on clinical and non-clinical factors [10].

Location

Transplant centers (TC) are locations that receive organs and patients for transplantation, and the most important as hospitals conforme Fig. 6. They are responsible for storing and transporting the organ, as well as performing the transplant. Studies focus on their location, organ/patient movement, and storage [1, 6, 14, 16, 22, 24, 27–36]. Hospitals play an important role in this supply chain, as their location needs to be strategic, and they must make the best decisions regarding patients. Not all hospitals specialize in organ transplants, so they need to refer patients to TCs [7, 14, 16, 24, 27–36, 47, 50]. The second most mentioned location was collection and search points (17%). These locations only search for, collect, and transport organs to TCs. This location was mentioned as it is responsible for moving organs by transport modes [13, 14, 23, 34, 35, 51]. Other study locations, representing 14% together, were logistics operation centers responsible for organ logistics [9, 39],Higher Education Institutions, for assisting in research on supply chain risk management [8, 21], and research laboratories for compatibility testing of donated organs with the patient [39].

4.2 (RQ2) What Strategies and Tools Are Being Used for Risk Management Initiatives in the Organ Donation Supply Chain?

A maioria dos autores utiliza a modelagem matemática para analisar os caminhos do ODSC como mostra a Fig. 7.

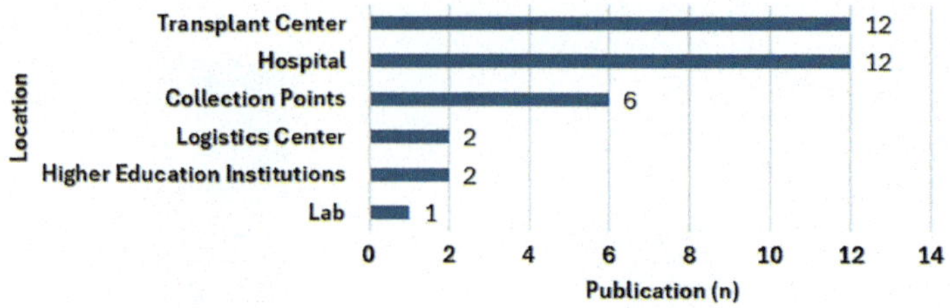

Fig. 6 Location. *Source* The authors (2024)

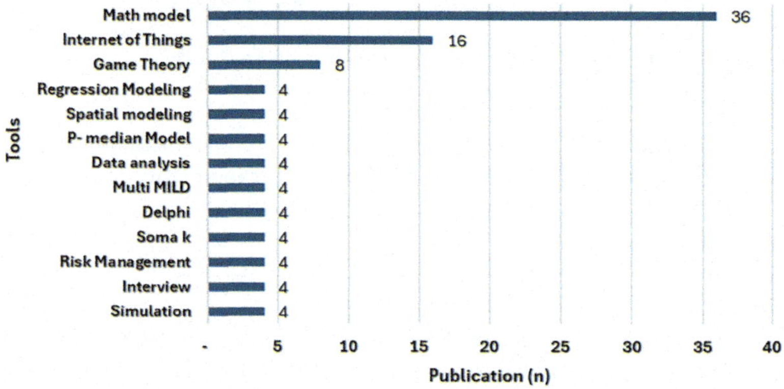

Fig. 7 Tools. *Source* The authors (2024)

Mathematical modeling was used to minimize costs [6, 21, 31], map flows and reduce movements [1, 14, 27–36], understand the interaction between team and donor [50], and increase the number of transplants [21]. The mathematical models used included network modeling [6], fuzzy models [1, 14, 31], linear and nonlinear progression models [21, 36, 50], multi-objective and multi-period models [34, 35].

Regarding IoT, the tools used included Artificial Intelligence (AI), Big Data, and Blockchain [2, 5, 30]. They employed AI within Big Data with a confidence level of 95% to minimize the supply chain in heart transplantation [30]. Blockchain was used to make processes transparent, improve governance, and overcome inequality in organ distribution [2, 5].

The game theory theoretical model was used to simulate different events and their consequences [24, 26]. Other tools and methodologies used included regression modeling [43], spatial modeling [7], p-median model [32], data analysis [39], multi MILD [51], Delphi, Soma k [9], risk analysis inventory [23], interviews [47], and simulation [38, 39].

4.3 (RQ3) What Are the Main Barriers and Facilitators Found in the Logistical Processes of Organ Transplantation?

According to the studies analyzed, the difficulty in analyzing data goes hand in hand with a lack of knowledge and both become a pressing barrier in ODSC, as shown in Fig. 8.

The difficulty was observed in obtaining data to analyze movement time between hospitals and transplant centers, identify the number of potential donors and patients who require transplantation, in addition to analyzing fragmented data on the costs involved in transplantation, and classify the results [14, 21, 26, 47]. Lack of knowledge is a barrier that impacts the aforementioned, as without prior knowledge of events, there may be a wrong interpretation. It was possible to identify the lack of knowledge as they were unable to identify what was a risk or adjust the distribution of organs to serve all those in need, they were unable to follow the implemented model, and little knowledge about the organ donation process [14, 31], A barrier that directly impacts the OD supply chain is cost, as transportation, storage, specialized and appropriate employees and locations are needed to carry out operations [7, 8, 24, 47]. Due to the few modes of transport (in some cases there is only land transport) and the distance between transplant centers and hospitals, logistics appears as a barrier [1, 10, 21, 32]. According to Palmieri et al. [30], Venanzi et al. [47], and Mikkelsen et al. [23], the lack of transparency about employees' opinions regarding the improvements implemented makes it difficult to understand whether the implementations were successful [23, 30, 47]. There is a shortage of organs for donation and a long queue of patients in need. According to Mahdi Aghazadeh [21] and Cole [7] one of the barriers to the low number of organs is the lack of public policies encouraging the practice of donation and for Misra et al. [24] and Dhakate and Joshi [9] is the family, which may prevent organ donation for religious reasons or lack of information about donation procedures. Misra et al. [24] and Sypek et al. [43] identified that the lack of information about

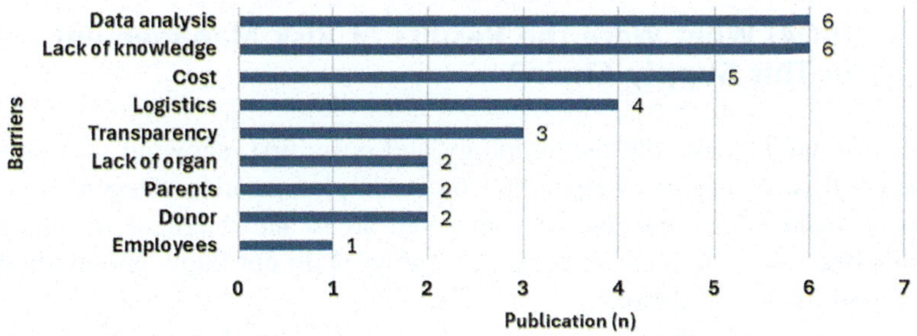

Fig. 8 Barriers. *Source* The authors (2024)

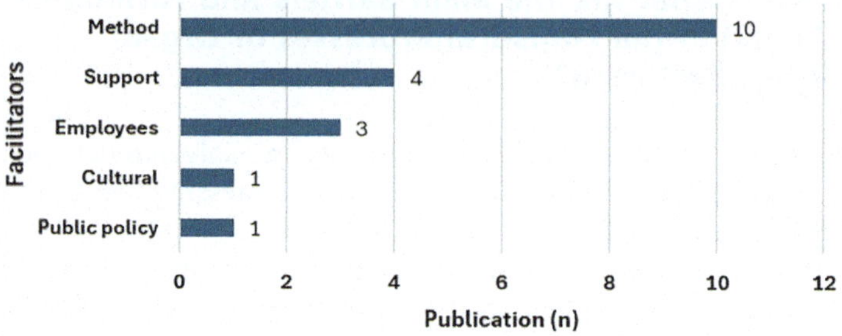

Fig. 9 Facilitators. *Source* The authors (2024)

donors makes it difficult to know about the compatibility of the donated organ with the patient. In Venanzi et al. [47], collaborators did not want to assist in the research, often omitting information and making the researchers' investigations impossible.

According to Fig. 9, the authors exposed more of the difficulties of implementation than the parts that helped to improve the ODSC. The method used can create a bottleneck in the supply chain when used incorrectly or if the choice is not appropriate for the situation. However, in research by Ahmadvand and Pishvaee [1], Rouhani et al. [34], Mantecchhini et al. [22], Nagurney [26], Venanzi et al. [47] and Anselmo et al. [2], the chosen method helped in the registration of patients in need of transplants, helped to understand the demand, identify which cases were most urgent, and to develop computational tools for recording and analyzing simple data, which do not require extensive training to use. The support, together with the implementation of the right methodology, helped to improve the OD supply chain and the participation of collaborators, providing clear information about the transplant processes [1, 8, 21, 26, 47]. Public policies helped to increase donations, as they create security for families to understand what will happen to the body of their loved one [21].

4.4 (RQ4) What Were the Results of Risk Management in This Supply Chain?

Figures 10 and 11 have the methodology and costs first, showing that its results can be positive or negative depending on its implementation. Depending on the decisions made, costs may increase in some areas and decrease in others. The same happens with the methodology, if employees do not know, the methodology applied will hinder operations.

After applying the improvements to the ODSC, it was possible to identify a 1.27% increase in taxes paid by the public network, a 1.3% increase in transportation costs in the case of rain or strong winds, the technology purchased to store the organs and increases their durability outside the human body has a high cost and

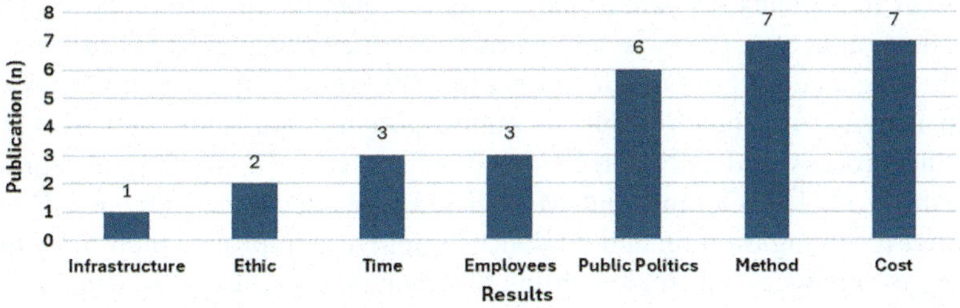

Fig. 10 Negative results. *Source* The authors (2024)

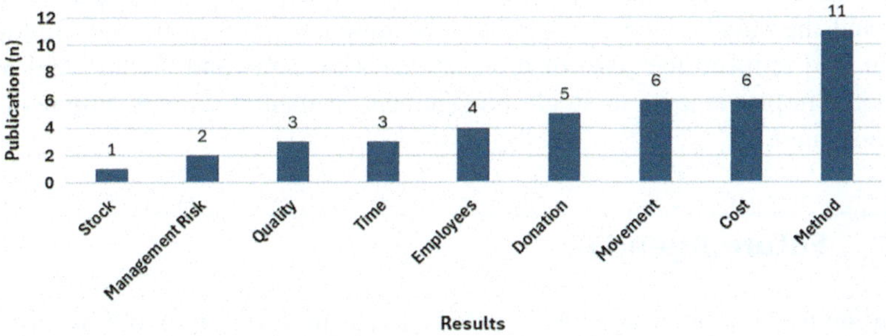

Fig. 11 Positive results. *Source* The authors (2024)

the training for the adaptation of collaborators in the improvements of the SC was expensive, and due to the high costs to improve the SC, the profit of the SC agents decreased [1, 24]; Regarding the methods used, Zhang et al. [51], Godino and Mizraji [13], de Vries [8], Mahdi Aghazadeh [21] identified that because it was complex, it required long training and its understanding was difficult and allowed the justification of the lack of organs, camouflaging the real situation. The public policies created on OD dealt superficially with regulations on the commercialization and storage of organs, due to the lack of transparency in the information collected [8, 10, 21, 22, 38]. Due to the high costs, there was no training for employees on the handling of the organs, which led to organ disposal [13, 22, 47]. Another negative result derived from the analysis was that the waiting time for a transplant often leads to the patient's death and the long duration of movements can damage the orga [21, 22, 47]. Palmieri et al. [30] identified that even after training there was a lack of professional ethics, a situation that prioritized patients with a good financial situation and Venanzi et al. [47] point out that even with improvements, hospitals remain without the infrastructure to serve as transplant centers.

It was possible to improve the supply chain through the methods used, which helped hospitals in decision-making and risk situations, identifying bottlenecks and locating the institutions that needed the donated organ [9, 10, 14, 24, 30]. There were cases in which the government reimburse hospitals that incurred additional costs with transplants, in others there was a reduction in transportation costs, a 20% reduction in storage costs, and an increase in company profits [24, 31]. It was possible to reduce excess OD movement by 20% through the use of nearby organs and an increase in donation due to public policies that addressed explanations about the process and encouraged the practice [1, 6, 7, 16, 38]. According to Colajanni et al. [6], Godino and Mizraji [13], Mantecchini [22], and Nagurney [26], after receiving training and guidance, employees improved their activities and handling of organs. After implementing the data analysis, it was possible to reduce the wait for a transplant from 16 to 2 years and the organ schematic time due to better storage conditions [8, 21, 38]. Due to improvements in storage quality, Salimian and Mousavi [36], Mantecchini et al. [22], and Vries et al. [8] noted improvements in organ quality by 17.8%, an increase in organ schematic time to 55 h, and the standardization of protocols. Jalilvand et al. [16] and Godino and Mizraji [13] reduced the risks of transparencies by 20%, and Godino and Mizraji [13] noted improvements in stock management of medicines and supplies needed for transplants.

5 Future Agenda

According to the articles analyzed, there is a growing need to model SC efficiently and sustainably, which is replicable and easy to adapt. The creation of frameworks will need to meet the needs of reducing movement time, and sharing organs through a common base for all countries [22, 32, 50]. To achieve this, Salimian and Mousavi [36] suggest using the Fuzzy tool, Colajanni et al. [6], the use of the Lagrange constant. Nagurney [26] considers it important to compare other CS with organ donation and Rouhani et al. [34] and Goli et al. [14], say it is necessary to compare cost and time in urgent and non-urgent situations. Mahdi Aghazadeh et al. [21] recommend using technologies such as AI and Machine Learning to optimize supply chains. The development of public policies that encourage organ donation and standardize procedures is a real need in many countries, requiring studies showing the best approaches and practices on how to talk to donors' families and how to act throughout the chain [9, 21]. A latent concern is regarding the storage of organs and their monitoring. De Vries et al. [8] show the importance of developing a computational model to monitor the quality of the organ while stored, and Ahmadvand and Pishavee [1] suggest the creation of a mathematical model that answers how many organs are discarded due to storage, how many people die and how many live after transplants. Many countries do not identify the patient's compatibility with the organ received, Rouhani and Amin [35] and Rouhani et al. [34] suggest taking into account the blood group of the donor and patient, creating a filter before transplantation due to the number of rejections. Anselmo et al. [2] says it is necessary to improve data analysis processes, and DLT innovation can be used. Cole [7] suggests the development of artificial organs created using a 3D printer. Study the administrative obstacles that a hospital faces when registering for organ collection [24].

6 Conclusion

This study aimed to map the state of the art of risk management initiatives in the organ donation supply chain. Therefore, bibliometric analysis was chosen as the method for this purpose. The criteria used were documents in English, in the Scopus and PubMed databases, between the years 2005 and 2023. Four research questions were investigated, and we sought to answer each RQ with appropriate methods and presented a final discussion summarizing the findings and implications.

Regarding the state of the art of risk management in the organ donation supply chain, the study identified the countries that published the most. An investigation was also conducted into the years with the highest publication rates, and despite the temporal cutoff of 2005–2023, articles addressing SCRM and OD were identified from 2013 onwards, indicating an increase in publications between 2013 and 2023. Furthermore, the study revealed the main tools and methodologies used for risk management initiatives in the organ donation supply chain, including Mathematical modeling, Internet of Things (IoT), game theoretical models, Artificial Intelligence (AI), Big Data, Blockchain, among others.

The main barriers encountered in organ transplant logistics processes included data scarcity, lack of knowledge, limited public policies, and lack of transparency in methodologies regarding information and opinions about improvements and implementations. The primary facilitator was the implemented method, which enabled the registration of patients in need of transplants, the development of computational tools, new technologies, and simpler models for data analysis. Implementation was facilitated in some institutions thanks to the support of the participating institutions themselves (hospitals, transplant centers, educational institutions), which provided an understanding of the needs, infrastructure for collection, transportation, and transplantation sites, as well as funding to improve organ supply chains. Other facilitators were the collaborators, who, due to their experience, were able to provide information about transplants.

Regarding the positive outcomes achieved, the methodologies used stood out as they enabled specialized knowledge in mathematical modeling and the complexity of methods. Cost and movement savings also emerged as positive results. As for negative outcomes, it was observed that untrained collaborators mishandled organs. Other negative results include waiting times, which can lead to patient death, or transit times, which can damage organs, lack of ethics, choosing patients based on financial status or location rather than need, and lack of hospital infrastructure to be transplant centers, leading to increased organ loss.

No similar bibliometric study was found in our search, hence this work provides a unique contribution. Having mapped the main articles, a comprehensive Systematic Literature Review with rigorous content analysis is recommended as future research. It is believed that the results obtained in this study will contribute promisingly to the scientific community and to risk management initiatives in the organ donation supply chain.

References

1. Ahmadvand S, Pishvaee MS (2018) Design and planning of organ transplantation networks. Int Ser Oper Res Manage Sci 262:211–240. https://doi.org/10.1007/978-3-319-65455-3_9
2. Anselmo A, Materazzo M, Di Lorenzo N, Sensi B, Riccetti C, Lonardo MT, Pellicciaro M et al (2023) Implementation of blockchain technology could increase equity and transparency in organ transplantation: a narrative review of an emergent tool. Transplant Int 36. https://doi.org/10.3389/ti.2023.10800
3. Berrang-ford L, Pearce T, Ford JD (2015) Abordagens de revisão sistemática para pesquisa de adaptação às mudanças climáticas. Mudança Ambiental Regional 15:755–769
4. Bowersox DJ, Stank TP, Daugherty P (1999) Lean launch: managing product introduction risk through response based logistics. J Prod Innov Manage 16(6):557–568
5. Chavez N, Kendzierskyj S, Jahankhani H, Hosseinian A (2020) Securing transparency and governance of organ supply chain through blockchain. Adv Sci Technol Secur Appl. https://doi.org/10.1007/978-3-030-50613-1_4
6. Colajanni G, Daniele P, Sciacca D (2022) Reagents and swab tests during the COVID-19 pandemic: an optimized supply chain management with UAVs. Oper Res Perspect 9. https://doi.org/10.1016/j.orp.2022.100257
7. Cole H (2021) The organ supply chain: geography and the inequalities of transplant logistics. Trans Inst Br Geogr 46(4):1008–1021. https://doi.org/10.1111/tran.12458
8. de Vries RJ, Yarmush M, Uygun K (2019) Systems engineering the organ preservation process for transplantation. Curr Opin Biotechnol 58:192–201. https://doi.org/10.1016/j.copbio.2019.05.015
9. Dhakate N, Joshi R (2020) Inhibitors in the recycling of organs and implications to the environment: an emerging economy context. Manage Environ Qual Int J 31(5):1183–1206. https://doi.org/10.1108/MEQ-10-2019-0211
10. Dhyankumar Chellappa T, Muthurathinasapathy R, Venkatesh VG, Shi Y, Islam S (2023) Location of organ procurement and distribution organization decisions and their impact on kidney allocations: a developing country perspective. Ann Oper Res 321(1–2):755–781. https://doi.org/10.1007/s10479-022-04956-1
11. Fan Y, Stevenson M (2018) Uma revisão da gestão de riscos da cadeia de suprimentos: definição, teoria e agenda de pesquisa. Jornal internacional de distribuição física e gerenciamento de logística
12. Filser LD, Silva FF, Oliveira OJ (2017) State of research and future researchtendencies in lean healthcare: a bibliometricanalysis. Scientometrics 112(2):799–816
13. Godino MM, Mizraji R (2023) Self-assessment tool and clinical audits: a way to manage organ donation and transplantation in hospital settings. Transpl Proc 55(6):1458–1462. https://doi.org/10.1016/j.transproceed.2023.02.042
14. Goli A, Ala A, Mirjalili S (2023) A robust possibilistic programming framework for designing an organ transplant supply chain under uncertainty. Ann Oper Res 328(1):493–530. https://doi.org/10.1007/s10479-022-04829-7
15. Hallikas J, Virolainen VM, Tuominen M (2002) Risk analysis and assessment in network environments: a dyadic case study. Int J Prod Econ 78(1):45–55
16. Jalilvand S, Heidari S, Mohammadnazari Z, Aghsami A, Rabbani E, Rabbani M (2023) A bi-objective organ transplant supply chain network with recipient priority considering carbon emission under uncertainty, a case study. Process Integr Optim Sustain 7(4):709–727. https://doi.org/10.1007/s41660-023-00314-1
17. Juttner U (2005) Supply chain risk management: understanding the business requirements from a practitioner perspective. Int J Logistics Manage 16(1):120–141
18. Leiras A, Brito I, Peres EQ, Bertazzo TR, Yoshizali HTY (2014) Literature review of humanitarin logistics reseach: trends and challenge. J humanitarian logistics and supply chain management, pp 95–130

19. Lewis A, Koukoura A, Tsianos GI, Gargavanis AA, Nielsen AA, Vassiliadis E (2021) Organ donation in the US and Europe: the supply vs demand imbalance. Transpl Rev. W.B. Saunders, 1 April. https://doi.org/10.1016/j.trre.2020.100585
20. Lonsdale C (1999) Effectively managing vertical supply relationships: a risk management model for outsourcing. Supply Chain Manage Int J 4(4):176–183
21. Mahdi Aghazadeh S, Mohammadi M, Naderi B (2018) Robust bi-objective cost-effective, multi-period, location-allocation organ transplant supply chain. Int J Logistics Syst Manage 29
22. Mantecchini L, Paganelli F, Morabito V, Ricci A, Peritore D, Trapani S, Montemurro A et al (2016) Transportation of organs by air: safety, quality, and sustainability criteria. Transpl Proc 48(2):304–308. https://doi.org/10.1016/j.transproceed.2015.12.050
23. Mikkelsen C, Mori G, van Walraven SM, Castrén J, Zahra S, MacLennan S, Seidel K et al (2021) How donor selection criteria can be evaluated with limited scientific evidence: lessons learned from the TRANSPOSE project. Vox Sanguinis 116(3):342–350. https://doi.org/10.1111/vox.13028
24. Misra A, Saranga H, Tripathi RR (2022) Channel choice and incentives in the cadaveric organ supply chain. Eur J Oper Res 302(3):1202–1214. https://doi.org/10.1016/j.ejor.2022.01.041
25. NEXXTO. Disponível em. https://nexxto.com/supply-chain-gestao-inteligente-de-suprimentos-para-o-setor-de-saude/. Acesso em: 12 mar. 2024
26. Nagurney A (2022) Supply chain networks, wages, and labor productivity: insights from Lagrange. Analysis and computations. J Global Optim 83(3):615–638. https://doi.org/10.1007/s10898-021-01122-y
27. Nascimento IT et al (2021) Aplicação de ferramentas de gestão enxuta na indústria 4.0: uma revisão sistemática. Jornal Independente de Gestão e Produção 12(9):s856–s864
28. Natarajarathinam M, Capar I, Narayanan A (2009) Managing suply chains in times of crisis: are views of literature and insights. Int J Phys Distrib Logistics Manage 39(7):535–573
29. Norrman A, Jansson U (2004) Ericsson´s proactive supply chain risk management approach after a serious sub-supplier accident. Int J Phys Distrib Logistics Manage 34(5):434–456
30. Palmieri V, Montisci A, Vietri MT, Colombo PC, Sala S, Maiello C, Coscioni E et al (2023) Artificial intelligence, big data and heart transplantation: actualities. Int J Med Inform. https://doi.org/10.1016/j.ijmedinf.2023.105110.
31. Rabbani M, Talebi E (2019) A comprehensive mathematical model for designing an organ transplant supply chain network under uncertainty. Int J Eng Trans B 32(6):835–841. https://doi.org/10.5829/ije.2019.32.06c.06
32. Rajmohan M, Theophilus C, Sumalatha MR, Saravanakumar S (2017) Facility location of organ procurement organisations in Indian health care supply chain management. S Afr J Ind Eng 28(1):90–102. https://doi.org/10.7166/28-1-1508
33. Rassias T, Pardaloss P (n.d.) Springer optimization and its applications, vol 167. Nonlinear analysis and global optimization
34. Rouhani S, Pishvaee MS, Zarrinpoor N (2021) A fuzzy optimization approach to strategic organ transplantation network design problem: a real case study. Decis Sci Lett 10(3):195–216. https://doi.org/10.5267/j.dsl.2021.5.001
35. Rouhani S, Amin SH (2022) A robust convex optimization approach to design a hierarchical organ transplant network: a case study. Expert Syst Appl 197. https://doi.org/10.1016/j.eswa.2022.116716
36. Salimian S, Mousavi SM (2023) A robust possibilistic optimization model for organ transplantation network design considering climate change and organ quality. J Ambient Intell Humaniz Comput 14(12):16427–16450. https://doi.org/10.1007/s12652-022-03863-4
37. Santos ACG, Reis AC, Souza CG, Santos IL, Ferreira LAF The first evidence about conceptual vs analytical lean health care research studies
38. Shoaib M, Prabhakar U, Mahlawat S, Ramamohan V (2022) A discrete-event simulation model of the kidney transplantation system in Rajasthan, India. Health Syst 11(1):30–47. https://doi.org/10.1080/20476965.2020.1848355

39. Shrestha S, Bradbury L, Boal M, Blackmur JP, Watson CJE, Taylor CJ, Forsythe JLR et al (2016) Logistical factors influencing cold ischemia times in deceased donor kidney transplants. Transplantation 100(2):422–428. https://doi.org/10.1097/TP.0000000000000844
40. Silva MEA et al (2021) Systematic review of lean thinking in education institutions. Independent J Manage Prod 12(9):s865–s882
41. Sorensen LB (2005) How risk and uncertainty is used in supply chain management: a literature study. Int J Integr Supply Manage 1(4):387–409
42. Sotoudeh-Anvari A (2022) The applications of MCDM methods in COVID-19 pandemic: a state of the art review. Appl Soft Comput 126. https://doi.org/10.1016/j.asoc.2022.109238
43. Sypek MP, Ullah S, Hughes PD, Clayton PA, McDonald SP (2019) Examining the increased rates of deceased donor kidney nonutilization in Australia: what has changed? Transplantation 103(12):2582–2590. https://doi.org/10.1097/TP.0000000000002761
44. Tang CS (2006) Perspectives in supply chain risk management. Int J Prod Econ 103(2):451–488
45. Teschke M, Naujokat H (2023) Indications for alloplastic temporomandibular joint replacement in maxillofacial surgery for benign lesions: a review of the literature and clinical cases. Front Oral Maxillofacial Med. https://doi.org/10.21037/fomm-22-41
46. Theophilus Dhyankumar C, Joe Arun C (2021) Review of organ donation and transplantation: a healthcare supply chain management perspective. SCMS J Ind Manage 18(3):39–52
47. Venanzi D, Roque Da Silva O, Palmisano A (2013) Supply chain of human organs: a case study in hospital complex in sorocaba. In: IFAC Proceedings volumes (IFAC-PapersOnline), vol 6, pp 183–189. https://doi.org/10.3182/20130911-3-BR-3021.00015
48. Wilkes DS, Egan TM, Reynolds HY (2005) Lung transplantation: opportunities for research and clinical advancement. Am J Respir Crit Care Med 172(8):944–955. https://doi.org/10.1164/rccm.200501-098WS
49. Yan Y, Liao Z, Chen X (2018) Fixed-income securities: bibliometric review with network analysis. Scientometrics 116(3):1615–1640
50. Zahiri B, Tavakkoli-Moghaddam R, Pishvaee MS (2014) A robust possibilistic programming approach to multi-period location-allocation of organ transplant centers under uncertainty. Comput Ind Eng 74(1):139–148. https://doi.org/10.1016/j.cie.2014.05.008
51. Zhang Y, Li Z, Zhao Y (2023) Multi-mitigation strategies in medical supplies for epidemic outbreaks. Socio-Econ Plan Sci 87. https://doi.org/10.1016/j.seps.2023.101516
52. Zsidisin G, Panelli A, Upton R (2000) Purchasing organization involvement in risk assessments, contingency plans, and risk management: an exploratory study. Supply Chain Manage Int J 5(4):187–198

Maria Eduarda Alves da Silva Master's student in Production and Systems Engineering at the Federal Center for Technological Education Celso Suckow da Fonseca (CEFET-RJ), in the line of research using Lean Six Sigma in supply chain Risk management. Currently, researcher at the Rio de Janeiro State Research Support Foundation (FAPERJ), developing research at the InstruLab of the Industrial Production Management department of the Federal University Institute of Education, Science and Technology of Rio de Janeiro (IFRJ), in the line Reverse Logistics research project: Development of PET filament for 3D printers.

Ingrid Teixeira do Nascimento Master's student in Production and Systems Engineering at the Federal Center for Technological Education Celso Suckow da Fonseca (CEFET-RJ), in the line of research Risk management in the health supply chain. Currently, researcher at the Rio de Janeiro State Research Support Foundation (FAPERJ), developing research at the InstruLab of the Industrial Production Management department of the Federal University Institute of Education, Science and Technology of Rio de Janeiro (IFRJ), in the line Reverse Logistics research project: Development of PET filament for 3D printers.

Fernanda Pinto Torres is a Master's student in Production and Systems Engineering at the Federal Center for Technological Education Celso Suckow da Fonseca (CEFET-RJ), specializing in Supply Chain Risk Management. Also holds a specialization in International Business Management from IBMEC in Rio de Janeiro (2014) and a Bachelor's degree in International Relations (2008). Currently, she works as a Project Control Specialist at SBM Offshore. She has experience in Project Management and Supply Chain (Procurement, International Logistics, Import, Export, and Customs compliance) in the Oil and Gas industry.

Pedro Senna holds a doctoral degree from the CEFET-RJ, in Industrial Engineering at the CEFET-RJ, Brazil. He has experience in the area of Supply Chain Management, Supply Chain Risk Management and Data Science. Professor at CEFET-RJ, Postgraduate Programme in Production Engineering and Systems (PPPRO), Department of Industrial Engineering (DEPRO). He is currently a postdoctoral researcher in industrial engineering in COPPE/PEP UFRJ under the supervision of professor Lino Guimar~aes Marujo.

Ana Carla de Souza Gomes dos Santos Holds a Ph.D. in Industrial and Systems Engineering at Federal Centre for Technological Education Celso Suckow da Fonseca (CEFET/RJ) in the lean healthcare line of research and a professor at the Federal Institute of Education, Science, and Technology of Rio de Janeiro (IFRJ), campus Niter oi. Her general field of research and experience is in Industrial Engineering, focussing on Production Management, Lean Managment, Lean Healthcare, and Service Quality.

Lino G. Marujo Received a B.Sc. degree in industrial metallurgy engineering from the Federal Fluminense University, Volta Redonda, Brazil, in 2000.

He was awarded an M.B.A. from Get ulio Vargas Foundation, Sao Paulo, Brazil in 2002, and an M.Sc.in Operations Research and Technology, from CEFET/RJ, Rio de Janeiro, Brazil, in 2003. His doctorate was completed in 2008 in naval engineering from COPPE/UFRJ, Rio de Janeiro, Brazil. He has been coordinating a research track with SCALE-MIT focussed in sustainable supply chains, He worked as a Visiting Scholar with Megacity Logistics Lab at MIT, Cambridge, MA in 2014–2015, developing models to assess cargo freight over public transport networks. He is currently an Associate Professor of Logistics and Simulation with the Department of Industrial Engineering at Polytechnic School of UFRJ, Brazil. He is also a Professor with Operations Research Program and collaborate with the Transportation Engineering Program at COPPE/UFRJ, Rio de Janeiro, Brazil. His research focuses on stochastic modelling, optimisation via simulation, data-driven decision making, and uncertainty quantification.The application areas of interest include supply chain management, logistics and transportation, urban operations research, health care services, and sustainable operations management.

Leonardo Mangia Rodrigues Ph.D. student in Production Engineering from the Federal University of Rio de Janeiro—COPPE/UFRJ, master's degree in Production Engineering from the Federal University of Rio de Janeiro—COPPE/UFRJ (2017), degree in Production Engineering from the Federal Center for Technological Education Celso Suckow da Fonseca—CEFET-RJ (2012). He is currently a professor of the Production Engineering course at Cândido Mendes University (UCAM). Has experience in the area of Production Engineering with an emphasis on Project Management and Business Process Management and Governance.

The Blood Product Supply Chain and Transfusion Network

Lamia Triqui

11

With every heart beat we live to see the sunset, with each drop of blood donated; another precious life will live to see the sunrise.

Wayne Chirisa

Abstract

The blood supply chain is a complex system that covers all the processes required to ensure a continuous, safe supply of blood from donors to patients. It encompasses several key stages: the collection of blood from donors, either in fixed collection centers or via mobile units, followed by sorting, storage, distribution, and an inventory management system to avoid shortages or excesses, taking into account the perishability of blood products. Human blood, a rare and precious resource, can only be produced by humans; no other substance or chemical method can replace it (Attari and Jami in J Intell Fuzzy Syst 35(2):2015–2033; [6]) Özener et al. in Comput Oper Res 102:10–21, [32]). It is essential for the proper functioning of the human body and vital for the maintenance of life Hamdan and Diabat (Comput Oper Res 101:130–143, [22]). However, the demand for blood by patients is uncertain and varies according to a number of unpredictable factors, such as accidents or surgical emergencies. The aim of this supply chain is to ensure that blood is available in sufficient quantity and in good condition to meet patients' needs. To ensure this availability, the hospital chain resorts to mobile collection, while minimizing losses and optimizing system efficiency. In this chapter, the author aims to propose a benchmark that takes into account all the steps involved in setting up a blood network, starting with the determination of the most important collection points

L. Triqui (✉)
Manufacturing Engineering Laboratory of Tlemcen (MELT), Abou Bekr Belkaid University of Tlemcen, Tlemcen, Algeria
e-mail: Lamia.triqui@univ-tlemcen.dz

F. Jawab (ed.), *Hospital Supply Chain*, Integrated Science 27,
https://doi.org/10.1007/978-3-031-70292-1_11

to visit and then proposing the optimal schedule of visits by introducing various constraints such as time windows, perishability characteristics, and the uncertain demands of healthcare facilities. A practical example serves as an applicative framework for the implementation of the proposed benchmark, namely the hospital logistics network of the city of Tlemcen, which serves as a support for real data. The structure of the document is given by the bellow flowchar.

Keywords

Blood donor network • Mobile blood collection • Fixed blood collection • Transfusion network optimization

Abbreviations

CPLP	Capacitated plant location problem
CRTS	Regional Transfusion Center of Casablanca
GIS	Geographic information system
GRASS	Geographic resources analysis support system
SCIR	Selective covering inventory routing

1 Introduction

Blood collection is crucial for the resilience of the chain to ensure continuity of healthcare, particularly in periods of emergency. It enables the hospital system to withstand, adapt, and recover quickly from disruptions. Specifically, regular and efficient blood collection is essential to maintain a constant supply of blood products needed for transfusions and medical treatments, ensuring blood availability in times of crisis or emergency. By responding rapidly to situations such as natural disasters or pandemics, a resilient blood supply chain ensures continued blood availability even in the most difficult circumstances. Well-organized, mobile blood collection enables operations to be rapidly adapted to changing needs, while effective inventory and demand management ensure appropriate blood levels, reducing the risk of shortages or surpluses, thereby strengthening the resilience of the hospital chain. Efficient, well-organized blood collection is a fundamental element in the resilience of the hospital chain, ensuring continuous blood availability for patients, even in emergency or crisis situations. This is why obtaining this product has become a collective priority, and the principle of blood donation and collection is in great demand and regularly renewed.

2 What Is Blood?

Blood is a vital liquid circulating in the body's blood vessels, playing an essential role in various biological functions. It is composed of several elements that can be mechanically separated into different components (cells). These include three families: white blood cells, which are part of the immune system; red blood cells, which transport oxygen; and platelets, which repair the body in case of injury or hemorrhage, all immersed in a liquid called plasma. The lifespan of blood components is very limited and varies from case to case. For example, platelets can be stored for up to five days before deteriorating, making them highly perishable. Red blood cells, the second most perishable blood component, can be stored for forty-two days [2]. The perishability of blood products complicates and increases the complexity of the supply chain, making it difficult to determine the optimal quantities of blood available for medical treatments. Knowing that blood not consumed in time will not be used and will have to undergo a respected destruction procedure, the supply of human blood remains a major challenge and must be efficient and sustainable to guarantee blood requirements, from the collection of blood from donors to the transfusion of blood to patients. In this context, we proposed a benchmark that takes into account all the stages involved in setting up a blood network. In the following sections, before presenting the proposed benchmark, we will first describe the various stages of collection and the procedures to be followed to ensure a good blood supply and an effective response to strengthen the resilience of the hospital supply chain.

3 The Blood Supply Chain

Obtaining blood is known by the concept of blood donation, which is a process by which a blood donor volunteers to have blood taken which will be stored in a blood bank before being transfused to a patient. During a blood transfusion the chain of blood products goes through several stages which can be arranged in three actions: a first action for collection, which will be carried out either in a fixed blood center (fixed collection), or through mobile collection. Then the samples obtained are sent directly to the analysis area to be sorted and stored before being supplied to a requesting establishment. This deduces that the blood product chain is described by three concatenated phases: collection, analysis and storage and finally distribution as represented by Fig. 1.

The problem encountered in the blood supply chain is highly restrictive. On one hand, it is necessary to maximize collection, as this is the only way to obtain this precious component. On the other hand, it is essential to minimize shortages and waste of blood, both in the hospital and at blood centers. Due to the perishable nature of blood, which becomes obsolete if not used within its predetermined duration, and the uncertain and unpredictable factors affecting patient consumption such as accidents and emergency surgical procedures, it is essential to avoid storing an excessive number of blood units.

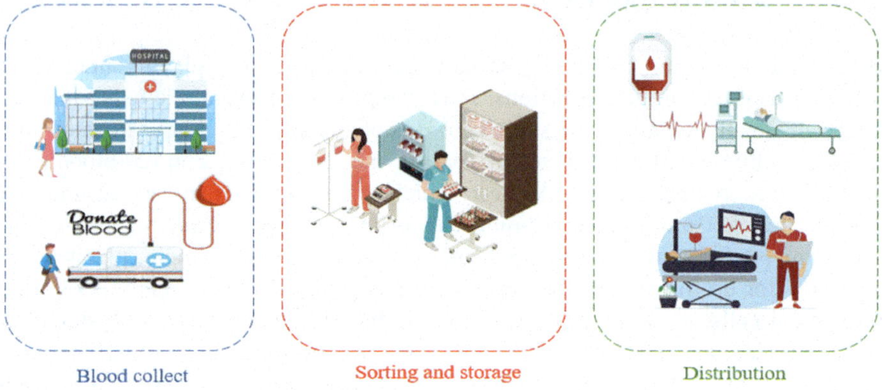

Fig. 1 The stages of the supply chain for labile blood products

3.1 The Internal Functions of the Blood Supply Chain

Blood donation generally comprises several stages starting with pre-registration, where potential donors fill in forms to check their eligibility, followed by the pre-donation interview, where the donor receives a medical consultation so that the doctor can ensure that the donor is not taking any risk, either to himself or to the receiver. Next, blood collection takes place, involving a blood sample taken from a vein in the patient's arm, and follow-up to ensure the safety and well-being of blood donors and receivers. As shown in Fig. 2

Although the blood collection lasts no more than 12 min, you have to wait 45 min between the arrival and departure of the donor to allow for administrative preparation, the pre-donation interview, the blood collection process itself, as well as the recovery time, according to information provided by the CHU of Tlemcen. However, this time may differ from system to system and from individual to individual. This information is vital for predicting the collection time windows in a given area.

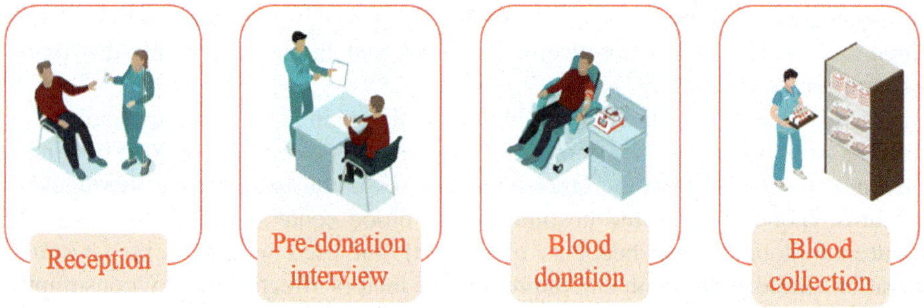

Fig. 2 Blood collection

There are criteria for giving blood, regardless of the donor's gender. Any healthy individual aged between 18 and 65 can donate blood up to 4 times a year for men and 3 times a year for women, Eskandari-Khanghahi al. [16], Rabbani et al. [35] with a minimum interval of 2 months between two consecutive donations. Each sample receives approximately 430–470 ml of blood, which is then divided into three distinct substances: packed red blood cells, packed platelets, and plasma. Once collected, blood is never transfused directly to a patient, regardless of where it is collected and its transfusion destination. Each collected bag is returned to the blood bank, which follows a standard procedure to ensure its safety from collection to prescription to the patient.

3.1.1 Analysis and Storage

Once collected, blood, it will be sent to the blood bank, which is an establishment, responsible for collecting, preparing, biologically qualifying, managing and distributing human blood and/or blood products intended for transfusion. Ganesh et al. [17], Lowalekar and Ravichandran [27], Masoumi et al. [28]. In fact, whole blood is never transfused directly to the patient, but only the component they need. After preparation, the collected sample tubes undergo a series of biological tests. Bags collected followed by product labeling to indicate compliance before being shipped and stored in appropriate locations in the blood bank for later use Blake et al. [8]. Managing this stage is a particular challenge, as it requires a large amount of information to sort out perishable products and products with high consumption and low availability.

3.1.2 Distribution/Blood Transport

When the hospital blood bank receives a specific request for blood, the blood bags are distributed to the various departments under close supervision. The blood must not change hands en route and must follow the most direct route in less than twenty minutes [12]. The counted blood is moved and stored in a designated area for transfusion to the patient. Unused blood is returned to the control unit for other purposes if it is not transfused [14, 41].

3.1.3 Destruction of Blood Products

As blood products are rare and fragile resources, it is imperative to limit their destruction as much as possible. However, destruction remains the only option for disposing of the product once it has expired or invalid product. The destruction of expired blood bags represents a bottleneck for the blood bank. This includes management tasks such as determining the type of blood product, transfusion service, start or collection date, blood product order, bag number, and cause of destruction. The destruction of blood products is unacceptable in today's transfusion-saving environment. Therefore, it is necessary to significantly reduce the proportion of blood products destroyed by implementing appropriate measures in terms of information, training, organization, and equipment.

3.2 The External Functions of the Blood Supply Chain

Blood logistics start with the collection process, which takes place upstream of the chain. Obviously, for the internal functions (analysis, sorting, and storage) to take place, it is first necessary to have the product processed and delivered, which is the blood. The only source of supply is the human being himself [28] in addition to the highly perishable characteristic, which puts more constraints on the blood product management sectors. This is why obtaining and recovering this product has become essential and must be carried out through rigorously planned plans and well-studied collection processes. In the following sections, we will define, present, and provide some information model, which helps researchers and suppliers to recover this substance while respecting vital constraints, technical constraints, and environmental constraints relating to the collection process.

3.2.1 Collection Process

The blood collection process can be carried out in two modes: either in a fixed blood center (fixed collection), or through mobile collection. The fixed centers such as hospitals, the blood transfusion post or even the health sectors where the donor presents himself to the blood banks, which are generally located near the hospitals or even inside a hospital. Which welcome the donors volunteers with completely random human cadences, it can go from zero donors for day x and around ten patients for the following day. For mobile collection, a team travels using specific trucks specially designed for collection in places, with high traffic at predetermined locations such as: town halls, schools, universities, shopping centers, etc. respecting a certain routing and a precise schedule in order to collect massive quantities of blood. Then the samples obtained are sent directly to the analysis area to be sorted and stored in appropriate locations in the blood bank for later use. Before being supplied to a requesting establishment. In this context, the distribution center is equipped with a supply regulation unit, which assesses needs and manages stocks of blood products on a daily basis. In this context, the major challenge for managers is to find the balance between the collection and consumption (distribution) of blood throughout this chain. This has prompted several researchers to invest in the supply of blood in logistics chains.

The first work on the management of the supply chain of perishable products, particularly blood products, dates back to Van Zyl [1]. In this work, the author examined the time required for blood to become obsolete and out of use for transfusion. He defined, with equations, the forecast of optimal stock in relation to stochastic demand. Cohen et al. [13] studied decision-making to determine an optimal stock level by considering two factors: the number of units of blood allocated to patients and the number of units of blood compatible with patients. [10] proposed a prototype using a Markov chain to minimize the number of expired blood units. Nahmias [30] initially studied perishable products globally and then adapted his analysis to blood products in the blood bank. His work was particularly focused on inventory management in blood banks. Prastacos [34] provides an overview of the theory and practice of blood stock management and has shown that there are advantages and disadvantages in maintaining a blood stock. Pierskalla [33] proposed strategic models, using algorithms and simulations to coordinate supply and demand, and determined optimal allocation of hospitals and donor areas to Blood Banks. Beliën and Forcé [7] have compiled the work that has been accomplished for the blood chain, with the aim of establishing traceability and providing documents in each link of the blood chain. Alfonso et al. [3] proposing different scenarios to accommodate donors at fixed sites and mobile collections, with a minimum waiting time to avoid donor abandonment. Hosseinifard and Abbasi [24] studied the stock level of a blood supply chain composed of two levels. The first level is represented by a blood bank, and the second level represents the number of hospitals. The goal was to centralize a certain number of hospitals and to analyze, the impact of costs on performance measurement. Duan and Liao [15] were particularly interested in platelets, which are one of the most perishable and least experienced components. They proposed a simulation and optimization approach with metaheuristics aiming to find the best supply policy under different scenarios to reduce the expiry rate and maintain optimal stock. Idriss et al. [25] proposed models of a complex hospital system (the regional transfusion center of Casablanca CRTS) under several possible scenarios. They valuate their performance using the EasyFit software. Gunpinar and Centeno [20] presented deterministic and stochastic integer programming models to minimize the costs of waste and shortage for red blood cells and platelets, which are the most perishable components. Rusman and Rapi [38] focused on the distribution of blood from two blood banks to seventeen hospitals in the city of Makassar in Indonesia. They presented two models taken from the CPLP problem (capacitated plant location problem), the two models aiming to minimize the total cost of the distance traveled between the two blood banks and the seventeen hospitals. Kazemi et al. [26] developed several model of inventory management in the blood bank located in Iran in several cities in order to deal with the various uncertain parameters related to blood. An iterative Branch-and-cut (B & C) was proposed to solve a certain number of numerical examples. Torrado and Barbosa-Póvoa [42] provided a literature review regarding blood bank inventory management from collection to distribution. They aimed to identify the most efficient way to supply blood based on the decision-making structure of the blood bank, whether centralized or decentralized.

Through the work in this field, scientists have deduced a taboo point concerning the quantity collected since blood is a highly perishable product, and its rarity requires massive recovery. Since the donors and recipients are not known with certainty in advance. The question arises: should we recover the maximum number of blood bags knowing that it requires special management of outdated and shortage products, generating high prices associated with the acquisition of blood with a great risk of not being transfused and subsequently being destroyed, or should collection be minimized with the risk of product unavailability Osorio et al [31]. Scientists and researchers have concluded that each geographical area needs to be equipped with a minimum number of fixed and mobile (blood-mobile) collection centers for effective and efficient management, ensuring optimal satisfaction of demand while minimizing losses and improving patients' quality of life. This problem can be characterized by mobile blood collection and by the location of blood donation vehicles within existing fixed sites. Mobile blood collection is established by locating blood collection vehicles in predefined locations based on demographic statistics, disease zones, etc.

3.2.2 Location of Mobile Collection

A team travels using specific trucks or special vehicles equipped with beds for donors and devices specially for collection in places with a high population density in predetermined locations such as: town halls, schools, universities, shopping centers, respecting a certain routing and a precise schedule as shown in Fig. 3.

The objective of mobile collection is to gather large quantities of blood while considering the anticipated demands of future periods. Given that the demands for various paradigms requiring human blood are unpredictable and vary significantly from day to day and from one period to another, mobile collection must be meticulously planned to ensure sufficient quantities are available when needed. It is imperative to monitor unused products closely as they will be automatically discarded if not consumed within their specified time interval. This dual constraint adds complexity to the system, requiring robust optimization of the blood network.

Mobile collection is an effective means of blood supply as it enhances donors' access to collection sites by strategically locating bloodmobiles close to donors' residences. This also fosters donor loyalty, ensuring regular and high-quality supply of labile blood products, as the requirement for regular visits to a site is integrated into the primary tour planning. To establish a collection network, collection points must first be identified in a region using coordinate information systems to pinpoint areas of high density and availability. Subsequently, planning must be undertaken to determine the areas to be visited. As each zone comprises several potential sites, planning must establish the optimal routing within a zone,

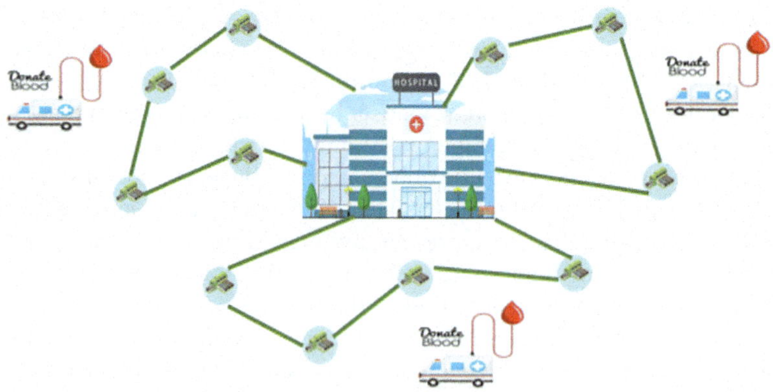

Fig. 3 Mobile collection

considering time windows for operational tasks such as directly transporting collected blood to the blood bank. Another temporal constraint involves scheduling regular visits spaced out over time for the same region. The time between two successive visits to the same site is significant, considering that donors can only donate every three months. Hence, this constraint plays a crucial role in planning different routing strategies for blood mobiles between zones and within a zone. Given these considerations, the location of mobile donation sites has been a topic of interest for several researchers, including Chaiwuttisak [11], Alfonso et al. [4], Zahiri et al. [43], Ramezanian and Behboodi [36], and Arvan et al. [5]. For instance, Alfonso et al. [3] examined both mobile and fixed blood collection and used Petri net models to describe various blood collection processes, donor behaviors, and human resource requirements. They also employed simulation approaches to determine appropriate planning and donor nomination strategies. Additionally, Fahiminia et al. studied emergency blood supply during natural disasters, considering blood transfusion centers, donation sites, and hospitals with stochastic demands. Various authors have also explored the problem of routing mobile donation sites, including Mobasher et al. [29], Şahinyazan et al. [40], Ganesh et al. [17], Ghandforoush and Sen [18], and Gunpinar and Centeno [21].

Furthermore, the problem of locating and routing mobile donation sites has been examined by, Rabbani et al. [35] and Zahiri et al. [43]. Zahiri et al. [43] formulated the problem using a mixed integer linear program, considering that the quantity of donations and demand are stochastic parameters. Rabbani created a fuzzy mathematical programming model to obtain solutions for small instances and proposed simulated annealing for larger instances. Şahin et al. [39] were among the first to advocate for the systematic use of blood mobiles in Turkey and used integer programming models to create a mathematical model of regionalizing blood transfusion services for the Turkish Red Crescent population. Heidari-Fathian and Pasandideh [23] conducted research in 2017 with the aim of proposing a mathematical model for the creation of a reliable blood supply chain network. Three main levels make up this network: main blood transfusion centers, demountable collection centers, and mobile blood transfusion centers. Rabbani et al. [35] published two mathematical models to cover the blood collection scheduling problem. The first model is a multi-objective fuzzy mathematical program in which mobile blood locations are taken into account with the aim of minimizing operational costs and maximizing the potential amount of blood collected. The second model is a vehicle routing problem with time windows that studies the routing of shuttles. Ramírez and Labadie [37] represented the mobile blood collection system as a problem with benefits for vehicle routing. The aim is to reduce costs, waste, and total routing. The problem is represented using a two-stage scenario-based stochastic model. Finally, in 2018, Ghasemi and Bashiri [19] assumed that the number of blood collection vehicles was determined in the first stage before determining the rest. To verify model validation, SCIR (selective covering inventory routing) was introduced to supply whole blood.

3.2.3 Identification of Collection Points in a Region (City)

To organize and manage the blood drive over a specific planning horizon, you need to determine the location, dates, and times that match the potential of the collection site and the donors. First of all, you need to select all the blood collection points in a region (city), known as donation sites. To do this, you need to start by drawing a map of the city using Geographic Information System (GIS) software. This provides a detailed and more global view of the city and makes it easier to read the elements relating to a collection, such as locations and their density, the characteristics of their immediate environment, and the potential for donors. In the second stage, bloodmobiles are assigned to the right places (collection points) at the right time. Each collection point must be visited once and only once by a single bloodmobile. And each vehicle must visit one or more collection points. To obtain a conjunction (collection point-mobile site) taking into account a maximum duration of visit and a predefined importance given to each site according to the population rate in the sampling area. Questions of location and routing are first linked to the identification of blood collection points. The second part consists of proposing an optimal routing plan for blood collection vehicles over a planning horizon.

In this chapter, we intend to propose a benchmark that takes into account all stages of blood network establishment, starting with the determination of the most important collection points to visit and then proposing the optimal schedule of visits by introducing various constraints such as time windows, perishability characteristics, and uncertain demands from healthcare facilities.

a. **System geographic coordinate systems by GIS**

The geographic coordinate system provides both a detailed and a more global view of the city. Originally, Quantum GIS was intended as a visualization tool for GRASS (Geographic Resources Analysis Support System) data. Today, this GIS has developed into a computerized system for collecting, organizing, managing, manipulating, processing, analyzing, combining, developing, and presenting geographically localized information from a variety of sources, with a particular emphasis on spatial management. GIS can contain a vast amount of cartographic data, making it quick and easy to search. It enables localized data to be captured, stored, retrieved, queried, analyzed, and displayed.

These points are then evaluated according to a set of predefined criteria. These criteria can include site visibility, site accessibility, security, etc., and are the main conditions that must be met at each collection point. Then, assign an importance (weight) to each criterion on a predefined scale for the final selection of collection points. Based on the mesh technique, which involves the division of geographical space into several contiguous single units. These units are all adjacent to each other and do not overlap. To visualize a simple mesh, we can imagine a grid. The mesh can be regular, with meshes of identical shapes and dimensions as shown in Fig. 4, or irregular, with meshes of heterogeneous shapes and dimensions [9].

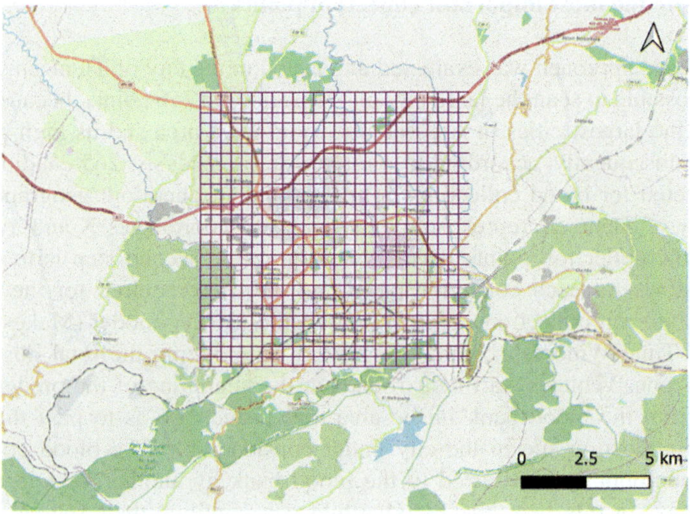

Fig. 4 Map representing the city of Tlemcen with mesh

The final selection of collection points, which can be schools, universities, employers in the public and private sectors, community organizations, public establishments such as centers sports, places of worship and shopping centers (Fig. 5).

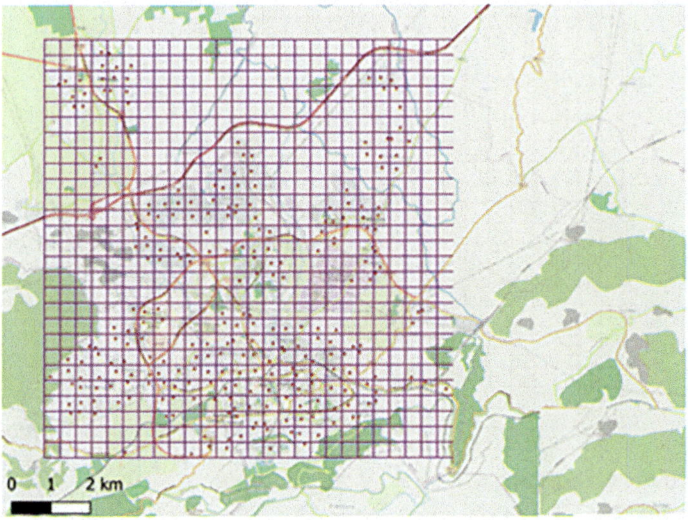

Fig. 5 Map represents the chosen collection points

b. **Example the most important collection points**

The proposed approach was evaluated and tested in the city of Tlemcen. The mesh made it possible to scan the large city of Tlemcen over 756 points, because this city is one of the largest cities in Algeria, due to its large area and its high population density. Subsequently, according to a multi-criteria analysis, 265 candidate points were selected for blood collections. These points are therefore geographical sites of the city of Tlemcen, represented by points with coordinates X and Y (Fig. 6).

Once the collection points have been chosen, the second step is to define the time windows for each collection point and the time required for the collection operation at each collection point. Based on the MPTW model (Makespan Problem with Time Windows), which consists of minimizing the total duration of a tour in a zone. Vehicles start their rounds at the beginning of the predefined time horizon from the blood bank in the area under study, so as to pass through any candidate collection site in the city under consideration. The blood collected by each bloodmobile is transferred to the blood bank by another vehicle at the end of each day. In this way, the bloodmobile can continue their rounds and don't need to return to the blood bank until the end of the predefined horizon. All the while respecting time windows and travel time. Once the available points have

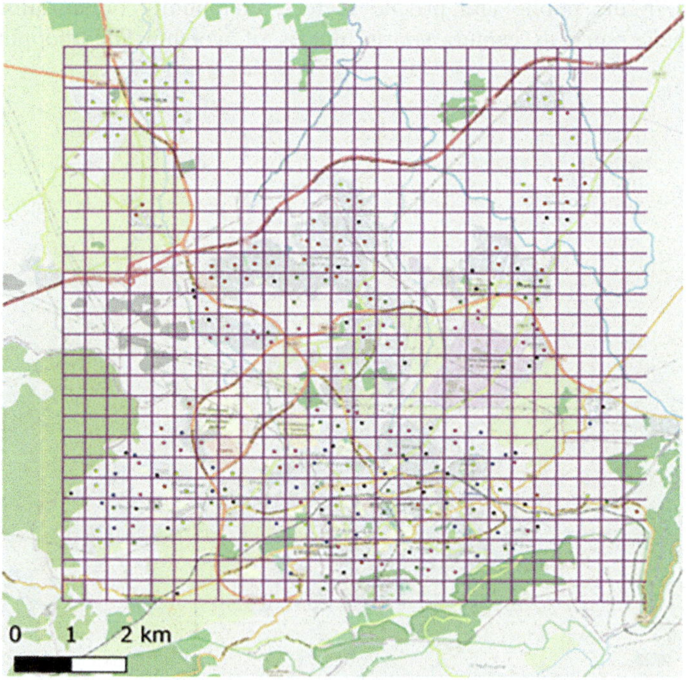

Fig. 6 Map represents most important collection points

been selected, each vehicle has the maximum amount of time to carry out its visits and collections, while respecting the service time at each point and the delivery deadlines.

3.2.4 Location/Allocation of Blood Mobiles

Consider an undirected graph G = (V, E), where V = {0, 1, ..., n} is the set of n + 1 nodes. Node 0 represents the blood bank and the set V corresponds to the locations of the collection sites. Each node is associated with an importance Imp_i, $\forall\, i \in V$ and the system has a fleet K of vehicles. Initially the blood bank can meet the demand from collection points. Each vehicle $k \in K$ can only visit a subset $Vk \subset V^+$. A routing is assigned to each vehicle a route such that: (a) the nodes visited by vehicle $k \in K$ are found in the set Vk; (b) each node must be visited exactly once; and (c) the importance of assigned nodes is maximized. We formulate a mixed integer program for the VRPCC as follows:

- **Mathematical modeling**

i	**index of the blood** collection point where $i \in \{1,...n\}$.
k	vehicle index (mobile site) where $k \in \{1,...m\}$.
not	Number of collection points.
m	Number of vehicles (mobile site).
cm	Number of vehicles available in the system.
Imp_i	The multi-criteria value of collection point i (importance).
t_i	Service time required to operate a collection at point i (number of collection days for collection point).
Td_i:	Downtime of collection points i.
$_{Max}T$:	Maximum vehicle time (maximum visit time).
w_i:	The variable that takes the value 1 if the collection site is considered very essential.
X_i	$\begin{cases} 1 \text{ if site i is visited} \\ 0 \text{ else} \end{cases}$
Z_k	$\begin{cases} 1 \text{ if vehicle k is chosen to visit collection point i} \\ 0 \text{ else} \end{cases}$
Y_i^k	$\begin{cases} 1 \text{ if site i is visited by vehicle k} \\ 0 \text{ else} \end{cases}$

- **Objective function**

$$\text{Max } F1 = \sum_{i=1}^{n} \text{Imp}_i * x_i \qquad (1)$$

- **Under the constraints**

$$\sum_{k=1}^{m} y_i^k = x_i \quad \forall\, i \in \{1, \ldots n\} \tag{2}$$

$$\sum_{i}^{n} t_i \, * \, y_i^k \le T_{\max} \, * \, z_k \quad \forall j \in \{1, \ldots k\} \tag{3}$$

$$\sum_{k=1}^{m} Td_i \, * \, y_i^k \le T_{\max} * z_k \quad \forall j \in \{1, \ldots k\} \tag{4}$$

$$\sum_{k=1}^{k} y_i^k \ge w_i \, * \, x_i \quad \forall\, i \in \{1, \ldots n\} \tag{5}$$

$$\sum_{k=1}^{m} z_k = Cm \tag{6}$$

$$x_i \in \{0, 1\}, y_i^k \in \{0, 1\}, z_k \in \,, \; z_k \in \{0, 1\} \quad \forall\, i \in \{1, \ldots n\}, \quad \forall j \in \{1, \ldots k\} \tag{7}$$

The mathematical model is made up of an objective function given by Eq. (1), the latter makes it possible to maximize the importance of a donor site (collection points).

The Constraint (2) imposes that each point is visited only once. Each mobile site can visit multiple points. This constraint therefore makes it possible to determine the coupling (vehicle point). The Constraint (3) makes it possible not to exceed the maximum time of the visit to point i with the satisfaction of the necessary service time of a point. Constraint (4) makes it possible to take into account a certain time of unavailability of the points and not to exceed the maximum time for visiting these points. Constraint (5) consists of forcing the visit of points which may not be available at a certain time but which are very essential. Constraint (6) indicates that only available vehicles are chosen to visit the points. Constraint (7) imposes non-negativity and binary restrictions.

3.2.5 Localization of Mobile Sites Content of Fixed Sites

To address the major challenge for managers, which is to find a balance between collection and consumption in both mobile and fixed collection modes. The network considered is made up of a blood bank and several candidate blood collection sites the starting point will be the blood bank, and the vehicles will circulate from one site to another respecting the time windows. While respecting that a site already used it will not be used in the following period; obviously, the collected bags will be transferred or to the blood bank and at the end of the circuit the Bloodmobile returns to the starting point, which is the blood bank. Thus, the model is formulated as follows:

- **Mathematical modeling**

t	Set of periods indexed by t where t ϵ T.
Bo	Set of localized (open) bloodmobiles during period t.
Bff	Set of non-localized (closed) bloodmobiles in period t.
i	Set of potential sites for locating bloodmobiles indexed by i such that: ∀ t : i= Bo+Bf.
L	Set of blood donor locations indexed by l.
T	Number pf points t.
Nbl	Number of bloodmobiles located.
Nt_t	Number of bloodmobile trips to the blood bank in period t.
Dist1	Distance between the bloodmobile i and the blood bank.
$Dist2_{i,i'}$	Distance between bloodmobiles i and i′.
D_t	The blood bank demand at period t.
Sci	Unit storage cost in the bloodmobile i.
Scb	Unit storage cost in the blood bank.
This	Storage capacity of the bloodmobile i.
Cb	Storage capacity of the blood bank.
Qc_i^t	Quantity of blood collected in bloodmobile i during period t.
Qb^t	Quantity of blood collected in blood bank during period t.
X_i^t	$\begin{cases} 1 \text{ if bloodmobile i is located in period t} \\ 0 \quad \text{else} \end{cases}$
$Y_{i,i'}^t$	$\begin{cases} 1 \text{ if bloodmobile i is moved to location i}' \text{ during period t} \\ 0 \quad \text{else} \end{cases}$

- **Objective function**

$$\text{Min } F3 = \sum_{t\in T}\sum_{i\in I} Qc_i^t * Sc_i + \sum_{t\in T} Qb^t * Scb + 2 * Nt_t * \sum_{t\in T}\sum_{i\in I} Dist1_i * X_i^t + \sum_{t=2}^{T}\sum_{i\in Bo^{t-1}}\sum_{i'\in Bf^{t-1}} Dist2_{i\,i'} * Y^t_{i\,i'} \tag{8}$$

The objective function (8) is to minimize the total cost, which includes the storage cost and the cost of moving the bloodmobiles from their location to the blood bank.

- **Under the constraints**

$$\sum_{i\in I} X_i^t = Nbl \quad \forall t \tag{9}$$

$$Qc_i^t \leq C_i * X_i^t \quad \forall i, \forall t \tag{10}$$

$$Qb^t \leq Cb \quad \forall t \tag{11}$$

$$\sum_{i \in I} Qc_i^t + Qb^t \geq D_t \quad \forall t \tag{12}$$

$$X_i^t = 1 - X_i^{t-1} \quad \forall i \in Bo^{t-1}, \quad \forall t \geq 2 \tag{13}$$

$$\sum_{i \in Bo^{t-1}} Z^t_{i\,i'} \leq X_{i'}^t \quad \forall i' \in Bf^{t-1}, \quad \forall t \geq 2 \tag{14}$$

$$\sum_{i' \in Bf^{t-1}} Z^t_{i\,i'} = 1 \quad \forall i \in Bo^{t-1}, \quad \forall t \geq 2 \tag{15}$$

$$\sum_{i \in Bo^{t-1}} \sum_{i' \in Bf^{t-1}} Y^t_{i\,i'} = 1 \quad \forall t \geq 2 \tag{16}$$

$$Z^t_{i\,i'} = 0 \quad \forall i \in I, \quad \forall i' \in Bo^{t-1}, \quad \forall t \geq 2 \tag{17}$$

$$Qb^t \in N, \quad Qc_i^t \in N \quad \forall i, \quad \forall t \tag{18}$$

$$X_i^t \in \{0, 1\}, \quad Y^t_{i\,i'} \in \{0, 1\} \quad \forall i, \forall i', \quad \forall t \tag{19}$$

Constraints (9), (10) and (11) ensure the optimal selection of the number of vehicles by determining their positions at the sites to be visited during period t, as well as the quantity of blood bags collected by either the fixed or mobile center, thereby ensuring the satisfaction of demand as expressed by constraint (12). Once a site has been visited, it must remain inactive during the following period, as mandated by constraint (13). The movement of collection vehicles from one location to another is guaranteed by constraint (14). Constraints (15), (16), and (17) specify that each vehicle is assigned to a single open site during period t. Constraints (18) and (19) define the nature of the decision variables.

Various challenges were identified and addressed, highlighting the characteristics of the modeling aspects of collection circuits, taking into account the risk of uncertainty, and reducing the negative impact on the patient (for example: delays). Respecting the strategic, tactical and operational decisions of the blood chain. The design of the blood collection network, and the allocation of optimal locations with rotary routing and planning, represents an economic and social pillar by excellence that greatly improves human survival and provides care units with more favorable conditions for saving lives.

4 Conclusion

Blood is a perishable product, where the demand and supply of these products are highly uncertain. These factors contribute to the complexity of modeling and managing the labile blood chain, which aims to enhance the design and planning of collection networks. Generally, poor management of blood supply chains leads to shortages, as the quantity collected in blood centers often remains insufficient. The management of the blood product supply chain and the persistent reliance on fixed collection influences this. Although it is widely acknowledged that blood is a precious resource that cannot be replaced, the costs of collection are often overlooked and disregarded. However, concerning the mobile system for this valuable product, ensuring suitable conditions and timely delivery are crucial to enhancing network performance.

In this chapter, the author underscores the importance of strategically locating both fixed and mobile blood collection sites within a defined time frame. Precise planning of blood transfusion sites is vital in hospital chains, as blood availability is critical for saving lives. However, patient blood consumption remains uncertain and unpredictable, highlighting the primary mission of the blood supply chain: to collect and process blood to meet patient needs.

Based on the analysis provided, the author concludes that for optimal effectiveness, mobile sites must be strategically located in public areas according to defined criteria such as density, security, accessibility, and visibility. The primary objective is to identify the best locations for bloodmobiles to meet the stochastic demand of patients while adhering to constraints related to capacity, storage, and blood distribution. To determine the required number of bloodmobiles circulating daily in various locations to collect necessary blood, the author presents several models aimed at ensuring blood supply in a given region while minimizing travel distances a significant challenge in the literature. Additionally, due to the perishable nature of blood, an effective inventory policy seeks to maximize satisfaction and minimize expired blood.

References

1. Van Zyl GJ (1963) Inventory control for perishable commodities. North Carolina State University, Department of Statistics
2. Abbasi B, Hosseinifard SZ (2014) On the issuing policies for perishable items such as red blood cells and platelets in blood service. Decis Sci 45(5):995–1020
3. Alfonso E, Augusto V, Xie X (2015) Mathematical programming models for annual and weekly bloodmobile collection planning. IEEE Trans Autom Sci Eng 12(1):96–105. https://doi.org/10.1109/TASE.2014.2329571
4. Alfonso E, Xie X, Augusto V, Garraud O (2013) Modelling and simulation of blood collection systems: improvement of human resources allocation for better cost-effectiveness and reduction of candidate donor abandonment. Vox Sang 104(3):225–233
5. Arvan M, Tavakkoli-Moghaddam R, Abdollahi M (2015) Designing a bi-objective, multiproduct supply chain network for blood supply. Uncertain Supply Chain Manag 3:57–68. https://doi.org/10.5267/j.uscm.2014.8.004

6. Attari MYN, Jami EN (2018) Robust stochastic multi-choice goal programming for blood collection and distribution problem with real application. J Intell Fuzzy Syst 35(2):2015–2033
7. Beliën J, Forcé H (2012) Supply chain management of blood products: a literature review. Eur J Oper Res 217(1):1–16
8. Blake JT, Hardy M, Delage G, Myhal G (2013) Déjà-vu all over again: using simulation to evaluate the impact of shorter shelf life for red blood cells at Héma-Québec. Transfusion 53(7):1544–1558. https://doi.org/10.1111/j.1537-2995.2012.03947.x
9. Bozon N, Mohammadi B (2009) GIS-based atmospheric dispersion modelling: forecasting the pesticide atmospheric spray drift from a vineyard plot to a watershed. Appl Geomatics 1:59–74
10. Brodheim E, Prastacos GP (1979) The Long Island blood distribution system as a prototype for regional blood management. Interfaces 9(5):3–20
11. Chaiwuttisak P (2015) Blood supply chain and logistics: a case study in Thailand (Doctoral dissertation, University of Southampton)
12. Cloutier MS, Apparicio P, Dubé J, Charbonneau J, Delage G (2012) Regional variation in the modeling of donation frequency: the case of Héma-Québec, Canada. Transfusion 52(11):2329–2338
13. Cohen MA, Or I, Pierskalla WP, Yen H (1978) Regionalization and regional management strategies for the blood banking system: an overview. In: The logistics of blood transfusion therapy: symposia proceedings, vol 1, p 219. Department of Health, Education, and Welfare, Public Health Service, National Institutes of Health
14. Dehghani M, Abbasi B (2018) An age-based lateral-transshipment policy for perishable items. Int J Prod Econ 198:93–103
15. Duan Q, Liao TW (2013) A new age-based replenishment policy for supply chain inventory optimization of highly perishable products. Int J Prod Econ 145(2):658–671
16. Eskandari-Khanghahi M, Tavakkoli-Moghaddam R, Taleizadeh AA, Amin SH (2018) Designing and optimizing a sustainable supply chain network for a blood platelet bank under uncertainty. Eng Appl Artif Intell 71:236–250
17. Ganesh K, Narendran TT, Anbuudayasankar SP (2014) Evolving cost-effective routing of vehicles for blood bank logistics. Int J Logist Syst Manage 17(4):381–415
18. Ghandforoush P, Sen TK (2010) A DSS to manage platelet production supply chain for regional blood centers. Decis Support Syst 50(1):32–42. https://doi.org/10.1016/j.dss.2010.06.005
19. Ghasemi E, Bashiri M (2017, February) A selective covering-inventory-routing problem to the location of bloodmobile to supply stochastic demand of blood. In: 13th International Conference on Industrial Engineering (IIEC2017)
20. Gunpinar S, Centeno G (2015) Stochastic integer programming models for reducing wastages and shortages of blood products at hospitals. Comput Oper Res 54:129–141
21. Gunpinar S, Centeno G (2016) An integer programming approach to the bloodmobile routing problem. Transp Res Part E Logistics Transp Rev 86:94–115
22. Hamdan B, Diabat A (2019) A two-stage multi-echelon stochastic blood supply chain problem. Comput Oper Res 101:130–143
23. Heidari-Fathian H, Pasandideh SHR (2018) Green-blood supply chain network design: robust optimization, bounded objective function & Lagrangian relaxation. Comput Ind Eng 122:95–105
24. Hosseinifard Z, Abbasi B (2018) The inventory centralization impacts on sustainability of the blood supply chain. Comput Oper Res 89:206–212
25. Idriss B, Saadi J, Bellabdaoui A (2014) Apport de la simulation dans les Centres de transfusion sanguine transfusion sanguine
26. Kazemi SM, Rabbani M, Tavakkoli-Moghaddam R, Shahreza FA (2017) Blood inventory-routing problem under uncertainty. J Intell Fuzzy Syst 32(1):467–481
27. Lowalekar H, Ravichandran N (2017) A combined age-and-stock-based policy for ordering blood units in hospital blood banks. Int Trans Oper Res 24(6):1561–1586

28. Masoumi AH, Yu M, Nagurney A (2017) Mergers and acquisitions in blood banking systems: a supply chain network approach. Int J Prod Econ 193:406–421. https://doi.org/10.1016/j.ijpe.2017.08.005
29. Mobasher A, Ekici A, Özener OÖ (2015) Coordinating collection and appointment scheduling operations at the blood donation sites. Comput Ind Eng 87:260–266
30. Nahmias S (1982) Perishable inventory theory: a review. Oper Res 30(4):680–708
31. Osorio AF, Brailsford SC, Smith HK (2018) Whole blood or apheresis donations? A multi-objective stochastic optimization approach. Eur J Operat Res 266(1):193–204
32. Özener OÖ, Ekici A, Çoban E (2019) Improving blood products supply through donation tailoring. Comput Oper Res 102:10–21
33. Pierskalla WP (2004) Supply chain management of blood banks. Operations research and health care: a handbook of methods and applications, pp 103–145
34. Prastacos GP (1984) Blood inventory management: an overview of theory and practice. Manage Sci 30(7):777–800
35. Rabbani M, Farrokhi-Asl H, Asgarian B (2017) Solving a bi-objective location routing problem by a NSGA-II combined with clustering approach: application in waste collection problem. J Ind Eng Int 13:13–27
36. Ramezanian R, Behboodi Z (2017) Blood supply chain network design under uncertainties in supply and demand considering social aspects. Transport Res Part E Logist Transp Rev 104:69–82
37. Ramírez AP, Labadie N (2017, October) Stochastic inventory control and distribution of blood products. In: Proceedings of the international conference on industrial engineering and operations management Bogota, Colombia
38. Rusman M, Rapi A (2014) Blood banks location model for blood distribution planning in Makassar city. In: Proceedings of the Asia Pacific industrial engineering & management systems conference 2014
39. Şahin G, Süral H, Meral S (2007) Locational analysis for regionalization of Turkish Red Crescent blood services. Comput Oper Res 34(3):692–704
40. Şahinyazan FG, Kara BY, Taner MR (2015) Selective vehicle routing for a mobile blood donation system. Eur J Oper Res 245(1):22–34
41. Seheult JN, Shaz B, Bravo M, Croxon H, Devine D, Doncaster C, Field S, Flanagan P, Germain M, Grégoire Y, Kamel H, Karafin M, Kelting N, Lewis M, O'Brien C, Murphy MF, Rossmann S, Sayers M, Shinar E, Takanashi M, Titlestad K, Yazer MH (2018) Changes in plasma unit distributions to hospitals over a 10-year period. Transfusion 58(4):1012–1020. https://doi.org/10.1111/trf.14526
42. Torrado A, Barbosa-Póvoa A (2022) Towards an optimized and sustainable blood supply chain network under uncertainty: a literature review. Cleaner Logis Supply Chain 3:100028
43. Zahiri B, Torabi SA, Mohammadi M, Aghabegloo M (2018) A multi-stage stochastic programming approach for blood supply chain planning. Comput Ind Eng 122:1–14. https://doi.org/10.1016/j.cie.2018.05.041

Lamia Triqui is currently an Associate Professor in the Faculty of Technology within the Industrial Engineering Department at Aboubekr Belkaïd University of Tlemcen. She obtained her Doctorate degree from the Laboratory for Sciences of Information and Systems (LSIS) in Marseille, France, and another Doctorate in Manufacturing Engineering. Her current degrees include HDR from the University of Tlemcen. Her main research interests lie in the field of supply chain management, Operations Research, and Game Theory. Her research aims to propose new learning management systems integrating cutting-edge technologies such as artificial intelligence (AI), machine learning (ML), blockchain, and mixed reality (MR) to design and implement intelligent industrial systems.

Medical Waste Management: From a Literature Review to a Conceptual and Multidimensional Framework

12

Ahmed Chtioui, Imane Bouhaddou, and Asmaa Benghabrit

Abstract

Medical Waste Management (MWM) is one of the most critical processes in the Hospital Supply Chain (HSC). This criticality was revealed during the Covid-19 crisis, as Medical Waste (MW) can be a factor favoring infection if they are poorly managed. In developing countries, this logistical activity is generally managed in a hazardous manner, posing a real danger to patients, healthcare staff, the population and, above all, the environment. The aim of this paper is to present an analysis of existing literature on MWM, before proposing a conceptual and multidimensional Framework for managing this type of waste. To do this, we will first delineate the MWM process in HSC, then carry out a literature review to identify research gaps, particularly in relation to the dimensions targeted by the study namely sustainability, digitalization, risk management, integration, performance, and resilience, which will enable us to develop a Conceptual and Multidimensional Framework for MWM. Which Framework provides considerable background in this area and will therefore serve as a roadmap for subsequent research work, but also a practical guide for practitioners and managers wishing to implement integrated, safe, efficient and responsible management methods for their MW.

A. Chtioui (✉) · I. Bouhaddou
L2M3S Laboratory ENSAM, Moulay Ismail University, Meknes, Morocco
e-mail: ahmed.chtioui79@gmail.com

I. Bouhaddou
e-mail: i.bouhaddou@umi.ac.ma

A. Benghabrit
LMAID Laboratory, L2M3S Laboratory, ENSMR, Rabat, Morocco

F. Jawab (ed.), *Hospital Supply Chain*, Integrated Science 27,
https://doi.org/10.1007/978-3-031-70292-1_12

Keywords

Medical waste management • Hospital supply chain • MWM literature review • MWM conceptual framework

Abbreviations

AHP	Hierarchical analytical process
AI	Artificial intelligence
CREA	Clinical risk and error analysis
EPI	Environmental performance index
FMEA	Failure mode and effects analysis
FTA	Fault tree analysis
GPS	Global positioning system
GA	Genetic algorithm
HACCP	Hazard analysis critical control point
HDI	Human development index
HSC	Hospital supply chain
ISM	Interpretive structural modeling
IOT	Internet of things
MWM	Medical Waste Management
MW	Medical waste
PHA	Process hazard analysis
RFID	Radio frequency identification
ResNeXt	Residual networks next
US EPA	United States Environmental Protection Agency
WHO	World Health Organization

1 Introduction

Medical waste management (MWM) is a vital process in all healthcare establishments that requires effective techniques to prevent health risks, comply with regulations, and reduce environmental damage [1]. Medical waste (MW) is considered the world's second most hazardous waste, following radiation. Sharps, human body and tissue pieces, blood, chemicals, pharmaceutical rubbish, and medical devices, both hazardous and non-hazardous, radioactive materials add to the amount of waste generated in healthcare institutions [2]. Thus, mismanaged MW poses significant dangers to human health and the environment. The dilemma is worse in underdeveloped countries, where neither resources nor technologies are adequate to address the situation. Furthermore, MW has not received enough attention in many nations, where it is still handled and disposed of simultaneously with domestic waste, presenting significant health risks to health-care staff, municipal workers, the public, and the environment [3]. The medical business has grown significantly over the last decade, resulting in a huge increase in MW overall [4]. The unanticipated COVID-19 pandemic has compounded the issue with a projected rise in COVID-19 associated MW of 3.4 kg cap–1d–1 globally [5].

Faced with these worrying facts, the research work that has dealt with MWM remains, to date, inadequate, particularly as regards the development of theories and concepts. Most of the contributions are case studies practically evaluating the medical waste process (production rates, costs and expenses incurred, means of waste treatment and disposal, etc.) in countries, regions and cities around the world.

The aim of this paper is to present an analysis of existing literature on MWM, before proposing a Conceptual and Multidimensional Framework for managing this type of waste. To do this, we will first delineate the MWM process in HSC, then carry out a literature review to identify research gaps, particularly in relation to the aspects targeted by the study namely sustainability, digitalization, risk management, integration, performance, and resilience, which will enable us to develop the target Framework.

The remaining sections of this work are organized as follows. Section 2 describes the position of the MW process within the Hospital Supply Chain (HSC). Section 3 explains the method used in this research. Section 4 reviews the literature on MWM, with particular reference to the aspects covered by the study. Section 5 discusses the results of the literature review, deduces research gaps and presents the MWM Conceptual and Multidimensional Framework. Section 6 closes this study by summarizing our contribution and outlining future directions.

2 Medical Waste Management: A Major Process in the Hospital Supply Chain

2.1 Hospital Supply Chain (HSC): Features, Processes, Flows ...

HSC is characterized by its complexity, its particularity which lies in its criticality in relation to the Global Supply Chain, but also and above all by the extremely high hospital costs it generates and which it is called upon to reduce in the most optimal way. It's for this reason that a number of researchers have taken an interest in this branch of logistics, which has been approached in a methodical and scholarly manner since the 1990s.

Through our previous work, we still consider that Chow and Heaver [6] are the first to explicitly characterize logistics activities within the hospital, of which there are three:

- Procurement, which involves purchasing and inventory management for diverse products.

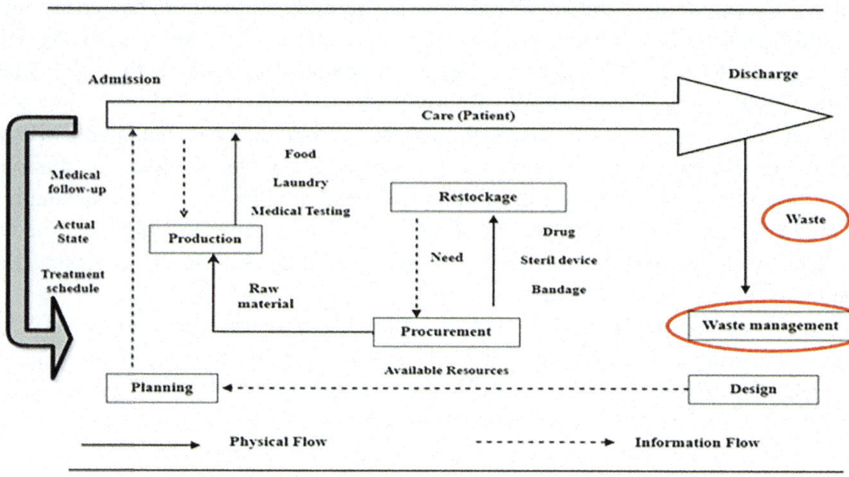

Fig. 1 Hospital Supply Chain processes and flows according to Ibn Elfarouk [9]

- Production, which oversees the numerous processing processes such as lingerie, kitchens, and sterilization.
- Distribution, which guarantees that items are carried from storage facilities to various points of usage, or garbage is transported to shipping areas.

According to Landry et al. [7], hospital logistics is described as a set of design, planning, and execution operations for the purchase, inventory management, and replenishment of goods and services used in the delivery of medical care to patients.

For Sampieri et al. [8] hospital logistics is "the technology of controlling physical flows and the trajectory of patients through information flows".

From these definitions of HSC, we can see that Chow and Heaver are the only authors to have mentioned "waste transport" in reference to the medical waste process, the subject of this study. Ibn Elfarouk [9], on the other hand, explicitly integrated medical waste as a process in its own right within the hospital logistics chain, as shown in Fig. 1.

Although the medical waste process is a fundamental link in the HSC chain, it is not considered as such in the literature. The following sub-section focuses on this process.

2.2 Medical Waste Process

All waste that comes from diagnostic, monitoring, preventive, palliative, or curative treatment activities in the fields of human or veterinary medicine, as well as any waste that comes from the operations of public hospitals, clinics, scientific

Table 1 Classification of medical and pharmaceutical waste according to the Moroccan Ministry of Public Health [12]

Categories	Nature/characteristics
CAT1	• Waste that poses an infection risk due to the presence of unidentifiable human or animal organs and tissues, as well as viable germs or toxins that can infect humans or other living things • Sharps that are meant to be used extensively, regardless of whether they have come into contact with a biological substance • Blood products and derivatives that have been partially utilized, spoilt, or have expired for medical use
CAT2	• Unused, rotten, or out-of-date chemicals, biologicals, and medications • Waste from cells
CAT3	Comprises tissues and organs, either human or animal, that are easily recognized by a non-specialist
CAT4	Is equivalent to home trash as long as it is produced in a medical facility

research facilities, analysis labs working in these fields, and all similar establishments, can be categorized as medical waste [10]. The World Health Organization defines waste material (WM) as any residue left over after extraction, exploitation, transformation, production, consumption, use, control, or filtration. In general, WM includes any abandoned object or material that the owner must dispose of to protect the environment or public health. Healthcare facilities generate two types of waste: high-risk waste and waste that is treated as household waste [11].

According to the Moroccan Ministry of Public Health [12], medical and pharmaceutical waste can be classified according to its nature and characteristics as follows (Table 1):

According to the WHO [13], there are 8 major types of medical waste:

- **Infectious waste**: waste tainted with blood or other bodily fluids (such as samples obtained for diagnosis and subsequently discarded), stocks and cultures of infectious agents used in labs (such as autopsy residue and contaminated lab animals), refuse from hospitalized patients kept in isolation, and supplies (such as bandages, swabs, and disposable medical devices).
- **Anatomical waste**: bodily fluids, human organs and tissues, and tainted animal corpses.
- **Sharp objects**: needles, syringes, razor blades, and disposable scalpels, among other items.
- **Chemicals**: such as batteries, heavy metals in medical equipment (mercury in broken thermometers), and solvents used in laboratory preparations.
- **Pharmaceuticals**: medicines, vaccinations, and sera that are tainted, outdated, and unutilized.
- **Genotoxic waste**: very dangerous, mutagenic, carcinogenic, or teratogenic substances, such as cytotoxic drugs used to treat cancer, as well as their metabolites.

- **Radioactive waste**: items such as radioactively contaminated medical or radiation equipment, among other products.

Other waste that doesn't specifically pose a risk to human health, the environment, radioactivity, or biology.

According to the WHO again [13], the main sources of healthcare waste are:

- Hospitals and other healthcare facilities;
- Laboratory and research centers;
- Morgues and autopsy centers;
- Research facilities and laboratories that conduct animal testing;
- Blood banks and blood collecting services.
- Senior care facilities.

The lack of a comprehensive and internationally recognized definition of medical waste, however, makes comparisons difficult because differing definitions cause different countries -or even different areas within the same country- to comprehend the notion differently. Additionally, medical waste streams and disposal containers are not standardized as a result of the absence of a common definition for medical waste [14].

3 Research Methodology

Any academic project must include a review of earlier, pertinent material. An efficient review establishes a solid basis for knowledge advancement. It opens up areas where there is a dearth of study and reveals places where research is needed, all while facilitating the formation of theories [15].

The method adopted in this work is generally the same as that found in literature reviews, which lead to a conceptual or practical Framework, obviously with specificities that differ from one study to another depending on the nature and scope of the work. Our method is the result of cross-referencing some of the most relevant research found in the literature, including the following references: [16–18], while taking into account the specificity and purpose of the present study.

Medical waste management, as we shall see, is a relatively recent field of research. Contributions in this area have been appearing consistently since the year 2000. Most of these works are case studies evaluating the practical management of medical waste in countries, regions and cities around the world. Theoretical work seeking to develop concepts and methods likely to optimize MWM is very limited. Indeed, the choice of eligible articles for the literature review was somewhat restrictive. To overcome this constraint, we chose keywords according to the aspects and dimensions targeted by the study.

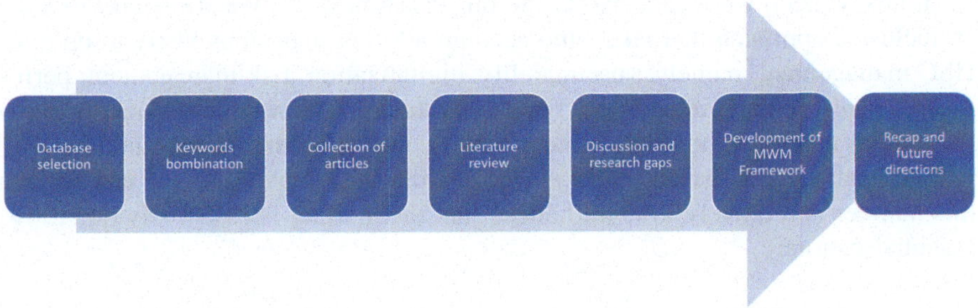

Fig. 2 Overview of research approach

After using several databases such as: Elsevier, Scopus, Inderscience, Emerald, Springer, Google Scholar etc., the keywords and terms we used to search for the most relevant articles for this literature review combine MWM and the different dimensions covered by the study, in particular: sustainability, digitalization, risk management, performance, resilience and integration. These keywords are as follows:

- Medical Waste Management (MWM);
- Sustainable MWM;
- Digital MWM;
- Risk management and MWM;
- Performance and MWM;
- Integration and MWM;
- Resilience and MWM.

The period chosen for the literature review extends from 1990 to 2023, since, as mentioned above, HSC in general and MWM in particular have been consistently addressed since the 1990s. The literature review was carried out using a variety of sources, including journal papers, book chapters, indexed conferences and theses.

After analyzing the selected documents, we have highlighted the research gaps in relation to the study objective, before proposing the target Framework and suggesting some directions for future research. Figure 2 illustrates and summarizes the method adopted.

4 Literature Review

The objective of this study is to propose a conceptual and multidimensional MWM Framework. To achieve this, we first conducted a literature review on MWM, focusing on the aspects and dimensions that will serve as the basis for the target Framework.

In this respect, we recall that during our research work, we always try to adopt an inclusive approach that takes into account all the dimensions likely to optimize HSC management, namely: sustainability, digitalization, risk management, performance, resilience and integration. For this literature review which concerns one of the critical processes of HSC, namely MWM, we proceeded in the same way.

The analysis was based on 92 works dealing with MWM, so we can see that this number is relatively low, we believe that this finding is essentially due to two essential factors:

- The HSC, of which the MW process is a part, is an offshoot of the Global Supply Chain, which takes up the lion's share of research work.
- MWM is a subdivision of Waste Management, and is therefore naturally less well covered than the latter.

Figure 3 shows the distribution of articles consulted during the study period.

The nature of the study and the insufficient number of works dealing with our subject led us to divide up the selected documents as follows:

- 50 papers on the state of the art of MWM in various countries around the world;
- 17 papers dealing with MWM in Morocco (our focus is more on the national context, since our aim is to optimize HSC in Moroccan public hospitals);
- 10 articles dealing with sustainability in MWM;
- 03 literature reviews on MWM;
- 04 papers dealing with digitalization in MWM;
- 03 papers dealing with risk management in the MWM process;
- 01 paper on performance improvement in MWM;
- 04 theses on MWM.

The results of this distribution are shown in Fig. 4.

MWM around the world is neither produced nor managed in the same way, hence the interest in discovering which countries are investing more in this field,

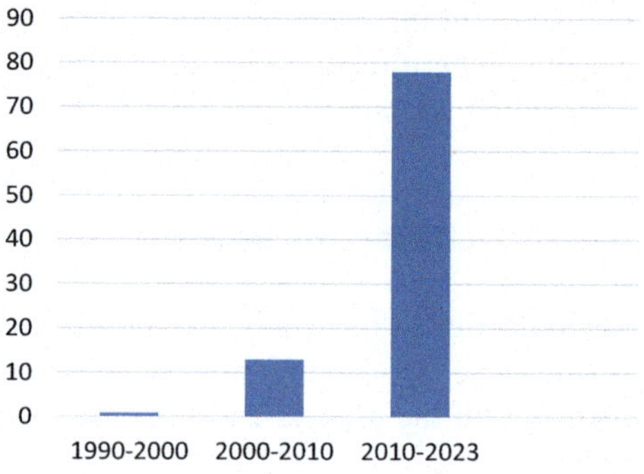

Fig. 3 Number of publications during the study period

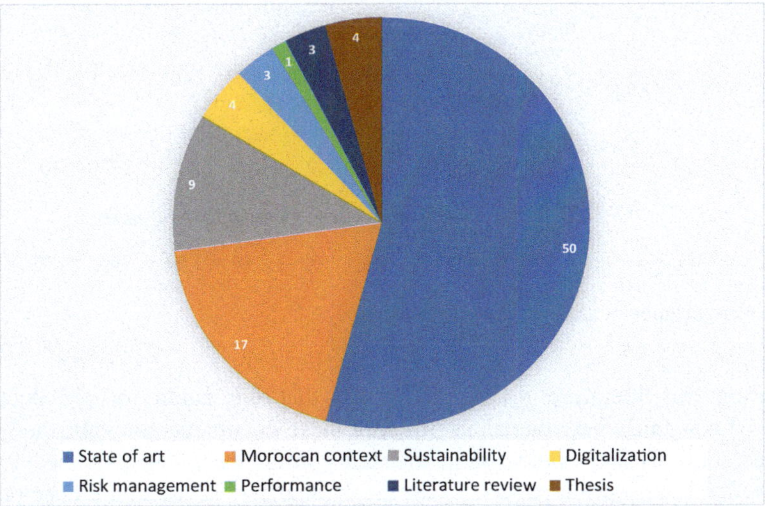

Fig. 4 Distribution of publications by theme

both academically and practically. But we found that the distribution of contributions by country was not relevant, as there are no countries that stand out clearly from others in terms of number of publications. For this reason, geographical distribution was based on continents. Figure 5 shows the geographical distribution of authors dealing with MWM between 1990 and 2023. the geographical analysis shows that Asia comes first with 36 contributions, notably thanks to China (07 publications), India (06 publications) and Bangladesh (05 publications). Then Africa with 29 publications of which Morocco is the first contributor with 17 research works. America occupies third place with 15 contributions thanks in particular to Brazil, the United States and Canada. Europe comes in fourth place with 12 contributions distributed equally among several European countries.

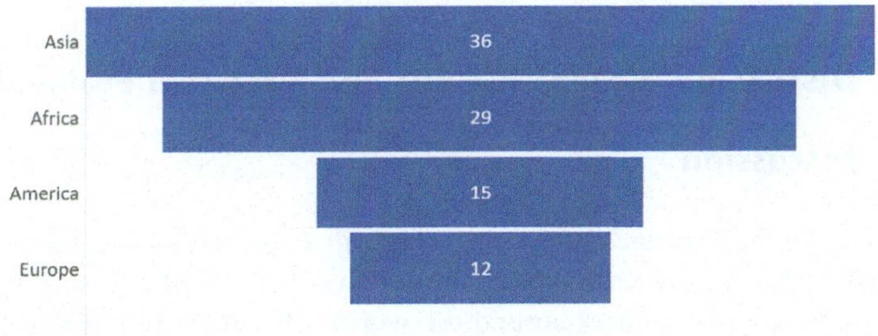

Fig. 5 Geographical distribution of analyzed documents

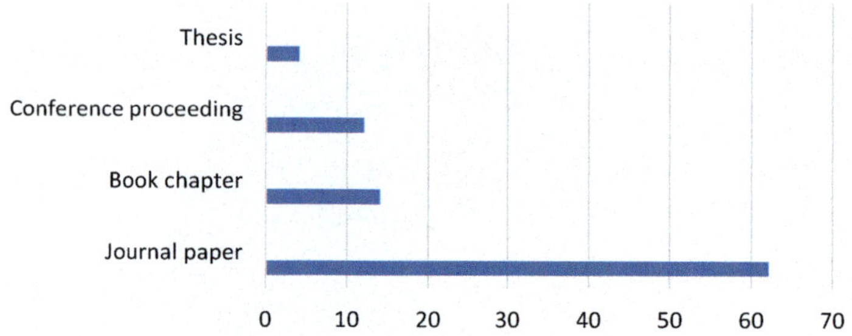

Fig. 6 Classification of analyzed documents by type

During this literature review, we noted that the nature of the documents analyzed was fairly heterogeneous. Most of these documents are published in specialized journals and books, or in indexed conferences. Thus, of the 92 works reviewed, 62 are journal papers, 14 are book chapters, 12 are conference proceedings and 4 are theses. Figure 6 shows the classification of analyzed documents by type.

To achieve the objectives of this research, we have focused on works that deal with the aspects targeted by the study. Among the 92 works analyzed, we selected 15 that deal respectively with sustainability, digitalization, risk management, performance, integration and resilience in MWM. Figure 7 shows the number of articles per aspect. Indeed, the most discussed aspect in the literature is sustainability with 10 articles, which can be explained by a set of issues such as environmental preservation, circular economy etc. Then, we find the risk management dimension with 03 articles: MWs present a potential and permanent risk, whether for patients, healthcare staff, the population or the environment. The same applies to digitalization, with 04 articles dealing with the use of new technologies in MWM. The least discussed aspect is performance, with 01 article. Integration and resilience were not addressed.

The contributions of works that have dealt with MWM, in particular in the above-mentioned aspects, are classified in Table 2.

5 Discussion, Research Gaps and Proposal Framework

5.1 Discussion

After analyzing the various works that have dealt with MWM, we can deduce that the majority of them are case studies evaluating the MWM process in hospitals in cities, regions and countries around the world. The evaluation covers the entire process, from waste generation in the care units to treatment in dedicated facilities. These assessments also focus on MW production rates, the means, procedures and techniques used to manage and dispose of this waste, the behavior and level of

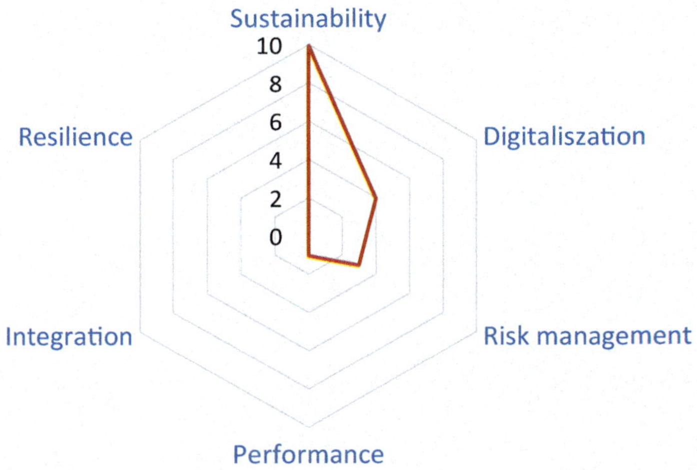

Fig. 7 Distribution of publications by dimensions

knowledge of the staff responsible for waste management within care facilities, etc.

Moreover, the target dimensions of our study have been treated differently in the literature. Indeed, referring to Table 2, we note that the "Sustainability" aspect is the most dealt with 10 articles, this is mainly due to the challenges of sustainable development and circular economy faced by the international community as a whole. Authors have approached sustainability in different ways, e.g. Lee et al. [19] identify key factors for MW reduction. Chtioui et al. [20] propose a MWM model to automate the process of sustainable MW management. Sisdyani et al. [21] encourage MW personnel to adopt environmentally-friendly behaviors. Singh et al. [23] show the importance of knowledge and awareness of MW personnel for responsible and sustainable management. Zamparas et al. [24] used the AHP method to assess sustainability in MWM. Finally, Chisholm et al. [27] show the role of environmentally-friendly technologies for effective MW treatment and disposal methods.

Concerning the "Risk management" aspect, of the 03 articles analyzed, 02 [29, 30] focus on the impact of Covid-19 on MWM, meaning that the emergence of the pandemic has had a trigger effect on the actions to be put in place to manage MW in the event of major crises. The third article [31] employs the fault tree analysis (FTA) method to analyze individual risks but also analyze the relationships and interdependencies between risks in MWM.

As for the "Digitalization" aspect, the 04 articles that dealt with it did so respectively through Artificial Intelligence (AI), in particular the deep learning approach, and other technologies such as blockchain, IoT, GPS etc. Indeed, Boudanga et al. [1] use a collaborative approach and technological advances in medical waste management, such as GPS and Artificial Intelligence. They also use genetic algorithms

Table 2 Overview of relevant documents dealing with MWM in the areas covered by the study

Reference	Article type	Studied aspect	Method	Contribution
Lee et al. [19]	Journal paper	Sustainability	Case study	The study offers theoretical and practical recommendations for putting into practice efficient medical waste management with an eye toward a sustainable and ecological healthcare environment through a case study (a survey of personnel managing medical waste). Priorities among the important elements found were established using the hierarchical analytical process (AHP), and the real application of the AHP's conclusions was evaluated by consulting expert viewpoints. The study found that medical waste management (26.6%), operational management issues (21.7%), medical waste management process training (17.8%), awareness-raising (17.5%), and environmental evaluation (16.4%) have the greatest influence on reducing medical waste
Chtioui et al. [20]	Book chapter	Sustainability	Modeling	This work makes a contribution by putting out a medical waste management model that addresses the issues of circular economy and sustainable development, particularly with regard to environmental preservation and hospital cost reduction. In order to characterize and eventually automate the process, the proposed model carefully defines the multi-agent method, which is one of the most successful paradigms for controlling complex systems
Sisdyani et al. [21]	Journal paper	Sustainability	Case study	The study demonstrates how the intention to adopt an ecological behavior affects the significance of using the four eco-control mechanisms—beliefs, limits, diagnosis, and interactive eco-control—through a case study (questionnaire survey of a randomly selected sample of 125 senior managers from Indonesian public hospitals). Put differently, the greater the intention, the greater the probability that the actual behavior will occur as a result of the use of limitative eco-control

(continued)

Table 2 (continued)

Reference	Article type	Studied aspect	Method	Contribution
Rolewicz-Kalińska [22]	Conference proceeding	Sustainability	Research	By analyzing the legal framework and organizational structure of the medical waste management system in Poland, the paper shows that the latter suffers from major limitations affecting the sustainability aspect
Singh et al. 2021 [23]	Journal paper	Sustainability	Research	Based on statistical relationships between the Human Development Index (HDI), life expectancy (LE), health expenditure (HE) per capita of GDP, and the Environmental Performance Index (EPI), the paper contributes to identifying barriers and challenges to integrating medical waste management into a forward-looking circular economy. This is accomplished through a meta-analysis of medical and healthcare waste management techniques from 78 nations. The findings highlight how crucial it is for staff members to be knowledgeable about the best methods for preventing infections and injuries in medical waste management
Zamparasa et al. [24]	Journal paper	Sustainability	Case study	This paper demonstrates how implementing the AHP (Analytic Hierarchy Process) approach can assist each hospital unit in verifying its environmental position and identifying areas and processes that need to be changed for environmental sustainability
Koo et al. [25]	Journal paper	Sustainability	Research	By analyzing four techniques—steam sterilization (SL), microwave disinfection (M), incineration (I), and incineration with heat recovery (ID50)—this research helps to improve sustainability in medical waste management. According to the findings, ID50 has less of an effect on the production of oxidants during conversion. The biggest impact on the potential for acidity is from incineration. Microwave disinfection and steam sterilization release certain harmful contaminants. Burning is the method that has the biggest effect on environmental danger when factored in

(continued)

Table 2 (continued)

Reference	Article type	Studied aspect	Method	Contribution
Cesaro et al. [26]	Journal paper	Sustainablility	Case study	This study makes a contribution by evaluating the medical waste management system's sustainability across five various-sized healthcare facilities. The findings demonstrate that accurate classification of medical waste types was acknowledged as a crucial component of the put into place waste management system, which adversely affected the system's overall sustainability
Chisholm et al. [27]	Journal paper	Sustainability	Review	The findings of an evaluation of medical waste management in developing African nations are presented in this research. The research's conclusions present policies, recommendations, and solutions related to medical waste management and sustainability. These can help decision-makers create sustainable strategies by utilizing environmentally friendly technologies for effective medical waste treatment and disposal techniques. They can also act as a conduit between the healthcare system, stakeholders, and decision-makers when it comes to creating health policies and programs
Tushar et al. [28]	Journal paper	Sustainability	Modeling	To assure environmental sustainability as well as community health and safety, this study proposes an integrated method to identifying, assessing, and prioritizing the critical barriers to the MWM program's successful implementation. Using literature studies and expert commentary, 12 problems were chosen for ISM-MICMAC examination. The results suggest that "insufficient financial support from investors and government" and "lack of proper law enforcement" are the two most prominent obstacles. The work has significant theoretical, practical, and environmental ramifications

(continued)

Table 2 (continued)

Reference	Article type	Studied aspect	Method	Contribution
Kalantary et al. [29]	Journal paper	Risk management	Case study	This paper examines how the Covid-19 epidemic has affected medical waste management through a case study analysis. The Covid-19 pandemic has resulted in an increase in the generation of medical waste. The amount of waste generated per bed per day in the hospitals under study ranges from 0.95 to 3.51 kg. Furthermore, due to an increase in patients in the infectious ward and staff use of personal protective equipment in the hospitals under study, a 9% increase in the ratio of infectious waste in the medical waste mass was observed. Hospitals now have the right high-capacity disinfection technology, which has made it possible to properly handle the increased amount and possibility for infection in medical waste. However, the absence of separate containers for disposing of gloves and face masks in hospitals raises the risk of contamination and sickness from medical waste. The separation of Covid-19 trash from other medical waste, as well as the daily cleaning of Covid-19 waste and infectious waste generated in other wards, have minimized the likelihood of disease transmission through the waste mass
Chtioui et al. [30]	Conference proceeding	Risk management	Case study	This article contributes by analyzing the impact of Covid-19 on the Hospital Supply Chain, and consequently on the Medical Waste Management process. The article shows that the risk of infection from waste generated in Covid-19 isolation units is extremely high, both inside and outside the hospital. This risk is omnipresent, from the sorting and packaging operations (at the isolation site), through the storage rooms at hospital level, to the transport vehicle that carries them to the processing units (generally outside the hospital)
Makajic-Nikolic et al. [31]	Journal paper	Risk management	Research	The authors of this study provide an application for infectious medical waste management risk assessment at the Clinical Centre of Serbia, the largest hospital in South-East Europe. The fault tree analysis (FTA) method was chosen because it allows for the examination of individual hazards as well as risk linkages and interdependencies, much like the majority of risk assessment techniques used in medical waste management, such as FMEA, HACCP, PHA, and CREA. Based on the results, we were able to pinpoint the fundamental flaws in medical waste management systems, the mitigation of which or prevention of which has the greatest impact on the system improvement that has been shown

(continued)

Table 2 (continued)

Reference	Article type	Studied aspect	Method	Contribution
Boudanga et al. [1]	Journal paper	Digitalization	Research	In light of technical advancements in MWM, such as smart containers, identity labels, object recognition sensors, air and ground monitoring sensors, global positioning system (GPS)-equipped trucks, artificial intelligence, etc., this study suggests a novel strategy. Smart and effective medical waste management starts with the integration of these state-of-the-art technology. The paper also discusses how genetic algorithms, or GAs, can be used to solve vehicle routing models, optimize garbage collection routes, and reduce the amount of time that waste is transported to treatment facilities
Zhou et al. [32]	Scientific Reports	Digitalization	Modeling	The deep learning method for the detection and categorization of medical waste is put forth in this study. The technique is based on deep learning, where transfer learning techniques are used to enhance classification outcomes. ResNeXt is a deep neural network that is appropriate for practical application. The method had a 97.2% accuracy rate in properly identifying 8 different forms of medical waste. Thus, there are advantages to using AI to medical waste management
Le et al. [33]	Journal paper	Digitalization	Modeling	In order to simplify waste handling procedures for used medical supplies and equipment between the parties concerned, this study proposes a decentralized blockchain system called the medical waste blockchain. It is made up of four parts: garbage centers, recycling plants, sorting plants, and medical supplies and equipment. Medical-Waste Chain securely communicates relevant data with stakeholders by fusing decentralized medical equipment and supply data storage with blockchain-based Hyperledger Fabric technology. In order to minimize the production of medical waste, the system's design and stakeholder interactions are described in this study
Kassou et al. [34]	Conference proceeding	Digitalization	Research	In order to properly manage, organize, and track the removal of waste, this article makes a contribution by suggesting the construction of a system based on Blockchain and IoT. Additionally provided are the system's preliminary design and a performance assessment
Kerdsuwan et al. [35]	Chapter book	Performance	Research	The study carried out in this paper recommends the use of small-scale incineration as a suitable technology for on-site medical waste disposal in developing countries. According to the performance testing, the incineration facility could be efficiently operated. The medical waste destruction rate achieved the designed value of 50 kg/h and the temperature in both the primary and secondary combustion chambers ranged from 650 to 780 °C and 900 to 1080 °C, respectively. In addition, the pollutants in flue gas from the stack were able to meet the requirements of the US EPA for small-scale medical waste incineration

(GA) to optimize MW collection routes. Zhou et al. [32] demonstrated the value of AI in MWM by using deep learning to classify 08 types of MW with an accuracy of 97.2%. Le et al. [33] proposed a decentralized system based on blockchain with centralized storage of information on medical equipment and supplies, and secure sharing of the corresponding data with stakeholders. Finally, Kassou et al. [34] proposed the design of a system, based on Blockchain and IoT, which ensures the control of this waste in order to effectively manage, coordinate and monitor its elimination.

For the only article with the "Performance" aspect [35], it was interested in MWM in developing countries, it recommends the use of small-scale incineration, performance tests have shown that pollutants resulting from combustion meet US EPA requirements for small-scale MW incineration.

5.2 Research Gaps

Through the literature review, we can first see that the MWM has not been treated sufficiently before, at least in the context of our context which is interested in the above-mentioned dimensions, the proof as shown in Table 2, the majority of articles are very recent: 02 articles published in 2023, 03 in 2022, 04 in 2021, 02 in 2020, 01 in 2019, 02 in 2016 and 02 in 2015.

Then, the "Integration" and "Resilience" dimensions have not been explicitly treated in any previous work.

Furthermore, the thematic analysis indicates that to date, no study has treated MWM taking into account the different dimensions, hence the interest in developing a conceptual and multidimensional Framework, which we will undertake in the following subsection.

5.3 Proposal Framework

From the theoretical analysis that we have carried out and especially thanks to our expertise in the field in a hospital environment, we propose a conceptual framework integrating the different dimensions likely to optimize the MW process and consequently the HSC. Figure 8 illustrates the proposed Framework:

Although the literature does not propose an integrated management of MW in healthcare facilities, the above Framework includes all possible dimensions likely to guarantee optimal MWM. For the aspects of sustainability, digitalization, risk management and performance, the literature has provided some guidance, which we have improved thanks to our presence in the hospital environment. For the two aspects that have not been addressed in the literature, namely integration and resilience, we propose a few lines of thought, as indicated on the Framework, in the hope that they will be well exploited in future research work.

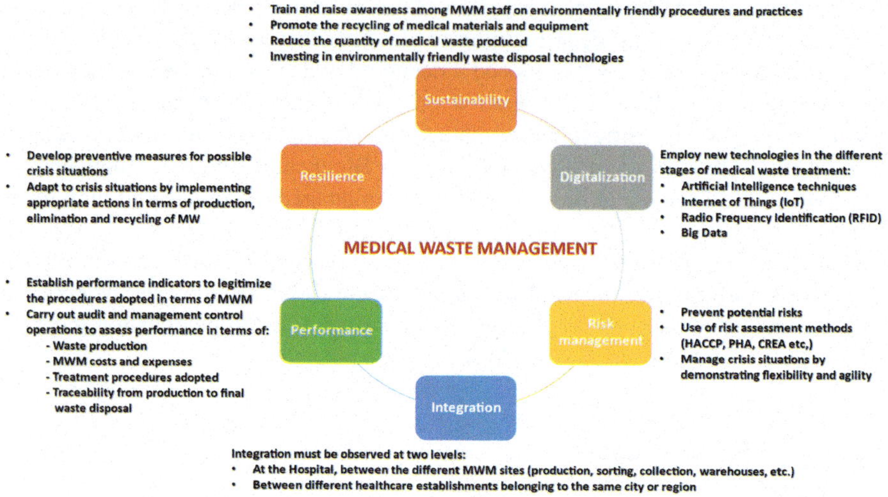

Fig. 8 Framework for the development of an integrated and multidimensional MWM

6 Conclusion

The MW process is considered one of the most critical activities within healthcare facilities. If not properly treated and disposed of, residues from this process represent a potential danger for patients, healthcare staff, logistics personnel, the population and the environment. This is particularly true in developing countries, where MW continues to be managed in a hazardous manner. In addition, research work that has addressed the issue of MW remains insufficient. The majority of these works are case studies evaluating the MW process in regional and city hospitals around the world. Contributions relating to research aimed at developing theories and concepts in this area remain very limited.

These facts motivated us to examine the research work that addressed the issue of MW through a rigorous literature review. The results showed that the aspects targeted by the study have been treated differently in the literature.

To help fill the research gap in this area, we propose a Conceptual and Multidimensional Framework for MWM. Which Framework provides considerable background in this area and will therefore serve as a roadmap for subsequent research work, but also a practical guide for practitioners and managers wishing to implement integrated, safe, efficient and responsible management methods for their MW.

References

1. Boudanga Z, Benhadou S, Medromi H (2023) An innovative medical waste management system in a smart city using XAI and vehicle routing optimization. https://doi.org/10.12688/f1000research.138867.1
2. Das AK, Islam MN, Billah MM, Sarker A (2021) COVID-19 pandemic and healthcare solid waste management strategy—a mini-review. Sci Total Environ 778:146220. https://doi.org/10.1016/j.scitotenv.2021.146220
3. Khandelwal H, Dhar H, Thalla AK, Kumar S (2019) Application of life cycle assessment in municipal solid waste management: a worldwide critical review. J Clean Prod 209:630–654. https://doi.org/10.1016/j.jclepro.2018.10.233
4. Kenny C, Priyadarshini A (2021) Review of current healthcare waste management methods and their effect on global health (2021). Healthcare 9:284. https://doi.org/10.3390/healthcare9030284
5. Yoon CW, Kim MJ, Park YS, Jeon TW, Lee MY (2022) A review of medical waste management systems in the Republic of Korea for hospital and medical waste generated from the COVID-19 pandemic. Sustainability 14:3678. https://doi.org/10.1016/j.jenvman.2015.08.013
6. Chow G, Heaver T, Henriksson L (1994) Logistics performance: definition and measurement. Int J Phys Distrib Logist Manage 24(1)
7. Landry S, Beaulieu M (2000) Étude internationale des meilleures pratiques de logistique hospitalière. Cahier de recherche n° 00-05, HEC Montréal
8. Sampieri N, Bongiovanni I (2009) Enjeux et perspectives des pratiques logistiques : pour une amélioration globale de la performance – Le cas de l'hôpital public français. RIRL 2000 – Les Troisièmes Rencontres Internationales de la Recherche en Logistique, Trois-Rivières, CRET-LOG.19P
9. IBN ELFAROUK.I « Chaîne logistique hospitalière : définition, état de l'art et pistes d'amélioration » (2012) GIGIM, 18–19 Avril 2012, Fès/Maroc
10. Maroc. Ministère de justice. Loi n ° 28–00 relative à la gestion des déchets et à leur élimination. 2006; Available from: http://aut.gov.ma/pdf/Loi_n2800_relative_a_la_gestion.pdf
11. WHO (World Health Organization) (1999) Safe management of wastes from health-care activities, Genève
12. Ministère de la santé (MS) (2010) Les professionnelles de la santé au cœur de l'environnement et du développement. Guide des déchets
13. WHO (World Health Organization) (2018) https://www.who.int/fr/news-room/fact-sheets/detail/health-care-waste
14. Insa E, Zamorano M, Lopez R (2010) Critical review of medical waste legislation in Spain. Resour Conserv Recycl 54 :1048–1059. https://doi.org/10.1016/j.resconrec.2010.06.005
15. Webster J, Watson RT (2002) Analyzing the past to prepare for the future: writing a literature review. MIS Quart 26(2):13–23. https://www.jstor.org/stable/4132319
16. Kannan D, Khademolqorani S, Janatyan N, Alavi S (2024) Smart waste management 4.0: the transition from a systematic review to an integrated framework. Waste Manage 174:1–14. https://doi.org/10.1016/j.wasman.2023.08.041
17. Büyüközkan G, Göçer F (2018) Digital supply chain: literature review and a proposed framework for future research. Comput Ind 97:157–177. https://doi.org/10.1016/j.compind.2018.02.010
18. Nord JH, Koohang A, Paliszkiewicz J (2019) The internet of things: review and theoretical framework. Expert Syst Appl 133:97–108. https://doi.org/10.1016/j.eswa.2019.05.014
19. Lee SM, Lee DH (2002) Effective medical waste management for sustainable green healthcare. Int J Environ Res Public Health 19:14820. https://doi.org/10.3390/ijerph192214820
20. Chtioui A, Bouhaddou I, Benghabrit A, Benabdellah AC (2023) A multi-agent system for the optimization of medical waste management. https://doi.org/10.1007/978-3-031-43520-1_12

21. Sisdyani EA, Subroto B, Saraswati E et al (2022) Levers of eco-control and green behavior in medical waste management Int J Energy Econ Policy (IJEEP). https://doi.org/10.32479/ijeep.9342
22. Rolewicz-Kalińska A (2016) Logistic constraints as a part of a sustainable medical waste management system. https://doi.org/10.1016/j.trpro.2016.11.044
23. Singh N, Ogunseitan OA, Tang Y (2022) Medical waste: current challenges and future opportunities for sustainable management. Crit Rev Environ Sci Technol 52(11). https://doi.org/10.1080/10643389.2021.1885325
24. Zamparasa M, Kapsalisb VC, Kyriakopoulosc GL, Aravossisb KH, Kanterakid AE, Vantarakisd A, Kalavrouziotis IK (2019) Medical waste management and environmental assessment in the Rio University Hospital, Western Greece. Sustain Chem Pharm. https://doi.org/10.1016/j.scp.2019.100163
25. Koo J-K, Jeong S-I (2015) Sustainability and shared smart and mutual-green growth (SSaM-GG) in Korean medical waste management. Waste Manage Res 33(5):410–418. https://doi.org/10.1177/0734242X15574561
26. Cesaro A, Belgiorno V (2016) Sustainability of medical waste management in different sized health care facilities. Waste Biomass Valor. https://doi.org/10.1007/s12649-016-9730-y
27. Chisholm JM, Zamani R, Negm AM, Said N, Abdel Daiem MM, Dibaj M, Akrami M (2021) Sustainable waste management of medical waste in African developing countries: a narrative review. Sagepub.com/journals-permissions https://doi.org/10.1177/0734242X211029175
28. Tushara SR, Bin Alama Md.F, Mainul Baria ABM, Karmaker CL (2023) Assessing the challenges to medical waste management during the COVID-19 pandemic: implications for the environmental sustainability in the emerging economies. https://doi.org/10.1016/j.seps.2023.101513
29. Kalantary RR, Jamshidi A, Golbini Mofrad MM, Jafari AJ, Heidari N, Fallahizadeh S, Arani MH, Torkashvand J (2021) Effect of COVID-19 pandemic on medical waste management: a case study. J Environ Health Sci Eng. https://doi.org/10.1007/s40201-021-00650-9
30. Chtioui A, Bouhaddou I, Benghabrit A, Benabdellah AC (2020) Impact of Covid-19 on the hospital supply chain. In: IEEE 13th International colloquium of logistics and supply chain management (LOGISTIQUA). https://doi.org/10.1109/LOGISTIQUA49782.2020.9353868
31. Makajic-Nikolic D, Petrovic N, Belic A, Rokvic M, Radakovic JA, Tubic V (2015) The fault tree analysis of infectious medical waste management. J Cleaner Prod. https://doi.org/10.1016/j.jclepro.2015.11.022
32. Zhou H, Yu X, Alhaskawi A, Dong Y, Wang Z, Jin Q, Hu X, Liu Z, Kota VG, Abdulla MH, Abdullah Ezzi SHA, Qi B, Li J, Wang B, Fang J, Lu H (2022) A deep learning approach for medical waste classification. https://doi.org/10.1038/s41598-022-06146-2
33. Le HT, Quoc KL, Nguyen TA, Dang KT, Vo HK, Luong HH, Van HL, Gia KH, Phu LVC, Quoc DNT, Nguyen TH, Son HX, Duong-Trung N (2022) Medical-waste chain: a medical waste collection, classification and treatment management by blockchain technology. Computers 11:113. https://doi.org/10.3390/computers11070113. https://www.mdpi.com/journal/computers
34. Kassou M, Bourekkadi S, Khoulji S, Slimani K, Chikri H, Kerkeb ML (2021) Blockchain-based medical and water waste management conception. In: E3S Web of Conferences 234, 00070 (ICIES 2020). https://doi.org/10.1051/e3sconf/202123400070
35. Kerdsuwan S, Laohalidanond K (2015) Efficiency improvement for medical waste management. In: Handbook of clean energy systems. Wiley, New York. https://doi.org/10.1002/9781118991978.hces19

Ahmed Chtioui is an Engineer in Manufacturing Systems Management of the Ecole Nationale Supérieure des Mines de Rabat (ENSMR), Morocco. Currently, he is head of the IT department of the Moulay Ismail Hospital, Meknes, Morocco. At the same time, he is a Ph.D. student in the

MOSI research team at the Ecole Nationale Supérieure d'Art et Métiers (ENSAM-Meknes). His research work focuses on the integration and optimisation of the Hospital Supply Chain (HSC).

Imane Bouhaddou is a Professor at ENSAM Meknes, University of Moulay Ismail, Morocco. She received her Ph.D. in Industrial Engineering from University of Le Havre, France and Moulay Ismail University, Meknes, Morocco in 2015. Her research work is dealing with supply chain optimisation, product life cycle management and complex systems.

Asmaa Benghabrit has been a lecturer-researcher in Industrial Engineering since 2017 in the Industrial Engineering Department of the Ecole Nationale Supérieure des Mines de Rabat (ENSMR). She is a permanent member of the Laboratory of Applied Mathematics and Business Intelligence (LMAID) at ENSMR and Associate Member of the research team Modelling and Optimisation of Industrial Systems (MOSI) at the Ecole Nationale Supérieure d'Art et Métiers (ENSAM-Meknès). Her research work focuses on Modeling, Extraction and Knowledge Management from Industrial Data and the Impact of Data Science and Artificial Intelligence on Manufacturing and Service Industries.

Inventory Management Performance of Medical Analysis Laboratory in a Public Hospital

13

Imen Mejri, Safa Bhar Layeb, Najla Aissaoui, and Mohamed Yassine Kaabar

Abstract

Healthcare decision-makers are increasingly prioritizing the measurement and enhancement of performance in order to deliver high-quality care efficiently in the face of escalating demand, rising costs, and limited resources. In this context, this study was conducted by an interdisciplinary team within a medical analysis laboratory of a Tunisian university hospital. More than 50,000 samples are collected per year, under the responsibility of medical biologists. The project aimed at optimizing inventory management for reagents and consumables. Initiating with modeling and analyzing existing supply processes using Business Process Model and Notation and Ishikawa diagrams, the team evaluated the current state based on collected data, pinpointing deficiencies hampering inventory management. These included layout issues, storage area organization, underutilization of Decision Support System (DSS), and lean inventory practices. Efforts were channeled towards implementing a new DSS and guiding staff in its adoption, acknowledging the substantial shift from manual to computerized inventory management. The adoption of the ADKAR methodology facilitated the transition, alongside a focus on optimizing storage areas and developing

I. Mejri · S. B. Layeb (✉) · N. Aissaoui
LR-OASIS, National Engineering School of Tunis, University of Tunis El Manar, Tunis, Tunisia
e-mail: safa.layeb@enit.utm.tn

I. Mejri
e-mail: imen.mejri@enit.utm.tn

I. Mejri
National Higher Engineering School of Tunis (ENSIT), University of Tunis, Tunis, Tunisia

N. Aissaoui
National Engineering School of Carthage, University of Carthage, Ariana, Tunisia

M. Y. Kaabar
Medical Analysis Laboratory of the Tahar Maamouri Hospital, Nabeul, Tunisia

F. Jawab (ed.), *Hospital Supply Chain*, Integrated Science 27,
https://doi.org/10.1007/978-3-031-70292-1_13

a just-in-time inventory system. These comprehensive interventions culminated in significant improvements in laboratory performance, demonstrating the effectiveness of strategic improvements in healthcare operations.

Keywords

Optimization • Health facilities • Laboratory • Lean practices • Quality

1 Introduction

Medical laboratories employ a variety of biological specimens (including whole blood, serum, plasma, urine, stool, sputum, and exudates) along with medical instruments, equipment, materials, and reagents (chemicals) to conduct diagnostics and investigations. They aim to detect, treat, and evaluate diseases through the analysis of biological samples [38]. These complex mechanisms are the backbone of healthcare systems globally, fulfilling a crucial function in diagnosing illnesses, monitoring treatments, and providing preventive care, thus ensuring the delivery of high-quality services [9]. According to Alharbi et al. [3], these facilities are vital components of healthcare. The authors asserted that medical laboratories function as silent drivers influencing clinical decision-making across the broad spectrum of healthcare. Their significance resonates throughout various medical fields, spanning from routine blood tests to advanced molecular diagnostics, encompassing a range of crucial services essential for patient care. However, their effectiveness heavily relies on the consistent availability of essential supplies, chemicals, and reagents, coupled with functional equipment and facilities. As highlighted by Boche et al. [10], effective inventory management is paramount for achieving desired outcomes in healthcare settings.

Moreover, inventory management (IM) plays a pivotal role in overseeing the supply chain within healthcare, acting as a safeguard against disruptions in service provision [19]. Nevertheless, healthcare supply chains encounter a significant challenge in balancing efficient inventory management with the maintenance of satisfactory service levels. Addressing the escalating demand for healthcare products necessitates the development of efficient strategies by professionals within healthcare supply chains. Additionally, the limited shelf-life of many healthcare products poses substantial challenges to healthcare supply chain management. These challenges are further compounded by existing managerial practices and conflicts among stakeholders, underscoring the critical importance of effective inventory management strategies [26].

In this context, this study aims to evaluate the performance of inventory management for laboratory products within a public university hospital in Tunisia. We opted for public hospitals due to their extensive reach in serving communities, while the selection of medical laboratories was influenced by their complexity, their crucial role, and their significant allocation of the annual health facility budget. Through empirical investigation, a framework was crafted to enhance logistical processes, scrutinize their management, conduct an in-depth analysis of the current scenario, and pinpoint inefficiencies in inventory management within the investigated laboratory services. In this study, various challenges were identified, significantly impacting both efficiency and patient satisfaction. Overall, inadequate inventory management was observed, evidenced by subpar storage practices, frequent stockouts, poor inventory control, product wastage leading to financial losses, a disorganized system, and inaccuracies in data recording. Therefore, several improvement initiatives were recommended and carried out accordingly to enhance the quality of laboratory services.

The rest of this chapter is structured as follows. Section 2 delves into a literature review focused on healthcare inventory management practices. Following that, Sect. 3 provides an in-depth analysis of the problems encountered in the management of laboratory inventory. In Sect. 4, we undertake a detailed examination of the current flow of inventory within the case study research, exploring bottlenecks and identifying root causes of inefficiencies. Section 5 offers recommendations aimed at enhancing laboratory management through optimal inventory practices. Finally, the chapter concludes with a summary of key findings and insights drawn from the preceding sections.

2 Healthcare Inventory Management: A Literature Review

The healthcare sector has encountered numerous hurdles in enhancing both the quality of care and patient satisfaction, all while striving to lower costs [5]. Inventory management represents a significant portion of the expenses for healthcare organizations [32].

Effective inventory management serves as a crucial tool for achieving productivity enhancements, such as cost reduction, waste minimization, and mitigating the risk of product obsolescence, all while meeting healthcare service standards. It significantly influences financial outcomes by ensuring cost control, optimizing supply chains, and enhancing patient experience. Nonetheless, supply chain administrators often face challenges due to the absence of measurable information concerning supply utilization, stock levels, product redundancy, and procedural expenses, hindering their ability to inform key stakeholders about the economic, medical, and logistical impacts of supply chain practices. Beier [7] suggested that by effectively managing inventory logistics, approximately 50% of the expenses associated with logistics in hospitals can be reduced. In contrast to various sectors, hospital management research has historically accorded lower importance to material management and logistics. This trend may stem from the intricate nature of healthcare supply chains and their secondary role in the primary objective of hospital management: the efficient treatment of patients [52].

The authors in Nachtmann and Pohl [34] outlined numerous approaches to enhance healthcare supply chain efficiency, including standardization levels, inventory management, waste minimization, data analytics, and enhanced management of physician preference cards. Nevertheless, there remains a deficiency in metrics for evaluating the performance of healthcare logistics in terms of both cost and quality. This underscores the notion that effective management is impossible without proper measurement, highlighting the importance of quantifiable assessment in decision-making processes. To contextualize their issue, Bijvank and Vis [8] provided a concise overview of replenishment policies applicable to hospital inventory systems. De Vries [13] offered a comprehensive introduction to inventory management, while Rosales et al. [41] commenced their research with a broad review of inventory models, touching upon relevant quantitative models within hospital environments.

Nojiyeza and Mkutshulwa [36] emphasized the necessity for efficient inventory control systems within the investigated public National Health Laboratory Services. They highlighted that reliance on manual inventory control systems contributes to both understocking and overstocking issues. Furthermore, they pointed out that optimizing the allocation of inventory items and balancing supply with demand could significantly improve patient satisfaction levels. Ahmadi et al. [1] conducted a survey among hospitals in the United States to gather data on blood product utilization, wastage, and inventory management practices. This included examining stock levels, rates of expiration, and instances of shelf life extension. Notably, the survey shed light on the challenges hospitals face in ensuring an adequate supply of blood products and how this impacts patient care. Recently Legese et al. [27] conducted a three-year inventory analysis of health commodities, including medicines, medical supplies, and laboratory reagents and chemicals, within a large teaching hospital. Their findings underscored the imperative of implementing effective inventory management practices. Specifically, they observed that the procurement of certain commodities, particularly those used for laboratory diagnosis, deviated from the hospital's standardized procurement guidelines, indicating the need for improved coordination between the laboratory unit and the Drug and Therapeutic Committee of the hospital.

According to De Vries [13] observations, it is common practice for healthcare organizations to structure their inventory systems around four key domains to achieve the necessary performance standards: (i) the physical infrastructure, (ii) the planning and control mechanisms, (iii) the information systems, and (iv) the organizational structure. The physical infrastructure of an organization pertains to its methods of distributing and storing various products and goods internally. Hospitals, for instance, handle a diverse array of items such as office supplies, apparel, medical-surgical supplies, devices, health aids, and pharmaceuticals. The supply chains within hospitals are notably intricate, as evidenced by Towill and Christopher [51], with products being managed through diverse distribution and storage strategies. The configuration of inventory systems encompasses various considerations, such as deliberations on implementing "stockless schemes" and managing the procurement of goods for planned versus emergency needs. Moreover, a multitude of strategic, tactical, and operational decisions must be made at different levels to synchronize the demand and supply of deliveries for diverse products within the organization. Hence, the efficacy of the inventory system in hospitals is largely influenced by the planning and control framework, alongside its associated information system. While some researchers contend that adopting planning and control methodologies from the industrial sector into healthcare is feasible [12, 24], others argue against it, citing the challenges posed by the critical consequences of stock shortages and the interplay between planned and emergency care [18, 31, 43, 54]. The integration of the inventory system within the organizational structure emerges as a significant factor that profoundly impacts inventory performance overall, especially within healthcare settings. The organizational setup concerning stock levels, along with the delegation of responsibilities and authorities, tends to be decentralized within hospitals. This contrasts with industrial firms due to the presence of various stakeholders and less clearly defined entities such as Sales and Production [13]. Moons et al. [32] presented relevant literature on the optimization of inventory management in healthcare settings. They discussed critical performance indicators across (i) quality, (ii) timeliness, (iii) financial dimensions, and (iv) productivity within the healthcare supply chain, seeking to optimize operational efficiency. A significant hurdle in healthcare supply chain management lies in striking the balance between costs and maintaining optimal inventory levels to ensure quality and timely patient care. Hospital decision-makers are tasked with weighing numerous factors, including costs, service levels, storage capacity, product availability, and expiration dates, to effectively manage stocking levels [15, 48, 49]. Current strategies within healthcare organizations often involve excessive resource planning to address the intricacies of last-minute changes in schedules, resulting in stock wastage due to inadequate planning, insufficient comprehension of appropriate inventory levels, and lax monitoring of budgetary constraints [44, 46].

Various factors significantly impact healthcare inventory control systems, ranging from fully observable to partially observable for decision-makers. Among these factors, demand and supply dynamics play a pivotal role [46]. While traditional forecasting methods can handle stationary demand, the non-stationary nature of healthcare item consumption, influenced by patient conditions and treatment stages, requires advanced modeling techniques. Additionally, supply-side risks, such as variable lead times and uncertain quantities due to supplier unavailability, further underscore the complexity of healthcare inventory management and necessitate comprehensive modeling approaches [29, 45].

Another significant factor influencing healthcare inventory management is the replenishment policy employed, which is broadly classified into continuous review, periodic review, or a combination of both. These policies are evaluated based on inventory-related costs and service levels [16]. Healthcare systems often blend continuous and periodic review strategies, alongside joint replenishment criteria for multiple items, to optimize inventory control [42].

Saha and Ray [46] introduced another pivotal factor in healthcare systems: ensuring maximum service level becomes imperative to promptly address patient demand and minimize stock-out risks. While backordering is generally discouraged due to its potential to delay fulfillment, expediting offers immediate access to alternative sources like nearby hospitals or local suppliers. However, frequent expedite orders may incur higher emergency ordering costs, thus discouraging their frequent use [28].

This chapter provides an in-depth exploration of supply chain processes in a medical analysis laboratory, with a specific focus on optimizing inventory management for laboratory products in the public health setting. The goal is to ensure the availability of necessary supplies while containing costs and guaranteeing access to quality medical laboratory services for all stakeholders.

3 Problem Description

Managing laboratory commodities presents considerable challenges within the healthcare system due to factors such as the short shelf life of many products, specialized storage requirements, diverse needs for different tests, and the packaging of items in bulk, including kits, consumable liquids, and dry chemicals [10]. Studies conducted in this field have highlighted challenges in managing laboratory inventory effectively. Issues such as constrained human resources, inadequate skills, limited funding, poor data quality at healthcare facilities, weak IT infrastructure, and insufficient storage capacity contribute to problems like product shortages, inaccurate diagnoses, service disruptions, and patient dissatisfaction [6, 20, 30, 37, 53].

This study focuses on inventory management of laboratory products at a public Tunisian hospital. This university hospital comprising 13 departments, including an emergency department, 18 outpatient clinics, a clinical laboratory, an anatomopathology laboratory, a radiology department, and a pharmacy, serves as the centerpiece of this investigation. With two fully equipped operating rooms for surgical procedures and annual handling of roughly 133,000 outpatient examinations, the hospital's medical laboratory encounters the challenge of processing over 50,000 samples annually from patients across various departments, leading to a complex multi-stage process. The laboratory is located at the heart of the hospital, comprising a registration and waiting area, a sample collection room, 7 analysis rooms, 4 offices, a laundry room, and 2 storage rooms. The successful execution of its tasks requires the staff to effectively handle a considerable volume of reagents, governed by the terms of public contracts, with meticulous attention to batch numbers and expiry dates. However, the inventory management system under investigation showed significant weaknesses, primarily due to inadequate information for procurement decisions, insufficient availability of necessary supplies, and wastage resulting from overstocking, expiration, and damage. These challenges led to frequent stock-outs of essential items, disrupting the continuity and quality of patient testing services.

4 Current Flow Analysis, Bottleneck Exploration, and Root Cause Identification

The initial phase involves a thorough examination of the existing laboratory system. This entails assessing various aspects such as the inventory composition, classification methods, replenishment strategies, distribution processes, resource allocation, and pertinent constraints like space limitations and service requirements. These observations offer valuable insights into the intricate challenges faced by the system, their underlying causes, and potential areas for enhancement.

Following this assessment, the subsequent step entails modeling the workflow for laboratory products, which serves as the primary focus of our inquiry. Gathering the requisite data for this modeling endeavor involves meticulously tracking these products, engaging in interviews with personnel, and observing operations over an extended period, utilizing the Gemba Walks technique [2]. Figure 1 depicts the BPMN model showcasing the process flow of the examined products, specifically Reagents and Consumables. Undoubtedly, the flow of these products entails numerous steps and involves various stakeholders. It's noteworthy that the products undergo five sub-processes as they transition through the subsequent stages: (i) Order processing, (ii) Acquisition and receipt, (iii) Storage and inventory management, (iv) Distribution.

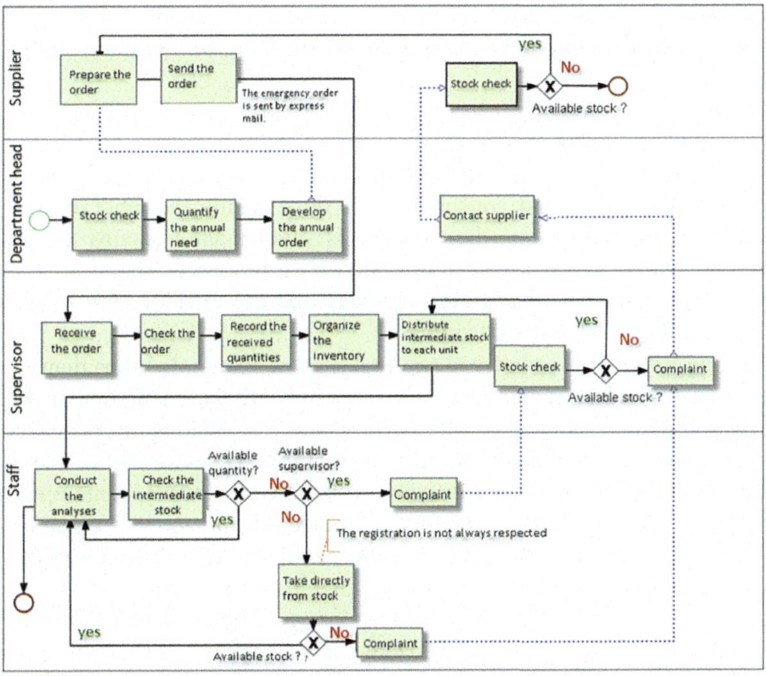

Fig. 1 BPMN model for the laboratory products process flow

- Order Processing

In the laboratory, the head of the department is solely responsible for selecting the quantities of reagents and consumables needed and for placing orders. The ordering process for reagents and consumables takes place annually at the end of December, based on rough estimates. The determination of needs is not based on any precise information regarding consumption or morbidity. According to the head of the department, she relies on her experience and observations of consumption throughout the year. After evaluating the stock status, she makes some adjustments to the previous order. Generally, the quantity to be ordered exceeds that of the previous year by a percentage of 10%. During our interviews with laboratory staff, we noted significant occurrences and durations of stockouts. This can be attributed to the lack of a general procurement plan and inaccurate estimations of departmental needs. Faced with the issue of stockouts, the head of the department resorts to advancing orders for the following year.

- Acquisition and Receipt

The receipt of orders delivered by suppliers to the laboratory is handled by the head of the department or by the supervisor according to their availability. Generally, the order is delivered in multiple shipments. Upon receiving the order, a product inspection is conducted. Indeed, the quantity, condition of the products, and expiration dates are verified. Since the laboratory department does not have an inventory management software system, all stock entries are manually recorded on entry forms.

- Storage and Inventory Management

The storage of reagents and consumables is done within the laboratory (Fig. 2). There are two storage rooms: the first one is smaller and contains a cold room. The second room also has a cold room but with a large area reserved for storage at room temperature. The remaining reagents and consumables are stored in the supervisor's office and in the corridors.

In storage room 2, we observed the presence of materials other than reagents, leading to a loss of storage space and hindered circulation of items. Additionally, heavy boxes are stored on the highest shelves, making them inaccessible. Moreover, there are no means provided to facilitate access to these boxes. Storage conditions in the corridors are inadequate. Some boxes containing fragile items, such as glass bottles of reagents, are placed in the corridor on steel sheets. However, shelves on the other side are underutilized, with empty spaces. In the supervisor's office, reagent boxes are in direct contact with the floor, risking moisture damage. The space allocated for storage is not reserved solely for laboratory consumables; some are used in other departments, such as the emergency department. Furthermore, significant areas in the corridor and supervisor's office are designated for archiving pathology samples, further reducing storage space

Fig. 2 Storage laboratory area

for laboratory consumables. As the laboratory lacks stock management software, recording stock movements is not always followed, resulting in unclear stock status. Additionally, stock levels of reagents and consumables are not determined.

- Distribution

The supervisor is responsible for distributing intermediate stocks of reagents. During their presence, they oversee the allocation of reagents to the analysis units for testing. They rely on their experience to estimate the demand from the analysis units. However, since the supervisor has multiple tasks in the laboratory, they are not always available. Consequently, when intermediate stock is unavailable, technicians directly access the storage rooms to obtain their needs. At this stage, many management problems arise due to the lack of traceability. Indeed, the laboratory does not have a consumption history of reagents and consumables since stock withdrawals are rarely recorded. The traceability method used relies on binders containing stock sheets for all reagents and consumables. Upon examination of these binders, several sheets were found to be incomplete, and the gap between two stock withdrawal records is several months. This method was not efficient as the binder was cluttered, and it took time to find the relevant reagent. Consequently, stock withdrawals are not indicated every time. In case an item is not available in stock, technicians or the supervisor request it from the head of service. She contacts the relevant supplier to obtain the required quantity. In such cases, it's mentioned that sometimes the shortage can last up to a month due to the unavailability of the required quantity of reagent or consumable from the supplier.

We have detected various anomalies within the reagents and consumables inventory management system in the laboratory. To categorize the diverse causes behind these deficiencies, we've conducted a root cause analysis. The fishbone diagram resulting from this analysis is presented in Fig. 3. This graphical representation, often referred to as the cause-and-effect diagram, serves as a practical method for examining potential problem sources and organizing causal connections [4]. Through the utilization of this technique, we've discerned five distinct categories (Manpower, Environment, Methods, Materials, and Management), which encapsulate the primary causes contributing to the deficiencies in laboratory inventory management.

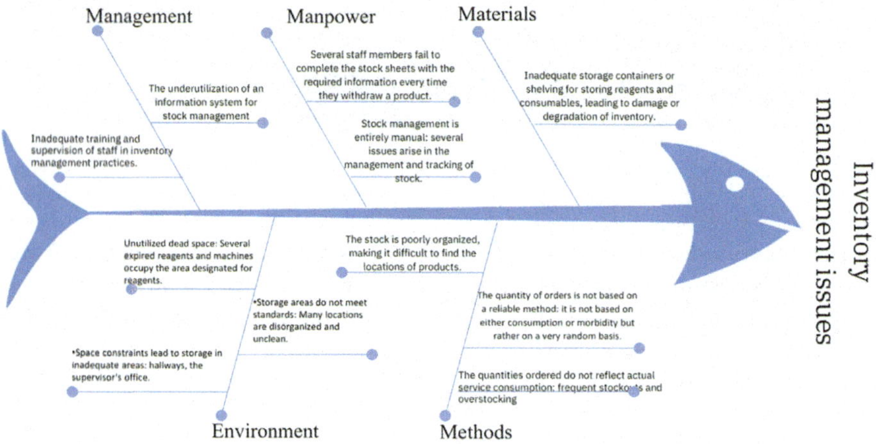

Fig. 3 Root cause analysis

5 Enhancing Laboratory Management: Recommendations for Optimal Inventory Practices

After pinpointing the root causes of inventory management issues and laboratory flow deficiencies, we delve into opportunities for enhancement to achieve cost-effective management. Building upon the findings of Odhiambo and Kihara's [39], Saha and Ray's [46], and Essila's [17] studies, which highlighted the pivotal role of lean inventory practices, inventory records accuracy, and information technology systems in enhancing supply chain performance within healthcare settings. Consequently, targeted solutions were developed for each root cause identified, facilitated through the coordination of brainstorming sessions and ongoing dialogues with stakeholders directly involved in the laboratory process flow. The principal best practices recommendations for the envisioned future state encompass:

- Decision Support System

The implementation of a suitable Decision Support System holds the potential to address numerous challenges within the existing laboratory framework. We have proposed the establishment of an inventory management information system to oversee procurement, stock management, and requisition orders for the medical analysis laboratory. This computerized system enables better tracking of orders and deliveries, monitoring of reagents and consumables consumption, stock status tracking, and provision of decision indicators (Fig. 4). The initial step in utilizing the software involves recording the initial stock. To accomplish this, an inventory was planned and conducted, determining the available quantities of reagents and consumables, along with their batch numbers and expiration dates. Subsequently, laboratory personnel undertook the data entry process into the software.

The transition from manual stock management to computerized stock management represents a significant shift for all laboratory personnel. Consequently, numerous operations and adjustments must be made to adapt to this change within the laboratory environment. To facilitate this transition effectively, we have chosen to implement the ADKAR methodology. As outlined in Hiatt and Creasey [21], the ADKAR change management model is rooted in the analysis of successful and unsuccessful organizational changes over several years [11, 23]. This model provides a structured framework for understanding and managing individual transitions within the context of organizational change. The **ADKAR** model outlines the individual change process through five essential steps [50]: **Awareness** (Recognizing the need for change); **Desire** (Cultivating willingness to participate in and endorse the change); **Knowledge** (Acquiring the understanding of how to change); **Ability** (Developing the capacity to implement new skills and behaviors); **Reinforcement** (Sustaining the change over time to ensure its permanence). The ADKAR model in our case study context is depicted in Fig. 5.

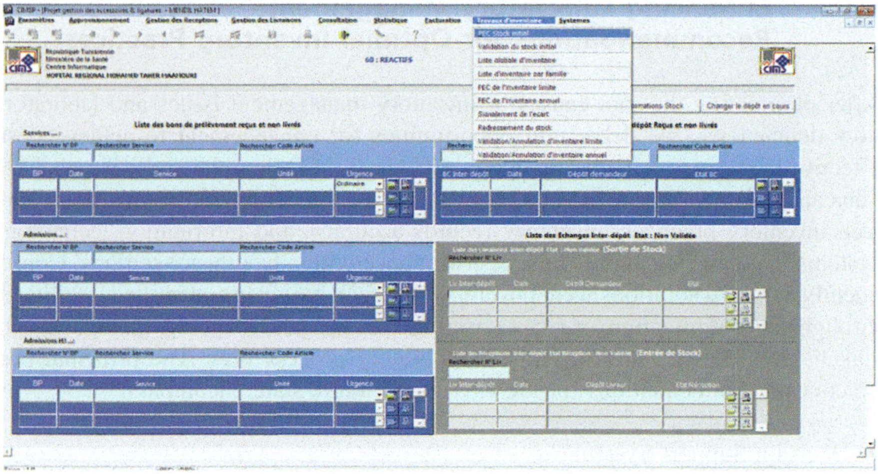

Fig. 4 Decision support system for the laboratory medical analysis

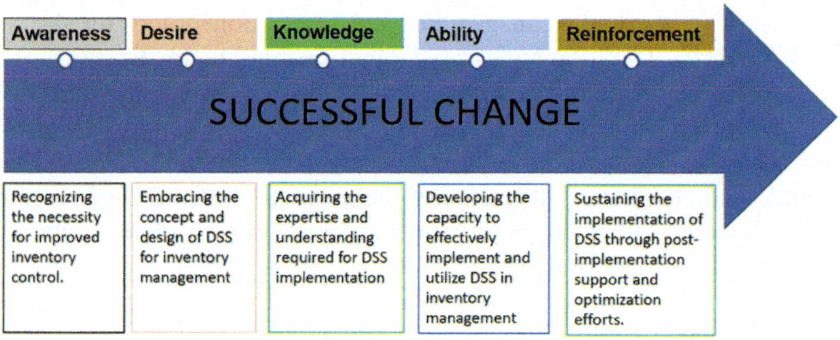

Fig. 5 The ADKAR model for the laboratory change

- Lean Inventory Practices

Odhiambo and Kihara's [39] study explored the impact of lean inventory practices on the supply chain performance of healthcare facilities. Specifically, their investigation centered on Just-in-Time (JIT), 5S lean practices, and the involvement of both customers and suppliers. The study posited that the organization, standardization, and maintenance of medical and non-medical supplies in healthcare facility stores contribute to the elimination of wasted time, effort, and expired resources. The research findings suggest that lean inventory practices are widely adopted among government health facilities in Kisumu County, aiming to enhance supply chain performance. Many other studies have consistently demonstrated the positive impact of lean practices on both operational and business performance metrics. For instance, Nawanir et al. [35] found that lean practices led to improvements in product quality, inventory management, timely delivery, cost reduction, as well as enhanced profitability, sales, and customer satisfaction. These findings underscore the importance of implementing lean inventory strategies to optimize supply chain performance in healthcare settings. In a recent study by Lanza-León et al. [25], a collection of articles detailing the application of the Kanban system in healthcare was examined. This comprehensive review shed light on both the barriers and benefits associated with implementing this lean practice in healthcare settings. The Kanban system, a method known for its ability to reduce inventory holding, was found to offer numerous advantages when applied in healthcare contexts. Mouaky et al. [33] explored the application of a Kanban system in managing pharmaceutical inventory and enhancing information sharing across a multi-echelon supply chain. Their study yielded two key findings: firstly, the implementation of the Kanban system strategically benefits the organization, enhancing service quality and facilitating information sharing across the supply chain. Secondly, it serves as a platform for innovation in pharmaceutical supply chains, enabling a transition from traditional push delivery systems to more effective logistics strategies, empowering frontline caregivers.

Drawing from these findings, our approach initially involved implementing the 5S continuous improvement lean practice to standardize laboratory inventory processes, enhance ergonomics, and bolster safety, among other advantages. Originating from Takashi Osada in the early 1980s [47], the 5S technique played a pivotal role in the Japanese manufacturing revolution of that era and has since been widely embraced across various sectors, including healthcare [14, 22]. During the establishment of the 5S methodology, we observed a disregard for the FEFO method during stock withdrawal. We found boxes of green tubes and cuvettes with varying expiration dates being opened simultaneously. Additionally, a batch of phenotyping cards, expiring in 2026, had already been consumed, while those expiring in 2024 remained untouched. These issues arose due to unrestricted access to the storage area by all personnel, as it was shared with consumption spaces, leading to negligence of expiration dates. At this point, we opted to implement the Two-Bin Kanban system to address the outflow of items, optimize inventory sizes, and move towards achieving a just-in-time inventory system.

The original kanban system, integral to Just In Time (JIT) manufacturing and Lean Production, emerged in Japanese manufacturing to efficiently manage repetitive small-batch production. Toyota Motor Company notably pioneered this system in the 1950s, spawning extensive literature and reports. Various companies have adapted the kanban system to align with their unique operations and management principles. This concept finds application in the healthcare industry as well, serving to minimize waste across its inventory processes [40].

We attempted to adapt the principles of the Two-Bin Kanban system in the laboratory inventory management context. In this system, two bins are utilized: the front bin contains the operational quantity of an item for daily use, while the back bin serves as a reserve stock. When the first bin is emptied, it is removed, causing the second bin to slide forward for use. An empty bin prompts the retrieval of a labeled reminder for replenishment. We adapted this principle in the laboratory by designating empty shelves with a green color code. These shelves house open containers of consumables for daily use, ensuring technicians access only the designated green areas for stock retrieval. The initial bins contain pre-opened cartons, while the rest of the stock serves as reserve stock in the second bin, accessed only by the supervisor for replacement. Each open container in the green zones is labeled with relevant information such as item name, code, quantity, location, and opening and expiration dates. When the last item is taken, the label is moved to a pouch on the stock room door, signaling the supervisor to replace the empty bin and update the label accordingly.

6 Conclusion

In recent years, there has been a growing interest among researchers in exploring inventory management within healthcare supply chains, reflecting the recognition of its critical role in ensuring efficient and effective healthcare delivery. While considerable progress has been made in identifying solutions to various challenges encountered in healthcare supply chains, there remains ample room for further research and innovation in this domain. Our study focused specifically on laboratory supply chain management, shedding light on prevalent issues, best practices, and strategies for optimizing inventory management processes. Moving forward, it is imperative to delve deeper into understanding how uncertainties in product demand impact the quality of laboratory services. This avenue of inquiry holds significant potential for enhancing healthcare supply chain resilience and performance in the face of dynamic and evolving healthcare landscapes.

Acknowledgements The authors express their gratitude to the staff at the Tunisian hospital for their support during the research. The engineering students Olfa Mezlini and Oumayma Laouini also deserve recognition for their efforts. The authors appreciate and acknowledge everyone involved for their support.

References

1. Ahmadi E, Masel DT, Metcalf AY, Schuller K (2019) Inventory management of surgical supplies and sterile instruments in hospitals: a literature review. Health Syst 8(2):134–151
2. Aissaoui NO, Ben Mbarek H, Layeb SB, Hadj-Alouane AB (2022) A BPMN-VSM based process analysis to improve the efficiency of multidisciplinary outpatient clinics. Prod Plann Control 1–31
3. Alharbi MSS, Alharbi AAF, Alotaibi RJ, Alyami MSA, Kindasa TMA, Maglia AIA et al (2023) Exploring the role of medical laboratories in modern healthcare: a comprehensive overview. J Namib Stud Hist Polit Cult 36:1893–1904
4. Andersen B, Fagerhaug T (2002) Root cause analysis: simplified tools and techniques. J Healthc Qual (JHQ) 24(3):46–47
5. Balkhi B, Alshahrani A, Khan A (2022) Just-in-time approach in healthcare inventory management: does it really work? Saudi Pharm J 30(12):1830–1835

6. Beheshti HM, Grgurich D, Gilbert FW (2012) ABC inventory management support system with a clinical laboratory application. J Promot Manag 18(4):414–435
7. Beier FJ (1995) The management of the supply chain for hospital pharmacies: a focus on inventory management practices. J Bus Logist 16(2):153
8. Bijvank M, Vis IF (2012) Inventory control for point-of-use locations in hospitals. J Oper Res Soc 63:497–510
9. Birx D, de Souza M, Nkengasong JN (2009) Laboratory challenges in the scaling up of HIV, TB, and malaria programs: the interaction of health and laboratory systems, clinical research, and service delivery. Am J Clin Pathol 131(6):849–851
10. Boche B, Temam S, Kebede O (2022) Inventory management performance for laboratory commodities and their challenges in public health facilities of Gambella Regional State, Ethiopia: a mixed cross-sectional study. Heliyon 8(11)
11. Chen C, Osei WA, Göransson B (2018) Implementing change in organisations
12. Chletsos M, Saiti A, Chletsos M, Saiti A (2019) Strategic planning in the health-care sector. In: Strategic management and economics in health care, pp 69–88
13. De Vries J (2011) The shaping of inventory systems in health services: a stakeholder analysis. Int J Prod Econ 133(1):60–69
14. Ebuetse M, Doggett M (2018) Analysis of the 5S technique: case study of a surveying laboratory. J Qual Manag Syst Appl Eng Technol Manage 3(1)
15. Epstein RH, Dexter F (2000) Economic analysis of linking operating room scheduling and hospital material management information systems for just-in-time inventory control. Anesth Analg 91(2):337–343
16. Esmaili N, Norman BA, Rajgopal J (2019) Exact analysis of (R, s, S) inventory control systems with lost sales and zero lead time. Nav Res Logist (NRL) 66(2):123–132
17. Essila JC (2023) Strategies for reducing healthcare supply chain inventory costs. Benchmark Int J 30(8):2655–2669
18. Fox ER, Sweet BV, Jensen V (2014) Drug shortages: a complex health care crisis. Mayo Clin Proc 89(3):361–373
19. Getele GK, Li T, Arrive JT (2020) The role of supply chain management in healthcare service quality. IEEE Eng Manage Rev 48(1):145–155
20. Hailu HA, Desale A, Yalew A, Asrat H, Kebede S, Dejene D et al (2020) Patients' satisfaction with clinical laboratory services in public hospitals in Ethiopia. BMC Health Serv Res 20:1–9
21. Hiatt J, Creasey T (2012) Change management. The people side of change, p 2
22. Ishijima H, Eliakimu E, Mshana JM (2016) The "5S" approach to improve a working environment can reduce waiting time: findings from hospitals in Northern Tanzania. TQM J 28(4):664–680
23. Jaaron AA, Hijazi IH, Musleh KIY (2022) A conceptual model for adoption of BIM in construction projects: ADKAR as an integrative model of change management. Technol Anal Strateg Manag 34(6):655–667
24. Jahangirian M, Naseer A, Stergioulas L, Young T, Eldabi T, Brailsford S et al (2012) Simulation in health-care: lessons from other sectors. Oper Res Int J 12:45–55
25. Lanza-León P, Sanchez-Ruiz L, Cantarero-Prieto D (2021) Kanban system applications in healthcare services: a literature review. Int J Health Plann Manage 36(6):2062–2078
26. Leaven L, Ahmmad K, Peebles D (2017) Inventory management applications for healthcare supply chains. Int J Supply Chain Manag 6(3):1–7
27. Legese N, Teshome D, Gedif T (2022) Inventory management of health commodities in a tertiary teaching hospital in Ethiopia. Front Pharmacol 13:763909
28. Lu H, Shi JJ (2019) Stockout risk of production-inventory systems with compound Poisson demands. Omega 83:181–198
29. Maestre JM, Fernández MI, Jurado IJCEP (2018) An application of economic model predictive control to inventory management in hospitals. Control Eng Pract 71:120–128
30. Mesfin EA, Taye B, Belay G, Ashenafi A, Girma V (2017) Factors affecting quality of laboratory services in public and private health facilities in Addis Ababa, Ethiopia. eJIFCC 28(3):205

31. Modisakeng C, Matlala M, Godman B, Meyer JC (2020) Medicine shortages and challenges with the procurement process among public sector hospitals in South Africa; findings and implications. BMC Health Serv Res 20:1–10
32. Moons K, Waeyenbergh G, Pintelon L (2019) Measuring the logistics performance of internal hospital supply chains—a literature study. Omega 82:205–217
33. Mouaky M, Berrado A, Benabbou L (2019) Using a kanban system for multi-echelon inventory management: the case of pharmaceutical supply chains. Int J Logist Syst Manag 32(3–4):496–519
34. Nachtmann H, Pohl EA (2009) The state of healthcare logistics: cost and quality improvement opportunities. Center for Innovation in Healthcare Logistics, University of Arkansas
35. Nawanir G, Kong Teong L, Norezam Othman S (2013) Impact of lean practices on operations performance and business performance: some evidence from Indonesian manufacturing companies. J Manuf Technol Manag 24(7):1019–1050
36. Nojiyeza S, Mkutshulwa L (2012) Inventory control systems for National Health Laboratory Services: the case of the KZN Health Department. J Manage Adm 10(2):37–81
37. Nyogea DS, Said H, Mwaigomole G, Stoeckle M, Felger I, Hatz C et al (2015) An assessment of the supply chain management for HIV/AIDS care and treatment in Kilombero and Ulanga districts in southern Tanzania. Tanzania J Health Res 17(2)
38. Obeta MU, Maduka KM, Ofor IB, Ofojekwu NM (2019) Improving quality and cost diminution in modern healthcare delivery: the role of the medical laboratory scientists in Nigeria. Int J Bus Manag Invent (IJBMI) 8(03):08–19
39. Odhiambo MO, Kihara AN (2018) Effect of inventory management practices on supply chain performance of government health facilities in Kisumu county in Kenya. J Int Bus Innov Strateg Manag 1(6):145–166
40. Raguramsingh M, Janarthanan V, Karthikeyan K (2012) Implementation of Kanban in pharmacy to achieve just in time inventory system using RFID. In: International conference on challenges and opportunities in mechanical engineering, industrial engineering and management studies (ICCOMIM-2012), July 2012, pp 11–13
41. Rosales CR, Magazine M, Rao U (2015) The 2Bin system for controlling medical supplies at point-of-use. Eur J Oper Res 243(1):271–280
42. Rosales CR, Magazine MJ, Rao US (2019) Dual sourcing and joint replenishment of hospital supplies. IEEE Trans Eng Manage 67(3):918–931
43. Rowan NJ, Laffey JG (2020) Challenges and solutions for addressing critical shortage of supply chain for personal and protective equipment (PPE) arising from coronavirus disease (COVID19) pandemic—case study from the Republic of Ireland. Sci Total Environ 725:138532
44. Rubigha K (2020) Sustainability in healthcare inventory management: a seven-dimensional review framework. J Contemp Manag Res 14(1):18–30
45. Saedi S, Kundakcioglu OE, Henry AC (2016) Mitigating the impact of drug shortages for a healthcare facility: an inventory management approach. Eur J Oper Res 251(1):107–123
46. Saha E, Ray PK (2019) Modelling and analysis of inventory management systems in healthcare: a review and reflections. Comput Ind Eng 137:106051
47. Shaikh S (2015) Review of 5S technique
48. Supeekit T, Somboonwiwat T, Kritchanchai D (2015) Linking hospital supply chain processes and performance to identify key performance indicator. In: Industrial engineering, management science and applications 2015. Springer Berlin Heidelberg, pp 927–938
49. Supeekit T, Somboonwiwat T, Kritchanchai D (2016) DEMATEL-modified ANP to evaluate internal hospital supply chain performance. Comput Ind Eng 102:318–330
50. Tang KN, Tang KN (2019) Change management. In: Leadership and change management, pp 47–55
51. Towill DR, Christopher M (2005) An evolutionary approach to the architecture of effective healthcare delivery systems. J Health Organ Manag 19(2):130–147
52. Volland J, Fügener A, Schoenfelder J, Brunner JO (2017) Material logistics in hospitals: a literature review. Omega 69:82–101

53. Weinstein W, Wenk RE (1985) Hospital laboratory inventory management. Clin Lab Med 5(4):753–760
54. Zuma SM (2022) Assessment of medicine stock-outs challenges in public health services. Afr Public Serv Deliv Perform Rev 10(1):578

Imen Mejri holds a Ph.D. in Industrial Engineering from the National Engineering School of Tunis, University of Tunis El Manar, Tunisia. Currently, she serves as an assistant professor at the National Higher Engineering School of Tunis, University of Tunis, and is affiliated with the OASIS lab at the National Engineering School of Tunis. Her research interests include industrial engineering, applied mathematics, operations research, healthcare optimization, and artificial intelligence.

Safa Bhar Layeb is currently a professor of industrial engineering and an active member of the OASIS Laboratory at the National Engineering School of Tunis, Tunisia. Safa holds a Polytechnic Engineering degree, a Master's degree in Mathematical Engineering, a Ph.D. in Applied Mathematics, and a university habilitation (HDR) in Industrial Engineering. She is the founding chair of the African Working Group in Health Systems and a member of the Executive Committee of the African Federation of Operations Research Societies (AFROS). She has served as guest editor and reviewer for over twenty international journals. She is an active member of the editorial, organizing, and scientific committees of several international conferences. She has supervised over thirty Master and Ph.D. theses in collaboration with several international institutes. Her teaching and research interests include Operations research, optimization, and data science approaches and their applications in healthcare organizations, industrial engineering, logistics, and supply chain management.

Najla Aissaoui received her Industrial Engineering degree, her M.S. and Ph.D. from the National Engineering School of Tunis (ENIT). She is currently an assistant professor of industrial engineering at the National Engineering School of Carthage and a member of OASIS Lab at the National Engineering School of Tunis, Tunisia. Her area of expertise and interest are production planning and control, supply chain optimisation, lean healthcare, health systems and performance measurement systems.

Mohamed Yassine Kaabar biologist pharmacist graduated in France from the University of Paris V and Rennes 1, he has been working since 2016 in Tunisian public hospitals. He specializes in biological hematology. Currently, he works as an Associate Professor at the Faculty of Pharmacy in Monastir and at the Mohamed Taher Maamouri University Hospital in Nabeul. His areas of interest include hematology and hospital governance.

Medicines Strategic Sourcing in Moroccan Public Hospital: Development of Purchasing Portfolio and Strategies

14

Imane Ibn El Farouk, Fatima Zahra Majidi, and Fouad Jawab

Abstract

The efficient management of the supply of medicines is of crucial importance for Moroccan public hospitals. Because of budgetary constraints and the need to provide quality care to a large number of patients, it is essential to design optimal purchasing strategies. These ensure a sufficient supply of medicines, minimize costs and ensure the quality and availability of pharmaceutical products. The objective of the following chapter is to focus on the design of an effective drug procurement strategy in the specific context Moroccan Hospital, witch facing particular challenges related to the acquisition and management of drugs. Our research question here is which purchasing strategy is more suitable for each medicine category in hospital? The aim of this article is to map the medicine purchasing with a portfolio model in order to make purchasing strategy in a public hospital using. To do this, we mobilized the strategic sourcing approach by opting for an action research and a case study of a university public hospital in Morocco. Kraljic Matrix Model (KMM) and AHP method were used as tools to map the hospital's medication purchasing portfolio. Through our research, we have highlighted an interesting concept; "reverse marketing".

I. Ibn El Farouk (✉) · F. Z. Majidi
Laboratory for Studies and Research in Economics and Management Sciences, LERSEM, ENCGJ, Chouaib Doukkali University, El Jadida, Morocco
e-mail: ibnelfarouk.i@ucd.ac.ma

F. Z. Majidi
e-mail: majidi.f@ucd.ac.ma

F. Jawab
Laboratory of Technologies and Industrial Services, Higher School of Technology, Sidi Mohamed Ben Abdellah University, Fez, Morocco
e-mail: Fouad.jawab@usmba.ac.ma

F. Jawab (ed.), *Hospital Supply Chain*, Integrated Science 27,
https://doi.org/10.1007/978-3-031-70292-1_14

In this context, the need to design purchasing systems to establish the perfect match between the needs of a buying company and the supply market has emerged.

Keywords

Kraljic matrix • Medicine • Drug • Reverse marketing • AHP

Abbreviations

AHP	Analytic Hierarchy Process
CHU	Centre Hospitalier Universitaire/University Hospital Center
DEA	Data Envelopment Analysis
KPM	Kraljic Portfolio Matrix
MCDM	Multiple Criteria Decision Making
PPM	Purchasing Portfolio Model
SI	Strategic impact
SR	Supplier risk
TCO	Total cost of ownership
TOPSIS	Technique for Order of Preference by Similarity to Ideal Solution

1 Introduction

Compelling evidence confirm that the strategic purchasing management can provide an important and sustainable competitive advantage for companies [26]. Purchasing plays an important and vital role in generating savings and ensuring the financial robustness of companies. In this context, strategic sourcing aims to sustain profitable growth by optimizing the supplier base, reducing linking cost in the supply chain, and maximizing the value of goods for the users [1, 13].

In Morocco, the availability of medicines at hospital level is a national priority, and this with regard to provided and mobilized to ensure the availability of the act of care. The drug is a critical element, given its high price, the complexity of the actors involved in its management, its diversity and its regulatory side serious [4, 17]. All of these elements make buying the drug in the hospital a big challenge. It is a question of making the constant match between availability and purchase cost. This equation finds its solution in the design of personalized purchasing start-ups for each category of drug. A purchasing strategy is used to show how to buy, how to well match the purchaser's need with the supplier's market offer.

Given the diversity of medical molecules managed by a hospital pharmacy, all these molecules should not be purchased in the same way [2]. In this sense, our objective in this work is to be able to model the drug purchasing portfolio within a Moroccan public hospital in order to design adapted and personalized purchasing strategies for each purchased molecule. This approach would not only ensure that the hospital is able to procure the necessary medications in a cost-effective manner, but also guarantee that the patients receive the best quality of care. By analyzing the purchasing patterns and requirements of different medical molecules, the hospital pharmacy can tailor their procurement strategies to meet specific needs and optimize their inventory management. Furthermore, by understanding the market dynamics and trends related to each type of medication, the hospital can negotiate better deals with suppliers and potentially reduce costs. This personalized approach to drug purchasing would ultimately benefit both the hospital and its patients, ensuring efficient and effective healthcare delivery. Ultimately, our goal is to create a model that can be replicated in other healthcare settings to improve medication management practices across the board.

To answer our question, we have adopted a strategic sourcing approach and the AHP method. In concrete terms, we will mobilize the strategic purchasing part of this process. This part begins with a segmentation of purchasing needs, identifies potential purchasing risks for each segment, through which a portfolio modeling is designed and which classifies each segment according to specific criteria. To ensure a faithful representation, these criteria must be weighted; here the use of a multicriteria analysis method such as AHP is essential. Strategic recommendations are then formulated according to the profile of each segment. The empirical side was a case study of a university hospital in Morocco.

We have structured our paper into three primary sections; initially, we introduce the concept of strategic sourcing as a reverse marketing strategy and detail its workings. Following this, we outline our research methodology, and lastly, we analyze and discuss the outcomes before wrapping up.

2 Background

2.1 Strategic Sourcing as Reverse Marketing Practice

The expenditure on procurement in the industrial sector has witnessed a substantial rise in the past few decades. Consequently, the significance of supply chain management and purchasing in determining the competitiveness of enterprises is being increasingly acknowledged. Consequently, it is imperative to customize and adapt supplier relationship management based on the characteristics of the purchased items. It is crucial to refrain from adopting a uniform management approach, be it the conventional "arm's-length model" or the "partner model of supplier management". Both models possess their own merits and drawbacks. Hence, it becomes essential to categorize the purchasing portfolio in order to select the appropriate model for each specific type of purchase [16].

Strategic sourcing reflects the change that the purchasing function has undergone, from a support function to a strategic function that provides a competitive advantage [13]. Historically, sourcing was seen as a purely administrative act, which consisted of satisfying the needs of an internal user, and nobody in the company believed that one day we would be able to create value and make a profit through sourcing [27].

Strategic sourcing can be defined as the process of configuring and managing the supply network in perfect harmony with the company's performance objectives. It is measured by the four sub-constructs of (1) strategic purchasing, (2) internal integration, (3) information sharing, and (4) supplier development [12, 18]. The principal call for strategic sourcing is to fit purchasing strategy to the business strategy [20] in order to enhance stakeholders value [31]. The main goal of strategic sourcing is to build a long term relationship with suppliers [40].

In their book about the strategic sourcing [1], authors consider that the development of strategic sourcing is linked to the question of how to reduce the total cost of ownership (TCO). This has given rise to four levels through which supply management has moved from a traditional, purely transactional vision to one of creating value for all. These levels are as follows:

- **level 0 "user buy"**: any strategic value for procurement, while user is satisfied, contract conditions are not optimal, and price is sometimes high.
- **level 1 "buy for less"**: buyer work closely with the user, centralization of needs, supplier are selected basing on price and terms.
- **level 2 "linked buy"**: the procurement organization takes an external view of the supply chain and develop a "win/win" relationship with suppliers. Streamlining bidding processes, optimization of logistic flows, stable commitment to lead supplier efficient investment. In this level, the aim is to reduce the TCO by better understanding the supplier market.
- **level 3 "value buy"**: the focus here is to optimize the total cost life cycle and the consumer value. Value engineering, reducing complexity, supplier involvement in product design, are examples of how supplier and buyers con work together to enhance procurement value added.
- **level 4 "integrated sell"**: a significant procurement innovation which allows company to sell better. Such situations are when a specific product has a high level of procurement risks and profit impact and subsequently the role of the supplier becomes central and decisive in maintaining a competitive position of the company.

Strategic sourcing is a process at the end of which it is decided to whom outsource, which relationship format and type to adopt with suppliers. It consists on making sourcing strategy by category purchased. Category is a homogeneous group of products or services to which the same form of contract, the same performance indicators, the same price range and the same approach to negotiation can be attributed. The exact definition of the categories is the key to the success of the strategic sourcing process. The strategic sourcing process is cross-functional and brings together several profiles of professionals from different areas in the company [31]. The sourcing process is described below and is shown in Fig. 1:

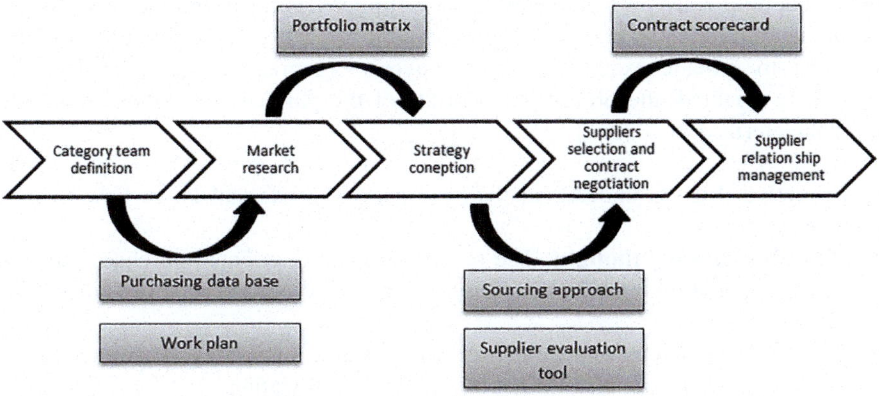

Fig. 1 Strategic processes, adapted from Monczka [31]

1. ***Category team definition***: This team is led by purchasing staff, and is made up of staff from a range of different areas, including engineering, quality, logistics and manufacturing. The output of this step is to clarify what we're working on and how we're organized.
2. ***Market research***: It aims to understand the category market. This is an internal and external analysis which aims to map the positioning of the company's needs in relation to the structure of the supplier market. It involves identifying the strengths and weaknesses of the company that need to be addressed, also the opportunities offered by the purchasing market and the threats they pose. This stage enables the portfolio model to be designed, like the KRALJIC matrix.
3. ***Strategies conception***: Once he purchasing needs have been mapped out, it is advisable to adopt a specific, personalized strategy for each category. Strategy recommended by each the category's purchasing profile is explained in the Kraljic Matrix section below.
4. ***Supplier selection and contract negotiation***: The aim is to select suppliers for each category in line with the agreed strategy. This involves selecting suppliers for each category in line with the agreed strategy. The selection criteria must respect the defined sourcing approach. For example, if the approach is to minimize supply risks, the supplier's production capacity becomes a very important criterion.
5. ***Supplier relationship management***: The strategic sourcing process is not limited to signing the agreement with the supplier, but extends to performance management of the relationship between buyer and seller, using performance indicators derived from the contract itself. This relationship management is the strength point of strategic sourcing, and the success factor of the company.

Strategic sourcing is also viewed as "reverse marketing". This concept was defined in Blenkhorn and Banting [7] and Dwyer et al. [15] as "*an imaginative approach to achieving supply objectives*". It involves a revolution and reversal in basic buyer–supplier roles. While, initially, the supplier has taken the initiative to persuade buyer, in reverse marketing approach, the buyer tries to interest the supplier in order to provide exactly what the buyer's organization needs. In Reverse-marketing-oriented, the profile and attitude of the purchasers is transformed and are characterized as follow [7]

- **Proactive**: Buyers understand their company's needs and know how to meet them.
- **Multidimensional thought**: The reverse-marketing oriented purchaser develop an integrated thinking about the implications of a purchase on several difference planes.
- **Creative approach**: The purchaser with reverse marketing posture thinks in multiple area at a time and aims to a global optimization.
- **Cooperative partnership**: Here, buyer looks for a long-term relationship with their suppliers.
- **Long-term perspective**: Purchaser develops the ability to assess effect of a current purchasing action on the firm's long-term future.
- **Continuing and optimizing**: Purchaser focuses on long-term sustainable gains rather than momentary gains.
- **Assertive**: Purchaser approaches purchasing in project terms, and won't accept inflexible suppliers who aren't interested in the project's long-term benefits.
- **Motivation**: Highly motivated to achieve their objectives, and despite the likely reluctance and non-cooperation of their suppliers, buyers are constantly on the lookout for new solutions, substitutes and new approaches to purchasing.

2.2 Medicine and Purchasing in Hospital

The public hospital is an organization whose primary purpose is to meet a public health objective. Its strategic objectives are: Meet the health needs expressed in its territory, ensure the quality of its activity, Optimize its economic and organizational efficiency. The hospital is also a particular and complex socio-technical system. Researchers such as Moons et al. [32], and Bélanger et al. [9] have highlighted these challenges. The main complexity factors of hospital systems as follows:

- The mobilization of a large number of flows, activities, services around the main mission of the hospital, namely the management of patients.
- Compartmentalization and too strong segmentation of activities.
- The diversity of functions and actors that come into play for the performance of the act of care. In addition to medical skills, catering and maintenance professionals, purchases interact in order to bring the care services to fruition.
- The singularity and specificity of each patient; the act of care may differ from one patient to another for the same pathology.

- Technological innovation; rapid evolution has a strong impact on how to perform an act of care.
- The particular decision-making system; hospital systems suffer from the absence of a clear hierarchical line. The administrative body does not have sufficient power to orchestrate the operational centers made up of groups of doctors with significant decision-making power. In such a context, the antagonism of the interests of the two groups makes decision-making a very difficult task.

The public hospital is facing pressure from the wards who are seeking to rationalize the spending allocated to health while wanting to maintain or even change the level of quality of care. In the same time, drug plays a crucial role in the availability of the act of care, at the lowest cost and at the best quality, which is why, to address a problem that affects the management of drug purchases and is of extreme importance. Globally, pharmaceutical expenditure is a major concern, with estimates suggesting it makes up 20–30% of total healthcare spending [21].

In hospitals, the purchase of the various items needed to carry out the act of care mobilizes enormous financial and human resources. Hospital purchasing is a complicated act, given the variety of products, their fragility and their impact on patient care act [2, 30]. Importance of purchasing within hospital area enhance with the fact that purchasing expenses for a hospital have accounted for up to 45% of its total costs [5, 30]. However, the variety of items means that they cannot be purchased in the same way, and the purchasing process needs to be personalized in order to build an adequate purchasing strategies [2]. A number of studies have looked at the issue of purchasing strategy in hospitals. The most famous are those dealing with purchasing groups. The purchasing group is an horizontal cooperation between two or more organizations which aims to build up a negotiating force vis-à-vis manufacturers. By consolidating their purchasing volumes, these groups have more scope to obtain attractive prices, thanks to economies of scale [5, 8, 36].

2.3 Kraljic Matrix

To guarantee the performance of the procurement process, not all items purchased need to be managed in the same way and with the same degree of importance [24]. For this reason, many classification models have been developed to help professionals classify purchases and allocate personalized strategies to them. Among those models; we find the "Kraljic Matrix". Although criticized, the Kraljic matrix is still the most portfolio mode widely used [26, 41]. The Kraljic Matrix is a model developed by Kraljic in 1977 and further refined in Kraljic [28]. It is a tool that helps purchasing managers to recognize their weaknesses in relation to a supplier market and to find the right approach to overcome these weaknesses and establish a match between their needs and the supplier market. The Kraljic Matrix, known as the Purchasing Portfolio Matrix (KPM) is a tool used to classify purchased items based on their "strategic importance" and "supply risk. This portfolio model

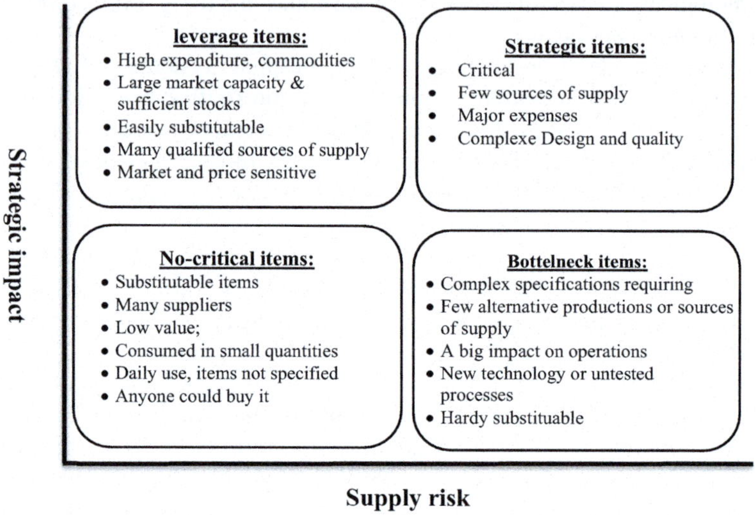

Fig. 2 Kraljic matrix [28]

is used by purchasing practitioners to manage supplier relations and developed appropriate purchasing strategies [10]. The matrix provides for four classes as show in Fig. 2 [25]: (1) non-critical, (2) leverage, (3) bottleneck, and (4) strategic. Each category requires specific tactics for effective management. Each quadrant is associated with specific tactics for managing the supply chain effectively [26].

The strategic importance reflects the financial impact. Such as: (1) the value contributed by the product, (2) the proportion of raw material costs in the overall expenses, (3) influence on profitability, (4) effect on product quality and business expansion. The supply risk is related to the purchasing difficulty or intricacy leverage. These are assessed through factors like (1) supply scarcity, (2) the rate of technological advancements, (3) materials substitution, (4) entry barriers, (5) logistics intricacies and costs, (6) presence of monopoly or oligopoly conditions, (7) numbers of suppliers, (8) availability [19, 28].

Therefore, the categorizing items or products involved in the KPMs based on their strategic importance (SI) and supply risk leading to four distinct categories, and each on requires a specific purchasing strategy [14, 19, 22, 34]: the four categories are described as follow:

- **Leverage items**: characterized by a high business share, significant strategic impact, and low or mitigated supply risk, typically follows a mature and well-established supply process. The recommended purchasing strategy for leverage items involves competitive bidding and the exploration of buying power to secure favorable deals.
- **Strategic items**: possess high business impact, high strategic importance, and an elevated supply risk. Managing these items successfully requires specific

practices such as fostering long-term relationships, involving suppliers early in the process, and strategic planning, given their critical role in the company's survival.

- **Bottleneck items**: with low business impact but a high supply risk, are susceptible to interruptions and delays. Strategies for bottleneck items include establishing alternative suppliers, maintaining safety stocks, and having backup plans in place. Finally,
- **Non-critical items**: characterized by low business and strategic impact, as well as low supply market complexity (supply risk), call for a focus on high performance and cost reduction. Strategies for non-critical items often involve standardization and cost-effective bidding processes to optimize efficiency and minimize expenses.

The Kraljic matrix has been widely used in different sectors and for a variety of purposes. Table 1 summarizes the various applications.

2.4 AHP

AHP is a method/approach used for decision-making. It is a tool that helps in representing overall priorities, comprised of products, sums of criteria weights, and the relative weights of alternatives. AHP is valuable when verbal judgments alone are insufficient for capturing the complexity of decision factors, and it emphasizes the use of a numerical and semantic scale within the AHP framework to refine and analyze these judgments more effectively. In essence, AHP is a structured methodology for decision analysis that involves a combination of numerical estimation and verbal expression [35].

The Analytic Hierarchy Process (AHP) is used as a decision-making tool in a Purchasing Portfolio Model (PPM). It is used to prioritize criteria related to Key Purchasing Measures (KPM), specifically strategic impact and supply risk [2].

In the health care sector, [2] the AHP model (AHP) was applied in developing a Purchasing Portfolio Model (PPM) to prioritize criteria in the Key Purchasing Measures (KPM) dimensions of strategic impact and supply risk. Using a four-level hierarchy, pairwise comparisons on a "1–9" scale determined criteria weights, while direct measurements simplified (classes of medicine items) CMIs scores. The AHP model, known for handling complex decisions, ensured consistency, and accommodated qualitative criteria, making it a valuable tool for rationalizing purchasing portfolio decisions. The approach involves pairwise comparisons and a relative importance scale for criteria weighting.

The Multiple Criteria Decision Making (MCDM) model is the predominant choice, constituting 62% of cases. Notably, the Analytical Hierarchy Process (AHP) emerges as the most widely recognized decision-making method, featured in 160 papers. Additionally, the Data Envelopment Analysis (DEA) model was applied in 122 studies, and the Technique for Order of Preference by Similarity to Ideal Solution (TOPSIS) ranked third with 101 studies [42]. According to Seth

Table 1 Use of Kraljic matrix by researchers

References	Sector	Purposes
Arantes et al. [2]	Hospital	Classification of different classes of medicines and define differentiated purchasing strategies
Bianchini et al. [6]	Manufacturing (production of street lamps)	Classification of suppliers to reduce lead time
Caniëls and Gelderman [10]	General	Study the relationship between customer and supplier for the four quadrant of the Kraljic matrix
Chancasanampa-Mandujano et al. [11]	Consumer goods company	Enhance stock monitoring and avoid raw materials stockouts and overstock
Ferreira et al. [19]	Construction sector	Defining purchasing strategies
Gangurde and Chavan [22]	General	Defining appropriate purchasing strategies in order to reduce profit impact and supply risk
Garzon et al. [23]	Chemical sector	A green procurement approach to choice suppliers
Ghanbarizadeh et al. [25]	Construction sector	Rsolve classification issue in Kraljic matrix by using hybrid MCDM
Hesping and Schiele [26]	General	Define tactical sourcing levers for each quadrant of Kraljic matrix
Medeiros and Ferreira [30]	Hospital	Conception of a purchasing portfolio
Padhi et al. [33]	Rural development department of a state government in India	Commodities classification
Tip et al. [41]	Hospital	Assess hospital purchasers' procurement strategies during the COVID-19 pandemic

et al. [39] researchers favor AHP, citing its robust framework for handling Multiple Criteria Decision Making (MCDM) requirements. This endorsement underscores AHP's reliability in addressing challenges associated with item classification across diverse studies. AHP also has the ability to handle complex problems and offers the advantage of being flexible and simple in its implementation.

3 Material and Method

3.1 Methodology Approach

According to the above, it is vital that the management of medicines in hospitals requires the design of a personalized purchasing strategy for each category of article. In this sense, our objective here is to design a purchasing strategy for groups of medicines in a public hospital in Morocco. To do this, we have adopted a strategic sourcing approach, which is presented as shown in Fig. 3.

1. **Criteria identification**: according to the strategic sourcing methodology, presented above, the first step in making purchasing strategy is the market analysis witch led to the purchasing portfolio. The aim of market analysis is to identify supply constraints, i.e. any obstacles that will prevent the company from matching its purchasing needs to the market situation. This is why this analysis is based on certain criteria. The constraints in question may be internal or external. The internal constraint is one that emanates from the purchasing company, for example: "unreliable purchasing forecasts" or "local regulatory constraints". The external constraint emanates from the external environment; from suppliers and also competitors who have the same need to buy as the company. This is what is called "competition in purchase". This competition has contributed to the emergence of the "reverse marketing" concept.
2. **Criteria prioritization**: prioritization of criteria is made according to a principle that not all criteria may have the same importance. To ensure a reliable representation of reality, it is essential to weigh each criterion. For this step, we used the AHP method. Following a network with experiences in the pharmaceutical field, we were able to assign weights to each criterion.
3. **Selection of categories**: this step consists in selecting from among all the molecules bought by the pharmacy, the one that we will conduct our analysis. This choice was made in agreement with the head pharmacist taking into

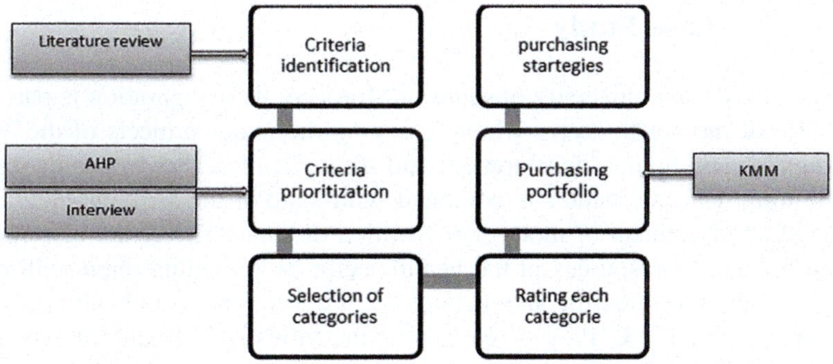

Fig. 3 Research methodology (authors)

account the challenges that some molecules have in terms of importance and financial impact.

4. **Rating each categories**: to rate each criterion by categories, we have chosen an evaluation scale as follow: 4: very high impact, 3: medium impact, 2: low impact, 0: no impact. By impact, we mean, the impact of the constraint on the category.
5. **Making the portfolio with Kraljic Matrix Model (KMM)**: to represent the different categories on the matrix, we need to calculate the coordinates according to the formula in Eq. (1).

Equation 1: Coordinates calculation

$$X_{(c)} = \left(\sum R(SRIi) * W(SSIi)/4\right) * 100\%$$

$$Y_{(c)} = \left(\sum R(SSIi) * W(SSIi)/4\right) * 100\%$$

With:

(c)	Category
X	abscissa (SR)
Y	ordinate (SI)
R(SRIi), R(SSIi)	rating of criterion
W(SSIi), W(SRIi)	weight of criterion.

6. **Making purchasing strategy**: to make personalized strategies, we follow the KMM recommendations. For example, working towards partnership and collaboration with the supplier for strategic categories, supporting the role of suppliers for the bottleneck categories, maximize commercial advantage for leveraged categories and delegate and minimize purchase effort for simple purchases.

3.2 The Case Study

The case study is an university hospital in Morocco, its inauguration is part of the promotion of the health sector which is among the major projects of the Moroccan kingdom and human development and the right of access to health services. This training and care center is equipped with state-of-the-art equipment; it has mobilized an investment of more than 1 billion dirhams. The center also provides training for human resources in the health sector by providing them with quality training, adapted to scientific and technological developments in health prevention and management. The CHU was realized by the Ministry of Health, it occupies an area about 50,000 m^2. It has a capacity of 500 beds, and it includes: (1) specialty hospital, (2) mother and child hospital, (3) Hassan II oncology center, (4) mental health and psychiatric hospital.

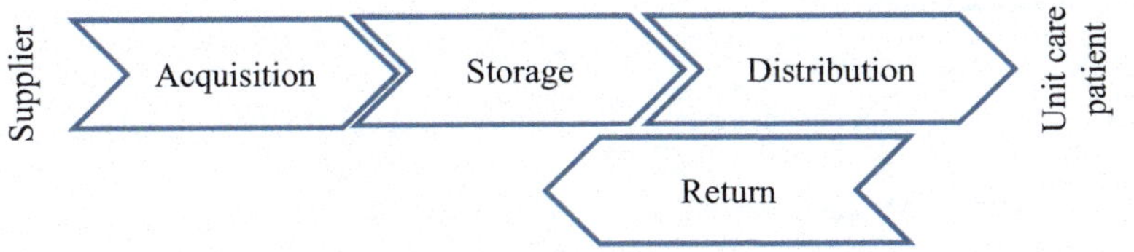

Fig. 4 Medicine supply chain in the hospital (authors)

The hospital has a central pharmacy, which is responsible for supplying health units with all medicines and medical devices. The pharmacy is under the management of a pharmacist designated by the Ministry of Health and who reports directly to the director of the hospital. Medicine supply chain (Fig. 4) goes from purchase (acquisition) to storage, distribution and management of returns. All drugs managed by the pharmacy are in the national nomenclature of medicines.

For the acquisition of medicine, the responsibility and autonomy of the hospital director is complete. This is done in several stages as follows:

- **Selection**: it is a question of fixing the list of medicines to be acquired. This selection takes into account several criteria: policies, techniques, and pharmacotherapeutics, national policy, the context and global situation.
- **Quantification**: a crucial and essential step in the management of hospital pharmacy. A fair quantification guarantees the availability of medicines for acts of care and avoids waste.
- **Acquisition**: this includes purchasing methods (tender, placing of orders), selection of suppliers, quantitative and qualitative control, and order tracking.

4 Results

4.1 Criteria Selection

According to what is explained in the paragraph of Kraljic Matrix, next to supply constraints, which we call supply risk (SR), it is also necessary to identify the financial impact of purchased items called strategic impact (SI). To identify and select the SR and SI we have used a literature review, after which we have identified the criteria cited and used by different authors who have designed a portfolio of purchases. The results are visible on Tables 2 and 3. Through interviews with stakeholders (pharmacists, pharmacist assistant, preparer, doctor, nurse), we were able to select the significant criteria for the purchase of drugs, the results are on Table 4. We limited ourselves to eight criteria in full; five in supplier risk and three in strategic impact.

Table 2 Selected criteria

Category	Code	Criteria	Signification
Supplier risk	SR1	Suppliers number	Number of supplier in the market
	SR2	Molecule substitution	If we can use another molecule
	SR3	Difficulty in switching the supplier	If it's easy or not to suite to another supplier
	SR4	Regulatory constraint	If there is any regulatory constraint witch make the purchasing difficult
	SR5	Supplier flexibility	If hospital can easily obtain added quantity
Strategic impact	SI1	Criticality of the molecule	If the patient care act cannot be accomplished without this molecule
	SI2	Growth in consumption	If the molecule consumption growth in future
	SI3	% in medicine expenditure	The share in medicine spending

4.2 Criteria Weighting

After applying the AHP prioritization methodology, we obtained the results contained in Table 5.

SR1. Substitution (0.30): This is the most important constraint in our analysis. Drug substitution refers to the possibility of exchanging one drug for another that has a similar or the same effect. If a drug is not available due to out-of-stock or production issues, the ability to substitute another drug can significantly reduce the risk of disruption to patient treatment. This is why this constraint has the greatest importance in risk management.

SR2. Regulatory constraints (0.28): These constraints are almost as important as the possibility of substitution. Regulation in the pharmaceutical sector is often strict and complex, aimed at ensuring patient safety and treatment effectiveness. This includes regulating the production, distribution, import and export of drugs. Non-compliance with these regulations can result in severe penalties and damage to the hospital's reputation, hence the importance of these constraints in risk management.

SR3. Number of suppliers (0.15) and SR4. Flexibility of supplier (0.15): These two constraints are equally important in our analysis. The number of providers refers to the amount of different sources from which a hospital can obtain its medications. The more suppliers, the easier it is to manage the risk of a stock shortage. Supplier flexibility refers to a supplier's ability to adapt to changes in demand, production problems, or other disruptions. A flexible supplier can increase or decrease production quickly, which can help manage risk.

Table 3 Literature review of supply risk criteria (authors)

Authors/criteria	Numbers of supplier	Monopole	Diversity	Financial instability of suppliers	Substitution	Scarcity	Availability	Technology peace	Entry barriers	Competitive demand
Hesping and Schiele [26]			√	√	√					√
Kraljic [28]		√			√	√	√	√	√	
Vijaya Dixit [14]	√				√	√	√			√
Arantes and Alhais[3]		√			√			√	√	
Sanchez et al. [37]	√				√	√				√
Ghanbarizadeha et al. [25]	√				√			√		
Pretell et al. [34]					√					√
Sanjaykumar and Amol [38]	√				√	√	√			
Ferreira et al. [19]	√	√			√			√	√	

Table 4 Strategic impact SI criteria from literature review (authors)

Authors	The volume purchased	Percentage of total purchase cost	Price variation	Impact on product quality	Business growth	Cost of raw material/ total cost	Profitability profile	Impact on scheduling operations	Cash flow	Economic factors	Information cost
Kraljic [28]	√	√	√	√	√	√	√				
Vijaya Dixit [13]	√	√	√	√	√						
Arantes [3]	√	√	√	√	√						
Sanchez et al. [37]	√	√	√	√	√						
Ghanbarizadeha et al. [25]	√							√	√	√	
Pretell et al. [34]	√	√	√								√
Sanjaykumar [38]	√	√	√								
Ferreira et al. [19]	√			√	√						

Table 5 Weighted criteria

Category	Code	Criteria	Weight
Supplier risk	SR1	Suppliers number	0.15
	SR2	Molecule substitution	0.3
	SR3	Difficulty changing the supplier	0.09
	SR4	Regulatory constraint	0.28
	SR5	Supplier flexibility	0.15
Strategic impact	SI1	Criticality of the molecule	0.52
	SI2	Growth in consumption	0.28
	SI3	% in medicine expenditure	0.2

SR5. Difficulty in switching providers (0.09): This constraint is the least important in our analysis. It refers to the challenges that can arise when switching suppliers. This can be due to long-term contracts, quality or compliance issues, or high change costs. Although this constraint is the least important of our analysis, it remains an essential consideration in risk management in pharmaceutical logistics.

4.3 Category Selection

Several criteria were selected to determine the categories for our study. Initially, the significance of each molecule in patient care was a key factor. Some molecules are essential for treating various medical conditions, and their availability directly impacts the quality of care. For instance, FENTANYL (Molecule 2) was identified as crucial for patient care, justifying its inclusion in the study. Additionally, we considered the proportion of total drug expenditures spent on each molecule. Molecules like FENTANYL (Molecule 2) and Nicardipine (Molecule 3) that contribute significantly to expenses can affect the hospital budget and supply chain efficiency. Lastly, we analyzed the monthly drug consumption. Molecules with high consumption rates pose challenges in inventory management. For example, Molecule 3 indicated potential future consumption growth, requiring special attention in supply chain planning. The selection of molecules for the study does not indicate their overall importance in the hospital's drug portfolio but focuses on logistical challenges and opportunities based on relevant criteria. We have identified 12 molecules for analysis, as detailed in Table 6.

4.4 Kraljic Matrix

To design the Kraljic matrix and map the positioning of the 12 molecules, he noted each molecule according to the risk and financial impact criteria. A grid of questions was administered to pharmacy staff, mainly the pharmacist, whose

Table 6 Selected categories

Number	Denomination	Therapeutic class
Molecule 1	Povidone iodeé	Antiseptic
Molecule 2	Fentanyl	Anaesthesia
Molecule 3	Nicardipine	Cardiology
Molecule 4	Paracetamol	Analgesic
Molecule 5	Methylprednisolone	Anti inflammatory
Molecule 6	Métoclopramide	Antiemetic
Molecule 7	Chlorure de sodium	Vitamin
Molecule 8	Albumin	Blood-derived drug
Molecule 9	Insulin	Diabetology
Molecule 10	Diazepam	Psychotropic
Molecule 11	Métalyse	Thrombolytic
Molecule 12	Omeprazole	Gastrology

answers were used to score each molecule against the different criteria. A rating scale of 0–4 was used as follows:

- 4: the impact of the important criteria
- 3: significant impact
- 2: average impact
- 1: average impact
- 0: no impact.

Example: for on Molecule 1, there is a single supplier, so the criterion "number supplier" and noted 4, it can be substituted by another molecule, so the criterion "substitution" is noted 0. Table 7 gives rating and coordinates for each molecule and Fig. 5 visualize the portfolio.

In fine, the resulted obtained as 42% of molecule are strategic, 33% are bottleneck, 17% are non-critical and just 8% are leverage effect (Table 8).

4.5 Purchasing Category Strategies

The purchasing strategies conception marks the ultimate phase in our methodology. Prior to this conception, it is crucial to have a thorough comprehension of the factors that influence the positioning of the molecule on the Kraljic quadrant. The position of each molecule is provided in Table 9. The mapping of the molecule in the Kraljic matrix can be elucidated as follows:

- **Strategic**: It accounts for 41% and pertains to five molecules. Molecules M1, M2, M9, and M11 face risks due to the scarcity of suppliers and the challenges associated with changing suppliers. Meanwhile, M7 poses a high supply risk as

Table 7 Molecule rating and coordinate

Category	Code	Criteria	Weight	M1	M2	M3	M4	M5	M6	M7	M8	M9	M10	M11	M12
Supplier risk	SR1	Suppliers number	0.15	4	3	4	0	3	1	2	4	4	4	4	0
	SR2	Molecule substitution	0.3	0	1	0	1	4	4	4	4	4	0	4	0
	SR3	Difficulty changing the supplier	0.09	4	0	0	0	4	0	0	4	4	4	4	0
	SR4	Regulatory constraint	0.28	4	4	4	4	4	4	4	4	4	4	4	4
	SR5	Supplier flexibility	0.15	1	1	1	1	1	1	1	1	1	1	1	1
Total															
Percentage (%)				56	51	47	39	82	66	69	86	86	56	86	32
Strategic impact	SI1	Criticality of the molecule	0.52	4	4	4	0	2	0	4	0	4	2	4	2
	SI2	Growth in consumption	0.28	2	0	1	0	1	0	1	0	1	0	0	0
	SI3	% in medicine expenditure	0.2	2	2	1	2	2	2	3	3	2	3	3	2
Total															
Percentage (%)				76	62	64	10	43	10	74	15	69	41	67	36

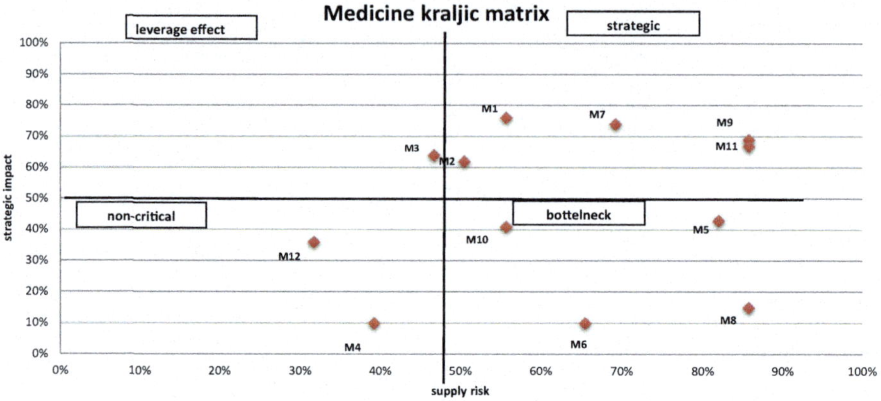

Fig. 5 Molecule position in the Kraljic matrix

Table 8 Distribution of the purchased amount among the four categories

Classes	Strategic	Leverage effect	Bottleneck	Non critical
Percentage of categories (%)	42	8	33	17

Table 9 Molecule mapping in the Kraljic matrix

Molecule	Denomination	Therapeutic class	Position in Kraljic matrix	Share %
Molecule 5	Methylprednisolone	Anti inflammatory	Bottleneck	33
Molecule 6	Métoclopramide	Antiemetic		
Molecule 8	Albumin	Blood-derived drug		
Molecule 10	Diazepam	Psychotropic		
Molecule 3	Nicardipine	Cardiology	Leverage effect	8
Molecule 12	Omeprazole	Gastrology	Non critical	17
Molecule 4	Paracetamol	Analgesic		
Molecule 2	Fentanyl	Anaesthesia	Strategic	42
Molecule 1	Povidone iodeé	Antiseptic		
Molecule 7	Chlorure de sodium	Vitamin		
Molecule 9	Insulin	Diabetology		
Molecule 11	Métalyse	Thrombolytic		

it cannot be replaced by another molecule. From a financial perspective, these molecules are crucial as they play a critical role in the provision of care.

- **Bottleneck**: This section represents 33%, and the molecules present here pose a significant supply risk but a low profit impact. Molecules M5, M6, and M8 cannot be replaced by any other molecule, and the limited number of suppliers,

along with the challenges in switching suppliers, contribute to the high supply risk. However, these molecules are not crucial for the care act and their consumption is relatively low.
- **Leverage effect item**: There is only one molecule situated in this quadrant, specifically molecule M3. This molecule plays a vital role in the operation of the car, however, there is no significant risk to the supply chain despite the limited number of suppliers available.
- **No critical item**: It is consistent that these two molecules are positioned in non-critical, it is a gastrology M12 molecule and an analgesic M4 well known, they are available on the market and substitutable.

The objective following the modeling of the drug purchasing portfolio is to transfer a maximum number of purchases to more manageable areas or implement strategies that simplify their management. According to Gelderman and Van Weele [24], within each category, two distinct types of strategic directions can be identified:

(1) Efforts focused on attaining new positions in the matrix,
(2) Initiatives aimed at maintaining current positions within the matrix.

Therefore, it is essential to analyze the placement of each molecule on the matrix to identify those that can easily be relocated to more accessible zones (e.g. from the strategic zone to leverage zone). Subsequently, appropriate strategies and tactics should be implemented to streamline management. In the subsequent discussion, we shall initially examine the molecules that exhibit effortless emigration, followed by the presentation of distinct strategies tailored to each respective domain.

1. **Strategies for streamlining of the purchasing portfolio**: *attaining new position in the matrix*

Depending on the placement of the various molecules on the Kraljic matrix, it is evident that the simplification process can be effectively applied to M1, M2, and M10. M1 and M2 are positioned in the strategic quadrant, with an abscissa very close to 50% (56% for M1 and 51% for M2), indicating an opportunity to transition them towards leveraged purchases. Upon analyzing the responses received while evaluating the different criteria associated with supply risks, it is apparent that the uniqueness of the supplier is the criterion that heightens the supply risk for M1. The pharmacist mentioned during the interview that purchases for M1 are exclusively made from a single supplier in Morocco, making it challenging to switch suppliers. Since this molecule is substitutable, enhancing the development of substitution could decrease reliance on sole suppliers. Leveraged purchases align well with M1, an antiseptic widely used in healthcare procedures that should ideally not pose any supply risks. As for M2, a pain-relief molecule categorized as opioids, there are two suppliers in the local market, but substitution is less straightforward. Given its high consumption rate in various care procedures, promoting substitution could facilitate its transition towards leveraged purchases.

The M10 molecule functions as an anxiolytic and sedative. It is identified as a bottleneck with a 56% abscissa and a 41% ordinate, indicating a potential for shifting towards non-essential purchases. To achieve this, addressing the supply risks is imperative. As per the interviews carried out, these risks primarily stem from the supplier's exclusivity. Given the challenges in establishing new suppliers in the pharmaceutical sector, substitution emerges as the primary strategy to diminish reliance and potentially phase out this molecule.

2. **Strategies for holding and maintaining current positions within the matrix**

Holding a position implies an acceptance of the existing circumstances [24]. It entails acknowledging the placement of a segment within a quadrant and responding accordingly. The objective of this response is to effectively oversee the category. The startup suggestions provided here are derived from the subsequent research studies [2, 10, 16, 19, 24]:

Strategic item: It is recommended to uphold partner relationships, which should encompass mutual trust, mutual commitment, and an open exchange of information. The supplier must be viewed as a crucial partner with whom there is a satisfactory strategic relationship. The supplier's performance is outstanding. Both parties must keen on maintaining the relationship. Sharing information is essential to the success of this partnership.

Bottleneck position: Contingency planning, along with risk analysis, consignment systems, long-term contracts focusing on quality and ensuring a stable supply, and maintaining surplus inventory.

Leverage effect: Negotiations are intense. It's recommended to prioritize suppliers who offer the lowest price, ensure quality, and deliver promptly. Employing competitive bidding is one of strategies, short-term contracts are preferred.

Non-critical: When it is not feasible to consolidate purchasing needs, the sole alternative is to resort to individual ordering, such as utilizing a purchase card. The procurement approach focuses on minimizing indirect purchasing expenses associated with administrative tasks like ordering, invoicing, and procurement processes.

Implementing these principles to the collection of molecules under investigation, we achieve the subsequent outcomes (Table 10).

5 Discussion and Further Research Issues

After conducting this research and analyzing the data gathered in the field, it is evident that drug procurement in Moroccan public hospitals is hindered by various external and internal factors. External constraints refer to limitations imposed by the supplier market that affect all purchasers, such as agreements between suppliers. On the other hand, internal constraints arise from the purchaser themselves,

Table 10 Strategic recommendation for molecules

Molecule	Denomination	Therapeutic class	Position in Kraljic matrix	Strategic recommendations
Molecule 5	Methylprednisolone	Anti inflammatory	Bottleneck	Maintain inventory, develop substitution look for alternative sources of procurement
Molecule 6	Métoclopramide	Antiemetic		
Molecule 8	Albumin	Blood-derived drug		
Molecule 10	Diazepam	Psychotropic		
Molecule 3	Nicardipine	Cardiology	Leverage effect	Consolidate order and maximize purchased volume
Molecule 12	Omeprazole	Gastrology	Non critical	Minimize effort in purchasing, delegate purchasing to users, simplify management
Molecule 4	Paracetamol	Analgesic	Non Critical	
Molecule 2	Fentanyl	Anaesthesia	Strategic	Maintain inventory, develop substitution, share information with suppliers, build collaborative relationships
Molecule 1	Povidone iodeé	Antiseptic	Strategic	
Molecule 7	Chlorure de sodium	Vitamin	Strategic	
Molecule 9	Insulin	Diabetology	Strategic	
Molecule 11	Métalyse	Thrombolytic	Strategic	

such as import restrictions. The internal constraint further exacerbates the impact of this limitation, as hospitals are obligated to obtain supplies within Morocco. Consequently, this geographical restriction restricts the available sources of supply and intensifies hospitals' reliance on laboratories.

The primary external limitation arises from the restricted pool of suppliers and the monopolistic control exerted by a handful of laboratories. In the case of 50% of the molecules under investigation, there exists just a solitary supplier within the Moroccan market, which serves as the sole source for this particular molecule.

While it is common in the private manufacturing sector for the purchasing company to develop suppliers [29], helping them become more efficient and master new technologies, this is not evident in the public sector. In Moroccan public hospital, this initiative can only be taken by the Ministry of Health. Currently, there is no research studying this type of initiative. This raises a very relevant research question regarding supplier development by the Ministry of Health in order to diversify sources of drug supply.

The other important constraint is the possibility of substituting one molecule for another. Our results perfectly match those obtained by Arantes et al. [2]. Both studies have resulted in a weighting of 30%. Alternative medicines, like other unconventional remedies, have the potential to address common challenges encountered by managers on a day-to-day basis, including issues like delayed deliveries, damaged goods, and supplier shortages. In this aspect, the main driver is the pharmacist who has all the skills to find the right substitutes for molecules. This must be done in consultation with the medical profession, as the end user. Here, we also identify a second research question, namely the impact of developing molecule substitution on dependence on suppliers.

6 Conclusion

To ensure adequate supply, efficient resource management, and optimal quality of care in a Moroccan public hospital, it is crucial to develop effective drug procurement strategies. Several key aspects need to be taken into consideration to achieve this objective. Firstly, establishing close collaboration between health professionals, purchasing managers, and hospital pharmacists is essential. This collaboration will enable a better understanding of the hospital's specific drug needs and an accurate evaluation of potential suppliers' performance and quality.

Subsequently, a thorough evaluation of suppliers must be conducted to select those offering the best products, competitive prices, and reliable delivery. Evaluation criteria may encompass drug quality, compliance with regulatory standards, supply capacity, and suppliers' reputation and track record.

Simultaneously, leveraging appropriate information systems and technologies can significantly enhance inventory management, drug traceability, stock-out prevention, and expiry date monitoring. Tools like computerized inventory management systems can optimize orders, minimize waste, and prevent shortages.

Furthermore, long-term strategic planning is vital to anticipate future drug requirements and formulate consistent purchasing policies. This may involve establishing long-term contracts with dependable suppliers, identifying essential medicines for priority storage, and creating contingency plans to address crisis situations.

References

1. Anderson MG, Katz PB (1998) Strategic sourcing. Int J Logist Manag 9:1–13. https://doi.org/10.1108/09574099810805708
2. Arantes A, Alhais AF, Ferreira LMDF (2022) Application of a purchasing portfolio model to define medicine purchasing strategies: an empirical study. Socioecon Plann Sci 84:101318. https://doi.org/10.1016/j.seps.2022.101318
3. Arantes A, Alhais A (2021) Development of a purchasing portfolio model for the health sector: a case study of a central hospital, pp 329–337. https://doi.org/10.5220/0010225903290337
4. Benazzouz T, Auhmani K (2023) Digital maturity assessment model for pharmaceutical supply chain: a patient and hospital-centred development. Int J Healthc Manag 1–24. https://doi.org/10.1080/20479700.2023.2177584
5. Bentahar O (2018) Key success factors for implementing purchasing groups in the healthcare sector. Supply Chain Forum Int J 19:90–100. https://doi.org/10.1080/16258312.2018.1433437
6. Bianchini A, Benci A, Pellegrini M, Rossi J (2019) Supply chain redesign for lead-time reduction through Kraljic purchasing portfolio and AHP integration. Benchmark Int J 26:1194–1209. https://doi.org/10.1108/BIJ-07-2018-0222
7. Blenkhorn DL, Banting PM (1991) How reverse marketing changes buyer—seller roles. Ind Mark Manag 20:185–191. https://doi.org/10.1016/0019-8501(91)90016-9
8. Burns LR, Lee JA (2008) Hospital purchasing alliances: utilization, services, and performance. Health Care Manage Rev 33:203–215. https://doi.org/10.1097/01.HMR.0000324906.04025.33
9. Bélanger V, Beaulieu M, Landry S, Morales P (2018) Where to locate medical supplies in nursing units: an exploratory study. Supply Chain Forum Int J 19:81–89. https://doi.org/10.1080/16258312.2018.1433438
10. Caniëls MCJ, Gelderman CJ (2007) Power and interdependence in buyer supplier relationships: a purchasing portfolio approach. Ind Mark Manag 36:219–229. https://doi.org/10.1016/j.indmarman.2005.08.012
11. Chancasanampa-Mandujano J, Espinoza-Poblete K, Sotelo-Raffo J, Alvarez JM, Raymundo-Ibañez C (2019) Inventory management model based on a stock control system and a Kraljic matrix to reduce raw materials inventory. In: Proceedings of the 2019 5th international conference on industrial and business engineering, pp 33–38. https://doi.org/10.1145/3364335.3364382
12. Chiang C, Kocabasoglu-Hillmer C, Suresh N (2012) An empirical investigation of the impact of strategic sourcing and flexibility on firm's supply chain agility. Int J Oper Prod Manag 32:49–78. https://doi.org/10.1108/01443571211195736
13. Ching-Tung Chan T, Chin K, Lam P (2007) Strategic sourcing in the Hong Kong toy industry. Int J Qual Reliab Manag 24:776–799. https://doi.org/10.1108/02656710710817081
14. Dixit V (2020) Risk assessment of different sourcing contract scenarios in project procurement. Int J Constr Manag 22:1537–1549. https://doi.org/10.1080/15623599.2020.1728610
15. Dwyer FR, Leenders MR, Blenkhorn DL (1989) Reverse marketing: the new buyer-supplier relationship. J Mark 53:129. https://doi.org/10.2307/1251420
16. Dyer JH, Cho DS, Cgu W (1998) Strategic supplier segmentation: the next "best practice" in supply chain management. Calif Manage Rev 40:57–77. https://doi.org/10.2307/41165933
17. El Farouk II, Jawab F (2020) Improving sustainability in public hospital through medicines supply chain management. In: 2020 IEEE 13th international colloquium of logistics and supply chain management (LOGISTIQUA). Presented at the 2020 IEEE 13th international colloquium of logistics and supply chain management (LOGISTIQUA). IEEE, Fez, Morocco, pp 1–5. https://doi.org/10.1109/LOGISTIQUA49782.2020.9353937
18. Eltantawy R (2015) Towards sustainable supply management: requisite governance and resilience capabilities. J Strateg Mark 24:118–130. https://doi.org/10.1080/0965254X.2015.1011201

19. Ferreira LMDF, Arantes A, Kharlamov AA (2014) Development of a purchasing portfolio model for the construction industry: an empirical study. Prod Plan Control 1–16. https://doi.org/10.1080/09537287.2014.906679
20. Formentini M, Ellram LM, Boem M, Da Re G (2019) Finding true north: design and implementation of a strategic sourcing framework. Ind Mark Manag 77:182–197. https://doi.org/10.1016/j.indmarman.2018.09.006
21. Franco C, López-Santana ER, Figueroa-García JC (2018) A mathematical model under uncertainty for optimizing medicine logistics in hospitals. In: Figueroa-García JC, Villegas JG, Orozco-Arroyave JR, Maya Duque PA (eds) Applied computer sciences in engineering, communications in computer and information science. Springer International Publishing, Cham, pp 53–60. https://doi.org/10.1007/978-3-030-00353-1_5
22. Gangurde SR, Chavan AA (2016) Benchmarking of purchasing practices using Kraljic approach. Benchmark Int J 23:1751–1779. https://doi.org/10.1108/BIJ-01-2015-0011
23. Garzon FS, Enjolras M, Camargo M, Morel L (2019) A green procurement methodology based on Kraljic matrix for supplier's evaluation and selection: a case study from the chemical sector. Supply Chain Forum Int J 20:185–201. https://doi.org/10.1080/16258312.2019.1622446
24. Gelderman CJ, Van Weele AJ (2003) Handling measurement issues and strategic directions in Kraljic's purchasing portfolio model. J Purch Supply Manag 9:207–216. https://doi.org/10.1016/j.pursup.2003.07.001
25. Ghanbarizadeh A, Heydari J, Razmi J, Bozorgi-Amiri A (2019) A purchasing portfolio model for the commercial construction industry: a case study in a mega mall. Prod Plan Control 30:1–22. https://doi.org/10.1080/09537287.2019.1612110
26. Hesping FH, Schiele H (2016) Matching tactical sourcing levers with the Kraljič matrix: empirical evidence on purchasing portfolios. Int J Prod Econ 177:101–117. https://doi.org/10.1016/j.ijpe.2016.04.011
27. Ketchen DJ, Crook TR, Craighead CW (2014) From supply chains to supply ecosystems: implications for strategic sourcing research and practice. J Bus Logist 35:165–171. https://doi.org/10.1111/jbl.12057
28. Kraljic P (1983) HBR. Harvard business review
29. Krause DR, Scannell TV (2002) Supplier development practices: product-and service-based industry comparisons. J Supp Chain Manag 38(1):13–21
30. Medeiros M, Ferreira L (2018) Development of a purchasing portfolio model: an empirical study in a Brazilian hospital. Prod Plan Control 29:571–585. https://doi.org/10.1080/09537287.2018.1434912
31. Monczka RM (ed) (2009) Purchasing and supply chain management, 4th edn. South-Western, Mason, OH
32. Moons K, Waeyenbergh G, Pintelon L (2019) Measuring the logistics performance of internal hospital supply chains—a literature study. Omega 82(C):205–217
33. Padhi SS, Wagner SM, Aggarwal V (2012) Positioning of commodities using the Kraljic portfolio matrix. J Purch Supply Manag 18:1–8. https://doi.org/10.1016/j.pursup.2011.10.001
34. Pretell G, Carvallo E, Del Carpio C, Macassi I (2020) Application of Kraljic and stowage techniques to define purchasing strategies to reduce cost overruns in a food service company. In: Proceedings of the 18th LACCEI international multi-conference for engineering, education, and technology: engineering, integration, and alliances for a sustainable development. https://doi.org/10.18687/LACCEI2020.1.1.90
35. Saaty TL (1991) Response to holder's comments on the analytic hierarchy process. J Oper Res Soc 42:909. https://doi.org/10.2307/2583423
36. Safaei AS, Heidarpoor F, Paydar MM (2017) A novel mathematical model for group purchasing in healthcare. Oper Res Health Care 15:82–90. https://doi.org/10.1016/j.orhc.2017.09.005
37. Sanchez F, Enjolras M, Camargo M, Morel L (2019) A green procurement methodology based on Kraljic Matrix for supplier's evaluation and selection: a case study from the chemical sector. Supp Chain Forum Int J 20. https://doi.org/10.1080/16258312.2019.1622446

38. Sanjaykumar RG, Amol AC (2016) Benchmarking of purchasing practices using Kraljic approach. Benchmark Int J 23(7):1751–1779. https://doi.org/10.1108/BIJ-01-2015-0011
39. Seth D, Nemani VK, Pokharel S, Al Sayed AY (2018) Impact of competitive conditions on supplier evaluation: a construction supply chain case study. Prod Plan Control 29:217–235. https://doi.org/10.1080/09537287.2017.1407971
40. Talluri S, Narasimhan R (2004) A methodology for strategic sourcing. Eur J Oper Res 154:236–250. https://doi.org/10.1016/S0377-2217(02)00649-5
41. Tip B, Vos FGS, Peters E, Delke V (2022) A Kraljic and competitive rivalry perspective on hospital procurement during a pandemic (COVID-19): a Dutch case study. J Public Procure 22:64–88. https://doi.org/10.1108/JOPP-11-2020-0081
42. Tronnebati I, El Yadari M, Jawab F (2022) A review of green supplier evaluation and selection issues using MCDM, MP and AI models. Sustainability 14:16714. https://doi.org/10.3390/su142416714

Imane Ibn El Farouk graduated in Supply Chain Management and obtained her Ph.D. in Public Hospital Medicine supply chain management. Currently, she is Professor of supply chain management in Chouaib Doukkali University of EL JADIDA. Her research activities are mainly focused on the study of upstream supply chain, supply chain performance monitoring, supplier's relationship and hospital logistic. She has published numerous articles in this field. His research activity is documented by publications in peer-reviewed international scientific journals and several communications in international and national congresses.

Fatima Zahra Majidi holder of a specialized Master's degree in Logistics Management and Transport, currently pursuing a doctoral thesis on sustainable strategic sourcing, member of the Research Laboratory [LERSEM] of the ENCGJ, Chouaib Doukkali University in Morocco, conducted various works in line with the theme of the thesis.

Fouad Jawab professor of Supply Chain at the Higher School of Technology of the Sidi Mohamed Ben Abdellah University of Fez, Morocco.

He has held several scientific and administrative responsibilities. He founded the International Conference on Logistics and Supply Chain Management (LOGISTIQUA), which he continues to develop with the support of several research teams in Morocco and abroad.

He is the author and co-author of more than 180 publications in national and international journals and proceedings. His research focuses on modeling, simulation and optimization of the supply chain, hospital supply chains and urban logistics. He is also an expert with several renowned organizations and a reviewer for prestigious journals.

Logistics of Local Produced Food for Increased Health

15

Andrej Lisec and Jabir Arif

Abstract

The healthcare industry is undergoing a paradigm shift in its approach to hospital supply chains (HSC), with increasing recognition of the crucial role that logistics, agriculture, and dietary choices play in patient care and overall well-being. This chapter explores the intersection of these factors within hospital supply chains, focusing on the integration of local food logistics (LFL), the importance of self-care practices, and the urgent need to address the pervasive threat of ultra-processed foods (UPF) in healthcare settings. The chapter examines the emerging trend of integrating local food systems into hospital supply chains, emphasizing the benefits of sourcing fresh, nutritious foods from nearby farms and producers. In addition, the chapter underscores the importance of self-care practices in healthcare delivery, emphasizing the holistic approach to patient well-being that extends beyond medical treatment alone. From nutrition education and culinary training to stress management and physical activity promotion, hospitals are increasingly embracing self-care initiatives to empower patients in their health journey. Insights from healthcare professionals and patient testimonials highlight the transformative effects of self-care interventions on patient engagement, recovery rates, and long-term health outcomes. Subsequently, the chapter delves into the pervasive threat of UFP in healthcare environments, exploring the detrimental effects of these products on patient health and well-being. From excessive sugar and salt content to harmful additives and preservatives, ultra-processed foods contribute to a range of

A. Lisec
Landscape Governance College GRM Novo mesto, Sevno 13, 8000 Novo mesto, Slovenia
e-mail: andrej.lisec@vsgrm.unm.si

J. Arif (✉)
Laboratory of Technologies and Industrial Services, Higher School of Technology, Sidi Mohamed Ben Abdellah University, Fez, Morocco
e-mail: Jabir.arif@usmba.ac.ma

F. Jawab (ed.), *Hospital Supply Chain*, Integrated Science 27,
https://doi.org/10.1007/978-3-031-70292-1_15

chronic diseases and undermine the therapeutic goals of healthcare facilities. Strategies for reducing the consumption of ultra-processed foods, such as menu reformulation, nutrition labeling, and culinary skill-building programs, are discussed in the context of promoting healthier food environments and fostering a culture of wellness within hospitals.

Keywords

Healthcare industry • Hospital • Supply chains • Patient • Sourcing fresh • Nutritious

Abbreviations

BMJ	British Medical Journal
CAP	Common Agricultural Policy
CFP	Carbon Footprint
COVID	Coronavirus
DLPF	Distribution of Locally Produced Food
EU	European Union
FAO	Food and Agriculture Organization
FGI	Fruit-Growing Industry
FLWP	Food Loss and Waste Prevention
FP	Food Products
FSC	Food Supply Chain
GFM	Global Food Model
GL	Global Logistics
GLV	Global Logistics Variability
GSC	Global Supply Chains
HS	Health System
JRC	Joint Research Center
LFL	Local Food Logistics
LFSS	Local Food Supply Systems
LPF	Local Produced Food
MAFF	Ministry of Agriculture, Forestry and Food
SCM	Supply Chain Management
SFC	Sustainable Food Consumption
SFP	Sustainable Food Production
SFPD	Sustainable Food Processing and Distribution
SGS	Sustainable Growth Strategy
SORS	Statistical Office of the Republic of Slovenia
SQ	Selected Quality
UPF	Ultra-processed foods

1 Introduction

Logistics is an interdisciplinary science, which is why it is necessary to constantly research, develop, integrate and implement it in supply chains. Even in the field of agriculture and food supply, the implementation and application of logistic skills and behaviours are very important [17].

In order to fulfil the needs of the customer, logistic enterprises want to create the maximum difference between revenue and operating costs, however, they are often restricted by mandatory standards or standards guaranteed by competition [16].

Specifically, logistics is the study of a set of activities that are related to the accompanying activities in the movement of goods from one point to another. The planning, implementation, and control of goods, people, information, ideas and financial flows are necessary to ensure that these elements are delivered at the right time, at the right place, and in the right quantity and quality. In doing so, planning and management must be such that they correspond to predetermined criteria of optimality. These can be different: minimum operating costs of the system, maximum net present value of returns, added values or, even better, profit. These goals can generally be achieved with careful management of all activities in supply systems [4, 15].

Because e-commerce is developing rapidly, the flow of parcels of food is increasing [31]. This is the reason why Central European countries are reconstructing their postal services [16].

The Common Agricultural Policy (CAP) is constantly adapting to the challenges facing European agriculture. The general objectives of the common agricultural policy are the promotion of food security and strengthening of care for the environment and climate measures and the strengthening of rural areas (Food and Agriculture Organization of the United Nations, FAO) [11]. One of the significant challenges in the process of planning the consumption of food is how to properly determine the design elements of food capacity [17].

There is a permanent change to the world as a result of human activities. Among the consequences are continuously confronting new and constantly changing problems and their resolution; both are characterized by complexity (intricacy arising from relationships) and dynamic development. A competent understanding of the theory of systems can be used to investigate and manage such phenomena [16].

In the era of global business, it is evident that intuition alone is not sufficient for decision-making. Managers must therefore have sufficient knowledge capital at their disposal.

With its production, Slovenia does not provide a sufficient quantity of agricultural products for its own needs. Slovenia also imports certain food from abroad. The country has a higher level of self-sufficiency in animal products, but a lower level in plant products. In Slovenia, we are the least self-sufficient in vegetables, potatoes and cereals.

In order to quantify and monitor the cost-benefits and other consequences of all for health and welfare, society, culture, employment, and the environment, we need to determine the most efficient ways to control and minimize ultra-processing food and use more locally produced food [3].

The chapter presents an opportunity to elucidate the alignment of our chapter with the overarching theme of hospital supply chains. Our chapter delves into the critical nexus between logistics and healthcare, particularly emphasizing their pivotal role in ensuring food stability and self-sufficiency within hospital settings. By scrutinizing the interconnectedness between logistical challenges and the imperative to maintain effective supply chains, our work sheds light on the paramount importance of efficient logistics in securing timely access to fresh and nutritious food for patients.

Furthermore, the chapter underscores the global shifts towards recognizing locally produced food as a viable alternative to traditional supply chains, especially within healthcare contexts. Through this lens, we provide valuable insights into the strategic imperatives for enhancing logistics management within healthcare facilities, particularly amidst the backdrop of global uncertainties. By addressing the essential components of self-sufficiency and food stability, our chapter contributes significantly to the broader discourse on hospital supply chains, offering practical implications for optimizing logistics practices to ensure optimal patient care outcomes.

2 Methodology

The methodology consists of a two-stage process designed to investigate the evolving role of logistics in agriculture and its implications for health and food distribution. In the first stage, we select articles representing different perspectives on logistics in agriculture. At this level, we try to come up the comparison of logistical approaches over time and an examination of their impact on health and food distribution.

The second stage involves a comparative study among the selected articles, focusing on their methodologies, findings, and implications. Each researcher interprets aspects of logistics in agriculture through various research methods, such as qualitative content analysis or thematic coding. This comparative analysis aims to identify commonalities, differences, and emerging trends in logistics practices, self-care, the threat of ultra-processed food, and the distribution of locally produced food. The findings are integrated and synthesized to develop practical recommendations for improving logistical practices in agriculture and promoting healthier food systems.

Constructive feedback is incorporated to refine and strengthen the analysis and recommendations, ensuring their relevance and applicability to diverse stakeholders. The chapter concludes by summarizing the key findings and implications for logistics in agriculture, emphasizing the importance of addressing logistical challenges to enhance health outcomes and food distribution efficiency.

3 Logistics in Agriculture

Logistics in agriculture is a specific field that covers every inhabitant of the world because it is impossible to live without food. It is important to have food close by, so the key to success is self-sufficiency in the territory of the country, namely for as many agricultural products as possible [17].

Food production and the mechanization associated with it are crucial for meeting all the food needs of every inhabitant of the world. Every day, farms face challenges and are also shifting to organic farming, as the demand for organic products is increasing every day. This requires the fulfilment of appropriate conditions and special requirements, with a smaller yield compared to conventional agricultural production. As a rule, organic crops are less burdened with costs, but their quantity per unit area is smaller, and they achieve a higher selling price [17].

Before agricultural products reach the store shelves, most products need to be properly stored. For the storage of some products, it is necessary to establish a controlled temperature regime and maintain this regime even during transport to the points of sale [17].

Delivery logistics have advanced to the point where we can get products delivered in less than an hour from ordering. This is especially true for larger cities and not for rural areas. Elsewhere in Slovenia, or more broadly in Europe and the world, food delivery is not so simple [17].

To have a comprehensive knowledge of logistics in agriculture, it is necessary to know logistics in connection with agriculture, historical development, logistics in individual segments of agriculture, distribution of locally produced food, maintenance of the temperature regime, circular economy in agriculture and what are the challenges of logistics in agriculture in the future, it is also covered in Slovenia's CAP 2023–2027 Strategic Plan. The basic principles of agricultural policy are coordinated at the level of the European Union (EU) and Slovenia implements them sensibly [17].

Coordinating the effective movement of people and products over time and space is known as logistics. From the perspective of effective agricultural logistics, we would like to have the shortest path from the produce in the field to the fork. The Slovenian countryside occupies approximately 80% of Slovenia's territory, which is a great potential in Slovenia; it is similar also abroad (Austria, Germany) [17].

In the case of logistics supply to customers in agriculture (customers) who are engaged in the transfer of various types of goods or food, farmers are frequently constrained by regulations or by standards set by the competition, which means that they seek to serve clients in a way that maximizes the difference between the revenue from the service and the operational costs (quality schemes) [18]. Supply means providing goods or services to users at the right time and in the right place [19].

To be able to understand the distance or journey made by goods (agricultural products), it is necessary to understand supply chains, which include:

- Suppliers;
- Component manufacturers;
- Workers;
- Intermediaries;
- Warehouses;
- Places for loading;
- Packaging;
- Logistic characteristics (trucks, ships, trains and planes).

Understanding each of these components and how they interact within the supply chain is crucial for effectively managing the journey of agricultural products from farm to market. It enables stakeholders to optimize efficiency, minimize waste, ensure product quality, and meet consumer demand effectively. In logistics, it is important that food waste is low. In 2022, there was almost 2% more food waste in Slovenia than in 2019, as the inhabitants of Slovenia threw away an average of 72 kg of food [30].

Example of Global Logistics Variability GLV: Figure 1 showcases an illustrative example of egg transport in Egypt. This depiction highlights the diverse logistical practices observed across different regions of the world, where standards and regulations vary significantly from country to country. Notably, in the Republic of Slovenia, such transportation methods do not align with legislative requirements. This example underscores the complexities inherent in global logistics (GL) and emphasizes the importance of understanding and adhering to local regulations to ensure compliance and minimize risks in food transportation practices.

Fig. 1 Egg transport in Egypt

4 Fields of Logistics in Agriculture

Logistics in agriculture encompasses a range of activities and processes involved in the production, distribution, and marketing of agricultural products. It plays a critical role in ensuring the efficient and timely movement of agricultural goods from farm to fork, encompassing various stages of the agricultural supply chain. Here are some key areas where logistics in agriculture is divided:

- logistics in fruit growing;
- logistics in horticulture;
- logistics in viticulture;
- logistics in forestry.

In the fruit-growing industry (FGI), logistics refers to all the operations that are part of fruit production. The production of vegetables involves logistics that are crucial in terms of planning and the impact of weather to be efficient. Logistics in viticulture is extremely important, especially in autumn, but of course also in other seasons. Logistics in forestry has recently become the most important because, during the energy crisis, the supply of heating was absolutely necessary [17].

Only appropriate logistics of production, processing and transport of products will be able to ensure long-term quality products on the shelves of retailers or online portals [17].

Safe food, which is also of good quality, is one of the guarantees for maintaining a person's state of health, which at the same time helps to relieve the burden on the health system (HS) since individuals do not need medical care if they eat healthily [17].

5 Evolution of Logistics in Agriculture: Tracing the Journey from Traditional Practices to Modern Innovations

In the past, food was used where it was produced. Throughout history, goods have been traded for goods, one type of food for another. With the advancement of technology and the development of agriculture and logistics, today we can consume food from practically the whole world. All this is made possible by the connection between logistics and agriculture [17].

In the past, food was stored in earthenware containers (Fig. 2), in cut logs and thus enabled food to be transported from one place to another [17].

Figure 3 shows how the cow was milked. As a rule, milk was used where it was produced. Even today, we strive for this.

In the past, all goods were predominantly local. We humans were foragers and consequently dependent on the local environment. The local environment provided everything necessary for survival. With the advent of civilization, everything began to change. Gradually, trade began between houses, villages, in short between the

Fig. 2 Pottery

Fig. 3 Milking in the past

countryside and cities and between individual countries. People who had a lot of property could afford to order products from distant places. But it was necessary to wait a long time for these goods. Today, everything is reachable, even from the most remote places in the world. Before the emergence of the coronavirus (COVID), we had everything at our fingertips, whatever we wanted. We got what we ordered online quickly. Today, logistics routes have become significantly more complicated.

Today, the most advanced technology is used to transport agricultural products, but we are returning to the segment of locally produced food, because we want to enjoy good, safe and high-quality food, and at the same time we want to cover as few journeys or kilometres as possible, thus saving on fuel and having a lower carbon footprint, as this is the way of protecting the environment.

Figure 4 shows a market in Africa, which is something unusual for us, but a reality for Africa.

We can learn a lot from history, including the area of self-sufficiency and food production.

6 The Importance of Self-care

The current situation in the world and Slovenia is unique. No one probably imagined that nowadays we could be limited by food and other products. There is a rapid increase in online sales, in the past we went to stores with masks. What will happen tomorrow is hard to predict. We can only hope that it will not be worse (a new wave of the epidemic or a protracted war in Ukraine and its surroundings) [20].

Fig. 4 Market in Africa

Thus, day by day, consumers better recognize the benefits of locally produced food, which represents an alternative to the global food model (GFM), where food is transported over great distances before reaching the consumer. At a time when the world has not only changed but also slowed down considerably when it is no longer so obvious that fresh vegetables from all over the world will be on the shelf the next day, the importance of self-sufficiency is even greater. Broken logistics routes and, the protectionism of certain countries cause food instability [20].

Self-sufficiency is the supply of goods (food products FP) that we need for life. Current data show that self-sufficiency in Slovenia is somewhere around 70%, only for vegetables and pork around 40%. Self-sufficiency increases the gross domestic product of each country. It would be good if, first of all, individuals were as self-sufficient as possible. This is especially important for places and areas of the world where the possibilities for growing your own fruit or vegetables in your home garden or breeding animals are great. In doing so, it is also important to take advantage of nature's gifts in all seasons, especially in spring and autumn, which also offers opportunities to prepare seasonal or winter dishes, because there are many possibilities and gifts in nature, you just need to take the time, collect and take advantage of them [20].

Locally produced food also has a wider social meaning, and the most important thing is that the food supply chain (FSC) is significantly shortened (Fig. 5). Short supply chains are crucial for preserving jobs and lowering the nation's need for social transfers, increasing consumption of repro material for production, increasing the purchasing power of the population and more intensive consumption, maintaining rural population and a lower carbon footprint CFP [1, 5]. Self-sufficiency increases the gross domestic product of each country. Locally produced food ensures the health of its citizens. The option of purchasing via websites is safe, easy and the right choice in today's emergency situation. In this way, providers of tourist services can also offer tourists healthy, locally produced food that is of higher quality and more nutritious [20].

Fig. 5 Production of locally produced food

Another option is to buy directly from the farmer. We have fresh milk, eggs, and meat, and we are familiar with their local origin and the way of production. In this way, we also support the farmers and the regional economy. The following are some benefits of eating food that is produced nearby [17]:

- Environmental function (preserving the quality of water, soil, air and biotic diversity),
- It preserves the image of the cultural landscape,
- Under the condition of product safety, it is one of the guarantees for ensuring people's health,
- It maintains the vitality and population of the countryside,
- The food has a better taste and aroma,
- Higher biological and nutritional value of locally produced food,
- Organic food is produced in the most environmentally friendly way,
- Local food shouldn't contain dangerous pesticides—this means less environmental pollution.

It also has a wider social significance, but most importantly, the food supply chain is greatly shortened (see Fig. 6). A short supply chain is crucial for maintaining employment and lowering the nation's need for social transfers, increasing consumption of raw materials for production, increasing the purchasing power of the

Fig. 6 Farm to fork strategy

population and more intensive consumption, maintaining rural population and a lower carbon footprint. Self-sufficiency increases the gross domestic product of each country. Locally produced food ensures the health of its citizens. The option of purchasing via the website is safe, easy and the right choice in each situation.

Healthy locally produced food is also increasingly important in tourism. This is not just one of the tourist trends, but the recognition of the quality of products and services, which is also included in the Sustainable Growth Strategy (SGS) of Slovenian Tourism, whose goal is to make Slovenia a "boutique five-star destination". The latter undoubtedly includes healthy food, which represents one of the key pillars of the destination's development and recognition, to which the action of Slovenia—the gastronomic region also contributed. The importance of healthy food is also recognized by Sevnica, which in recent years, through various projects, training and the increased interest of domestic and foreign tourists in Melanija's town, has planned to raise awareness about healthy food, which is the basis of a healthy life for everyone, the local population and tourists. The project focuses on buckwheat as a grain [27].

In fact, shortening supply chains has never been more urgent than it is today. On the one hand, we have ecological pressure, which clearly shows us the way to a grey future if we ignore it, and on the other hand, it has shown itself in the latest epidemic crisis of global proportions. Due to the well-developed logistics in Slovenia, there have been no major shortages in the supply of foodstuffs, but even a few years ago these were real potential challenges. Suddenly, we started looking for ways to source local food so that we could be supplied even if global supply chains were to break [21].

The world is shaken by remarkable occurrences once more after the COVID-19 epidemic; this time, they are connected to the Ukrainian crisis and the battle in Gaza. This is evident in many aspects of our lives, but in Slovenia primarily manifests as exorbitant costs for energy and consumer goods. Compared to levels before the Ukrainian crisis, food prices have significantly increased due to shortages, high pricing for certain goods, high fertilizer costs, and restrictions on the export of various commodities. According to the Statistical Office of the Republic of Slovenia (SORS), food waste per capita is still significant, but consumers are starting to realize how important it is to have access to good-quality food. We have also made progress toward digitizing agriculture with the rise of online marketplaces, which surged during the COVID-19 pandemic [2].

The notion of locally produced foods refers to foods that are produced, sold and consumed in a certain geographical area (Risku-Norja et al. [28] in Šinko and Lisec (2021)). Different countries of the world interpret the term local differently, mainly in terms of the size of the country or the territory in which they are observed. In the United States, the definition of locally grown food is food that is sold within 400 miles (about 644 km) of the nation where the food is produced, or its place of origin [22]. Food that is cultivated and sold inside a province or territory, or that is sold across provincial borders up to 50 km from the province of origin or territory, is referred to as locally grown food in Canada [12]. Joint Research Center in the European Union JRC [13] considers locally produced food as food that is produced, processed and sold within the geographical area between the place of origin up to a maximum distance of between 20 and 100 km. In Slovenia, the general definition is that the local market is an environment that is up to 60 km away from the consumer ("Local food supply and gardening" [NIJZ], 2020). Agriculture Act defines the local market as the entire area of the Republic of Slovenia (applies to agricultural products and foodstuffs) [2].

In Slovenia, the local production and purchase of food have been encouraged for a long time with the national project "Our superfood" (Fig. 7), which "encourages consumers to choose home-grown, locally produced food in their choice, rather than others" [23]. With this aim, a quality scheme has been established in Slovenia since 2014, which defines domestic, local, Slovenian-grown and processed food [24]. For growers to obtain the "Selected Quality SQ" certificate, intended for agricultural produce or food with special properties, they must meet certain stricter criteria. These standards could include things like composition, ecologically friendly production, raw material quality, animal welfare, special care for sick animals, feeding practices, transportation routes' length, raw material processing speed, or minimal post-processing during storage and transit. The label "Selected quality—Slovenia" indicates crops and products that are grown and processed in Slovenia and undergo additional, stricter controls. As such, the "Selected quality" certificate doesn't mean organic production at the same time, which was encouraged by the additional awareness campaign Organic and local is ideal [25]. Also, in 2020, the European Commission set out a "Farm to Fork" strategy, which states that "to increase the resilience of regional and local food supply systems LFSS, it will support reducing dependence on long-distance transport to create

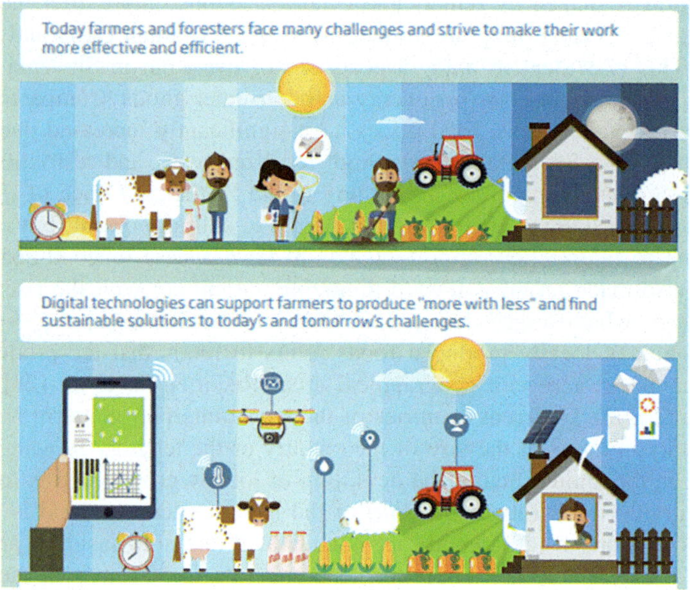

Fig. 7 Today and in the future

shorter supply chains" [10]. It is clear, therefore, that countries are striving hard to achieve as much local self-sufficiency as possible since in this way producers and consumers stimulate the local economy in addition to other possible beneficial effects [2].

The basic goods of life are food and drink, without which we cannot live, so we can produce them ourselves at home or import them. However, we must not leave everything to global markets and allow long global supply chains to dominate. Shortening supply chains has never been more urgent than in the current period of economic emergency. On the one hand, there is an ecological pressure that paves the way to a grey future if we ignore it, and on the other hand, it has been shown in the latest epidemic crisis of global proportions. To maintain self-sufficiency, it is important to buy raw materials, foodstuffs, crops and products from local farms, where the journey 'from forks to forks' is short. Additionally, advancements in delivery technologies and logistics depicted in Fig. 8 may offer opportunities to further strengthen local sourcing initiatives and reduce dependency on long global supply chains. This requires a great deal of connection, cooperation, networking and permanent orientation both between providers and the population because we want people to live in coexistence and mutual creativity so that we can be self-confident, sovereign and decisive even in the international arena—that's why we have to be independent and equipped with knowledge [6].

Fig. 8 Delivery in the future

7 Ultra-processed Food Is a Big Threat to Our Health

Food that has been overly processed has no place in our food supply. Ultra-processed foods (UPF) include extremely refined breads, fast food, sugary drinks, cereals, cookies, and other packaged snacks. These are some of the more popular examples. They frequently have low levels of fiber and micronutrients such vitamins and high levels of salt, sugar, fat, and calories.

Food that has undergone excessive processing is generally considered detrimental to our food supply and overall health [8]. These UPFs undergo extensive refinement and often contain additives, preservatives, and artificial ingredients. Examples of ultra-processed foods include highly refined bread, fast food items, sugary drinks, cereals, cookies, and various packaged snacks. Despite their convenience and popularity, these products typically offer little nutritional value and may even contribute to various health issues when consumed excessively.

Ultra-processed foods are often characterized by their low levels of essential nutrients such as fiber, vitamins, and minerals. Fiber, which is abundant in whole foods like fruits, vegetables, and whole grains, is essential for digestive health and helps regulate blood sugar levels and cholesterol. However, in UPF, fiber content is typically minimal or completely absent, contributing to poor digestive function and potential health problems.

Moreover, these products are typically high in unhealthy additives such as salt, sugar, and fats. Excessive salt intake has been linked to hypertension and cardiovascular diseases, while high sugar consumption is associated with obesity, type 2 diabetes, and dental issues [29]. Additionally, the high levels of unhealthy fats found in ultra-processed foods can contribute to weight gain, inflammation, and increased risk of chronic diseases.

Furthermore, UPFs are often calorie-dense but nutrient-poor, meaning they provide a significant amount of energy but little to no essential nutrients. This imbalance can lead to overconsumption of calories without meeting the body's nutritional needs, potentially resulting in weight gain, nutrient deficiencies, and various health complications over time.

In contrast, whole, minimally processed foods such as fresh fruits, vegetables, whole grains, lean proteins, and healthy fats offer a wealth of essential nutrients, including vitamins, minerals, antioxidants, and phytonutrients [7]. These foods support overall health, help maintain a healthy weight, and reduce the risk of chronic diseases when consumed as part of a balanced diet.

According to the results of the largest-ever review in the field, eating foods high in processing can have up to 32 negative health effects, such as an increased risk of heart disease, cancer, type 2 diabetes, poor mental health, and early mortality [14].

Fast food, protein bars, carbonated drinks, prepared meals, and other highly processed foods are being consumed at an exponentially high rate worldwide. Ready-to-eat meals, fizzy drinks, packaged baked goods and snacks, sugary cereals, and processed foods all go through a number of industrial processes and frequently include additives like flavourings, emulsifiers, colorants, and others. These goods typically have minimal vitamin and fiber content and high added sugar, fat, and salt content [14].

Greater than half of the average person's diet in the US and the UK is made up of highly processed foods. For some, such a diet makes up as much as 80% of their food intake, particularly those who are younger, poorer, or from underserved areas (Guardian). Scientists have conducted the largest review of this field to date, and the findings are devastating. According to a significant study, eating a diet high in ultra-processed foods can be quite hazardous to your health. Experts from numerous prestigious health institutions participated in the review, including the University of Sydney, the Sorbonne University in France, and the Johns Hopkins Bloomberg School of Public Health in the United States [14].

The review of UPF was published in the scientific journal British Medical Journal (BMJ). As summarized by the Guardian, the results showed a general correlation between 32 health indices (such as cancer, mortality, and digestive, respiratory, cardiovascular, and mental health issues) and the consumption of ultra-processed meals. More ultra-processed food consumption has been linked to a higher risk of negative health outcomes, including mental and metabolic illnesses as well as early mortality [14].

A higher consumption of these foods is linked, among other things, to a 48–53% increased risk of anxiety and other common mental illnesses, a 12–13% increased risk of type 2 diabetes, and a roughly 50% increased risk of mortality from cardiovascular disease. Additionally, they discovered that consuming more of these items was linked to a 21% increased risk of dying from any cause, a 40–66% increased risk of dying from heart disease, obesity, type 2 diabetes, and sleep disorders, as well as a 22% increased risk of depression [14].

It is very important to have short supply chains for a better and healthier life for everybody in our world.

8 Distribution of Locally Produced Food

The distribution of locally produced food (DLPF) is crucial to the price of food. This applies to both key customers and catering establishments [17].

The DLPF is approached in different ways around the world—through sales at markets, sales at growers, mobile stores, sales via vending machines, online sales and door-to-door sales. These ways of selling food are growing day by day, and awareness of locally grown food is also growing, as supply chains are shorter, food reaches the consumer fresh and at the time of natural maturity [17].

Of course, the producer and the consumer of the product must cooperate successfully during the business process. Successful cooperation is not only a source of current income, but it is necessary to strive for a long-term business process, which allows the producer of the product on the one hand a constant source of income, and the consumer of the product the desired goods in the desired form and at a satisfactory price [17].

A constant source of income is undoubtedly related to a constant number of customers with the same purchasing power. It is easier for a vegetable grower or a livestock farmer involved in meat processing if he can predict the amount of goods needed in advance. Demand and supply on the market determine the prices of agricultural products, which fluctuate from year to year mainly due to weather influences. The market for agricultural products can be saturated in a very short time, for example: with salad in just a few days, so the producer is forced to either throw the product away or offer it at a significantly lower price [17].

In addition, the DLPF plays a crucial role in determining the price and accessibility of food within a region. This holds true for both individual consumers and catering establishments alike [9, 26].

- Price Stability: Local food distribution can contribute to price stability within the market. By sourcing food locally, consumers and businesses can avoid the volatility of prices associated with long-distance transportation, import/export costs, and fluctuations in global markets. This stability benefits both consumers, who can enjoy more predictable prices for their groceries, and catering establishments, which can better manage their food costs and pricing strategies.

- Reduced Transportation Costs: Locally produced food typically requires shorter transportation distances from farm to market or restaurant. This reduces transportation costs, including fuel expenses, maintenance, and logistical overhead. As a result, the overall cost of locally sourced food can be lower compared to imported or long-distance products, which often incur additional transportation fees that are passed on to consumers.
- Fresher and Higher Quality Products: Local food distribution ensures that products reach consumers and catering establishments quickly after harvest or production, preserving freshness and quality. Freshly harvested fruits and vegetables retain their nutritional value, flavor, and texture, enhancing the dining experience for consumers and allowing chefs to create dishes with superior taste and visual appeal. Additionally, locally sourced meats, dairy, and other perishable goods are less likely to spoil during transit, reducing food waste and associated costs.
- Support for Local Economy: By purchasing locally produced food, consumers and catering establishments support local farmers, producers, and businesses within their communities. This promotes economic resilience, fosters job creation, and strengthens local food systems. Moreover, dollars spent on local food tend to circulate within the community, benefiting other local businesses and contributing to overall economic development.
- Environmental Sustainability: Local food distribution systems often have lower environmental impacts compared to long-distance transportation of food. By reducing the distance food travels from farm to plate, local sourcing helps minimize carbon emissions, air pollution, and fossil fuel consumption associated with transportation. Additionally, supporting local agriculture encourages sustainable farming practices, biodiversity conservation, and stewardship of natural resources, contributing to environmental preservation and resilience.

The risk of losing of income is lower for the growers if they have an agreement with a permanent customer, such as a public institution or a company that sells locally produced products. This type of agreement has the following advantages [32]:

- The public institution is a permanent customer, as food must be provided daily during its operation in kindergartens, primary schools, hospitals, prisons, and homes for the elderly;
- The growers can more easily plan the necessary volume of production based on public data on the number of meals distributed in the institute. It is necessary to take into account that relations between sellers and buyers in public institutions are regulated through contracts and public procurement, where quantities are defined in advance;
- The absence of food in the above-mentioned public institutions is easier to predict than in the specific case of door-to-door marketing in the countryside; for example, educational institutions do not need food during the summer holidays;

- Logistics costs are lower for the growers and the consumer since there is only one delivery address;
- The costs of packaging, sorting and sorting, which arise when the product is shipped, are lower since it is a one-time purchase in a larger quantity;
- If we assume that a certain public institution is supplied by farms from its immediate surroundings, it is important to highlight the environmental protection aspect: the emissions of propellant fuels are lower due to shorter distances; a predictable and familiar route makes time planning easier; the local proximity of the provider and the consumer enables orders to be changed in a short time (for example: in the morning, the catering manager informs the producer of a cancellation or the purchase of something new);
- Food imported from far away (from, for example, Spain) requires a long transport, which has negative consequences for the product: the product is no longer fresh, and damage may occur during transport, which affects the final quality of the product in the kitchen, and thus the amount of waste (biological) as well as packaging (longer transport requires better protection). At the same time, the public institution is obliged to properly sort all generated waste and take care of its removal, which is a paid service.

9 Conclusion

In conclusion, logistics in agriculture has emerged as a critical component in ensuring the global supply of food to all inhabitants of the world. As emphasized throughout this chapter, self-sufficiency in food production is paramount for the development and sustenance of any nation. The ability to grow food efficiently and effectively relies heavily on the utilization of appropriate agricultural machinery, as elaborated in the fifth section. However, the journey of food from farm to table doesn't end with production, it also entails the distribution of locally produced goods.

Effective distribution requires suitable vehicles, ideally ones that are environmentally friendly, to transport food from producers to consumers. Moreover, addressing waste management in agriculture is crucial. Recognizing the potential value in waste products, a thorough understanding of reverse logistics is essential for managing agricultural waste effectively. Given the substantial amount of waste generated within the agricultural sector, implementing strategies to minimize waste and extract value from bioproducts can lead to significant economic and environmental benefits.

In summary, logistics in agriculture encompasses not only the efficient production of food but also its distribution and waste management. By optimizing these logistical processes, countries can enhance their food security, promote sustainable agricultural practices, and contribute to the well-being of both their populations and the planet as a whole.

References

1. Abatekassa G, Peterson HC (2011) Market access for local food through the conventional food supply chain. Int Food Agribus Manag Rev 14:20
2. Bencak P, Lisec A, Šinko S (2022) Potrošnja lokalno pridelane hrane v Sloveniji v času ukrajinske krize. In: XVI. International conference on logistics in agriculture 2022: conference proceedings. Univerzitetna založba Univerze v Mariboru
3. Bimbo F, Bonanno A, Nardone G, Viscecchia R (2015) The hidden benefits of short food supply chains: farmers' markets density and body mass index in Italy. Int Food Agribus Manag Rev 18(1):1–16
4. Born B, Purcell M (2006) Avoiding the local trap: scale and food systems in planning research. J Plan Educ Res 26(2):195–207
5. Carino S, Porter J, Malekpour S, Collins J (2020) Environmental sustainability of hospital foodservices across the food supply chain: a systematic review. J Acad Nutr Diet 120(5):825–873
6. Colarič JLM (2022) Samooskrba in trajnostni razvoj podeželja kot priložnost po pandemiji globalnih razsežnosti: Primer dobre prakse v Sloveniji
7. Draper A, Green J (2002) Food safety and consumers: constructions of choice and risk. Soc Policy Adm 36(6):610–625
8. Edwards-Jones G, Canals LM, Hounsome N, Truninger M, Koerber G, Hounsome B et al (2008) Testing the assertion that 'local food is best': the challenges of an evidence-based approach. Trends Food Sci Technol 19(5):265–274
9. Enthoven L, Van den Broeck G (2021) Local food systems: reviewing two decades of research. Agric Syst 193(C)
10. European Commission (2020) Communication from the commission to the European parliament, the council, the European economic and social committee and the committee of the regions: a farm to fork strategy for a fair, healthy and environmentally-friendly food system. https://ec.europa.eu/food/horizontal-topics/farm-fork-strategy_en
11. Food and Agriculture Organization of the United Nations (FAO) (2016) Influencing food environments for healthy diets. [Internet]. Available from: https://www.fao.org/3/a-i6484e.pdf
12. Government of Canada CFIA (2022) Origin claims on food labels [fact sheet, guide, reference material]. https://inspection.canada.ca/foodlabels/labelling/industry/origin-claims/eng/1626884467839/1626884529209
13. Kneafsey M, Venn L, Schmutz U, Balázs B, Trenchard L, Eyden-Wood T, Bos E, Sutton G, Blackett M (2013) Short food supply chains and local food systems in the EU. A state of play of their socio-economic characteristics. JRC scientific and policy reports, 123, 129
14. Lane MM et al (2024) Ultra-processed food exposure and adverse health outcomes: umbrella review of epidemiological meta-analyses. BMJ
15. Lisec A (2006) Optimizacija logistike paketov v hierarhični prostorski zasnovi poštne mreže. Doktorska disertacija, Ekonomska fakulteta, Ljubljana
16. Lisec A (2016) Reorganization of the postal system: the case of the parcel network in Slovenia. Pearson, Harlow
17. Lisec A (2022) Logistics in agriculture. Faculty of Logistics
18. Lisec A, Bogataj M (2002) Optimalno delovanje bencinskih servisov. Transp Ljubljana 2:1
19. Lisec A, Rihter A, Radinja B (2005) Logistical characteristics of postal operations. In: Marina Z, Daša F, Peter J (eds) Mednarodno posvetovanje o prometni znanosti. 9th international conference on traffic science—ICTS 2005, ur. 9, Portorož, Slovenija, 14–15 Nov 2005. Promet v znanosti in praksi. Zbornik referatov. Conference proceedings. Fakulteta za pomorstvo in promet, Portorož
20. Lisec A, Petek V et al (2022) Logistika v specifičnih okoljih: vpliv epidemije na logistiko v turizmu: učno gradivo. Fakulteta za turizem, Univerza v Mariboru, Brežice

21. Low SA, Vogel S (2011) Direct and intermediated marketing of local foods in the United States. Economic research report no. 128. Economic Research Service, U.S. Department of Agriculture, Washington, DC
22. Martinez S, Hand M, Da Pra M, Pollack S, Ralston K, Smith T, Vogel S, Clark S, Lohr L, Low S, Newman C (2010) Local food systems: concepts, impacts, and issues. https://www.ers.usda.gov/webdocs/publications/46393/7054_err97_1_.pdf?v=0
23. Ministry of Agriculture, Forestry and Food. Izbrana kakovost—Slovenija. Naša super hrana—Izbrana kakovost. https://www.nasasuperhrana.si/za-potrosnike/sheme-kakovosti/izbrana-kakovost/
24. Ministry of Agriculture, Forestry and Food (2020) Vseslovenska kampanja ozaveščanja—Ekološko in lokalno je idealno! https://www.nasasuperhrana.si/clanek/vseslovenska-kampanja-ozavescanja-ekolosko-inlokalno-je-idealno/
25. Ministry of Agriculture, Forestry and Food (2021) Strateški načrt skupne kmetijske politike 2023–2027 za Slovenijo
26. Morland K, Wing S, Roux AD (2002) The contextual effect of the local food environment on residents' diets: the atherosclerosis risk in communities study. Am J Public Health 92(11):1761–1767
27. Richardson S, McSweeney L, Spence S (2022) Availability of healthy food and beverages in hospital outlets and interventions in the UK and USA to improve the hospital food environment: a systematic narrative literature review. Nutrients 14(8):1566
28. Risku-Norja H, Hietala R, Virtanen H, Ketomäki H, Helenius J (2008) Localisation of primary food production in Finland: production potential and environmental impacts of food consumption patterns. Agric Food Sci 17:127–145. https://doi.org/10.2137/145960608785328233
29. Salois MJ (2012) Obesity and diabetes, the built environment, and the 'local' food economy in the United States, 2007. Econ Hum Biol 10(1):35–42
30. Surs (2022) Odpadna hrana. https://www.stat.si/StatWeb/News/Index/11387
31. Wierda JJ, de Vet E, Troost E et al (2024) Characterizing food environments of hospitals and long-term care facilities in the Netherlands: a mixed methods approach. BMC Health Serv Res 24:31. https://doi.org/10.1186/s12913-023-10399-6
32. Zadružna zveza Slovenije (2021) Zadružnik

Andrej Lisec, Ph.D. is an Associate professor of logistics at the Landscape Governance College GRM Novo Mesto. Pedagogic and research field is packaging, reverse logistics, logistics in tourism, distribution, post and logistics in agriculture. He has been involved in the coordination and implementation of several international and national projects, focusing on sustainability, reduction of logistics cost and environment. He was member of the expert group by the European commission in the field Smart, green and integrated transport for the H2020 in the Member States. He was also in the Expert group for the Strategic Transport Research and Innovation Agenda (STRIA) governance.

Jabir Arif received the M.Sc., Engineering, Ph.D., HdR degrees in Industrial Engineering and Logistics from the National School of Applied Sciences Tangier, Faculty of Sciences and Technologies Fez, in 2008, 2010, 2016, and 2020 respectively. He is currently serving as an Associate Professor at Sidi Mohamed Ben Abdellah University, Morocco.

He began his career as a Production Planner within a multinational company operating in the automotive wiring harness. Afterward, he was appointed as State Engineer at the Ministry of Public Services and Modernization of Administration where he was in charge of the national major projects. Jabir Arif's main research area is Supply Chain Management and Logistics, Outsourcing of Logistic Activities, Risk Assessment, IoT, Artificial Intelligence, and Industrial engineering.

Apart from teaching and research, he is acting as a reviewer in many ranked journals and conferences. He served as a Technical Committee member of several international conferences, tracks, and workshops.

Part III

Patient Flow Optimization and Transport Logistics for Healthcare Services

A Multi-objective Programming Model for Physician Scheduling: A Case Study

16

Khadija Werghi, Jihene Jlassi, Ines Rekik, and Abderrahman El Mhamedi

Abstract

In this research, we have constructed a multi-objective programming framework for organizing physician schedules. This article introduces a goal programming (GP) model designed to address both hard and flexible constraints within a monthly planning timeframe. The rigid constraints demand strict compliance, while the flexible constraints may be relaxed when required. The significance of the flexible constraints is determined through the Analytical Hierarchy Process (AHP) and is incorporated as coefficients reflecting deviations from these constraints in the objective function. The proposed model has been implemented based on real data taken from the "Dermatology and Venereology" department's Sfax Tunisian Hedi Chaker's hospital. The obtained results show the efficiency of the presented integrated AHP-GP model compared to the physician schedules adopted in this department.

Keywords

Mathematical formulation • Goal programming (GP) • Analytical Hierarchy Process (AHP) • Healthcare problems • Physician scheduling • Patient satisfaction

K. Werghi · J. Jlassi (✉) · I. Rekik
OLID Laboratory, Higher Institute of Management Industrial of Sfax (ISGIS), University of Sfax, Sfax, Tunisia
e-mail: jihene.jlassi@isgis.usf.tn

K. Werghi
e-mail: khadijawerghi.olid@isgis.usf.tn

I. Rekik
e-mail: ines.rekik@isgis.usf.tn

A. El Mhamedi
QUARTZ Laboratory, IUT Montreuil University Paris 8, Paris, France
e-mail: a.elmhamedi@iut.univ-paris8.fr

F. Jawab (ed.), *Hospital Supply Chain*, Integrated Science 27,
https://doi.org/10.1007/978-3-031-70292-1_16

1 Introduction

Healthcare optimization problems have obtained a significant interest to offer a good service and to decrease cost.

Efficient healthcare scheduling is a crucial mission due to the multitude of constraints and preferences involved, such as personnel requirements and resource limitations. Unlike some other institutions, hospitals operate 24/7. Nevertheless, the challenges posed by staffing shortages and irregular working shifts can significantly impact patient satisfaction.

The Dermatology and Venereology (DV) department is consequently a 24 h/ 24 h service. In this department physicians are obligated to work day, night, and weekend shifts.

So, physician scheduling presents a formidable and time-intensive challenge. The goal is to formulate daily shift assignments for each physician within a specified horizon of time.

In the Dermatology and Venereology (DV) Department at Sfax Hospital, the process of scheduling physicians is currently done manually, taking about one workday each month for the head of the department to create the schedule. In the studied real case, the head Department generates individually schedules. Unfortunately, this operation is a very time and effort consuming. Also, it does not take into account physicians' preferences, resulting in frequent frustration and elevated stress levels among the medical staff. This, in turn, has the potential to adversely affect the quality of healthcare services provided by the doctors. Therefore, the primary aim of the present study is to develop and implement a computerized physician scheduling system. This paper specifically concentrates on addressing the Physician Scheduling Problem (PSP) through the application of a multi-objective mathematical programming approach.

In general, the constraints associated with the Physician Scheduling Problem (PSP) can be categorized into two main groups: hard and soft constraints. First, hard constraints are nonnegotiable and must be met without any exceptions, whereas soft constraints can be relaxed to produce a feasible solution. The PSP involves the consideration of multiple objective functions, including but not limited to maximizing physician preferences, minimizing violations of coverage and/ or time-related constraints, and so on.

The paper will be organized as follows: Sect. 2 will provide a comprehensive review of existing literature related to healthcare scheduling, particularly focusing on physician scheduling problems and optimization approaches. It will explore various methodologies, algorithms, and technologies employed in previous studies to address similar challenges. The review will highlight both strengths and limitations of prior research, providing a foundation for the proposed approach in this paper. Section 3 introduces the real case study and the problem description, in this section, the specific context of the Dermatology and Venereology Department at Sfax Hospital will be outlined. Details regarding the department's operations, staffing requirements, and current scheduling practices will be provided. Additionally, the challenges and limitations associated with the manual scheduling process will be discussed, emphasizing the need for a more efficient and effective solution. The problem of physician scheduling will be formally defined, including the objectives, constraints, and key performance indicators.

Section 4 presents the proposed mathematical model of the Physician Scheduling Problem (PSP) using a multi-objective optimization approach. The model will consider various factors such as physician preferences, coverage requirements, shift durations, and resource constraints. Both hard and soft constraints will be incorporated into the formulation, ensuring that the generated schedules meet operational requirements while maximizing staff satisfaction and minimizing disruptions to patient care. The model will be designed to produce feasible and high-quality schedules within a reasonable computational period.

Section 5 conducts implementation and obtained computational results. This section will focus on the practical implementation of the proposed scheduling system. Details regarding software development, data collection, and integration with existing hospital systems will be discussed. Computational experiments will be conducted to evaluate the performance of the scheduling model using real-world data from the Dermatology and Venereology Department. Metrics such as schedule quality, adherence to constraints, and computational efficiency will be analyzed to assess the effectiveness of the proposed approach. The section will conclude with a discussion of the findings, potential limitations, and avenues for future research.

Finally, Sect. 6 gives the concluding remarks and future research.

2 Literature Review

Physician scheduling, while a subset of personnel scheduling within healthcare institutions, possesses distinct characteristics that set it apart from other scheduling problems. One crucial aspect is the pivotal role that physicians play as the primary and most valuable resource within hospitals. As noted by Santos and Eriksson [8], physicians not only represent a cornerstone of healthcare delivery but also constitute a significant portion of the operational costs for healthcare facilities.

Despite this, research on physician scheduling, in comparison to nurse scheduling, has received less attention in the literature. Nurse scheduling problems have been the focus of numerous studies in healthcare personnel scheduling due to the sheer volume of nursing staff in healthcare settings and the complexity of their scheduling requirements.

However, several notable studies have addressed the unique challenges of physician scheduling. For instance, Beaulieu et al. [1] were pioneers in proposing a mathematical programming approach for scheduling physicians in the emergency room. Their model, based on multi-objective integer programming theory, aimed to optimize various objectives while satisfying a range of constraints. These constraints were categorized into four main groups: compulsory constraints, ergonomic constraints, distribution constraints, and goal constraints, reflecting the diverse considerations involved in physician scheduling.

Similarly, Van Huele and Vanhoucke [10] tackled the physician scheduling problem within the operating theatre environment, with a specific focus on minimizing overtime costs for the department. Their mathematical model aimed to efficiently allocate physician shifts while ensuring adequate coverage and minimizing resource utilization. The authors utilized a CPLEX solver to effectively solve the optimization problem, demonstrating the applicability of mathematical programming techniques in addressing complex physician scheduling challenges.

El-Rifai et al. [3] addressed the Physician Scheduling Problem (PSP) within the context of the emergency department, where the planning horizon is limited to 24 h. This short-term scheduling focus is crucial in emergency settings where staffing needs must be dynamically adjusted to accommodate fluctuating patient arrivals and acuity levels. By considering the unique challenges of emergency medicine, such as unpredictable patient flow and urgent care demands, El-Rifai et al. developed a scheduling framework tailored to the specific requirements of emergency physicians, ensuring timely and efficient allocation of resources to meet patient needs.

Gunawan and Lau [4] tackled the PSP from a tactical planning perspective, focusing on assigning physician duties to predefined time slots or shifts over an extended time horizon. Their approach incorporated a multitude of constraints and complex physician preferences, aiming to satisfy as many preferences as possible while ensuring operational efficiency. By developing a mathematical programming model, the authors provided a systematic framework for optimizing physician schedules, demonstrating its effectiveness in a real-case scenario within the Surgery Department.

Hidri and Labidi [5] addressed the physician scheduling problem within the Intensive Care Unit (ICU), where the objective was to minimize total overtime while adhering to complex constraints. Their study involved two simultaneous phases: composing teams and assigning workload to each team, reflecting the unique dynamics of ICU staffing and patient care needs. By formulating the scheduling problem as an integer linear program, Hidri et al. provided a rigorous optimization approach tailored to the specific requirements of ICU physicians, ultimately enhancing operational efficiency and staff satisfaction.

Cildoz et al. [2] focused on physician scheduling within the Emergency Room (ER), considering the real calendar and including holidays to ensure accuracy and realism in the scheduling process. By formulating a mathematical model without simplifications, the authors addressed the complexity of physician-demand coverage in the ER, aiming to optimize resource allocation while meeting patient care needs. Through linear programming techniques, Cildoz et al. provided a robust scheduling framework capable of accommodating the dynamic nature of emergency medicine, ultimately enhancing patient care delivery in the ER setting.

Hidri et al. [6] presented a mathematical model formulated as an integer linear program to minimize total overtime, a critical objective in healthcare settings aiming to optimize resource utilization and mitigate staff burnout. By leveraging state-of-the-art optimization techniques and software, the authors demonstrated the effectiveness of their approach in minimizing overtime while meeting operational

Table 1 Summary of previous work

Author	Problematic	Methodology	Result
Gunawan and Lau [4]	Assignment of physician duty in surgery department	Linear programming + heuristic	Optimum solution achieved
Van Huele and Vanhoucke [10]	Optimizing PSP in operating theatre	Linear programming + heuristic	Meta heuristic is recommended to generate good result
El-Rifai et al. [3]	PSP of emergency room	Linear programming + simulation	Minimize waiting time
Hidri and Labidi [5]	Intensive care unit PSP	Linear programming	Reduction of the over time is 50%
Hidri et al. [6]	Optimization of the procedure of physician scheduling	Integer linear programming	Reduction of the over time by about 69.23%
Cildoz et al. [2]	Optimization PSP in emergency room	Linear programming + hybrid algorithm	Model assignment is optimal than manual schedule

constraints. Experimental tests conducted on real data showcased the performance and practical applicability of the proposed scheduling procedure, highlighting its potential to improve operational efficiency and staff satisfaction in healthcare organizations.

The existing literature reviewed in this paper (summarized in Table 1) underscores several limitations in current scientific research studies within the field of healthcare resource scheduling. One notable gap is the predominant focus on nurses' scheduling, with limited attention given to the equally critical aspect of physician scheduling. While nurses play a vital role in healthcare delivery, physicians represent another essential component of the healthcare workforce, yet their scheduling challenges have not received commensurate attention in the literature.

Furthermore, there is a noticeable absence of studies aimed at minimizing deviations between soft constraints in healthcare resource scheduling to enhance both physician and patient satisfaction. Soft constraints, such as physicians' preferences for certain shifts or days off, are often overlooked in optimization models, leading to suboptimal schedules that may impact the well-being of medical staff and the quality of patient care. Addressing these soft constraints is crucial for improving overall satisfaction and performance in healthcare settings.

Moreover, the integration of different methodological approaches, such as Goal Programming (GP) multi-objective methods and Analytic Hierarchy Process (AHP)-based multi-criteria methods, is rarely seen in solving healthcare human resources scheduling problems. GP methods are effective for optimizing multiple conflicting objectives, while AHP provides a structured approach for determining the relative importance of different criteria. Combining these approaches can offer a comprehensive and systematic framework for addressing the complexities of healthcare resource scheduling.

In response to these identified limitations, this paper proposes a two-step method for solving the physician scheduling problem. In the first step, a GP mathematical model is developed to minimize deviations between soft constraints, thereby improving schedule adherence and satisfaction among medical staff. In the second step, an AHP-based method is employed to determine the importance weights of each soft constraint, allowing for a more nuanced understanding of their relative significance in the scheduling process. By integrating these two approaches, the proposed method aims to enhance the efficiency, fairness, and effectiveness of physician scheduling in healthcare organizations.

3 Case Study

The context of this study is rooted in a challenging scenario within the Dermatology and Venereology Department of the Hedi Chaker Hospital in Sfax, Tunisia. This scenario is characterized by a multitude of dissatisfaction indicators, affecting both patients and physicians alike. Patients have expressed discontent, likely due to prolong waiting times, difficulties in accessing timely care, and potentially suboptimal treatment experiences. Similarly, physicians within the department have voiced dissatisfaction, likely stemming from excessive workloads, irregular schedules, and high levels of stress caused by inadequate scheduling practices.

One of the prominent issues exacerbating these challenges is the presence of high deviations between physicians' workloads and their capacity to manage them effectively. This misalignment can lead to inefficiencies, compromised patient care, and increased frustration among both patients and healthcare providers. Additionally, the lack of a well-structured scheduling system likely contributes to prolonged waiting times, exacerbating patient dissatisfaction and potentially influencing patient outcomes.

In response to this unsatisfactory situation, the departmental authorities recognize the urgent need for intervention. They are compelled to seek an efficient physician scheduling solution that can address the underlying issues and restore balance within the department. The primary objective is to achieve a certain equilibrium between the various soft constraints inherent in physician scheduling. These soft constraints encompass a range of factors, including physicians' preferences for shifts, time off, workload distribution, and the equitable allocation of duties.

By addressing these soft constraints effectively, the aim is not only to improve the satisfaction and well-being of healthcare providers but also to enhance the overall patient experience within the Dermatology and Venereology Department. Achieving this balance is crucial for optimizing operational efficiency, reducing waiting times, and ultimately, elevating the quality of care provided to patients.

Therefore, the study seeks to develop and implement a comprehensive physician scheduling system that can navigate these complexities and foster a more harmonious and effective healthcare environment within the department.

3.1 Presentation of the "Dermatology and Venereology" Department

The Hedi Chaker Hospital stands as a cornerstone of healthcare in Tunisia, boasting a rich history that dates back to the early twentieth century. Established through law n° 74–83 on December 11, 1929, the hospital is named in honor of the esteemed Tunisian physician Hédi Chaker. Originally classified as a public administrative establishment (EPA), the hospital underwent a significant transformation in 1992, transitioning into a category A public health establishment (E.P.S). Operating under the dual supervision of the Ministry of Higher Education and Scientific Research and the Ministry of Public Health, the hospital serves as a prominent public higher education and research institution.

The hospital's commitment to excellence in healthcare is evident in its strategic redirection of surgical facilities to new premises initially intended as an extension of the University Hospital. These facilities were later reconfigured into an independent entity, now known as the University Hospital H. Bourguiba. The Dermatology and Venereology Department, situated at the heart of the facility alongside the administration, rheumatology, and neuro-pediatrics departments, plays a vital role in promoting overall well-being within the community.

Spanning two efficiently organized floors, the Dermatology and Venereology Department's first floor houses consultation rooms, reception areas, doctors' offices, archives, treatment rooms, an operations block with a recovery room, a phototherapy and allergology unit, as well as secretarial and administrative offices. The department head's office, supervisor's office, nurses' office, meeting room, and other essential facilities are also located on this floor.

Ascending to the second floor (level 1), separate spaces for women and men are equipped with doctor's offices, nurses' offices, treatment preparation rooms, and other essential facilities to cater to patients' specific needs.

A dedicated team, including 19 nurses and technicians, 11 support staff, and 1 supervisor, staffs the department. Additionally, there are 9 residents and 9 academic staff members, including 1 senior (head of department), 4 associate professors, 1 associate professor, and 3 assistants. This diverse team collaborates to deliver exceptional medical services through treatment rooms and an operating theater, serving approximately 150–180 patients daily in the outpatient department.

The patient journey within the department is well structured and organized, with individuals checking in at the reception counter upon arrival. Patients then wait in the designated waiting room before being directed to one of three residents' offices for initial sorting through a pre-consultation process. Subsequently, based on individual needs, a second assignment is made to a specialist professor, available during the day shift, to conduct a detailed consultation and provide a specific diagnosis. This patient-centric approach reflects the department's commitment to providing high quality, personalized care to its patients.

3.2 Problem Description

The scheduling challenge within the Dermatology and Venereology Department at Hedi Chaker Hospital is a multifaceted endeavor, requiring the effective organization of teams comprising doctors and medical residents. At the core of this challenge lies the imperative to align scheduling practices with the department's operational demands, spanning a 24 h period throughout the designated workweek.

Ensuring optimal scheduling within the department involves meticulous planning to meet the diverse needs of patients while maximizing the efficiency of medical staff utilization. The primary objective is twofold: to allocate resources judiciously to provide comprehensive coverage across all shifts and to accommodate the varying skill sets and expertise of medical personnel to meet the department's clinical requirements.

Given the round-the-clock nature of healthcare delivery, the scheduling process must address the unique demands of each day of the week, taking into account factors such as patient volume, complexity of cases, and the availability of specialized services. From routine consultations to emergency interventions, the scheduling framework must be flexible and adaptable to accommodate the dynamic nature of patient care.

Moreover, the scheduling challenge extends beyond merely assigning shifts to doctors and medical residents. It encompasses considerations such as ensuring adequate supervision for medical trainees, facilitating continuity of care for patients, and optimizing resource allocation to minimize downtime and maximize productivity.

Additionally, the scheduling process must adhere to regulatory guidelines and professional standards, ensuring compliance with laws governing working hours, rest periods, and duty rotations. This necessitates careful monitoring of workload distribution and the implementation of safeguards to prevent staff fatigue and burnout.

Ultimately, the goal of effective scheduling within the Dermatology and Venereology Department is to optimize patient outcomes by ensuring timely access to high-quality care while promoting the well-being and professional development of medical staff. By aligning scheduling practices with the department's operational requirements and leveraging innovative approaches to resource management, Hedi Chaker Hospital can enhance its capacity to deliver exceptional healthcare services to the community it serves.

Table 2 presents the daily schedule of doctors, including seniors and professor.

Physicians are obligated to adhere to the suggested daily schedule for conducting both internal and external consultations, as well as surgical procedures, in

Table 2 Presentation of the daily schedule of doctors

Horizon	Week						
Physician	Day						
	Monday	Tuesday	Wednesday	Thursday	Friday	Saturday	Sunday
1	C	B	C	C	B	*V*	*R*
2		C		C	B	*V*	*R*
3	C		B		C	*V*	*R*
4		C		C		*V*	*R*
5	C	B		C		*V*	*R*
6		C	C	B		*V*	*R*
7	B	C			C	*R*	*R*
8	C		C	B		*V*	*R*
9	B	C	C		C	*R*	*R*
10	C	B	C	B	C	*V*	*R*
11	C	B	C	B	C	*V*	*R*
12	B	C	C			*V*	*R*
13	C	B		C		*V*	*R*
14		C	B	C	B	*V*	*R*
15	B		C		C	*V*	*R*
16	C	C	B	C		*V*	*R*
17		B		C	C	*V*	*R*
18	B	C	C		B	*V*	*R*

C consultation, *B* operating bloc, *V* visit, *R* rest

alignment with their individual preferences. It is crucial to highlight that the existing schedule does not accommodate the preferences of all physicians. For instance, Doctor 1 prefers not to have days off during the week.

In fact, Table 3 presents the duty plan of June month. It is poorly planned night shifts.

Usually, physician called to participate to specific number of night shift separated for long a month but it is noticed in Table 3 that total number of duty for Doctor 1 is 6 nights included 3 nights consecutively planed but doctor 2 and 9 not scheduled for night shift.

To address this complexity, we propose a comprehensive scheduling model that takes into account a multitude of constraints, each requiring careful consideration to achieve satisfaction. These constraints are systematically categorized into two classes: hard constraints, which are non-negotiable and must be strictly adhered to, and soft constraints, which can be violated to a certain extent without compromising the overall schedule integrity.

Table 3 Example of night shift for June month

Date	1	2	3	4	5	6	7	8	9	10	11	12	13	14	15	16	17	18
	Physician																	
01/06						*				*								
02/06	*										*							
03/06				*								*						
04/06				*									*					
05/06				*										*				
06/06							*				*							
07/06								*									*	
08/06					*										*			
09/06						*						*						
10/06	*										*							
11/06	*															*		
12/06	*														*			
13/06				*									*					
14/06							*										*	
15/06								*						*				
16/06					*						*							
17/06			*															*
18/06			*									*						
19/06						*				*								
20/06	*												*					
21/06				*											*			
22/06							*			*								
23/06								*								*		
24/06					*									*				
25/06					*												*	
26/06					*					*								
27/06						*												*
28/06	*														*			
29/06				*														*
30/06						*							*					
Total	6	0	2	6	5	5	3	3	0	4	4	3	4	3	4	2	3	3

Our model is specifically designed to minimize deviations from the designated targets of these soft constraints, thereby enhancing schedule adherence and accommodating physicians' preferences to the greatest extent possible. By leveraging the Analytical Hierarchy Process (AHP), we assign weights to these deviations within the objective function, allowing for a systematic and data-driven approach to prioritize constraints and optimize scheduling outcomes.

Through this integrated approach, we aim to develop a scheduling framework that not only ensures operational efficiency and patient satisfaction but also enhances physician well-being and job satisfaction by accommodating their preferences and minimizing disruptions to their work-life balance. By addressing the unique challenges of physician scheduling within the Dermatology and Venereology Department, we strive to foster a more harmonious and effective healthcare environment at Hedi Chaker Hospital.

4 Proposed Mathematical Model

4.1 The AHP Approach

AHP, introduced by Saaty [9], is concerned with determining the relative importance of a set of activities in a multicriteria decision problem. This procedure makes it possible to include the evaluation of intangible qualitative criteria in addition to specific quantitative criteria. This method uses pairwise comparisons of both alternatives and criteria to facilitate the decision-making process. This approach offers significant advantages, as highlighted by Wilson [11], particularly when collecting data from decision-makers.

Pairwise comparisons allow decision-makers to focus on comparing only two objects or criteria at a time. This structured approach minimizes cognitive load and reduces the potential for bias or distortion in observations. By breaking down complex decision-making tasks into simpler pairwise comparisons, decision-makers can more effectively evaluate the relative importance or preference of each alternative or criterion.

Moreover, pairwise comparisons enable decision-makers to provide more nuanced and precise assessments, as they can carefully weigh the relative strengths and weaknesses of each option or criterion against one another. This granularity in evaluation enhances the accuracy and reliability of the decision-making process, leading to more informed and robust outcomes.

Furthermore, pairwise comparisons help mitigate the impact of external influences or biases that may arise when considering multiple alternatives or criteria simultaneously. By isolating comparisons to only two objects or criteria at a time, decision-makers can focus their attention more effectively and make clearer, more objective judgments.

Overall, the adoption of pairwise comparisons in our methodology enhances the efficiency, accuracy, and objectivity of the decision-making process. By providing decision-makers with a structured framework for evaluating alternatives and criteria, pairwise comparisons facilitate more informed and robust decision-making, ultimately leading to better outcomes.

4.2 Proposed Mathematical Model

4.2.1 Notation and Variables

To formulate the proposed model, the following notations are used.

- i index of the physician, $i = 1, \ldots, I$
- j index of the monthly planning period days, $j = 1, \ldots, J$
- k index for the shift type, $k = 1$ for the day shift (7 a.m.–5 p.m.) and 2 for the night shift (5 p.m.–7 a.m.)
- s index of the physicians specialty, $s = \{1, 2\}$
- S set of all Saturdays within the planning period.

4.2.2 Objective Function

In our study, we employ a comprehensive approach to measure deviations in various soft constraints within the scheduling process. This approach is rooted in the concept of assigning importance weights to each constraint, reflecting their relative significance compared to one another. This methodology, as highlighted by Jlassi et al. [7], provides a structured framework for quantifying the impact of each constraint on the overall scheduling objectives.

By assigning importance weights to individual constraints, we can effectively prioritize them based on their relative importance and influence on the scheduling outcomes. For example, constraints related to physician preferences or patient satisfaction may be assigned higher importance weights than constraints related to resource availability or operational efficiency.

The importance weights serve as a quantitative measure of the relative significance of each constraint, allowing us to gauge their impact on the scheduling process accurately. Deviations from these constraints can then be measured and evaluated based on their respective importance weights, providing valuable insights into areas where the scheduling model may need further refinement or optimization.

By incorporating importance weights into our deviation measurement framework, we can ensure that the scheduling process is aligned with the overarching goals and objectives of the department. This structured approach to constraint prioritization enables us to focus our efforts on addressing the most critical constraints first, thereby maximizing the efficiency and effectiveness of the scheduling model.

$$Min\, 0.744 \sum_{m-1}^{M} \sum_{j-1}^{J-1} night1_{mj} + 0.192 \sum_{m-1}^{M} \sum_{j-1}^{J-2} day1_{mj}$$
$$+\, 0.064 \sum_{m-1}^{M} wkd_m$$

4.2.3 Constraints

Hard Constraints

The hard constraints include the staffing requirements of both the day and the night shifts as well as the physicians' working hours restrictions.

A physician cannot work both the day and night shifts in a workday.

$$\sum_{k=1}^{2} X_{pjk} \leq 1 \quad p = 1, \ldots, I,\ j = 1, \ldots, J$$

A physician assigned to a night shift can not be assigned to a day shift on the next day.

$$X_{pj2} + X_{p(j+1)} \leq 1 \quad p = 1, \ldots, I,\ j = 1, \ldots, J - 1$$

Each physician should be assigned to his number of day and night shifts during the scheduling period.

$$\sum_{j=1}^{J} X_{pj1} = DS_{ij} \quad p = 1, \ldots, I$$

$$\sum_{j=1}^{J} X_{pj2} = NS_{ij} \quad p = 1, \ldots, I$$

The overall number of physicians assigned to a day or night shift should be in the specified range.

$$LD \le \sum_{p=1}^{I} X_{pjk} \le UD \;\; j = 1, \ldots, J, \;\; k = 1, 2$$

Soft Constraints

The soft constraints relate to physicians' preferences for the scheduling of shifts.

A physician should not work two consecutive night shifts.

$$X_{pj2} + X_{i(i+1)2} + \text{night } 1_{ij} \le 1 \; p = 1, \ldots, P, \;\; j = 1, \ldots, J - 1$$

A physician should not work three consecutive day shifts.

$$X_{pj1} + X_{p(j+1)1} + X_{p(j+2)1} + \text{day } 1_{ij} \le 2 \quad p = 1, \ldots, P, \;\; j = 1, \ldots, J$$

Each physician should take at least one weekend off during the scheduling period

$$\sum_{j \in S} Y_{pj} + wkd_p \ge 1 \quad p = 1, \ldots, P$$

5 Implementation and Results

The integration of the CPLEX solver into our scheduling model represents a significant advancement in healthcare operations management. By leveraging the computational power and optimization capabilities of CPLEX, we were able to address the intricate challenges of physician scheduling with unprecedented efficiency and precision.

Executing the model with the CPLEX 22.1.1 solver not only highlighted the critical importance of assigning physicians to shifts but also underscored the necessity of adopting a data-driven approach to achieve departmental objectives. The solver's ability to rapidly process complex scheduling constraints and preferences for all 18 doctors within the department was instrumental in streamlining the scheduling process and mitigating the inherent conflicts that arise from manual scheduling methods.

One of the key advantages of using the CPLEX solver was its capacity to generate an optimal solution within a reasonable timeframe, with an instance resolution time of 3584 s. This rapid turnaround time significantly reduced the administrative burden associated with manual scheduling, allowing for more timely and effective decision-making in resource allocation.

Furthermore, the optimized solution produced by the CPLEX solver redefined the assignment of senior doctors and residents based on the dynamic needs of the department. By strategically distributing day and night shifts, as well as weekend rotations, among the medical staff, the solver ensured equitable workload distribution while accommodating individual preferences and constraints.

For example, the scheduling algorithm intelligently reduced the number of night shifts assigned to Doctor 1, thereby alleviating the burden of successive shifts and promoting a healthier work-life balance. Moreover, by limiting day shifts to two consecutive days, the solver enhanced the overall management and organization of medical planning, minimizing the risk of fatigue and burnout among the medical staff.

In summary, the implementation of the CPLEX solver revolutionized physician scheduling within the Dermatology and Venereology Department, paving the way for more efficient resource allocation, improved staff satisfaction, and enhanced patient care delivery. By harnessing the power of advanced optimization techniques, we have successfully navigated the complexities of healthcare scheduling, driving operational excellence and innovation in healthcare management.

The results obtained from the CPLEX 22.1.1 solver shed light on the significant improvements brought about by our scheduling model, particularly in the realm of shift planning and the allocation of rest days. By meticulously analyzing the data matrices generated by the solver, we gain valuable insights into the optimized scheduling outcomes that our model has produced.

One of the key highlights of our model is its ability to create an on-call schedule that ensures doctors on duty have the following day off. This strategic approach to scheduling not only promotes a healthier work-life balance for medical staff but also contributes to enhanced patient safety and quality of care. By providing doctors with adequate rest periods following their on-call shifts, we mitigate the risk of fatigue-related errors and ensure that physicians are refreshed and capable of delivering optimal care to patients.

A detailed comparison between the initial on-call schedule proposed by the department head and the outcomes derived from our scheduling model reveals significant disparities. In the initial schedule, certain doctors were burdened with consecutive night shifts and excessive working days, leading to potential fatigue and burnout. However, our model addresses these shortcomings by distributing on-call and working days more equitably among medical staff, thereby optimizing workload distribution and enhancing overall departmental efficiency.

Furthermore, the results obtained from our model adhere to soft constraints, indicating that it provides a more efficient solution for managing on-call schedules while minimizing constraints for doctors. This emphasis on flexibility and adaptability ensures that the scheduling model can accommodate the diverse preferences and needs of medical staff, ultimately leading to higher levels of job satisfaction and morale.

The utilization of the CPLEX solver for modeling purposes has proven to be advantageous, allowing us to optimize scheduling outcomes with unparalleled efficiency and accuracy. By leveraging advanced optimization techniques, we have been able to create a scheduling framework that not only meets the operational needs of the department but also prioritizes the well-being of medical staff and the quality of patient care.

However, the results obtained from our scheduling model (see Table 4) demonstrate a notable enhancement in the distribution of on-call and working days, contributing to a more balanced and sustainable workload allocation within the Dermatology and Venereology Department. Moving forward, we anticipate that our scheduling model will continue to serve as a valuable tool for enhancing operational efficiency and improving the overall quality of care provided to patients.

The comparative graph depicted in Fig. 1 serves as a visual representation of the scheduling outcomes generated by our proposed model, allowing for a comprehensive assessment of the distribution of on-call shifts, including weekends, among department doctors. The graph clearly illustrates that in an ideal scenario, every doctor should participate in at least one Sunday shift, as indicated by the green bars. This equitable distribution of weekend shifts aims to ensure a well-balanced involvement of all medical staff within the department, promoting fairness and reducing the burden on individual physicians.

However, upon closer examination of the real-case data, a discrepancy emerges between the proposed scheduling model and the actual on-call schedule implemented within the department. Contrary to the ideal scenario depicted in the graph, the data reveals that on-call weekends are disproportionately restricted to a select group of doctors, namely doctors 1, 3, 4, 5, 12, 13, 16, and 17. This discrepancy highlights the challenges inherent in translating theoretical scheduling models into practical implementation, underscoring the importance of continuous refinement and adaptation of scheduling practices based on real-world constraints and considerations. Table 5 contains a comparative state of real case data with the proposed model result.

In conclusion, the results obtained from our scheduling model demonstrate a notable reduction in the deviation of soft constraints compared to the planning adopted in the case study. Despite the discrepancies observed between the proposed model and the real-case data, the performance of the model remains commendable, as it provides valuable insights and optimization opportunities for scheduling practices within the Dermatology and Venereology Department. Moreover, the validation of the presented model by the department head signifies a vote of confidence in its efficacy and utility in addressing the scheduling challenges

Table 4 Obtained results

Day	K	Physicians																	
		1	2	3	4	5	6	7	8	9	10	11	12	13	14	15	16	17	18
1	1	*	*		*				*	*	*	*					*	*	
	2						*								*				
2	1		*	*		*			*	*		*	*	*					*
	2							*										*	
3	1	*		*	*	*	*				*			*	*		*		
	2								*							*			
4	1	*	*		*		*			*	*		*		*				*
	2					*						*							
5	1		*	*				*	*	*				*		*	*		*
	2						*						*						
6	1	*		*	*	*			*		*	*			*			*	
	2									*									*
7	1							*									*		
	2						*							*					
8	1	*	*	*				*		*					*		*	*	*
	2				*							*							
9	1	*		*		*			*	*			*		*	*			*
	2							*									*		
10	1		*		*	*	*		*		*	*		*				*	
	2			*												*			
11	1	*			*		*	*		*		*	*		*				*
	2								*									*	
12	1	*	*	*		*				*	*			*	*	*			
	2						*						*						
13	1		*	*	*			*	*		*	*						*	*
	2	*												*					
14	1									*						*			
	2		*										*						
15	1	*			*	*		*	*			*			*		*		*
	2						*									*			
16	1	*	*	*		*				*	*	*		*				*	
	2							*							*				
17	1		*	*			*		*	*	*						*	*	*
	2	*												*					

(continued)

Table 4 (continued)

Day	K	Physicians																	
		1	2	3	4	5	6	7	8	9	10	11	12	13	14	15	16	17	18
18	1				*	*	*	*	*			*	*		*		*		
	2			*												*			
19	1	*	*		*	*				*	*			*				*	*
	2						*										*		
20	1		*	*				*	*	*		*	*			*			*
	2					*								*					
21	1	*									*								
	2			*															*
22	1	*	*			*			*	*	*	*			*		*		
	2							*					*						
23	1		*	*	*		*			*				*		*		*	*
	2					*					*								
24	1	*		*			*	*	*				*		*		*		*
	2				*							*							
25	1	*	*			*			*	*				*	*		*	*	
	2							*			*					*			
26	1		*	*		*	*			*		*	*	*					*
	2				*												*		
27	1	*		*			*	*	*		*		*					*	*
	2		*													*			
28	1								*									*	
	2					*									*				
29	1	*	*	*				*		*	*	*	*			*			
	2				*														*
30	1	*					*	*	*	*	*				*	*		*	
	2			*		*						*							

faced by the department. Moving forward, ongoing refinement and adaptation of the scheduling model will be essential to ensure its continued relevance and effectiveness in meeting the evolving needs of both medical staff and patients within the department.

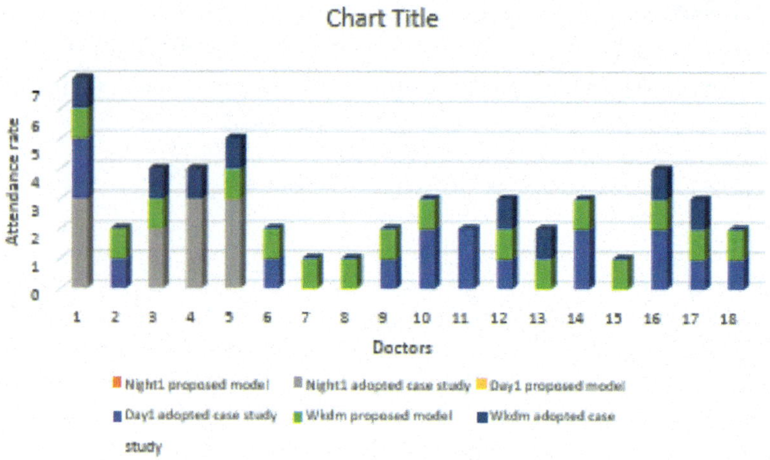

Fig. 1 Graph of comparison of real data with the obtained result

Table 5 Comparative state of real case data with model result proposed

Physician	Night		Day		Weekend	
	Proposed model	Real case adopted	Proposed model	Real case adopted	Proposed model	Real case adopted
1	**0**	**3**	**0**	**2**	1	1
2	0	0	**0**	**1**	**1**	**0**
3	**0**	**2**	0	0	1	1
4	**0**	**3**	0	0	**0**	**1**
5	**0**	**3**	0	0	1	1
6	0	0	**0**	**1**	**1**	**0**
7	0	0	0	0	**1**	**0**
8	0	0	0	0	**1**	**0**
9	0	0	**0**	**1**	**1**	**0**
10	0	0	**0**	**2**	**1**	**0**
11	0	0	**0**	**2**	0	0
12	0	0	**0**	**1**	1	1
13	0	0	0	0	1	1
14	0	0	**0**	**2**	**1**	**0**
15	0	0	0	0	**1**	**0**
16	0	0	**0**	**2**	1	1
17	0	0	**0**	**1**	1	1
18	0	0	**0**	**1**	**1**	**0**

the bold values signify the different between result obtained by the proposal model and the real case adopted

6 Conclusion and Future Work

In this study, we have introduced an integrated AHP-GP approach for the planning of the scheduling process within the Dermatology and Venereology Department. This innovative approach combines the strengths of AHP in prioritizing constraints and preferences with the optimization capabilities of GP to generate high-quality monthly schedules efficiently.

The presented GP model demonstrates remarkable capability in producing schedules that adhere to both hard and soft constraints within the scheduling process. By considering factors such as physician preferences, departmental requirements, and patient satisfaction metrics, the model ensures that scheduling decisions are aligned with the overarching goals of the department while optimizing resource allocation and workload distribution.

The execution of the linear program with the CPLEX solver has yielded satisfactory results, effectively minimizing gaps between physicians' charges and meeting departmental requirements. This optimization not only enhances operational efficiency but also contributes to improved patient satisfaction by ensuring timely access to care and continuity of treatment.

As we look towards future work, our focus will be on measuring the degree of satisfaction of both patients and physician resources to validate the efficiency of the presented model. By conducting surveys and collecting feedback from stakeholders, we aim to assess the impact of the scheduling model on various aspects of healthcare delivery, including patient wait times, physician workload, and overall departmental performance.

Additionally, future iterations of the model can incorporate uncertainties and imprecise information to enhance its robustness and adaptability in real-world scenarios. By accounting for factors such as unexpected fluctuations in patient volume, staff availability, and resource constraints, the model can better accommodate the dynamic nature of healthcare operations and improve decision-making in scheduling processes.

Overall, the integration of AHP-GP methodology represents a significant advancement in healthcare scheduling practices, offering a systematic and data-driven approach to optimize resource allocation and enhance operational efficiency within the Dermatology and Venereology Department. As we continue to refine and expand upon this approach, we remain committed to driving innovation and excellence in healthcare management.

Acknowledgements We're grateful to the anonymous reviewers for constructive comments and suggestions.

The authors thank the Dermatology and Venereology Department of the Hedi Chaker Hospital in Sfax, Tunisia.

References

1. Beaulieu H, Ferland JA, Gendron B, Philippe M (2000) A mathematical programming approach for scheduling physicians in the emergency room. Health Care Manage Sci 3:193–200
2. Cildoz M, Mallor F, Mateo PM (2021) A GRASP-based algorithm for solving the emergency room physician scheduling problem. Appl Soft Comput 103
3. EL-Rifai O, Garaix T, Augusto V, Xie X (2015) A stochastic optimization mod-el for shift scheduling in emergency departments. Health Care Manag Sci 18:289–302
4. Gunawan A, Lau HC (2013) Master physician scheduling problem. J Oper Res Soc 64(3):410–425
5. Hidri L, Labidi M (2016) Optimal physicians schedule in an Intensive Care Unit, IOP Conf. Series: Mater Sci Eng 131
6. Hidri L, Gazdar A, Mabkhot M (2020) Optimized Procedure to Schedule Phy-sicians in an Intensive Care Unit: A Case Study, Mathematics 8:1976
7. Jlassi J, Chabchoub H, El Mhamedi A (2011) A combined AHP-GP model for nurse scheduling. 2011 4th International Conference on Logistics
8. Santos M, Eriksson H (2014) Insights into physician scheduling: A case study of public hospital departments in Sweden. Int J Health Care Qual Assur 2:76–90
9. Saaty TL (1988) What is Analytical Hierarchy Process?, NATO ASI Ser Math Model Decis Support F48:109–122
10. Van Huele C, Vanhoucke M (2014) Analysis of the integration of the physi-cian rostering problem and the surgery scheduling problem topical collection on systems-level quality improvement. J Med Syst 38
11. Wilson DM (2001) Public and private health-care systems: what the literature says. Canadian Public Administration/Administration Publique Du Canada 44(2):204–231

Khadija Werghi is a Master student on Sciences of logistics and transport at the Higher Institute of Industrial Management of Sfax (ISGI Sfax, University of Sfax, Tunisia).

Jihène Jlassi is an assistant professor of science in logistics and transport at the Higher Institute of Industrial Management of Sfax (ISGI Sfax_University of Sfax). She got her Ph.D. in Industrial Engineering from the Paris 8 University. She was also member of scientific committees of many conferences. In addition, she served as a reviewer for several referred conferences and journals in her field. As a member of OLID research lab, her main research interests are logistics and optimization. She has published many papers in international journals and presented several communications.

Ines Rekik is an associate professor on Sciences of logistics and transport at the Higher Institute of Industrial Management of Sfax (ISGI Sfax, University of Sfax, Tunisia). She has obtained her Ph.D. in computer science from the University of Sfax (Tunisia). Her research interest focuses on the real time decision making in logistics and transportation systems. She uses some techniques issued from the artificial intelligence for the development of decentralized and intelligent decision making for the supply chain management.

Abderrahman El Mhamedi is professor at the Department of Industrial Logistics Quality and Organization of the Paris 8 University (France). He is the founder and director of the research group "MGSI—Modeling and Engineering of Industrial Systems" at the University of Paris 8—Laboratory Quartz. He is involved in several industrial and scientific projects in the area of integrated Product Lifecycle and supply chain management in order to link the academic and the industrial world. He is author of more than 160 papers that have been published on national and international proceedings and journals. His research works are related to the logistic system and healthcare, product lifecycle management, simulation and optimization in supply chain.

17 Use of Participatory Ergonomics to Ensure the Safety of Patients and Healthcare Workers in Cancer Care Settings; PECS Framework

Safa Elkefi and Roa Sabra

An ounce of prevention is worth a pound of cure.

—Benjamin Franklin

Abstract

In contemporary cancer care settings, ensuring the safety of patients and healthcare workers is paramount. This study introduces the Participatory Ergonomics for Cancer Safety (PECS) framework, which emphasizes the involvement of all stakeholders in enhancing work environments and safety protocols. By integrating participatory ergonomics, the study aims to address both process-related and organization-related safety issues, which are often overlooked in traditional safety culture methodologies. Our approach focuses on the micro (individual interactions with tasks), meso (team interactions), and macro (organizational and system features) levels to foster a comprehensive safety culture. The findings highlight the potential of participatory ergonomics to mitigate risks such as hazardous drug exposure, radiation, and psychological stress among healthcare workers, as well as to improve patient safety by reducing medication errors and treatment complications. This study contributes to the existing literature

S. Elkefi (✉)
Nursing School, Columbia University, New York, USA
e-mail: se2649@columbia.edu

HPHACTORS Lab, New York, USA

R. Sabra
Faculty of Health Sciences, University of Ottawa, Ottawa, ON, Canada
e-mail: Rsabr047@uottawa.ca

F. Jawab (ed.), *Hospital Supply Chain*, Integrated Science 27,
https://doi.org/10.1007/978-3-031-70292-1_17

by showcasing how a participatory approach can lead to more sustainable and effective safety practices in high-risk environments like cancer care settings.

Keywords

Human factors • Work environment • Oncology • Workplace wellbeing

1 Introduction

Cancer is a challenging setting of care, where hospitals have a fast pace, a complex system, and exigent workplaces [1]. The hospital, the patients, and the clinical staff, thus, face continuous pressuring deadlines, routines, and schedules [2]. The ever-increasing demands for cancer services add more workload and pressure on the hospital staff to deliver more efficient cancer care services in less time, which threatens both the quality of cancer care delivered and the well-being of the workers [2] and the quality of services delivered to the patients. In addition, most of the studies addressing safety cultures' challenges in cancer care focus on the patient's experience rather than the employee's experience, which remains poorly investigated [3].

The American Safety Council defines organizational safety culture as a combination of individual and group values, attitudes, perceptions, competencies, and behavioral patterns that are key aspects of an organization's health and safety management [4]. Implementing safety cultures has been associated with better healthcare workers, patients, and organizational outcomes such as fewer injuries, more job satisfaction, better staff retention rates, less burnout, fewer adverse events, and better quality of care in cancer care settings and primary care [5–7]. To account for good work and care environments in healthcare settings, Human Factors and Ergonomics (HFE) efforts have been known to promote the involvement of all stakeholders in the redesign of spaces, processes, and tools, also known as participatory ergonomics (PEs) [8]. End-user participation in workplace safety management is often cited as essential for improving and maintaining safe workplace behavior and conditions and fostering functional and adaptive safety cultures [9].

As a result of focusing on and involving stakeholders at all system levels, HFE also promotes a micro, meso, and macro perspective through participatory ergonomic approaches [10]. Taking a slightly broader perspective at a group or team level and how they interact with work, the micro level would look at individuals' interactions with their tasks. In contrast, the meso level would look at group or team interactions [10]. As a last step, the macro level considers the system's features and organizational factors [10]. These approaches have been used extensively in promoting safety in complex healthcare systems [11]. Although cancer care is suffering from many safety-related challenges, participatory ergonomics has shown efficiency in addressing safety concerns in other settings [12, 13]. It remains unclear what participatory ergonomics offers regarding cancer care safety issues. Our study tries to address that gap by identifying process-related and organization-related safety issues in cancer care and exploring how participatory ergonomic approaches could potentially help.

2 Safety Issues in Cancer Care

2.1 Safety Issues Encountered by Healthcare Workers and Providers

2.1.1 Exposure to Hazardous Drugs and Radiation Exposure

Healthcare professionals who operate in cancer settings encounter several safety hazards. These issues highlight the necessity of strict safety protocols and strong support networks. For instance, they are exposed to risky substances, such as chemotherapy and other cytotoxic medicines, in cancer rooms [12]. Exposure to these substances occurs when healthcare workers inhale vapors or touch contaminated surfaces.

2.1.2 Infectious Diseases

Studies have found that nurses who reported handling hazardous drugs had twice the risk of reproductive problems [12]. These risks can unintentionally result in major health concerns, including cancer and reproductive disorders [13]. In a similar vein, individuals receiving radiological therapy run the danger of being exposed to ionizing radiation, which could result in long-term health problems like cancer and radiation sickness [14]. Furthermore, cancer patients' weakened immune systems make them more susceptible to infections, which is extremely dangerous for medical personnel who routinely interact closely with these patients.

2.1.3 Psychological Stress and Burnout, Physical Strain

In addition to the risks to their physical health, cancer specialists frequently experience high levels of emotional stress from overseeing the treatment of patients who are very sick [15]. Caring for patients with cancer can be taxing for frontline healthcare providers. The growing intensity of treatment protocols, in conjunction with staff shortages, reduced hospital stays, and broader pressures on the cancer care system, may exacerbate these challenges, leading to an increased risk for burnout [16].

2.2 Safety Issues Encountered by Patients

2.2.1 Medication Errors

Patients with cancer face enormous problems related to medication errors [17]. A review of data about medication errors among cancer patients by Weingart et al. indicated that 1–3% of patients experienced a medication error during treatment [17]. Only in the USA the incidence of medication errors among cancer patients reached a rate of 7.1% among adults and 18.8% among pediatric patients [18]. Although chemotherapy is a well-established treatment modality, chemotherapy errors represent a potentially serious risk of patient harm, with an occurrence rate of one to four per 1000 orders [17]. Systems that are designed to prevent these medication errors are often inadequate because of factors such as lack of recognition of errors, communication problems, and fragmentation of care [18]. Outpatient chemotherapy regimens are particularly complex because of the intense monitoring required, unanticipated and frequent changes in medication doses based on clinical changes, body-surface area-based dosing calculations, and medications taken only on certain days of the week or month [19].

2.2.2 Infections

Cancer patients have weakened immune systems [20]. While cancer treatments such as chemotherapy, radiotherapy, and surgery have been known to improve malignancy morbidity and mortality, they also have the potential to weaken immune defenses and induce periods of severe cytopenia [21]. These adverse effects pave the way for opportunistic infections to complicate a hospitalized cancer patient's clinical course [21]. The vulnerability of hospital-acquired infections can complicate treatments and result in worse health outcomes [20]. Infections could be due to various factors, including local tumor effects, complex cancer treatments, disruption of physical barriers, neutropenia, humoral and/or cellular dysfunction, asplenia, and the presence of foreign devices [20].

2.2.3 Treatment Complications

Many treatment modalities have side effects and complications that can pose additional risks to patient safety, including severe reactions and long-term health issues [22]. As high as 34% of cancer patients experience one or more adverse events, a much higher rate in comparison with the general patient population [22, 23]. Side effects may include damaging healthy cells, organ removal during surgery, deficiency in white blood cells, hair loss, memory issues, nausea and vomiting, and blood clots [24]. Additionally, patients often face complications from navigating the transitions between different treatment environments and communicating with different healthcare providers throughout their long journey, which could result in misunderstandings and different care standards [25]. In the realm of cancer care, it is becoming increasingly apparent that the resilience of the system has a significant impact on patient safety [26]. The system's capacity to react, monitor, anticipate, and learn has a direct effect on the quality of care patients receive [26].

2.3 Safety Issues Encountered by Organizations

2.3.1 Data Security, Privacy Concerns, and Regulatory Compliance

Healthcare organizations deal with very sensitive cancer patients' data, which requires stringent safeguards against breaches. In addition to patient privacy protocols, they must also adhere to numerous regulations and procedures to handle hazardous materials and treatment protocols safely. Non-compliance can result in legal penalties and jeopardize patient safety.

2.3.2 Resource Allocation

Oncology is persistently marred by an array of resource constraints that continue to challenge the delivery of optimal cancer care [27]. These constraints include unavailability of key cancer therapies, drug shortages, overburdened imaging machines, operating rooms, and radiotherapy machines, limited blood supply, private sector costs that are prohibitive to most people, and inadequate numbers of trained oncology clinicians [27, 28]. Ensuring sufficient resources, including staffing, equipment, and space, is critical for safe cancer care. The impact of these constraints is felt across the entire spectrum of cancer care, from diagnosis to treatment and follow-up care. Inadequate resources can lead to treatment delays, increased errors, and staff burnout. Addressing these persistent challenges will require innovative solutions and collaborative efforts from stakeholders across the healthcare continuum [27, 28].

2.3.3 Emergency Preparedness

Cancer care facilities must have plans for emergency preparedness. Emergencies include but are not limited to, power outages, natural disasters, and other unexpected events that could disrupt the care delivery for vulnerable patients. One of the latest emergencies that cancer care settings were vulnerable to was the COVID-19 pandemic. Patients with cancer were reported to have an increased risk for morbidity and mortality from COVID-19, and active treatment was suggested to increase these risks further [29]. During the early days of the pandemic, addressing these challenges became a top priority. As a result, several studies were initiated to determine the best approach for patients with cancer. One study found that cancer patients have a higher risk of all-cause mortality and need for Intensive Care Unit admission compared to the general population [30]. Another study showed that immunocompromised states make cancer patients more vulnerable to infection [31]. A third study analyzed 218 individuals with COVID-19 and cancer, revealing a significant increase in COVID-19-related mortality in cancer patients compared to non-cancer patients [32]. Similarly, another analysis of 928 patients with COVID-19 and cancer showed increased mortality and morbidity [33]. To account for the safety challenges, providers accommodated short-term adjustments to cancer care delivery, such as temporarily discontinuing nonemergent cancer screenings, shifting the delivery to telehealth, and delaying surgeries and other in-office services to reduce the transmission risk, building hospital capacity in anticipation of increasing rates of infections, and comply with regulations and guidelines from organizations, societies, and governments [34].

3 Potential Role of Participatory Ergonomics in Supporting Safety Challenges in Cancer Care Settings

Participatory ergonomics is a proactive approach to addressing the complex safety and health challenges in cancer care for patients, healthcare workers, and the organizations in which they operate. The approach involves the collaborative design and adjustment of work tasks, environments, and systems by including those who directly interact with them. This method has been found to be particularly effective in mitigating risks and enhancing the overall quality of care and work life in oncology settings. By incorporating participatory ergonomics, organizations can proactively address safety and health concerns, improve the work environment, and provide better-quality care to patients. The challenges, as well as the potential role of participatory ergonomics in safety insurance, are summarized in Fig. 1.

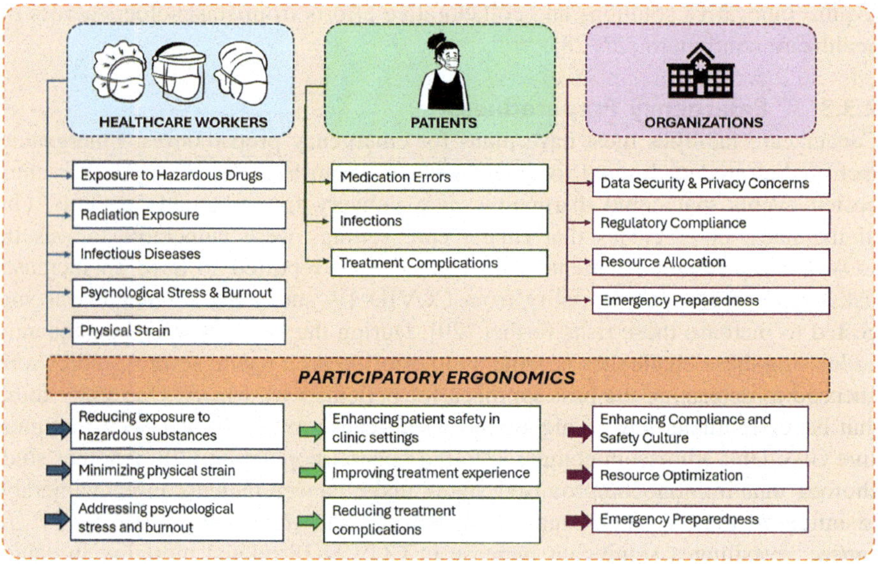

Fig. 1 PECS framework (Participatory Ergonomics for Cancer Safety)

3.1 For Healthcare Workers

Participatory ergonomics is a critical element in mitigating the risks associated with exposure to hazardous drugs and radiation. By engaging healthcare workers in the creation and execution of safety protocols, Participatory ergonomics promotes the development of more pragmatic and efficient solutions. This might involve improving the use of personal protective equipment (PPE), optimizing the layout of pharmacy mixing rooms, and establishing safer procedures for drug administration and disposal. Furthermore, Participatory ergonomics can be employed to redesign work tasks and physical workspaces to reduce the physical strain associated with tasks such as lifting and transferring patients. This might include ergonomic modifications to patient handling practices, the introduction of mechanical aids, and the creation of training sessions that address explicit risks and requirements. Additionally, participatory ergonomics facilitates the creation of initiatives such as peer support groups, stress management training, and work schedule adjustments, which contribute to addressing psychological stress and burnout among staff.

3.2 For Patients

The implementation of participatory ergonomics plays a crucial role in bolstering patient safety by fostering secure and comfortable treatment settings. Patient involvement is instrumental in the creation of spaces that cater to their physical and emotional requirements, mitigating potential hazards such as falls and infections. Moreover, the integration of patient feedback concerning their treatment encounters empowers healthcare establishments to revamp treatment procedures, making them less daunting and more accommodating. This not only elevates patient comfort but also augments adherence to treatment schedules and overall contentment.

3.3 For Organizations

Incorporating participatory ergonomics into organizational policies and procedures can have significant benefits, such as enhancing compliance and fostering a culture of safety. By involving staff in the process, safety becomes an integral part of the organizational culture. Participatory ergonomics can also help optimize resource allocation by engaging stakeholders in discussions about where to prioritize investments in safety and ergonomics. Furthermore, involving employees in the development and refinement of emergency preparedness plans can increase the likelihood of a coordinated and effective response during emergencies.

The successful implementation of participatory ergonomics in cancer care requires several crucial steps. It is essential to engage all stakeholder groups, including frontline workers, management, and patients, to ensure that the ergonomic process is comprehensive and practical. Continuous feedback and iterative improvements play an integral role in participatory ergonomics, leading to lasting and effective changes. Educating stakeholders about the principles of ergonomics and the benefits of a participatory approach is also crucial in ensuring their active and effective involvement in the ergonomic process. By adopting these strategies, cancer care facilities can create a safer, more efficient, and supportive environment for all involved.

4 Discussions

This study suggests a framework that summarizes the safety issues faced by the different stakeholders of cancer care. It also suggests participatory ergonomics approaches as a solution to these different issues. The safety challenges stated in the framework are related to the patients' experience, doctors' and staff's experience, and the organization itself. This approach makes our study inclusive of all the stakeholders, which strengthens the scope of the framework suggested. It also covers the role of participatory ergonomics in supporting the safety of all the stakeholders.

4.1 Theoretical Implications

This framework has several theoretical implications, such as the following.

4.1.1 Human Factors and Ergonomics Theory

Adaptive Systems

The PECS framework supports the theory that ergonomic interventions should be adaptable to specific contexts. This permits more flexibility and customization to the unique contexts, which ensures that the intervention is tailored to meet the specific needs of the end-users, such as the patients. When the end-users are actively involved in the design process, the framework facilitates the identification of any potential challenges, preferences, and opportunities for improvement, which allows for more effective and user-friendly solutions. This increases the likelihood of successful implementation and sustainable, ergonomic interventions since they are catered to the specific needs of the users and the complex environment. This allows for improved outcomes in cancer safety.

Socio-technical Systems

The PECS framework acknowledges that healthcare is inherently socio-technical. The complex interactions between healthcare providers, patients, organizations, and technology play a major role in the success of healthcare delivery. PECS takes a holistic approach that ensures a comprehensive view of both the social and technical aspects of healthcare, thus improving the safety and ergonomics of cancer care settings. For example, Munoz and colleagues [35] involved ergonomists in designing a software workflow tool for radiotherapy that supports communication between professionals while producing a treatment plan to enhance patient safety. This recognizes that human interactions with technology and processes are key determinants of system effectiveness.

4.2 Healthcare Quality and Safety

4.2.1 Systems Approach to Quality of Care

PECS demonstrates a practical and complete use of the systems approach to healthcare quality. This approach sees patient safety and quality of care as the result of complex interactions within healthcare systems. It also recognizes that increasing patient safety and quality necessitates a comprehensive understanding of how various components of the healthcare system interact with one another and influence results. For example, it can be used to assess the ergonomic design of a chemotherapy administration process by taking into account a variety of criteria, such as equipment usability, workflow efficiency, and staff communication patterns. This evaluation allows us to identify areas for improvement. PECS, when combined with stakeholder participation, can be utilized to construct safe and efficient processes that contribute to improved quality of patient care.

4.2.2 High-Reliability Organization (HRO)

HROs are organizations that operate in high-risk and complex environments yet prioritize high levels of safety and reliability. The PECS framework aligns with this by promoting the involvement of stakeholders in designing and implementing ergonomic interventions. Stakeholders such as healthcare professionals, patients, and administrators can then be actively involved in maintaining a safety culture as a collaborative process with shared responsibility. PECS also recognizes that health safety includes multiple contributing factors, such as technology, process, and organizational culture. HROs share this view by highlighting the interactions within complex systems in order to predict any plausible failures.

4.3 Organizational Behavior

4.3.1 Engagement and Culture

According to the PECS framework, participative techniques have the potential to boost employee engagement and happiness, which in turn can foster a positive organizational culture that prioritizes safety and continuous improvement. Participatory approaches guarantee that the diverse viewpoints, expertise, and concerns of the stakeholders are taken into account, resulting in more sustainable and successful solutions. PECS encourages accountability, teamwork, and a sense of ownership by including the stakeholders. Promoting open communication, trust, and shared accountability for the safety of all people working in the organization helps to foster a positive safety culture. In this culture, learning is respected, and errors are freely discussed, resulting in continuous progress by placing safety as the top priority.

4.3.2 Change Management

The PECS framework offers a model for implementing change in healthcare organizations, highlighting stakeholder involvement as a critical factor for successful change adoption. The PECS framework does this through engaging the stakeholders, assessing needs and identifying the problem, designing and planning the intervention, communicating and training, and finally, evaluating and providing feedback. Engaging the stakeholders permits the identification of the appropriate needs of the users and identifying any relatable problems those in the organization are actively facing. Once these are determined, an appropriate intervention can be designed and implemented to reduce resource waste and promote sustainability. To further encourage its permanence, evaluations, and adjustments are made to the intervention.

4.4 Management Science

4.4.1 Resource Optimization

The framework implies that resource optimization in healthcare settings should be a dynamic and participatory process, leading to more efficient and effective resource use. PECS leads to reduced resource wastage by directly targeting the concerns and the gaps that the users are actively facing with methods in which stakeholders are enthusiastic to take part. By addressing the concerns of healthcare professionals, patients, and administrators, the resources can be better allocated in the appropriate areas to achieve desired outcomes, leading to enhanced patient safety. Active participation of stakeholders also leads to the sustainability of the intervention, which also promotes resource usage on effective methods.

4.4.2 Decision-Making

PECS supports theories of decentralized decision-making, suggesting that involving frontline workers in decision processes can lead to better outcomes. Encouraging frontline workers in the decision-making process can promote a safety culture and habits for the same workers to which the methods will be applied. Furthermore, it allows for addressing any concerns they may have, which they see firsthand in the organization daily. PECS encourages the involvement of the patients and administrators in this process as well to ensure that the intervention achieves the desired outcomes for the end-users.

4.5 Policy Implications

4.5.1 Policy Formulation

The framework theoretically supports the idea that safety and ergonomics rules should be developed collaboratively rather than imposed from above. The framework can be used to develop guiding principles or guidelines for ergonomic design and healthcare safety. It can also be utilized to lobby for laws that encourage good ergonomic treatments and safety precautions. PECS assesses and monitors efforts to establish policy success and identify areas for improvement, which leads to evidence-based adjustments. The framework emphasizes stakeholder involvement in policy development, which allows policies to be informed by real-life experiences, viewpoints, and needs, boosting their relevance, acceptability, and efficacy.

4.5.2 Regulatory Compliance

PECS aligns with the theory that compliance is not just a matter of meeting regulations but of integrating regulatory requirements into the fabric of organizational practice through stakeholder engagement. The framework provides a structured participatory approach to ergonomic interventions and safety initiatives. Engaging stakeholders and end-users of initiatives increases the likelihood of compliance since they have been involved in the design and implementation of the intervention that meets their specific needs and concerns. PECS also promotes a safety culture, thus encouraging regulatory compliance among organization members. PECS also facilitates the development of an action plan for implementing ergonomic interventions and safety initiatives that can be in line with regulatory requirements, thus encouraging regulatory compliance.

By integrating these theoretical implications, the PECS framework can guide future research in these areas and inform the development of models and hypotheses for empirical testing.

4.6 Practical Implications

The practical implications of the PECS framework are the following.

4.6.1 For Healthcare Workers

Practical Training

The framework can be used for implementing specialized training programs on handling hazardous drugs and dealing with radiation that are tailored to the feedback from staff. Practical training sessions on the proper usage of ergonomic equipment and tools can be incorporated to encourage a culture of safety and compliance. PECS encourages stakeholders' involvement in developing real-life scenarios to be used in simulation exercises to practice ergonomic techniques in a controlled environment. These can include medication administration, surgical procedures, and patient handling. This allows providers to refine their skills in realistic situations and encourages hands-on learning experiences, preparing them for the demands of their role.

Ergonomic Workspace

PECS allows the improvement of ergonomic workspaces by optimizing the layout, equipment, and tools to minimize physical strain and reduce musculoskeletal injuries, leading to enhanced comfort and productivity for healthcare workers. A needs assessment would also be done to identify any challenges that healthcare professionals encounter that are physically demanding or placing their safety at risk. PECS ensures that the intervention is tailored to the end-user's needs by involving them in the process and catering to their preferences. This also means providing training and education to empower healthcare workers with the appropriate knowledge and skills to identify ergonomic risks, use ergonomic equipment and tools properly, and adopt ergonomic work practices.

Mental Health Programs

Understanding the individual pressures of oncology workers allows you to use the framework to create mental health support structures and stress management programs. PECS' collaborative approach to include healthcare practitioners in the development of these programs helps generate feelings of teamwork, communication, and social support among peers, thereby increasing resilience and promoting mental health well-being. PECS can help to reduce stigma, raise awareness, and promote self-care among healthcare workers by encouraging interaction and transparency. The promotion of a safety culture can extend to mental health programs, ensuring that employees feel supported, respected, and empowered to seek help when necessary.

4.6.2 For Patients

Safety-First Approach

PECS encourages designing clinic settings with patient safety as a priority, potentially reducing falls, infections, and other complications. This promotes cultural safety and patient-centered care within healthcare organizations. Furthermore, incorporating ergonomic interventions to enhance patient safety during a variety of healthcare activities allows healthcare providers to deliver safer and more efficient care to patients. PECS includes patient engagement, which can provide a sense of empowerment in their healthcare provision and a sense of their needs and concerns being met. This sense of control over one's health encourages compliance with safety regulations and optimizing safety culture amongst patients.

Patient-Centered Care

PECS invites patients to provide feedback about their experiences, preferences, and suggestions for improvement. This allows us to customize therapeutic experiences depending on patient feedback, resulting in higher satisfaction and outcomes. The input gathered can also be utilized to analyze their needs and indicate any areas for change that are of genuine concern to the patients. This puts patients at the center of the healthcare intervention, ensuring their needs are satisfied. By engaging patients, we encourage inclusivity and accessibility to all patients, allowing us to make healthcare decisions that are relevant to different patients by providing alternate options and adjustments to meet their requirements. Healthcare organizations will provide services that are responsive, respectful, and compassionate to patients, hence improving patient outcomes.

Reducing Complications

Patients' experiences can help to inform methods for monitoring and managing potential treatment problems. PECS facilitates open communication and collaboration to obtain varied viewpoints and insights into the underlying causes of difficulties. Conducting a risk assessment of probable consequences can help to identify relevant ergonomic solutions to prevent or mitigate them. These can include redesigning workflows, optimizing equipment and technology, strengthening communication procedures, and increasing patient education and empowerment.

4.6.3 For Organizations

Policy Development

It is vital to engage stakeholders from the various levels of the organization, such as healthcare providers, administrators, patients, caregivers, and other regulatory bodies, in developing policies that meet the organization's ergonomic needs, challenges, and priorities. Through this engagement and collaboration, any gaps and complexities in the system can be identified, which can aid in developing the appropriate policies and protocols that address these needs while being feasible for the members. The PECS framework highlights this teamwork effort and provides a systematic approach to integrate ergonomic principles while improving adherence and fostering a proactive safety culture. These new policies on improving patient safety and reducing ergonomic risks will need to be monitored and evaluated to ensure that the desired outcomes are being achieved.

Resource Management

PECS begins with a comprehensive needs assessment by consulting staff and patients to identify the specific resources required to deliver high-quality cancer care. Once these needs have been determined, then PECS helps healthcare organizations allocate resources strategically to address these unique challenges and demands of cancer care. This could look like prioritizing resources for cancer screening programs, diagnostic imaging equipment, oncology treatment centers, palliative care services, and so on. PECS supports effective staffing and workforce training to ensure that the necessary personnel are present with the right skills and training to deliver cancer care. This may involve investing in training programs for oncologists, nurses, radiologists, and support staff to enhance expertise in cancer diagnosis, treatment, and supportive care.

Robust Emergency Plans

PECS includes stakeholders in the development and testing of preparedness plans to guarantee their practicality and readiness. Organizations can ensure that emergency plans are comprehensive, realistic, and responsive to the demands of all stakeholders by bringing together different viewpoints and experiences. A detailed risk assessment could be conducted to detect potential risks and vulnerabilities, particularly among sensitive populations like cancer patients. This would necessitate a thorough examination of various emergencies that could disrupt cancer treatment delivery, such as the COVID-19 pandemic, natural disasters, or security concerns. Understanding these risks allows organizations to establish targeted methods for mitigating them and improving preparation. PECS emphasizes the value of effective communication and information sharing. Thus, in emergency preparedness, this would entail creating strong communication networks and leveraging technology to transmit important information to providers. This includes the implementation of emergency alerting systems, telemedicine platforms, and electronic health record systems.

4.7 Future Directions

4.7.1 Empirical Validation and Longitudinal Research

Conducting empirical validation studies is critical for determining the success of the PECS framework in improving safety in cancer care settings. Furthermore, conducting longitudinal research can provide insights into the long-term viability and impact of participatory ergonomic solutions on both healthcare professionals' well-being and patient safety. Researchers can better understand the effectiveness and long-term viability of ergonomic interventions in enhancing safety and quality of care by gathering empirical evidence and tracking outcomes over time.

4.7.2 Cross-Cultural Studies and Technology Integration

Understanding the PECS framework's global relevance requires investigating its cross-cultural applicability and modification in a variety of healthcare scenarios. Concurrently, research into how technology, such as electronic health records and patient monitoring systems, might be integrated into the PECS framework is critical. Healthcare organizations can improve safety, efficiency, and communication by leveraging technology within participatory ergonomics, particularly in complex and dynamic healthcare contexts.

4.7.3 Education and Interdisciplinary Collaboration

Creating and assessing focused educational programs will be critical for providing stakeholders with the requisite knowledge and skills in participatory ergonomics. Furthermore, encouraging multidisciplinary research collaborations can bring together insights from healthcare, ergonomics, organizational behaviour, and safety engineering. This partnership may result in the development of comprehensive approaches to addressing ergonomic difficulties and promoting a safety culture within healthcare organizations.

4.7.4 Economic Analysis and Policy Impact Studies

Cost–benefit studies will provide useful information on the economic implications of using participatory ergonomics in cancer care. Simultaneously, evaluating the impact of participatory ergonomic interventions on policy formulation and regulatory compliance within healthcare organizations is critical. By proving the effectiveness and utility of ergonomic techniques, researchers can influence policy decisions and advocate the incorporation of participatory ergonomics into healthcare rules and standards.

4.7.5 Scalability Assessment and Technology-Assisted PE

Evaluating the scalability of participatory ergonomic treatments in larger or more complicated healthcare settings is critical for widespread adoption. Furthermore, investigating the impact of digital tools and virtual platforms in promoting participatory ergonomic processes, particularly in remote or resource-constrained contexts, is critical. Leveraging technology can improve the accessibility, speed, and effectiveness of ergonomic treatments, allowing for more adoption and implementation of the PECS framework.

4.8 Strengths and Limitations

The safety of cancer care environments is crucial for ensuring optimal patient outcomes and healthcare worker well-being. In this section, we assess the strengths and limitations of the Participatory Ergonomics for Cancer Safety (PECS) framework, a systematic approach aimed at enhancing safety in cancer care settings.

4.8.1 Strengths

The PECS framework offers several notable strengths that contribute to its effectiveness in improving safety in cancer care environments.

Stakeholder Engagement

PECS prioritizes the active involvement of stakeholders, including healthcare providers, administrators, patients, and community partners. This participatory approach ensures that interventions are tailored to meet the specific needs and preferences of those directly affected by cancer care.

Holistic Approach

PECS takes a comprehensive approach to safety, addressing physical, psychosocial, and organizational factors. By considering multiple dimensions of safety, PECS promotes sustainable improvements in cancer care environments.

Evidence-Based Practices
Grounded in evidence-based practices and principles of ergonomics, PECS draws on established research findings and best practices to inform safety interventions. This ensures that interventions recommended by PECS are grounded in scientific evidence and have a strong theoretical foundation.

Adaptability
PECS is adaptable to diverse healthcare settings and contexts, allowing for flexibility in implementation based on the unique needs and resources of individual organizations. This adaptability makes PECS suitable for a wide range of cancer care settings, from small community clinics to large academic medical centers.

Continuous Improvement
PECS fosters a culture of continuous improvement by encouraging regular evaluation and refinement of safety initiatives. By fostering a cycle of assessment, feedback, and adjustment, PECS supports ongoing learning and optimization of safety practices in cancer care.

4.8.2 Limitations

While the PECS framework offers valuable insights and guidance, it also has several limitations that warrant consideration.

Resource Intensive
Implementing PECS may require significant resources, including time, funding, and expertise. Stakeholder engagement, training programs, and infrastructure improvements can be resource-intensive, particularly for organizations with limited resources or competing priorities.

Complexity
The multidimensional nature of PECS can make it complex to implement and sustain over time. Coordinating efforts across multiple stakeholders and addressing diverse aspects of safety requires careful planning and coordination, which may present challenges for some organizations.

Cultural and Organizational Barriers
Cultural and organizational barriers may hinder the effective implementation of PECS in some healthcare settings. Resistance to change, lack of buy-in from key stakeholders, and existing organizational structures or practices can impede efforts to adopt participatory ergonomics principles.

Long-Term Sustainability
Ensuring the long-term sustainability of PECS interventions may pose challenges for healthcare organizations. Maintaining momentum, sustaining stakeholder engagement, and integrating safety practices into routine workflows require ongoing commitment and support from organizational leadership.

Generalizability

While PECS has been developed and tested in specific healthcare settings, its generalizability to other contexts remains to be fully established. Variations in organizational culture, resources, and patient populations may influence the effectiveness and feasibility of PECS implementation in different settings.

5 Conclusions

In conclusion, the PECS framework offers valuable insights and guidance for improving safety in cancer care environments. PECS values integrating participatory ergonomic interventions while engaging stakeholders from various levels like healthcare professionals, patients, and organizations. The use of this collaborative approach promotes safety culture, sustainability, and resource management, increasing the likelihood of achieving desired outcomes. However, healthcare organizations need to consider both the strengths and limitations of PECS when planning and implementing safety initiatives. By addressing these factors thoughtfully, organizations can maximize the potential of PECS to enhance the safety and quality of care for cancer patients and healthcare workers alike.

Together, we can do better.

—Safa Elkefi

References

1. Braithwaite J et al (2018) The goldilocks effect: the rhythms and pace of hospital life. BMC Health Serv Res 18:1–5
2. Barrett AK (2014) Breaking boundaries: temporality and work–life practices in hospital organizations. West J Commun 78(4):441–461
3. Wagner A, Schöne L, Rieger MA (2020) Determinants of occupational safety culture in hospitals and other workplaces—results from an integrative literature review. Int J Environ Res Public Health 17(18):6588
4. Health and Safety Commission (1993) ACSNI human factors study group third report: organising for safety. HMSO, London
5. Hessels AJ, Wurmser T (2020) Relationship among safety culture, nursing care, and standard precautions adherence. Am J Infect Control 48(3):340–341
6. McHugh MD et al (2011) Nurses' widespread job dissatisfaction, burnout, and frustration with health benefits signal problems for patient care. Health Aff 30(2):202–210
7. Hannisdal E et al (2013) A risk analysis of cancer care in Norway: the top 16 patient safety hazards. Jt Comm J Qual Patient Saf 39(11):511-AP1
8. Noro K, Imada AS (1991) Participatory ergonomics. Taylor & Francis
9. Rost KA, Alvero AM (2020) Participatory approaches to workplace safety management: bridging the gap between behavioral safety and participatory ergonomics. Int J Occup Saf Ergon 26(1):194–203

10. Dagliana G et al (2021) From theory to real-world integration: implementation science and beyond. In: Textbook of patient safety and clinical risk management. Springer, Cham, pp 143–157
11. Carayon P et al (2021) Human factors and ergonomics in health care and patient safety from the perspective of medical residents. In: Donaldson L et al (eds) Textbook of patient safety and clinical risk management. Springer, Cham, pp 81–89
12. Friese CR et al (2020) Oncology nurses' exposure to hazardous drugs in ambulatory settings: case report analysis from a prospective, multi-site study. Clin J Oncol Nurs 24(3):249
13. Graeve CU et al (2017) Occupational exposure to antineoplastic agents: an analysis of health care workers and their environments. Workplace Health Saf 65(1):9–20
14. Elshamy K et al (2010) Health hazards among oncology nurses exposed to chemotherapy drugs. Afr J Haematol Oncol 1(3)
15. Guveli H et al (2015) Oncology staff: burnout, job satisfaction and coping with stress. Psychooncology 24(8):926–931
16. Sherman AC et al (2006) Caregiver stress and burnout in an oncology unit. Pall Supp Care 4(1):65–80
17. Weingart SN et al (2018) Chemotherapy medication errors. Lancet Oncol 19(4):e191–e199
18. Walsh KE et al (2009) Medication errors among adults and children with cancer in the outpatient setting. J Clin Oncol 27(6):891–896
19. Hartigan K (2003) Patient education: the cornerstone of successful oral chemotherapy treatment. Clin J Oncol Nurs 7
20. Seo SK, Liu C, Dadwal SS (2021) Infectious disease complications in patients with cancer. Crit Care Clin 37(1):69–84
21. Delgado A, Guddati AK (2021) Infections in hospitalized cancer patients. World J Oncol 12(6):195
22. Norton PG, Baker GR (2007) Patient safety in cancer care: a time for action. Oxford University Press, pp 579–580
23. Lipitz-Snyderman A et al (2017) Preventable and mitigable adverse events in cancer care: measuring risk and harm across the continuum. Cancer 123(23):4728–4736
24. Centers for Disease Control and Prevention (2023) Side effects of cancer treatment. Available from: https://www.cdc.gov/cancer/survivors/patients/side-effects-of-treatment.htm
25. Martin HM, Navne LE, Lipczak H (2013) Involvement of patients with cancer in patient safety: a qualitative study of current practices, potentials and barriers. BMJ Qual Saf 22(10):836–842
26. Tillbrook D et al (2022) What do patients and their carers do to support the safety of cancer treatment and care? A scoping review. J Patient Saf 18(8):779–787
27. DeBoer RJ et al (2020) Applying lessons learned from low-resource settings to prioritize cancer care in a pandemic. JAMA Oncol 6(9):1429–1433
28. Lindgren P, Jönsson B, Wilking N (2017) Assessment of value for resource allocation in cancer care. J Cancer Policy 11:12–18
29. Lee LY et al (2020) COVID-19 mortality in patients with cancer on chemotherapy or other anticancer treatments: a prospective cohort study. Lancet 395(10241):1919–1926
30. Giannakoulis VG, Papoutsi E, Siempos II (2020) Effect of cancer on clinical outcomes of patients with COVID-19: a meta-analysis of patient data. JCO Glob Oncol 6:799–808
31. Dignani MC et al (2014) Pandemic 2009 Influenza A (H1N1) virus infection in cancer and hematopoietic stem cell transplant recipients; a multicenter observational study. F1000Research 3
32. Mehta V et al (2020) Case fatality rate of cancer patients with COVID-19 in a New York hospital system. Cancer Discov 10(7):935–941
33. Kuderer NM et al (2020) Clinical impact of COVID-19 on patients with cancer (CCC19): a cohort study. Lancet 395(10241):1907–1918
34. Patt D et al (2020) Impact of COVID-19 on cancer care: how the pandemic is delaying cancer diagnosis and treatment for American seniors. JCO Clin Cancer Inform 4:1059–1071

35. Munoz MI, Bouldi N, Barcellini F, Nascimento A (2012) Designing the safety of healthcare. Participation of ergonomics to the design of cooperative systems in radiotherapy. Work 41(Supplement 1):790–796

Safa Elkefi obtained a Ph.D. in Engineering Management with research in Human factors from Stevens Institute of Technology in 2023 and a master's degree from the National Engineering School of Tunisia in 2019. He is now a project director at Columbia University and an Adjunct Professor at Stevens.

Roa Sabra has a Master of Health Sciences (Audiology) degree and is currently a Ph.D. candidate in the Population Health program at the University of Ottawa. Her research focus is on sexual and reproductive health in marginalized communities.

Critical Analysis of the Evolution of Methods for Calculating Costs of Patient-Centered Health Services

18

Abdelaziz Zerka and Fouad Jawab

Abstract

In the healthcare sector, obtaining accurate information on costs for decision-making and reimbursement rates is a fundamental challenge for healthcare facility decision-makers and researchers in hospital cost accounting. This chapter aims to study the mechanisms and evolution of cost calculation for healthcare services in hospital logistics practice. The calculation of healthcare service costs is becoming increasingly important within hospital facilities. This importance stems from the crucial role that cost calculation plays in resource allocation, hospital financing, and accurate pricing of care delivery. In this perspective, we have approached models for calculating healthcare service costs from different dimensions: healthcare services provided and activities that result in hospitalization. We searched for scientific literature at the international level, particularly from the Scopus database, which was explored for its relevance to healthcare. The results show that studies that have sought to estimate and model the cost of healthcare services are numerous, and the methodologies used are varied. Although authors who have worked on questions related to this modeling in research areas such as surgery, radiology, and hospital transport are numerous, they do not agree on a precise cost calculation method, to the extent that one could say there are as many researchers as there are approaches. However, the current state of research highlights the effectiveness of TD-ABC in evaluating healthcare service costs.

A. Zerka (✉)
Faculty of Sciences Dhar El Mahraz, Industrial Technologies and Services Laboratory, Sidi Mohamed Ben Abdelah University, Fez, Morocco
e-mail: abdelaziz.zerka@usmba.ac.ma

F. Jawab
High School of Technology, Industrial Technologies and Services Laboratory, Sidi Mohamed Ben Abdellah University, Fez, Morocco
e-mail: fouad.jawab@usmba.ac.ma

F. Jawab (ed.), *Hospital Supply Chain*, Integrated Science 27,
https://doi.org/10.1007/978-3-031-70292-1_18

Keywords

Hospital • Logistics • Patient • Radiology • Transport TDABC

Abbreviations

CCR	Cost/charge ratio
RVU	Relative Value Unit
ABC	Activity-Based Costing
TD-ABC	Time-Driven Activity-Based Costing

1 Introduction

Healthcare represents a crucial issue for the well-being of a country at all levels and is considered one of the most essential sectors. This field is rapidly evolving, transitioning from a traditional approach to modern and therapeutic treatments. This evolution comes with challenges such as population growth, high administrative costs, the complexity of care, and more advanced treatments, leading to rising healthcare costs. These increasing costs are a major concern for patients, as well as decision-makers, funders, and other stakeholders in the healthcare sector. Faced with these challenges, hospital logistics proves to be an essential management tool, not only in other industries but also in the healthcare supply chain. The application of modern logistics practices in the healthcare sector can help reduce delays, costs, and improve the quality of patient care services. Hospital logistics can have a direct impact on cost control and the quality of care. Therefore, implementing efficient hospital logistics is necessary to improve the overall performance of hospitals.

Certainly, Healthcare service costs provide hospital and healthcare system decision-makers with valuable information on various decision-making issues, such as their institutions' capacity to meet patient needs, assessing the resources required to provide a specific service, and the effectiveness of the financing system implemented by healthcare facilities.

Understanding the actual costs of healthcare services will help healthcare providers make more informed decisions on how to efficiently utilize resources [1, 2], as well as determine which tasks in the care journey do not add value for patients. However, establishing actual costs is a challenge in hospital logistics practice. Without a grasp of the actual costs of services, managers will be unable to manage patient expectations and also determine which pathways could enhance value for their patients; thus, an accurate cost calculation system is also necessary. Generally, as Pierre Mévellec suggests, cost calculation allows us to understand how consumption occurs. Furthermore, it provides information for better resource utilization [3] and accurately captures the cost (of a product, of care provision, etc.) for relevant decision-making. However, evaluating the cost of the latter is not an easy task. However, cost calculation in the healthcare field is limited by the problem of allocating indirect costs and becomes challenging given the complexity of healthcare activities themselves, as confirmed by Kaplan and Porter [4]. Added to this complexity is the fragmentation of medical care for patients with different risk factors and requiring various medical treatments, as well as the development of technology in the healthcare sector, etc. [1, 2]. For example, a patient's hospitalization journey may involve multiple services (emergency, diagnosis, treatment, radiology), none of which have a standard care pathway for patients suffering from the same disease case. Today, the challenge for hospitals worldwide is to adapt to patient expectations, available financial resources, demographic constraints, patient case diversification, and technological advancements in this field, etc. [5]. To achieve this, they rely on cost calculation practices and optimize the performance of hospital logistics.

Today, the cost of patient care continues to increase due to the development of new technologies and treatment protocols. It is therefore important to improve the financial performance of hospitals and to define new methods of cost calculation that are modern and adaptable to the complex environment of healthcare services. These cost calculation methods enable a better understanding of the cost composition of various services and treatments provided to patients.

While the primary focus in the evolution of logistics cost calculation systems has been on setting prices for healthcare facility tariff systems, the increase in healthcare expenditures has shifted the focus to cost management. Indeed, cost information supports decisions regarding resource allocation and the healthcare services provided to patients. In fact, in the current international pricing environments, there are indications that some hospitals are now implementing more advanced cost calculation systems in hospital practice [1].

In a context where healthcare organizations lack hospital cost accounting, accurately assessing the total cost of patient care is challenging. However, the field of hospital logistics employs cost calculation methods to estimate healthcare service tariffs by comparing outcomes and costs [6]. Although the importance of accurately pricing healthcare service costs and its implementation pose a challenge in hospital practice, given the absence of precise healthcare service tariffs, researchers have experimented with cost calculation methods in hospital logistics capable of determining healthcare service costs and the resulting services [7].

It's worth noting that there are several research works in the scientific literature focusing on modeling the costs of logistics activities within hospitals, whether they are public or private (which is the aim of our work). After systematic filtering in the mentioned database (Scopus), we found a lack of comprehensive view regarding tools for calculating healthcare service costs for patients. In this study, we aim to fill this gap by delving into the subject of calculating healthcare service costs for patients and the resulting support activities.

Through a literature review, we analyze the mechanisms and evolution of cost calculation tools in the field of hospital logistics. The problematic questions guiding this research can be formulated as follows:

Are there cost calculation methods for patient healthcare services modeled and calculated using hospital cost accounting methods? If so, what conclusions can be drawn from them?

What are the mechanisms driving the evolution of patient healthcare service cost calculation methods?

What is the most recognized method currently in the healthcare field?

In this work, we will first examine the theoretical framework of the study; then, we will outline the methodology employed. Next, we will study the evolution and mechanisms of cost calculation in the healthcare field. We will then present how the current cost establishment is useful compared to traditional cost calculation systems.

2 General Context

2.1 The Issue of Cost Calculation in Logistics Activities

The hospital provides medical care and services in the interest of the patient, who, like any other client, should be able to assess the quality of the care received and express satisfaction, or choose to change physicians or facilities if possible. Like any service-oriented business, the hospital is committed to improving the quality of services provided to patients. Healthcare facilities must identify the requirements and needs of the population in terms of quality, as a lack of quality can result in immeasurable costs. Indeed, hospital logistics is integrated into an approach to overall performance improvement, where activities are organized and structured to satisfy patients in terms of quality, quantity, timeliness, safety, and at the lowest cost possible.

The function of hospital logistics ensures the management and synchronization of physical and informational flows for healthcare services, using resources optimally to provide patient care at a lower cost. It represents a comprehensive and integrated approach across various hospital functions, with the ultimate goal of patient satisfaction. The patient is considered the central pillar around which all hospital activities revolve.

Many countries allocate a significant portion of their available resources to healthcare financing. This is one of the reasons why studying the healthcare sector to improve its efficiency is important. However, healthcare systems are among the most complex systems in contemporary society. In particular, hospitals are considered extremely complex organizations [1]. Care chains are complex and involve many interdependent parts that contribute to solving health problems, such as those encountered by different categories of patients. When multiple care units (care services and support services) are involved in solving a health problem, there is a risk of sub-optimization, especially when these units are constrained to optimize their own outcomes.

The fundamental function of a hospital, one of the most important systems in every country, is to provide healthcare to patients. It is worth noting that hospitals are distinguished from other service businesses by their degree of complexity and the variety of activities they perform [8]. Considering all available resources and aiming for a more efficient accomplishment of the fundamental function, each hospital requires logistics. Numerous types of flows are present in a hospital every day. The complexity of activities, patient flows, and participants in hospital logistics necessitates thorough research to improve service and reduce costs [9, 10]. The literature contains various definitions and explanations of hospital logistics, whereby either the traditional definition of logistics is simply applied to hospital systems, or various supports of hospital logistics are essential for the proper functioning of a hospital [11].

Hospital logistics is focused on the efficiency of medical activity, so it is essential for hospitals to realize that logistics is part of the organizational process. For example, this includes managing healthcare services and support activities, managing the information system, standardizing databases, and calculating the costs of healthcare services to achieve optimal quality of care.

In the healthcare sector, logistical activities are aimed at creating value for patients, providers, and other stakeholders involved in this field. The ability of healthcare facilities to produce and deliver value depends on their ability to provide consumers (patients) with products and services where and when they want them, at competitive prices and the lowest total cost. Therefore, logistics cost is increasingly recognized as a tool for calculating actual costs, not only in the healthcare sector but also in other sectors, as logistics cost is key to logistics performance management. Recently, the healthcare industry has begun to invest in a more adopted cost management system. However, the function of logistics is to ensure better coordination between supply and demand at the lowest cost. In healthcare facilities, estimating logistics costs is paramount. On the other hand, the concept of cost reduction is complementary to that of the quality of healthcare services. In this perspective, logistics in hospital settings aims to provide the right product at the right time and place. It is part of a dynamic search for patient satisfaction in terms of quality, quantity, safety, and timeliness at the lowest cost. Today, the challenge for hospitals worldwide is to adapt to patient expectations, available financial resources, demographic constraints, patient case diversification, and technological advancements in this field, etc. To achieve this, they rely on cost control practices and optimize the performance of hospital logistics.

From the perspective of hospital logistics, a patient's treatment plan at the hospital may involve multiple hospital services (care and related services). Consequently, they incur various costs: ambulance, emergency, radiology treatment, medical expenses, care services, catering, accommodation, operating room, administrative services, etc. Estimating the costs of these services can be based on the costs of consumed supplies [1]. To manage these elements, they rely on cost calculation practices to optimize the performance of hospital logistics.

It is important to note that analyzing the costs of patient care services becomes complex due to the different types of care and the complexity of health situations [12]. Therefore, current mechanisms for evaluating costs in hospital logistics often focus on cost pricing for independent activities, such as separate tasks or activities [13]. It is therefore prudent to consider certain imperfections of a hospital cost verification system. One of the main difficulties is related to standardizing costs per care. Indeed, patients differ due to their sex, age, and reactions to medical procedures, resulting in different costs depending on the demand for services necessary for the patient's full health recovery. Therefore, researchers have explored and experimented with hospital logistics systems capable of determining healthcare service costs.

2.2 Healthcare Cost Calculation

In general, as Pierre Mévellec suggests, cost calculation allows us to understand how consumption occurs. Furthermore, it provides information for better resource utilization [3] and also enables the precise capture of costs for relevant decision-making. However, evaluating the cost of these decisions is not an easy task.

Costs consist of all expenses and fees (consumed resources) incurred by a healthcare organization during the provision of a healthcare service. The cost of a service or procedure does not exist. Instead, it is a calculation based on conventions and theory or methods [14]. The cost of treatment is a sum expressed in monetary units of all the repercussions that a given pathology can have on society [14].

In healthcare, a cost is characterized by its object (a patient admission, a day of care, a homogeneous group of patients suffering from the same diseases, a treatment stage, etc.). It is also characterized by its content (direct costs of the service, costs directly attributable to the patient, quasi-total costs, general administrative expenses, total costs, etc.). Two elements are determining in cost calculation: the perspective taken (that of the hospital, the state, health insurance, society, etc.) and the moment at which it is calculated [14].

In the healthcare field, cost objects have significant financial importance throughout the entire care pathway [15], as they form the basis for billing for healthcare services and tracking actions to be taken for patients. The lack of a clear definition of cost objects makes comparison between units/services difficult and sometimes even impossible. Hence the need to find a common definition of cost objects, i.e., a common language for recording, billing, pricing, and tracking healthcare treatments. For patient healthcare, cost objects are possible at different levels depending on the patient's health status. Table 1, which we have developed, provides several healthcare procedures related to patient healthcare services and services related to patient healthcare.

When using cost accounting in the healthcare field, determining the cost object is not an easy task, even though there is a standard vocabulary internationally, as it depends on several influential factors [15], such as the importance of viewing

Table 1 Examples of cost objects for patient care services

	Patient healthcare	
	During the transport	To the hospital
Patient healthcare services	• Resuscitation • Oxygenation • Urgent care	• Consultation • Surgery • Radiology
Patient healthcare related services	• Hospital transport service	• Catering • Accommodation • Cleaning • Administrative services • Operating room

Source Elaborated by the author

the care pathway (cancer disease, chronic disease, etc.) as a series of well-defined care activities and the availability of a reliable information system. In this regard, it is important to note the level of detail represented by the cost object, as the better these objects are mastered, the more cost elements can be directly attributed to them.

In healthcare, cost calculation allows for understanding the actual costs of a healthcare service or a specific support service (such as catering, accommodation, cleaning, etc.). It also helps managers make more effective decisions on how to allocate and utilize budgetary resources dedicated to healthcare, as well as determine services that do not add value to the patient's care pathway. However, cost calculation in the healthcare field is limited by the issue of allocating indirect costs and becomes challenging due to the complexity of healthcare activities themselves, as confirmed by Kaplan and Porter [4]. Adding to this complexity is the fragmentation of medical care for individuals with different risk factors and responses to medical treatments, as well as the development of technology in the healthcare sector, etc. [16]. For example, a patient's care pathway may involve various hospital services, none of which have the same treatment plan. Therefore, Kaplan et al. [17] specify that this difficulty can be overcome by providing information allowing for precise allocation of resources to patients using a cost calculation method that considers the complexity of healthcare activities in general.

It is important to emphasize that the concept of cost, as provided by hospital cost accounting, is present in all healthcare facilities, whether public or private. However, its relevance depends on the integrated calculation model, the provided pricing systems, and the levels of decision-making involved. Indeed, the same healthcare facility may need to estimate the cost of several different care activities (such as radiology, emergency care, intensive care, etc.), as well as the cost of support activities (such as intra and extra-hospital transport, administrative services, etc.). The diversity and multiplicity of cost objects will influence the construction of the information system, which forms the basis of decision-making.

Moreover, in the healthcare field, costs play a crucial role in decision-making. These decisions can be strategic, such as deciding whether to launch a new medical specialty, or operational, such as deciding whether to outsource a support activity. The importance of costs in the decision-making process raises questions about how they are calculated and their impact on the decisions made.

Ideally, in the healthcare field, these decisions should be made by comparing the potential social health benefits, the fees set for services rendered, and the actual costs of each healthcare intervention. Physicians, patients and their families, third-party payers, and other healthcare decision-makers all face the challenge of gathering the necessary information to make optimal healthcare decisions.

It is important to note that decision-makers in the healthcare field are often faced with complex questions. They must make decisions on the pricing of treatments and diagnostics, as well as the costs of the support activities that result from them, such as accommodation, catering, cleaning, etc. To address these questions, careful cost calculation is necessary to manage the trade-offs between the social benefits, drawbacks, and costs associated with health policies or interventions. This allows for determining the optimal choice in these delicate situations.

3 Research Method

The approach adopted to address the evolution and mechanisms of calculating healthcare service costs for patients relies on leveraging cost calculation models in the field of hospital logistics, spanning the patient care journey from transport to admission and discharge. This utilization of models is based on synthesizing scientific articles to identify cost calculation models applicable to healthcare services for patients. Specific keywords were developed to collect a maximum of scientific articles, particularly from the Scopus database, offering cost calculation models for patient healthcare services. This database was chosen for its relevance in the healthcare domain. The objective is to study the scientific evolution and mechanisms of calculation methods in the field of hospital logistics. The research strategy we adopted involves cross-referencing specific keywords related to our research objective: "cost calculation - healthcare," "cost calculation - patient," and "cost calculation - hospital logistics." These keywords were chosen because they encompass the possible services patients receive in their care journey. Our research strategy is detailed in Fig. 1.

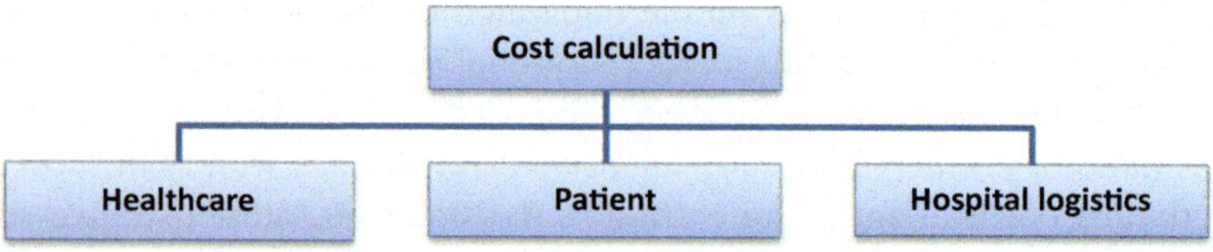

Fig. 1 Keywords used for document collection. *Source* Elaborated by the author

From a literature review, the main foundational documents on cost calculation in the field of hospital logistics were subjected to content analysis using a developed methodology. This analysis aimed to determine the cost calculation methods used in hospital logistics. For example, this led us to consider both patient care treatment services and the support activities derived from hospitals, as well as more operational processes of analytical accounting such as cost calculation tools.

As a methodological limitation, we did not scientifically diagnose the content of the articles, nor did we account for the number of articles corresponding to our research objective. If the researcher is satisfied with a cost calculation method, other research documents corresponding to the same method are excluded because our goal was to search for cost calculation methods in the healthcare domain (healthcare services and support services), and not the results of cost modeling. Therefore, there is a possibility of extracting research documents presenting inaccurate results or proposing multiple cost calculation models in the field of hospital logistics.

4 Evolution of Cost Calculation Methods in Healthcare Services

The scientific literature contains several cost modeling tools in the healthcare domain. After examining the database (Scopus) on this subject, four main cost calculation systems have been scientifically studied and utilized in the field of hospital logistics. Figure 2 summarizes the evolution of these cost calculation methods (cost/charge ratio: CCR, Relative Value Unit: RVU, Activity-Based Costing: ABC, and Time-Driven Activity-Based Costing: TD-ABC).

4.1 Method: Relative Value Unit (RVU)

Cost calculation methods rely on Relative Value Units (RVUs) [18], which attempt to assess the complexity and time required for hospital treatment or performing a care activity. However, it is common for costs not to be determined taking into account all the resources used for treatment [4]. Many healthcare providers employ the Relative Value Unit (RVU) method to allocate costs of clinical services to treatments and care procedures, leading to significant distortions in cost estimation. Since RVUs only consider reimbursed procedures and treatments, and not those

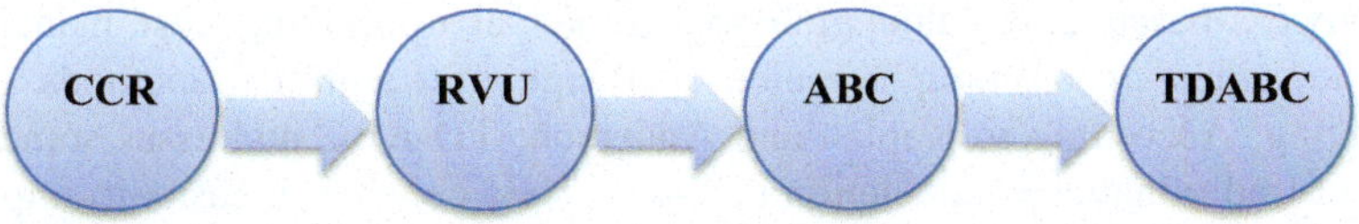

Fig. 2 The evolution of costing methods for healthcare services. *Source* Elaborated by the author

that are not reimbursed, they do not account for differences in staff compensation and thus conflate the issue of procedures with the resources needed to perform them.

4.2 Method: Cost/Charge Ratio (CCR)

In the scientific literature, the Cost-to-Charge Ratio (CCR) method is widely used in many developed countries, probably due to its familiarity and simplicity of use. In the 1960s, the CCR was developed as a "top-down" approach to costs [19]. This system is based on three types of costs: expenses related to medical practice, physician labor, and malpractice insurance. A "Relative Value Unit" (RVU) is used to assess each category of costs [20]. Physician labor is evaluated based on the time, effort, and level of skill required. Medical expenses include costs (direct and indirect) related to a provider's practice. However, direct costs correspond to expenses directly related to the provision of healthcare services, such as supplies, direct provider labor, materials, etc. Thus, indirect costs refer to overhead expenses that contribute to maintaining healthcare activity, such as rent and office expenses. Physicians and hospitals are not reimbursed based on the use of a patient's resources.

This cost calculation system presents significant challenges. Firstly, the cost of care activities is determined based on the amount of reimbursement rather than the actual resources devoted to healthcare services [21]. Secondly, costs are assessed based on information gathered about services rather than the cost of care related to a specific patient [22]. Although this approach is simple, it generates inaccurate cost information, limiting healthcare professionals' ability to assess strategic cost savings and improvements in care processes. While healthcare is reimbursed using value-based payment models, current practices of calculating costs of healthcare services must consider other financial models in hospital logistics such as (ABC) and (TD-ABC).

4.3 Method: ABC and TD-ABC

In today's competitive healthcare environment, there has been a significant shift. Competition is fierce and demands up-to-date and more concrete information on costs. Time-Driven Activity-Based Costing (TD-ABC), which has seen some success in the industry and service sectors [23], was established by Anderson and Kaplan in 2004 as an evolution of Activity-Based Costing (ABC) [17]. TD-ABC is a process-based cost calculation tool aimed at optimizing cost management efficiency, thus overcoming a major challenge of traditional methods of cost accounting. According to Kaplan and Anderson, TD-ABC addresses some drawbacks of traditional cost calculation methods. They consider it easier to implement and more flexible in adapting to internal and external changes within the organization [17]. Additionally, it offers various possibilities to design cost models tailored to organizations where activities are complex, such as healthcare facilities [24]. "Indeed, it is a method of cost calculation, but since costs are calculated based on time, this naturally leads to concrete actions to reduce costs [17]," hence its designation as "time-driven" [17, 25]. Despite previous attempts to develop process-oriented cost calculation methods in healthcare, in the 1980s, Robin Cooper and Robert Kaplan (1991) developed the ABC method, which is a variant of traditional methods, particularly concerning the information it provides.

Traditional cost calculation systems indeed have the ability to accurately measure operational and support services but do not precisely measure costs at the patient level [4]. As a result, there was a trend towards adopting activity-based costing (ABC) by healthcare organizations, which became well-established in the mid-1990s, especially in developed countries [26]. Competition in healthcare performance became a driving force for implementing the ABC method in healthcare. However, ABC has shown its limitations [7, 17]. We observe this trend in service activities, particularly in hospitals, where the application of ABC has been flourishing since the early 1990s [26]. Despite the initial advantages and the problems that the ABC model theoretically solved compared to traditional methodologies, issues [7, 17] have been detected when applying this model in healthcare organizations:

- It is a lengthy process as the interviews and surveys conducted with the responsible individuals for each activity are extensive and challenging to comprehend.
- Non-productive time is not accounted for during the surveys.
- This method is considered highly imprecise due to the complexity of calculations. To create an adequate ABC model, numerous activities had to be included, making the model very complex and also increasing uncertainty because estimating time was much higher due to the large number of activities.
- It is challenging to implement and update.

For these reasons, Anderson and Kaplan (2008) developed the TD-ABC method. The TD-ABC method was devised to address the issues encountered when applying the ABC method [27, 28]. One of the main criticisms of the activity-based costing method is that it requires a lot of information to perform cost calculations, it is a costly process to transform data, and sometimes the results obtained are not accurate [9, 29]. The TD-ABC cost calculation system provides more precise information than the traditional model [17, 30], because in the activity-based costing system, the tasks performed can be expressed in time equations.

The fundamental difference between the two methods is that TD-ABC does not involve interviews and surveys with employees for cost allocation to activities but considers the actual time required to perform the activities and calculates the cost from real-time data [31]. Another fundamental difference between the two models is that the ABC model uses many different cost drivers, whereas TD-ABC only uses time as a cost driver. Thus, the complexity added to the ABC method by using many cost drivers has been eliminated, as only one driver, time, is used.

Indeed, Time-Driven Activity-Based Costing (TD-ABC) allows for an enhancement of the cost management system in healthcare systems, enabling cost managers to obtain information on costs and profitability to improve care processes and relationships between patients and care organizations in a mutually beneficial manner.

The TD-ABC model, or Time-Driven Activity-Based Costing, enables healthcare organizations to understand the cost of resources used in producing care for each activity in the care pathway. The primary driver of the method is time, which is the measure used to quantify this approach.

5 Discussions

The precision in calculating healthcare service costs is impeded by the fragmentation of medical care and the complexity of managing patients with varying risk levels and diverse treatment needs. Treatment plans may involve multiple hospital services and related services, without standardization for patients with similar conditions [12]. In the absence of standards, accurately assessing the costs associated with delivering care is crucial. Consequently, current cost pricing tools often focus on measuring and controlling costs for restricted units such as a service or individual and separate activities [1, 13]. Scientific literature suggests that reimbursement systems, such as Relative Value Units and cost-to-charge ratio (RVU and CCR), are not based on an understanding of the actual costs of care for an individual patient or for patients suffering from similar diseases [1, 13]. The complexity of cost calculation is further exacerbated by reimbursement systems and accounting practices prevalent in many healthcare organizations worldwide.

Traditional cost structures pose a barrier to implementing management cost calculation models in the healthcare field [18]. Calculating healthcare service costs is challenging due to the complexity and diversity of patients and care provisions. Patients require multiple revenue sources, all of which need to be considered (technological, supply, etc.). Additionally, management preferences of various physicians or providers, based on their respective specialties, can sometimes lead to increased variability and complicate healthcare delivery. A values-based care program requires a transformation in the care continuum, with physicians aligned towards a common objective.

The findings of this study indicate that costings based on TD-ABC, although presented in comparative studies, are consistently more accurate and practical than those calculated using traditional cost calculation methods. The use of TD-ABC for cost calculations has primarily been observed with the aim of enhancing operational efficiency, enabling precise cost comparisons, and reducing risks associated with bundled payments. This method (TD-ABC) has also proven suitable for managing complex costs in healthcare facilities [21, 24, 32, 33]. However, despite its recent application in the healthcare domain, this approach should gradually be implemented in healthcare organizations and easily applicable in hospitals [34].

The results of this review suggest that studies on cost modeling using TD-ABC have primarily been published after 2015, highlighting that this method (TD-ABC) is likely to be applied in various healthcare-related domains, such as emergency care, chronic diseases, cancer, hospital transport, support activities, etc. [1, 16].

Based on the analysis of the selected literature, three main dimensions regarding the application of TD-ABC in healthcare have been identified: improving the outcome of different healthcare services, developing hospital financing and reimbursement modes, and identifying cost reduction opportunities [35].

TD-ABC is widely regarded as the most accurate method for assessing costs and resources allocated to managing healthcare facilities, whether public or private [1]. It is recognized for its effective adaptation to evaluating the complexity of healthcare service costs, thereby enabling establishments to compare their costs with pre-established reimbursement rates. A major advantage of TD-ABC in healthcare is its ability to precisely estimate resource utilization for specific care activities, such as surgical interventions for given patients [1]. However, its application in this domain is extensively documented in the scientific literature post-2013. We reiterate here that a recent systematic review on the use of TD-ABC in general healthcare shows that 80% of studies were published during or after 2013 [34]. The authors recommend a progressive integration of TD-ABC into healthcare systems and its easy application in care organizations [34]. In summary, TD-ABC is considered the most accurate tool for assessing the health value of certain medical conditions.

It is crucial to note that providing healthcare services in hospitals worldwide requires the adoption of advanced technologies and developed care services to add value and ensure service quality at a reasonable cost. However, the development of these technologies and care services is one of the main drivers of the considerable increase in costs within hospitals. Faced with this rise in healthcare expenses, it is essential to improve the management of healthcare facility cost accounting and implement reliable analytical accounting tools to better manage this cost increase. In this context, the use of analytical accounting tools, particularly the TD-ABC method, is proposed as a solution to the cost crisis in the healthcare field.

Research highlights several limitations in calculating healthcare service costs. The first limitation concerns the number and fragmentation of healthcare services received by patients. The second limitation is the difficulty in obtaining certain necessary information to accurately track, describe, and measure process mapping and various cost calculations following care standards and protocols.

Patient healthcare costs significantly influence overall hospital logistics costs. To ensure comprehensive control of healthcare service costs, future research should focus on pricing all logistics activities. TD-ABC can be used to assess the costs of processes currently used in patient care pathways. This method provides a methodology for accurately calculating actual costs based on total resource utilization, allowing decision-makers to understand, among other things, the value of patient service costs. When actual healthcare service costs are known, it becomes possible to address other support activities processes in future research (such as catering, cleaning, accommodation, etc.).

The findings of this study suggest that TD-ABC could be an effective cost calculation method to support value-based initiatives in healthcare. Implementing this method (TD-ABC) can provide decision-makers and care managers with a precise understanding of cost distribution throughout a patient's comprehensive care trajectory. Additionally, this method can enrich decision-making processes regarding resource allocation, care process control, procedure optimization, and the establishment of new financing modes.

The importance of the TD-ABC approach, aimed at significantly improving value for patients, also opens up new perspectives for other areas of healthcare, including home care, pharmacy, and support activities. Just as in other sectors (such as the hospitality industry), TD-ABC will enable healthcare facilities to model and implement best practices to enhance value for patients and optimize their care pathways.

6 Conclusion

In a competitive environment, efforts in the healthcare sector are increasingly focused on streamlining and better utilizing care providers' resources to reduce costs while maintaining or improving outcomes for patients. Indeed, patient healthcare represents a significant cost for an already burdened healthcare system. Healthcare facilities worldwide, operating in multifaceted supply chain environments, are under pressure to manage their care activities and cost reduction effectively. Although the importance of activity-based costing systems for healthcare facility financing has been recognized, hospital analytical accounting remains a significant challenge due to the complex competitive environment involving numerous factors such as patients, external stakeholders, materials and supplies, healthcare providers, etc.

The fundamental questions for today's healthcare management must consider the cost of healthcare services and the resulting activities. Based on these pressures, there is a need to allocate financial resources to public hospitals and clinics in new ways, compelling institutions to reconsider their cost calculation structures and analyze corresponding activities. Cost evaluation methods thus become tools for better managing human, financial, and material resources in care pathways to which they are applied, as they first allow an understanding of the cost structure and promote awareness regarding resource allocation to deliver care within a specified time frame and at a lower cost.

References

1. Zerka A, Jawab F (2020) Calculation of the costs of health care services for road accident victims in TDABC: a systematic review of the literature. In: 2020 IEEE 13th international colloquium of logistics and supply chain management (LOGISTIQUA). IEEE, pp 1–7
2. Zerka A, Fouad JAWAB (2023) TDABC: an efficient system for calculating the costs of health care services for road accident victims. Altern Managériales Economiques 5(3):162–181

3. Mévellec P (1995) Le calcul des coûts dans les organisations. Éditions La Découverte
4. Kaplan RS, Porter ME (2011) How to solve the cost crisis in health care. Harv Bus Rev 89(9):56–61
5. Frichi Y, Jawab F, Boutahari S (2020) Modeling the impact of hospital logistics on quality of care and patient satisfaction: results of a survey in three public healthcare facilities in Fez-Morocco. J Ind Eng Manag 13(2):296–320
6. Finkler SA, Ward DM (2007) Essentials of cost accounting for health care organizations. Jones & Bartlett Learning
7. Kaplan RS, Anderson SR (2007) Time-driven activity-based costing: a simpler and more powerful path to higher profits. Harvard Business School Press
8. Frichi Y, Jawab F, Aboueljinane L, Boutahari S (2022) Development and comparison of two new multi-period queueing reliability models using discrete-event simulation and a simulation–optimization approach. Comput Ind Eng 168:108068
9. El Farouk II, Talbi A, Jawab F (2011) Modeling and simulation of hospital supply chain: state of the art and research perspectives. In: 2011 4th International conference on logistics. IEEE, pp 287–291. Kaplan RS, Witkowski M, Hohman J (2013) Boston Children's hospital: measuring patient costs. Harvard Business School Case
10. Frichi Y, Jawab F, Boutahari S (2019) The mixed-method 5W2D approach for health system stakeholders analysis in quality of care: an application to the Moroccan context. Int J Environ Res Pub Health 16(16):2899
11. Frichi Y, Jawab F, Boutahari S (2019) An exploratory qualitative study of the influence of hospital logistics factors on quality of care and patient satisfaction at public hospitals in Morocco. Adv Sci Technol Eng Syst J 4(6):414–422
12. Zerka A, Jawab F, Frichi Y (2022) Mapping's process of the Trajectory of pre-hospital transport by basic ambulance for road accidents' victims in TDABC. In: 2022 14th international colloquium of logistics and supply chain management (LOGISTIQUA). IEEE, pp 1–6
13. Oklu R et al (2015) Time-driven activity-based costing in IR. J Vasc Interv Radiol 26(12):1827–1831
14. Launois R, Vergnenègre A, Garrigues B (2003) Notions et Mesure Des Coûts En Fonction de La perspective Choisie. Bull Cancer 90(11):946–954
15. Boker Z (2009) Implementation of actvity based based costing in logistics. Acta Tech Jaurinensis 2(3):337–343
16. Zerka A, Jawab F (2022) Modelling the costs of pre-hospital transport service for victims of road accidents in TDABC. Arch Transp 61(1):89–101
17. Kaplan RS, Anderson SR (2004) Time-driven activity-based costing. Harvard Business School Press
18. Allin O et al (2020) Using time-driven activity-based costing to demonstrate value in perioperative care: recommendations and review from the society for perioperative assessment and quality improvement (SPAQI). J Med Syst 44(1):1–8
19. Kaplan RS, Witkowski ML, Hohman JA (2012) Boston Children's hospital: measuring patient costs. Harv Bus Rev 3(1):e28
20. Kaplan MJ (2013) Role of neutrophils in systemic autoimmune diseases. Arthritis Res Ther 15:1–9
21. Porter ME (2010) What is value in health care? N Engl J Med 363:2477–2481
22. Azoulay A et al (2007) The use of the transition cost accounting system in health services research. Cost Eff Resour Alloc 5(11)
23. Sophie H, Werner B (2010) Identifying operational improvements during the design process of a time-driven ABC system: the role of collective worker participation and leadership style. Manag Acc Res 21(3):185–198
24. Demeere N, Stouthuysen K, Roodhooft F (2009) Time-driven activity-based costing in an outpatient clinic environment: development, relevance and managerial impact. Health Policy 92(2–3):296–304
25. Kaplan RS, Haas D (2017) Defining, measuring, and improving value in spine care. WB Saunders 30(2):80–83

26. Baker JJ (1998) Activity-based costing and activity-based management for health care. Gaithersburg, Md. Aspen
27. Tang D, Loze MT, Zeh HJ, Kang R (2010) The redox protein HMGB1 regulates cell deathand survival in cancer treatment. Autophagy 6:1181–1183
28. Udpa S (1996) Activity-based costing for hospitals. Health Care Manage Rev 21(3):83–96
29. Lipscomb J et al (2009) Health care costing: data, methods, current applications. Med Care 47(7)
30. Ostadi B, Daloie RM, Sepehri MM (2019) A combined modelling of fuzzy logic and time-driven activity-based costing (TDABC) for hospital services costing under uncertainty. J Biomed Inform 89:11–28
31. Öker F, Özyapici H (2013) A new costing model in hospital management. Health Care Manag 32(1):23–36. https://journals.lww.com/00126450-201301000-00004
32. Au J, Rudmik L (2013) Cost of outpatient endoscopic sinus surgery from the perspective of the Canadian government: a time-driven activity-based costing approach. Int Forum Allergy Rhinol 3(9):748–754
33. Campanale C, Cinquini L, Tenucci A (2014) Time-driven activity-based costing to improve transparency and decision making in healthcare: a case study. Qual Res Account Manag 11(2):165–186
34. Keel G, Savage C, Rafiq M, Mazzocato P (2017) Time-driven activity-based costing in health care: a systematic review of the literature. Health Policy 121:755–763
35. Chan YC (1993) Improving hospital cost accounting with activity-based costing. Health Care Manage Rev 18:71–7

Abdelaziz Zerka Holds a Ph.D. in management sciences and serves as an assistant professor at the Faculty of Sciences Dhar El Mahraz in Fez, he is a member of the Industrial Technologies and Services Laboratory at Sidi Mohammed Ben Abdellah University, specializing in hospital logistics research.

Fouad Jawab Professor of Supply Chain at the Higher School of Technology of the Sidi Mohamed Ben Abdellah University of Fez, Morocco.

He has held several scientific and administrative responsibilities. He founded the International Conference on Logistics and Supply Chain Management (LOGISTIQUA), which he continues to develop with the support of several research teams in Morocco and abroad.

He is the author and co-author of more than 180 publications in national and international journals and proceedings. His research focuses on modeling, simulation and optimization of the supply chain, hospital supply chains and urban logistics. He is also an expert with several renowned organizations and a reviewer for prestigious journals.

Optimization of a Meal Distribution Circuit in a Hospital: Vehicle Routing Problem

19

Jihene Jlassi, Ines Rekik, and Habib Chabchoub

Abstract

Healthcare establishments present many problems of layout, sizing, and especially optimization of logistics flows. As part of a study on the reorganization of hospital logistics, we focus on the distribution of meal trays between the different sectors as a vehicle routing problem (VRP). We focus on catering since it plays an essential role in the smooth running of the patient's stay in the hospital. The meal takes on a very special dimension, given the fragile situation of hospitalized people. In this paper, we propose a mathematical modelling of this problem to improve the performance of the process studied using a Cplex solver.

Keywords

Meal distribution • Vehicle routing problem • Patient satisfaction • Hospital logistics • Healthcare • Distribution time

J. Jlassi (✉) · I. Rekik
OLID Laboratory, Higher Institute of Management Industrial of Sfax (ISGIS), University of Sfax, Sfax, Tunisia
e-mail: jihene.jlassi@isgis.usf.tn

I. Rekik
e-mail: ines.rekik@isgis.usf.tn

H. Chabchoub
College of Business, Al Ain University, Abu Dhabi, United Arab Emirates
e-mail: habib.chabchoub@aau.ac.ae

F. Jawab (ed.), *Hospital Supply Chain*, Integrated Science 27,
https://doi.org/10.1007/978-3-031-70292-1_19

1 Introduction

The decreasing food intake among hospitalized patients is often associated with adverse consequences for the health as the quality of hospital food service directly affects the hospitalized patients.

The provision of hospital meals is a highly sophisticated operation. The quality of the food served during the hospital stay can significantly impact the patients' satisfaction.

Hospital meals are considered as part-and-parcel of In-patients' management, which facilitates recovery and improves patient satisfaction regarding the overall treatment experience.

Provision of meals is a part of the daily in-patient care, making the service more 'hospitable'. A large part of the overall satisfaction of hospital stay is linked with the hospital diet. An important number of hospitalised patient depend solely on hospital food for their nutritional needs.

Therefore, hospitals are obligated to uphold a high standard of quality and nutritional value in the food they serve. The way patients feel about the food and food service can even affect the way they rate other services.

The food distribution in hospitals has been the subject of many researches and it is more and more becoming a matter of great concern. However, the research in this field is not yet well adopted. As far as the authors' knowledge, the meal distribution to patients in a given hospital is not yet treated in the literature. There is also no research study considering this problem as a Vehicle Routing Problem (VRP).

The Vehicle Routing Problem (VRP) involves determining the optimal sequence of visited nodes by a vehicle to minimize both the total travelled distance and transportation costs.

This problem contains diverse variants. For example, the Capacitated Vehicle Routing Problem (CVRP)involves transporting goods from a central depot to a designed set of customers considering their demand and by the mean of a fleet of vehicles while respecting their uniform capacity. The Multi-Trip VRP (MTVRP) is another well-known variant of VRP, and which consists on a possible using multiple trips by each vehicle.

The Vehicle Routing Problem with Pickups and Deliveries (VRPPD) is another important type of VRP. It refers to transport goods, instead of from a central depot, between Pickups and Deliveries locations.

The aim of this study consists on developing a food distribution model tailored to the context of a Tunisian hospital, using a specific case study approach. The objective is to suggest a new approach so as to reduce the meal distribution time which will influence not only the patient's meal waiting time but also the quality of care related to each patient face to its specific diet in terms of both the related type and time of meal.

The paper is structured as follows. In the second section, a literature review is represented, focusing on hospital food service. In Sect. 3, the case study is depicted and shown in details, and the mathematical formulation of the model is discussed.

In Sect. 4, the results are demonstrated. In Sect. 5, conclusions and future research directions are ultimately displayed.

2 Literature Review

Catering services in a hospital is an essential component of caregiving that can be examined in order to find out ways to improve a patient-centred experience.

In the literature, many issues related to Hospital Food Service Practices have been taken into consideration such as the Quality of food service.

Numerous studies have investigated the effects of different food service delivery methods on quality indicators of inpatient food. These surveys commonly assess quality indicators such as cost, temperature, texture, menu style, and flavour. For instance, one study conducted by Hartwell et al. in [1] found that a "bulk trolley" system, involving the serving of food from a portable heated system, led to enhanced texture across all foods, improved temperature acceptability for certain items, and better flavour compared to the traditional "plated" system [1].

The restaurant-style system can offer significant benefits to patients. Patients have greater meal time options, can receive food at their preferred times, and can order meals closer to consumption compared to other traditional systems.

In the same context, Nettles et al. [2] conducted a study focusing on paediatric oncology patients, which found that implementing a restaurant-style food delivery system resulted in improved dietary and caloric intake, along with increased patient satisfaction. Additionally, the study showed that the restaurant-style service enhanced the efficiency of meal delivery, as patients ordered meals less frequently but consumed more food at each meal.

Hartwell et al. [1] confirmed that providing choice at the point of consumption (using a trolley system) enhances patient satisfaction, with portion size being less critical. The most important attributes affecting patient satisfaction with food were found to be temperature and texture, which should guide hospital food service managers in their focus. A predictive model for patient satisfaction with food quality as served has not yet been proposed, making this work a valuable addition to existing knowledge in the field. This report contributes new insights into service styles for dishes aimed at improving food quality and thereby enhancing patient satisfaction.

Cronk and Medeiros [3] formulated operational recommendations for implementing an on-demand meal delivery system for inpatients. They examined various combinations of meal delivery cart capacities and dispatching strategies using a discrete event simulation model to assess effectiveness. This model incorporated facility routing considerations. Based on their analysis, the researchers recommended a specific delivery strategy that satisfied operational performance and service level requirements.

Safarian et al. [4] emphasized the importance of patient satisfaction with hospital food service as a key measure of the effectiveness of implemented strategies. Their study identified several factors significantly associated with overall patient satisfaction regarding food services at Ghaem Hospital and Imam Reza Hospital in Mashhad, Iran. These factors included food temperature, quantity, taste, appearance, availability of replacement meals, and diet compatibility. These findings provide valuable insights for dieticians, enabling them to prioritize specific indicators to enhance hospital food catering services and optimize patient satisfaction with hospital food.

Table 1 outlines a summary of the research centred on the quality of food within the hospital sector.

Some studies dealing with hospital meals management concern essentially meals waste management in order to reduce both waste and costs [5–7].

Some other hospital healthcare problems are considered as VRP problems. These problems are classified into four main groups: healthcare waste transportation problem, distribution of vaccines and certain medicaments problem and Home Healthcare Routing Problem.

For healthcare waste transportation problems, Ben-Romdhane et al. [8], for example, treated the transport of healthcare waste, which comprises infectious and toxic materials, from facilities to treatment centers in order to ensure safe management during the transport of these substances which are threatening not only to humans but also to environment. They proposed to classify waste into hazardous and non-hazardous all along the routing. They formulated this problem as a multi-compartment vehicle routing problem with the aim of minimizing the total distance travelled. For solving this problem, they applied an adaptive genetic algorithm. For

Table 1 Literature review on food quality

Authors	Objective	Method	Result
Hartwell et al. [1]	Assess patient satisfaction by comparing plate service with bulk trolley food delivery systems in hospital settings	Binary logistic regression analysis	This study validates that offering choice at the point of consumption (through the trolley system) contributes to enhanced patient satisfaction
Hartwell et al. [1]	Offer fresh perspectives on food serving methods designed to enhance food quality	A model predicting patient satisfaction based on food quality	Enhancing food quality to improve patient satisfaction
Cronk and Medeiros [3]	Explored different combinations of meal delivery cart capacities and dispatch strategies	A discrete event simulation model was employed to assess effectiveness	The researchers suggested a particular delivery strategy that fulfils both operational performance and service level criteria
Safarian et al. [4]	Identified several factors strongly correlated with overall patient satisfaction regarding food services	Prioritize specific indicators to improve hospital catering services	Maximize patient satisfaction with hospital food

testing the efficiency of the proposed approach, comparisons with both benchmark instances and real data instances have been adopted.

In the same context, Ouertani et al. [9] extended their study of [8] by minimizing not only the travelled distance but also the total routing cost. They proposed an adapted multi-compartment vehicle routing problem MILP (Mixed Integer Linear Programming) model to the context of healthcare waste. For the resolution of this problem, they presented an adaptive evolutionary algorithm. The obtained results are also compared to both instances taken from the literature and real data instances to draw the managerial insights related to the studied problem.

Nikzamir and Baradaran [10] developed a new perspective for healthcare waste location-routing problem essentially in Coronavirus Disease 2019. In their study, they integrated the stochastic emission of contamination. They introduced a multi-objective model with two goals: minimizing total cost and reducing contamination emissions. To solve this problem, the authors applied the Multi-Objective Water-Flow like Algorithm (MOWFA) based metaheuristic. This algorithm uses in a first step the Analytical Hierarchy Process (AHP) multi-criteria method to rank the archived non-dominated solutions. Then, this algorithm uses the best archived ranked solutions to produce new solutions. To test the effectiveness of the presented method, test experimentations have been made compared with Multi-Objective Simulated Annealing (MOSA) and the Multi-Objective Imperialist Competitive Algorithm (MOICA).

The second group of VRP based hospital healthcare problems concerns the distribution of vaccines, Testers and certain medicaments. Recently, Maleki et al. [11] treated the direct and the reverse COVID-19 vaccine medical supply chain network. They considered both the vaccine distribution phase and the health care waste management related to the vaccination process. The problem described has been modelled as a capacitated and multi-depot vehicle routing problem (VRP) involving heterogeneous vehicles. In their research work, the authors proposed a sustainable fuzzy multi-objective model considering multi-product and multi-period aspects. The fuzzy version appears when considering the time-window aspect and which integrates both priority of the nodes to be visited and the satisfaction level. The obtained results demonstrate the effectiveness of the proposed model.

Benini et al. [12] introduced recently Mixed Integer Linear Programming models (MILP) along with a Hybrid Adaptive Large Neighborhood Search (H-ALNS) metaheuristic to address the transportation of biological samples from blood draw centers to the main laboratory, treating the problem as a Vehicle Routing Problem (VRP). The study was based on real-world data from the Local Healthcare Authority in Bologna, Italy. Experimental results demonstrated the effectiveness of the proposed algorithms in optimizing this transportation process.

The third manner to integrate VRP in healthcare problems consists on Home Healthcare Management. In the literature, there exist numerous studies related to this field. Frifita et al. [13] introduced a General Variable Neighborhood Search algorithm (GVNS) to address the home healthcare routing and scheduling problem, focusing on synchronized visits and time windows. The primary objective was to generate assignment plans for nurses to home caregivers and optimize the sequence of visits. To evaluate the performance of their method, the authors used benchmark instances obtained from existing literature. The results demonstrated that the proposed algorithm outperformed existing methods in approximately half of the tested cases.

Shiri et al. [14] introduced a three-step methodology to address home health care routing and scheduling under uncertainty. In the first step, they identified a set of candidate health care facilities through a combinatorial evaluation process that combines grey relational analysis and fuzzy analytic hierarchy process. The second step consists on proposing a multi-objective model focusing on minimizing the total network cost, minimizing the overqualified skill levels and maximizing the qualitative factors of healthcare facilities. Finally, the third step concerns the conversion of the three presented objective functions into a scalar-valued optimization problem by using the Nimbus method. For the validation of the proposed approach, a real case study from Iran country is applied.

Guo and Bard [15] examined the home care routing and scheduling problem. They formalized this problem as a modified TSP (Travelling Salesman Problem) model in order to balance a set of factors including the traveled distance, the overtime, the productivity points, the need to have breaks and the daily workload. The authors incorporated additional metrics summarized as patient time windows, the nurse skill qualifications and the continuity of care. They proposed a three-step based algorithm for solving this problem. The first step uses the k-means clustering technique for grouping locations of demanded visits and assign then each visit to a provider. The second step consists on formulating and solving a modified traveling salesman problem in order to find optimal solutions. The third step concerns the development of a swapping and gap adjustments based local search heuristic and while adding the lunch break to schedules.

Alkaabneh and Diabat [16] approached home health care delivery as a combined routing and assignment problem. They developed a Mixed Integer Programming (MIP) model that simultaneously addressed the assignment of nurses to patients, the routing of nurses between patients, and the scheduling of nurses' workdays. This problem was formulated as a multi-objective problem with the objectives of maximizing the compatibility between nurses and patients, minimizing the healthcare-associated service and minimizing the routing costs. In their paper, the authors demonstrate the value of the combination between the assignment, the scheduling and the routing problems compared with solving each problem sequentially. For solving this problem, they developed two approaches. The first approach is based on a Branch and Cut algorithm whereas the second approach consists on a two-stage based Tabu search meta-heuristic.

Yang et al. [17] presented the home healthcare routing and scheduling problem considering the uncertainty of the environment. The uncertainty appears in both the travel times and the service times. They considered this problem as multi-objective integrating two conflicting goals: minimizing the routing cost, workload balance and improving service consistency. For the resolution of this problem, an improved multi-objective artificial bee colony (IMOABC) metaheuristic has been developed.

Shahnejat-Bushehri et al. [18] considered the in-home delivery COVID-19 test services face to the spread of the pandemic COVID-19.The problem consists on managing the transport activities from laboratories to patients face to unprecedented requests. In addressing this problem as a Vehicle Routing Problem with Time Windows (VRPTW), a mixed-integer programming (MIP) model was developed to optimize the balancing of testers' workload. The model was solved using the CPLEX solver for small instances, while an adaptive large neighborhood search algorithm was implemented for larger instances to obtain results efficiently. To test the effectiveness of the suggested methods, comparisons have been made based on a real world laboratory.

Tohidifard et al. [19] formulated a mathematical model for the Multi-Depot Vehicle Routing Problem (VRP) with Time Windows and Fuzzy Demands to address the home care routing problem. In this problem, the goal is to efficiently visit patients using multiple vehicles stationed at various depots while considering time constraints and uncertain demands represented by fuzzy logic. The objectives were to minimize distance, traveling time, the number of vehicles, and transportation costs.

To solve this complex problem, the authors proposed using Genetic Algorithm (GA) and Particle Swarm Optimization (PSO) based metaheuristics.

Recently, Santa González et al. [20] adopted a new strategy for home healthcare, known as the planning of mobile clinics operations. This strategy consists on reaching populations which are cut off from the local health services in order to deliver primary healthcare. This problem is considered as a multiperiod location-routing problem (MLRP). In their research paper, the authors presented a mathematical formulation.

Riazi et al. [21] expressed the Home Healthcare Scheduling and Routing Problem as a vehicle routing problem with time windows (VRPTW). They applied a distributed Gossip based algorithm for solving this problem. They then developed an extension of this algorithm named n-Gossip which is responsible for balancing between optimality and computational speed.

Salehi-Amiri et al. [22] proposed the use of Internet Of Things (IOT) for designing a real-time home healthcare routing system considering uncertain demand. They considered this problem as a Green Split Pick-up Vehicle Routing Problem (GSPVRP). They developed a two-phase based modeling approach for selecting the number of used vehicles by identifying in a first step the potential patients; and collect, in a second step, their biological samples for sending them to the analyze. The objective consists on the maximization of the total occupancy rate of the vehicles, the minimization of both the total costs and the greenhouse gas emissions by optimizing the number of trips. Four multi-objective metaheuristic based algorithms are then proposed to solve this problem. The computational tests are based on real world data taken from Montreal, Canada case study.

The literature conducted in this chapter reveals several limitations related to the existing studies. First of all, in integrated healthcare-VRP problems, the most works are concentrated in Home Healthcare Management. There is a notable lack of treatment of the distribution of medical equipment and medicaments in hospitals. Second, despite the importance of the healthcare waste management problem face to the harmful effects of the healthcare either to human or to environment, studies in this field still limited and very restricted. More in-depth research studies should be performed again and with more details either in the waste transportation or in the waste treatment. Then, there is no research study, as far as we know, treated the meal distribution inside hospitals. There is also no work considering this problem as an adapted VRP. Most of existing papers investigating Meals management present this problem as waste management problem.

3 Context of the Study

3.1 Presentation of the Center for Traumatology and Major Burns

Founded in 2008, this center mainly specialises in treating serious burns and injuries from work and accidents.

It is situated in Ben Arous, near the highway, at the southern entrance to the city of Tunis. It covers an area of six hectares. It has a capacity of 168 beds. There are seven floors and ten operating rooms.

Other departments in Ben Arous Center for Trauma and Burn include Orthopedics, Burn resuscitation, Aesthetic surgery, Emergency Medicine, General Medicine, Neurosurgery, Anesthesia, Physiotherapy, Radiology, Medical biology, a blood bank and a pharmacy.

We are going to inspect in more detail the service that our study revolves around.

3.2 The Catering Service

Hospital catering "covers meals for patients, staff and children of staff, in the event of the existence of a creche. The whole range of meals is concerned, from breakfast to dinner, including snacks for night staff.

More broadly, hospital and social catering, together with school catering and company catering, make up collective catering. This can be defined as the provision of meals to people working or living in a community.

"Restoration plays an essential role in the smooth running of a patient's stay in hospital. A personal analysis has enabled us to assign the four following roles to it:

- A feeding role: This is the primary objective of catering; it consists of feeding each patient, despite the obstacles that the initial physical state or the dietary changes induced by the pathology may constitute.

- A supportive role for medical treatment: This role is still sometimes underestimated. But it has now been proven that a good diet reduces the average duration of the hospital stay and decreases the risk of nosocomial illnesses.
- A well-being-related role: hospital stays can be mundane and for many patients, both physical pain and the isolation from family or friends can negatively impact their overall health and well-being. In this view, the patient is often pleased, satisfied and reassured when he/she is awarded a successful meal.
- A role in raising awareness of a balanced diet".

In the CTGB, the catering policy is oriented towards outsourcing. On the one hand it is designed to reduce budget. On the other hand, specialized companies are more efficient and they save the time required to properly train agents.

3.3 The Meal Tray Distribution System

Hospital catering has a meal distribution system that is specific to it: unloading of orders requested from the caterer, assembly and constitution of meal trays in a dedicated room (known as an allotment), transport of meal trays to hospital ward naves using three carts and three servers.

With the increasing number of hospitalized patients, the number of meats to be distributed is more and more elevated and while respecting several criteria related to the type of meal distributed to each patient, the meal time for several patients, the available carriages to distribute meals... in this context the hospital manager suffer from a huge time in the distribution of meals which can cause delays for taking meal for certain patients. This waste of time can deteriorate the quality of the care in the hospital and influence the health and also the satisfaction of several patients.

The organization of the catering served nearly 640 meals in this environment each day while guaranteeing four objectives: health safety, quality of service, organoleptic and nutritional quality, and productivity. The duration of the distribution of meal trays to patients is relatively identical regardless of the department. It is between 20 and 30 min, with a median of 25 min.

The present study is concerned with monitoring the distribution time of these meals while trying to minimize it in order to guarantee patients satisfaction.

To solve this problem by determining the distribution plan for each trolley, this problem is considered in this research as a Capacitated VRP. This variant of VRP integrates the constraint of the capacity of each trolley.

The Vehicle Routing Problem (VRP) is typically represented as a graph, where customer locations are represented by vertices, and travel routes between them are depicted as arcs. One vertex serves as the "depot," from which vehicles start their routes and return after completing them (as shown in Fig. 1). The objective of the VRP is to assign each customer to one vehicle exactly once, aiming to minimize travel times, costs, and distances.

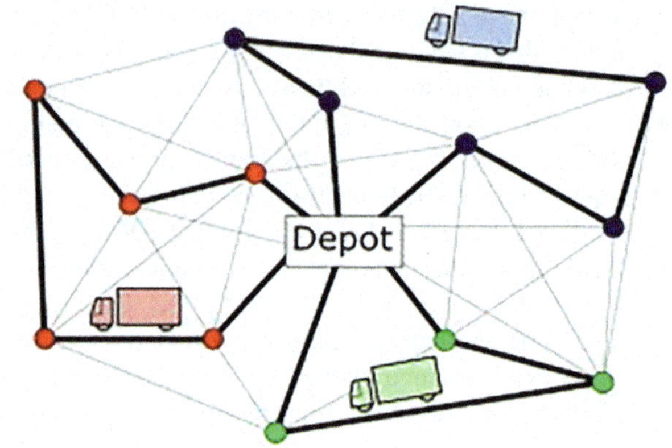

Fig. 1 Vehicle routing problem (VRP) presentation

In addition to the basic VRP formulation, various constraints can be incorporated to model real-world scenarios more accurately. Common constraints include vehicle capacity limits, route duration constraints, and time window constraints, among others. These additional constraints have led to several classifications of the VRP, each tailored to specific problem scenarios and requirements.

Vehicle Routing Problems (VRPs) involve the challenge of determining the most efficient routes for vehicles travelling from one or multiple depots to a specified set of locations or customers. These problems have numerous practical applications in distribution and logistics, where optimizing transportation routes can lead to significant cost savings and improved efficiency in supply chain operations.

In the context of meal distribution problem, the vehicles represent the trolley, the nodes represent the different sectors of the hospital department and the depot relates to the restaurant. The problem consists on determining the sectors visited by each trolley and the corresponding routing, in each shift, in order to minimize the meat total distribution time.

Section 4 will present the proposed mathematical modelling of the meal distribution problem.

4 Proposed Mathematical Model

In this section, we present the mathematical model proposed to formulate the problem of meal distribution in a university hospital center. To do this, we define then the decision variables as well as the fixed parameters. We assume in this study that each sector will be served by only one trolley.

- **Decisions variables**
- $X_{ij}^{rt} = \begin{cases} 1, \text{if trolley r goes from sector i to sector j} \\ \text{at time period t} \\ 0, \textit{sinon} \end{cases}$

- q_{ij}^{rt} = Total quantity of meals delivered by trolley r from sector i to sector j at time period t
- **Parameters**
- T : Plan horizon
- n: Number of sectors
- m: Nombre of trolley
- TP_{ij}: Travel time from sector i to sector j
- S_j^t: Service time in sector j at time t
- Q^r : The capacity of trolley r in terms of number of dishes
- dem_j^t: Demandof sector j at time period t
- T_{max}: Maximum service time
- M : Great number
- $p = n - m$
- **Indices**
- r: Trolley index
- i, j: Sector Index
- t: time index
- **Objective function**

$$\min \sum_{i=1}^{n} \sum_{j=1}^{n} \sum_{r=1}^{m} \sum_{t=1}^{T} \left(TP_{ij} + S_j^t\right) X_{ij}^{rt}$$

The objective of the proposed model is to minimize the total time for distributing meals to the various departments in order to satisfy the patients.

- **Contraints**

The various constraints that must be taken into account and respected to model our problem are summarized as follows:

- Constraint (1) ensures that each sector must be visited at least once every instant t.

$$\sum_{i=0}^{n} \sum_{r=1}^{m} X_{ij}^{rt} \geq 1, \forall j \in n, t \in T$$

- Constraint (2) guarantees that each trolley entering a sector must leave it

$$\sum_{j=0}^{n} X_{ji}^{rt} = \sum_{j=0}^{n} X_{ij}^{rt}, \forall i \in n, r \in m, t \in T$$

- Constraint (3) ensures that the total quantity of dishes delivered by a handler (trolley) to all sectors must not exceed the capacity of the corresponding trolley.

$$\sum_{i=0}^{n}\sum_{j=0}^{n} q_{ij}^{rt} \leq Q_r, \forall r \in m, t \in T$$

.

- Constraint (4) ensures that the total duration of a tour will never exceed its maximum total duration.

$$\sum_{i=0}^{n}\sum_{j=0}^{n} S_j^t X_{ij}^{rt} + \sum_{i=0}^{n}\sum_{j=0}^{n} TP_{ij} X_{ij}^{rt} \leq T_{\max}, \forall r \in m, t \in T$$

- Constraint (5) ensures that the total quantity of dishes distributed to each sector at time period t should respect the demand of this sector at this time period

$$\sum_{i=0}^{n}\sum_{r=1}^{m} q_{ij}^{rt} = dem_j^t, \forall j = \{1, \ldots, n\}, t \in T$$

- Constraint (6) ensures that each trolley should return to the restaurant empty

$$\sum_{i=1}^{n} q_{i0}^{rt} = 0, \forall r \in m, t \in T$$

- Constraint (7) forbids having intermediate nodes

$$X_{ij}^{rt} + X_{ji}^{rt} \leq 1, \forall i = \{0, \ldots, n\}, j = \{1, \ldots, n\}, r \in m, t \in T$$

- Constraint (8) ensures that each trolley must start its tour from restaurant

$$\sum_{j1=1}^{n} X_{0j1}^{rt} \geq X_{ij}^{rt}, i = \{1, \ldots, n\}, j = \{1, \ldots, n\}, r \in m, t \in T, i \neq j$$

- Constraint (9) guarantees that for each cart the starting point differs from the ending point

$$i \neq j, \forall r \in m, t \in T$$

- Constraint (10) indicates that each trolley contains meal only if it is assigned

$$X_{ij}^{rt} \leq q_{ij}^{rt}, \forall i = \{0, \ldots, n\}, j = \{1, \ldots, n\}, r \in m, t \in T$$

- Constraint (11) guarantees that if a trolley is not assigned, it can't deliver meal

$$q_{ij}^{rt} \leq MX_{ij}^{rt}, \forall i = \{0, \ldots, n\}, j = \{1, \ldots, n\}, r \in m, t \in T.$$

- Constraint (12) guarantees that the decision variables are of binary type

$$X_{ij}^{rt} \in \{0, 1\}, \forall r \in m, t \in T.$$

- Constraint (13) ensures the non-negativity of the decision variable

$$q_{ij}^{rt} \geq 0, \forall i \in n, j \in n, r \in m, t \in T$$

5 Implementation and Computational Results

This part firstly gives a brief overview of the hospital's distribution mechanism. Then we examine the new rounds released using the software. Our conclusion is finally drawn.

5.1 Implementation

Computational experiments were conducted using real and simulated case instances on a personal computer equipped with an Intel® Core 2 Duo CPU running at 2.0 GHz. The calculations were also performed on a Windows cluster.

For modelling, ILOG OPL 6.1 was used as the modelling language, and the mixed integer solver from CPLEX 10.1 was employed for solving all variants of the problem. Additionally, algorithms were implemented in C++using Microsoft Visual Studio 6.0.

CPU times are reported in seconds, reflecting the computational efficiency and performance of the implemented algorithms and solver in solving the meal distribution optimization problem.

The experimentations are based on the data related to the real case study. In the Center for Traumatology and Major Burns, there are 9 sectors and 3 carriages. The tested instance is taken from historical hospital data at the edge of October 2019.

The demand of each sector is represented in Table 2.

The matrix of the travel time between sectors and between the restaurant and sectors is represented as follows:

Table 2 Demand of each sector

Sector 1	Sector 2	Sector 3	Sector 4	Sector 5	Sector 6	Sector 7	Sector 8	Sector 9
10	20	10	50	10	26	10	10	50

Table 3 Real case carriage orientation

Carriage 1	Carriage 2	Carriage 3
Sector: 3-8-9	Sector: 2-5-6	Sector: 1-4-7

```
TPij=[[0, 3, 5, 5, 5, 5, 5, 5, 5, 5],
[3, 0, 4, 5, 5, 4, 5, 5, 3,4],
[5, 4, 0, 3, 5, 3, 5, 5, 4, 4],
[5, 5, 3, 0, 5, 4, 5, 5, 5, 4],
[5,5,5,5,0,4,5,5,5,4],
[5,4,4,4,4,0,3,4,5,4],
[5,5,5,5,5,3,0,5,3,3],
[5,5,5,5,5,4,5,0,3,3],
[5,3,4,5,5,5,3,3,0,3],
[5,4,4,4,4,4,3,3,3,0]];
```

The service time at each sector is about 25.8 s per meal.

Table 3 shows the assignment of sectors to carriages as well as the routing order for each carriage in the Center for Traumatology and Major Burns.

5.2 Computational Results

In the real case study, there is no strategy for planning the meal distribution. The assignment of the sectors to carriages is done according to the rule First Come First Served (FCFS). In addition, the routing plan for each carriage is done randomly.

In the Center for Traumatology and Major Burns, This assignment is static and doesn't take into consideration neither the number of dishes distributed to each sector nor the routing time between sectors. Table 4 summarizes the distribution of meals by trolleys as well as the distribution time accorded by each trolley. This table reveals a remarkable imbalance in both the distribution of meals by the trolleys and the trolley's distribution time. Consequently, this imbalance generates a swelling in the distribution time.

For further investigation; we opt to a graphic presentation shown in Fig. 2. This graph corroborates a considerable imbalance between the distribution of meals and therefore an imbalance in the distribution time. We observe that the unbalanced distribution of the trolleys brings about an increase in terms of service time which

Table 4 Real case distribution of meals by trolleys

Trolley	Service time (min)	Routing time (min)	Total distribution time
Trolley 1	30.1	18	48.1
Trolley 2	24.08	16	40.08
Trolley 3	30.1	18	48.1

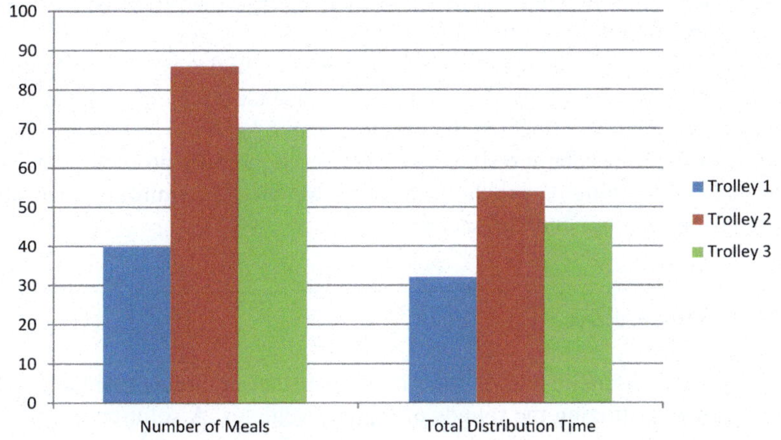

Fig. 2 Imbalance of distribution of meals by trolleys

takes nearly 37 min, on the other hand the first trolley ends its round in 17 min. In this case, the total distribution time is about 136.28.

We approach this problem as a routing problem while trying to minimize the total distribution time by finding a new distribution that guarantees the improvement of the circuit, using the proposed mathematical model. The obtained distribution plan as well as the distribution time are summarized in Tables 5 and 6 respectively.

Table 5 explores the new direction provided by our model while trying to reduce distribution and service time. Consequently, the distribution time, after applying the proposed mathematical model, becomes 134.28.

We can state that our model has given rise to a notably distinguished new orientation:

The first trolley visits sectors (in the order) 6, 5 and 3, while the second serves sectors 1, 8 and 4, and the third visits sectors 7, 9 and 2.

Table 5 The obtained trolley orientation

Trolley1	Trolley 2	Trolley3
Sectors: 6-5-3	Sectors: 1-8-4	Sectors: 7-9-2

Table 6 The obtained distribution of meals by trolleys

Trolley	Service time (min)	Routing time (min)	Total distribution time
Trolley 1	19.78	17	36.78
Trolley 2	30.1	16	46.1
Trolley 3	34.4	17	54.1

Finally, we can notice that the distribution related to the proposed model seems to perform much better than the oldone.

As a conclusion, the results obtained showed the efficiency and the adaptability of the proposed model. However, the tests are provided for only one shift. When we increase the number of shifts, the execution time becomes very huge and when the number of shifts is about 6 shifts, we obtained a memory problem. For this reason, to make a planning of one day and more, we should require to other methods as artificial intelligence based methods.

6 Conclusion

This paper sheds lights on solving the meal distribution circuit problem, as a hindrance against optimizing the rounds of logistic vehicles. A solution method based on linear programming has been proposed to solve this problem using a Cplex solver so as to find out a best distribution of vehicle routes between the various departments. This resolution enables us to suggest a revised and enhanced solution for cart rounds that is both reliable regarding the diminution of distribution time and adequate to meet the patient needs, which proves the efficiency and the applicability of our model.

Acknowledgements We're grateful to the anonymous reviewers for constructive comments and suggestions.

The authors thank Center for Traumatology and Major Burns in Ben Aous Tunisia.

References

1. Hartwell HJ, Edwards JSA, Beavis J (2007) Plate versus bulk trolley food service in a hospital: comparison of patients' satisfaction. Nutrition 23:211–218
2. Nettles MF, Canter DD, Gregoire MB (1997) Analysis of the decision to select a conventional or cook-chill system for hospital foodservice. J Am Diet Assoc 97(6):626–631
3. Cronk C, Medeiros DJ (2013) Development of operational strategies for on-demand meal delivery. In: . Krishnamurthy A, Chan WKV (eds) Healthcare proceedings of the 2013 industrial and systems engineering research conference
4. Safarian M, Alinezhad-Nameghi M, Vafisani F, Asadi Z, Seyedhamzeh S (2018) Patient satisfaction with hospital food in the hospitals affiliated to mashhad university of medical sciences. Iran J Nutrition Fasting Health 6(4):191–197
5. Arriz-Jorquiera M, Acuna A, Rodríguez-Carbó JM, Zayas-Castro JL (2024) Hospital food management: a multi-objective approach to reduce waste and costs. Waste Manage 175:12–21
6. Cook N, Porter J, Goodwin D, Collins J (2023) Diverting food waste from landfill in exemplar hospital foodservices: a qualitative study. J Acad Diet
7. Hoteit M, Antar E, Malli D, Fattouh F, Khattar M, Baderddine N, El Cheikh J, Chalak A, Abiad GM, Hassan FH (2024) A review on hospital food waste quantification, management and assessment strategies in the eastern Mediterranean region. J Agric Food Res 15
8. Ben-Romdhane H, Ouertani N, Krichen S, Nouaouri I (2023) On optimizing healthcare waste routing systems using waste separation policies: a case study. Appl Soft Comput 146

9. Ouertani N, Ben-Romdhane H, Nouaouri I, Allaoui H, Krichen S (2023) A multi-compartment VRP model for the health care waste transportation problem. J Comput Sci 72
10. Nikzamir M, Baradaran V (2020) A healthcare logistic network considering stochastic emission of contamination: Bi-objective model and solution algorithm. Transp Res Part E Logistics Transp Rev 142
11. Maleki A, Hemmati V, Abazari SR, Aghsami A, Rabbani M (2024) Optimal distribution and waste management of Covid-19 vaccines from vaccination centers' satisfaction perspective—A fuzzy time window-based VRP. Transp Res Part E: Logistics Transp Rev 183
12. Benini M, Detti P, Manrique de Lara GZ (2022) Mathematical programming formulations and metaheuristics for biological sample transportation problems in healthcare. Comput Oper Res 146
13. Frifita S, Masmoudi M, Euchi J (2017) General variable neighborhood search for home healthcare routing and scheduling problem with time windows and synchronized visits. Electron Notes Discrete Math 58:63–70
14. Shiri M, Ahmadizar F, Mahmoudzadeh H A three-phase methodology for home healthcare routing and scheduling under uncertainty. Comput Ind Eng 158
15. Guo J, Bard FJ (2023) A three-step optimization-based algorithm for home healthcare delivery. Socio-Econ Planning Sci 87
16. Alkaabneh F, Diabat A (2023) A multi-objective home healthcare delivery model and its solution using a branch-and-price algorithm and a two-stage meta-heuristic algorithm. Transp Res Part C: Emerg Technol 147
17. Yang M, Ni Y, Yang L (2021) A multi-objective consistent home healthcare routing and scheduling problem in an uncertain environment. Comput Ind Eng 160
18. Shahnejat-Bushehri S, Kermani A, Arslan O, Cordeau J-F, Jans RA (2022) Vehicle routing problem with time windows and workload balancing for COVID-19 testers: a case study, IFAC-PapersOnLine, 55(10):2920–2925
19. Tohidifard M, Tavakkoli-Moghaddam R, Navazi F, Partovi MA (2018) Multi-depot home care routing problem with time windows and fuzzy demands solving by particle Swarm optimization and genetic algorithm. IFAC-PapersOnLine 51(11):358–363
20. Santa González R, Cherkesly M, Crainic TG, Rancourt M (2023) Multi-period location routing: An application to the planning of mobile clinic operations in Iraq. Comput Oper Res 159
21. Riazi S, Chehrazi P, Wigström O, Bengtsson K, Lennartson B (2014) A Gossip algorithm for home healthcare scheduling and routing problems. IFAC Proc Volumes 47(3):10754–10759
22. Salehi-Amiri A, Jabbarzadeh A, Hajiaghaei-Keshteli M, Chaabane A (2022) Utilizing the Internet of Things (IoT) to address uncertain home health care supply chain network. Expert Syst Appl 208

Simulation Optimization Models for Reducing Inequities in Ambulance Coverage

20

Youness Frichi and Fouad Jawab

Abstract

Inequity in access to ambulance services is a well-recognized issue in the literature. Most studies have focused on the efficiency objective of maximizing ambulance coverage, paying little attention to the equitable distribution of this coverage among the served population. This chapter proposes coverage models that seek both to maximize overall coverage and distribute it equitably across the areas of the studied territory. To this end, several multi-objective simulation optimization (SO) models are developed and compared using data from the Fez-Meknes region in Morocco. These SO models were built using the weighted sum method and the ϵ-constraint method and were solved by deploying the *OptQuest* engine. The simulation results show that efficiency and equity objectives are conflicting. Additionally, SO models developed using the weighted sum method achieved better results than those developed using the ϵ-constraint method in terms of both coverage and equity.

Keywords

Emergency medical systems • *OptQuest* • Discrete-event simulation • Equity • Gini coefficient • What-if analysis

Y. Frichi (✉) · F. Jawab
Technologies and Industrial Services, High School of Technology, Sidi Mohamed Ben Abdellah University, Fez, Morocco
e-mail: youness.frichi@usmba.ac.ma

F. Jawab
e-mail: fouad.jawab@usmba.ac.ma

F. Jawab (ed.), *Hospital Supply Chain*, Integrated Science 27,
https://doi.org/10.1007/978-3-031-70292-1_20

1 Introduction

Out-of-hospital emergency services worldwide coordinate their operations to enhance their performance, often measured by ambulance response times (RT). Evidence from numerous studies showed a strong relationship between RT and patient survival. Byrne et al. [1] observed that US counties with an RT of 12 min or more had a mortality rate of 11.9 per 100,000 population/year, compared to 4.9 in counties with an RT of 7 min or less. The success of resuscitation and survivability are severely impacted by extended RT, according to studies on cardiac arrest patients in Germany, when the RT increases by one minute, the probability of survival drops by 5% [2]. Another study in Sweden examined RT's effect on 30-day survivability after cardiac arrest [3]. According to the results, survival rates drop as response times rise, from 19.5% when RT is less than 6 min to 9.4% when RT is 10 min or greater. Therefore, RT is the most frequently used metric to assess emergency medical services (EMS) performance [4–6]. In this regard, many countries have defined target RT for EMS. For instance, the RT threshold value in the US is 10 min in urban areas and 30 min in rural areas [7]. In the UK, 95% of critical requests should be served within 14 min in urban areas and 19 min in rural areas [8]. In Portugal, the threshold values are 15 and 30 min in urban and rural areas, respectively [8]. 90% of most urgent calls in Norway should be served within 12 min [9].

RT is often expressed in coverage rate, the percentage of emergency transport requests served within an RT below a defined threshold. Therefore, EMS actions are only concerned with efficiently locating ambulances to maximize the coverage rate. However, maximizing ambulance coverage is a global indicator, and the obtained performances can vary significantly from one geographic region to another within the same served territory. Indeed, maximizing the overall coverage results in coverage disparities, where more densely populated regions benefit from higher coverage at the expense of less populated areas [10]. Efficient solutions can be unacceptable to the community since they favor densely populated regions over others [11]. The trade-off between efficiency and equity is challenging for EMS because efficient solutions introduce inequalities [12]. Therefore, it is essential for public services, mainly EMS services, to consider fairness in distributing resources, as equity is a crucial indicator for assessing the performance of public services [13]. Furthermore, equity in public services is one of the sustainable development goals adopted by the United Nations (i.e., Goal 10: Reduce inequality within and among countries) [14].

Researchers resort to operational research techniques to locate ambulance stations and deploy and redeploy ambulances [15]. Mathematical programming models maximizing ambulance coverage have seen increased development over the past fifty years. Initially, deterministic single-coverage models were developed, followed by deterministic multiple-coverage models, probabilistic models, and subsequently, multi-period redeployment and dynamic redeployment models [5]. The objective has been to suggest analytical models that approximate the real system being modeled. The achievements in terms of improving coverage are undeniable. However, the models more they attempt to account for the various constraints and dependencies in the EMS system, the more complex and untraceable they become, which results in models with simplifying assumptions. Researchers turn to descriptive techniques such as simulation to overcome the limitations of analytical models. It allows for modeling the system under scrutiny by closely mimicking its operation as faithfully as possible [16]. Once verified and validated, the simulation model enables measuring the system's performance [17]. However, simulation alone does not optimize the system's configuration since it does not generate optimal solutions. For this reason, it is preferable to use simulation–optimization (SO), which integrates optimization techniques with simulation to leverage the advantages of both approaches. The SO generates a solution for the system, measures its performance using the simulation model, and, based on the results, proposes another solution to improve the system's performance, continuing until a certain number of iterations are reached [18].

This chapter aims to improve not only the EMS efficiency but also the equity in distributing EMS resources (i.e., ambulances) through a multi-objective optimization approach: maximizing coverage and minimizing coverage disparities among regions. The SO method is used to propose ambulance location solutions that improve coverage and reduce coverage disparities. This study employs *OptQuest*, an SO engine developed by OptTek. *OptQuest* is a commercial optimization software integrated as a module into several simulation software. It combines various simulation–optimization approaches, such as neural networks, evolutionary algorithms, Tabu search, and scatter search methods. Combining all these metaheuristic methods in a single software results in a powerful and user-friendly tool [19]. *OptQuest* is widely applied in the fields of logistics and supply chain [20] as well as in the healthcare sector [5, 18, 19, 21].

The study area covers the Fes-Meknes region of Morocco, composed of nine provinces. The selection of the study area is justified by the disparities in healthcare access between its various provinces (see Sect. 3). The remainder of this chapter is structured into six distinct sections. Section 2 offers a background to the study, providing context and relevance. Section 3 delves into the disparities in healthcare access in Morocco, shedding light on the pertinent issues. In Sect. 4, the methodology employed in this study is comprehensively detailed. The research findings are presented in Sect. 5. Section 6 conducts a comprehensive discussion, interpreting and analyzing the results. Section 7 encompasses the conclusion, summarizes the key findings and insights, and presents potential avenues for future research.

2 Background

The equity of public services is a crucial issue that impacts all facets of individuals' lives within societies. Nevertheless, there is no universally agreed-upon definition of equity; instead, the concept of equity often varies depending on its application within different domains [10]. In healthcare, from the patient perspective, equity is a way of assessing the fairness of resource allocation to patients. McLay and Mayorga [12] stated that resource distribution should be balanced among individuals to establish equity. Marsh and Schilling [22] asserted that equity is achieved "*when each group receives its fair share of the effect of the facility siting decision.*" For Grot et al. [23], an EMS system is equitable if it covers every part of the territory equally, guaranteeing that any patient, no matter where they are in the territory, has the same probability of receiving an ambulance within the RT threshold. More definitions and discussions of equity in the healthcare context can be found in [24].

Despite the widespread demand from citizens and government commitments to ensure equitable access to healthcare, including ambulance services, it is noteworthy that this topic is seldom addressed within operations research. Indeed, developing decision-support tools to enhance equity in ambulance services has garnered limited interest from the scientific community [25]. Most work on ambulance location problems has focused on improving ambulance coverage with little consideration given to equity in the distribution of coverage between geographical areas and populations [26]. Akdogan et al. [25] studied and compared the performance of several mathematical programming models concerning the equity of ambulance services, measured by mean waiting time and the Gini coefficient. The authors conclude that the models developed in the literature primarily aim to maximize overall performance and significantly overlook equity among demand zones.

One of the classical location models that consider equity in facility location, not necessarily ambulances, is the *p*-center problem [27]. It aims to position *p* facilities to minimize the maximum distance between a demand area and its closest facility. However, the *p*-center problem focuses on the least-served patient. It does not consider the quantity of demand in each demand zone or the coverage optimization. Chanta et al. [28] proposed the Minimum *p*-Envy Location Problem, which aims to locate ambulances to increase equity in ambulance service. The authors defined envy as the difference in patients' dissatisfaction between demand zones. Their model considered that an ambulance could not answer a call by embedding the hypercube queueing model. The findings demonstrate that, compared to other equity models, the suggested model produces the lowest total weighted envy and efficient solutions in terms of coverage. Jagtenberg and Mason [26] proposed sharing ambulance service time to improve EMS system fairness. The authors employed a nonlinear optimization model that maximizes the Bernoulli–Nash social welfare function. McLay and Mayorga [12] have dealt with equity by concentrating on ambulance dispatching to prioritized patients. They formulated an equity-constrained Markov Decision Process to dispatch ambulances to maximize efficiency. Aringhieri et al. [29] considered the issue of equity in ambulance tours in post-disaster situations. The problem was modeled as a variant of the Team Orienteering Problem and solved by a new hybrid algorithm based on machine learning and neighborhood search. Luo et al. [30] formulated a multi-optimization model to locate EMS stations in order to reduce inequalities in accessibility and coverage between rural and urban populations. The authors employed the ϵ-constrained method to find the Pareto-optimal solutions. Li et al. [31] proposed two models to optimize EMS station locations and capacities for equal accessibility. The first model aims to minimize the standard deviation of EMS accessibility, while the second model seeks to minimize the weighted average EMS response time and the number of unserved demands within the maximum mandatory RT. Grot et al. [23] considered the EMS efficiency and fairness in a location-allocation model. They have used the ϵ-constrained method to simultaneously consider both objectives, and have employed the Gini coefficient and Rawlsian criterion to measure the EMS fairness.

The previously mentioned works focused on examining equity from the perspective of patients. Other studies have explored equity from the EMS staff's viewpoint, particularly concerning workload distribution. In this context, Pirkul and Schilling [32] revealed that EMS stations in densely populated areas experience heavier workloads than those in less densely populated areas. The authors developed the Capacitated Maximal Covering Location Problem (CMCLP) to address the inequity in workload distribution. The CMCLP model establishes a maximum workload capacity for each EMS station. Xu et al. [33], recognizing that workload imbalance can lead to dissatisfaction among workers, investigated the fairness of workload distribution among EMS workers. In their study, the authors formulated five workload balancing models based on five distinct workload balance measures: total pairwise absolute difference, total mean absolute deviation, maximum mean absolute deviation, range, and maximum workload. Li and Saydam [34] proposed an ambulance dispatching policy to balance the EMS crew workload. Their approach consists of dispatching the nearest ambulance only for high-priority patients and the least utilized ambulance for medium and low-priority patients. The results showed improved workload balance with no adverse effect on survival rate. Enayati et al. [35] introduced a real-time approach for ambulance redeployment aimed at maximizing coverage for emergency call requests while considering the workload of EMS providers. Their method involved redeploying idle ambulances based on the workload restrictions of EMS providers. The results demonstrated that this approach significantly improves coverage while limiting the workload. Essus et al. [36] proposed a real-time ambulance relocation and dispatching optimization framework to maximize the survivability of patients experiencing life-threatening emergencies while ensuring a balanced workload among EMS providers. Their approach integrated an optimization model into a discrete-event simulation model. The findings indicate that this approach enhances patients' survivability and achieves workload balance by taking into account real-time information about the EMS system's state provided by the simulation model.

Within the existing literature, various measures of service equity are documented, including variance, mean absolute deviation, the sum of absolute deviations, range, Gini coefficient, etc. [10, 22]. For instance, Li et al. [31] measured equity in ambulance allocation using the Theil index and the Gini coefficient. The results, which were closely aligned, indicated severe inequities in ambulance allocation. McLay and Mayorga [12] and Sreekanth and Roy [37] used four measures of equity, two from the patients' perspective and two from the providers' perspective. Equity measure 1 refers to the percentage of patients served by ambulances from the patient's base location or district. Equity measure 2 is the percentage of patients who survived with the help of EMS. The equity measure 3 relates to the distribution of workload among the ambulances. The last equity measure maintains a balance in the ambulances' service of high priority patients. Xu et al. [33] have employed five equity measures among EMS workers: total pair-wise absolute difference, total mean absolute deviation, maximum mean absolute deviation, range, and maximum workload.

3 Disparities in Healthcare Access in Morocco

The distribution of healthcare provision in Morocco is characterized by striking spatial disparities between regions, prefectures, and provinces, as well as between urban and rural areas [38]. Healthcare access proves to be highly challenging for a significant proportion of the population. Studies have shown that physical access to healthcare remains a major concern for the Moroccan population [39, 40]. At the national level, 21.2% of households are required to spend more than an hour to reach the nearest healthcare facility. This rate is 41.4% in rural areas compared to 11.1% in urban areas [41].

The imbalanced distribution of healthcare provision leads to significant inequalities in life expectancy, maternal mortality rates, and child mortality rates by area of residence. Indeed, the urban population can expect to live five years longer than those in rural areas; the infant mortality rate is 47% higher in rural areas (21.6‰) than in urban areas (14.7‰), and the maternal mortality rate is two and a half times higher in rural areas (111.1 per 100,000 live births) than in urban areas (44.6 per 100,000 live births) [42, 43].

The relationship between transportation and healthcare accessibility is well-documented in the literature [44, 45]. Transportation plays a significant role in healthcare accessibility [38, 45, 46]. Indeed, an efficient transportation system facilitates access to healthcare, while an inadequate or inefficient transportation system could pose an obstacle [47]. Therefore, promoting healthcare accessibility depends on a transportation system that effectively fulfills its missions. The lack of transportation represents 46.2% of the reasons women do not access maternal care services [48]. Thus, it is among the primary factors contributing to maternal mortality [49].

The transportation system is characterized by an imbalanced distribution of resources, particularly in the number of ambulance stations and ambulances per province [45, 50]. This results in inequity in the provision of ambulance services. Hence, this chapter focuses on reducing inequalities in ambulance services by addressing the geographic distribution of ambulances.

4 Methods

This chapter aims to mitigate disparities in ambulance coverage within the Fez-Meknes region in Morocco. We employ discrete-event simulation (DES) to model the EMS system in the Fes-Meknes region. DES is one of the operational research tools that enables accurate modeling of the studied system [51]. It has been extensively applied to study various issues in the healthcare sector and has proven to be an effective tool for analyzing such systems [16, 52]. Afterward, a set of SO models is developed to improve coverage and reduce inequity in the coverage distribution between the provinces in the region under consideration.

4.1 Conceptual Simulation Model

Emergency out-of-hospital transport services in Morocco are provided by the Civil Protection (CP) Services [45]. These services are responsible for transporting individuals in need, including casualties from public road incidents such as road accidents, as well as patients from their residences or incident locations during emergencies such as intoxication or fires [6, 53]. To gain a comprehensive understanding of how this system operates, we conducted interviews with the management team of the CP in the Fez-Meknes region, Morocco. The insights obtained from these interviews revealed the following key operational details:

- The CP services have established an emergency call reception center where callers are required to specify the incident's location, the number of injured individuals, and their conditions. Upon receiving this information, the center dispatches ambulances from the closest ambulance station.
- Patient pick-up is executed by the nearest available CP team to respond to the request.
- The ambulance transports the patient to the nearest public hospital within their territorial jurisdiction, corresponding to the prefecture or province. However, when the patient's condition at the incident site indicates that the nearest hospital lacks the required specialization to address the case, the CP services initiate the evacuation of the patient to the closest and most suitable hospital, even if it is located outside their usual territorial jurisdiction.
- After completing their service, ambulances return to their original station.

The simulation conceptual model of Fig. 1 is constructed in light of the details mentioned above and the work of [5, 54].

4.2 Simulation–Optimization Models

This chapter aims to locate ambulances in a way that maximizes the overall coverage (efficiency) and minimizes coverage inequalities between regions. It is a

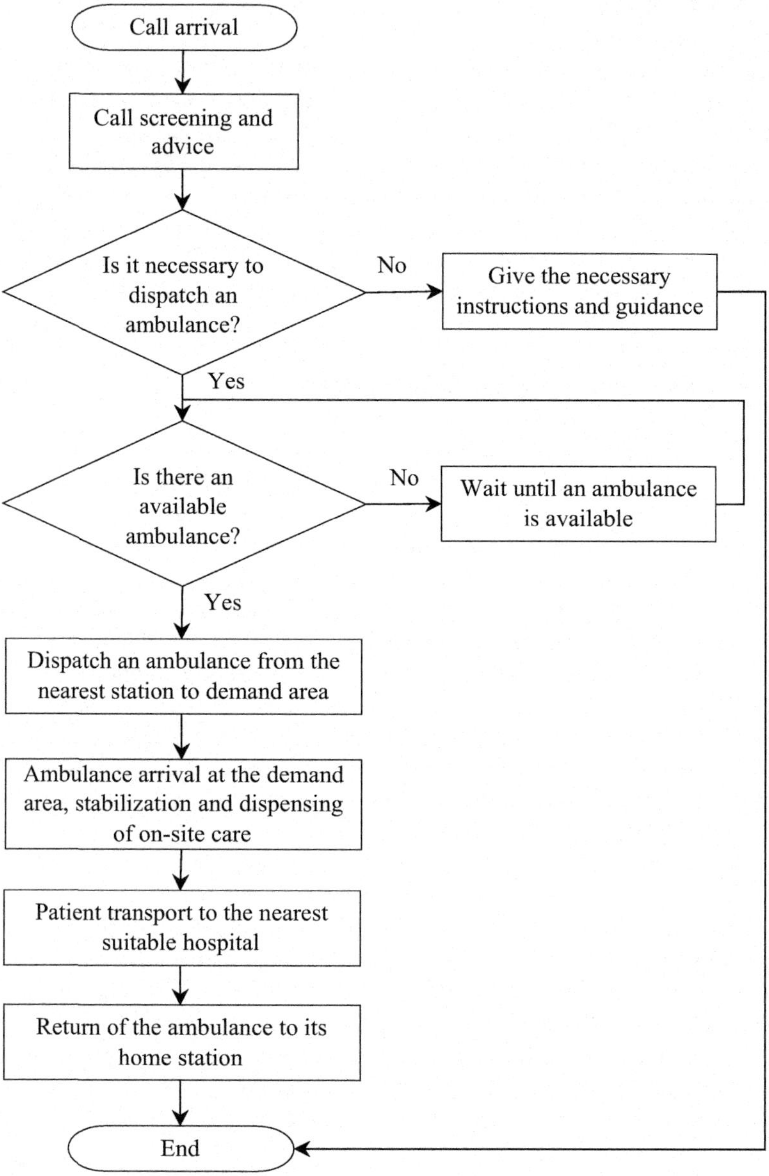

Fig. 1 Simulation conceptual model

multi-objective optimization problem. To formulate this problem, we have opted for the weighted sum method and the ϵ-constraint method. The first method involves formulating an objective function that incorporates both objectives by assigning a weight to each objective. Meanwhile, the second method keeps a single objective in the objective function and constrains the second objective to a specific value [30].

The following notation is used to formulate SO models:

I	The set of provinces
i	Index of provinces
T	The set of periods
t	Index of periods
CR	Overall coverage rate
CR_i	Coverage rate in province $i \in I$
x_{it}	Decision variable representing the number of ambulances in province $i \in I$, in period $t \in T$
P	Total number of ambulances
P_t	Number of ambulances available in period $t \in T$
α_1	Weighting coefficients for coverage maximization objective
α_2	Weighting coefficients for coverage disparities minimization objective
ε	Accepted tolerance of coverage inequity.

In the following, we formulate ten SO models. The first two models are efficiency models, maximizing coverage without considering equity in the modeling. The remaining models are equity models considering both coverage and equity.

4.2.1 Efficiency SO Models

Efficiency SO Model 1

$$\max f(X, \omega) = E[CR(X, \omega)] \tag{1}$$

$$S.t \quad \sum_{i \in I} x_{it} \leq P_t \quad \forall t \in T \tag{2}$$

The objective function (1) maximizes the average overall coverage. Where X is the vector of decision variables x_{it}, and ω is the randomness of the DES model. The expression E[$CR(X, \omega)$] represents the average overall coverage. The objective function (1) does not consider regional coverage in each province. Constraint (2) restricts the number of ambulances in each province not to exceed the total available number of ambulances available in period $t \in T$. This constraint also applies to all the subsequent models.

Efficiency SO Model 2

$$\max f(X, \omega) = \sum_{i \in I} E[CR_i(X, \omega)] \tag{3}$$

The objective function (3) maximizes coverage across all provinces. The Efficiency SO Model 2 reduces disparities in coverage, given that the objective function comprises coverage rates from all provinces, thereby not favoring one province over another.

4.2.2 Equity SO Models

In this section, Efficiency SO Models 1 and 2 are adapted to seek a balance between efficiency and equity in coverage across provinces. Integrating both objectives, maximizing coverage and minimizing coverage disparities, within the same SO model could be achieved through two different approaches: the weighted sum method and the ϵ-constrained method [55]. In the following, eight models are presented; the first four (Equity SO Models 1, 2, 3, and 4) describe the first method, while the last four (Equity SO Models 5, 6, 7, and 8) illustrate the second method.

Equity SO Model 1

$$\max f(X,\omega) = \alpha_1 E[CR(X,\omega)] - \alpha_2 \sum_{i \in I} |E[CR(X,\omega)] - E[CR_i(X,\omega)]| \quad (4)$$

The objective function (4) consists of two terms: the first term is the maximization of the average overall coverage, while the second is the minimization of the mean absolute deviation. In facility location, the mean absolute deviation indicates the coverage rate that exceeds what would let each province have equitable access to ambulances [22]. The mean absolute deviation measures the difference between the overall coverage and the coverage of each province. The two terms of (4) are weighted using the coefficients α_1 and α_2.

Equity SO Model 2

$$max f(X,\omega) = \alpha_1 E[CR(X,\omega)] - \alpha_2 \sum_{i \in I} \sum_{j \in I} \left| E[CR_i(X,\omega)] - E\left[CR_j(X,\omega)\right] \right| \quad (5)$$

The objective function (5) contains two terms: the first maximizes the average overall coverage, and the second represents a penalty for coverage disparities between provinces. Ideally, the second term would equal zero, indicating uniform coverage across all provinces.

Equity SO Model 3

$$\max f(X,\omega) = \alpha_1 \sum_{i \in I} E[CR_i(X,\omega)] - \alpha_2 \sum_{i \in I} |E[CR(X,\omega)] - E[CR_i(X,\omega)]| \quad (6)$$

Equity SO Model 4

$$\max f(X,\omega) = \alpha_1 \sum_{i\in I} E[CR_i(X,\omega)] - \alpha_2 \sum_{i\in I}\sum_{j\in I} \left| E[CR_i(X,\omega)] - E\left[CR_j(X,\omega)\right] \right| \tag{7}$$

Objective functions (6) and (7) are similar to (4) and (5), respectively, apart from the first term, which maximizes coverage in each province rather than average overall coverage.

Equity SO Model 5

$$\max f(X,\omega) = E[CR(X,\omega)] \tag{8}$$

$$S.t \quad |E[CR(X,\omega)] - E[CR_i(X,\omega)]| \leq \epsilon \quad \forall i \in I \tag{9}$$

The objective function (8) maximizes overall coverage. Constraint (9) ensures that the absolute difference between overall coverage and the coverage in each province does not exceed a limit value ϵ.

Equity SO Model 6

$$\max f(X,\omega) = E[CR(X,\omega)] \tag{10}$$

$$S.t \quad \left| E[CR_i(X,\omega)] - E\left[CR_j(X,\omega)\right] \right| \leq \epsilon \quad \forall i,j \in I \tag{11}$$

The objective function (10) is the same as (8). Constraint (11) requires the absolute difference between coverage rates in the provinces to be less than ϵ.

Equity SO Model 7

$$\max f(X,\omega) = \sum_{i\in I} E[CR_i(X,\omega)] \tag{12}$$

$$S.t \quad |E[CR(X,\omega)] - E[CR_i(X,\omega)]| \leq \epsilon \quad \forall i \in I \tag{13}$$

The objective function (12) maximizes coverage in each province. Constraint (13) is the same as (9), restricting the absolute difference between global coverage and coverage in each province.

Equity SO Model 8

$$\max f(X,\omega) = \sum_{i\in I} E[CR_i(X,\omega)] \tag{14}$$

$$S.t \quad \left| E[CR_i(X,\omega)] - E\left[CR_j(X,\omega)\right] \right| \leq \epsilon \quad \forall i,j \in I \tag{15}$$

The objective function (14) is the same as (12). Constraint (15) is the same as (11), restricting the absolute variation in coverage between provinces.

4.3 Software

The conceptual model of Fig. 1 was built using Rockwell Automation Arena 14.0 simulation software. This tool is widely used in industry and scientific research applied to healthcare [56]. Furthermore, according to a comparison of 19 simulation software packages by Dias et al. [57], Arena is the most popular tool due to its qualities, notably its comfortable development environment and flexibility.

We used OptQuest for Arena to generate optimal or near-optimal solutions to efficiency SO models 1 and 2, and equity SO models 1 to 8. The obtained solutions are then simulated using the simulation model of Fig. 1 to measure the coverage. OptQuest is oriented towards optimizing a simulation model, i.e., a simulation model is developed for a given system, and then OptQuest is used to optimize the system's control parameters. It operates as follows: OptQuest loads its data from the Arena simulation model when launched. It then modifies the values of control variables (decision variables) and resource capacities (constraints) according to the parameters set by the user. It calls Arena to run the first replication (the number of replications is specified by the user). After each replication, OptQuest retrieves the evaluation of the proposed solution (value of the objective function) from the simulation model. Based on this evaluation, OptQuest is guided to generate new solutions. This sequence is repeated until the number of simulations is reached [58].

In this study, 1000 iterations are used for SO models. The last solution obtained is retained after this number of iterations. The performance of each solution in terms of coverage and equity is assessed using the simulation model, which was run for a 3-month simulation duration with a warm-up period of 2 days and a number of replications of 100.

4.4 Equity Measures

In this chapter, we used the Gini coefficient (GC), also known as the Gini index, to assess the inequity in ambulance coverage among provinces. The GC is the most well-known summary measure of inequity in the literature on economic and social welfare [22]. It is simple and widely employed [25, 26]. The GC computation expression is given in (16), where N is the number of provinces, and $\overline{CR}$ is the arithmetic mean coverage rate. A GC of zero indicates a perfect equity, while a GC of one reflects total inequity.

$$GC = \frac{1}{2 \times \overline{CR} \times N^2} \sum_{i \in I}^{N} \sum_{j \in I}^{N} \left| CR_i - CR_j \right| \tag{16}$$

Table 1 Scenarios of efficiency SO models

Models	Scenario	$P_{t=1}$	$P_{t=2}$
Efficiency SO Model 1	Eff1_Sc1	200	250
	Eff1_Sc2	300	350
Efficiency SO Model 2	Eff2_Sc1	200	250
	Eff2_Sc2	300	350

4.5 Scenarios

To evaluate the ten models developed within this study, several scenarios were tested by varying the number of ambulances to be deployed, the values of the weighting coefficients α_1 and α_2, and the value of accepted tolerance of coverage inequity ϵ.

The retained scenarios for efficiency SO models 1 and 2 are presented in Table 1. We varied the number of ambulances in each period. For the first scenario, we considered 200 ambulances for the first period t = 1 and 250 for the second period t = 2. As for the other scenario, we considered using 300 ambulances in the first period and 350 in the second period.

We tested ten scenarios per model for equity SO models using the weighted sum method, as shown in Table 2. These scenarios use different ambulance fleet sizes and different values for the weights α_1 and α_2 ranging from 0.5 to 0.9.

As for equity SO models employing the ϵ-constraint method, we evaluated eight scenarios per model, as illustrated in Table 3. We used four different ϵ values: 0.15, 0.2, 0.25, and 0.3, all for different ambulance numbers.

4.6 Data Collection

We used open-access data from [5, 54, 59] to assess the SO models. These include data on emergency transport in the provinces of the Fez-Meknes region, such as ambulance base locations, demand zones, demand value, ambulance travel time, etc

5 Results

All solutions from the SO models were assessed based on coverage and equity. Figure 2 presents the performance of efficiency SO models 1 and 2. The two evaluated scenarios exhibit considerable similarity, implying that adding ambulances has no significant impact. Instead, it might be more effective to consider increasing the number of ambulance bases.

Simulation of all scenarios of the equity SO models 1 to 4 yielded the results shown in Fig. 3. We note that equity SO model 3 gives better results in terms of coverage and equity for all scenarios. The equity SO model 2, on the other

Table 2 Scenarios of equity SO models—weighted sum method

Models	Scenario	α_1	α_2	$P_{t=1}$	$P_{t=2}$
Equity SO model 1	Eq1_Sc1	0.5	0.5	200	250
	Eq1_Sc2	0.6	0.4		
	Eq1_Sc3	0.7	0.3		
	Eq1_Sc4	0.8	0.2		
	Eq1_Sc5	0.9	0.1		
	Eq1_Sc6	0.5	0.5	300	350
	Eq1_Sc7	0.6	0.4		
	Eq1_Sc8	0.7	0.3		
	Eq1_Sc9	0.8	0.2		
	Eq1_Sc10	0.9	0.1		
Equity SO model 2	Eq2_Sc1	0.5	0.5	200	250
	Eq2_Sc2	0.6	0.4		
	Eq2_Sc3	0.7	0.3		
	Eq2_Sc4	0.8	0.2		
	Eq2_Sc5	0.9	0.1		
	Eq2_Sc6	0.5	0.5	300	350
	Eq2_Sc7	0.6	0.4		
	Eq2_Sc8	0.7	0.3		
	Eq2_Sc9	0.8	0.2		
	Eq2_Sc10	0.9	0.1		
Equity SO model 3	Eq3_Sc1	0.5	0.5	200	250
	Eq3_Sc2	0.6	0.4		
	Eq3_Sc3	0.7	0.3		
	Eq3_Sc4	0.8	0.2		
	Eq3_Sc5	0.9	0.1		
	Eq3_Sc6	0.5	0.5	300	350
	Eq3_Sc7	0.6	0.4		
	Eq3_Sc8	0.7	0.3		
	Eq3_Sc9	0.8	0.2		
	Eq3_Sc10	0.9	0.1		
Equity SO model 4	Eq4_Sc1	0.5	0.5	200	250
	Eq4_Sc2	0.6	0.4		
	Eq4_Sc3	0.7	0.3		
	Eq4_Sc4	0.8	0.2		
	Eq4_Sc5	0.9	0.1		
	Eq4_Sc6	0.5	0.5	300	350

(continued)

Table 2 (continued)

Models	Scenario	α_1	α_2	$P_{t=1}$	$P_{t=2}$
	Eq4_Sc7	0.6	0.4		
	Eq4_Sc8	0.7	0.3		
	Eq4_Sc9	0.8	0.2		
	Eq4_Sc10	0.9	0.1		

hand, can be considered the worst performer, particularly in terms of coverage, which does not exceed 10% for all scenarios. As for equity SO models 1 and 4, the best results in terms of coverage and equity are obtained when the weight assigned to the first term of the objective function (α_1) is greater and the number of ambulances is higher.

Results of simulating solutions of equity SO models 5 to 8 are presented in Fig. 4 for all scenarios. We note that the performance of these models is relatively poor in terms of coverage and equity compared to equity SO models 1–4. When the value of ϵ is small, the results are even worse. A slight improvement is observed as the value of ϵ increases.

6 Discussion

Equity in healthcare concerns two main aspects: patient equity, ensuring equitable access to care, and healthcare personnel equity, ensuring equitable workload distribution. In this study, our focus was on patient equity, specifically regarding access to Emergency Medical Services (EMS). The performance of EMS is often measured by coverage rate, which is the percentage of requests served within a specific response time limit. Response time is the interval between receiving a call to attend to a patient and the ambulance's arrival at the patient's location.

Consequently, scientific literature has expanded with works aiming to maximize overall coverage in a given territory through mathematical modeling, simulation, and queueing theory, among other methodologies. However, little attention has been paid to equity in the distribution of overall coverage [11]. In the literature, equity is measured by several indicators, such as variance, mean absolute deviation, sum of absolute deviations, range, Gini coefficient, etc. [10, 22]. For an indicator to be accepted, it should be defined by all health system stakeholders [24, 60]. In this study, we have retained the Gini coefficient (GC) to assess equity in coverage distribution.

A fundamental point emerging in discussions of public service equity is efficiency [13]. When addressing disparities in access to healthcare services, efficiency becomes a concern [26]. Equity implies resource distribution so everyone has equal access with the same degree of ease, but this pursuit of equity does not necessarily ensure greater efficiency. In this chapter, we investigated equity in coverage. Efficiency is represented by the objective of maximizing the overall coverage,

Table 3 Scenarios of equity SO models, ϵ-constraint method

Models	Scenario	ϵ	$P_{t=1}$	$P_{t=2}$
Equity SO model 5	Eq5_Sc1	0.15	200	250
	Eq5_Sc2	0.2		
	Eq5_Sc3	0.25		
	Eq5_Sc4	0.3		
	Eq5_Sc5	0.15	300	350
	Eq5_Sc6	0.2		
	Eq5_Sc7	0.25		
	Eq5_Sc8	0.3		
Equity SO model 6	Eq6_Sc1	0.15	200	250
	Eq6_Sc2	0.2		
	Eq6_Sc3	0.25		
	Eq6_Sc4	0.3		
	Eq6_Sc5	0.15	300	350
	Eq6_Sc6	0.2		
	Eq6_Sc7	0.25		
	Eq6_Sc8	0.3		
Equity SO model 7	Eq7_Sc1	0.15	200	250
	Eq7_Sc2	0.2		
	Eq7_Sc3	0.25		
	Eq7_Sc4	0.3		
	Eq7_Sc5	0.15	300	350
	Eq7_Sc6	0.2		
	Eq7_Sc7	0.25		
	Eq7_Sc8	0.3		
Equity SO model 8	Eq8_Sc1	0.15	200	250
	Eq8_Sc2	0.2		
	Eq8_Sc3	0.25		
	Eq8_Sc4	0.3		
	Eq8_Sc5	0.15	300	350
	Eq8_Sc6	0.2		
	Eq8_Sc7	0.25		
	Eq8_Sc8	0.3		

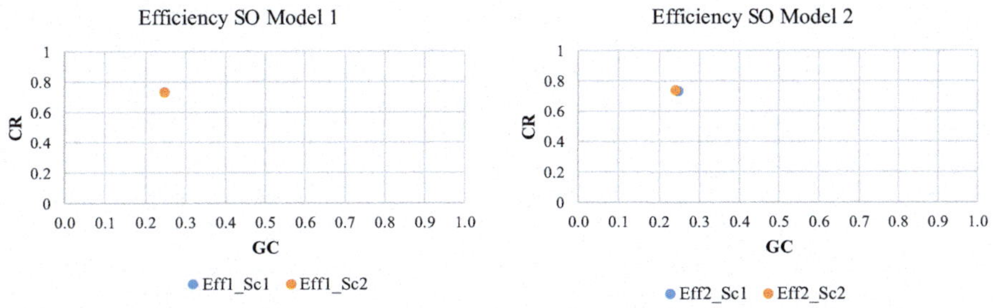

Fig. 2 CR and GC of scenarios of Efficiency SO models 1 and 2

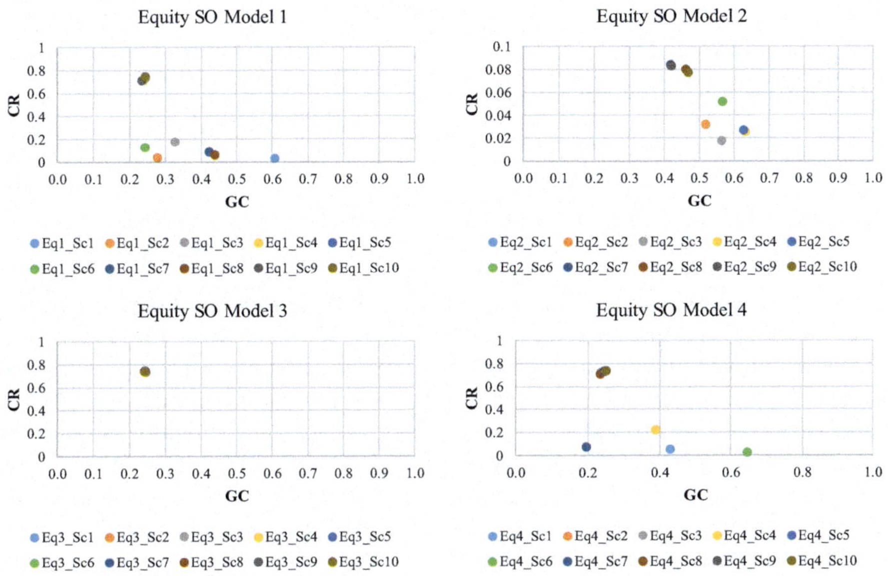

Fig. 3 CR and GC of scenarios of Equity SO models using the weighted sum method

while equity is represented by minimizing coverage disparities between provinces within the study territory. We established a discrete-event simulation model capturing the operations of the EMS services in the Fez-Meknes region, Morocco. Subsequently, we proposed a series of 10 Simulation–Optimization (SO) models. The first two SO models aimed solely at maximizing overall coverage without considering equity. Conversely, the remaining eight models combined coverage maximization with reducing coverage disparities between provinces within the study territory. This pertains to a multi-objective optimization, given that our research problem encompasses two distinct objectives: the first is the maximization of coverage across all provinces, while the second entails the maximization of equity in coverage by minimizing disparities among provinces.

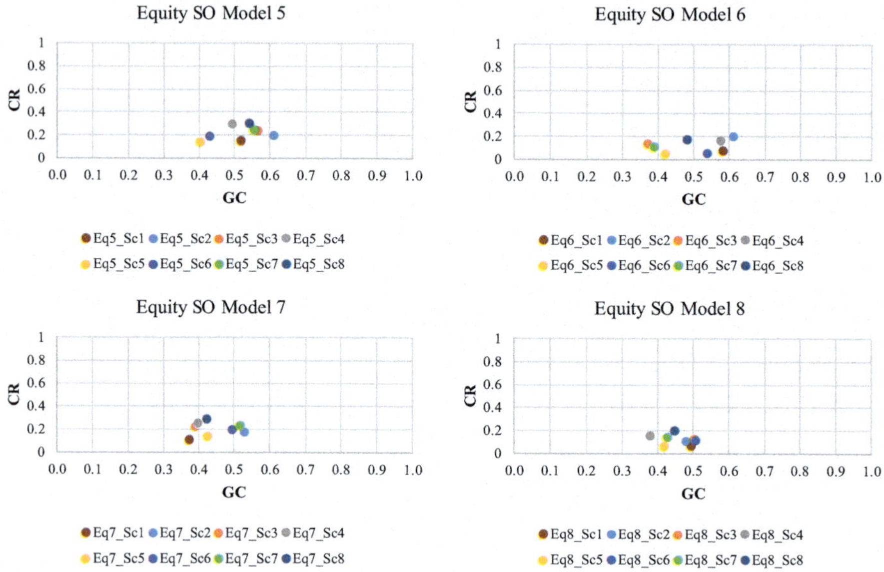

Fig. 4 CR and GC of scenarios of Equity SO models using the ϵ-constraint method

To solve the SO models, we utilized the *OptQuest* tool, considering two distinct methods. The first method is the weighted sum method. It formulates both objectives of maximizing coverage and minimizing coverage disparities within the same objective function. It assigns a weight to each term of the objective function [30]. However, this method has shortcomings, notably the difficulty in choosing weights for the terms of the objective function. There is no consensus in the literature regarding the values of weights for each objective. For this reason, we employed multiple scenarios, varying the weights. The second method is the ϵ-constraint method. It retains one objective in the model's objective function and places the second objective as a constraint [30].

The simulation model evaluated the solutions of the SO models in terms of coverage and equity. The results demonstrated that the SO models designed using the weighted sum method outperformed those developed using the ϵ-constraint method. Specifically, the results in Fig. 3, pertaining to the models of the weighted sum method, showed relatively high coverage rates (*CR*) and small values of *GC*, indicating less disparity in coverage distribution. In contrast, the results in Fig. 4, regarding the models of the ϵ-constraint method, displayed moderate values of coverage and equity. For the weighted sum SO models, it was observed that when the equity objective is given high weights, it leads to unexpected location decisions. SO models, in seeking to reduce coverage disparities, locate ambulances in bases that make coverage low. This finding was highlighted by Chanta et al. [28] and McLay and Mayorga [12].

A surprising result of this study is that the efficiency SO models 1 and 2 provided satisfactory equity levels, sometimes much better than those obtained by SO equity models (Fig. 2).

In this study, it was noted that the addition of ambulances has not significantly contributed to increasing coverage or reducing inequities. This is because the initial number of ambulances is already large enough, and all ambulance bases are saturated. On the other hand, we propose to increase the number of ambulance bases so that the increase in the ambulances would have a significant effect. This has been confirmed in previous studies [6, 61].

7 Conclusion

In this chapter, we have attempted to address the issue of equity in EMS ambulance coverage, as much of the literature has focused on maximizing overall coverage (efficiency) without paying sufficient attention to the distribution of this coverage across the entire territory (equity). To this end, we have formulated several multi-objective SO models to investigate the efficiency and equity of EMS coverage. The results have shown that efficiency and equity are two conflicting objectives. When seeking to improve one objective, it is done at the expense of the other. Furthermore, the results have also shown that models formulated using the weighted sum method are more effective than those developed using the ϵ-constraint method.

We conclude from this study that increasing the number of ambulances is not enough to improve efficiency and equity. It is essential to expand the number of ambulance bases to improve coverage and ensure equity in the distribution of resources.

This study has some limitations, which we summarize in the following points:

- The measure of equity only considered differences in coverage between the provinces in the studied territory. However, disparities in access to EMS services may exist between individuals within the same province. For this reason, it is recommended that future work focus on measuring equity between individuals and not just between geographical areas.
- Equity has been measured by the Gini coefficient alone, which is a well-known indicator for measuring equity in wealth distribution. It would be useful to compare the Gini coefficient with other indicators, whether already developed in the literature or proposed exceptionally for EMS services.
- The SO models were solved using *OptQuest*, a powerful optimization simulation engine. However, *OptQuest* requires several simulation iterations to approach the optimal solution, which is time-consuming. The number of iterations used in this chapter is likely not sufficient. We recommend trying out other faster and more efficient optimization simulation tools.

References

1. Byrne JP, Mann NC, Dai M, Mason SA, Karanicolas P, Rizoli S, Nathens AB (2019) Association between emergency medical service response time and motor vehicle crash mortality in the United States. JAMA Surg 154(4):286–293. https://doi.org/10.1001/jamasurg.2018.5097
2. Bürger A, Wnent J, Bohn A, Jantzen T, Brenner S, Lefering R, Seewald S, Gräsner JT, Fischer M (2018) The effect of ambulance response time on survival following out-of-hospital cardiac arrest: an analysis from the German resuscitation registry. Deutsches Arzteblatt Int 115(33–34):541–548. https://doi.org/10.3238/arztebl.2018.0541
3. Holmén J, Herlitz J, Ricksten SE, Strömsöe A, Hagberg E, Axelsson C, Rawshani A (2020) Shortening ambulance response time increases survival in out-of-hospital cardiac arrest. J Am Heart Association 9(21). https://doi.org/10.1161/JAHA.120.017048
4. Boujemaa R, Jebali A, Hammami S, Ruiz A (2020) Multi-period stochastic programming models for two-tiered emergency medical service system. Comput Oper Res 123:104974. https://doi.org/10.1016/j.cor.2020.104974
5. Frichi Y, Jawab F, Aboueljinane L, Zerka A, Benkacem A (2022) Assessing and improving ambulance coverage in the prefecture of Fez using discrete-event simulation. In: 14th international colloquium of logistics and supply chain management (LOGISTIQUA), pp 1–6. https://doi.org/10.1109/LOGISTIQUA55056.2022.9938091
6. Zerka A, Jawab F, Frichi Y (2022) Mapping's process of the trajectory of pre-hospital transport by basic ambulance for road accidents' victims in TDABC. In: 2022 IEEE 14th international conference of logistics and supply chain management, LOGISTIQUA , pp 25–27. https://doi.org/10.1109/LOGISTIQUA55056.2022.9938108
7. Takeda RA, Widmer JA, Morabito R (2007) Analysis of ambulance decentralization in an urban emergency medical service using the hypercube queueing model. Comput Oper Res 34(3):727–741. https://doi.org/10.1016/j.cor.2005.03.022
8. Nelas J, Dias J (2021) Locating emergency vehicles: Modelling the substitutability of resources and the impact of delays in the arrival of assistance. Operations Res Perspectives 8. https://doi.org/10.1016/j.orp.2021.100202
9. Andersson H, Granberg TA, Christiansen M, Aartun ES, Leknes H (2020) Using optimization to provide decision support for strategic emergency medical service planning—Three case studies. Int J Med Inf 133(March 2019):103975. https://doi.org/10.1016/j.ijmedinf.2019.103975
10. Shehadeh KS, Snyder LV (2023) Equity in stochastic healthcare facility location. In: Eiselt HA, Marianov V (eds) Uncertainty in facility location problems. International series in operations research & management science. Springer, Cham. https://doi.org/10.1007/978-3-031-32338-6_12
11. Enayati S, Mayorga ME, Toro-Díaz H, Albert LA (2019) Identifying trade-offs in equity and efficiency for simultaneously optimizing location and multipriority dispatch of ambulances. Int Trans Oper Res 26(2):415–438. https://doi.org/10.1111/itor.12590
12. McLay LA, Mayorga ME (2013) A dispatching model for server-to-customer systems that balances efficiency and equity. Manuf Serv Oper Manag 15(2):205–220. https://doi.org/10.1287/msom.1120.0411
13. Savas ES (1978) On equity in providing public services. Manage Sci 24(8):800–808. https://doi.org/10.1287/mnsc.24.8.800
14. United Nations (2015) Goal 10: Reduce inequality within and among countries. https://www.un.org/sustainabledevelopment/inequality/
15. Frichi Y, Jawab F (in press) A review and classification of ambulance deployment and redeployment models in emergencies. Int J Logistics Syst Manag https://doi.org/10.1504/IJLSM.2022.10045194
16. Currie CSM, Fowler JW, Kotiadis K, Monks T, Onggo BS, Robertson DA, Tako AA (2020) How simulation modelling can help reduce the impact of COVID-19. J Simulation 14(2):83–97. https://doi.org/10.1080/17477778.2020.1751570

17. Amorim M, Antunes F, Ferreira S, Couto A (2019) An integrated approach for strategic and tactical decisions for the emergency medical service: exploring optimization and metamodel-based simulation for vehicle location. Comput Industrial Eng 137(September). https://doi.org/10.1016/j.cie.2019.106057
18. Aboueljinane L, Frichi Y (2022) A simulation optimization approach to investigate resource planning and coordination mechanisms in emergency systems. Simul Model Pract Theory 119(April):102586. https://doi.org/10.1016/j.simpat.2022.102586
19. Niessner H, Rauner MS, Gutjahr WJ (2018) A dynamic simulation–optimization approach for managing mass casualty incidents. Operations Res Health Care 17:82–100. https://doi.org/10.1016/j.orhc.2017.07.001
20. Chiadamrong N, Piyathanavong V (2017) Optimal design of supply chain network under uncertainty environment using hybrid analytical and simulation modeling approach. J Ind Eng Int 13(4):465–478. https://doi.org/10.1007/s40092-017-0201-2
21. Zeinali F, Mahootchi M, Sepehri MM (2015) Resource planning in the emergency departments: a simulation-based metamodeling approach. Simul Model Pract Theory 53:123–138. https://doi.org/10.1016/j.simpat.2015.02.002
22. Marsh MT, Schilling DA (1994) Equity measurement in facility location analysis: a review and framework. Eur J Oper Res 74(1):1–17. https://doi.org/10.1016/0377-2217(94)90200-3
23. Grot M, Nagel L, Becker T, Fiebrandt PM, Werners B (2022) Fairness or efficiency-managing this conflict in emergency medical services location planning. Comput Ind Eng 173(November 2021):108664. https://doi.org/10.1016/j.cie.2022.108664
24. Leclerc PD, McLay LA, Mayorga ME (2012) Modeling equity for allocating public resources. In: Community-based operations research: decision modeling for local impact and diverse populations, Vol. 167. Springer, Berlin, pp 97–118. https://doi.org/10.1007/978-1-4614-0806-2_4
25. Akdogan MA, Bayındır ZP, Iyigun C (2023) An analysis of ambulance location problem from an equity perspective. Soc-Econ Planning Sci 90(November 2022):101737. https://doi.org/10.1016/j.seps.2023.101737
26. Jagtenberg CJ, Mason AJ (2020) Improving fairness in ambulance planning by time sharing. Eur J Oper Res 280(3):1095–1107. https://doi.org/10.1016/j.ejor.2019.08.003
27. Calik H, Labbé M, Yaman H (2015) p-Center problems. In: Laporte G, Nickel S, Saldanha da Gama F (eds) Location science. Springer, Cham, pp 79–92. https://doi.org/10.1007/978-3-319-13111-5_4
28. Chanta S, Mayorga ME, Kurz ME, McLay LA (2011) The minimum p-envy location problem: a new model for equitable distribution of emergency resources. IIE Trans Healthcare Syst Eng 1(2):101–115. https://doi.org/10.1080/19488300.2011.609522
29. Aringhieri R, Bigharaz S, Duma D, Guastalla A (2022) Fairness in ambulance routing for post disaster management. CEJOR 30(1):189–211. https://doi.org/10.1007/s10100-021-00785-y
30. Luo W, Yao J, Mitchell R, Zhang X, Li W (2022) Locating emergency medical services to reduce urban-rural inequalities. Socio-Econ Plann Sci 84(July 2021):101416. https://doi.org/10.1016/j.seps.2022.101416
31. Li M, Wang F, Kwan MP, Chen J, Wang J (2022) Equalizing the spatial accessibility of emergency medical services in Shanghai: a trade-off perspective. Comput Environ Urban Syst 92(August 2021):101745. https://doi.org/10.1016/j.compenvurbsys.2021.101745
32. Pirkul H, Schilling DA (1991) The maximal covering location problem with capacities on total workload. Manage Sci 37(2):233–248. https://doi.org/10.1287/mnsc.37.2.233
33. Xu J, Murray AT, Church RL, Wei R (2023) Service allocation equity in location coverage analytics. Eur J Oper Res 305(1):21–37. https://doi.org/10.1016/j.ejor.2022.05.032
34. Li X, Saydam C (2016) Balancing ambulance crew workloads via a tiered dispatch policy. Pesquisa Operacional 36(3):399–419. https://doi.org/10.1590/0101-7438.2016.036.03.0399
35. Enayati S, Mayorga ME, Rajagopalan HK, Saydam C (2018) Real-time ambulance redeployment approach to improve service coverage with fair and restricted workload for EMS providers. Omega 79:67–80. https://doi.org/10.1016/j.omega.2017.08.001

36. Essus Y, De La Fuente R, Venkitasubramanian A (2023) Real-time optimization for relocation and dispatching of Emergency Medical Services with balanced workload and outsourced ride-hailing services. Comput Ind Eng 111045. https://doi.org/10.1016/j.cie.2023.109823
37. Sreekanth VK, Roy RB (2017) Equity-constrained dispatching models for emergency medical services. Team Performance Manage 23(1–2):28–45. https://doi.org/10.1108/TPM-10-2015-0051
38. Jawab F, Frichi Y, Moufad I (2021) Logistique hospitalière et accès aux soins de santé. Cas du transport sanitaire au Maroc. In Naciri A, Paché G, Savy M (eds) Penser le Maroc logistique : une perspective pluridisciplinaire. Presses universitaires d'Aix-Marseille, pp 315–336
39. Frichi Y, Jawab F, Boutahari S.(2019a) An exploratory qualitative study of the influence of hospital logistics factors on quality of care and patient satisfaction at public hospitals in Morocco. Adv Sci Technol Eng Syst J 4(6):414–422. https://doi.org/10.25046/aj040652
40. Frichi Y, Jawab F, Boutahari S (2020) Modeling the impact of hospital logistics on quality of care and patient satisfaction: results of a survey in three public healthcare facilities in Fez-Morocco. J Ind Eng Manag 13(2):296–320. https://doi.org/10.3926/jiem.3143
41. HCP (2016) Les indicateurs sociaux du Maroc 2013–2014
42. Frichi Y (2021) Modélisation de l'impact de la logistique hospitalière sur la qualité des soins et la satisfaction des patients. Optimisation du déploiement et du redéploiement des ambulances. Sidi Mohamed Ben Abdellah University
43. Ministère de la Santé (2019) Sante En Chiffres—2016
44. American Hospital Association (2017) Social determinants of health series: transportation and the role of hospitals. https://www.aha.org//ahahret-guides/2017-11-15-social-determinants-health-series-transportation-and-role-hospitals
45. Frichi Y, Jawab F, Boutahari S (2020b) Diagnosis of the main issues of extra-hospital medical patient transportation: case of Morocco. In: 2020 13th international colloquium of logistics and supply chain management, LOGISTIQUA 2020. https://doi.org/10.1109/LOGISTIQUA49782.2020.9353883
46. Frichi Y, Ibn El Farouk I, Jawab F, Boutahari S (2020) Hospital logistics' effect on patient satisfaction. Int J Sci Technol Res 9(04):210–216
47. Higgs G, Zahnow R, Corcoran J, Langford M, Fry R (2017) Modelling spatial access to general practitioner surgeries: does public transport availability matter? J Transp Health 6:143–154. https://doi.org/10.1016/j.jth.2017.05.361
48. Ministére de la Santé (2008) Plan d'action santé, 2008–2012
49. Yaakoubd A-I (2010) La dimension sociale de la santé au Maroc. In: Aboussad A, Cherkaoui M, Vimard P (eds) Santé et vulnérabilité au Maroc, p 43
50. Frichi Y, Ben Kacem A, Jawab F, Kamach O, Chafik S (2020) Improving interhospital medical patient transportation in Morocco: a forecasting collaborative approach. In: Euchi J (ed) Transportation, logistics, and supply chain management in home healthcare: emerging research and opportunities. IGI Global, pp 136–162. https://doi.org/10.4018/978-1-7998-0268-6.ch008
51. Frichi Y, Aboueljinane L, Jawab F (2023) Using discrete-event simulation to assess an AHP—based dynamic patient prioritisation policy for elective surgery. J Simulation. https://doi.org/10.1080/17477778.2023.2284145
52. Frichi Y, Ben Kacem A, Jawab F, Boutahari S, Kamach O, Chafik S (2021) The contribution of reduced COVID-19 test time in controlling the spread of the disease: a simulation-based approach. J Public Health Africa 12(2). https://doi.org/10.4081/jphia.2021.1455
53. Zerka A, Jawab F (2022) Modelling the costs of pre-hospital transport service for victims of road accidents in TDABC. Arch Transp 61(1):89–101. https://doi.org/10.5604/01.3001.0015.8197
54. Frichi Y, Jawab F, Aboueljinane L, Boutahari S (2022) Development and comparison of two new multi-period queueing reliability models using discrete-event simulation and a simulation-optimization approach. Comput Ind Eng 168:108068. https://doi.org/10.1016/j.cie.2022.108068

55. Khodaparasti S, Maleki HR, Bruni ME, Jahedi S, Beraldi P, Conforti D (2016) Balancing efficiency and equity in location-allocation models with an application to strategic EMS design. Optimization Lett 10(5):1053–1070. https://doi.org/10.1007/s11590-015-0929-9
56. El Oualidi MA, Bellabdaoui A, Saadi J (2016) Simulation de flux de patients et optimisation des infirmiers. Cas du service d'accueil des urgences de CHU Ibn Rochd de Casablanca. GISEH
57. Dias LMS, Vieira AAC, Pereira GAB, Oliveira JA (2016) Discrete simulation software ranking—a top list of the worldwide most popular and used tools. In: Proceedings of the 2016 winter simulation conference, pp 1060–1071
58. Rockwell Automation (2012) Opt quest for Arena : user's guide
59. Frichi Y, Jawab F, Aboueljinane L (2022) Dataset on optimizing ambulance deployment and redeployment in Fez-Meknes region, Morocco. Data Brief 42:108178. https://doi.org/10.1016/j.dib.2022.108178
60. Frichi Y, Jawab F, Boutahari S (2019b) Identification of health system stakeholders in Morocco. In: Proceedings of the international conference on industrial engineering and operations management, 5–7 Mar, 1193–1199
61. Savas ES (1969) Simulation and cost-effectiveness analysis of New York's emergency ambulance service. Manage Sci 15(12):B608–B627. https://doi.org/10.1287/mnsc.15.12.b608

Youness Frichi is a researcher at the Higher School of Technology of Sidi Mohamed Ben Abdellah University. He holds a doctorate in industrial engineering. His primary research interests include supply chain management, healthcare supply chain, and operations research. He is co-author of several articles published in international indexed journals.

Fouad Jawab Professor of Supply Chain at the Higher School of Technology of the Sidi Mohamed Ben Abdellah University of Fez, Morocco.

He has held several scientific and administrative responsibilities. He founded the International Conference on Logistics and Supply Chain Management (LOGISTIQUA), which he continues to develop with the support of several research teams in Morocco and abroad.

He is the author and co-author of more than 180 publications in national and international journals and proceedings. His research focuses on modeling, simulation and optimization of the supply chain, hospital supply chains and urban logistics. He is also an expert with several renowned organizations and a reviewer for prestigious journals.

Part IV

Major Health Crises; Maturity and Resilience of Hospital Supply Chains

21 Healthcare Supply Chain: Resilience Qualitative Evaluation

Naima Rahiel, Abderrahman El Mhamedi, and Khalid Hachemi

Abstract

Hospital resilience is a pivotal factor in determining the effectiveness of healthcare supply chains, particularly in the face of diverse disruptions and challenges. This chapter conducts a rigorous examination of hospital resilience by undertaking a comprehensive literature review to analyze and synthesize the prevailing definitions across scholarly works. By scrutinizing a variety of sources, the chapter aims to construct a comprehensive understanding of hospital resilience, emphasizing its multidimensional nature and contextual variations. Furthermore, a detailed overview of the frameworks used for the qualitative evaluation of hospital resilience is provided, drawing from a wide array of literature in this domain. By presenting a panel of these frameworks, this chapter equips healthcare practitioners, researchers, and policymakers with valuable insights to enhance the resilience of healthcare supply chains. Ultimately, this study contributes to the advancement of knowledge in the field, facilitating more effective strategies for managing and enhancing hospital resilience in healthcare supply chains by identifying the key factors influencing hospital resilience.

Keywords

Healthcare supply chain • Hospital resilience • Resilience evaluation

N. Rahiel (✉) · A. El Mhamedi
QUARTZ, Paris 8 Vincennes-Saint-Denis University, Saint-Denis, France
e-mail: n.rahiel@iut.univ-paris8.fr

A. El Mhamedi
e-mail: a.elmhamedi@iut.univ-paris8.fr

K. Hachemi
LGPMI, Oran 2 University, Oran, Algeria
e-mail: hachemi.khalid@univ-oran2.dz

F. Jawab (ed.), *Hospital Supply Chain*, Integrated Science 27,
https://doi.org/10.1007/978-3-031-70292-1_21

Abbreviations

4Rs	Robustness, rapidity, resourcefulness, redundancy
BHDRA	Baseline hospital drought resilience assessment
CHDRA	Comprehensive hospital drought resilience assessment
DRM	Disaster resilience management
HSI	Hospital safety index
RAG	Resilience analysis grid.

1 Introduction

Healthcare services play an invaluable role in safeguarding public health and curbing the effects of disasters [1]. Hospitals, as pivotal components of healthcare systems, play a central role in ensuring community well-being during crises [2]. This includes managing surges in demand, providing continuous services, and adapting swiftly to unforeseen challenges [3].

The frequency and intensity of disasters have risen significantly in recent years, presenting new challenges for healthcare systems worldwide. While traditional disaster preparedness focuses on scenarios such as earthquakes and floods, emerging threats like pandemics and cybersecurity breaches require novel approaches to resilience planning [4]. The COVID-19 pandemic, in particular, exposed vulnerabilities in healthcare systems globally, testing hospitals' abilities to manage patient flows, secure essential supplies, and protect healthcare workers while maintaining quality care.

Despite growing awareness of the importance of hospital resilience, defining and operationalizing resilience metrics remain contentious issues [5]. The multifaceted nature of resilience, spanning organizational dynamics, resource management, and community engagement, complicates efforts to develop standardized assessment frameworks. Hospital resilience goes beyond mere disaster response; it encompasses proactive measures such as capacity building, interagency collaboration, and continuous learning from past incidents [3].

The COVID-19 pandemic highlighted systemic weaknesses in healthcare delivery, especially in resource-constrained and conflict-affected settings [6]. Hospitals in these contexts face compounded challenges, including political instability, infrastructure deficits, and limited access to critical resources such as medical personnel and equipment.

Enhancing hospital resilience necessitates collaboration across disciplines, sectors, and stakeholders. Integrating insights from health systems management, disaster risk reduction, and engineering can inform comprehensive resilience frameworks tailored to diverse hospital settings [7]. However, bridging the gap between theoretical models and practical implementation remains a key challenge [5]. Developing standardized metrics, fostering knowledge sharing among healthcare institutions, and leveraging technology for real-time data analytics are promising avenues for advancing hospital resilience in the face of evolving threats.

The evolving landscape of disasters and pandemics underscores the urgent need for resilient healthcare systems anchored by adaptable and proactive hospitals. By addressing the complexities of defining, measuring, and enhancing hospital resilience, stakeholders can better prepare for future crises, safeguard public health, and promote sustainable healthcare delivery worldwide.

2 Hospital Resilience

Resilience has gained remarkable attention and importance across a wide range of disciplines over the past four decades (Fig. 1). This bar chart shows the number of publications on resilience across various research categories. Social sciences, engineering, and health sciences published the most articles on resilience, with over 28,000 publications each. Conversely, research areas like philosophy and religious studies, and mathematical sciences published far fewer articles, under 3000 each. This distribution suggests a focus on resilience in applied fields that deal with human systems and health, potentially reflecting the realworld challenges these fields grapple with. Figure 2 visually demonstrates the growing interest in resilience. We can observe a significant upsurge in discussions, research, and practical applications within this field. Notably, the number of documents published in 2023 alone surpasses 39,000. The exponential growth depicted in the statistics mirrors the increasing recognition of resilience as a fundamental concept.

Recognizing the importance of robust health systems in the face of diverse external threats, scholars have proposed a wealth of frameworks to comprehend and bolster health system resilience. Figure 3 illustrates the evolution of the number of studies addressing hospital resilience. This figure illustrates the increasing interest and attention devoted to understanding and improving resilience within the healthcare sector in recent years. The surge in publications notably evident since 2016, can be attributed in part to the simultaneous escalation of climate change effects, including extreme weather events. This trend has become even more pronounced since 2020, primarily due to the COVID-19 pandemic, which has heightened awareness of the vulnerabilities and resilience needs of healthcare systems worldwide.

Hospital resilience is far from a monolithic concept. As evidenced by Fig. 4, numerous publications explore hospital resilience from different fields. Notably, health sciences lead the pack with 6,051 publications, followed closely by biomedical and clinical sciences (2354 publications), psychology (997 publications), and human society (831 publications).

This breadth of research highlights the multifaceted nature of hospital resilience. It's not simply a singular concept, but rather a complex issue examined from diverse perspectives across different domains [4, 8].

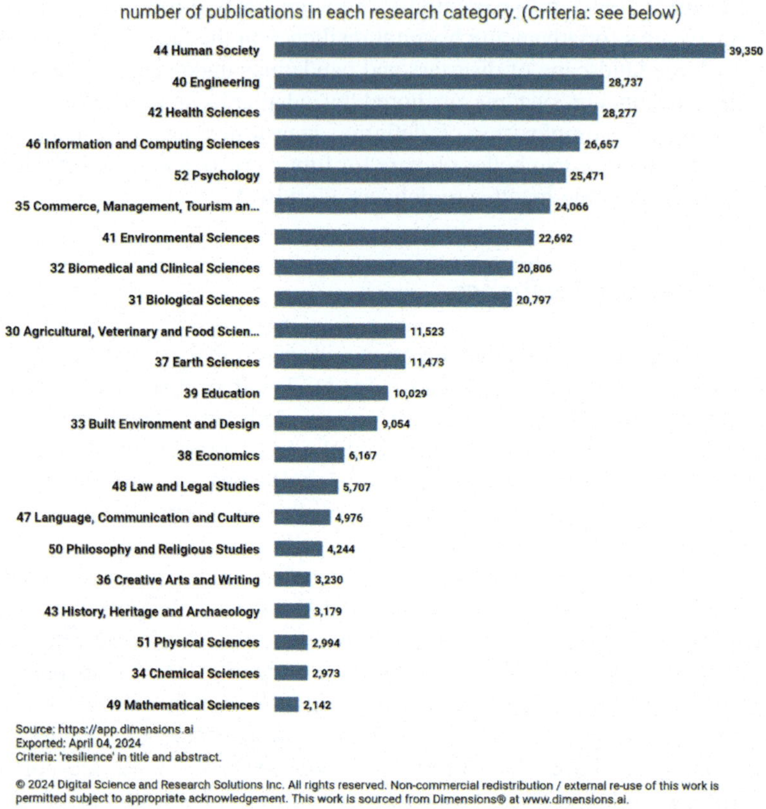

Fig. 1 Previous research domains addressing resilience number of publications

The distribution of research types within the literature review (Fig. 5) reveals interesting insights into the methodologies employed in the study of improvement strategies and evaluations within the healthcare sector.

A predominant focus on improvement strategies is evident, representing 39.53% of the articles analyzed [9–12]. This suggests a concerted effort within the research community to identify and implement strategies aimed at enhancing resilience in healthcare settings. Concurrently, qualitative evaluation methods constitute a notable proportion at 19.77%, indicating a recognition of the importance of in-depth qualitative analysis in understanding the intricacies of healthcare resilience [13–15]. Furthermore, the significant presence of quantitative evaluation methods, comprising 24.42% of the articles, underscores the emphasis placed on rigorous statistical analysis and empirical evidence in assessing resilience initiatives [8, 16–18]. Interestingly, the utilization of mixed evaluation methods, though representing a smaller percentage at 5.81%, highlights the recognition of the complementary nature of both qualitative and quantitative approaches in providing a comprehensive understanding of resilience dynamics in healthcare [4]. Additionally, reviews

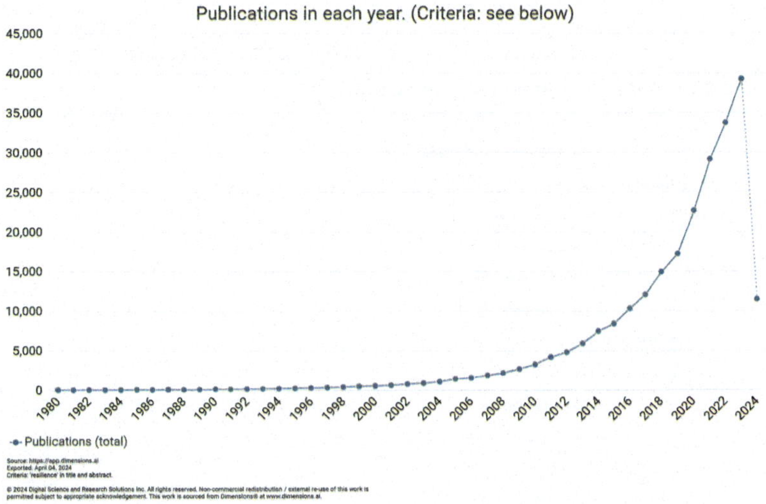

Fig. 2 Number of publications related to resilience published in four last decades

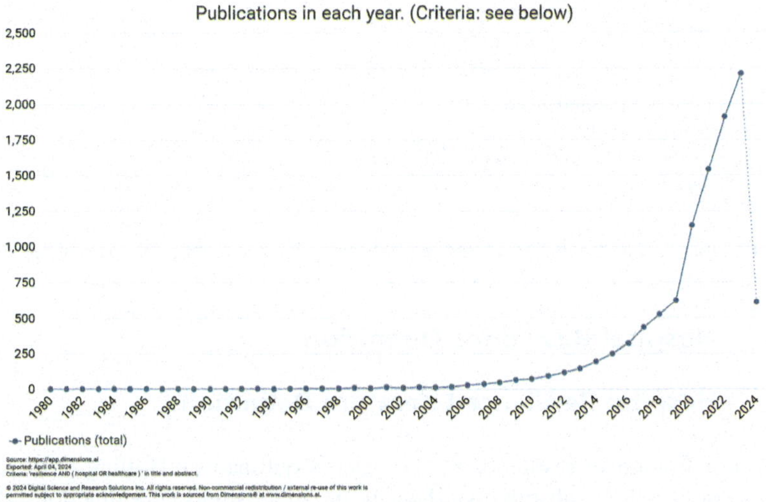

Fig. 3 Number of publications related to hospital resilience published in four last decades

constitute 10.47% of the articles, indicating a concerted effort to synthesize existing knowledge in this field [5]. This diverse array of research types reflects a multifaceted approach to addressing the complexities of resilience enhancement in healthcare systems, thereby contributing to a more nuanced understanding and effective implementation of resilience strategies.

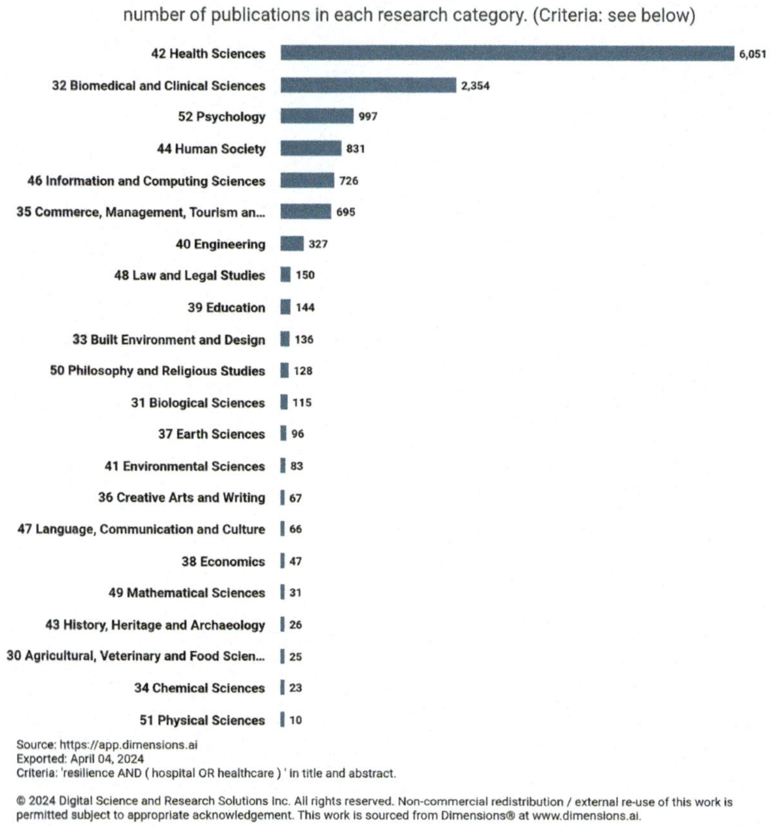

Fig. 4 Previous research domains addressing hospital resilience number of publication

3 Hospital Resilience Definition

3.1 Hospital Resilience Literature Definition

A classic definition of resilience in ecology, as outlined by Holling [19], focuses on a system's ability to absorb disturbances and maintain its core functions, despite changes in its components. This concept, often termed ecological resilience, underscores a system's ability to endure and remain in its initial state despite disturbances. Expanding on his earlier work, Holling [20] further refined the concept of resilience by introducing two distinct forms. Engineering resilience emphasizes how quickly a system can bounce back to its original state. In contrast, ecological resilience focuses on a system's ability to adapt and absorb disturbances without transitioning to a fundamentally different and potentially less desirable state. Thus, according to Holling's definition, we can initially view resilience in two

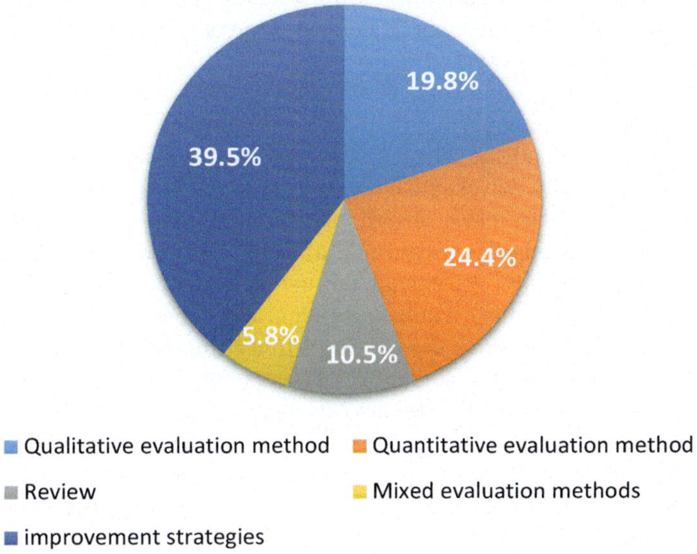

Fig. 5 Studies by research type

parts: first, recovery, which aligns more closely with engineering resilience; and second, resistance, which is more associated with ecological resilience.

A literature review conducted in 2011 [21], highlighted 14 distinct definitions of resilience across domains such as disaster management, engineering, ecological systems, psychology, and organizational resilience, all emphasizing a system's return to stability. Aldea and all [1] synthesized 23 recent definitions of resilience across 18 intervention domains, shedding light on the multifaceted nature of the concept. These varied perspectives highlight the complexity and significance of resilience across different domains, underlining the ongoing efforts to develop comprehensive frameworks for enhancing resilience in critical sectors.

In the healthcare sector, resilience manifests in various ways. Public health focuses on a hospital's ability to maintain operations and deliver essential services during public health emergencies, while disaster management emphasizes preparedness for natural disasters and large-scale emergencies [22, 23]. Additionally, healthcare management examines how effective leadership, resource management, and decision-making contribute to building resilience within hospitals [24]

The varied interpretations of hospital resilience in scientific literature collectively provide a nuanced and comprehensive understanding of the concept. Health systems resilience has been viewed through different lenses as a process, capacity, ability, outcome, attributes, and even as a policy objective [5]. Essentially, hospital resilience encompasses a multifaceted ability that includes resistance, absorption, and recovery from shocks and disruptions. Bruneau and all [25] established the foundation by defining seismic resilience, emphasizing not only the system's ability to minimize shock likelihood but also to absorb its impact and swiftly return to normal functioning. This threefold framework serves as a guiding principle echoed in subsequent research, reflecting a holistic approach to managing unforeseen events within hospital settings.

Building upon this groundwork, Cimellaro and all [17] and Zhong and all [8] expand the scope of resilience, emphasizing the preservation of critical functionality during disasters and the adaptation to new post-disaster states. Sharma and Sharma [13] specifically delves into emergency-resilient hospitals, emphasizing the necessity for hospitals to resist, absorb, and respond while maintaining essential functionality, highlighting the critical role of healthcare during emergencies.

Paz de Sousa and all [16] extend the concept to health systems, considering impacts from epidemics, natural disasters, and economic crises. De Araujo Oliveira and all [26] introduce the notion of transformation in response to unexpected changes, while Ahizoune and all [9] stress proactive measures to reduce vulnerability. Ravaghi and all [10] dissects hospital resilience into components and capacities.

The visualization presented in Fig. 6 showcases a word cloud illustrating the diverse range of terminologies and concepts associated with hospital resilience as identified in the literature review. This visual representation vividly encapsulates the varied perspectives adopted by different authors in defining hospital resilience. While all definitions emphasize maintaining essential functions during disruptions, the sheer number of interpretations highlights the multifaceted nature of the hospital resilience system.

Despite the wide variance in definitions and terminology used, a coherent trend emerges as a shared theme unifies the various interpretations. The consistent utilization of terms such as'capacity' and'ability' across the literature collectively portrays hospital resilience as a fundamental capability. This overarching theme underscores the resilience's essence in enabling hospitals to sustain their essential functions and adapt effectively to challenges and uncertainties.

Fig. 6 Hospital resilience definitions word cloud

Additionally, Fig. 7 illustrates the proportions of words in definitions of hospital resilience identified through the literature review. The dominant theme (over 74%) centered on reactive capabilities—the ability to resist disruptions, absorb their impact, and ultimately recover employing terms such as "resist," "absorb," "recover," or "bounce back". This focus on withstanding and bouncing back underscores the foundational role these elements play in building resilient hospitals. However, a significant portion (21%) emphasized proactive measures, using terms like "plan" and "reduce probabilities", highlighting the importance of planning and mitigating vulnerabilities before a crisis strikes. This proactive stance suggests efforts to fortify hospital systems against potential shocks, building resilience through preparedness.

Further enriching the understanding of hospital resilience, 26% of definitions embraced the concept of learning and adaptation, as evidenced by the inclusion of terms such as "learn" and "new state". This viewpoint posits that resilience goes beyond mere recovery; it involves leveraging disruptions as opportunities to improve system functionality. By learning from past challenges, hospitals can emerge stronger and more adaptable. Additionally, the temporal dimension emerged as crucial for 37% of definitions, underscoring the need for a swift and efficient recovery after an event. A rapid bounce back minimizes the disruption's impact on patient care and overall hospital operations. Interestingly, a minority of definitions acknowledged the cost dimension, recognizing the importance of economic constraint considerations in building resilience.

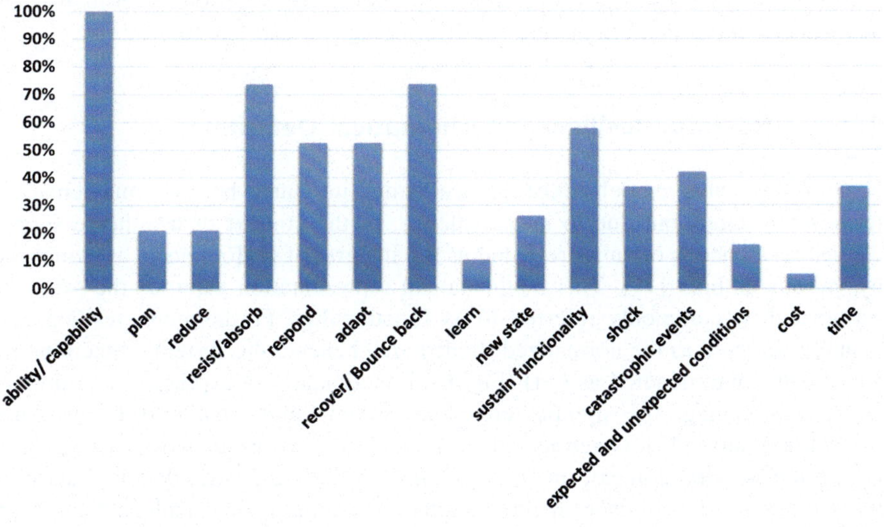

Fig. 7 Proportions of words in hospital resilience definitions

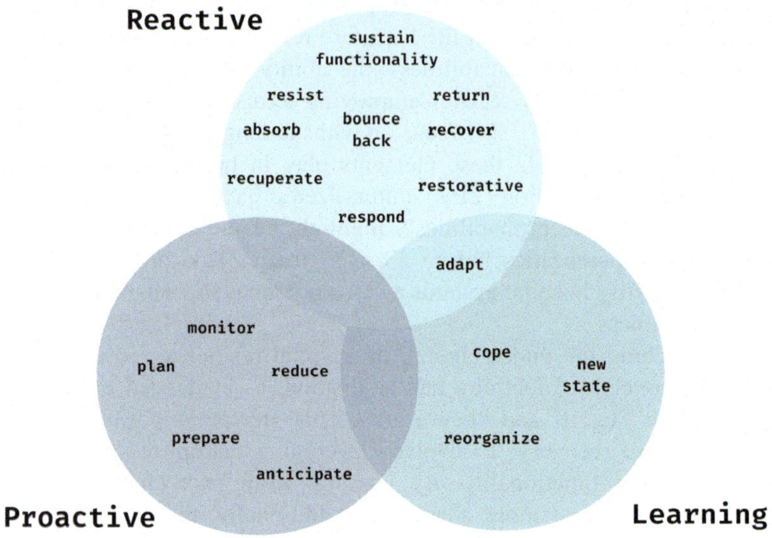

Fig. 8 Classification of terms found in the definitions according to different resilience capacities

Analyzing hospital resilience definitions reveals a multifaceted concept encompassing reactive capabilities like resistance and recovery, proactive measures like planning and mitigation, and even the potential for post-disruption improvement. Figure 8 further illustrates this complexity with a classification of terms used in hospital resilience definitions into reactive, proactive, and learning facets.

3.2 Hospital Resilience Mathematical Definition

Various resilience models exist in academic literature, but one mathematical framework stands out due to its prevalence. In the context of healthcare supply chains, resilience is often represented as the integral of performance, as evidenced by various authors [17]. This mathematical representation captures the system's serviceability, commonly referred to as functionality. Furthermore, resilience is visually depicted as the normalized shaded area beneath the system's functionality curve over time, denoted as Q(t) (Fig. 9). Functionality is expressed as a dimensionless percentage 0% signifies complete system failure, while 100% indicates perfect operation [17]. Given its extensive adoption in various works, particularly within the hospital context, this mathematical modeling is regarded as a defining representation of resilience in this chapter. In addition, this mathematical characterization is commonly attributed to the work of Bruneau and all [25], who

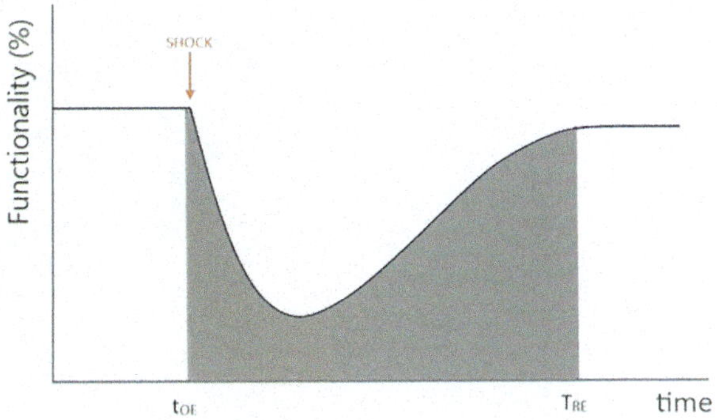

Fig. 9 Resilience—system functionality over time

introduced the following equation:

$$R = \int_{t_{OE}}^{t_{OE}+T_{RE}} Q(t)dt \quad (1)$$

R	Resilience
Q(t)	Functionality
t_{OE}	Disruption time
T_{RE}	Recovery time.

4 Hospital Resilience Evaluation

Measurement is essential for identifying areas that require improvement [18]. The assessment of resilience plays a crucial role in shaping strategies for the development of resilient healthcare facilities [18]. Recognizing its significance, many previous studies on healthcare facility resilience have concentrated on quantifying or evaluating resilience, each employing various methods, perspectives, and responses to different disruptions. Figures 10 and 11 illustrate; respectively, the distribution of studies according to the type of disruption and the distribution based on the scope of resilience assessment.

This distribution in Fig. 10 highlights the diverse range of challenges that healthcare facilities face. Among the evaluation articles analyzed, a significant emphasis is placed on seismic events, with 33% of the studies specifically addressing this type of natural hazard [8, 27, 28]. Moreover, the COVID-19 pandemic emerges as another prominent area of study, with 22%. Such attention underscores the urgency and importance of evaluating and improving healthcare facility resilience in the face of infectious disease outbreaks [9, 10, 16, 26]. Interestingly, a small percentage (8%) of the studies explore resilience in the context of other

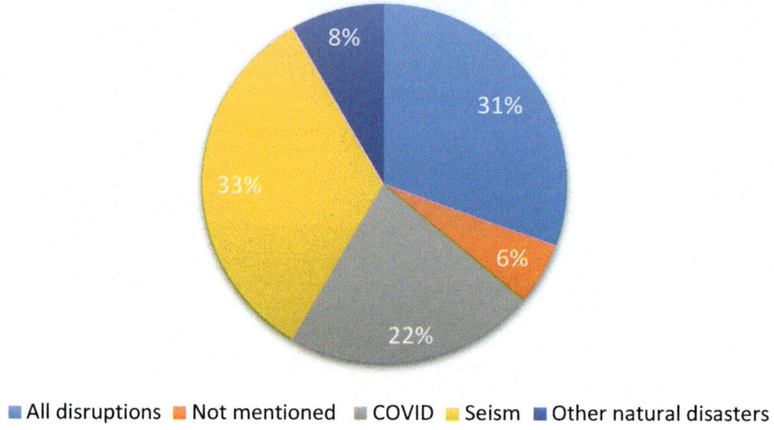

Fig. 10 Studies by type of disruption

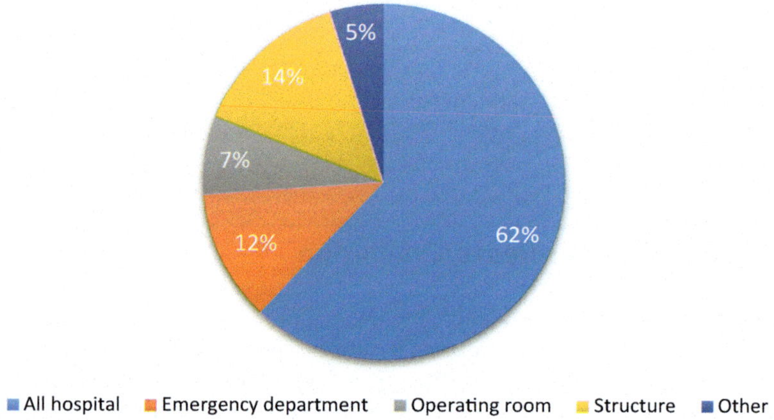

Fig. 11 Studies by resilience assessment scope

natural disasters, indicating a broader scope of research beyond seismic events and pandemics [11, 14]. Additionally, it is notable that a few studies (6%) did not specify the type of disruption they addressed [15, 29].

Figure 11 provides insights into the scope of resilience assessment in the reviewed studies. The majority of the articles (62%) examine resilience at the level of the entire hospital, indicating a comprehensive approach to understanding and enhancing overall organizational resilience [9–12, 26]. This broad focus suggests a recognition of the interconnectedness of various hospital departments and functions in maintaining effective healthcare delivery, especially during times of crisis. Moreover, a significant portion of the studies (12%) focus on assessing the resilience of emergency departments, recognizing their role as the frontline in disaster response [15]. Similarly, a smaller yet significant number of articles (7%) assess resilience specifically within the operating room environment, highlighting the importance of surgical services in maintaining continuity of care [29]. In addition to departmental resilience, some studies (14%) examine the structural resilience of healthcare facilities, underscoring the significance of robust infrastructure in ensuring operational continuity and patient safety, particularly in seismic events [17, 27]. Interestingly, a few articles (5%) explore resilience in other specific areas, indicating a diverse range of research interests and focal points within the broader context of healthcare facility resilience [28].

Furthermore, a variety of studies have investigated different methodologies and frameworks for assessing hospital resilience, taking into account factors ranging from organizational dimensions to economic indicators. In this comprehensive overview, we present key studies, each employing distinct methodologies and approaches to evaluate hospital resilience. Through an extensive literature review, we identify two main evaluation approaches: qualitative and quantitative, as well as mixed methods.

Due to space constraints, this chapter will prioritize a detailed exploration of qualitative methodologies employed in hospital resilience evaluation. Below, a closer examination of the specific qualitative methods applied:

Modified Delphi Study In a three-round, modified Delphi study conducted by Zhong and all [30], a panel of 33 Chinese experts endeavored to construct a comprehensive framework for assessing hospital resilience. Through iterative rounds of deliberation and feedback, potential measures were meticulously refined to encompass the broad spectrum of factors influencing hospital resilience. Using a five-point Likert scale, experts systematically scored the importance of these measures. Ultimately, the study identified 43 indicators spanning eight overarching domains and 17 subdomains pertinent to hospital resilience. These indicators ranged from the availability of on-site rescue equipment to the efficacy of medication management strategies and the initiation of emergency plans. However, the study's findings are tempered by certain limitations, notably the constrained external validity stemming from a lack of comparable studies for validation and the potential for bias in the prioritization of measures by participating experts.

Healthcare System Index The Hospital Safety Index (HSI) provides a structured method for evaluating a hospital's ability to withstand and function during emergencies. Luke and all [31] utilized the HSI framework in a hospital setting. The HSI checklist, typically divided into modules: hazard assessment, structural safety, non-structural safety, and functional capacity, was employed. In Luke and all's [31] study, each hospital underwent a self-assessment using this checklist, identifying potential hazards, building resilience, ensuring equipment functionality during emergencies, and evaluating operational capacity. An independent HSI-trained team then verified these assessments. By combining document review, on-site observations, and interviews, a comprehensive picture emerged. Each element within the checklist received a score (often 0–2 for lowhigh safety), and these scores were aggregated and weighted to generate a final Hospital Safety Rating (low, average, or high) based on the World Health Organization (WHO) guidelines. This rating, as seen in the study of Luke and all [31], offers a snapshot of the hospital's overall resilience. More importantly, the detailed breakdown within each module highlights specific areas for improvement. This allows hospitals to prioritize interventions and ultimately enhance disaster preparedness, safeguarding patient well-being during critical situations. The HSI thus serves as a valuable tool for continuous improvement in hospital resilience.

However, the HSI doesn't fully assess hospital resilience to specific hazards like pandemics. Elements such as air handling system isolation and negative pressure areas are inadequately covered. Similarly, pandemic-related capacity needs lack specific capacity ratings.

Organizational Resilience Ahizoune and all [9] evaluated hospital resilience utilizing a questionnaire tailored to gauge essential components of organizational resilience: Preparation, Adaptation, and Recovery. Preparedness serves as the foundation, with pre-existing crisis plans and learnings from past experiences providing a roadmap for resource allocation and response protocols during unforeseen circumstances. Adaptation emerges as the engine driving resilience during a crisis. Hospitals demonstrate remarkable flexibility by reorganizing operations, modifying workflows, and implementing new protocols. This adaptation is fueled by dedicated and adaptable human capital, clear leadership through crisis management and disease management committees, and effective communication that fosters collaboration among staff. Recovery is the ability of hospitals to bounce back and restore normalcy after a disruptive event. Their research highlights recovery as the culmination of preparedness and adaptation efforts. It's the return to normal operations and services, and it requires effective communication, flexible decision-making, strong leadership, and continuous learning from the disruption. The assessment encompassed strategies such as crisis preparedness plans, professional engagement, and rapid care organization. While the questionnaire offered valuable insights into organizational resilience, there remains potential for further refinement and validation to better capture the dynamic and multifaceted nature of hospital resilience.

Disaster Resilience Management Ravaghi and all [10] investigated hospital resilience during COVID-19 using a multi-method approach anchored in the Disaster Resilience Management (DRM) framework. This framework assessed hospitals' capabilities at various pandemic stages. Qualitative interviews explored experiences mapped to each DRM phase (response, recovery, mitigation). A key component of the study involved a quantitative survey design with a two-pronged approach [10]. First, hospital managers rated their preparedness for different risks using a 5-point Likert scale, providing a baseline understanding of prepandemic readiness. Second, they rated their hospitals' responses to non-COVID emergencies on a 10-point Likert scale. These ratings offered insights into four crucial resilience capacities: absorb (withstanding initial impact), adapt (adjusting practices during the event), transform (making lasting improvements), and learn (incorporating knowledge for future preparedness). By linking these capacities with the DRM stages, the study design allowed researchers to compare hospitals' pre-pandemic and pandemic resilience. It is important to acknowledge, however, that the study's reliance on self-reported data and a limited sample size may affect the generalizability of the findings. Additionally, the high workload of frontline personnel during the pandemic may have influenced their responses.

Fuzzy Analytic Network Process Fallah and all's [4] framework utilizes a three-phase approach that integrates expert opinion and Fuzzy Analytic Network Process to analyze and reduce a large pool of indicators. In Phase I, a systematic review identified 108 potential indicators categorized into 27 sub-domains and 3 domains (constructive, infrastructural, administrative resilience). Phase II employed a series of expert panel sessions to refine this list through discussion and consensus building. Panelists with diverse backgrounds in healthcare management, engineering, and crisis management reviewed and categorized indicators. Finally, Phase III addressed the challenge of complex interdependencies between factors in traditional decision-making methods by implementing Fuzzy Analytic Network Process. This fuzzy analytical technique utilizes triangular fuzzy numbers to account for ambiguity in expert judgments during pairwise comparisons. Experts rated the relative importance of domains, sub-domains, and individual indicators using linguistic scales converted to fuzzy numbers. **The Fuzzy Analytic Network Process** software then integrated these fuzzy weights to calculate the overall weight and ranking of each factor contributing to hospital resilience. This framework provides a robust method for qualitative hospital resilience evaluation by incorporating expert knowledge and addressing inherent uncertainties in decision-making. While this method provided valuable insights, its reliance on expert opinions and the time-consuming nature of the survey may limit its applicability in busy clinical settings.

Resilience Analysis Grid The Resilience Analysis Grid (RAG) framework offers a systematic methodology for evaluating a system's resilience potential, as exemplified in both the Chuang and all [15] and Yin and all [12] studies. Focusing on four crucial capabilities - responding, anticipating, monitoring, and learning RAG employs a set of dedicated questions tailored to the specific domain under investigation.

Chuang and all [15] demonstrate the adaptability of RAG by customizing it for emergency departments. They translated the original RAG questionnaire into Chinese and refined it based on emergency department specific policies and procedures. This ensured the questions addressed the unique challenges faced by emergency department staff. For instance, "responding" capabilities might be assessed through questions on resource mobilization or communication during a mass casualty incident. Similarly, "anticipating" might delve into how the emergency department identifies potential surges in patient volume or prepares for equipment failures. Through piloting with medical professionals, Chuang and all [15] further ensured the clarity and applicability of the Emergency Department

RAG (ED-RAG) in the fast-paced emergency department environment. This iterative process even led to the removal of questions on "time horizon" which were deemed irrelevant. Finally, they developed a new scoring method to analyze the ED-RAG results.

Yin and all [12] applied RAG to analyze ethnographic observations of hospital staff coping with a crisis. The RAG framework, with its focus on the four key abilities, helped them categorize observed behaviors like staff improvisations and workarounds. This categorization provided valuable insights into the hospital's resilience strengths and weaknesses across different levels (organization, teams, individuals). Essentially, RAG allowed them to move beyond documenting actions to understanding the "why" behind them, revealing how the hospital achieved successful outcomes under pressure.

Hence, both studies highlight the strengths of RAG. It offers a structured and systematic approach to assess resilience, while also being adaptable for tailoring to various contexts. This adaptability makes RAG a valuable tool for evaluating resilience across different healthcare systems. It is important to acknowledge the limitations of the RAG approach, however. The studies capture only snapshots of system activity, and the long-term repercussions of decisions and trade-offs made during crisis situations may not be immediately observable.

4Rs Framework Moitinho de Almeida and all [7] employed a qualitative framework rooted in system resilience, specifically the 4Rs model (Robustness, Rapidity, Resourcefulness, Redundancy), offering a comprehensive lens to examine how organizations endure and bounce back from disruptions. This framework unpacks resilience into two key objectives (ends) and two corresponding methods (means) to achieve them. The ends, robustness and rapidity, represent the organization's ability to maintain its core function during a crisis (robustness) and to recover swiftly afterwards (rapidity). Resourcefulness and redundancy, the means, delve into the organization's existing strategies for adapting to unforeseen challenges (resourcefulness) and for having backups for critical elements (redundancy). Furthermore, the study examined individual staff resilience through the lens of safety, meaningfulness, and sense of belonging, highlighting the interconnectedness between individual and system resilience. The 4Rs framework acknowledges that a resilient workforce is instrumental for organizational resilience. When examining robustness, for instance, the framework considers not just the organization's ability to maintain functionality but also how individual staff members cope with the pressure and emotional toll of a crisis. Their sense of safety, purpose, and belonging significantly impacts their ability to effectively contribute to maintaining core operations. Similarly, rapidity is influenced by individual resilience. Staff who can adapt quickly and manage stress effectively are better equipped to contribute to swift recovery efforts. Resourcefulness, a key means of organizational resilience, is often fueled by individual initiative and problem-solving skills during a crisis. When faced with disruptions, resourceful employees can identify creative solutions and find alternative ways to complete tasks, ultimately bolstering the organization's adaptability. In conclusion, the 4R framework, coupled with a focus on individual resilience, provides a powerful approach to understanding and enhancing an organization's ability to weather disruptions and emerge stronger.

Drought Resilience Assessment The study by Wijesekara and all [14] utilized a framework consisting of two questionnaires, the Baseline Hospital Drought Resilience Assessment (BHDRA) and the Comprehensive Hospital Drought Resilience Assessment (CHDRA), to assess and improve hospital resilience against drought. The BHDRA focused on essential aspects like water sources, storage capacity, and electricity availability, while the CHDRA provided a more in-depth evaluation by including water quality monitoring, alternative energy sources, and disaster preparedness plans. The researchers developed these tools after reviewing existing tools and considering their limitations, such as a broader hazard focus or lack of regional relevance. The BHDRA and CHDRA were piloted and refined before large-scale implementation. Data collection employed both questionnaires and field visits to hospitals across five districts. Finally, minimum water requirements were calculated, and hospitals were ranked based on their storage capacity relative to these needs. This framework highlights the importance of incorporating drought preparedness into hospital disaster plans to safeguard essential healthcare services during emergencies.

Kruk Framework Rios and all [11] employed qualitative methods to evaluate hospital resilience in a disaster scenario. Their approach centered on the Kruk framework [32], which defines hospital resilience through five key domains: Aware (recognizing risks and vulnerabilities), Diverse (having a variety of resources and perspectives), Self-Regulating (adapting to changing conditions), Integrated (functioning as a cohesive unit), and Adaptive (learning and improving from experiences). By conducting in-depth interviews with key stakeholders at a purposefully chosen case study hospital, the researchers aimed to understand "why" and "how" the hospital's resilience impacted patient outcomes. This analysis not only identified strengths and weaknesses in the hospital's response, but it also yielded valuable insights applicable to broader healthcare systems. This framework emphasizes the importance of measuring health system resilience capacity ahead of crises. The proposed resilience index takes a balanced approach, considering both slow-changing factors (reflected by existing health system metrics) and fast-evolving elements (captured by newly proposed measures). Additionally, it integrates relevant metrics from other disciplines to provide a nuanced picture of a system's resilience. Unlike traditional health security frameworks, many indicators in this index reflect characteristics of "everyday" resilience, supporting daily function and proactively reducing the likelihood of rising threats.

Other de Araújo Oliveira and all [26] employed a case study approach to analyze hospital resilience during the COVID-19 pandemic. Data were collected and organized using pre-defined conceptual categories, including infrastructure adaptations for increased patient capacity, management of personal protective equipment, equipment, and supplies, and staff management strategies to mitigate healthcare worker exposure risks [26]. The study highlighted the importance of considering the specific context of each hospital and emphasized three key dimensions of the resilience process: effects, implemented strategies, and the resulting impacts. They identified absorption, adaptation, and transformation strategies as key factors contributing to hospital resilience.

Besides, Sharma and Sharma [13] addressed a critical gap in disaster preparedness research by proposing a framework to assess hospital resilience against unforeseen disasters like COVID-19. This framework goes beyond basic clinical skills to delve into the transitions healthcare providers experience during emergencies. It emphasizes the importance of not only possessing knowledge of disaster protocols but also having the competencies to navigate the crucial transformations within the hospital environment. The framework focuses on four key aspects: (1) Public Health Emergency Preparedness which evaluates understanding of general protocols, (2) Training which assesses completion of programs equipping them with essential response skills, (3) Capacity to Deal with an Emergency which examines resource availability for patient surges, and (4) Prior Experience in Managing an Emergency which explores past involvement in similar situations to understand potential impact on confidence and effectiveness. By analyzing these core areas through surveys and interviews, the study aimed to identify strengths and weaknesses in hospital resilience. This information could then be used to develop targeted interventions to improve overall preparedness for future emergencies.

5 Conclusion

The resilience of healthcare supply chains, especially within hospitals, is crucial due to its direct impact on public health and safety. Enhancing hospital resilience ensures continuous healthcare quality or performance, manages patient flow during crises, and maintains system integrity during disruptions. This is increasingly important with the rise of natural disasters, pandemics, and global warming.

This chapter explored hospital resilience in the healthcare supply chain, analyzing literature to define it as the capacity to resist, absorb, and recover from shocks while maintaining essential functions and adapting to new circumstances. This includes both reactive capabilities and proactive measures, along with the ability to learn and adapt from past incidents.

Across the literature review, numerous resilience evaluation methods exist. In this chapter, we examined the qualitative methods for evaluating hospital resilience. These methods provide valuable insights into organizational resilience, leadership, communication, and learning. They develop practical frameworks, identify critical indicators, and offer actionable recommendations for enhancing resilience adapted to specific settings and challenges.

Research in hospital resilience focuses on refining frameworks, conducting empirical studies, integrating technology, and translating theoretical models into practical applications. Future research should develop standardized metrics, investigate cost-effectiveness, and explore the potential of real-time data analysis during disruptions. Further integration of diverse disciplines, advanced analytics, global comparisons, longitudinal studies, and community engagement are promising areas for advancing hospital resilience.

References

1. Aldea A, Vaicekauskaite E, Danevaand M, Piest JS (2020) Assessingresilience in enterprise architecture: a systematic review. In: IEEE 24th international enterprise distributed object computing conference (EDOC). Eindhoven, Netherlands, pp 1–10
2. Rahiel RN et al (2024) Towards developing a model for the evaluation of hospital resilience. 25ème édition du congrès annuel de la Société Française de Recherche Opérationnelle et d'Aide à la Décision ROADEF. https://roadef2024.sciencesconf.org/512898
3. Paulikiene˙B (2022) Hospital disaster resilience: a conceptual framework. Reg Formation Dev Stud 2:121–131
4. Fallah-Aliabadi S, Ostadtaghizadeh A, Fatemi F, Ardalan A, Rezaei E, Raadabadi M, Heydari A (2022) Hospital disaster resilience: development of an assessment tool using expert panel and fuzzy analytical network process. Int J Disaster Resilience Built Enviro 13(5):554–567
5. Khalil M, Ravaghi H, Samhouri D, Abo J, Ali A, Sakr H, Camacho A (2022) What is "hospital resilience"? A scoping review on conceptualization, operationalization, and evaluation. Front Public Health 10:1009400
6. World Health Organization (2021) Health service continuity planning for public healthemergencies: a handbook for health facilities: interim version for field testing. World Health Organization, Geneva
7. Moitinho de Almeida M, van Loenhout JAF, Singh Thapa S, Kumar KC, Prakash Mahara D, Guha-Sapir D, Aujoulat I (2021) Hospital resilience after the 2015 Earthquake in Nepal: Results from semi-structured interviews with hospital staff. Front Public Health 9:602509
8. Zhong S, Clark M, Hou XY, Zang Y, FitzGerald G (2014) Validation of a framework for measuring hospital disaster resilience using factor analysis. Int J Environ Res Public Health 11(6):6335–6353
9. Ahizoune S, Alaoui AM, Belrhiti Z (2023) La résilience des hôpitaux pendant covid-19: Une seule étude de cas à m'éthodes mixtes au Maroc. Kinésithérapie La Rev 23(258):3–10
10. Ravaghi H, Khalil M, Al-Badri J, Naidoo AV, Ardalan A, Khankeh H (2022) Role of hospitals in recovery from covid-19: reflections from hospital managers and frontliners in the eastern Mediterranean region on strengthening hospital resilience. Front Public Health 10:1073809
11. Rios C, Ling E, Rivera Gutierrez R, Gonzalez J, Bruce J, Barry M, de Jesus Perez V (2020) Puerto Rico health system resilience after hurricane maria: implications for disaster preparedness in the COVID-19 Era. medRxiv: Prepr Server Health Sci 20198531, 20 Sept 2020
12. Yin S, Chong CY, Ng KC, Lee KP (2020) Resilience engineering inpractice: reflecting on a pediatric hospital's preparation for unknown coronavirus outbreak. J Hosp Adm 9(6):Article 6
13. Sharma SK, Sharma N (2020) Preparedness and resilience in public health emergencies at district hospitals and community health centers. J Health Manag 22(2):146–156
14. Wijesekara NW, Wedamulla A, Perera S, Pesigan A, Ofrin RH (2020) Assessment of drought resilience of hospitals in Sri Lanka: a cross-sectional survey. WHO South-East Asia J Publ Health 9(1):66
15. Chuang S, Ou J-C, Hollnagel E, Hou S-K (2020) Measurement of resilience potential—Development of a resilience assessment grid for emergency departments. PLoS ONE 15(9):e0239472

16. Paz de Sousa KM, Rosana de Ara ujo Oliveira S, Alencar Sousa Macau Furtado BM, Ribeiro de Vasconcelos AL, Gomes de Medeiros S, Cazarin G, Soares Sampaio A, Ridde V (2023) Hospital resilience in three covid-19 referral hospitals in Brazil. Health Syst Reform 9(2):2205–2726
17. Cimellaro GP, Piqué M (2016) Resilience of a hospital emergency department under seismic event. Adv Struct Eng 19(5):825–836
18. Jin A, Li G, Yu Y, Wang J, Nie Q (2022) Establishment of hospitalresilience framework in urban China: Insight from Wuhan city. Comput Urban Sci 2(1):31
19. Holling CS (1973) Resilience and stability of ecological systems. Annu Rev Ecol Syst 4:1–23
20. Holling CS (1996) Engineering resilience versus ecological resilience. In: Schulze PC (ed) Engineering within ecological constraints. National Academy Press, Washington, DC, pp 31–44
21. Bhamra R, Dani S, Burnard K (2011) Resilience: the concept, a literaturereview and future directions. Int J Prod Res 49(18):5375–5393
22. Arji G, Ahmadi H, Avazpoor P, Hemmat M (2023) Identifying resiliencestrategies for disruption management in the healthcare supply chain during COVID19 by digital innovations: a systematic literature review. Inform Med Unlocked 38:101199
23. Wright AM, Snowdon A, Saunders M, Trampas D (2023) The necessityof healthcare supply chain resilience for crisis preparedness. Healthc Manage Forum
24. Lau Y-Y, Dulebenets MA, Yip H-T, Tang Y-M (2022) Healthcare supply chain management under COVID-19 settings: the existing practices in Hong Kong and the United States. Healthc 10(8)
25. Bruneau M, Chang SE, Eguchi RT, Lee GC, O'Rourke TD, Reinhorn AM, Shinozuka M, Tierney K, Wallace WA, von Winterfeldt D (2003) A framework to quantitatively assess and enhance the seismic resilience of communities. Earthq Spectra 19(4):733–752
26. de Araujo Oliveira SR, Cazarin G, Soares Sampaio A, Ribeiro de Vasconcelos AL, Furtado B, Gomes de Medeiros S, Correia Paes Zacarias A, Reis Andrade AC, Paz de Sousa KM, Zinszer K, Ridde V (2023) Potential strengths and weaknesses in hospital resilience in the context of the COVID-19 pandemic in Brazil: a case study. Health Syst Reform 9(2):2177–2242
27. Shang Q, Wang T, Li J (2022) A quantitative framework to evaluate theseismic resilience of hospital systems. J Earthquake Eng 26(7):3364–3388
28. Hansapinyo C (2018) Hospital resilience to earthquake-induced lifeline interruptions. IOP Conf Ser Mater Sci Eng 453(1):012059
29. Azizi F, Tavakkoli-Moghaddam R, Hamid M, Siadat A, Samieinasab M (2022) An integrated approach for evaluating and improving the performance of surgical theaters with resilience engineering. Comput Biol Med 141:105148
30. Zhong S, Clark M, Hou X-Y, Zang Y, FitzGerald G (2015) Developmentof key indicators of hospital resilience: a modified Delphi study. J Health Serv Res Policy 20(2):74–82
31. Luke J, Franklin RC, Dyson J, Aitken P (2023) Building toward adisaster resilient health system: a study of hospital resilience. Disaster Med Public Health Prep 17:e219
32. Kruk ME, Ling EJ, Bitton A, Cammett M, Cavanaugh K, Chopra M, ElJardali F, Macauley RJ, Muraguri MK, Konuma S, Marten R, Martineau F, Myers M, Rasanathan K, Ruelas E, Soucat A, Sugihantono A, Warnken H (2017) Building resilient health systems: a proposal for a resilience index. BMJ 357:j2323

Naima Rahiel is a doctoral candidate at the University of Paris 8 (France) specializing in Industrial Engineering and Production. She holds an engineering degree in Industrial Engineering from the University of Oran 2 (Algeria). Her thesis focuses on optimizing the resilience of hospital supply chains in emergency services during health crises. She is involved in the ANR project "Resilience to Global Crises through Supply Chain Reconfigurability (SC-Reborn)." Her current research interests include healthcare supply chain resilience.

Abderrahman El Mhamedi is professor at the Department of Industrial Logistics Quality and Organization of the Paris8 University (France). He is the founder and director of the research group "MGSI - Modeling and Engineering of Industrial Systems" at the University of Paris 8-Laboratory Quartz. He is involved in several industrial and scientific projects in the area of integrated Product Lifecycle and supply chain management in order to link the academic and the industrial world. He is author of more than 160 papers that have been published on national and international proceedings and journals. His research works are related to the logistic system and healthcare, product lifecycle management, simulation and optimization in supply chain.

Khalid Hachemi Received his Engineer Degree (1995) and a Master's Degree (1999) from the University of Tlemcen, Algeria. He obtained his Doctorate Degree (2008) from the Tlemcen University in Manufacturing Engineering. He is currently a full professor at the Institute of Maintenance and Industrial Safety and a researcher at the Production Engineering and Industrial Maintenance laboratory at the University of Oran 2, Algeria. His current research interests focus on automated drug dispensing systems and healthcare management.

Hospital Medicines Supply Chain Maturity Assessment Tool Based on Processes Modeling: Case Study of a Public Hospital in Morocco

22

Imane Ibn El Farouk, Amine El Asri, and Fouad Jawab

Abstract

Improving process maturity is essential for enhancing performance. One of the key processes that require improvement is the supply chain. This chapter focuses on studying Supply Chain Maturity Models (SCMM) with the goal of developing a specific SCMM for the supply chain of medicines in Moroccan public hospitals. A thorough review of existing literature on various models was conducted to identify the key characteristics of a maturity process model. Action research was utilized to model the supply chain processes and determine the scope of evaluation. A Moroccan hospital's medicine supply chain was used as a case study.

Keywords

Logistic • Healthcare • Drug • SCOR model • ARIS • FTA

Abbreviations

AMO	Assurance Maladie Obligatoire/Mandatory Health Insurance
ARIS	Architecture of integrated information systems

I. Ibn El Farouk (✉) · A. El Asri
Laboratory for Studies and Research in Economics and Management Sciences, LERSEM. ENCGJ, Chouaib Doukalli El Jadida University, El Jadida, Morocco
e-mail: ibnelfarouk.i@ucd.ac.ma

A. El Asri
e-mail: elasri.a@ucd.ac.ma

F. Jawab
Laboratory of Technologies and Industrial Services, Higher School of Technology, Sidi Mohamed Ben Abdellah University, Fez, Morocco
e-mail: Fouad.jawab@usmba.ac.ma

F. Jawab (ed.), *Hospital Supply Chain*, Integrated Science 27,
https://doi.org/10.1007/978-3-031-70292-1_22

DPRF	Direction de planification et ressources financière/Financial planning and resources management department.
FTA	Fault tree analysis
HMSC	Hospital medicine supply chain
SCMM	Supply chain maturity model
SCOR	Supply chain operations references model
SD	Supply division.

1 Introduction

The hospital is an organization with the main mission of meeting public health objectives [1]. Its strategic objectives include meeting the health needs expressed in its area, ensuring the quality of its activities, optimizing economic and organizational efficiency, providing community services, promoting health, and engaging in training and research [2].

However, there are numerous constraints that hinder the achievement of these objectives. Public hospitals are currently under pressure from supervisory bodies that aim to rationalize healthcare expenditure while also improving the quality of care. Additionally, hospitals have unique characteristics compared to other organizations, such as the absence of profit maximization, the coexistence of stakeholders with conflicting interests, and massive public intervention [3].

Like all service companies, hospitals must manage seasonal demand and a lack of visibility on future consumption. Hospitals also lack the authority to set charges, as they are determined by supervisory authorities. The provision of care is characterized by the intangibility and indivisibility of care production, relying on the work of care providers and the contribution of patients.

In Morocco, there is a strong commitment to improving the quality of patient care, particularly with the plan to make AMO medical coverage universally available from December 2022 [4, 5]. Hospital pharmacies play a crucial role in realizing this plan, as quality care cannot be provided without access to medications.

In this particular scenario, the public hospital pharmacy in Morocco is confronted with the task of guaranteeing the availability of medication at a suitable cost. The achievement of this objective heavily relies on the performance of the supply chain. Utilizing Supply Chain Maturity Models (SCMM) is considered as one of the most effective methods to enhance this performance. Therefore, the main focus of this chapter is to analyze SCMM in order to create a tailored model for the supply chain of pharmaceuticals in public hospitals in Morocco.

The subsequent contribution is structured into three primary sections. Initially, we provide an overview of the hospital supply chain and SCMM to highlight the key concepts related to maturity processes. Subsequently, we outline our research methodology prior to discussing the results.

2 Background

2.1 Hospital Supply Chain Management

Logistics management plays a crucial role in controlling both the physical and information flows within a network, all with the ultimate goal of meeting the needs of the end consumer. This satisfaction must be achieved under optimal conditions of cost, lead time, and quality. These flows move in various directions within a chain, encompassing all stages involved in delivering a product or service to consumers, as outlined by Chopra et al. [6]. The supply chain includes not only the producer and their suppliers, but also carriers, service providers, retailers, and the customers themselves. While supply chain and logistics management are distinct concepts, they are closely intertwined. Logistics management specifically focuses on managing flows and counter-flows throughout the supply chain to ensure consumer needs are met effectively. The strategic positioning of logistics management has gained significance due to the competitive advantage it offers companies in terms of cost efficiency and customer service. This advantage extends beyond the primary upstream and downstream flows to encompass return flows as well. By recognizing the importance of logistics management in enhancing overall supply chain performance, companies can better position themselves for success in today's competitive marketplace.

Hospitals are undergoing a significant transformation, with logistics management emerging as a crucial focus area. The efficient delivery of patient care relies on various activities such as procurement, inventory management, distribution to care units, and product returns. Hospital logistics encompasses a range of design, planning, and execution activities that facilitate the procurement, inventory management, and replenishment of goods and services essential for medical service provision to patients [7, 8]. The scope of logistics management within hospitals is extensive, encompassing various aspects such as resource allocation, activity planning, procurement, inventory management, in-house production, supply chain management, internal and external transport, and waste management [7–10].

Hospital logistics management is known for its high degree of complexity compared to other industries. This complexity arises from various factors, including the diversity of needs, users, products, and distribution channels, as well as unpredictable demand and the sensitive nature of healthcare. Researchers such as Moons et al. [10], and [11] have highlighted these challenges.

The increasing importance of supply chain management in public hospitals can be attributed to its critical role in managing costs and ensuring service quality. Balancing these objectives presents a significant challenge for hospital logistics management. Hospitals are expected to deliver high-quality care while controlling rising expenses. Logistics costs typically make up a substantial portion of hospital budgets, accounting for approximately 30–45% of total expenditures. These costs encompass labor expenses for handling, moving, and processing materials, asset costs, information management expenses, infrastructure costs, and procurement-related labor costs, as noted by Gonzalez et al. [12], Moons et al. [10]. To achieve the dual objectives of maximizing patient care and controlling costs, hospitals may need to adopt multiple supply chain policies.

2.2 Medicine Hospital Supply Chain

In the hospital setting, medications are classified as pharmaceutical products, representing a specialized category with specific requirements [13]. It is imperative for Hospital Pharmacies to ensure the availability of all pharmaceutical products in adequate quantities at all times. This availability is a direct reflection of the alignment between the services provided by the healthcare system and the needs of the population [14]. Medications, or drugs are the cornerstone of pharmaceutical products, and effective drug management within hospitals is a critical aspect. This management involves adhering to the "five rights": ensuring the right drug is administered at the correct dose, through the appropriate route, at the proper frequency, to the right patient [15]. The availability of medications in hospitals directly impacts the quality of service, leading to reduced mortality rates and increased patient satisfaction [16]. While prioritizing medication availability, the pharmaceutical supply chain must also prioritize safety, traceability, and compliance with regulations during dispensation [17]. Kabera and Mukanyangezi [18] have established a correlation between the availability of emergency obstetric drugs and the reduction of maternal mortality rates. Overall, the management and availability of pharmaceutical products within hospital settings are crucial components in ensuring optimal patient care and outcomes.

Ensuring availability is crucial in the healthcare industry, but another key factor that cannot be overlooked is cost. Pharmaceutical expenses represent a significant portion of hospital budgets, typically accounting for 25–30% of total costs. Logistic costs associated with medicines, including moving, conditioning, handling, and dispatching, can make up 35–40% of total logistic costs. Globally, pharmaceutical expenditure is a major concern, with estimates suggesting it makes up 20–30% of total healthcare spending [19].

In the Moroccan healthcare system, the importance of medicines is evident, as they alone make up 31.7% of total healthcare expenditure [13]. Managing drugs in hospitals is a significant cost driver due to the high cost of products, as well as the storage and control requirements [20]. Medicines in hospitals follow two distinct but interconnected circuits. The clinical circuit focuses on the pharmacotherapy of hospitalized patients, from admission to discharge. The logistical circuit, on the other hand, deals with the procurement and delivery of drugs to care units [13, 21–23].

Logistics operations for medicines in hospitals are complex and differ significantly from other industries. Factors contributing to this complexity include (1) pricing, (2) replenishment frequency, (3) vitality level, (4) diversity of actors, (5) regulation, (6) demanding requirements, and (7) criticality for human health. Stock management in healthcare does not follow the same principles as in other industries, as a stock out can have life-threatening consequences [13, 15, 19].

In Morocco, the management of drugs in public hospitals is a top national priority, with the primary objectives being to ensure availability, accessibility, and control of expenditures [21]. This commitment is also evident within the scientific research community in Morocco, where numerous academic studies have been conducted to enhance the reliability of the medicine supply chain in public hospitals [13, 14, 16, 21, 22, 24, 25]. The interest in addressing medicine-related issues is driven by the challenges faced by public hospitals in Morocco, including: (1) Insufficient specialized pharmacists (2) Management of certain medicines outside the hospital pharmacy (3) Inadequate storage conditions for medicines (4) Failure and irregularity in delivery times of medicinal products (5) Frequent stock deviations for specific drugs (6) Problematic management of psychotropic and narcotics (7) Challenges with centralized medicine supply management for regional hospitals [13, 14]. Efforts to address these issues are crucial for ensuring the effective and efficient management of medicines in public hospitals in Morocco.

2.3 Supply Chain Maturity Model

2.3.1 Definitions and Concepts

The concept of process maturity serves as a key indicator of how well a process is performing [26]. This concept is closely tied to quality management, with Crosby being one of the first to discuss "Maturity" in his book "Quality is Free" [27]. According to Hammer [28], maturity involves the systematic enhancement of an organization's skills and processes to achieve higher levels of productivity. Maturity models utilize criteria to evaluate and depict an organization's readiness level, aiding managers in assessing process readiness and implementing improvements. These models serve as a framework for understanding the various stages of maturity within a specific domain [29].

By defining the current stage that best represents a company, maturity enables positioning within the market. The maturity model facilitates the identification of necessary capabilities to reach desired levels [30]. Zouaghi [31] defines maturity as the level of cognitive development at which a company can systematically perceive, evaluate, and act appropriately with limited rationality, developing necessary capabilities. He distinguishes between performance and maturity, with performance focusing on competition and achievement relative to specific objectives or competitors, while maturity emphasizes cognitive achievement and mastery of a situation or environment. Maturity serves as a measure for evaluating an organization's capabilities within a particular discipline [32].

The level of maturity in a company's supply chain is directly linked to the maturity of its logistics processes [33]. Process maturity is a key concept used to assess a company's ability to fulfill its responsibilities and enhance its overall performance [34]. This concept refers to how well a company has implemented processes that are clearly defined, managed, measured, controlled, and continuously improved [35]. Improving performance in the long term is a crucial goal for any organization [36]. In their research, Lefort et al. [37] developed a maturity model for supply chain process management that includes 90 maturity indicators grouped into 13 categories. This model provides a comprehensive framework for assessing and improving the maturity of supply chain processes within an organization.

According to Zouaghi [31], supply chain maturity refers to the level of cognitive development at which a company systematically perceives, evaluates, and acts appropriately with limited rationality to achieve a satisfactory solution. This is achieved by developing various capabilities such as (1) understanding the market, (2) managing market uncertainty, (3) aligning supply chain strategy with capacity and demand, (4) monitoring the supply chain with key performance indicators, (5) ensuring a cross-functional approach, integrating the company's main stakeholders in decision-making, (6) identifying the structure of the supply chain, coordinating and organizing the supply chain, (7) dedicating necessary human resources to supply chain management, (8) ensuring synchronized multi-level operational management, (9) sharing information and enhancing visibility among partners, (10) jointly managing technologies and information systems, (11) identifying and managing risks inherent in the supply chain, (12) ensuring resilience of the supply chain, (13) considering sustainable development and social responsibility within the supply chain.

2.3.2 Supply Chain Maturity Models

The current state of the art in maturity models reveals a plethora of repositories within the realm of logistics and operations management. These models categorize referees based on their academic and professional backgrounds. One such model that stands out is the Supply Chain Management Maturity Model (SCMM). Let us delve into a detailed description of this particular model.

- **Supply Chain Management Maturity Model (SCMM)"**

It's based on BPO (business process orientation) model, according what; firms can improve their performance through a "process view". BPO can minimize conflict, support connectedness within an organization, and enhance business performance [38]. Originally, SCMM was the SCOR (Supply-Chain Operation Reference) introduced by the Supply-Chain Council in 1996. It combines the processes description framework from SCOR Model and the BPO. As shown in Fig. 1, the model is organized in five levels of maturity:

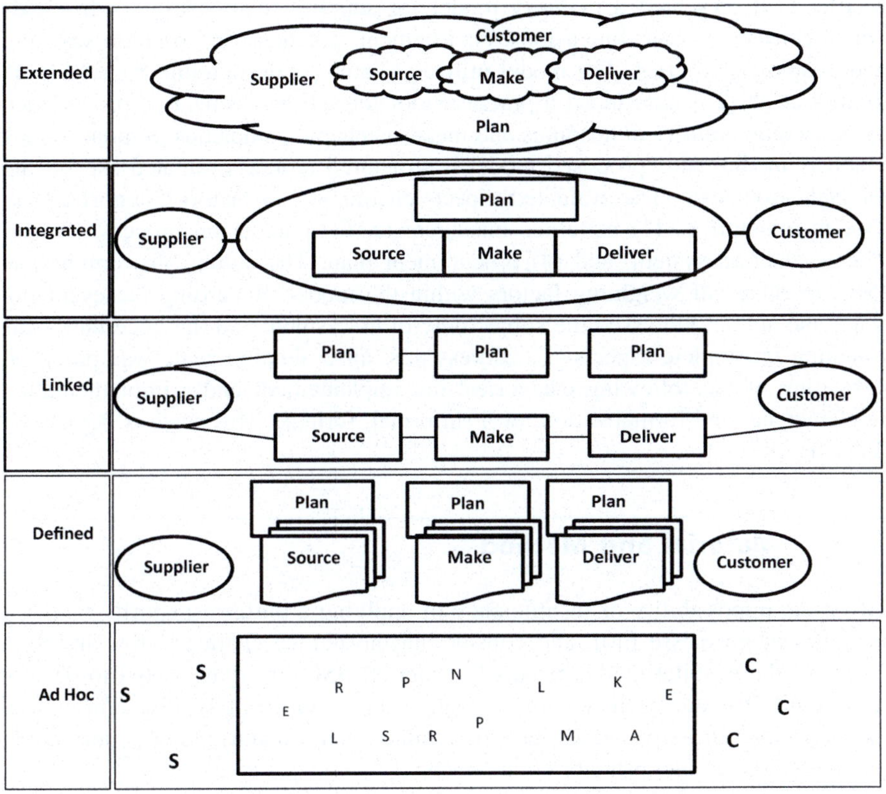

Fig. 1 Supply chain maturity model SCMM [38]

- **Level 1 (ad hoc)**: the supply chain is unstructured; there is no processes view, high cost on supply chain and low customers satisfaction.
- **Level 2 (defined)**: Basic supply chain processes are well determined and documented. Jobs and organization are still traditional.
- **Level 3 (linked)**: the internal supply chain and processes approach are in place. Cooperation across functions, and with customers and suppliers around common objectives. Reduced Supply chain costs and continuous improvement mind.
- **Level 4 (integrated)**: integration with partners becomes collaboration and practices such as CPFR and VMI are in place.
- **Level 5 (extended)**: collaboration has reached its peak; competition is now between supply chains and not between companies.

2.3.3 Supply Chain Maturity Evaluation in Hospital

At the conclusion of our research, it was observed that there is limited research on the co-design of a maturity model specifically tailored to the hospital supply chain.

Mettler [39] presented a maturity model for supplier relationships in hospitals, which consists of four dimensions: environment, practices, information structure, and people capabilities. The model utilizes a rating scale ranging from “0 to 4”. Tontini et al. [27] introduced a practical tool for self-assessment of procurement management maturity in hospitals and metal-mechanic companies. Similar to most maturity models, this proposed model is structured around evaluated aspects and an evaluation scale. The evaluated aspects encompass 14 factors categorized into four main families: (1) materials management, (2) purchasing process, (3) supplier evaluation system, and (4) procurement plan. The author also emphasized the importance of weighting factors within the model. Regarding the evaluation scale, the author addressed the subjectivity of assessment and the uncertainty surrounding incomplete aspects. To address this, an evaluation scale was proposed, consisting of the following categories: not implemented, under implementation, implemented, and formalization level (informal, formal). This scale is depicted in Table 1.

3 Material and Method

Given the impossibility or insufficiency of applying a uniform maturity model to all types of businesse [40], and considering the unique characteristics and intricacies of the hospital medicine supply chain (HMSC), we have opted to develop a customized maturity model for evaluating the maturity of HMSC. Through an extensive literature review, we have determined that a maturity assessment model should consist of two primary components:

1. **The aspects or axes to be assessed**: these axes come from the description of the processes making up the supply chain. To map the processes of HMSC, we have combined theory and practice.
2. **Rating system or evaluation scale**: For each axis, a score is given for each possible situation.

To meet these two requirements, we had to gain a thorough understanding of how the supply chain under study operates and identify the various possible situations, from the most degraded to the most sophisticated. To achieve this, we used an approach combining process modeling, performance and risk analysis. In practical terms, the success of our maturity model depends on answering these five questions:

- Q1: what are the supply chain processes, activities and players?
- Q2: how is supply chain performance measured?
- Q3: what are the disruptive factors that can hinder performance?
- Q4: What are the best practices to implement in a supply chain?
- Q5: What are the KPI to check in a supply chain?

Table 1 Maturity model (Tontini 2016)

	The price and budget process includes	Formalization and implementation Stage			
		Do not have or started to implementer informally	Formally implementing	Formally impleaded	Effectively deployed and running
Basic → Advanced	Prioritization of the participation of the largest number of participants in the quote /budgeting process				
	Adoption of formal quotation and budget that aim to identify the best proposals of the market and guide the purchasing system				
	Evaluation of proposals based on clearly defined commercial and technical criteria, aided by computerized system				
	Adoption of electronic quotation tools in order to optimize and streamline the buying process				
	Company participation in buying groups, aiming to reduce the total cost of purchase				

To answer those questions, an approach with five steps has been deployed (Fig. 2).

Implementation of our approach required the use of three tools and is: **SCOR Model, ARIS, FTA.**

SCOR Model [41] is a recognized model worldwide for its application to supply chains. It dates back to 1996, when the Supply Chain Council (SCC) created the first supply chain reference model. SCOR was developed to describe the activities associated with all the phases involved in satisfying customer requirements. It is a tool for analysis, evaluation and improvement. SCOR Model is the most suitable for our study, for the following reasons:

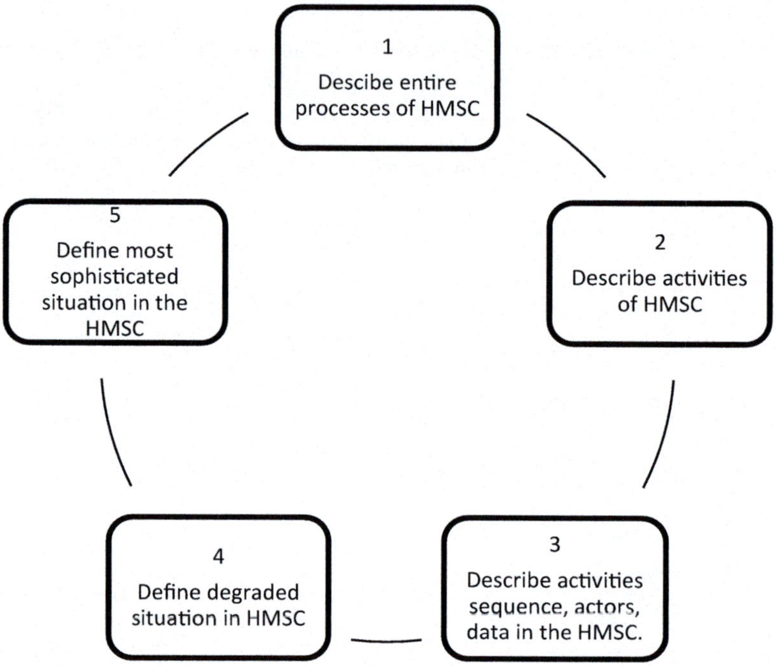

Fig. 2 Approach for HMSC maturiy assessement model (authors)

- A Supply Chain Reference Model
- An architecture based on the process approach
- An architecture that includes a performance measurement component
- Strategic and tactical supply chain modelling
- Modeling from three views: process, data, functions.
- Perfect application to internal supply chains.
- Hospital use [42], demonstrating applicability to the case.
- It provides the best practices and performance indicators of the supply chain and which serve us to identify the performance situations of the supply chain

At a basic level, the SCOR model offers three functionalities:

1 Process and activity modeling
2 Best practices
3 Performance attributes and metrics.

For processes modeling, SCOR Model proposes to break down the overall supply chain process into five main processes: PLAN, SOURCE, MAKE, DELIVER, and RETURN:

- **PLAN**: These are the processes to balance the demand and the means implemented to satisfy it (load/capacity balancing) and to define the actions to be taken in order to best match the strategy of the company. This includes business processes such as resource assessment, inventory planning, distribution, production and supply requirements.
- **SOURCE**: These are the processes responsible for making available the goods or services needed to meet anticipated or actual demands. These include the raw material, components, transportation service, storage. This includes operational processes such as receiving, verifying, storing, and transferring raw materials and management processes such as setting up contracts and supplier certification, quality management and performance management.
- **MAKE**: These are the processes allowing the transformation of raw materials into a final state in order to meet anticipated or actual requests. This includes operational processes (such as raw material replenishment, product manufacturing and testing, packaging, storage and/or product shipping) and management processes such as equipment and facility management, quality management, inventory management, scheduling (short term).
- **DELIVER**: These are the processes that provide the goods and services in order to respond to forecast or actual requests. they include demand management (order entry, creation and maintenance of the customer database, management of the allocation of products/services, maintenance of a price database). The associated management processes are transport management, warehouse management (geographical optimization of warehouses, etc.), inventory management of finished products, quality management of finished products.
- **RETURN**: Return is both upstream and downstream. This is the return of raw materials (to suppliers), and the reception and management of returns of finished products (by customers). This includes return authorization, planning, receipt and refund as well as defining and maintaining return rules/conditions, return inventory management, network configuration (reverse logistics).

In summary, the SCOR model was used to model the processes and activities of the supply chain studied. This modeling identifies the axes and sub-axes to be audited. the model enabled us to identify situations of high maturity thanks to best practices and performance indicators.

ARIS is an IDS Scheer solution for modelling business processes. The usefulness of ARIS has gone beyond the link between economics and computer technology to be applied to purely economic subjects. The process approach is at the heart of the ARIS architecture, and is also closely linked to supply chain performance evaluation. Modeling with ARIS is highly appropriate for our case. It enables us to identify the supply chain's operational activities, the documents and the actors involved, thanks to the following features: functional view, functions tree, organizational view, data view flowchart, the model Entity -Relation Modeling, the process view, the process chain.

FTA (fault tree analysis), is a causes/effects analysis tool with what we search for and identify all possible combinations of causes behind an undesirable event (Xing and Amari 2008). Among all causes/effects analysis tool, we consider that FTA is the most suitable to establish our maturity model. It serves to identifying undesirable situations that will be considered as areas of poor maturity. Table 2 gives the correspondence between each step for our approach and mobilized tool.

Once, the axes and axes to be audited are identified, and according to any maturity assessment tool, it is vital to define a rating system to evaluate the maturity of each area. To do it, we adopted a notation system as mentioned in Table 3.

Table 2 Correspondence between approach steps and tool (authors)

	Step	Tool	Objectif
1	Descibe entire processes of HMSC	SCOR Model • TOP level (1) • Processes configuration (2)	• Define the dimensions to evaluate • Define normal situation in each activities wich will be noted "1"
2	Describe activities of HMSC	SCOR model • Processes element level (3)	
3	Describe activities sequence, actors, data in the HMSC	ARIS • Function view • Organization view • Data view • Processes view	
4	Define degraded situation in HMSC	FTA	Define situation wich will be noted "0"
5	Define most sophisticated situation in the HMSC	SCOR Best practices Performance Metric	Define situation wich will be noted "2" or "3"

Table 3 Rating system (authors)

Situation	Note
The activity mentioned in the SCOR model is not deployed	0
The activity mentioned in the SCOR model is deployed without KPI or bests practices	1
The activity mentioned in the SCOR model is deployed with KPI and one best practices	2
The activity mentioned in the SCOR model is deployed with KPI and more than one best practice	3

Example For activity ES.2[1] "***assess suppliers performance***", the good practice stipulates "all the indicators according to which this performance must be assessed", so we asked the question: Do you monitor the performance of your suppliers? If the answer is " not", we note "0", if yes, we note "1", if yes, with all the required indicators, we note "2".

Since the SCOR model gives the overall configuration of a supply chain, we had to extract the processes and activities that concern our HMSC. This is why it was vital to use an action research approach, through a case study of a public hospital in Morocco.

4 Results

The obtained results comprise of two components:

1. The design of the maturity audit grid of HMSC
2. The application of the grid to assess the maturity of an HMSC.

Our research-action methodology led us to conduct a comprehensive study at a regional hospital in Morocco, referred to as hospital X. This hospital has a capacity of 400 beds and is designed to cater to the needs of 800,000 individuals. It is staffed by 75 specialized doctors, several general practitioners, and approximately 170 nurses from various categories. Through observations and interviews, we were able to analyze and model the processes and activities of the HMSC. The management of medications within the hospital falls under the responsibility of the pharmacy department. This department is headed by a chief pharmacist, supported by a team of assistant pharmacists, nurse preparers, and a secretary. The pharmacy oversees a diverse range of drugs, with approximately 400 different molecules being managed. These molecules are utilized to varying extents by the different units of care.

The logistic circuit is initiated at the pharmacy and care services levels, its purpose is the supply of medicines to all the hospital services. At Hospital X, this circuit includes four basic steps and three supports. The basic steps are: drug selection, acquisition, distribution and use. The support steps are the steps that accompany the basic steps, it is: traceability of stock movements, inventories and management of expiry.

Selection: This document serves as the annual assessment of drug needs. It aims to answer two crucial questions: which articles should be purchased and how much should be bought. The selection process occurs on a yearly basis and involves

[1] Is the code provided by the SCOR model to this activity. the "E" corresponds to the ENABLE process, the "S" corresponds to the SOURCE process, and the "2" is the rank of this activity. ca means that the second activity in ENABLE SOURCE is vendor performance management.

collaboration among various stakeholders, including pharmacists, heads of care units, and the head of administrative affairs. The selection of drugs is based on the national nomenclature established by the Moroccan healthcare ministry. This nomenclature undergoes an annual review and is sent to hospital delegations by the procurement division.

In addition, Hospital X has a separate budget known as "SEGMA" (Service Managed Autonomously), which allows for the direct acquisition of medicines from laboratories. This budget is specifically allocated for three purposes: acquiring medicinal products that are not listed in the nomenclature, obtaining drugs that are urgently needed but currently out of stock, and procuring drugs that have not been successful in the market. These unsuccessful drugs are those managed under the nomenclature's International Nonproprietary Name (DCI) but for which the supply division has been unable to select a supplier.

The budget designated for acquiring products listed in the nomenclature is referred to as the operating budget. It is important to note that both the operating budget and the SEGMA budget cover all pharmaceuticals, not just medicines. However, the majority of the budget is allocated to medicines. Approximately 60% of the allocated budget is dedicated to drug purchases, while the remaining 40% is allocated for medical devices. Usually, the SEGMA budget constitutes approximately 5% of the total budget.

Acquisition: It' is the phase of drug purchase. There are two types of acquisition:

- Procurement from Supply Division, for drugs managed on operating budget.
- Acquisition from laboratories.

For both types of acquisition, the latter consists of:

- Forward the annual order to the Supply Division or Laboratory.
- Receiving medication.

Distribution: This is the provision of drugs to care units for administration to patients. Distribution is a shared task between the pharmacy and the care unit. There are several modes of distribution according to the type of the DCI and also the urgency of the need, these modes will be detailed further.

Use of medicines: We designate by use, the logistic treatment of the drug and not its modes of administration to patients, this is the job of doctors and nurses. After replenishment of the unit, drugs are stored in identified cabinets. Narcotics are stored in locked cabinets. The head nurse distributes them to the various teams of nursing assistants. The system adopted within the care units at Hospital X is the 3-day staffing distribution; the nursing aid teams must keep a stock movement record.

Traceability of movements: It's the postponement of all movements in and out of a stock. The information entered is: denomination, the quantity of the movement, the destination or origin, the expiry date. The points of capture of movements are multiple and are located at the borders between the stock areas. Within the hospital, we distinguish three stock areas:1. Pharmacy Inventory, 2. Care Unit Pharmacy Inventory, 3. Stock per shift.

Inventories: Inventory refers to the process of tallying the quantity of items present in the inventory at a specific moment. The management of inventory is an integral part of the medication cycle, and it is applicable in both the hospital pharmacy and the care units. There are three types of inventories: 1. *Monthly inventories*: These are conducted at the care unit level and serve as the basis for the monthly medication order.2. *Annual inventories*: These inventories are carried out at both the pharmacy and care unit levels. They play a crucial role in determining the annual order.3. *Periodic inventories*: Nurses conduct these inventories at the pharmacy level. Their purpose is to update the theoretical stock status by comparing it with the actual stock.

Management of expiry items: The purpose of expiry management is to handle medications that have either expired or are nearing their expiry date, which are referred to as "Near expired". This management is necessary at both the individual unit level and the pharmacy level. There are two distinct phases involved in expiry management: 1. Isolation of medications: Nurses isolate medications during inventories and gather them at the centralized pharmacy warehouse. 2. Medication Processing: The isolated medications are then centralized at the pharmacy level.

4.1 HMSC Maturity Assessment Tool

The utilization of the initial level of the SCOR Model in our modeling process yielded the subsequent outcomes:

1. **Plan**: The process of medication scheduling involves the development of an initial strategic annual plan by the DPRF and the Supply Division (SD). This plan includes determining the budgets for drug purchases and establishing the national drug nomenclature. The nomenclature outlines the specific drugs that pharmacists need to procure. The head pharmacist of each regional hospital then estimates the annual medication requirements based on consultations with medical officers and historical consumption data. Subsequently, the SD consolidates the medication needs of all regional hospitals to create a unified list of requirements.
2. **Source**: Following the consolidation of the annual medication requirements, the objective is to align these needs with the available resources in the national pharmaceutical market. This process encompasses various components such as:
   - *Supplier consultations*: The SD identifies potential suppliers through a tender process to secure the best prices. The tender serves the dual purpose of ensuring fairness among bidders and maximizing bids to enhance the selection and negotiation process.

- *Logistics*: This involves receiving and verifying the quality and compliance of drugs with standards, as well as storing medications in designated facilities.
- Payment processing

3. **Make**: While most drugs are procured externally, there is minimal in-house preparation conducted by pharmacists, which does not constitute a significant portion of the overall process.
4. **Distribution**: The delivery of medications from suppliers to healthcare units is coordinated by the DA, which establishes a delivery schedule with suppliers and transports the drugs to hospitals. Subsequently, the hospital pharmacy distributes the medications to various care units using different methods such as globalized distribution, nominative distribution, or advance distribution.
5. **Return**: The process of returning items is a significant aspect of the HMSC. It involves returning drugs that were delivered incorrectly (not ordered) or non-compliant. Additionally, care units return expired, surplus, or nearly expired medications.
6. **Enable**: Enablement processes are essential in providing the necessary resources for carrying out other processes. This includes inventory management, for instance.

By categorizing the processes in the HMSC (as shown in Fig. 3), all activities are clearly defined. Subsequently, each category was further analyzed using ARIS to identify key parameters, as outlined in Table 4.

By compiling all the information obtained so far, we have been able to determine the areas to be assessed:

1. **Demand management**: forecasting of annual need in medicine in order to satisfy the patient care
2. **Inventory management**: management of inventory in pharmacy and the unit care
3. **Purchasing management**: relationship between pharmacy and the procurement division
4. **Deliver management**: distribution of medicine to unit care
5. **Return management**: return medicine from unit care and how to manage this in order to increase efficiency.

The maturity assessment model is shown in Fig. 4. It shows the five axes to be evaluated, and the corresponding maturity scale. This scale consists of four levels, from 0 to 3 and which corresponds to the rating system already explained in the Table 2. In summary, the maturity assessment grid comprises five axes and 28 questions. An extract from this grid is shown in Table 5.

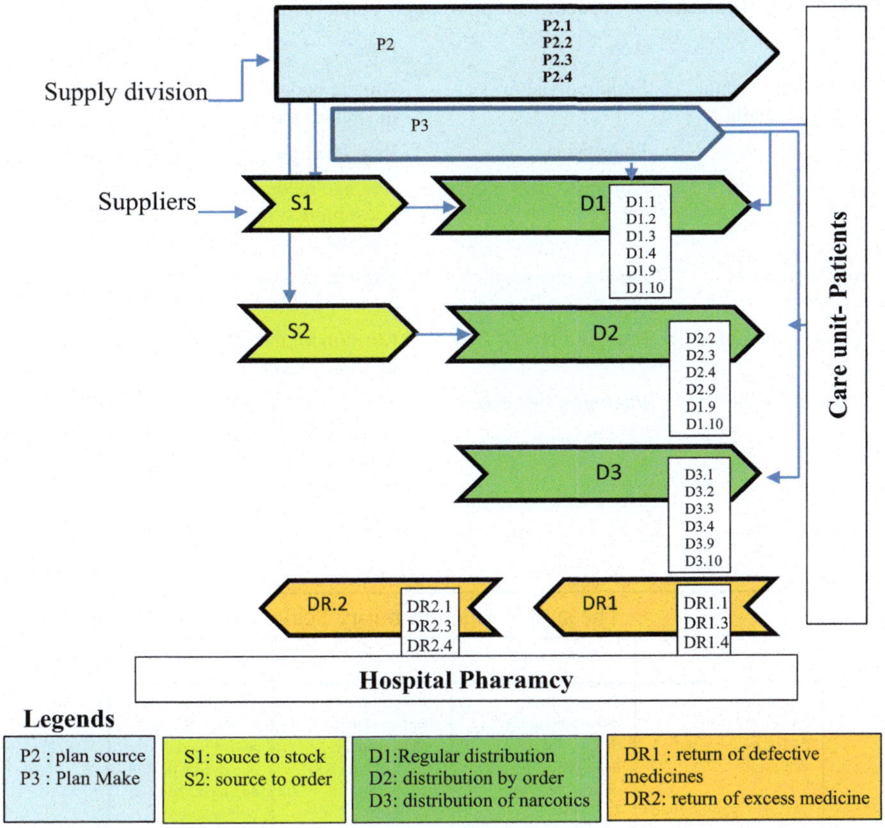

Fig. 3 Processes categories modeling (authors)

4.2 Hospital Medicine Supply Chain Maturity Evaluation

The maturity level of the studied HMSC is presented in this report. The supply chain has undergone an assessment using the maturity grid (Table 5) that was specifically designed for this purpose. Interviews were conducted with the identified actors (Table 4) to gather information. Based on the results obtained from the maturity audit (Fig. 5), it is evident that the HMSC has a very low maturity level. The maximum average score is less than 1. Further details regarding the maturity level are provided for each axis:

1. **Demand management**: The absence of a proper forecast for the demand of medicinal products has been identified as a significant issue in demand management. Annual planning of drug needs is solely based on past consumption data, lacking strategic planning which hinders effective drug inventory management.

Table 4 Key parameters of medicines hospital supply chain (authors)

Activités	Actors	Data	Documents
Estimate the anuual need of medicines	Supply division	Annual budget of medicines purchasing	Order form
Order medicines	Pharmacist	Real inventory	Prescription
Receive medicines	Administrative affairs chief	Average medicines consumption in the hospital	National list of medicines
Stock medicines	Doctor, pharmacist, nurses	Expiration date	Order wad
Distribute medicines	Care unit chief	Consumption level inventory level	Delivery sheet
Return medicines	Pharmacy dispenser	Medicines national classification	Order form
	Hade nurse	Address storage	Stock file
	Medicines committee		Narcotic register

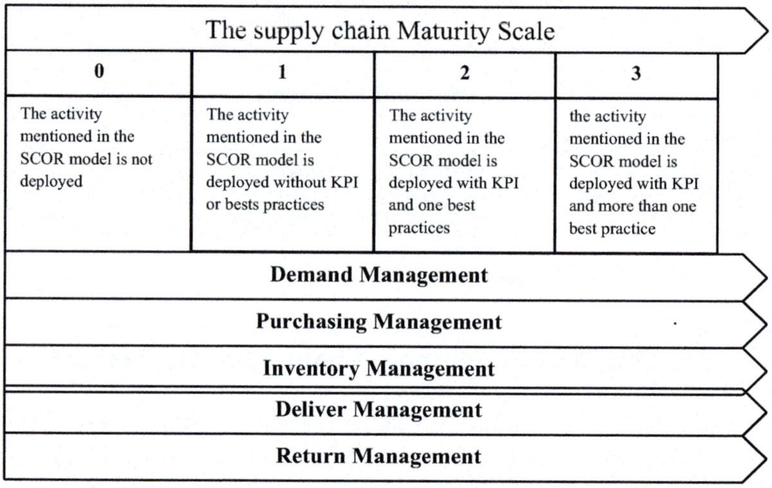

Fig. 4 Hospital medicine supply chain maturity model (authors)

2. **Purchasing**: The centralized drug purchasing process by the Supply Division aims to lower purchase costs, however, there is a lack of supplier relationships and monitoring systems for supplier performance. The volumes purchased are determined by inaccurate forecasts.
3. **Inventory management**: it faces challenges due to the lack of information integration. Manual stock updates result in significant stock discrepancies. Irregular

Table 5 Extract of hospital medicine supply chain maturity assessment tool (authors)

Maturity level/ questions		3	2	1	0
A	Demand management				
1	Do you forecast the medicine demand	Yes we use a specific workflow to have accuracy forecast	Yes, based on history of consumption and other calculation	Yes, based on history	No
2	What is the frequency of forecast?	1 month	6 month	1 year	Any forecasting activity
3	Do you calculate the forecast precision?	Yes, and we have a very high precision	Yes, but precision is precision is not yet good	Sometimes	No
4	Do you know the drug consumption?	It is update automatically	Yes	Not for all articles	No

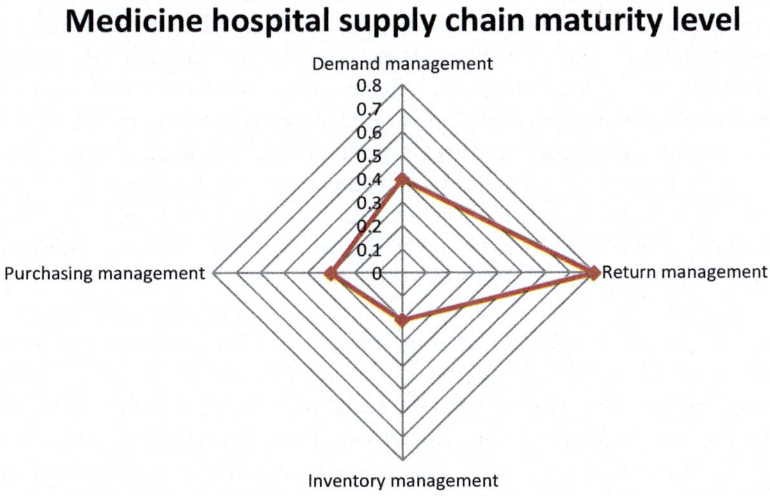

Fig. 5 Result of HMSC maturity assessment (authors)

stock checks lead to poor control over the stock situation. The fixed security stock level is not tailored to individual consumption variability or supply difficulties.

4. **Return management**: The efficiency of this axis appears to be unparalleled. Undoubtedly, the return of medications plays a vital role in the supply chain, particularly when dealing with perishable products. The return process involves transferring the medications from the treatment unit back to the pharmacy.

This process specifically targets drugs that are nearing their expiration date. It has been observed that this procedure incorporates a commendable practice, wherein returned drugs are exchanged for other medications within various healthcare facilities. This practice, initiated by the chief pharmacists across different health structures in Morocco, significantly enhances the cost optimization of medication returns.

Upon analyzing the factors contributing to the observed dysfunctions at the conclusion of the audit, we have identified several key areas where the maturity of the HMSC can be enhanced. These areas are outlined below:

1. **The centralization of drug purchases**: The strategy of centralizing purchases has been a long-standing and widely adopted approach. However, when it comes to procuring medicines for regional hospitals in Morocco, this practice presents a challenge. The Ministry of Health's supply division, which is responsible for these purchases, faces the issue at hand. Each year, this division consolidates the entire country's medication requirements and negotiates bulk purchasing agreements with suppliers. Additionally, they handle the logistics of delivery. Hospital pharmacies, on the other hand, do not have a direct relationship with the suppliers. Instead, they are required to confirm their annual medication needs, which contradicts the irregular and unpredictable patterns of drug usage. As a result, drug deliveries are unplanned and occur randomly.
2. **Medicines distribution**: Drug delivery is an essential component of the supply chain process. It is important to consider the method of drug delivery implemented in hospitals, where 90% of medications are distributed on a monthly basis. This monthly distribution involves providing each care unit with the necessary amount of drugs to meet the demand for a month, following the specific requirements of each unit; this process can be described as a "pushed flow". While this method, known as the "requisition" system, has its advantages, it has also demonstrated some limitations. The requisition system often leads to excessive stockpiling in care units to prevent shortages, which can actually result in shortages. Therefore, the requisition system is effective as a replenishment method, but only under certain circumstances:
   - Multi-functional molecules are typically consumed regularly in specific quantities and frequencies.
   - Small packaging units are used for these molecules, which are also cost-effective.
   - The pharmacy must implement a customized replenishment method based on the specific flow type, as the molecules they handle do not meet all these criteria.

5 Conclusion

In this chapter dedicated to evaluating the maturity of the drug supply chain at public hospitals in Morocco, we have developed a personalized and tailored tool for this assessment. Initially, we examined existing tools and identified the common features of any model used to measure process maturity. This included the areas that are evaluated and the scoring system. Consequently, the model we have created is based on process modeling using two main tools: the SCOR Model and ARIS. Additionally, the concept of risk management was employed to identify undesirable situations.

By applying this model to a regional hospital in Morocco, we were able to determine the level of maturity of its drug supply chain and identify the major issues that it faces. These issues primarily revolve around the centralized supply of medications and the standard distribution of drugs to the care units.

To improve maturity and enhance performance, it is essential to propose an action plan that addresses the observed dysfunctions. In terms of supply centralization, our proposal is to maintain this approach due to the advantages it offers in terms of streamlining flows and reducing costs. However, it should be revised to establish a relationship between the hospital's pharmacy and the supplier. This relationship would facilitate downstream flow and enable adjustments in medication deliveries to both the pharmacy and the care units.

Regarding the distribution of medicinal products, it is important to recognize that the current standardized method does not cater to the diverse consumption patterns of different molecules. Therefore, we recommend customizing the distribution process and adopting demand-driven modes based on the specific characteristics of each molecule.

References

1. Qin X, Wang BL, Zhao J, Wu P, Liu T (2023) Learn from the best hospitals: a comparison of the mission, vision and values. BMC Health Serv Res 23(1):792. https://doi.org/10.1186/s12913-023-09699-8. PMID: 37491237; PMCID: PMC10367322
2. Fonseca Pires J, Rey C, Más-Machuca M, Bastons M (2016) Management by missions in the healthcare sector. Rev Calid Asist 31:239–242. https://doi.org/10.1016/j.cali.2016.03.003. Epub 2016 Apr 8. PMID: 27068141
3. Bonvoisin F, Chaabane S, Sénéchal O, Tahon C (2014) Evaluation de la performance des blocs opératoires: du modèle aux indicateurs. Logistique & Manag 22:33–42. https://doi.org/10.1080/12507970.2014.11665666
4. Chahouati W (2021) La Qualité dans les hôpitaux publics marocains : Enjeux et pistes d'amélioration
5. Fariji K (2012) Comptes nationaux de santé 2010, principaux résultats des CNS et analyses des dépenses des principaux financements du système de santé au Maroc, Sept 2012
6. Chopra S, Sodhi M, Lücker F (2021) Achieving supply chain efficiency and resilience by using multi-level commons. Decis Sci
7. Frichi Y, Jawab F, Boutahari S (2019) SEM to analyze the interaction between hospital logistics and quality of care, a systematic review. Presented at (LOGISTIQUA 2019), IEEE, Montreuil, Paris, France, pp 1–5

8. Ibn El Farouk I, Jawab F, Talbi A (2018) Tableau de bord de la supply chain du médicament à l'hôpital public, 1. Auflage. ed, 2018. Éditions universitaires européennes, Saarbrücken
9. De Vries H, Jahre M, Selviaridis K, van Oorschot KE, Van Wassenhove LN (2021) Short of drugs? Call upon operations and supply chain management. Int J Oper Prod Manag
10. Moons K, Waeyenbergh G, Pintelon L (2019) Measuring the logistics performance of internal hospital supply chains—A literature study. Omega 82:205–217
11. Bélanger V, Beaulieu M, Landry S, Morales P (2018) Where to locate medical supplies in nursing units: an exploratory study. Supply Chain Forum Int J 19:81–89
12. Gonzalez M, Nachtmann H, Pohl E (2017) Time-driven activity-based costing for health care provider supply chains. Eng Econ 62:161–179
13. Ibn El Farouk I, Jawab F (2020) Improving sustainability in public hospital through Medicines Supply chain management. Presented at (LOGISTIQUA20), IEEE, Fez, Morocco, pp 1–5
14. Benazzouz T, Charkaoui A, Echchatbi A (2019) Risks related to the medical supply chain in public hospitals in Morocco: qualitative study. Pharm Hosp Clin 54:19–29
15. Law KMY (2016) How schedule issues affect drug logistics operations: an empirical study in hospitals in China. Ind Manag Data Syst 116:369–387
16. El Midaoui M, Qbadou M, Mansouri K (2021) Logistics chain optimization and scheduling of hospital pharmacy drugs using genetic algorithms: Morocco case. Int J Web-Based Learn Teach Technol 16:54–64
17. Halouani N, Dhouib N (2014) A linguistic approach to the organization of drug flows: the case of CHU Habib Bourguiba. In: Presented at the 2014 international conference on advanced logistics and transport (ICALT). IEEE, Hammamet, Tunisia, pp 281–285
18. Kabera JC, Mukanyangezi MF (2024) Influence of inventory management practices on the availability of emergency obstetric drugs in Rwandan public hospitals: a case of Rwanda Southern Province. BMC Health Serv Res 24:14
19. Franco C, López-Santana ER, Figueroa-García JC (2018) A mathematical model under uncertainty for optimizing medicine logistics in hospitals. Applied computer sciences in engineering communications in computer and information science. Springer International Publishing, Cham, pp 53–60
20. Postacchini L, Ciarapica FE, Bevilacqua M, Mazzuto G, Paciarotti C (2016) A way for reducing drug supply chain cost for a hospital district: a case study. J Ind Eng Manag 9:207
21. El Afia A, Mezouar H (2017) A global mapping of the Moroccan supply chain of hospital drugs, and a simulation of the dispensation process. In: Proceedings of the 2nd international conference on big data, cloud and applications. Presented at the BDCA'17: 2nd international conference on big data, cloud and applications, ACM, Tetouan Morocco, pp 1–8
22. Ouzayd F, Tamir M, Chiheb R (2017) Analysis of the logistic rate of the patient satisfaction in the drug supply chain: case of Moroccan hospital system. In: Rocha Á, Correia AM, Adeli H, Reis LP, Costanzo S (eds) Recent advances in information systems and technologies, advances in intelligent systems and computing. Springer International Publishing, Cham, pp 670–678
23. Pinna R, Carrus PP, Marras F (2015) The drug logistics process: an innovative experience. TQM J 27:214–230
24. El Asri A, El Farouk II, Jawab F, Arif J, Moufad I (2022) The drug supply chain at the public hospital in Morocco: a literature review. Presented at the (LOGISTIQUA22), IEEE, EL JADIDA, Morocco, pp 1–5
25. Ibn El Farouk I, Jawab F, Abdennebi T (2016) From modeling to logistic KPI Use of SCOR model and ARIS to build a dashbord to manage medicines supply chain in moroccan public hospital, Presented at (CIST), IEEE, Tangier, Morocco, pp 746–750
26. Dahlin G (2020) What can we learn from process maturity models?—A literature review of models addressing process maturity. Int J Proc Manag Benchmarking 10:495–519. https://doi.org/10.1504/IJPMB.2020.110285
27. Tontini G, De Carvalho LC, Schlindwein NFDC, Tomarevski V (2016) Maturity model of procurement and supply management in small and medium-size enterprises: a benchmarking of hospitals and metal-mechanic companies. Int J Qual Serv Sci 8:315–333. https://doi.org/10.1108/IJQSS-04-2016-0036

28. Hammer M (2007) The process audit. Harv Bus Rev 85(4):111
29. Akbar MA, Leiva V, Rafi S, Qadri SF, Mahmood S, Alsanad A (2022) Towards roadmap to implement blockchain in healthcare systems based on a maturity model. J Softw Evol Process 34:e2500
30. Crawford JK (2006) The project management maturity model. Inf Syst Manag 23:50–58
31. Zouaghi I (2013) Company supply chain maturity: Conception of an assessment model and implementation. Thesis Grenoble University
32. De Oliveira MPV, Bronzo MPK (2011) The supply chain process management maturity model—SCPM3. In: Onkal D (Ed) Supply chain management—Pathways for research and practice. InTech
33. McCormack K, Bronzo Ladeira M, Paulo Valadares De Oliveira M (2008) Supply chain maturity and performance in Brazil. Supply Chain Manag Int J 13:272–282
34. Röglinger M, Pöppelbuß J, Becker J (2012) Maturity models in business process management. Bus Process Manag J 18:328–346
35. Van Looy A, De Backer M, Poels G (2011) Defining business process maturity. A journey towards excellence. Total Qual Manag Bus Excell 22:1119–1137
36. Rosemann M, Vom Brocke J (2010) The six core elements of business process management. In: Brocke JV, Rosemann M (eds) Handbook on business process management 1. Springer, Berlin, pp 107–122
37. Lefort G, Servien R, Quesnel H, Billon Y, Canario L, Iannuccelli N, Canlet C, Paris A, Vialaneix N, Liaubet L (2020) The maturity in fetal pigs using a multi-fluid metabolomic approach (preprint). Dev Biol
38. Lockamy A, Mccormack K (2004) The development of a supply chain management process maturity model using the concepts of business process orientation. Supply Chain Manag: Int J 9:272–278. https://doi.org/10.1108/13598540410550019
39. Mettler T (2011) Transformation of the hospital supply chain: how to measure the maturity of supplier relationship management systems in hospitals? Int J Healthc Inf Syst Inform 6:1–13
40. Schweiger J (2014) A theory-based perspective on maturity models in purchasing and supply management
41. Morana J (2008) L'utilisation d'indicateurs logistiques: une étude exploratoire via le modèle SCOR. Logistique Manag 16:31–44
42. Hassan T (2006) Logistique hospitalière: organisation de la chaîne logistique pharmaceutique aval et optimisation des flux de consommables et des matériels à usage unique. Informatique [cs]. INSA de Lyon

Imane Ibn El Farouk Graduated in Supply Chain Management and obtained her Ph.D. in Public Hospital Medicine supply chain management. Currently, she is Professor of supply chain management in Chouaib Doukalli University of EL JADIDA. Her research activities are mainly focused on the study of upstream supply chain, supply chain performance monitoring, supplier's relationship and hospital logistic. She has published numerous articles in this field. His research activity is documented by publications in peer-reviewed international scientific journals and several communications in international and national congresses.

Amine El Asri Holder of a Master's degree in Supply Chain Management: "Optimisation of the warehousing and distribution logistics process", currently a Doctoral Researcher in Supply Chain Management, member of the Research Laboratory [LERSEM] of the ENCGJ_ University [Chouaib Doukkali] in Morocco, has professional experience as Supply Chain Coordination Manager in a multinational company. His research area is Supply Chain Maturity in the industrial sector in Morocco

Fouad Jawab Professor of Supply Chain at the Higher School of Technology of the Sidi Mohamed Ben Abdellah University of Fez, Morocco.

He has held several scientific and administrative responsibilities. He founded the International Conference on Logistics and Supply Chain Management (LOGISTIQUA), which he continues to develop with the support of several research teams in Morocco and abroad.

He is the author and co-author of more than 180 publications in national and international journals and proceedings. His research focuses on modeling, simulation and optimization of the supply chain, hospital supply chains and urban logistics. He is also an expert with several renowned organizations and a reviewer for prestigious journals.

Hospital Supply Chain Resilience: An Experimental Case Study from the Covid-19 Crisis

23

Ahmed Chtioui, Imane Bouhaddou, and Asmaa Benghabrit

Abstract

The health crisis of Covid-19 has affected all spheres of human activity hard. Because of the cruel lack of funding and resources, particularly at the height of the pandemic, health care sectors around the world, which were meant to fight the spread of the disease and restrict its extent, are out of breath. This raises concerns about the robustness of existing Hospital Supply Chain (HSC) models, designed to provide the necessary resources to ensure the delivery of high-quality medical treatment for patients. This paper aims to initially perform an empirical study through a field survey, revealing the impact of Covid-19 on the processes within the HSC of a public hospital actively engaged in patient care during the pandemic. Subsequently, a set of potential actions, encompassing both preventive and adaptive measures, to address the challenges faced by the pandemic are presented. The goal is to foster the resilience of the HSC, ensuring its capacity to effectively navigate potential future crises.

Keywords

Hospital supply chain • Crisis situation • Field survey • Resilience • Potential actions

A. Chtioui (✉) · I. Bouhaddou
L2M3S Laboratory, ENSAM, Moulay Ismail University, Meknes, Morocco
e-mail: ahmed.chtioui79@gmail.com

I. Bouhaddou
e-mail: i.bouhaddou@umi.ac.ma

A. Benghabrit
LMAID Laboratory, L2M3S Laboratory, ENSMR, Rabat, Morocco

F. Jawab (ed.), *Hospital Supply Chain*, Integrated Science 27,
https://doi.org/10.1007/978-3-031-70292-1_23

Abbreviations

CT	Crisis Times
FMECA	Failure Mode, Effects, and Criticality Analysis
FPP2	Filtering FacePiece2
GSC	Global Supply Chain
HACCP	Hazard Analysis Critical Control Point
HIS	Hospital Information System
HSC	Hospital Supply Chain
IOT	Internet of Things
JIT	Just in Time
MERS	Middle East respiratory syndrome
NT	Normal Times
RABC	Risk Analysis Bio-contamination Control
RBV	Resource-Based View
SARS	Severe Acute Respiratory Syndrome
SCM	Supply Chain Management
WHO	World Health Organization

1 Introduction

The World Health Organization (WHO) declared a public health emergency of international concern over the global outbreak of the novel virus SARS-CoV-2 (Covid-19) with origin in Wuhan, China—on 30th January 2020—[16]. It escalated to a global pandemic on 11th March 2020. The Covid-19 pandemic has been progressing rapidly [29], as shown by the reported statistics [13], with tragic consequences on a very large scale, whether in the economic, social, political, financial or other fields, but also and above all in the health sector. In this respect, the health care systems, which are supposed to be bulwarks against health crises, are finding it difficult to cope.

With the ongoing Covid-19 outbreak, healthcare systems across the world have been pushed to the brink. The approach of traditional healthcare systems to disaster preparedness and prevention has demonstrated intrinsic problems, such as failure to detect early the spread of the virus, public hospitals being overwhelmed, a dire shortage of personal protective equipment, and exhaustion of healthcare workers [38]. In the context of the effects of Covid-19 on the components of health systems, the Hospital Supply Chain (HSC), considered one of the performance levers of any hospital, as it determines the most efficient way of delivering care [14], has not escaped the impact of the crisis and has been greatly affected, which may have serious consequences on the care process (the medical care of patients).

Based on the thematic analysis we have conducted, to date, no study has addressed the impact of Covid-19 on the HSC as a whole, i.e. by conceiving the HSC as an entity integrating a set of processes and flows. For example, [23,

28, 39] have analysed the impact of Covid-19 on medical waste management, other researchers have looked at demand management in the HSC in the context of Covid-19 [19], while other researchers have assessed the psychological impact of Covid-19 on hospital logistics and administrative staff [27]. Therefore, existing studies have analysed the impact of Covid-19 in limited aspects of HSC, namely demand management and medical waste management, while other aspects (procurement, sterilization, catering, laundry, information flows, physical flows…) have not been addressed.

The objective of this study is to analyze the impact of Covid-19 on all the processes and flows of the hospital supply chain (HSC) of a public hospital directly involved in the care of patients suffering from the disease, but also to propose potential actions, whether preventive or adaptive, to cope with the pandemic and consequently to make the HSC more and more resilient in the face of possible future crises. In other words, we should answer the following research questions:

RQ1: How existing studies have addressed the impact of Covid-19 on HSC?

RQ2: Did Covid-19 impact the HSC processes to the same extent, or were some processes disrupted more than others?

RQ3: What are the actions to be taken in order to make the HSC more resilient in the face of not only Covid-19 but any crisis of similar magnitude?

To this end, we have adopted empirical research, and in particular a qualitative method based on semi-structured interviews with a relevant sample, composed of hospital staff, especially those in charge of logistics processes at the target hospital.

The remainder of this paper is organized as follows. Section 2 defines the key concepts of our study, particularly the Hospital Supply Chain and the Covid-19 disease. Section 3 presents the theoretical framework and the development of hypotheses. Section 4 describes the methodology adopted in this research. Section 5 discusses the results obtained from the interviews and draws up a conceptual framework encompassing the effects of Covid-19 on HSC. Section 6 proposes potential actions to prevent and mitigate the effects of the crisis on HSC from an approach based on dynamic capabilities theory. Section 7 presents the practical implications and limitations of this study. Section 7 presents the practical implications and limitations of this study. Section 8 concludes this study, recapitulating our contribution and highlighting future directions.

2 Theoretical Background

2.1 Hospital Supply Chain

In the literature, several authors have addressed the issue of hospital logistics. For example, Chow and Heaver [9] identify three main activities in hospital logistics (Fig. 1):

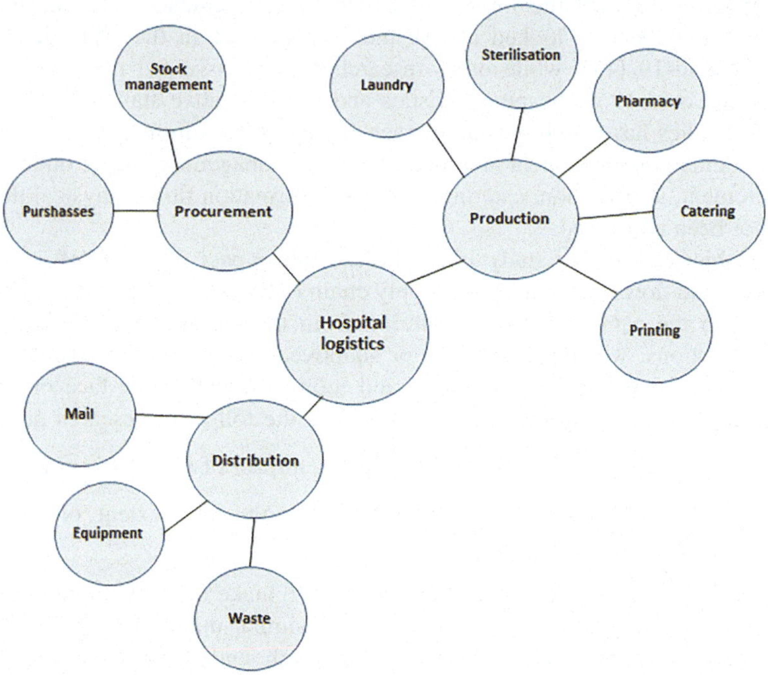

Fig. 1 The different functions of hospital logistics according to Chow and Heaver [9]

- Procurement, which includes purchasing and stock management of the various products.
- Production, which manages the various processing activities such as lingerie, kitchens, sterilization, etc.
- Distribution, which ensures that the different products are transported from the storage areas to the different points of use, or from the transport of waste to the shipping areas.

According to Landry et al. [25], hospital logistics is defined as a set of design, planning and execution activities for the purchase, inventory management and replenishment of goods and services surrounding the provision of medical services to patients.

Di Martinelly et al. [15] use the following model for the design and planning processes:

- At the design level, hospital logistics can intervene in the structuring of the main resources (technical platforms, medical imaging, etc.) and for implementation.
- At the planning level, hospital logistics contributes to the planning of resource requirements (nursing staff, medical equipment, etc.), the planning and scheduling of care activities, and the reorganization according to hazards.

For Sampieri and Bongiovanni [36] hospital logistics is "the technology of controlling physical flows and the trajectory of patients through information flows".

As a result, we can say that the logistical processes in the hospital are mainly: design, planning, procurement, production and distribution linked with physical and information flows.

Moreover, the concept of the HSC is broader and more complex in the sense that it implies inclusion and integration of the different logistic activities within the hospital, through the exchange of different types of flows between all logistic processes.

2.2 Covid-19 Disease

For World Health Organization (WHO) "coronaviruses are a large family of viruses that can be pathogenic in humans and animals. Several coronaviruses are known to cause respiratory infections in humans, ranging from the common cold to more serious illnesses such as Middle East Respiratory Syndrome (MERS) and Severe Acute Respiratory Syndrome (SARS). The latest coronavirus (SARS-COV-2) that has been discovered is responsible for coronavirus 2019 disease (COVID-19)".

"The disease is spread mainly through respiratory droplets expelled by people who cough. The risk of contracting COVID-19 from a person who has no symptoms is very low. However, many people with the disease have only mild symptoms. This is especially true in the early stages of the disease. It is, therefore, possible to contract COVID-19 from someone who has, for example, only a mild cough but does not feel sick. WHO is reviewing ongoing research on the transmission delay of COVID-19 and will continue to provide updated results". In the same context, epidemiologic data suggest that droplets expelled during faceto-face exposure during talking, coughing, or sneezing is the most common mode of transmission [22]. Prolonged exposure to an infected person (being within 6 feet for at least 15 min) and briefer exposures to symptomatic individuals (e.g., coughing) are associated with a higher risk for transmission, while brief exposures to asymptomatic contacts are less likely to result in transmission [11]. Contact surface spread (touching a surface with the virus on it) is another possible mode of transmission. Transmission may also occur via aerosols (smaller droplets that remain suspended in air), but it is unclear if this is a significant source of infection in humans outside of a laboratory setting [7, 26].

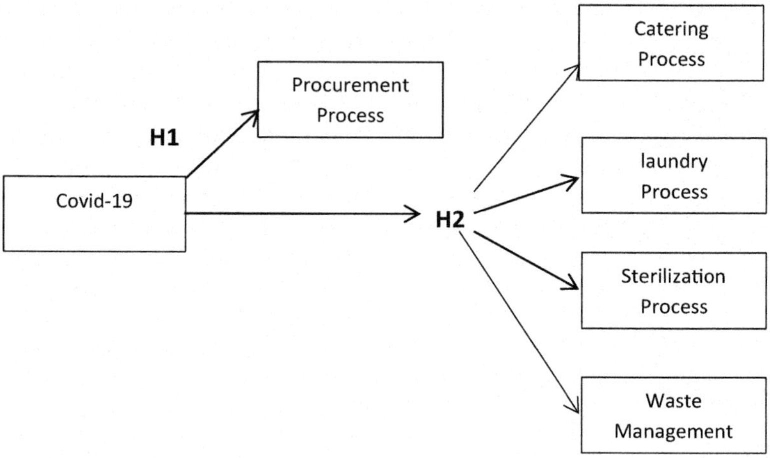

Fig. 2 Conceptual model of hypotheses

3 Theoretical Framing and Hypotheses Development

3.1 Theoritical Framinig

The objective of this study is to measure the impact of Covid-19 on HSC, from a practical case study in a hospital involved in the fight against the pandemic, to find adequate solutions to deal with this type of crisis or at least to mitigate its impact. To achieve this, we'll start with a concise thematic analysis of the impact of Covid-19 on the HSC and the Global Supply Chain (GSC), given their strong interdependence. The results of this analysis, combined with our theoretical and practical understanding of HSC processes, will then be used to develop our hypotheses.

In the next section, we derive the two hypotheses H1, H2 shown in Fig. 2.

3.2 Hypotheses Development

3.2.1 Impact of Covid-19 on the Global Supply Chain

The Covid-19 pandemic has disrupted all business operations worldwide [8, 34]. According to [21], this health crisis is the most serious in the last decade in that it has disrupted and dismantled supply chains globally. A review of the literature on the impact of Covid-19 on the GSC finds that research has addressed various aspects related to this issue. For example, Goel et al. [18] analyzed the link between supply chain performance and economic growth in the context of Covid-19 effects. On their side, Sharma et al. [37] provide an overview of the main issues facing the GSC in times of health crises, before proposing some recommendations to make it sustainable and resilient to crises. Similarly, Butt [5] explores how companies are coping with the supply chain disruptions caused by Covid-19, finding that companies are moving towards more agile production and that retailers are seeking alternative routes to manage the effects of the pandemic. More practically, Fonseca and Azevedo [16] identify the possible impacts of Covid-19 on the management and performance of the supply chain. Finally, Grida et al. [20] proposed a framework assessing the impact of measures taken by several countries to mitigate the effects of Covid-19 on SCM.

So, GSC has been greatly affected by the Covid-19 crisis, and as long as the procurement process is the gateway from HSC to GSC, or the link between the two chains, we consider that it will be the process most affected by the crisis.

H1: Procurement is the HSC process most affected by the pandemic because of its strong dependence on the global supply chain, i.e. if there is a disruption in the latter, it will be well observed in the HSC.

3.2.2 Impact of Covid-19 on the Hospital Supply Chain

About this aspect, the thematic analysis revealed that medical waste management is by far the most discussed process to show the impact of Covid-19 on the HSC. In this regard Tirkolaee et al. [39] proposed a decision support system to ensure the timely, regular, safe and efficient disposal of Covid-19 related medical waste taking into account sustainability. In China, Ma et al. [28] showed how municipal waste treatment facilities have undergone appropriate technological transformations to cope with the high infection risks of Covid-19 medical waste. Another study by Kalantary et al. [23] showed that infectious waste generation has substantially increased in hospitals, which is an additional challenge that needs to be properly managed by modifying routine activities. In addition to medical waste management, other aspects of HSC have been addressed, for example Govindana et al. [19] proposed a practical decision support system based on physician knowledge and a fuzzy inference system to manage demand in the context of Covid-19. Pharmacy, which is a strong link in the HSC, has not escaped the Covid-19 crisis, and the considerable impact of the pandemic on logistical procedures should encourage pharmacies to set up telepharmacy or remote services to best support patients during the epidemic [24]. Finally, Luo et al. [27] explored the suspected infection pathways and psychological impact of Covid-19 on hospital logistics and administrative staff.

Although the literature has focused on the medical waste management process to the detriment of other processes (catering, laundry, sterilization), our presence in the field suggests that these processes will be severely disrupted by the crisis, and may even be a vector for virus transmission if not properly controlled.

H2: Because they are part of the internal HSC, the other processes cannot escape the crisis; they can even be vectors of virus transmission if they are not properly controlled.

4 Research Design

In field surveys, the qualitative approach remains one of the most widely used data collection and analysis methods. [35] specifies that "the qualitative approach generally targets the relevant elements of the survey. It also seeks to uncover the hidden side of the survey through a policy of proximity to the respondents".

In this section, we first present the field of the study, then the sample selection technique, followed by data collection and analysis.

4.1 Experimental Field and Involvement of the Authors

The target hospital for this study is located in Meknes, a city in Morocco, a country substantially affected by the pandemic with 1,264,822 cases and a cure rate of 98,71% as of 21 September 2022 (Ministry of Public Health http://www.covidmaroc.ma). The Moulay Ismail Hospital is a medium to a large care facility (350 beds) belonging to the University Hospital of Fez, which will allow the results of this study to be generalized to a wide range of Moroccan and foreign hospitals, since the business processes in hospitals, whether medical or logistical, are practically thc same. The target departments of the survey are: procurement, finance, pharmacy, sterilization, catering, laundry and waste management.

The research team that carried out this study is composed of industrial engineers and a hospital engineer working in the target hospital. Therefore, fieldwork, access to data and interviews with the various stakeholders were not an obstacle to the conduct of the survey.

4.2 Sample Selection

The sample is made up of 28 hospital practitioners working in the various logistics departments covered by the study, i.e. procurement, catering, laundry, sterilization, medical waste management and financial services. When selecting the sample, care was taken to choose staff who are directly involved in each logistics process, diversifying the level of responsibility (senior manager, manager, logistics agent) in order to obtain relevant results.

The first criterion for selecting respondents was to have at least five years' experience in the logistics process concerned, whether in the study's target hospital or in another care facility. In addition, we required participants to have been present full-time at the hospital during the various waves of the pandemic. The profile of respondents is shown in Table 1.

To be open to other experiences relating to our subject, and above all to demonstrate the validity of our hypotheses, we chose two other hospitals belonging to the same university hospital center. We focused on the heads of the logistics departments concerned, or their representatives, and conducted the interviews by telephone, using simpler, clearly formulated questions.

Table 1 Respondent profiles in logistics processes affected by the crisis

	Procurement	Catering	Laundry	Sterilization	Medical waste management	Cash flow
Senior manager	1	1	1	–	1	1
Manager	2	2	3	1	1	2
Logistics agent	–	3	2	3	4	–
Total interviewees	3	6	6	4	6	3

4.3 Data Collection and Analysis

In our survey, we opted for one of the most frequently used qualitative methodological tools: the semi-structured interview. According to [32], the semi-structured interview is based on an interview guide, which consists of a questionnaire listing all the themes to be addressed in a certain order. Respecting this order is what differentiates it from the thematic interview. The difference with the classic questionnaire is the predominance of open-ended questions.

To this end, we began our study five months after the first Covid-19 cases were admitted to the study hospital. The surveys were conducted between August 2020 and November 2021, the duration of the survey is justified by the many waves of the crisis, but also by the availability of interviewees and especially by the complex and uncertain environment caused by the crisis.

Similarly, the interviews took place in the logistics departments concerned by the survey, and lasted between 40 min and an hour for each interviewee. Before the start of each interview, we specified that anonymity would be guaranteed to enable respondents to express themselves freely. In addition, our permanent presence at the hospital enabled us to contact interviewees whenever we needed additional data. This method provides a framework in which similar themes are addressed in each interview, while offering the flexibility to delve deeper into particular situations that seem to be rich in lessons and would not have been foreseen at the outset [3].

In addition, to carry out our survey, we first produced an interview guide comprising ten standardized questions, i.e. the same questionnaire was submitted to each respondent (Fig. 3). At the end of each interview, we drew up reports on the data provided by each respondent, in line with the qualitative data analysis method proposed by Miles and Huberman [31], which uses matrices to highlight the data collected from each respondent.

For the two remote hospitals, we opted for telephone interviews because of the crisis context. As mentioned above, the questions were simpler, more generic and clearly formulated such as: To what extent was your process disrupted by the Covid-19 crisis?; How did you adapt to the effects of the crisis?

1. Have you ever been disrupted in your duties in the same way as during the Covid-19 crisis?
2. Were you sufficiently prepared to deal with this kind of crisis?
3. Can you tell us more about how your service has been disrupted by the health crisis?
4. What aspects have been most affected in your department during the crisis?
5. To what extent has the crisis disrupted the aspect for which you are responsible?
6. How have you coped with the impact of the crisis while continuing to provide your services?
7. What vulnerabilities has the crisis revealed in the procedures you are adopting?
8. Do you think the Covid-19 crisis will cause organizational and procedural changes in your department?
9. What lessons have you learned from the crisis in relation to your duties?
10. Do you think your process will emerge from the crisis more resilient? If so, can you tell us how?

Fig. 3 Interview guide

Thus, we designed thematic analysis grids in which we considered each respondent's answer as a secondary idea, including answers obtained by telephone interviews from remote sites. The aggregation of secondary ideas enabled us to generate guiding ideas, i.e. more elaborate and relevant results transcribed and classified by theme or logistical process.

5 Results Discussion-Impact of Covid-19 on the Hospital Supply Chain

Before discussing the results of our study, we recall that the method we have adopted to show the impact of Covid-19 on HSC is based on an empirical study, from a public hospital directly involved in the care of patients with the disease. For this reason, the findings of this study are more the result of field experimentation and analysis than of a theoretical study. Thus, the analysis of the survey results combined with the operating procedures of hospital logistics processes and the health situation caused by the crisis lead to the following findings:

5.1 Impact of Covid-19 on the Procurement Process

The interviewees in the procurement process are unanimous, the health crisis caused by the Covid-19 pandemic has heavily impacted the HSC, especially in its supply chain aspect which has been severely disrupted by the substantial shortage of certain pharmaceutical products and medical equipment crucial in this situation, as it (supply chain) depends where it is located on the global supply chain, which is in turn greatly affected, thus highlighting the concept known among logisticians as the "bullwhip effect ". This concerns the products and equipment used by ordinary citizens to protect themselves against the disease as part of barrier measures (protective masks, hydroalcoholic gels), but also screening devices (sampling kits, test kits, etc.), and above all resuscitation and treatment drugs, as well as the more or less heavy medico-technical equipment needed to care for patients with complications resulting from the severe form of the disease, and requiring, for example, artificial ventilation (resuscitation beds, respirators, etc.). Not forgetting, of course, the medical devices necessary to comply with the safety protocol for the nursing staff, particularly those on the front lines, in direct contact with patients (FFP2 masks, waterproof gowns, glasses, gloves, hydroalcoholic solutions, etc.).

In this respect, it is appropriate to recall that the HSC is distinguished from the global supply chain by a much higher degree of criticality, as the unavailability of certain vital medical products or equipment is little or even not tolerated in certain cases, since the issue at stake could be not only the patient's health but also his or her survival.

From the answers of the interviewees, as well as the observations made in the field, we can deduce that the procurement process is the most affected by the crisis. The observed effects of its destabilization are due to both endogenous and exogenous factors. To be convinced of this, it is wise to return to the structure of the HSC to determine the levels likely to be affected by the crisis. Figure 4 presents the structure of the HSC according to Andersen [1].

We can deduce from this structure that HSC is split into two chains, an external chain including raw material suppliers, manufacturers or production units, distributors and intermediate suppliers, and an internal logistics chain, i.e. within the hospital, which concerns the depots and storage warehouses for the various products in use in the hospital, the functional units and even the places of care. Hence, we can say then that the impact of Covid-19 on the HSC is observed at two levels: an upstream level (external HSC), and a downstream level (internal HSC).

At the upstream level, the head of the procurement department ensures that the effects of the pandemic are largely related to the dependence of suppliers who are often far away and who in turn depend on the major distributors and/or manufacturers (local or foreign), the delivery times for hospital products, and equipment and the excessively competitive global demand, because it concerns a category of equipment specific to the disease (resuscitation beds, respirators,

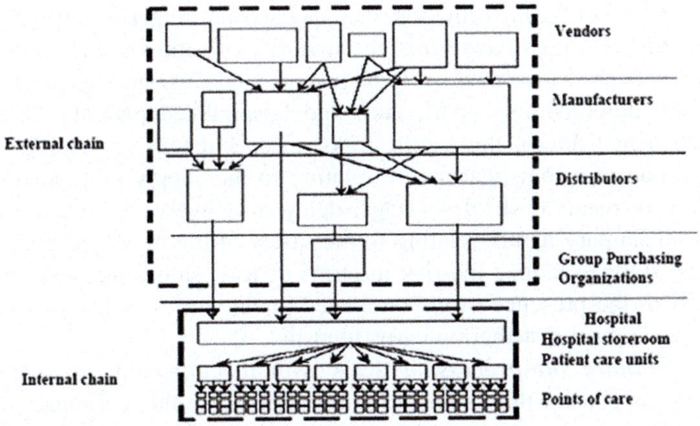

Fig. 4 The hospital supply chain according to Andersen [1]

masks, etc.) on the one hand, and on the other hand the "surprise" factor related to the pandemic (unforeseen phenomenon).

As for the downstream level, the answers of the interviewees converge towards the idea that the impact of Covid-19 on the procurement process will not be perceptible with the same intensity, it will differ from one establishment to another. It will depend on the internal management of each hospital, particularly in terms of purchasing policies (prioritization, rationalization, etc.), and stock management (safety stock, pull or push flows, JIT, etc.). What is certain, however, is that the majority of hospitals, even the most efficient and best-equipped ones, have been surprised by the pandemic, and at present, they are suffering severely from shortages or even stock shortages of certain products.

If the procurement process is proving to be the most affected by the Covid-19 crisis, what about other logistics activities?

5.2 Impact of Covid-19 on Other Hospital Logistics Processes

About ***design*** and ***planning***, it should first be recalled that these two processes take place at a strategic level and, as a result, we cannot see them being undermined by any crisis. However, it seems legitimate to question the models with which they have been approached and implemented, by asking, for example, whether during the construction of health care facilities (location, sizing) containment areas are planned to house patients suffering from highly contagious diseases, with a resuscitation service, dedicated technical platforms, etc. to avoid disrupting the normal functioning of the hospital, but above all to reduce the risk of infection. It is also questionable whether the organization of care activities (allocation of resources, scheduling of tasks) is sufficiently flexible to cope with hazards and crises (management of the unexpected), etc.

Concerning the ***production process***, it includes, as already mentioned, the logistical activities of transformation such as catering, lingerie, sterilization, etc.

First of all, in terms of ***catering***, the majority of infrastructure hospitals have collective kitchens whose mission is to prepare and distribute meals for hospital staff (nurses, administrative staff, etc.) and hospitalized patients. The interviewees confirm that during the health crisis, these kitchens are facing two major challenges: one of a logistical nature relating to the supply of foodstuffs for the manufacture of meals (risk of shortage, delay in delivery…), and the other of a hygienic and sanitary nature relating to the safety of the meals offered to patients and nursing staff, to reduce the risk in terms of food safety [the risk increases in the hospital in the presence of contaminated patients (possibility of transmission of the virus via meal distribution carts, utensils…)].

For the ***laundry sub-process***, it deals with the treatment of hospital linen. Respondents emphasize that in such circumstances, it could be a source of contamination insofar as hospital linen, whether clean or dirty, is a potential vector for nosocomial infections (hospital-acquired). They add that the infection or spread of the virus can occur either in the laundry if the rules in force are not respected (absence of process sheets, lack of disinfection equipment, incomplete drying, failure to observe the separation between clean and dirty linen, etc.), or during storage (non-ventilated premises, humidity, etc.).

Finally, for the ***sterilization sub-process***, it is recalled that it is normally responsible for ensuring the washing and disinfection of reusable medical devices after their use by the various health care services. Interviewees state that during the crisis, the workload in the department has ostensibly increased, because it has been assigned the task of sterilizing and disinfecting all hospital premises, particularly those through which suspect or infected Covid-19 patients have passed (corridors, lifts, screening rooms, technical platforms, etc.). In addition, as the sterilization department is generally part of the central pharmacy, it may be entrusted with the delicate task of managing and distributing FPP2 masks and hydroalcoholic solutions (products that are becoming increasingly rare these days).

We also have another logistical process that is not lacking in importance within the hospital, and which has been considerably shaken by the Covid-19 crisis, this process is none other than the management of ***medical and pharmaceutical waste***. Interviewees' answers confirm that the risk of infection through the waste generated in the Covid-19 isolation units is extremely high both inside and outside the hospital. This risk is omnipresent from the sorting and packaging operations (isolation site) through the storage rooms at the hospital level and the transport vehicle that takes them to the treatment units (usually outside the hospital).

In addition to the logistical processes mentioned above, this crisis context has had repercussions on the production of health care services and consequently on the cash flow of hospitals. Indeed, the financial managers interviewed point out that, due to the circumstances of the crisis, hospitals have limited their care activities to focus more on the fight against the pandemic. At the same time, health care institutions are obliged to incur substantial unforeseen expenses related to the massive acquisition of specific equipment and materials to counter the spread of the disease, changes to their structures (works, fitting out isolation units…), etc.

Figure 5 presents a framework encompassing the effects of covid-19 on all HSC processes.

This part allowed us to take a close look at the extent of Covid-19's impact on HSC. We can therefore affirm that it is not only a sanitary scourge but also a logistic crisis. It is therefore imperative to question the notion of HSC, to rethink it, to make it more agile, more reactive and sufficiently resilient to be able to face any phenomenon likely to have effects on medical activity. This is what we will try to describe in the following section through the proposal of a series of measures and actions to be undertaken in all logistical processes.

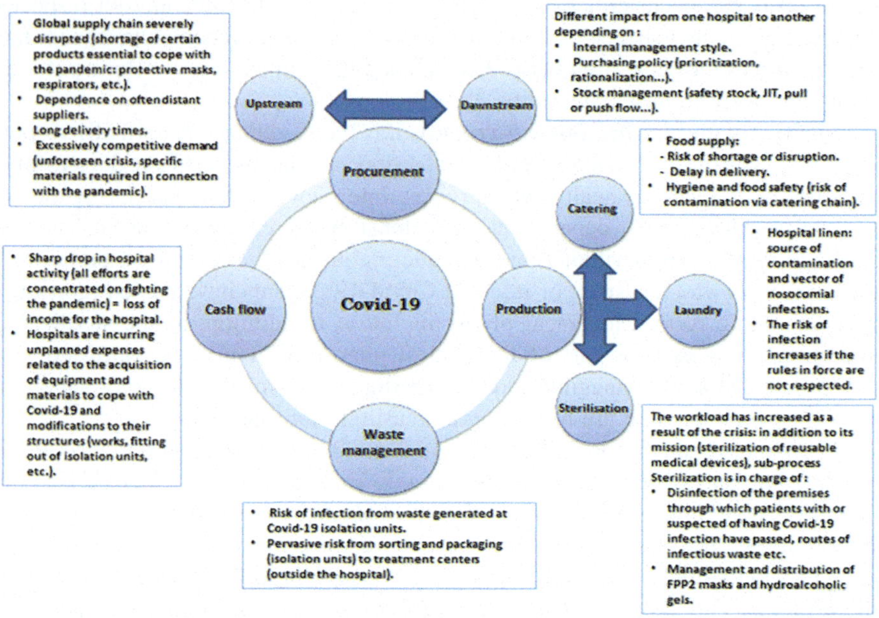

Fig. 5 A framework encompassing the impact of Covid-19 on HSC

6 Towards a Resilient Hospital Supply Chain: A Dynamic Capabilities Approach

Developing the capacity of any organization is a key factor in recovering from supply chain disruptions and building resilience. To reduce the impact and to be able to bounce back after the disruption requires a response and recovery ability. Failure to develop preparedness, response and recovery capabilities will make supply chains even more vulnerable [10].

This is all the more true in our case, insofar as the HSC suffered the same impact from Covid-19 as the overall supply chain, due to their interdependence, in addition to the serious disruption caused by the hospital's handling of patients suffering from the virus.

According to Burger and Frank [4], a dynamic capability can be defined in two ways:

- Either as a skill (Capabilites): the ability to integrate, build and above all reconfigure internal and external competencies;
- Or as the result of this ability (Capacities): capabilities held and mobilized, after the process of creation or reconfiguration.

Based on our interviews with logistics process managers in the field, we believe that the HSC could cope with Covid-19, or any potential crisis, through two fundamental capabilities: firstly, ***prevention*** by implementing preventive measures even before the crisis arises, and secondly, through ***adaptative actions*** undertaken during the crisis. The latter are likely to develop and, above all, reconfigure existing skills, thus offering greater flexibility to the HSC, and consequently a competitive advantage to the hospital in question.

The dynamic capabilities we have highlighted in this study are interwoven into all the HSC processes affected by the crisis. Thus, in light of the results of our survey concerning the effects of the pandemic on all HSC processes, and based on the opportunities offered by the dynamic capabilities considered, we propose in this section both preventive actions (in normal times) to prevent the risks related to HSC management, and adaptive actions (in times of crisis) to mitigate the impact not only of Covid-19, but of any eventual crisis of a similar magnitude on the HSC.

The conceptual model of these actions is illustrated in Fig. 6. Then, the way they should be implemented is explained in detail in Table 2.

In addition to the measures mentioned above that address, the impact of Covid-19 on the different processes of the HSC, another aspect that should not be overlooked is the flow of information. This is a cross-cutting aspect that enables the communication between processes and thus contributes to the integration of the HSC.

In this register relating to the management of information flows inherent to physical flows (people and materials), it should be stressed that hospitals are increasingly using Hospital Information Systems (HIS) to manage all information

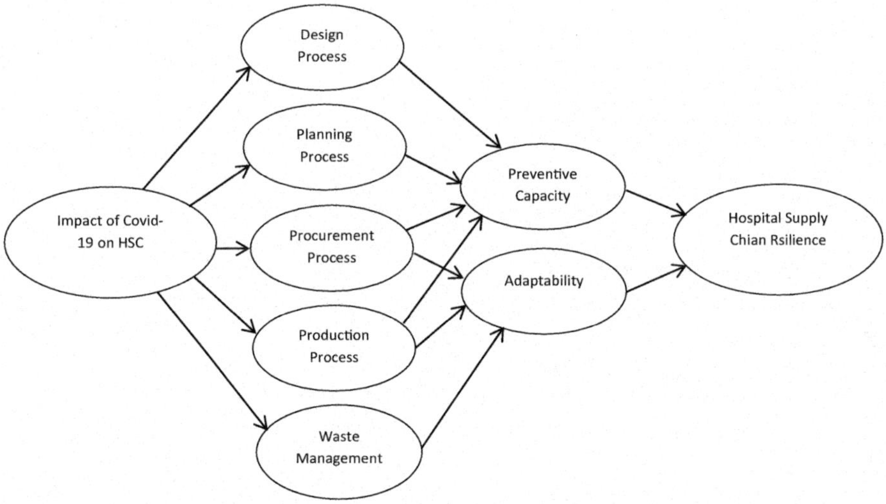

Fig. 6 Conceptual model of capabilities for a resilient HSC

Table. 2 Proposed actions to prevent and/or mitigate the impact of Covid-19 on HSC

Process	Potential actions	
Design	Preventive (normal times) N.T	• When sizing hospital structures, provide for remote isolation zones with resuscitation units and technical platforms dedicated to the care of patients suffering from a contagious disease, to reduce the risk of contamination and not disrupt the hospital's normal operations. In some hospitals, especially the most modern ones, there are departments physically separated from the hospital grounds, dedicated solely to infectious diseases, with medical staff qualified for this type of illness and equipment adapted to it. Otherwise, entire departments have to be evacuated and reserved for infected patients, prefabricated buildings or tents have to be erected within the hospital to house patients, as was the case in the hospital concerned by this study • The acquisition and packaging of mobile hospitals with large reception capacities (resuscitation beds, hospital beds, isolation wards, etc.) are designed to relieve congestion in infrastructure hospitals in the event of a mass influx caused by a crisis of any kind (pandemic, natural disaster…). In this respect, the hospital group to which the hospital under study belongs has mobile health structures that have been deployed in heavily contaminated areas to relieve the infrastructure hospitals and limit the movement of contaminated populations, which is a major vector of virus transmission

(continued)

Table. 2 (continued)

Process	Potential actions	
Planning	Preventive (normal times) N.T	• Planning must be fairly agile and flexible, both in terms of the organization of the care activity and in terms of the allocation of hospital resources (nursing staff, medical equipment, pharmaceutical products, etc.), due to the uncertain and complex context of the hospital environment and the hazards linked to medical activity (possible crises). In other words, there must always be an operational potential in terms of human resources (medical, paramedical and support staff), as well as resources in terms of pharmaceutical products and medico-technical equipment specific to crisis situations, to be deployed where necessary • The implementation of HSC risk management protocols (standardized and secure) to be operationalized in the event of a crisis. To achieve this, multidisciplinary committees (medical, administrative and logistical staff) must be set up within the hospital and reactivated through planned and coordinated actions to deal with any possible health crisis
Procurement	Preventive (normal times) N.T	• Diversify sources of supply • Increase the level of partnership with suppliers (business and support), favoring relationships based on trust and transparency • Seek to shorten supply circuits • Ensure computerized and smart supply management to have a clear and accurate view at all times of the stock levels of the various products in use in the hospital • To have traceability and perfect knowledge of the real needs of the services to reject abusive and unjustified requests and not to fall into over-consumption • Have intelligent systems capable of understanding the state of stock and predicting any shortages or out-of-stock

(continued)

Table. 2 (continued)

Process	Potential actions		
	Adaptation (crisis times) C.T	• Identify the products (medicines, medical devices, and equipment, etc.) that are essential to cope with the crisis and which are at risk of shortage or out of stock • Review the forecast of needs and the nature of orders (prioritize the materials and products used to deal with the crisis) • Seek alternative suppliers in the event of a shortage or out of stock • Set up crisis units to follow the circuit of products and medical devices along the supply process from acquisition to distribution (upstream-middle-downstream	
Production	Catering	N.T	• As in the procurement process, the partnership with suppliers must be consolidated and not be limited to a single source of supply • Ensure the strict application of hygiene rules and food safety control protocols based on prevention (HACCP method, forward motion, etc.)
		C.T	• Analysing the risks of contamination linked to the preparation and distribution of meals and taking steps to control them (use of disposable dishes for both nursing staff and patients, automation of the delivery process, etc.) • Strengthen the observation of prevention mechanisms and good practices in terms of hygiene and food safety
	Laundry	N.T	• To set up techniques for analyzing and controlling the risks of microbiological contamination of linen (e.g. RABC method) • Ensure compliance with hygiene and health safety standards relating to the management of hospital linen

(continued)

Table. 2 (continued)

Process	Potential actions		
		C.T	• Prefer single-use linen (sheets, pajamas, nurses' coats, etc.) and dispose of them after use with infectious medical waste • Reinforce treatment protocols for reusable linen (use of water-soluble bags, disinfection, complete drying after washing, etc.) • Ensure the protection of the personnel in charge of the linen management (masks, glasses, gloves…)
	Sterilization	N.T	• Use risk management tools related to the sterilization process for reusable medical devices (FMECA, HACCP, etc.) • Have decontamination materials and products available for use when necessary (disinfection of care services, sick rooms, etc.) according to pre-established operating procedures
		C.T	• Strictly comply with current procedures and practices regarding the processing of medical devices from a Covid-19 service • Reinforce the protection of the agents in charge of sterilizing medical devices and disinfection teams by wearing protective clothing (coveralls, protective glasses, masks, gloves…)

(continued)

Table. 2 (continued)

Process	Potential actions	
Waste management	N.T	• Prepare contingency plans to be implemented to deal with situations where the risk of infection from the medical waste generated is very high
	C.T	• Ensure the protection of personnel responsible for sorting and packaging operations at the level of health care units as well as those responsible for the collection, handling, transport and treatment of infectious waste • Disinfect the path of infectious waste from sorting and packaging in isolation units to treatment centers, including pre-collection, storage and transport by appropriate vehicles to treatment sites to limit the risk of contamination

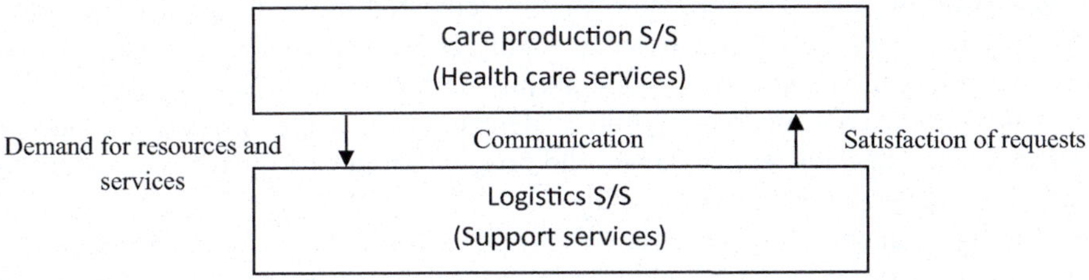

Fig. 7 Sub-systems of a HIS

relating to the hospital's business lines in an integrated and automatic manner, particularly the care production process. Usually these systems do not deal with the support or logistics process.

About our problem, we consider that a HIS should include, in addition to the care production sub-system (S/S), a logistics S/S enabling direct communication between the care services and the support services (pharmacy, sterilization, linen, kitchen, waste management, etc.), see Fig. 7.

Thus, a HIS designed in such a way would necessarily reduce the risk of Covid-19 infection, since the transfer of data between health care and logistics services (status of inpatients, requests for pharmaceuticals and medical devices, food vouchers, condition of hospital linen, medical equipment to be sterilized, feedback, etc.) would be automatic and secure instead of the traditional method (paper from hand to hand), highlighting the importance and relevance of the concept of dematerialization or "paperless" in more ways than one.

To implement this solution, we based ourselves on the Resource-Based View (RBV) theory developed by Jay Barney in 1991. RBV theory focuses on an organization's internal resources as a means of organizing processes and gaining competitive advantage. Barney [2] stated that, for resources to retain their potential as sources of sustainable competitive advantage, they should be valuable, rare, imperfectly imitable and non-substitutable. Resource-based view theory suggests that organizations need to develop unique, company-specific core competencies that will enable them to outperform their competitors by doing things differently [38].

In our context of Hospital Information Systems in particular, and information and communication technologies in general, RBV is irrelevant insofar as new technologies are increasingly characterized by a high degree of standardization using generic IT applications, and are therefore not inimitable [7]. In the same vein, the author points out that information technology, and in particular data, is now extremely reproducible at low cost, which deprives it of its scarcity and therefore of the possibility of offering a sustained competitive advantage.

However, the approach we've adopted allows us to highlight the RBV theory while remaining within the IT domain, by integrating the support module into the HIS, unlike healthcare software publishers who emphasize the business process (medical management of patients) to the detriment of the logistics process. We would point out that this approach was implemented in the hospital in question, but only in one process of the hospital supply chain, namely the pharmacy, which enabled it to gain a competitive edge during the period of the health crisis.

This approach has made it possible to dematerialize drug requests from medical departments and their delivery from the hospital pharmacy, thereby substantially reducing the spread of the virus.

The digitization of this process was possible thanks to the internal managerial and technical skills of the hospital group of which our hospital is a part, via an effective and efficient computer application because it was implemented in a short time given the urgency that implies the health crisis.

From what preceded, we can say that our study has highlighted the relevance of the RBV theory, giving the hospital an undeniable competitive advantage during the period of the crisis, through in particular:

- The proposal of an innovative HIS based on an architecture integrating a support module, which allowed the exchange of information flows between the care production process and the logistics process, in an integrated, instantaneous and secure manner.
- The capacity of the hospital group to which the target hospital of this study belongs, to implement a computer application which allows communication between the care production process and the hospital pharmacy, in a complex and uncertain environment generated by the Covid-19 crisis in order to reduce the spread of the virus within the hospital.

7 Practical Implications and Research Limitations

At the end of this work, it can be seen that preventive actions are as significant as adaptation measures, insofar as their observation would make it possible to absorb the shock wave caused by the pandemic in the various processes of the HSC. Hence the interest in rethinking the models and risk management tools relating to hospital logistics activities by integrating an aspect that is often overlooked or at least minimized in this case: the unforeseen emergence of large-scale health crises. Thus, the actions proposed to deal with Covid-19 can constitute for the various actors of the HSC (managers, logisticians, doctor, etc.), a reliable risk management tool specific to the HSC, particularly in the aspect relating to health crises, as long as we have a "framework" setting out the risks on the one hand and the solutions or actions to control them on the other.

However, although HSC is a generic concept, logistics practices may differ from one hospital to another depending on the resources and means used. Thus, other empirical analyses, from other hospitals at national or international level, may propose other solutions enriching those proposed in this study.

8 Conclusion

In sum, the health crisis caused by Covid-19 has dramatically disrupted health systems around the world. The resources needed to counter its disastrous effects were lacking, especially at the peak of the pandemic, which calls into question the central role of the HSC as essential support in the care process.

During this research, we were able to show the effects of the pandemic on all HSC processes and flows, through an empirical survey based on semi-structured interviews with a relevant sample, composed of hospital staff, especially those in charge of logistics processes at a Moroccan public hospital involved in the fight against Covid-19. This allowed us to confirm and validate the initial hypotheses, i.e. that procurement is the process most affected by the crisis because of its strong dependence on the GSC and that the other processes can constitute vectors of virus transmission if they are not properly controlled. After, and to face these findings, we have proposed potential actions likely to alleviate the effects of the pandemic on the HSC from an approach based on dynamic capabilities theory.

Moreover, the Covid-19 crisis has shown that, more than ever before, the HSC needs to be more resilient and sufficiently flexible. In this respect, we that the changing and complex nature of the hospital environment, the uncertainty of medical activity, the multidimensional management of the hospital supply chain (cost, quality, safety, lead times, etc.), the diversity and volume of data to be processed, etc., should encourage those involved in HSC management (managers, logisticians, pharmacists, doctors, etc.) to make greater use of digitization and new technologies (artificial intelligence, big data, new robotics, cloud, blockchain, Internet of Things "IoT" etc.), the deployment of which has produced impressive results in several industrial sectors, accelerating the transition to Hospital Supply Chain 4.0.

Disclosure Statement No potential conflict of interest was reported by the author(s).

References

1. Andersen A (1990) Stockless materials management, how it fits into the healthcare cost puzzle. HIDA Educational Foundation, Washington
2. Barney JB (1991) Firm resources and sustained competitive advantage. J Manag 17:99–120. https://doi.org/10.1177/014920639101700108
3. Baumard P et al (1999) La collecte de données et la gestion de leur source. In: Méthodologie de la recherche en gestion. Ed Thiétart, Nathan
4. Burger H, Frank L (2011) La création de rentes: une approche par les compétences et capacités dynamiques. Dans Innov 2(35):89–111
5. Butt AS (2021) Strategies to mitigate the impact of COVID-19 on supply chain disruptions: a multiple case analysis of buyers and distributors. Int J Logist Manag
6. Carr N (2003) IT doesn't matter. Harv Bus Rev 1–12
7. Chia PY, Coleman KK, Tan YK et al, Singapore 2019 Novel Coronavirus Outbreak Research Team (2020) Detection of air and surface contamination by SARS-CoV-2 in hospital rooms of infected patients. Nat Commun

8. Choi T-M (2020) Innovative ‘bring-service-near-your-home’ operations under corona-virus (COVID19/SARS-CoV-2) outbreak: can logistics become the messiah? Transp Res Part E Logist Transp Rev 101961. https://doi.org/10.1016/j.tre.2020.101961
9. Chow G, Heaver T, Henriksson L (1994) Logistics performance: definition and measurement. Int J Phys Distrib Logist Manag 24(1)
10. Chowdhury MMH, Quaddus M (2016) Supply chain readiness, response and recovery for resilience. Supply Chain Manag 21(6):709–731. https://doi.org/10.1108/SCM-12-2015-0463
11. Chu DK, Akl EA, Duda S et al (2020) COVID-19 systematic urgent review group effort (SURGE) study authors. Physical distancing, face masks, and eye protection to prevent person-to-person transmission of SARS-CoV-2 and COVID-19: a systematic review and meta-analysis. Lancet
12. Colenda C, Applegate B, Reifler V, Blazer G (2020) COVID-19: financial stress test for academic. Med Cent Acad Med 95(8)
13. Covid-19 Coronavirus pandemic, *Worldometer*, https://www.worldometer.info/coronavirus/#countries%3C
14. Dallery Y (2004) Les méthodes de la logistique industrielle au service de la santé: apports et limitations. Cours d’Ingénierie de la santé. Ecole Centrale de Paris, 2004
15. Di Martinelly C, Guinet A, Riane F (2005) Chaîne logistique en milieu hospitalier: modélisation des processus de distribution de la pharmacie. In: 6e Congrès international de génie industriel, 7–10 juin 2005. Besançon, France
16. Fonseca LM, Azevedo AL (2020) COVID-19: outcomes for global supply chains. Manag Mark Chall Knowl Soc
17. FuchsVR (2020) COVID-19: beyond tomorrow. Health care policy after the COVID-19 pandemic. JAMA. Published online 12 June 2020
18. Goel RK, Saunoris JW, Goel SS (2021) Supply chain performance and economic growth: the impact of COVID-19 disruptions. J Policy Model 43:298–316
19. Govindana K, Minac H, Alavid B (2020) A decision support system for demand management in healthcare supply chains considering the epidemic outbreaks: A case study of coronavirus disease 2019 (COVID-19). Transp Res Part E 138:101967
20. Grida M, Mohamed R, Zaied AH (2020) Evaluate the impact of COVID-19 prevention policies on supply chain aspects under uncertainty. https://doi.org/10.1016/j.trip.2020.100240
21. Ivanov D (2020) Predicting the impacts of pandemic outbreaks on global supply chains: a simulation-based analysis on the COVID-19 outbreak (COVID-19/SARS-CoV-2) case. Transp Res Part E Logist Transp Rev 136:101922
22. Joost Wiersinga W, Rhodes A, Cheng AC (2020) Pathophysiology, transmission, diagnosis, and treatment of coronavirus disease 2019 (COVID-19). JAMA
23. Kalantary RR, Jamshidi A, Mofrad M, Jafari A, Heidari N, Fallahizadeh S, Arani M, Torkashvand J (2021) Effect of COVID-19 pandemic on medical waste management: a case study
24. Koster E, Philbert D, Bouvy M (2020) Impact of the COVID-19 epidemic on the provision of pharmaceutical care in community pharmacies. Res Soc Adm Pharm
25. Landry S, Beaulieu M (2000) Étude internationale des meilleures pratiques de logistique hospitalière. Cahier de recherche n° 00-05. HEC Montréal
26. Lewis D (2020) Is the coronavirus airborne? Experts can’t agree. Nature
27. Luo L, Jin Y, Cai L, Pan Z, Zeng X, Wang X (2020) COVID-19: presumed infection routes and psychological impact on staff in administrative and logistics departments in a designated hospital in Wuhan. China. Front Psychol 11:1501. https://doi.org/10.3389/fpsyg.2020.01501
28. Ma Y, Lin X, Wu A, Huang Q, Li X, Yan J (2020) Suggested guidelines for emergency treatment of medical waste during COVID-19: Chinese experience. Waste Dispos Sustain Energy. Published online 03 June 2020
29. Mckinsey & Company (2020) Jump-starting resilient and reimagined operations. Retrieved from: https://www.mckinsey.com/business-functions/operations/ourinsights/jump-starting-resilient-and-reimagined-operations
30. Metzl M, Maybank A, De Mai F (2020) Responding to the COVID-19 pandemic the need for a structurally competent health care system. JAMA. Published online 4 June 2020

31. Miles MB, Huberman AM (2003) Analyse des données qualitatives. De Boeck Supérieur, Bruxelles, p 632
32. Pellemans P (1999) Recherche qualitative en marketing, Ed DeBoeck Université, Paris
33. Prahalad CK, Hamel G (2006) The core competence of the corporation. Harv Bus Rev 68(3):79–91
34. Queiroz MM, Ivanov D, Dolgui A, Fosso Wamba S (2020) Impacts of pandemic outbreaks on supply chains: mapping a research agenda amid the COVID-19 pandemic through a structured literature review. Ann Oper Res. https://doi.org/10.1007/s10479-020-03685-7
35. Samlak N (2020) L'approche qualitative et quantitative dans l'enquête du terrain: l'observation, l'entretien et le questionnaire. Rev Linguist Référ Intercult 1(1). https://doi.org/10.34874/IMIST.PRSM/liri-v1i1.21443
36. Sampieri N, Bongiovanni I (2009) Enjeux et perspectives des pratiques logistiques: pour une amélioration globale de la performance—Le cas de l'hôpital public français. RIRL 2000—Les Troisièmes Rencontres Internationales de la Recherche en Logistique, Trois-Rivières, CRET-LOG.19P
37. Sharma A, Adhikary A, Borah SB (2020) Covid-19's impact on supply chain decisions: strategic insights for NASDAQ 100 firms using Twitter data. J Bus Res. https://doi.org/10.1016/j.jbusres.2020.05.035
38. Sun S, Xie Z, Yu K et al (2021) COVID-19 and healthcare system in China: challenges and progression for a sustainable future. Global Health 17:14. https://doi.org/10.1186/s12992-021-00665-9
39. Tirkolaee et al (2020) Sustainable fuzzy multi-trip location routing problem for medical waste management during the COVID-19 outbreak. https://doi.org/10.1016/j.sctotenv.2020.143607

Ahmed Chtioui is an Engineer in Manufacturing Systems Management of the Ecole Nationale Supérieure des Mines de Rabat (ENSMR), Morocco. Currently, he is head of the IT department of the Moulay Ismail Hospital, Meknes, Morocco. At the same time, he is a Ph.D. student in the MOSI research team at the Ecole Nationale Supérieure d'Art et Métiers (ENSAM-Meknes). His research work focuses on the integration and optimisation of the Hospital Supply Chain (HSC).

Imane Bouhaddou is a Professor at ENSAM Meknes, University of Moulay Ismail, Morocco. She received her Ph.D. in Industrial Engineering from University of Le Havre, France and Moulay Ismail University, Meknes, Morocco in 2015. Her research work is dealing with supply chain optimisation, product life cycle management and complex systems.

Asmaa Benghabrit has been a lecturer-researcher in Industrial Engineering since 2017 in the Industrial Engineering Department of the Ecole Nationale Supérieure des Mines de Rabat (ENSMR). She is a permanent member of the Laboratory of Applied Mathematics and Business Intelligence (LMAID) at ENSMR and Associate Member of the research team Modelling and Optimisation of Industrial Systems (MOSI) at the Ecole Nationale Supérieure d'Art et Métiers (ENSAM-Meknès). Her research work focuses on Modeling, Extraction and Knowledge Management from Industrial Data and the Impact of Data Science and Artificial Intelligence on Manufacturing and Service Industries.

Calibrating Resilience Strategies for PPE: Lessons from the COVID-19 Pandemic

24

Reza Shahin, Martin Beaulieu, Valérie Bélanger, and Martin Cousineau

Abstract

This study addresses the critical issue of healthcare supply chain resilience in the context of personal protective equipment (PPE) shortages experienced during the COVID-19 pandemic. With the pandemic highlighting severe vulnerabilities in the healthcare supply chain, particularly in PPE procurement, the study emphasizes the necessity for robust resilience strategies. It outlines the dual crisis faced by the healthcare sector: an unprecedented demand surge and a disruption of supply chains, primarily due to containment measures impact on production. The paper critiques the limitations of conventional responses, such as stockpiling and diversification of supply sources, especially in industrialized nations where cost considerations often lead to offshoring production. By examining the Canadian experience and incorporating theoretical and practical insights, the study proposes a nuanced model for formulating infection prevention supplies resilience strategies. This model is tailored to the specific characteristics of the PPE supply chain and the varying nature of PPE items, offering a more sustainable approach to managing healthcare supply chain vulnerabilities in pandemic scenarios. This model will help decision-makers determine an ideal level of stock to keep, based on scenarios of rising demand and supply chain recovery time. To understand the assumptions underlying the

R. Shahin
COSYS-ESTAS, Université Gustave Eiffel, Villeneuve d'Ascq, France

M. Beaulieu (✉) · V. Bélanger · M. Cousineau
HEC Montréal, 3000 chemin de la Côte Sainte-Catherine, Montréal, QC H3T 2A7, Canada
e-mail: martin.beaulieu@hec.ca

V. Bélanger
e-mail: valerie.3.belanger@hec.ca

M. Cousineau
e-mail: martin.cousineau@hec.ca

F. Jawab (ed.), *Hospital Supply Chain*, Integrated Science 27,
https://doi.org/10.1007/978-3-031-70292-1_24

model, this chapter will present the findings of work carried out in the public health system of the province of Quebec concerning PPE management during the first months of the COVID-19 pandemic.

Keywords

Personal protective equipment • Healthcare supply chain • Inventory optimization • Purchasing strategies

Abbreviations

AIDS	Acquired Immunodeficiency Syndrome
DGBLA	Direction du génie biomédical, de la logistique et de l'approvisionnement (Biomedical Engineering, Logistics and Procurement Directorate)
IPS	Infection Prevention Supplies
LP	Linear Programming
PPE	Personal Protective Equipment
SC	Supply chains

1 Introduction

The COVID-19 pandemic has become a historical event for many industries. Yet, in the early stages, the search for personal protective equipment (PPE) became a significant challenge for several healthcare organizations [8]. Consequently, strengthening resilience in healthcare supply chains (SCs) has emerged as a critical concern across nations. It is imperative to acknowledge that the healthcare sector was concurrently grappling with a twofold crisis. First, a demand crisis, triggered by a marked escalation in PPE usage, an outcome anticipated in the wake of similar health emergencies [23]. Second, a supply crisis, due to a simultaneous disruption of SCs, notably in Wuhan (China), the initial epicenter of the pandemic, which experienced extensive lockdown measures in the early months of 2020. This region was responsible for half of the worldwide production of PPE [35]. Amid such disturbances, the healthcare sector cannot afford to merely await the stabilization of SCs, thereby delaying its operations and potentially endangering the wellbeing and survival of patients requiring medical attention [28]. In these circumstances, building up a PPE stockpile on a regional or national scale tends to be the solution that received the most attention [16]. However, such a solution will inevitably have its limitations. As Stein [30] points out, for the United States, it would be necessary to use all of the country's storage capacity if we wished to build up a stockpile sufficient to cope with a pandemic of the same magnitude as the Spanish flu of the late 1910s. Such a solution will tend to run up against available storage capacity, requiring choices to be made between the various products for which managers wish to build up a safety stockpile. Another frequently mentioned solution consists in diversifying the sources of supply, mainly by engaging local suppliers. Nevertheless, for industrialized nations, this approach is not sustainable over the long term. PPE represents a commodity for which the primary procurement goal is cost minimization [13]. This goal encourages suppliers to adopt strategies aimed at reducing expenses, such as relocating operations to countries with lower production costs. This trend was observed in Canada at the onset of the 1990s. The AIDS epidemic had led to an increase in the consumption of latex gloves in healthcare institutions. Canadian factories were set up to meet the demand, but quickly ceased operations in the face of reduced demand and significantly lower prices offered by foreign producers [7].

Therefore, there is a case for adopting more nuanced resilience strategies, calibrated according to the nature of the products. In fact, this approach is even more plausible given that PPE does not form a uniform category [12]. Thus, this chapter intends to propose a model for studying infection prevention supplies resilience strategies, drawing on qualitative and quantitative data gathered from a Canadian province. This model will help decision-makers determine an ideal level of stock to keep, based on scenarios of rising demand and supply chain recovery time.

This introduction outlines the critical questions this study seeks to answer. Throughout the pandemic, shortages of crucial items such as N95 respirators highlighted significant vulnerabilities, elevating the risk to healthcare personnel and patients alike. The urgent need for strategic PPE stockpile management has become evident, driving the necessity to develop robust models that ensure adequate supplies during health crises [15]. This study will focus on developing a Linear Programming (LP) formulation to optimize PPE stockpiles across varying demand scenarios. Specifically, it aims to explore strategies to mitigate future shortages, investigate correlations between PPE usage and pandemic metrics (hospitalizations, death rates, test positivity), and determine optimal stockpile levels for different types of PPE.

In the remainder of this chapter, we review the literature in Sect. 2 and outline the methodology in Sect. 3. Section 4 discusses the case study that was used to justify the assumptions underlying the model. This case study presents the findings of work carried out in the public health system of the province of Quebec concerning PPE management during the first months of the COVID-19 pandemic. The presentation of the mathematical formulation follows in Sect. 5. Finally, we conclude in Sect. 6.

2 Literature Review

This literature review delves into the management of PPE SCs during global health crises, particularly focusing on strategies to enhance supply chain resilience such as stockpiling, demand forecasting, and optimized distribution. Employing both deterministic and stochastic models, the review analyzes the complexities involved in managing SCs in crisis situations, aiming to outline effective practices and pinpoint areas requiring further research.

Key recent literature includes Jessop et al. [17], Galanis et al. [14], and Cook [10]. Jessop et al. [17] offer a systematic review of the use and distribution of PPE for surgeons during COVID-19, highlighting the need for evidence-based guidance and addressing global shortages and ethical issues, though it lacks specific advice on stockpiling strategies. Galanis et al. [14] analyze the physical health impacts on healthcare personnel from PPE use, providing insights into associated risks, yet not discussing mitigation strategies like stockpiling. Cook [10] focuses on the application of PPE in healthcare settings tailored to the modes of COVID-19 transmission, providing strategies to conserve PPE and maintain safety, but without preventive strategies for shortages. Jessop et al. [17] conducted a systematic review of the use and distribution of PPE for surgeons during the COVID-19 pandemic, synthesizing data from multiple studies to provide evidence-based guidance and addressing global shortages and ethical issues. The review highlights the need for strategic management and rationing of PPE but falls short of detailing specific strategies for the stockpiling of PPE types.

Our study seeks to build on these works by reviewing literature on optimal PPE stockpiling during the COVID-19 pandemic. We aim to synthesize lessons and practical implications from these experiences to enhance future crisis response strategies. The existing literature, published either early in the pandemic or during later waves, has yet to provide a comprehensive understanding of these improvements, underscoring the need for our focused analysis.

2.1 PPE and Resilience

PPE falls within the medical supply family, which can be broken down into three main market segments [31]. First, there is the high-tech segment, mainly comprising equipment (e.g., diagnostic equipment). Second, there is an intermediate technology segment, such as surgical instruments and ventilators. Finally, there is the low-tech segment, which includes PPE. This sector encompasses commodities and items characterized by technical specifications that are universally recognized and standardized across the industry. Likewise, the production methods are standardized.

Various definitions exist for the concept of supply chain resilience [32]. Resilience can be defined as the ability of an organization to survive, adapt and grow in the face of environmental turbulence [25]. Under these conditions, resilience will be embodied primarily by the presence of slack in the supply chain, e.g., excess production capacity, additional inventory, and diversification of supplier markets across multiple suppliers [19]. Reshoring is also considered a measure of resilience [33].

Moreover, in the specific case of PPE, the pandemic highlighted another reality of supply chain resilience. The schematization of the latter implies that turbulence limits production or transport capacities preventing market demand from being met [36]. Patel et al. [23] have demonstrated that a pandemic can escalate PPE consumption by a factor of up to ten. Therefore, the difficulties encountered in PPE supply during the COVID-19 pandemic are attributable to a confluence of two distinct phenomena. First, a disruption in the PPE supply chain at the outset of 2020, precipitated by the stringent lockdown measures imposed by Chinese authorities in the Wuhan region which reduces capacity. Second, there was a surge in demand for PPE as the virus proliferated across the northern hemisphere [5].

Another important dimension of supply chain resilience is recovery time following turbulence. For example, the tsunami that hit the coast of Japan in May 2011 had a significant impact on Toyota's supplier base and, more broadly, on the automotive industry. It took four months for the industry to return to its previous production levels [9]. The healthcare sector cannot easily adapt its activities in the event of turbulence among its suppliers, as the consequences for the health of its patients could be significant [28].

2.2 Studies on PPE Management During a Pandemic

The COVID-19 pandemic has severely challenged the robustness of SCs imposing numerous restrictions and impacting their worldwide effectiveness. Globally, shortages have occurred due to disruptions in SCs, potentially jeopardizing lives as essential items such as ventilators and PPE are vital for managing this international crisis. Lucas et al. [18] investigated mitigating the effects of the pandemic on crucial SCs by optimizing the distribution of essential materials and enhancing the resilience of these chains, filling a research gap where few studies have integrated simulation and optimization methods to address these challenges. Another study highlighted the inventory management tactics of healthcare providers, determining that while just-in-time delivery enhances efficiency and reduces surplus inventory and costs under normal conditions, it fails to meet the abrupt increase in demand during emergency situations [24]. Queiroz et al. [27] employed optimization techniques and epidemic models to explore the relationship between these areas in the context of resource allocation issues and the distribution of medical supplies. Alikhani et al. [1] developed a two-stage stochastic optimization model incorporating various resilience strategies to construct a robust retail SC, offering insights into cost-effectiveness and resilience. Das et al. [11] developed a resilient supply network suited for both local and global markets to accommodate consumer needs amidst disruptions such as pandemics. The overarching insight from the aforementioned studies is that systems designed to handle pandemics must be capable of swiftly adapting to rapidly evolving circumstances. Overall, in synthesizing the insights garnered from this review of the literature on the management of PPE SCs during pandemics, it becomes imperative to underscore the multifaceted nature of distribution and allocation strategies within the broader context of supply chain resilience. To effectively implement these strategies, there must be a foundational stock available for distribution, necessitating proactive upstream decision-making processes. Moreover, the composition of PPE, encompassing a diverse range of products, inherently possesses varying recovery times influenced by their technical complexity. This differentiation underscores the necessity for resilience strategies to be meticulously calibrated, acknowledging the distinct characteristics and requirements of each PPE component. Additionally, the significance of grounding these studies in empirical evidence cannot be overstated. Leveraging real data not only enhances the accuracy and relevance of research findings but also ensures that the proposed strategies are pragmatically viable and tailored to the nuanced realities of PPE supply chain management during health crises. Thus, it is through this lens of strategic foresight, technical discernment, and empirical rigor that we can advance toward more resilient and responsive PPE SCs in the face of future pandemics. Moreover, upon examining the current body of literature, it becomes evident that there exists a deficiency in optimization models that manage stockpile inventory levels for various PPE by incorporating suppliers under uncertainty.

Before resorting to such tools, we need to base our working hypotheses on the reality of observable practices in the healthcare supply chain. In this sense, the experience of the public health system in the province of Quebec (Canada) becomes a privileged study environment, thanks to the numerous research studies that have been carried out.

3 Methodology

This chapter presents a valuable opportunity to elucidate the underlying assumptions of the mathematical model that was developed to bolster strategies for PPE resilience within the healthcare sector. To concretely illustrate our hypotheses, we employ a case study as a methodological tool, aimed at addressing practical aspects. The use of a case study is recognized as an effective means for comprehending the dynamics of supply chain disruptions [26]. Furthermore, the formulation of this model is a component of a collaborative research endeavor [3], facilitated by gaining insights regarding supply chain resilience strategies from policymakers at the Ministry of Health in Quebec, Canada.

3.1 Case Study

Given the collaborative nature of the research, the case study is that of the public health system in the province of Quebec. The public health system in the province of Quebec includes 34 institutions since the spring 2015 reform. These institutions often operate on a regional scale and are made up of several dozen facilities. Compared to other Canadian provinces, a distinctive feature of Quebec's public health system is the presence of a Biomedical Engineering, Logistics and Procurement Directorate (DGBLA) within the Ministry of Health. This department is typically not directly involved in purchasing or inventory management decisions at the institutional level. Instead, it provides provincial guidance to institutions and suppliers on coordinated procurement and logistics strategies. This department is the research team's partner. The case study is mainly focused on the events surrounding crisis management during the first months of the COVID-19 pandemic in early 2020 until a stabilization phase in the spring of 2021. With its global view, the DGBLA can arbitrate between collective resilience measures for the 34 institutions of the health system in the province of Quebec, and local measures specific to each institution. The DGBLA can also deploy more concerted strategies and measures with suppliers, ensuring a more consistent message.

3.2 Data Collection

The case study combines data of different kinds: artifacts, interviews and databases. Artifacts mainly took the form of public reports, enabling us to understand certain decisions taken, public documents associated with PPE use standards, or press articles, enabling us to document the nature of decisions taken. The interviews cover many stakeholders associated with the supply chain in the public healthcare sector in the province of Quebec (see Table 1). The following points should be noted. In the healthcare sector, many contracts for PPE are concluded through a purchasing group, which consolidates the needs of several hospitals to generate a larger volume of purchases, thereby enabling price reductions [21]. Traditional suppliers are companies that offered one or more products to healthcare institutions on a regular basis before the pandemic and for whom these customers represent the mainstay of their sales. Non-traditional suppliers are rather made up of organizations that were approached by public decision-makers when they realized that their traditional suppliers could not meet the demand of the public health system. These were companies in the textile, alcoholic beverage or manufacturing sectors [2].

Table 1 Interviews conducted

Respondent category	Type of respondent	Time (min)	Data collection period
Institutions—logistics function	• 5 logistics managers • 5 assistant logistics managers • 2 logistics coordinators • 5 analysts	780	July–November 2020
Purchasing group	• 2 purchasing group executives	60	January and February 2021
Ministry of Health	• 3 advisors	120	February 2021
Traditional suppliers	• 8 companies	415	June and July 2021
Non-traditional suppliers	• 12 companies	510	October and November 2020

Two databases were also analyzed. The first database is associated with the impact of COVID-19 on the population of the province of Quebec. This database tracks, on a daily basis, the number of hospitalizations, the number of individuals testing positive for COVID-19, the number of deaths attributed to COVID-19, and the percentage of COVID-19 test positivity (number of positive cases out of the number of tests performed). The database covers the period from January 2020 to January 2024. The second database consolidates inventory levels across the province of Quebec for all public health system hospital storage sites. This database also shows consolidated deliveries from these warehouses to the care units of healthcare institutions. The data covers 30 different products associated with PPE (e.g., reusable gowns, latex gloves, vinyl gloves, nitrile gloves, tubing, N99 masks, N95 masks, medical masks, thermometer, hand disinfectant, disposable gowns, goggles, vaccination material). This second dataset is from February 2021 to the end of September 2022.

3.3 Data Analyses

PPE management during the first months of the pandemic in the province of Quebec has already been the subject of numerous analyses [2, 4–6]. Each of these articles has studied a specific aspect of PPE management: the management of healthcare institutions [5, 6], traditional and non-traditional PPE suppliers [2] or the dynamics of actors within an institution [4]. For the model development, six PPE are targeted in this chapter: N95 masks, medical masks, latex gloves, hand sanitizer, protective eyewear and reusable gowns. These items have been the subject of numerous government audits [20, 22, 34]. So based on the work of Beaulieu et al. [2, 4–6], we will extract conclusions that will validate the level of slack in the PPE supply chain, the reaction time of the supply chain to adjust to an extraordinary rise in demand and, finally, the predictability of the crisis.

4 Case Study

The description of the case study of PPE management in the public health system of the province of Quebec will be composed of four sections. The first section describes the slack in the PPE supply chain. The second section presents the state of demand for PPE. The third section describes reaction times for the various PPE studied. Finally, the last section assesses the possibility of anticipating an increase in demand.

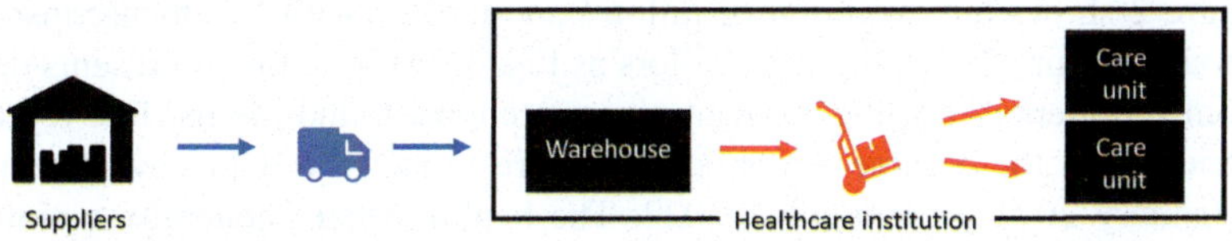

Fig. 1 Healthcare supply chain

4.1 The Presence of Slack in the Supply Chain

Canada was dependent on imports for its PPE needs in the healthcare sector. Furthermore, the contracts signed included clauses whereby the total quantities ordered may exceed the quantities stipulated in the agreement by 20%.

Figure 1 shows the simplified supply chain of the public health system. There are three main storage points: the supplier's warehouse, a warehouse associated with a healthcare institution, and finally a stockroom located in each care unit. We thus see two delivery segments: (1) deliveries from the supplier to the healthcare institution's warehouse (blue line) and (2) deliveries from the warehouse to the care unit stockroom (red line). Quebec's healthcare supply chain generally carries about around 12 weeks' worth of inventory: stock equivalent to three to four weeks' consumption can be found in unit care stockroom; the healthcare institution's central warehouse will also hold the equivalent of three to four weeks' consumption; suppliers whose products are generally manufactured in China will also have four to six weeks' stock, depending on normal consumption.

Although there were manufacturers with production capacity in North America, these companies offered their products to other sectors, such as construction or retail. At the start of the pandemic, when the needs of healthcare institutions became critical, these companies diverted their production from their traditional networks to the healthcare sector.

Also, in early March, when the Quebec provincial government declared a health emergency that also meant the closure of so-called non-essential economic sectors, garment manufacturers produced washable gowns to replace disposable gowns that had supply challenges, distilleries produced disinfectant gel and other manufacturers produced visors.

4.2 Trends in PPE Demand

The first case of COVID-19 in the province of Quebec was reported on February 22, 2020. The first death attributable to COVID-19 in the province of Quebec was recorded on March 16, 2020. Across Canada, the province of Quebec was the epicenter of the first pandemic wave. Quebec accounts for 22.5% of the country's population, but as of June 30, 2020, it accounted for 60% of deaths attributable to COVID-19.

Figure 2 shows the evolution of inflows and outflows for healthcare institution warehouse. Figure 2 uses the same colors as Fig. 1: the blue line represents deliveries from suppliers to healthcare institution warehouses, and the red line represents deliveries from these same warehouses to care units. The data cover the period from January 2021 to September 2022. The health system generally maintains a high level of inventory. This last one can be 10, 20, 30 or even more times the outflows in a given week. Figure 2 demonstrates that despite this stock, suppliers' obligation is not to meet consumption-related demand, but to be able to respond to orders placed by material managers in the province fo Quebec's public health system.

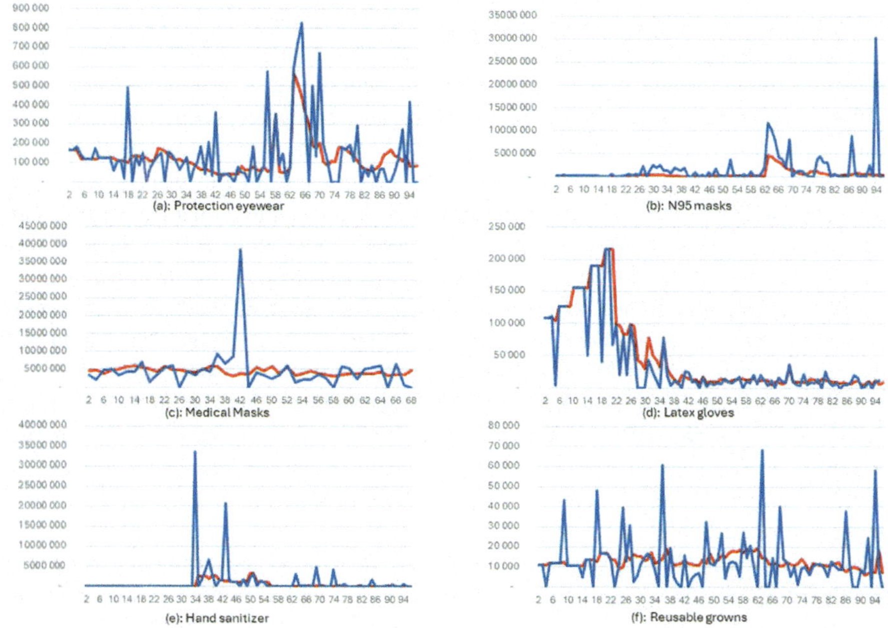

Fig. 2 Deliveries for different PPEs from January 2021 and September 2022

Table 2 Reaction times by product type

Product	Lower and upper lead times before first delivery
Eyewear	7–28 days
Hand Sanitazer	15 days
Gown level 1*	15 days
Gown level 2**	28–42 days
Masks	21–42 days

* Level 1 minimal water resistance (some resistance to splashing water)
** Level 2 low water resistance (resistance to water splashing and some resistance to water penetration under constant contact with increasing pressure)

Although the data selected is significantly further out in time than the first wave of the COVID-19 pandemic, it can be used to illustrate demand patterns. Our research partner indicated that orders placed in December 2021 were significantly higher than those placed in spring 2020. They can, therefore, be used to realistically illustrate supply issues that suppliers may have faced with respect to the health system.

4.3 Supply Chain Reaction Time

The experience with the first wave showed it took two to three months to turn around the PPE supply chain to meet the new ordering parameters. After that time, traditional suppliers were able to meet the quantities ordered by healthcare institutions in the province of Quebec. This is equivalent to the adjustment period that a supplier will require when awarded a new provincial contract.

For non-traditional suppliers, those who offered substitute products, Table 2 shows the times until different suppliers could deliver. There is a direct link between the technical complexity of the product and the reaction time. N95 masks require specific installations that would take several months to become operational [12].

4.4 Anticipating Turbulence

Healthcare organizations had anticipated the potential PPE crisis, ordering additional quantities of PPE and other critical supplies. This anticipation was more a matter of luck than a deliberate approach to monitoring risks within the supply chain.

Figure 3 illustrates four important measures from January 2021 to September 2022, encompassing: (1) hospitalization rate; (2) death rate; (3) proportion of positive COVID-19 test; and (4) positive case rate. These databases originate from the health system of Quebec province during the COVID-19 pandemic. The primary

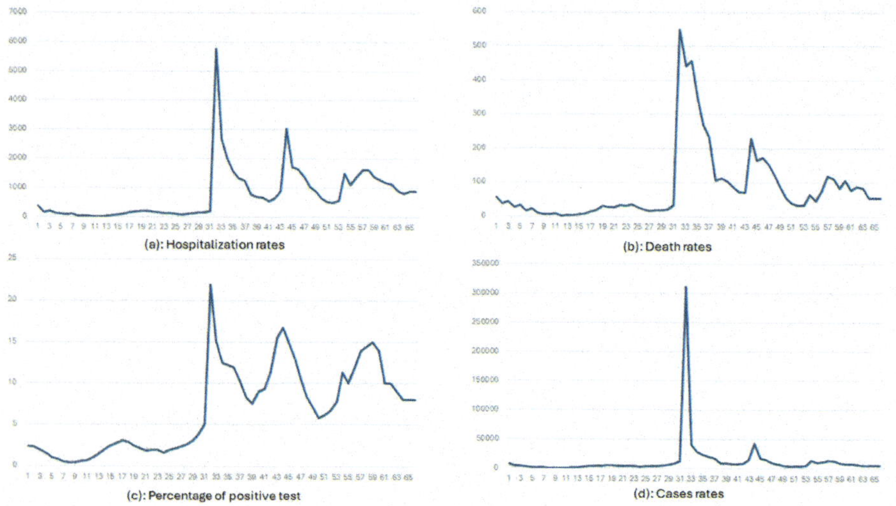

Fig. 3 Databases derived from Quebec case study

rationale for selecting these databases is their potential to facilitate a correlation analysis between the data they contain, and the demand and supply of the PPE being analyzed.

In Table 3, we systematically analyzed the congruence between demand and supply, as was shown in Fig. 3, for various PPE and degree of COVID-19 proliferation, particularly through: (1) hospitalization rate; (2) death rate; (3) proportion of positive COVID-19 test; and (4) Positive case rate. The analysis utilized Pearson correlation tests to examine the relationships among 48 variable clusters. Furthermore, for clarity, we highlight some specific results. In particular, moderate positive correlations (0.4–0.59) are marked in italic, while strong positive correlations (0.6 and above) are highlighted in bold. This approach highlighted a notable pattern: among all variables, only N95 masks and eyewear protection demonstrated a significant correlation, with death rates. Conversely, the examination also revealed that 16 variables were inversely related, showing negative correlations. This observation warrants further analyses as it suggests these variables diverge from expected patterns, potentially indicating unique influences or outliers within the dataset.

How might these results be elucidated? Initially, an organization dedicated to health and safety within Quebec's jurisdiction disseminated guidelines concerning the employment of PPE in healthcare settings. These guidelines were formulated to establish a baseline for PPE usage that would remain constant irrespective of the prevailing health circumstances. Table 4 shows the chronology of the main directives issued to healthcare institutions. Moreover, healthcare facilities were free to set their own PPE usage protocols, on the condition that these did not undermine the provincial benchmarks. Such a circumstance could exacerbate the impact of a crisis, as elucidated by a logistics manager: "One Friday afternoon, the

Table 3 Correlation test results

	N95 mask	Medical mask	Latex gloves	Hand sanitizer	Eyewear	Reusable gowns
Demand versus % of positive	***0.58***	– 0.18	– 0.69	– 0.60	***0.51***	0.16
Demand versus hospitalized	***0.43***	– 0.03	– 0.47	– 0.43	***0.40***	0.12
Demand versus death	**0.77**	0.09	– 0.47	– 0.37	**0.73**	0.32
Demand versus # of cases	0.09	0.15	0.05	– 0.17	0.08	0.01
Supply versus % of positive	0.32	0.05	– 0.35	– 0.23	0.2	0.30
Supply versus hospitalized	0.14	0.00	– 0.25	– 0.18	0.01	0.2
Supply versus death	0.26	0.12	– 0.17	– 0.12	0.31	0.28
Supply versus # of cases	0.00	0.02	– 0.02	– 0.07	– 0.04	0.18

health and safety department of our institution decided to impose the wearing of visors for professionals in contact with patients. Over the weekend, I had to find thousands of visors to meet the requirements of this standard!".

The public health sector's experience in the province of Quebec illuminates a complex scenario necessitating nuanced solutions. Specifically, PPE exhibits varied behaviors in terms of complexity, leading to different recovery times. Additionally, the consumption rates of these PPE items significantly diverge, further complicating the landscape. This variance in behaviors is particularly evident in the distinct impacts of eyewear and N95 masks, which stand out due to their heightened influence on the healthcare supply chain's resilience. Health professionals may have intuitively determined that these PPE offered the best protection against the virus, while being relatively simple to use. In light of these observations, the following section introduces a model aimed at calibrating resilience strategies.

5 Model Development

In the system under study, we consider a stockpile that is designed to store PPE received from suppliers. The supply side is represented by two distinct categories of suppliers. The first corresponds to traditional suppliers. These entities are directly connected to the demand side and primarily serve to fulfill immediate

Table 4 Chronology of directives concerning the use of PPE in healthcare institutions

Date	Guidelines
March 27, 2020	• Employees should wear medical masks during treatment
March 31, 2020	• Prioritize the use of disposable or reusable gowns for extended periods of time (without removing them) for care • Wear a medical mask for up to 4 h • Only use eye protection such as visors or shields that fully cover the face • Wear a respirator for extended periods (without removing it) for the care of several users
April 3, 2020	• All healthcare workers who provide care and are within two meters of a patient should wear a procedural mask continuously. Change the mask as needed if wet, soiled or at the end of the shift
April 7, 2020	• Any person providing personal assistance, body care or any other intervention to a non-sick person should wear a mask
July 17, 2020	• Medical masks must be worn by all users who consult us, whether or not they have COVID-19 symptoms • Masks are mandatory for all healthcare workers providing care • Masks must also be worn when healthcare workers are in close proximity to each other

requirements for PPE. In instances where traditional suppliers have excess production that surpasses current demand, the surplus PPE units are directed towards a centralized stockpile. The second category relates to non-traditional suppliers. These suppliers are capable of delivering the necessary items, albeit at a marginally higher cost relative to traditional suppliers. The underlying rationale for this cost increase is attributed to the fact that the non-traditional suppliers primarily focus on different product lines; however, in response to the crisis, they started the production of PPE as a measure to mitigate the scarcity issue. In cases where both traditional and non-traditional suppliers as well as stockpile storage are unable to meet the demand, a shortage situation arises. This represents a failure of the system to fulfill the demand for PPE and is considered an undesirable outcome. Prior to delineating the mathematical model, we provide our assumptions for the model:

1. Under normal circumstances, the production capability of traditional suppliers matches the demand level.
2. During a crisis, there exists an opportunity to augment the production capacity of traditional suppliers by 20%.
3. This enhancement in capacity can be implemented by suppliers within a timeframe of two to four weeks.
4. We take the stock level of a given week in the provincial warehouse minus the stock level of the previous week, to which we add the week's deliveries from suppliers.

5. The supply chain incorporates a reaction period of three months, during which suppliers adjust to the escalated demand levels, establishing a new standard. After this period, suppliers are expected to fulfill the demand.
6. The supply chain maintains an inventory equivalent to 70–90 days. On days of standard consumption, should demand surge exponentially, this inventory will be rapidly depleted.

Given the unpredictability of the situation, predicting the precise moment when demand will escalate becomes challenging. This is where the concept of demand scenarios, including the progression of demand and the duration of peak demand, becomes crucial. It necessitates accounting for demand uncertainty to accurately simulate crisis conditions where demand markedly increases, and suppliers are unable to meet such escalated demands.

We delineate the mathematical formulation of our proposed LP formulation aimed at integrating the stockpiling strategy of PPE. We consider T to be a set of time periods. Turning our focus to parameters, d_t is the demand at the end of time period t. We let $Q_{w,t}$ and $Q_{z,t}$ be the maximum delivery capacity during time period t by traditional and non-traditional suppliers, respectively. We define the maximum capacity of the stockpile to be Q_I. We let c_1, c_2, c_3, and c_4 to be costs for the different components of the objective functions. It is noteworthy that the cost associated with placing orders from traditional supplier is usually less than that incurred when engaging with non-traditional supplier. This discrepancy can be attributed to the fact that non-traditional suppliers do not manufacture PPE under normal circumstances, thereby incurring an additional setup cost to commence production of PPE during a crisis. Turning our focus to decision variables, we define I_t as the stockpile level at the end of time period t. We let S_t to be amount of shortage at the end of time period t, while the quantities ordered during time period t from traditional and non-traditional suppliers are defined as W_t and Z_t, respectively. It should be noted that the lead time is established as one week, and each period commences with the processing of orders received in the preceding period. Subsequently, demand is satisfied, and at the end of each period, the remaining inventory and any shortages are calculated. Having defined the notations, we provide the model of the problem as:

$$\min c_1 \sum_{t \in T} I_t + c_2 \sum_{t \in T} S_t + c_3 \sum_{t \in T} W_t + c_4 \sum_{t \in T} Z_t \tag{1}$$

Subject to:

$$I_t = W_{t-1} + Z_{t-1} - d_t + I_{t-1} + S_t \quad \forall t \in T \tag{2}$$

$$Z_t \le Q_{z,t} \quad \forall t \in T \tag{3}$$

$$W_t \le Q_{w,t} \quad \forall t \in T \tag{4}$$

$$\sum_{t \in T} I_t \leq Q_I \tag{5}$$

$$I_t, Z_t, W_t, S_t \geq 0, \quad \forall t \in T \tag{6}$$

The objective function of the model (1) consists of four components. The first component minimizes the inventory cost, while the second component minimizes the shortage cost. Components three and four minimize the ordering cost from traditional and non-traditional suppliers, respectively. Constraints (2) compute the inventory level at the end of each time period. Constraints (3) and (4) enforce the maximum ordering capacity from non-traditional and traditional suppliers. Constraint (5) enforces the maximum level of the stockpile. Constraints (6) are the non-negativity constraints.

Here we show the link between our assumptions and our LP model. The problem is formulated in a way that each PPE should be solved by the model independently, as the product index is omitted. This approach enables a focused analysis of the inventory management for each PPE type separately. To elucidate the connection between our initial assumptions and the LP formulation, we observe the following details reflected in the constraints. In alignment with the first assumption, the Constraints (2) calculate the stock level. Nevertheless, given that the ordering costs for both traditional and non-traditional suppliers, as well as the inventory cost are lower than the cost associated with shortages, the model advocates for fulfilling demand through these former avenues. During a crisis, situations where demand is higher than usual production and stock levels are identified as shortages or unmet demand, according to the second assumption. The modeling approach presupposes that suppliers can adjust their production across different periods, subject to a maximum production capacity denoted by $Q_{z,t}$. This represents the upper bound on the suppliers' capability to increase production, aligning with the flexibility mentioned in the assumptions. The $Q_{z,t}$ helps adjust production levels over different time periods, based on the principles in assumption three, and can be raised after two to four weeks of rising demand. Assumption four delineates the methodology for deriving demand levels from the empirical data pertinent to our case study. It posits that the establishment of a novel standard is feasible upon the augmentation of suppliers' production capacities over a trimester. Consequently, this emergent norm of production capacity is anticipated to surpass the former benchmark by 20%, achievable by modifying the upper limit of production for suppliers as delineated in Constraints (2)–(3). In the final assumption, the discourse extends to the potential repercussions in the event of a crisis.

6 Conclusion

The proposed model to calibrate resilience strategies for the PPE supply chain seeks to maximize available resources (financial or infrastructure) in order to minimize the risks of a disruption in healthcare services resulting from a shortage. The main hypotheses used in the study stems from prolonged observation of PPE management in the early months of the COVID-19 pandemic within the public health system of the province of Quebec (Canada). In addition, access to certain data is part of a collaborative approach with decision-makers at the Ministry of Health [3]. Moreover, although several studies attempt to derive insights from the experiences gathered during the COVID-19 pandemic, a systematic literature review remains notably absent [29].

To effectively manage public health crises, logistics managers must consider a multi-dimensional approach to PPE stockpile management, extending beyond mere inventory control. Prior to a crisis, anticipating potential disruptions enables proactive engagement with suppliers to secure necessary resources without the burden of long-term storage. During a crisis, it is imperative to establish clear PPE usage protocols to efficiently manage demand and ensure adequate supply. Following the crisis, collaborating with suppliers to enhance the adaptability of production processes can significantly improve response capabilities. Such strategic planning not only mitigates the immediate impacts of a crisis but also strengthens the overall resilience of health systems against future emergencies. This comprehensive framework addresses the initial shortcomings observed in the COVID-19 pandemic response, proposing a more dynamic and responsive approach to crisis management in public health logistics.

To prevent future shortages, it is essential to maintain a reserve of each type of PPE. To this end, policymakers should meticulously monitor the demand trends for PPE during the COVID-19 pandemic within their specific region to understand how demand patterns shifted. Once policymakers have a grasp on these demand patterns, they can apply our proposed LP formulation to determine appropriate stockpile levels for each type of PPE. By inputting their specific scenarios into the model, they can understand the necessary stockpile sizes should a similar or more severe pandemic occur. Our correlation analyses have identified strong links between the use of certain PPE and the number of deaths, although these findings are specific to Quebec and may not be applicable elsewhere. It would be beneficial for researchers in other regions to investigate whether similar correlations exist under their local conditions. In summary, while the concept of maintaining PPE reserves for future pandemics is universally applicable, the precise levels of these stockpiles might vary based on local demand scenarios. The proposed LP model provides a valuable tool for identifying these levels across various scenarios, but the applicability of our correlation findings may be limited to specific geographical contexts.

However, the proposed model has its limitations. For example, the model does not specify which actor will be responsible of the stockpile management. This could be done by a direct entity of the province of Quebec's public health system, or by one of its suppliers. Also, the model does not specify whether such a stockpile should contain finished products, such as reusable gowns, or raw materials (e.g., fabrics). Finally, the model assumes that non-traditional suppliers can compensate in the short term for supply chain failures. However, contractual arrangements will need to be considered for these very specific situations. It remains to be seen whether the market will be receptive to such arrangements in a post-pandemic environment. It will be necessary to translate the calibration of the resilience measures suggested by the model into procurement strategies that will achieve these objectives while reconciling the interests of suppliers.

Declaration of Interest The authors declare no conflicts of interest.

References

1. Alikhani R, Torabi SA, Altay N (2021) Retail supply chain network design with concurrent resilience capabilities. Int J Prod Econ 234:108042
2. Beaulieu M, Roy J, Rebolledo C, Landry S (2024) La contribution des fournisseurs à la résilience de la chaîne logistique d'équipements de protection individuelle. Can J Adm Sci 41(3):376–397
3. Beaulieu M, Rebolledo C, Lissillour R (2024) Collaborative research competencies in supply chain management: the role of boundary spanning and reflexivity. Int J Logist Manag 35(2):305–331
4. Beaulieu M, Roy J, Chenevert D, Rebolledo C, Landry S (2024) Lessons learned from the pandemic: expanding the collaboration between clinical and logistics activities in a hospital. J Health Organ Manag 38(2):286–304
5. Beaulieu M, Roy J, Rebolledo C, Landry S (2022) The management of personal protective equipment during the COVID-19 pandemic: the case of the province of Quebec. Healthc Manage Forum 35(2):48–52
6. Beaulieu M, Roy J, Snowdon A, Rebolledo C, Landry S, Wright A (2022) Managing personal protective equipment in a pandemic: lessons from the Canadian health sector. Logist Manag 30(4):213–229
7. Beaulieu M, Roy J, Snowdon A, Ruel S (2021) Les pièges à éviter avant la prochaine pandémie. Gest Hosp 603:70–71
8. Bhaskar S, Tan J, Bogers MLAM, Minssen T, Badaruddin H, Israeli-Korn S, Chesbrough H (2020) At the epicenter of COVID-19-the tragic failure of the global supply chain for medical supplies. Front Public Health 8:562882
9. Canis B (2011) The motor vehicle supply chain: effects of the Japanese earthquake and Tsunami. CRS Report for Congress, Washington
10. Cook TM (2020) Personal protective equipment during the coronavirus disease (COVID) 2019 pandemic—a narrative review. Anaesthesia 75(7):920–927
11. Das K, Annand A, Ram M (2021) A global supply network design model: a resilient management approach
12. Elsahn Z, Siedlok F (2021) 'Can we build it? Yes, we can!' Complexities of resource redeployment to fight pandemic. Ind Mark Manage 93:191–207
13. Fox HW, Rink DR (1978) Purchasing's role across the product life cycle. Ind Mark Manage 7(3):186–192

14. Galanis P, Vraka I, Fragkou D, Bilali A, Kaitelidou D (2021) Impact of personal protective equipment use on health care workers' physical health during the COVID-19 pandemic: a systematic review and meta-analysis. Am J Infect Control 49(10):1305–1315
15. Götz P, Auping WL, Hinrichs-Krapels S (2024) Contributing to health system resilience during pandemics via purchasing and supply strategies: an exploratory system dynamics approach. BMC Health Serv Res 24(1):130
16. Handfield R, Finkenstadt DJ, Schneller ES, Godfrey AB, Guinto P (2020) A commons for a supply chain in the post-COVID-19 era: the case for a reformed strategic national stockpile. Milbank Q 98(4):1058–1090
17. Jessop ZM, Dobbs TD, Ali SR, Combellack E, Clancy R, Ibrahim N, Whitaker IS et al (2020) Personal protective equipment for surgeons during COVID-19 pandemic: systematic review of availability, usage and rationing. J Br Surg 107(10):1262–1280
18. Lucas TC, Guimarães RD, Vasconcellos MSG, Lins ID, das Chagas Moura MJ, de Siqueira PGSC (2024) Resilience of critical supply chains in pandemics: A model proposal for health personal protective equipment socially optimal distribution. Oper Res Health Care 40:100420
19. Manikas AS, Patel PC (2016) Managing sales surprise: the role of operational slack and volume flexibility. Int J Prod Econ 179:101–116
20. National Audit Office (2020) The supply of personal protective equipment (PPE) during the COVID-19 pandemic. United Kingdom
21. Nollet J, Beaulieu M, Fabbe-Costes N (2019) Measuring purchasing groups performance in the health care sector. Can J Adm Sci 36(4):514–526
22. Northern Ireland Office Audit (2022) The COVID-19 pandemic: supply and procurement of personal protective equipment to local healthcare providers. https://www.niauditoffice.gov.uk/files/niauditoffice/documents/2022-03/niao-report-the-covid-19-pandemic-supply-and-procurement-of-ppe-to-local-healthcare-providers_web_final.pdf
23. Patel A, D'Alessandro MM, Ireland KJ, Burel WB, Wencil EB, Rasmussen SA (2017) Personal protective equipment supply chain: Lessons learned from recent public health emergency responses. Health Secur 15(3):244–253
24. Patrinley JR, Berkowitz ST, Zakria D, Totten DJ, Kurtulus M, Drolet BC (2020) Lessons from operations management to combat the COVID-19 pandemic. J Med Syst 44:1–2
25. Pettit TJ, Croxton KL, Fiksel J (2019) The evolution of resilience in supply chain management: a retrospective on ensuring supply chain resilience. J Bus Logist 40(1):56–65
26. Ponomarov SY, Holcomb MC (2009) Understanding the concept of supply chain resilience. Int J Logist Manag 20(1):124–143
27. Queiroz MM, Ivanov D, Dolgui A, Fosso Wamba S (2022) Impacts of epidemic outbreaks on supply chains: mapping a research agenda amid the COVID-19 pandemic through a structured literature review. Ann Oper Res 319(1):1159–1196
28. Scala B, Lindsay CF (2021) Supply chain resilience during pandemic disruption: evidence from healthcare. Supply Chain Manag 26(6):672–688
29. Shahin R, Hosteins P, Pellegrini P, Vandanjon PO, Quadrifoglio L (2024) A survey of flex-route transit problem and its link with vehicle routing problem. Transp Res Part C Emerg Technol 158:104437
30. Stein S (2020, December) The future of the U.S. National Stockpile isn't a bigger stockpile. https://www.bloomberg.com/news/articles/2020-12-10/the-future-of-u-s-national-stockpile-isn-t-a-bigger-stockpile
31. Torsekar MP (2018) China climbs the global value chain for medical devices. J Int Commer Econ
32. Tukamuhabwa BR, Stevenson M, Busby J, Zorzini M (2015) Supply chain resilience: definition, review and theoretical foundations for further study. Int J Prod Res 53(18):5592–5623
33. van Hoek R, Dobrzykowski D (2021) Towards more balanced sourcing strategies—are supply chain risks caused by the covid-19 pandemic driving reshoring considerations? Supply Chain Manag 26(6):689–701
34. Vérificateur général du Québec (2022) Gestion des équipements de protection individuelle pendant la pandémie. Assemblée Nationale, Québec

35. Wadhwa P (2020) Global annual spend on PPE can hit $50–80 bn; China key player: Jefferies. Business Standard
36. Wagner SM, Neshat N (2010) Assessing the vulnerability of supply chains using graph theory. Int J Prod Econ 126(1):121–129

Reza Shahin (Ph.D.) serves as a researcher at the University of Gustave Eiffel. His research interests encompass supply chain management, optimization, operations research, and transportation science. His Ph.D. focus was on integrating ad hoc stops into public transport in which the flexibility of demand responsive transit was merged with the low cost of public transportation, providing a door-to-door pick-up and drop-off to customers. He also serves as a reviewer for Transportation Research.

Martin Beaulieu (M.Sc.) is a Research Associate at HEC Montréal's Supply Chain Research Group. His research focuses on supply chain integration dynamics. He is a noted researcher on supply chain management and healthcare operations management with numerous articles and case studies published in the last two decades as well as government commissioned studies. Amongst other outlets, he has published in journals such as the International Journal of Operations and Production Management, Supply Chain Management: An International Journal, Journal of Purchasing and Supply Management, International Journal of Logistics Management or IEEE Transactions on Engineering Management.

Valérie Bélanger is a professor in the Department of Logistics and Operations Management at HEC Montréal. She holds a M.Sc. in mechanical engineering, as well as a Ph.D. in decision sciences. Her main research interests focus on health care logistics and emergency service management. She is working actively with various organizations from the health care sector on projects related to patient and material transportation, emergency care, and network design. Pr. Bélanger is affiliated with the Interuniversity Research Centre on Enterprise Networks, Logistics and Transportation (CIRRELT).

Martin Cousineau Ph.D., is an assistant professor in the Department of Logistics and Operations Management at HEC Montréal and a professor of the Institute for Data Valorization (IVADO). He is a co-head researcher of the Sustainable Health research theme of the International Observatory on the Societal Impacts of AI and Digital Technology (OBVIA) and a member of the Interuniversity Research Centre on Enterprise Networks, Logistics and Transportation (CIRRELT). He is specialized in methods at the intersection of operations research and artificial intelligence, with applications to logistics, transportation and healthcare.

Part V

Revolution of the Hospital Supply Chain: Information Systems; Artificial Intelligence; Digital Transition and Innovative Technologies

The Future of Healthcare Supply Chains: Integrating Industry 4.0 Technologies for Improved Resilience and Sustainability

25

Thomas K. Dasaklis and Giannis T. Tsoulfas

Abstract

The healthcare supply chain, a critical part of the healthcare sector, involves the planning, procurement, storage, and distribution of medical necessities. With the advent of Industry 4.0 technologies, there is an opportunity to transform and enhance the resilience and sustainability of these supply chains. The COVID-19 pandemic has laid bare the vulnerabilities within the system, accentuating the need for research into methods that leverage Industry 4.0 technologies to improve resilience. This article critically assesses the current state of healthcare supply chain operations, identifying weaknesses and areas for development, particularly in the context of integrating advanced technologies. It then investigates the factors that influence healthcare supply chain resilience, drawing insights from evidence-based cases and exploring the role of Industry 4.0 technologies. Based on this analysis, the paper offers recommendations for enhancing resilience and sustainability in healthcare supply chains through the adoption of Industry 4.0 solutions. By ensuring the continuous availability of essential medical supplies and equipment during disruptive events, the research contributes to the creation of more resilient and sustainable healthcare supply chains. The integration of Industry 4.0 technologies not only strengthens the supply chain but also positions healthcare organizations to improve patient outcomes and better prepare for future emergencies, minimizing potential interruptions.

T. K. Dasaklis
School of Social Sciences, Hellenic Open University, 26335 Patras, Greece
e-mail: dasaklis@eap.gr

G. T. Tsoulfas (✉)
Department of Agribusiness and Supply Chain Management, Agricultural University of Athens, 32200 Thiva, Greece
e-mail: giannis@aua.gr

F. Jawab (ed.), *Hospital Supply Chain*, Integrated Science 27,
https://doi.org/10.1007/978-3-031-70292-1_25

Keywords

Medical supplies • Vulnerabilities • Robustness • Redundancy • Flexibility • Agility

1 Introduction

The healthcare supply chain is an essential element of the healthcare industry, acting as the foundation that guarantees the smooth movement of medical items, equipment, and services from producers to final recipients, usually patients. This intricate network entails the synchronization of many entities, such as suppliers, manufacturers, distributors, and healthcare professionals. The main objective of the healthcare supply chain is to efficiently provide the appropriate items in the correct amounts, at the designated time and location, while minimizing expenses and guaranteeing superior quality and patient safety [21, 57].

The importance of resilience and sustainability in healthcare supply chains cannot be overstated due to various reasons. Resilience pertains to the capacity of the supply chain to foresee, plan for, react to, and bounce back from unfavorable occurrences, such as disasters, pandemics, or interruptions in the supply. A robust healthcare supply chain possesses the ability to adjust to obstacles, uphold its fundamental operations, and promptly restore normal functioning following a disturbance [31] In the healthcare sector, the presence of medical supplies is of utmost importance as it can be a matter of life and death.

Sustainability prioritizes the enduring feasibility of the supply chain. Supply chain sustainability comprises the environmental, social, and economic dimensions. Its objectives include minimizing the environmental effects of supply chain activities, promoting social responsibility, and achieving cost efficiency. Implementing sustainable practices in the healthcare supply chain can result in decreased waste, enhanced resource utilization, and improved public health outcomes [4, 39].

The COVID-19 pandemic has acted as a major driver for transformation in healthcare supply chains, revealing multiple weaknesses and inefficiencies. The pandemic underscored the necessity for supply chains that are more robust and environmentally-friendly, as healthcare providers encountered severe scarcities of personal protective equipment (PPE), ventilators, and other medical supplies. The exceptional worldwide demand for these products, along with delays in the supply chain, highlighted the significance of implementing resilient systems that can endure such unexpected events [10, 60].

The pandemic has expedited the process of digitizing supply chains, prompting healthcare businesses to reassess their plans and operations [37, 56]. Industry 4.0 technologies have emerged as effective instruments to improve the robustness and environmental friendliness of supply chains. These technologies have the capability to offer data in real-time, enhance transparency, optimize inventory management, and enable more effective decision-making.

This article provides a thorough assessment of healthcare supply chain operations, highlighting deficiencies and opportunities for enhancement, particularly through the integration of advanced technologies. It subsequently analyzes the resilience of the healthcare supply chain by utilizing evidence-based examples and Industry 4.0 technology.

2 Current State of Healthcare Supply Chain Operations

2.1 Main Healthcare Supply Chain Processes

The provision of healthcare services depends on a number of vital processes, all of which are part of the complex and dynamic healthcare supply chain. Planning, sourcing, storing, and distributing are some of the current procedures in this supply chain that need to work together harmoniously to guarantee the prompt delivery of medical supplies and services [2].

The fundamental process of planning involves evaluating the needs of healthcare providers and creating projections to ascertain what medical supplies are needed, when they are needed, and in what quantities. In order to complete this stage, past usage patterns must be examined, healthcare demand trends must be taken into account, and future needs must be projected. These needs may be impacted by disease outbreaks, demographic changes, or adjustments to medical procedures. Careful planning guarantees that the supply chain can satisfy the demands of the healthcare industry without suffering shortages that could jeopardize patient care or unnecessary expenditures from overstocking [67, 73].

Procurement follows planning and involves the selection and purchasing of medical supplies and equipment. Suppliers must be carefully chosen for this procedure based on their quality, reliability, and cost-effectiveness. Because healthcare products have to adhere to strict rules and standards to ensure patient safety and efficacy, procurement can be extremely challenging. Contract negotiations, relationship management, and ongoing performance evaluation of suppliers are all part of the procurement process, which makes sure that the requirements of the purchase are being fulfilled to a satisfactory degree [20, 40].

The next crucial step is storage, which entails managing the inventory and warehousing of medical supplies. In order to preserve the items' quality and utility, this stage must guarantee that they are stored under appropriate conditions. Certain drugs must be refrigerated, and others may need to be kept in a sterile environment. Effective inventory management in storage is essential for avoiding stockouts and product waste caused by outdated goods. It involves technologies that keep tabs on stock levels, keep an eye on expiration dates, and make it easier to rotate stock so that older products are used first [16, 69].

The last stage is distribution, in which medical goods are sent to the places they are supposed to go—like clinics, hospitals, or pharmacies. To guarantee that medical professionals obtain the materials they need to treat patients right away, this procedure needs to be timely and effective. Distribution needs to be adaptable enough to respond to last-minute demands or shifts in demand. It can be complicated, including several different transportation routes and modes. Medical product replacements, recalls, and returns are all handled as part of the distribution process [7, 48].

The seamless functioning of the healthcare supply chain depends on the interactions between these operations [17, 35, 63]. Every phase depends on the others; wise planning influences procurement choices, which influence storage needs and logistics of delivery. Inaccurate planning can result in either a shortage of resources, which could delay patient care, or an excess of goods, which would raise storage expenses and the possibility of waste. Similar to this, procurement and storage needs must coincide; buying a product in bulk without the space to store it appropriately might result in spoiling and financial loss. Furthermore, effective distribution must be supported by the storage process' design. Supplies can be delivered to healthcare providers more quickly by using sophisticated inventory management systems and selecting and packing procedures that are expedited in a well-organized warehouse. Distribution plans need to be adaptable and strong enough to meet regular supply demands and expand in the event of crises or unanticipated demand surges.

The capacity of healthcare supply chains to satisfy the demands of healthcare professionals and, eventually, patients is a key indicator of their efficacy. This entails offering top-notch medical equipment and supplies, preserving the integrity of goods (particularly those that need regulated conditions), and guaranteeing continuous availability of necessities.

2.2 Mature Technologies and Systems in Use

Currently, the healthcare supply chain makes use of a range of methods and technologies intended to improve efficiency, expedite processes, and guarantee the prompt and economical delivery of medical supplies. The management of the intricate logistics involved in the planning, acquiring, storing, and distribution of medical supplies depends heavily on these technologies. Systems and technologies aid in the automation of repetitive operations and lessen the possibility of human errors, which can cause supply chain discrepancies.

Maintaining ideal stock levels requires the use of sophisticated inventory management systems. These systems track inventory levels in real-time, forecast stock requirements, and send out warnings when replenishment is necessary using data analytics [1]. By lowering overstock and understock conditions, this system helps to minimize waste and guarantee that necessary medical supplies are available when needed.

Warehouse Management Systems (WMS) are used to regulate and oversee the transportation and storage of goods inside warehouses. They play a crucial role in overseeing the reception, storage, and retrieval of goods in the warehouse and assist warehouse workers in the effective picking, packing, and shipping of goods [46]. Radio Frequency Identification (RFID) technology and barcode scanners can be integrated into WMS to improve accuracy and lower the chance of errors. For the purpose of tracking and tracing products along the supply chain, RFID and barcode technologies are indispensable [9, 12]. These technologies aid in decreasing manual errors, improving operational efficiency, and automating the identifying process of medical supplies. The ability to scan many products at once and update inventory information in real-time is a benefit of RFID in particular.

The supply chain's transportation component is optimized through the use of Transportation Management Systems (TMS). These systems support cargo tracking, payment processing, freight auditing, and route planning. By offering real-time data and analytics on transportation operations, TMS may assist healthcare organizations in lowering shipping costs, expediting delivery, and improving service quality [14, 38].

Healthcare supply chains frequently employ Enterprise Resource Planning (ERP) to combine several corporate operations into a logical, cohesive system. Daily operations including purchasing, inventory control, finance, and human resources are managed by these systems [19]. ERP systems are useful in supply chain management because they facilitate demand forecasting, production scheduling, and supply and demand alignment. Better decision-making is made possible by this integration, which offers a comprehensive picture of supply chain processes.

3 The Rapidly Evolving External Environment

3.1 The Impact of Recent Global Events on Supply Chain Operations

The COVID-19 pandemic and other recent international events have had a significant impact on the operations of the healthcare supply chain by drawing attention to weaknesses and spurring changes towards more robust and sustainable procedures. These incidents have highlighted how important it is to maintain strong supply chains that can resist shocks to the world economy and guarantee the ongoing provision of necessary medical goods and services [15, 30].

The COVID-19 pandemic served as a significant stress test for healthcare supply chains worldwide. The pandemic caused previously unheard-of increases in demand for ventilators, medications, PPE, and other medical goods. Hoarding and panic buying, along with the abrupt spike in demand, rapidly depleted supplies and created serious shortages. Healthcare practitioners encountered significant difficulties in obtaining these vital supplies, which were necessary for treating COVID-19 patients and ensuring the safety of healthcare personnel [68, 72]. Due to the worldwide nature of healthcare supply chains, disruptions in one region of the world may spread to other parts of the world. Lockdowns and travel restrictions had a disastrous effect on logistics and manufacturing during the pandemic. Supply networks were severely disrupted by factory closures, especially in nations that are important hubs for the manufacture of medical products. Restrictions on air and sea travel also affected the distribution and transportation of products, causing delays and making shortages worse [22, 68]. It was discovered that a large number of healthcare supply chains lacked the flexibility and agility necessary to react quickly to changes in supply and demand. The use of just-in-time inventory techniques, which lower stock levels to cut expenses, wasn't wise in this situation. These procedures made it difficult to account for mistakes or unexpected changes in demand, which emphasizes the need for supply chain tactics that are more flexible and responsive [62, 72].

In addition to the pandemic, other global events have also impacted healthcare supply chains. Geopolitical unrest and trade disputes may result in limitations, tariffs, or embargoes that impact the supply of medical goods. Trade disputes between large economies have the potential to impair supply chains, raise prices, and restrict access to necessary medical supplies [25, 59]. Natural disasters like hurricanes, floods, and wildfires can cause supply chain disruptions both locally and internationally. These occurrences may result in abrupt increases in the demand for medical assistance and supplies in the impacted areas, damage to production facilities, and disruptions to logistics routes [23, 64]. Supply chain operations may be impacted by changes in regulations, especially those pertaining to international trade and healthcare products. For supply chain operators, new rules pertaining to the approval, production, or labeling of medical products may cause delays and extra expenses [11, 45].

3.2 Key Vulnerabilities in Healthcare Supply Chains

A significant portion of healthcare supply chains depend on a limited amount of suppliers, and in certain cases, even a solitary source, for critical items [29]. The high level of concentration amplifies the likelihood of substantial disruption in the event that a supplier encounters problems such as cessation of production, financial instability, or geopolitical crises.

Traditional supply chains are typically optimized for efficiency through the implementation of just-in-time inventory techniques, which aim to minimize stock levels in order to save expenses. Although this approach can save money, it also implies that there is limited flexibility to handle unexpected increases in demand or delays in supply [68].

Lacking immediate access to the supply chain, it becomes difficult to monitor inventory levels, anticipate shortages, and address disruptions. The absence of transparency can result in inefficiency and heightened susceptibility to unforeseen circumstances [74].

The healthcare sector is subject to rigorous regulations, and alterations in these standards can profoundly affect the functioning of supply chain activities. Adhering to many international, national, and local regulations can be intricate and expensive, resulting in delays and heightened chances of failing to meet the requirements [21, 55].

There is frequently a disparity in the extent to which technology is adopted in various segments of the supply chain. While certain regions may employ cutting-edge technologies, others may continue to depend on obsolete systems, resulting in inefficiencies and a lack of seamless integration [51].

3.3 Major Impacts

The risks and challenges present in healthcare supply chains might result in many negative repercussions [6, 27, 52]. Insufficient inventory levels can result in stock-outs, which occur when crucial items are not accessible when required. These circumstances can have significant consequences for the quality of patient care, perhaps resulting in delayed or less effective therapies. Conversely, excessive stockpiling or inadequate inventory management can lead to wastage caused by products expiring prior to consumption. This not only signifies a monetary deficit but also raises environmental and ethical apprehensions, as valuable resources are being wasted. Both instances of inventory shortages and instances of unnecessary waste can have a substantial financial effect on healthcare institutions. Stock-outs necessitate urgent purchase at elevated expenses, while wastage immobilizes money in idle inventory and incurs disposal expenditures. Ultimately, the most notable result of these vulnerabilities is their influence on the outcomes of patients. Supply chain inefficiencies can result in procedural delays, heightened infection rates due to inadequate PPE, and a general decline in the quality of healthcare.

4 Healthcare Supply Chain Resilience

4.1 Components of Supply Chain Resilience

Supply chain resilience encompasses the capacity of a supply chain to foresee, plan for, react to, and bounce back from disturbances while ensuring uninterrupted operations and protecting individuals, resources, and overall brand value. The resilience of healthcare supply chains is of utmost importance due to its direct influence on human lives and health outcomes. The constituents of supply chain resilience can be roughly classified into four primary areas [5, 28, 32, 44]:

- Robustness—The capacity of the supply chain to endure disturbances without experiencing substantial operational deterioration. This requires the implementation of solid and dependable procedures that are capable of managing unforeseen pressures.
- Redundancy—The incorporation of supplementary or alternative resources that do not actively contribute to normal functioning but can act as a contingency plan in the event of a disruption. This may encompass supplementary suppliers, inventory, stockpiling critical medical supplies, resource sharing among hospitals, and surplus production capacity.

- Flexibility—The adaptability to modify activities in response to disturbance. This may entail altering manufacturing methods, changing suppliers, or utilizing alternative transportation routes.
- Agility—The ability to promptly address disruptions and recover from them. Agility necessitates both the ability to respond operationally and the ability to react fast and effectively through decision-making.

4.2 External and Internal Factors Affecting Resilience

When it comes to analyzing the major factors that affect resilience, organizations should address both external and internal factors. Regarding the former, trade policies, tariffs, and political instability can impact the accessibility of vital supplies and the expenses associated with acquiring them [42]. Disruptions occurring at the level of a supplier, be it caused by financial issues, natural calamities, or other operational difficulties [13], can result in a chain reaction that impacts the healthcare supply chain. In addition, seasonal fluctuations can also significantly impact the demand for specific healthcare products, putting strain on the supply chain [36]. Moreover, the rapid advancements in technology might make old processes outdated or necessitate substantial adjustments, which can affect the resilience of the supply chain [61].

With respect to the internal factors, first of all the intricacy of the supply chain, the multitude of layers, and the concentration of decision-making power might influence the efficiency of its response to disturbances [34]. The resilience of the supply chain can be greatly affected by the company culture and leadership style. An organizational culture that promotes innovation, adaptability, and proactive risk mitigation can strengthen resilience [50]. Furthermore, insufficient financial resources or a lack of access to essential skills and technologies can restrict the ability to effectively address disruptions in the supply chain [68]. Additionally, the robustness and seamless integration of information technology systems utilized for supply chain management are of paramount importance. Ineffective reaction to disruptions might be impeded by systems that are poorly connected or outdated [33].

5 Industry 4.0 Solutions

5.1 Relevant Industry 4.0 Technologies

The emergence of Industry 4.0 has ushered in a revolutionary surge of technical progress that is set to change supply chain management. Industry 4.0 involves the use of digital technologies into production and supply chain operations [3]. This integration offers the potential to improve the effectiveness, clarity, and robustness of supply networks. Within the healthcare sector, the consequences are especially significant, as the supply chain has a direct influence on the quality of patient care and the resulting outcomes.

The Internet of Things (IoT) denotes a network of tangible items that are equipped with sensors, software, and other advanced technologies. The primary objective of IoT is to establish connections and facilitate the exchange of data with other devices and systems over the internet. IoT devices in supply chains may monitor the whereabouts and state of products across the supply chain, offering immediate visibility and facilitating proactive control of inventory and assets [49].

Artificial Intelligence (AI) refers to a variety of technologies that empower systems to see, understand, take action, and acquire knowledge with intelligence comparable to that of humans. AI can be utilized in supply chains to perform predictive analytics, estimate demand, and provide support for decision-making. AI algorithms have the capability to evaluate extensive quantities of data in order to detect trends and forecast future results, so assisting in the optimization of supply chain operations. Machine learning is a branch of AI that allows computers to learn from data and enhance their performance without the need for explicit programming. Its capacity to examine historical data and market trends makes it particularly pertinent to healthcare supply chains. This enables it to forecast future occurrences, such as probable backorders, and make well-informed decisions on inventory levels, procurement methods, and distribution logistics [8].

Blockchain is a decentralized system that enables data to be stored on a series of interconnected and protected blocks using cryptographic techniques. Blockchain technology can offer a secure and unchangeable record of transactions in supply chains, improving the ability to track products and decreasing the likelihood of fraudulent activities. Ensuring the validity and provenance of medicinal items is of utmost importance in the healthcare industry [26].

Big Data Analytics is the process of analyzing extensive and diverse datasets to discover concealed patterns, unfamiliar relationships, market trends, client preferences, and other valuable business insights. Big Data Analytics can be employed in healthcare supply chains to enhance the efficiency of supply chain operations by optimizing routes, forecasting demand, and improving overall performance [71].

Cloud computing offers users immediate access to computer system resources, such as data storage and computational power, without requiring direct user management. Cloud computing provides healthcare supply chains with scalable and flexible data storage options, as well as the capability to utilize software-as-a-service (SaaS) applications for different supply chain management activities [24].

Cyber-Physical Systems (CPS) refer to the amalgamation of computation, networking, and physical processes. Embedded computers and networks oversee and regulate physical processes, typically via feedback loops where the physical processes influence computations and vice versa. Within supply chains, the implementation of CPS can result in more efficient warehousing, automatic restocking, and enhanced adaptability to fluctuations in the supply chain landscape [54].

Additive manufacturing, also referred to as 3D printing, is the method of fabricating a tangible item by progressively depositing material layers based on a digital model until the object is fully formed. 3D printing can be utilized in healthcare supply chains to produce medical items as needed, resulting in decreased inventory expenses and shorter production times [53].

Robotics and automation encompass the utilization of robots and automated systems to execute jobs that pose risks, involve monotonous repetition, or need meticulous accuracy [65]. Robotics can be employed in healthcare supply chains to automate the processes of order picking and packing in warehouses, as well as in transportation through the use of automated guided vehicles.

A digital twin is an exact digital copy of a physical entity, whether it is a live organism or an inanimate object. Through the integration of the physical and virtual realms, data is effortlessly exchanged, enabling the coexistence of virtual and physical entities [47]. Supply chains can utilize digital twins to mimic and assess performance, allowing for the optimization of the supply chain prior to executing physical alterations.

Augmented Reality (AR) and Virtual Reality (VR) technology can improve the way supply chain processes are visualized and interacted with. AR can enhance warehouse operations by delivering workers with real-time information superimposed on their range of vision, while VR can be employed for training and simulating supply chain situations [58].

Edge computing is the act of analyzing data in close proximity to where it is generated, rather than in a centralized data-processing facility. Edge computing can be employed in supply chains to promptly process data from IoT devices, facilitating expedited and more effective decision-making [43].

5.2 Evidence from Reported Cases

VentilatorChallengeUK

Before the onset of the COVID-19 pandemic, the manufacturing of ventilators followed a consistent and foreseeable procedure. Manufacturers functioned under typical demand conditions without requiring fast expansion or extensive deployment of resources. The VentilatorChallengeUK consortium was established promptly to address the pressing need for ventilators, leading to the manufacture of 14,000 units during a span of only 12 weeks. This was accomplished through the cooperation of firms from many industries, employing Industry 4.0 technologies such as AR and 3D printing to accelerate the design, manufacturing, and assembly procedures [41].

NHS and Big Data Analytics

The conventional supply chain operations of the NHS relied on standard data collecting and processing techniques, which may have been ill-prepared to cope with the sudden increase in demand for medical goods and equipment during a pandemic [66]. The NHS successfully implemented a centralized platform for real-time data collecting and analysis by incorporating big data analytics and AI. This enhanced the efficiency of distributing crucial equipment and facilitated a more flexible deployment of resources throughout the pandemic.

Ford, 3M, and General Electric Healthcare Collaboration
Traditionally, automotive and industrial corporations such as Ford and 3M have not been involved in the production of medical equipment, specifically ventilators. Ford, 3M, and General Electric Healthcare made a significant shift in their operations by utilizing their manufacturing skills to make ventilators and PPE through the application of 3D printing technology [18]. This not only showcased the adaptability of Industry 4.0 technologies but also underscored the possibility of inter-industry cooperation during periods of emergency.

Sustainable Humanitarian Supply Chains
Humanitarian supply chains frequently encounter challenges related to sustainability, especially when confronted with climatic crises and disasters. The utilization of Industry 4.0 technology was employed to establish humanitarian supply chains that are more environmentally friendly and can be maintained for a longer period of time [70]. During the COVID-19 pandemic, big data analytics and AI were employed to enhance adaptability and durability. Additionally, the potential of utilizing drones as an alternative transportation system was investigated.

6 Discussion

6.1 Expected Benefits

Integrating Industry 4.0 technology into healthcare supply chains provides numerous advantages that can greatly enhance operational efficiency, enhance patient care, and ensure sustainability. These technologies play a distinct role in the evolution of healthcare supply chains. IoT devices have the capability to track products in real-time across the supply chain, improving visibility and enabling proactive management of inventories and assets. Blockchain technology promotes traceability and minimizes the risk of fraud in healthcare by providing a secure and unchangeable record of transactions. This is vital because the validity and origin of medical supplies are of utmost importance. AI is highly proficient in processing extensive quantities of data to forecast future demand with greater precision, resulting in enhanced efficiency in inventory management. This aids in minimizing occurrences of excessive inventory or shortages, guaranteeing that healthcare professionals possess the requisite resources when required. Cloud computing enables a connected, intelligent, scalable, and fast supply chain, which enhances agility and flexibility in enterprises. Cyber-physical systems combine physical processes with computer-based algorithms to improve automation and efficiency, especially in the fields of warehousing and logistics. Additive manufacturing enables the fabrication of medical equipment and customized prosthetics as needed, resulting in substantial reductions in inventory costs and lead times. This technology is especially advantageous for promptly addressing unique patient requirements and managing abrupt increases in demand, such as those experienced during health emergencies. Advanced robotics and automation optimize processes, ranging from the use of automated storage and retrieval systems in warehouses to the utilization of robotics-assisted surgical equipment that improves precision in medical treatments. These technologies diminish the dependence on human labor for monotonous activities, enabling healthcare personnel to dedicate more attention to patient care. Digital twins are virtual counterparts of physical systems or processes that allow for simulation and analysis, enabling the prediction of outcomes and optimization of operations. Within the healthcare sector, digital twins have the capability to replicate and model hospital processes as well as patient reactions to various treatments. This can be highly beneficial in terms of strategic planning and making informed clinical decisions. AR and VR are used in teaching medical personnel and strategizing intricate medical operations. These technologies enhance the abilities of healthcare practitioners and aid in the planning of procedures with greater accuracy, potentially decreasing the likelihood of mistakes, by offering immersive and interactive simulations. Edge computing fosters the processing of data created by IoT devices at the periphery of the network. This approach minimizes the delay in data transmission and enables immediate analysis of the data in real-time. Immediate data processing is essential in important healthcare applications as it can expedite decision-making and interventions. It is also important to point out that the utilization of Industry 4.0 technologies enhances sustainability by efficiently managing resources and minimizing waste. Additive manufacturing reduces material waste, while automation and efficient logistical routes decrease energy use. Systems' security is enhanced, and the safety of patients is improved, which is a solid piece of evidence regarding the social pillar of sustainability.

6.2 Barriers

Although Industry 4.0 technologies have the potential to bring about significant advantages, there are various obstacles that hinder their implementation in healthcare supply chains. First of all, the initial capital needed to incorporate Industry 4.0 technologies can be substantial. Healthcare organizations may exhibit reluctance in allocating funding towards new technology, particularly in cases where the return on investment is uncertain or long-term. In addition, the implementation of Industry 4.0 technology can be intricate, necessitating modifications to current processes and systems. The intricacy of the task can discourage organizations with fewer resources. On some occasions there is also a deficiency in the current workforce's abilities when it comes to the knowledge necessary for implementing and overseeing Industry 4.0 technology. Acquiring or instructing personnel with the requisite expertise can be a difficulty and can impede the pace of implementation.

In addition, data privacy and security are important considerations in healthcare supply chains, as they handle sensitive data. The implementation of digital technologies has raised worries about the protection and confidentiality of this data. Safeguarding patient information and other confidential data is a crucial issue that requires attention. Moreover, the healthcare sector is subject to extensive regulations, and any novel technologies must adhere to an intricate network of rules and requirements. Overcoming these laws and guaranteeing adherence can impede the implementation of Industry 4.0 technologies. Furthermore, cultural resistance can emerge as an obstacle to organizational culture. The reluctance to embrace change and a predilection for conventional approaches can impede the assimilation of novel technologies. To overcome this reluctance, it is necessary to have effective leadership and provide a clear illustration of the advantages that Industry 4.0 technology may offer. Additionally, the selected technologies must possess the capability to scale alongside the firm and adjust to evolving requirements within the supply chain. Cloud computing provides scalable solutions that may be easily altered according to demand. Stakeholders should also consider the use of modular technologies that have the capability to be expanded or upgraded according to requirements. In terms of continuity, it is crucial to emphasize that the seamless operation of the supply chain relies on the crucial integration with existing systems. Healthcare organizations should prioritize the adoption of technologies that can seamlessly integrate with their existing infrastructure, thereby reducing any potential disruptions and maximizing the utilization of their present assets. This may entail utilizing APIs, middleware, or other integration platforms to guarantee compatibility between legacy and contemporary systems.

7 Concluding Remarks

Examining the existing shortcomings in healthcare supply chains, with the potential advantages offered by Industry 4.0, results in a number of strategic suggestions. First and foremost, healthcare organizations should give priority to diversifying their supplier base in order to reduce the risks associated with relying on a single source. Organizations can enhance the resilience of their supply chain by utilizing AI and big data analytics to find and assess alternative suppliers. Furthermore, in order to tackle the rigidity of supply chain architecture, it is advisable for stakeholders to allocate resources towards the use of technologies that facilitate adaptability and expandability. The utilization of IoT and cloud computing has the potential to play a crucial role in establishing a supply chain that is highly adaptable to dynamic demands and situations. IoT devices can enable immediate and ongoing control of inventory, while cloud platforms can rapidly adjust the size of operations to meet specific requirements. In addition, it is imperative to improve transparency and visibility throughout the entire supply chain. Blockchain technology can be utilized to establish a clear and unchangeable record of transactions, facilitating the monitoring of the origin of medical supplies, and guaranteeing their genuineness. In addition, digital twins have the capability to replicate supply chain activities, enabling the detection of possible problems and the experimentation of remedies in a simulated setting. In order to address technological inequalities, healthcare organizations should prioritize the incorporation of systems and the establishment of uniform data formats. This would facilitate uninterrupted communication among diverse technologies and systems, enhancing the overall efficiency of the supply chain. Cyber-physical systems facilitate the integration of physical operations and digital information, resulting in enhanced coordination of supply chain activities.

Policy and regulations are crucial in promoting the implementation of Industry 4.0 technology in healthcare supply chains. Regulatory authorities should strive to establish a conducive atmosphere that fosters innovation while simultaneously safeguarding patient well-being and data integrity. One way to accomplish this is by establishing explicit protocols and criteria for the implementation of emerging technology in healthcare supply chains. Policymakers should additionally contemplate offering incentives to healthcare organizations for the purpose of encouraging investment in Industry 4.0 technologies. These incentives may encompass tax exemptions, financial grants, or subsidies that reduce the economic obstacles to the adoption of technology. In addition, rules should be formulated to possess sufficient adaptability to keep up with the swift rate of technological advancement, enabling healthcare companies to embrace novel solutions without encountering excessive regulatory obstacles. Moreover, it is imperative for legislation and law to specifically tackle issues pertaining to data privacy and cybersecurity. With the increasing digitization of healthcare supply chains, there is a growing risk of data breaches and cyber-attacks. Regulations should establish stringent cybersecurity requirements and mandate healthcare firms to adopt steps that safeguard sensitive data.

Healthcare supply chains must adapt to changing patient needs, illness prevalence, and medical technology to stay resilient. Industry 4.0 technologies can improve supply chain visibility, real-time monitoring, and data-driven decision-making. They offer proactive risk management and prompt response to evolving circumstances.

References

1. Abu Zwaida T, Pham C, Beauregard Y (2021) Optimization of inventory management to prevent drug shortages in the hospital supply chain. Appl Sci 11:2726. https://doi.org/10.3390/app11062726
2. AbuKhousa E, Al-Jaroodi J, Lazarova-Molnar S, Mohamed N (2014) Simulation and modeling efforts to support decision making in healthcare supply chain management. Sci World J 2014:1–16. https://doi.org/10.1155/2014/354246
3. Akbari M, Kok SK, Hopkins J et al (2023) The changing landscape of digital transformation in supply chains: impacts of industry 4.0 in Vietnam. IJLM. https://doi.org/10.1108/IJLM-11-2022-0442
4. Asif K (2022) The impact of procurement strategies on supply chain sustainability in the pharmaceutical industry. SAJSR 53–64. https://doi.org/10.57044/SAJSR.2022.1.1.2203

5. Aslam H, Khan AQ, Rashid K, Rehman S-U (2020) Achieving supply chain resilience: the role of supply chain ambidexterity and supply chain agility. J Manuf Technol Manage 31:1185–1204. https://doi.org/10.1108/JMTM-07-2019-0263
6. Atcha P, Vlachos I, Kumar S (2023) Inventory sharing in healthcare supply chains: systematic literature review and future research agenda. IJLM. https://doi.org/10.1108/IJLM-12-2022-0497
7. Awad A, Trenfield SJ, Pollard TD et al (2021) Connected healthcare: improving patient care using digital health technologies. Adv Drug Deliv Rev 178:113958. https://doi.org/10.1016/j.addr.2021.113958
8. Azadi M, Yousefi S, Farzipoor Saen R et al (2023) Forecasting sustainability of healthcare supply chains using deep learning and network data envelopment analysis. J Bus Res 154:113357. https://doi.org/10.1016/j.jbusres.2022.113357
9. Bendavid Y, Boeck H, Philippe R (2010) Redesigning the replenishment process of medical supplies in hospitals with RFID. Bus Process Manag J 16:991–1013. https://doi.org/10.1108/14637151011093035
10. Best S, Williams SJ (2021) What have we learnt about the sourcing of personal protective equipment during pandemics? Leadership and management in healthcare supply chain management: a scoping review. Front Public Health 9:765501. https://doi.org/10.3389/fpubh.2021.765501
11. Bhakoo V, Choi T (2013) The iron cage exposed: institutional pressures and heterogeneity across the healthcare supply chain. J Ops Manag 31:432–449. https://doi.org/10.1016/j.jom.2013.07.016
12. Borelli G, Orrù PF, Zedda F (2015) Performance analysis of a healthcare supply chain for RFID-enabled process reengineering. IJPM 8:169. https://doi.org/10.1504/IJPM.2015.066293
13. Burkhart D, Bode C (2024) On supplier resilience: how supplier performance, disruption frequency, and disruption duration are interrelated. J Purch Supply Manag 100921. https://doi.org/10.1016/j.pursup.2024.100921
14. Buttigieg SC, Bezzina F, Xuereb A, Dey PK (2020) Healthcare supply chain management: application in the Maltese healthcare system. Health Serv Manage Res 33:55–65. https://doi.org/10.1177/0951484819871003
15. Caniato F, Graham G, Roehrich JK, Vereecke A (2023) Impact pathways: a home for insights from relevant and impactful operations and supply chain management research. IJOPM 43:270–288. https://doi.org/10.1108/IJOPM-03-2023-0163
16. Castro C, Pereira T, Sá JC, Santos G (2020) Logistics reorganization and management of the ambulatory pharmacy of a local health unit in Portugal. Eval Program Plann 80:101801. https://doi.org/10.1016/j.evalprogplan.2020.101801
17. Chen DQ, Preston DS, Xia W (2013) Enhancing hospital supply chain performance: a relational view and empirical test. J Ops Manag 31:391–408. https://doi.org/10.1016/j.jom.2013.07.012
18. Chervenkova T, Ivanov D (2023) Adaptation strategies for building supply chain viability: a case study analysis of the global automotive industry re-purposing during the COVID-19 pandemic. Transp Res Part E Logist Transp Rev 177:103249. https://doi.org/10.1016/j.tre.2023.103249
19. De Vries J, Huijsman R (2011) Supply chain management in health services: an overview. Supply Chain Manag Int J 16:159–165. https://doi.org/10.1108/13598541111127146
20. Ding B (2018) Pharma Industry 4.0: literature review and research opportunities in sustainable pharmaceutical supply chains. Process Saf Environ Prot 119:115–130. https://doi.org/10.1016/j.psep.2018.06.031
21. Dobrzykowski D (2019) Understanding the downstream healthcare supply chain: unpacking regulatory and industry characteristics. J Supply Chain Manag 55:26–46. https://doi.org/10.1111/jscm.12195
22. Francis JR (2020) COVID-19: implications for supply chain management. Front Health Serv Manage 37:33–38. https://doi.org/10.1097/HAP.0000000000000092

23. Gerwig K (2022) Climate change and healthcare: a complicated relationship. Front Health Serv Manage 39:4–10. https://doi.org/10.1097/HAP.0000000000000148
24. Gonul Kochan C, Nowicki DR, Sauser B, Randall WS (2018) Impact of cloud-based information sharing on hospital supply chain performance: a system dynamics framework. Int J Prod Econ 195:168–185. https://doi.org/10.1016/j.ijpe.2017.10.008
25. Handfield RB, Graham G, Burns L (2020) Corona virus, tariffs, trade wars and supply chain evolutionary design. IJOPM 40:1649–1660. https://doi.org/10.1108/IJOPM-03-2020-0171
26. Jadhav JS, Deshmukh J (2022) A review study of the blockchain-based healthcare supply chain. Soc Sci Human Open 6:100328. https://doi.org/10.1016/j.ssaho.2022.100328
27. Jæger B, Menebo MM, Upadhyay A (2021) Identification of environmental supply chain bottlenecks: a case study of the Ethiopian healthcare supply chain. MEQ 32:1233–1254. https://doi.org/10.1108/MEQ-12-2019-0277
28. Kamalahmadi M, Shekarian M, Mellat Parast M (2022) The impact of flexibility and redundancy on improving supply chain resilience to disruptions. Int J Prod Res 60:1992–2020. https://doi.org/10.1080/00207543.2021.1883759
29. Kanyoma KE, Khomba JK, Sankhulani EJ, Hanif R (2013) Sourcing strategy and supply chain risk management in the healthcare sector: a case study of malawi's public healthcare delivery supply chain. JMS 4:16. https://doi.org/10.5430/jms.v4n3p16
30. Kashem MA, Shamsuddoha M, Nasir T (2024) Digital-era resilience: navigating logistics and supply chain operations after COVID-19. Businesses 4:1–17. https://doi.org/10.3390/businesses4010001
31. Katsaliaki K, Galetsi P, Kumar S (2021) Supply chain disruptions and resilience: a major review and future research agenda. Ann Oper Res. https://doi.org/10.1007/s10479-020-03912-1
32. Kazancoglu I, Ozbiltekin-Pala M, Kumar Mangla S et al (2022) Role of flexibility, agility and responsiveness for sustainable supply chain resilience during COVID-19. J Clean Prod 362. https://doi.org/10.1016/j.jclepro.2022.132431
33. Kopanaki E (2022) Conceptualizing supply chain resilience: the role of complex IT infrastructures. Systems 10. https://doi.org/10.3390/systems10020035
34. Küffner C, Kopyto M, Wohlleber AJ, Hartmann E (2022) The interplay between relationships, technologies and organizational structures in enhancing supply chain resilience: empirical evidence from a Delphi study. Int J Phys Distrib Logist Manage. https://doi.org/10.1108/IJPDLM-07-2021-0303
35. Kumar R, Kumar S (2020) Supply chain orientation, integration, sustainability and organizational performance in healthcare industry. J Comput Theor Nanosci 17:5174–5181. https://doi.org/10.1166/jctn.2020.9360
36. Lee J, Moon I (2024) An integrated model of supply chain resilience considering supply and demand uncertainties. Int Trans Oper Res (ITOR) 13459. https://doi.org/10.1111/itor.13459
37. Leite H, Lindsay C, Kumar M (2020) COVID-19 outbreak: implications on healthcare operations. TQM 33:247–256. https://doi.org/10.1108/TQM-05-2020-0111
38. Lele V, Nyathani R, Singh D (2023) Case study: role of supply chain & transportation in food and healthcare. EJTAS 1:54–62. https://doi.org/10.59324/ejtas.2023.1(6).06
39. Letunovska N, Offei FA, Junior PAJ et al (2023) Green supply chain management: the effect of procurement sustainability on reverse logistics. Logistics 7:47. https://doi.org/10.3390/logistics7030047
40. Lingg M, Wyss K, Durán-Arenas L (2016) Effects of procurement practices on quality of medical device or service received: a qualitative study comparing countries. BMC Health Serv Res 16:362. https://doi.org/10.1186/s12913-016-1610-4
41. Liu W, Beltagui A, Ye S, Williamson P (2022) Harnessing exaptation and ecosystem strategy for accelerated innovation: lessons from the VentilatorChallengeUK. Calif Manage Rev 64:78–98. https://doi.org/10.1177/00081256211056651
42. Liu W, Li X, Liu C et al (2023) Resilience assessment of the cobalt supply chain in China under the impact of electric vehicles and geopolitical supply risks. Resour Policy 80:103183. https://doi.org/10.1016/j.resourpol.2022.103183

43. Liu Z, Zhang X (2023) Multimedia and multimodal sensing with edge computing for personalized healthcare supply chain system data optimization. Pers Ubiquit Comput 27:955–972. https://doi.org/10.1007/s00779-022-01679-9
44. Mackay J, Munoz A, Pepper M (2020) Conceptualising redundancy and flexibility towards supply chain robustness and resilience. J Risk Res 23:1541–1561. https://doi.org/10.1080/13669877.2019.1694964
45. Marques L, Martins M, Araújo C (2020) The healthcare supply network: current state of the literature and research opportunities. Product Plann Control 31:590–609. https://doi.org/10.1080/09537287.2019.1663451
46. Moons K, Waeyenbergh G, Pintelon L (2019) Measuring the logistics performance of internal hospital supply chains—a literature study. Omega 82:205–217. https://doi.org/10.1016/j.omega.2018.01.007
47. Moshood T, Nawanir G, Sorooshian S, Okfalisa O (2021) Digital twins driven supply chain visibility within logistics: a new paradigm for future logistics. ASI 4:29. https://doi.org/10.3390/asi4020029
48. Nabelsi V, Gagnon S (2017) Information technology strategy for a patient-oriented, lean, and agile integration of hospital pharmacy and medical equipment supply chains. Int J Prod Res 55:3929–3945. https://doi.org/10.1080/00207543.2016.1218082
49. Nanda SK, Panda SK, Dash M (2023) Medical supply chain integrated with blockchain and IoT to track the logistics of medical products. Multimed Tools Appl 82:32917–32939. https://doi.org/10.1007/s11042-023-14846-8
50. Ndonye DM, Odiyo WJO (2022) Innovation, leadership and supply chain resilience. A theoretical review. J Procur Supply Chain 6:106–126. https://doi.org/10.53819/81018102t4092
51. Odimarha AC, Ayodeji SA, Abaku EA (2024) The role of technology in supply chain risk management: innovations and challenges in logistics. Magna Sci Adv Res Rev 10:138–145. https://doi.org/10.30574/msarr.2024.10.2.0052
52. Owolabi OR, Olatoye FO, Elufioye OA, Okunade B (2024) Reviewing healthcare financial management: strategies for cost-effective care. World J Adv Res Rev 21:958–966. https://doi.org/10.30574/wjarr.2024.21.2.0523
53. Özceylan E, Çetinkaya C, Demirel N, Sabırlıoğlu O (2017) Impacts of additive manufacturing on supply chain flow: a simulation approach in healthcare industry. Logistics 2:1. https://doi.org/10.3390/logistics2010001
54. Paksoy T, Deveci M (eds) (2023) Smart and sustainable operations and supply chain management in industry 4.0, 1st edn. CRC Press, Boca Raton
55. Phares J, Dobrzykowski DD, Prohofsky J (2021) How policy is shaping the macro healthcare delivery supply chain: the emergence of a new tier of retail medical clinics. Bus Horiz 64:333–345. https://doi.org/10.1016/j.bushor.2021.02.040
56. Pujawan IN, Bah AU (2022) Supply chains under COVID-19 disruptions: literature review and research agenda. Supply Chain For Int J 23:81–95. https://doi.org/10.1080/16258312.2021.1932568
57. Rego N, De Sousa JP (2009) Supply chain coordination in hospitals. In: Camarinha-Matos LM, Paraskakis I, Afsarmanesh H (eds) Leveraging knowledge for innovation in collaborative networks. Springer, Berlin, pp 117–127
58. Rejeb A, Rejeb K, Keogh JG (2021) Enablers of augmented reality in the food supply chain: a systematic literature review. J Foodserv Bus Res 24:415–444. https://doi.org/10.1080/15378020.2020.1859973
59. Roscoe S, Aktas E, Petersen KJ et al (2022) Redesigning global supply chains during compounding geopolitical disruptions: the role of supply chain logics. IJOPM 42:1407–1434. https://doi.org/10.1108/IJOPM-12-2021-0777
60. Rowan NJ, Laffey JG (2020) Challenges and solutions for addressing critical shortage of supply chain for personal and protective equipment (PPE) arising from coronavirus disease (COVID19) pandemic—case study from the Republic of Ireland. Sci Total Environ 725:138532. https://doi.org/10.1016/j.scitotenv.2020.138532

61. Sáenz MJ, Revilla E, Acero B (2018) Aligning supply chain design for boosting resilience. Bus Horiz 61:443–452. https://doi.org/10.1016/j.bushor.2018.01.009
62. Sathiya V, Nagalakshmi K, Jeevamalar J et al (2023) Reshaping healthcare supply chain using chain-of-things technology and key lessons experienced from COVID-19 pandemic. Soc Econ Plann Sci 85. https://doi.org/10.1016/j.seps.2023.101510
63. Setiawati M, Pasaribu A, Halim DP, Darmawan J (2023) Exploring hospital supply chain partnership factors and its impact on overall supply chain performance. Petra IJBS 6:213–225. https://doi.org/10.9744/petraijbs.6.2.213-225
64. Sherman JD, MacNeill AJ, Biddinger PD et al (2023) Sustainable and resilient health care in the face of a changing climate. Annu Rev Public Health 44:255–277. https://doi.org/10.1146/annurev-publhealth-071421-051937
65. Sodiya EO, Umoga UJ, Amoo OO, Atadoga A (2024) AI-driven warehouse automation: a comprehensive review of systems. GSC Adv Res Rev 18:272–282. https://doi.org/10.30574/gscarr.2024.18.2.0063
66. Sood SK, Rawat KS, Kumar D (2022) A visual review of artificial intelligence and Industry 4.0 in healthcare. Comput Electr Eng 101:107948. https://doi.org/10.1016/j.compeleceng.2022.107948
67. Soyiri IN, Reidpath DD (2013) An overview of health forecasting. Environ Health Prev Med 18:1–9. https://doi.org/10.1007/s12199-012-0294-6
68. Spieske A, Gebhardt M, Kopyto M, Birkel H (2022) Improving resilience of the healthcare supply chain in a pandemic: evidence from Europe during the COVID-19 crisis. J Purch Supply Manage. https://doi.org/10.1016/j.pursup.2022.100748
69. Sri Rezeki D, Girsang E, Silaen M, Nasution SR (2022) Evaluation of drug storage using FIFO/FEFO methods in Royal Prima Medan Hospital Pharmacy Installation. IJHP 2:9–17. https://doi.org/10.51601/ijhp.v2i1.8
70. Ülkü MA, Bookbinder JH, Yun NY (2024) Leveraging industry 4.0 technologies for sustainable humanitarian supply chains: evidence from the extant literature. Sustainability 16:1321. https://doi.org/10.3390/su16031321
71. Yu W, Zhao G, Liu Q, Song Y (2021) Role of big data analytics capability in developing integrated hospital supply chains and operational flexibility: an organizational information processing theory perspective. Technol Forecast Soc Chang 163:120417. https://doi.org/10.1016/j.techfore.2020.120417
72. Zamiela C, Hossain NUI, Jaradat R (2022) Enablers of resilience in the healthcare supply chain: a case study of U.S healthcare industry during COVID-19 pandemic. Res Transp Econ 93. https://doi.org/10.1016/j.retrec.2021.101174
73. Zhao AP, Li S, Cao Z et al (2024) AI for science: predicting infectious diseases. J Saf Sci Resil 5:130–146. https://doi.org/10.1016/j.jnlssr.2024.02.002
74. Zhu G, Chou MC, Tsai CW (2020) Lessons learned from the COVID-19 pandemic exposing the shortcomings of current supply chain operations: a long-term prescriptive offering. Sustainability 12:5858. https://doi.org/10.3390/su12145858

Thomas K. Dasaklis is currently an Assistant Professor at the Hellenic Open University, School of Social Sciences. He graduated from the University of Piraeus, Department of Industrial Management and Technology. He holds an M.Sc. degree in supply chain management and a Ph.D. in emergency supply chain management and disaster response, both from the University of Piraeus. His research interests lie in supply chain management, operational research, humanitarian logistics/disaster response, data analysis, and blockchain technology. He has participated in national and European research projects and has published more than 30 papers in books, peer-reviewed journals, and conference proceedings. He has worked for the European Commission (DG Humanitarian Aid and Civil Protection) and the University of Piraeus Research Centre. Additionally, he has three years of experience in the private sector as a supply chain director. He has served as a guest editor, program committee member, and reviewer for various international journals and scientific conferences.

Giannis T. Tsoulfas is an Associate Professor of "Supply Chain & Logistics" at the Department of Agribusiness and Supply Chain Management at the Agricultural University of Athens, Greece. He is also Tutor-Counselor at the Hellenic Open University and the Open University of Cyprus. In the past he was Assistant Professor at the Technological Education Institution of Sterea Ellada, Greece, Scientific Associate at the Presidency of the Hellenic Republic and he worked as Independent Contractor/Mechanical Engineer for several design and construction companies and organizations. He holds an integrated master's degree from the Department of Mechanical Engineering and Aeronautics, University of Patras, Greece. He holds a Ph.D. degree from the Department of Industrial Management and Technology, University of Piraeus, Greece. His research interests lie in supply chain management and sustainability. He has published more than 60 articles in international journals, books, and conference proceedings. He has participated in several research projects funded by European and Greek grants. He has served as a guest editor, program committee member, and reviewer for various international journals and scientific conferences.

Navigating the Future: AI-Driven Healthcare Supply Chains

26

Ivan Kudrenko

Abstract

The healthcare supply chain (HCSC) is a crucial part of the healthcare industry, ensuring the timely and efficient delivery of medical supplies and services. However, it is fraught with challenges such as demand unpredictability, inventory management complexities, sourcing issues, warehousing inefficiencies, and sustainability concerns. The COVID-19 pandemic has further underscored the vulnerability of HCSCs, highlighting the need for greater resilience and adaptability. This chapter explores the potential of advanced analytics and Artificial Intelligence (AI) in transforming HCSCs. It delves into real-world examples of AI implementation in HCSCs across various regions, including vaccine distribution in West Africa, supply chain management in India, and pharmaceutical companies' operations. The chapter also addresses the challenges of integrating AI into HCSCs, including data privacy, security concerns, and ethical considerations. By leveraging AI and advanced analytics, healthcare supply chains can enhance demand forecasting, optimize inventory management, improve sourcing strategies, streamline warehousing, and promote sustainability, ultimately leading to improved healthcare outcomes and supply chain efficiency.

Keywords

Logistics • Artificial intelligence • Advanced analytics • Operations • Inventory management • Warehousing

I. Kudrenko (✉)
The Boeing Company, Charleston, USA
e-mail: ivank@umich.edu

F. Jawab (ed.), *Hospital Supply Chain*, Integrated Science 27,
https://doi.org/10.1007/978-3-031-70292-1_26

Abbreviations

AI	Artificial Intelligence
ANN	Artificial Neural Networks
BT	Blockchain Technology
CSF	Critical Success Factors
GDPR	General Data Protection Regulation
HCSC	Healthcare Supply Chain
HIPAA	Health Insurance Portability and Accountability Act
IoT	Internet of Things
JIT	Just-in-Time
KNN	K-Nearest Neighbors
LSTM	Long Short-Term Memory
NN	Neural Network
PPE	Personal Protective Equipment
SCM	Supply Chain Management
SME	Small and Medium Enterprises

1 Introduction

Under cost pressure and volatile demand, healthcare supply chains (HCSC) have become interconnected and increasingly complex. Higher risks and vulnerability characterize such complex supply chains.

The COVID-19 crisis has highlighted the weaknesses of the global HCSC. The disruptions caused by the COVID-19 crisis represent a novelty as they differ considerably from other supply chain disruptions due to their scale, duration, and high levels of uncertainty [1]. During the pandemic, the situation was complicated by exponential demand, export restrictions, and impeded manufacturing capacities—every level of the supply chain was severely affected. Hospitals faced a significant increase in intensive care patients, leading to a sharp rise in demand for medical supplies. However, medical supply manufacturers and their sub-suppliers struggled to meet this increased demand, exacerbating the hospitals' dependence on their supply chain partners. Suppliers could not maintain previously negotiated production capacities due to COVID-19 cases among their workforce or infection prevention measures by public authorities. The general economic downturn also affected suppliers' financial stability, particularly those serving industries hit hard by the pandemic, such as the automotive industry. Hospitals faced uncertainty due to unreliable information on delivery dates, volumes, and critical bottlenecks from suppliers, impairing their operational capabilities and control over suppliers. The shutdown of passenger flights and border closures significantly reduced cargo capacities, shifting bargaining power towards logistics service providers who increased freight rates. Hospitals and pharmaceutical manufacturers extended their procurement beyond historical needs to meet the surge in demand for COVID-19-related products. Finally, governmental procurement and product distribution interventions, such as public authorities' export bans and direct procurement, led to higher prices and fewer procurement options, increasing competitive dependencies [2]. It is evident how mutually dependent the HCSC is.

The widespread impact of the pandemic has sparked a global debate on enhancing the resilience of healthcare supply chains. In fact, as distributors attempted to stabilize the availability of medical supplies, the discussions about how to increase supply chain resilience in HCSC has gained new momentum. Supply chain resilience is defined as the ability to return to its original or a better state after absorbing a supply chain disruption [3]. In a healthcare context, a supply chain disruption can be defined as "an unexpected event that can hinder the delivery of healthcare services to patients" [4]. Considering the direct implications for human lives and the inherent uncertainty, mitigation, preparation, and management of such disruptions are especially critical in the HCSC compared to other industries [5]. Indeed, it is important to remember that supply shortages in healthcare can put human lives at stake [4], and hence, the task of strengthening the HCSC stability goes beyond traditional cost-saving and service level performance and reiterates the objective of mitigating service interruptions at all costs. Like in the case of supply chain disruptions in other industries, COVID-19 has indicated the weakest link of the HCSC and spurred interest in improving the resilience of HCSC among professionals and researchers. The latter has identified a series of components of supply chain resilience: flexibility, collaboration, visibility, and redundancy [3, 6]. Product standardization and strategic sourcing can increase flexibility and redundancy, while vendor-managed inventory and active data sharing improve visibility and collaboration.

The COVID-19 crisis has demonstrated the vulnerabilities and complexities of HCSC, highlighting the need for greater resilience and adaptability. As we move forward, it is crucial to address specific challenges that have become evident. These challenges, including demand forecasting, inventory management, sourcing, warehousing issues, and sustainability, are critical for building a more robust and responsive HCSC. In this chapter, we will delve into each of these areas, using the recent COVID-19 crisis as a backdrop to illustrate their importance and the potential strategies involving advanced analytics and AI-powered solutions for improvement. By addressing these challenges, we can work towards a healthcare supply chain better equipped to handle future disruptions and ensure the continuous delivery of essential medical supplies and services.

Advanced analytics and AI have emerged as powerful tools to address these resilience challenges. They offer the potential to transform reactive approaches into proactive and predictive strategies, as we will explore in the following sections. Let's begin with understanding AI capabilities.

2 Fundamentals and Potential Application of Advanced Analytics and AI in HCSC

AI is the simulation of human intelligence in algorithms that are coded to think and learn like humans. The primary objective of AI is to equip machines with the capability to undertake activities traditionally associated with human intellect, including visual perception, speech recognition, decision-making, and translating languages. AI systems can process information, identify patterns, and execute decisions based on data analysis. Key branches of AI encompass machine learning, which focuses on algorithmic self-improvement from direct experience; natural language processing, facilitating the comprehension and production of human language; and robotics, integrating AI into tangible devices. AI is rapidly transforming the supply chain management landscape across various industries, serving as a pivotal tool in addressing both traditional and novel challenges. Its ability to process and analyze extensive datasets uncovers valuable insights, leading to significant advancements in areas such as demand forecasting and facility location optimization. By accurately predicting market trends, businesses can adjust their strategies to stay ahead, while AI-driven analysis assists in identifying optimal facility locations, enhancing operational efficiency, and minimizing costs. Furthermore, AI revolutionizes sourcing and supplier management by utilizing sophisticated algorithms to assess potential partners, ensuring collaborations are formed with suppliers who align with a company's criteria for reliability, quality, and sustainability.

As the supply chain navigates through uncertainties, AI's contribution to risk management becomes crucial, offering strategic insights to mitigate potential disruptions and maintain inventory at levels that meet demand efficiently. This shift towards more data-driven decision-making and automated processes underscores AI's role in refining inventory management practices. Concurrently, sustainability concerns within global supply chains are being addressed through AI's capabilities to promote environmentally friendly and ethical operations. By analyzing and optimizing supply chain practices, AI aids in reducing the environmental impact and advancing sustainable supply chain initiatives.

In the healthcare sector, the integration of AI with technologies like blockchain significantly bolsters the integrity of supply chains. This synergy ensures product authenticity, combats counterfeit goods, and upholds the verification of medical devices. AI's influence extends to establishing equitable pricing models and enhancing healthcare data management, pivotal aspects contributing to healthcare supply chains' efficiency and patient-centric focus. As organizations delve deeper into AI applications, particularly within healthcare, they stand to achieve unparalleled efficiency, resilience, and sustainability, marking a new era in supply chain management where technology drives progress and fosters a more sustainable future.

Widely used AI technologies in HCSC include Neural Networks (NN), K-Nearest Neighbors (KNN), Artificial Neural Networks (ANN), Decision Trees, and

Decision Forests. These tools are more sophisticated than traditional data analysis instruments due to their ability to learn from data, adapt to new information, and identify complex patterns that are not easily discernible through conventional methods. For instance, Neural Networks can model non-linear relationships and handle vast amounts of data, making them ideal for predicting demand and identifying supply chain risks. KNN is useful for classification and regression tasks, such as categorizing medical supplies based on their characteristics. ANNs, inspired by the human brain's structure, excel in tasks like forecasting and optimizing inventory levels. Decision Trees provide a clear visualization of decision paths, aiding in supplier selection and risk assessment. Lastly, Decision Forests, which are ensembles of Decision Trees, offer improved accuracy and robustness in predicting supply chain outcomes. These AI technologies enable more precise and efficient decision-making in HCSC, leading to enhanced performance and resilience in the face of uncertainties. While the booming market of AI solutions offers a myriad of platforms, small and medium enterprises (SME) can potentially employ AI models developed in Python and R customized to their needs.

3 Challenges in HCSC

3.1 Demand Forecasting

Demand forecasting in healthcare is associated with unpredictability due to sudden outbreaks, seasonal fluctuations in disease, and rapid changes in healthcare practices or policies. The COVID-19 pandemic has underscored the difficulty in predicting the scale and specificity of medical needs during a global health crisis, leading to either severe shortages or wasteful surpluses of medical supplies. Effective demand forecasting requires sophisticated models incorporating various variables, including epidemiological data, healthcare policy changes, and global supply chain dynamics. However, traditional models may not account for the rapid onset of pandemics or the sudden shifts in healthcare delivery practices, such as the move towards telehealth. This gap can result in either overstocking, which ties up valuable resources, or understocking, jeopardizing patient care [7]. Multiple analytic models are increasingly used to improve demand forecasting by analyzing historical data, trends, and external factors such as epidemiological data. However, as these models require high-quality, comprehensive data, they may struggle to predict sudden demand spikes due to unforeseen events (e.g., pandemics) accurately. In demand forecasting, incorporating AI (artificial intelligence) can significantly enhance the accuracy and adaptability of predictive models, effectively addressing the inherent unpredictability of healthcare demand. AI algorithms can analyze vast datasets, including epidemiological trends and historical demand patterns, to provide more precise forecasts, enabling better resource allocation and inventory management. AI models, such as Long Short-Term Memory (LSTM) networks, have been used to predict demand spikes in healthcare, incorporating variables such as epidemiological data, healthcare policy changes, and even social media trends to enhance accuracy. For instance, a Seattle (USA) hospital used AI-driven models to predict the demand for influenza vaccines. By incorporating local data on flu trends and social media activity, they could adjust their orders throughout the flu season, reducing waste by 30% while ensuring vaccines were available for every patient who needed one.

3.2 Inventory Management

Inventory management in healthcare must balance the need to maintain adequate stock levels of a wide range of items, from perishable vaccines to durable medical equipment, against the risk of obsolescence or expiry. The COVID-19 crisis has exposed vulnerabilities in managing inventories of critical supplies, such as PPE, where global demand outstripped supply. Efficient inventory management is critical for ensuring that healthcare providers have the necessary supplies without incurring excessive holding costs. The challenge is compounded by the need for specific storage conditions for many medical supplies and the high cost of certain medications and equipment. The pandemic has highlighted the need for dynamic inventory management systems to adapt to sudden changes in demand and supply chain disruptions. Just-in-time (JIT) inventory strategies and automated inventory management systems help reduce excess stock and shortages by ordering supplies based on actual demand. At the same time, JIT strategies can lead to vulnerabilities in the event of supply chain disruptions, and automated systems require significant initial investment and ongoing maintenance. Furthermore, JIT requires a high level of data sharing across the supply chain, visibility, and interdependence that are not possible in all industries. For inventory management, while JIT strategies are beneficial in reducing excess stock and associated costs, it's crucial to balance these with contingency planning. AI can mitigate some of the vulnerabilities of JIT strategies by using predictive analytics to create buffer stocks strategically during anticipated disruptions. This approach ensures that healthcare supply chains remain resilient despite disruptions, such as those experienced during the COVID-19 pandemic, by maintaining a safety stock or alternative sourcing options to prevent critical shortages. One supply chain manager at a large healthcare system in the US shares, "Implementing AI-driven inventory management transformed our operations. We moved from a reactive posture to a proactive one, where we anticipate needs before they become critical, ensuring no patient is left without essential supplies".

3.3 Sourcing

Sourcing in the healthcare supply chain involves finding reliable suppliers who can provide required products at a reasonable cost. The pandemic has shown the risks associated with relying heavily on single sources or geographic regions for critical supplies, leading to significant disruptions when those sources are compromised.

Diversifying sourcing strategies is essential for reducing risk in the healthcare supply chain. This involves identifying alternative suppliers and developing contingency plans for critical items. The challenge lies in ensuring the quality and compliance of products from diverse sources, requiring robust vetting processes and quality assurance measures. Additionally, geopolitical tensions and trade policies can complicate international sourcing strategies [8]. Diversifying suppliers and implementing strategic sourcing can reduce dependence on a single source and mitigate risks. That being said, identifying, qualifying, and managing new suppliers can be time-consuming and costly. Moreover, diversification may also lead to increased complexity in supply chain management. In sourcing practices, ethical considerations are paramount, impacting not only the sustainability of the HCSC but also its reputation and compliance with regulatory standards. Ethical sourcing ensures that products are obtained in a responsible manner, considering factors such as labor rights, environmental impact, and fair-trade practices. AI facilitates smarter sourcing by using machine learning algorithms to evaluate supplier performance, predict risks, and suggest alternative suppliers, enhancing the robustness of the sourcing strategy. In fact, the potential of AI applications in sustainable and strategic sourcing is immense.

3.4 Warehousing

Warehousing in healthcare must address unique challenges, including the need for specialized storage conditions (e.g., cold chain for vaccines) and the ability to scale operations in response to emergencies quickly. The COVID-19 pandemic has stressed warehousing systems, with the need for rapid distribution of vaccines and PPE to diverse geographic locations. Efficient warehousing solutions must be capable of handling a wide variety of healthcare products, each with its own storage requirements. This includes managing cold chain logistics for temperature-sensitive products and ensuring secure storage for controlled substances. The pandemic has underscored the importance of flexible warehousing strategies that can accommodate fluctuating inventory levels and facilitate the quick deployment of supplies to areas in need [9]. Automated warehousing solutions and adopting flexible warehousing strategies can optimize storage and improve efficiency, but such systems are usually quite expensive for most companies. Regarding warehousing issues, deploying AI and Internet of Things (IoT) technologies can significantly improve efficiency and accuracy in monitoring storage conditions. These technologies enable real-time tracking of inventory levels, temperature control for sensitive products, and automated replenishment systems, leading to optimized warehouse operations and reduced risk of product spoilage or loss. Moreover, AI-driven robots and drones can be used for automated picking and replenishment, which not only speeds up the process but also reduces errors and improves safety in warehousing.

3.5 Sustainability

Sustainability in the healthcare supply chain encompasses environmental, social, and economic dimensions, requiring adopting practices that minimize environmental impact, ensure ethical labor practices, and achieve cost-effectiveness. The challenge is to integrate sustainable practices without compromising the quality of care or increasing costs prohibitively. Integrating sustainability into the healthcare supply chain involves a multi-faceted approach that includes adopting green procurement policies, investing in renewable energy sources, and utilizing data analytics for efficient resource management. It also requires collaboration with stakeholders across the supply chain to align sustainability goals and practices. One significant barrier is the need for upfront investment in sustainable technologies and processes, which may have more extended payback periods. Despite these challenges, the push toward sustainability is driven by regulatory requirements, societal expectations, and the recognition of the long-term benefits of sustainable operations for the environment, society, and the bottom line [10]. Implementing green supply chain practices, such as eco-friendly packaging, renewable energy use in warehousing, and optimizing logistics to reduce carbon footprint. However, sustainable initiatives can incur higher upfront costs and require significant process changes. There may also be a trade-off between environmental benefits and operational efficiency. As organizations face increasing pressure from stakeholders, governments, and regulatory bodies while simultaneously demonstrating high operational and financial performance to stay competitive, securing buy-in to adopt sustainability policies poses a significant challenge for many companies. While sustainability initiatives are essential for reducing the environmental footprint of HCSC, they may sometimes conflict with operational efficiency. AI can play a crucial role in balancing these objectives by optimizing route planning to minimize fuel consumption, predicting the lifespan of medical equipment for effective recycling, and enhancing the efficiency of renewable energy use in warehouses.

4 Overview of Off-the-Shelf and More Affordable R and Python Tools for Implementing These Technologies

In the realm of HCSC, many off-the-shelf AI solutions promise to streamline operations and enhance decision-making. Platforms like IBM Watson, SAP Integrated Business Planning, and Oracle Supply Chain Management Cloud are renowned for their sophisticated analytics and AI capabilities. These solutions offer a range of functionalities, from demand forecasting to inventory optimization, tailored to the specific needs of the healthcare sector. However, the allure of these comprehensive systems often comes with a caveat for SMEs. The high licensing, implementation, and maintenance costs can be prohibitive for smaller organizations. Furthermore, the complexity and rigidity of these solutions may not align well with the dynamic and unique requirements of SMEs in the healthcare supply chain.

In this environment, the open-source programming languages R and Python emerge as powerful allies for SMEs. These languages offer various packages and libraries that enable the implementation of advanced analytics and AI at a fraction of the cost of commercial solutions.

R Packages for HCSC:

- "forecast" and "prophet": These packages are instrumental in time series analysis and demand forecasting. They allow for modeling complex seasonal patterns and trends in healthcare demand, providing accurate predictions that can inform inventory planning and resource allocation.
- "randomForest" and "xgboost": These packages are used for building predictive models that can anticipate supply chain disruptions, predict patient demand, or optimize resource allocation. They employ powerful ensemble learning techniques that enhance the accuracy and robustness of predictions.
- "shiny": This package enables the creation of interactive web applications for supply chain analytics. It allows supply chain professionals to visualize data, explore scenarios, and communicate insights in a user-friendly manner, facilitating informed decision-making.

Python Libraries for HCSC:

- "pandas" and "numpy": These libraries are foundational for data manipulation and numerical computations. They provide efficient structures for handling and analyzing large datasets, which is crucial for identifying trends, patterns, and anomalies in healthcare supply chain data.
- "scikit-learn": This library offers many machine learning algorithms for classification, regression, clustering, and more. It is a versatile tool for building models that can improve various aspects of HCSC, from demand forecasting to supplier evaluation.
- "tensorflow" and "keras": These libraries are used for deep learning applications, such as predictive analytics, natural language processing, and image recognition. They can be leveraged to develop advanced models that provide insights into complex supply chain dynamics and enhance decision-making processes.

Supply chain professionals must feed these tools with relevant historical data, such as sales figures, inventory levels, and supplier performance metrics, to effectively harness these tools. This data serves as the foundation for building and training models that can accurately predict future trends and optimize supply chain operations.

However, the flexibility and power of R and Python come with particular challenges. The open-source nature of these languages requires a degree of programming expertise to build and maintain models effectively. Moreover, the responsibility for data security and model accuracy rests with the organization, necessitating a vigilant and skilled team to navigate the nuances of data management and model validation.

While R and Python offer promising avenues for SMEs in HCSC to leverage advanced analytics and AI, success in this endeavor requires a careful balance between technical proficiency, data stewardship, and strategic vision. With the right approach, these tools can unlock new efficiency, resilience, and innovation levels in the healthcare supply chain. Of course, a specific solution should align with and support a company's strategy.

5 Real-World Examples of Healthcare Organizations Successfully Implementing AI in Their Supply Chains

To illustrate the transformative power of AI and advanced analytics in healthcare supply chains, let's explore some real-world examples where these various AI technologies have been successfully implemented. In this chapter, we delve into the transformative role of AI in enhancing healthcare supply chains across the globe. Through a series of case studies, we explore how leading pharmaceutical companies and healthcare systems in regions such as West Africa, India, and Turkey have successfully integrated AI technologies to address challenges in vaccine distribution, production optimization, quality control, and supply chain management. These examples illustrate the diverse applications of AI in improving efficiency, reducing costs, and ensuring the quality and timely delivery of healthcare products and services.

5.1 AI-Powered Supply Chain Management for Vaccine Distribution in West Africa

Addy [11] elaborates on Ghana's healthcare system. Like many in West Africa, it faces challenges in vaccine distribution due to limited resources, inadequate infrastructure, and geographical barriers. These issues are complicated even more by manual processes and a lack of technological advancements, leading to inefficiencies in reaching remote areas with life-saving vaccines.

The primary challenge in Ghana's vaccine distribution is the manual and inefficient supply chain management, which results in delays, inaccuracies in tracking vaccine supplies, and difficulties in reaching remote areas. These inefficiencies result in wasted resources and missed opportunities to protect vulnerable populations against preventable diseases.

Ghana has started incorporating AI into its supply chain management for vaccine distribution to address these challenges. AI technologies such as machine learning algorithms are utilized for real-time monitoring of vaccine stocks, optimizing delivery routes based on demand patterns and geographical factors, and providing predictive analytics for future demand trends. Additionally, AI-powered drone delivery company Zipline has partnered with the Ghana Health Service to transport vaccines and other medical supplies to remote areas, significantly improving access to healthcare services.

The implementation of AI in vaccine distribution has led to improved efficiency and effectiveness. Real-time monitoring and proactive inventory management have ensured timely restocking before shortages occur. Optimization of delivery routes has reduced transportation costs and ensured that vaccines reach even the most underserved communities promptly. Predictive analytics have enabled authorities to plan ahead by procuring an adequate supply of vaccines in anticipation of increased demand, thus preventing stockouts and ensuring a continuous flow of vaccines to healthcare facilities.

The successful integration of AI into Ghana's vaccine distribution highlights the potential of technology to overcome traditional supply chain challenges. It demonstrates the importance of leveraging AI for real-time data analysis, predictive modeling, and optimizing logistics to enhance healthcare outcomes. This approach can serve as a model for other countries facing similar challenges in their healthcare systems.

5.2 The Ghanian Medical Drones and AI

Damoah et al. [12] discuss the Ghanaian medical drone program, launched in April 2019, which is a partnership with Zipline, a San Francisco-based robotics manufacturer and logistics service provider. The program aims to supply emergency and essential medical supplies, including vaccines, blood, and lifesaving medical supplies, to healthcare centers across the country to reduce death rates related to childbirth, accidents, and snakebites.

Ghana's healthcare supply chain system faced challenges in promptly delivering essential medical supplies to remote areas, leading to increased mortality rates and healthcare inefficiencies.

The implementation of the medical drone program involves healthcare workers and drone operators. Healthcare practitioners place orders via text message to the drone distribution center, where supplies are packed into a padded box with a parachute and attached to a drone. The drone navigates to its destination using a military-grade GPS and releases the supplies at a designated location. The program operates with the expectation of doing 600 flights daily using four distribution centers nationwide. The medical drone program has delivered over 5000 essential medical supplies across over 1000 flights without accidents or problems. The timely delivery of medical supplies has reduced mortality rates, eased congestion at larger hospitals, and reduced referrals to teaching hospitals in cities. The program has also reduced costs by avoiding overstocking and reducing wastage of medical supplies.

The implementation of the medical drone program in Ghana's healthcare system has demonstrated the potential of AI and drone technology in enhancing supply chain efficiency and healthcare delivery. The program has highlighted the importance of collaboration between government agencies, technology providers, and healthcare workers in addressing healthcare challenges. Additionally, the program's success suggests that cutting-edge technology like AI can be appropriate in developing countries with infrastructural deficits, challenging the notion that advanced technologies are only suitable for developed nations.

5.3 The Indian Healthcare Supply Chain and AI Adoption Case

Kumar et al. [13] consider the Indian healthcare industry one of the largest and fastest-growing sectors in emerging economies that plays a vital role in the nation's economy. The industry is ripe for integrating disruptive technologies like AI, blockchain technology (BT), IoT, and machine learning (ML) to enhance healthcare operations and supply chain management. However, the adoption of AI in the healthcare supply chain (HSC) is still nascent in India due to challenges like the digital divide, disparities in healthcare access, and limited investment from authorities.

The primary challenge in implementing AI in India's HSC is the vast inequalities in healthcare infrastructure, the digital divide, and the geographical and population-related disparities in healthcare access and delivery between urban and rural areas.

The study uses a mixed-method approach to analyze AI adoption's critical success factors (CSFs) in the Indian healthcare industry, involving extensive literature review and expert opinions. Twenty experts, including supply chain managers, IT managers, and academic experts, were consulted to finalize the CSFs related to AI adoption in HSC. The study identified twenty-two CSFs of AI adoption in HSC, grouped into technological, organizational, environmental, institutional, and human dimensions. The technological dimension, particularly factors like technology sophistication, sustainable data quality and integrity, and interoperability, was the most influential in impacting AI adoption in HSC.

The successful implementation of AI in India's healthcare supply chain requires focusing on technological feasibility, data quality, competitive pressure, and government support. Organizational readiness, culture, and strategic alignment are also critical for AI adoption. The study highlights the need for healthcare providers, researchers, and the government to understand and address the CSFs for effective AI implementation in HSC, contributing to improved healthcare outcomes and supply chain efficiency.

5.4 The Turkish Healthcare Supply Chain and AI Adoption Case

Similarly, Deveci [14] examines the Turkish healthcare industry, which has seen accelerated growth in recent years, partly due to the increase in health tourism. The

Turkish government is ambitious in adopting technology and providing subsidies to organizations in the health, defense, and automotive industries. The healthcare industry in Turkey is an interesting case to study, especially in supply chain management, where the implementation of AI is relatively higher compared to other uses.

Despite the potential advantages of AI implementation in healthcare supply chains, such as efficiency improvements and cost reductions, some obstacles can prevent the implementation process. The study aims to identify these barriers and obstacles to enable a smooth and quick transformation process following the successful implementation of AI technologies.

The authors proposed a fuzzy Aczel–Alsina–based decision-making model to analyze the factors that enhance the diffusion of AI technologies in healthcare supply chain management. The model evaluates four dimensions: technical infrastructure, business environment, macroeconomic system, and social acceptance, along with 22 factors that may influence the diffusion of AI. The study found that technology intensity, trialability, and government support and policies are the most important AI success factors in the Turkish healthcare industry. These results highlight the significance of technical infrastructure and government support in facilitating the adoption of AI technologies.

The study suggests that a comprehensive approach considering various dimensions and factors is crucial for the successful diffusion of AI in healthcare supply chains. Government support is crucial in developing countries like Turkey, where the private sector may not be ready to bear the financial burden of new technology adoption. The study also emphasizes the importance of trialability, allowing adopters to test new technologies before full adoption and technology intensity, which prepares users for new technologies.

5.5 Pharmaceutical Companies' Supply Chain Management and AI

Guo [15] elaborates on how global pharmaceutical companies leverage AI in their supply chains. Pharmaceutical companies are increasingly leveraging AI to enhance their supply chain management and production processes. Pfizer, a leading pharmaceutical company, has developed an intelligent logistics platform that utilizes AI and analytics to optimize the transportation of goods across its entire supply chain. This platform helps predict demand, detect supply chain disruptions, and optimize inventory levels, ensuring timely delivery of products while minimizing transportation and logistics costs.

Amgen, another major player in the pharmaceutical industry, has implemented AI to optimize the production of biological drugs. By employing machine learning algorithms, Amgen can identify and rectify issues that previously went unnoticed, minimizing production costs and reducing the risk of product defects.

GSK has incorporated AI to improve its quality control process. The company has implemented tools that automate data analysis generated during manufacturing, enabling GSK to detect deviations in real time, reduce the likelihood of quality issues, and ensure that products meet regulatory requirements.

Merck, a multinational pharmaceutical company, leverages AI-powered predictive analytics to enhance its supply chain management. The company has developed an intelligent tool that can simulate the impact of different scenarios on its supply chain, enabling informed decisions about inventory levels, production schedules, and transportation logistics.

Roche, a Swiss multinational biopharmaceutical company, uses AI to optimize its warehouse operations. The company has developed a machine learning-based system that monitors and analyzes real-time data from sensors installed in its warehouses to optimize inventory management, reduce waste, and improve efficiency.

6 The Challenges of Integrating AI into Healthcare Supply Chains

Integrating AI into HCSC offers promising efficiency, accuracy, and patient care enhancements. However, this integration has challenges, particularly regarding data privacy, security concerns, and ethical considerations. This chapter delves into these challenges, underscoring the need for meticulous planning, regulatory compliance, and ethical foresight in deploying AI technologies in HCSC.

6.1 Data Privacy and Security Concerns

The healthcare industry is inherently data-intensive, relying on sensitive patient information to make critical supply chain decisions. As AI systems require access to vast amounts of data to function optimally, the risk of data breaches and unauthorized access becomes a significant concern. The sensitivity of healthcare data, including patient medical records, treatment histories, and insurance information, necessitates stringent data protection measures to ensure privacy and security. Regulatory mechanisms, such as the General Data Protection Regulation (GDPR) in the European Union and the Health Insurance Portability and Accountability Act (HIPAA) in the United States, provide a framework for data protection. However, ensuring compliance across the entire supply chain, especially among smaller firms with limited cybersecurity resources, remains a challenge.

6.2 Ethical Considerations

The deployment of AI in healthcare supply chains also raises profound ethical questions. One critical issue is the ethical use of AI in making decisions that can significantly impact human lives. For example, AI-driven systems for vaccine allocation need to be designed and operated with a keen awareness of potential biases and inaccuracies. These systems should complement human decision-making, with the final decisions resting with health authorities considering broader contextual factors and ethical standards. Moreover, there is an imperative to maintain transparency and accountability in AI operations, ensuring that AI technologies are used responsibly and in a manner that upholds the highest ethical principles.

6.3 Overcoming the Challenges

To address these challenges, it is crucial to develop robust data pre-processing mechanisms that enhance data accuracy and reliability, facilitating the effective use of AI algorithms in pharmaceutical supply chain management. Additionally, creating a secure data-sharing environment that protects patient data confidentiality while enabling the seamless exchange of information across supply chain partners is essential. This requires technological solutions and organizational and procedural changes to ensure data security and privacy compliance.

Furthermore, addressing ethical considerations necessitates a multidisciplinary approach that includes ethicists, technologists, healthcare professionals, and regulatory bodies. Developing ethical guidelines for AI use in healthcare supply chains, conducting regular ethical audits of AI systems, and fostering a culture of ethical awareness among stakeholders can help mitigate ethical risks.

Integrating AI into healthcare supply chains offers transformative potential but presents significant challenges in data privacy, security, and ethical considerations. Overcoming these challenges requires a concerted effort from all stakeholders, including technology developers, healthcare providers, regulatory authorities, and patients. Addressing these concerns head-on and establishing rigorous standards for AI use in healthcare makes it possible to harness AI's benefits while safeguarding patient welfare and maintaining public trust in healthcare systems.

6.4 Future Directions

The integration of AI and advanced analytics into supply chain management is on the brink of revolutionizing how global supply chains operate, promising to usher in an era of unprecedented efficiency and responsiveness. As we peer into the future, the interplay between AI and advanced analytics is poised to enhance predictive capabilities, enabling supply chains to anticipate disruptions and prescribe strategic responses that mitigate risks and optimize performance. The drive towards fully autonomous supply chains, where AI systems autonomously manage and execute a wide array of operations, marks a significant leap toward operational efficiency. This vision of self-orchestrating supply chains capable of making informed decisions in real time promises to drastically reduce manual intervention, thereby streamlining processes and enhancing decision-making.

The synergy between AI and blockchain technology is another frontier in SCM (supply chain management), offering a robust framework for ensuring data integrity, enhancing transparency, and fostering trust across supply chain networks. This integration is particularly pivotal in sectors where provenance, authenticity, and compliance are crucial. As environmental sustainability becomes a core concern for consumers and businesses alike, AI emerges as a key enabler of sustainable and circular supply chain practices. By leveraging AI to optimize resource utilization, reduce emissions, and facilitate the recycling or repurposing of products, supply chains can significantly reduce their environmental footprint while aligning with broader sustainability goals.

Moreover, the advent of AI-driven hyper-personalization represents a paradigm shift in customer engagement and satisfaction. By harnessing vast amounts of data to understand and predict individual customer preferences, AI enables supply chains to deliver tailored experiences, products, and services, thereby elevating customer satisfaction to new heights. The future landscape of SCM, characterized by resilience and agility, is where AI's potential to rapidly adapt to changing market dynamics and ensure business continuity comes to the fore. Collaborative ecosystems powered by AI will encourage seamless data sharing and coordination among all stakeholders, thereby dismantling silos and fostering a more integrated and innovative supply chain network.

In this emerging scenario, the customer-centric supply chain becomes a reality, with AI at the helm, guiding strategies to ensure that customer needs and expectations are met with unprecedented precision and care. Yet, this future is not devoid of challenges. The ethical, privacy, and security implications of deploying AI in SCM necessitate a thoughtful approach to technology adoption. Ensuring the ethical use of AI, safeguarding data privacy, and maintaining security standards are imperative to maintaining stakeholder trust and ensuring the responsible use of technology.

Looking to the future, we envision a world where AI manages supply chains and predicts patient needs, perhaps even before the patients themselves are aware. Picture a system where AI, using data from wearable health devices and environmental sensors, forecasts potential health issues and automatically adjusts medical supplies in anticipation. This could dramatically reduce emergencies, transforming reactive healthcare into a proactive wellness system.

As we contemplate the future of SCM, AI, and analytics will play a pivotal role in shaping supply chain strategies. From enhancing operational efficiencies and fostering sustainability to ensuring customer satisfaction and upholding ethical standards, the journey of integrating AI into supply chains is fraught with challenges but also brimming with transformative potential. The evolution of supply chains in this AI-driven era will undoubtedly redefine the landscape of global commerce, setting new benchmarks for innovation, resilience, and sustainability.

7 Conclusion

Integrating AI and advanced analytics into healthcare supply chain management heralds a new era of efficiency, resilience, and patient-centric care. As demonstrated through various case studies, AI-powered solutions offer promising avenues to address the myriad challenges faced by HCSC, from demand forecasting and inventory management to sourcing, warehousing, and sustainability. However, successfully implementing these technologies requires carefully considering data privacy, security, and ethical concerns.

Looking ahead, the future of HCSC lies in leveraging AI to create autonomous, collaborative, and sustainable supply chains that can adapt to changing market dynamics and ensure uninterrupted access to essential healthcare services. Embracing AI not only enhances operational efficiencies but also aligns with broader goals of sustainability and patient satisfaction. As we navigate this transformative journey, it is imperative to foster an environment of innovation, collaboration, and ethical responsibility to fully realize the potential of AI in revolutionizing healthcare supply chains.

In conclusion, the intersection of AI and HCSC presents a paradigm shift towards more agile, responsive, and patient-focused supply chains. By addressing the challenges and harnessing the opportunities presented by AI, healthcare providers can build a resilient and sustainable supply chain ecosystem that is equipped to meet future demands. It is essential to reflect on how these advancements in AI and analytics are more than technological achievements; they are steps toward a more humane, accessible, and responsive healthcare system. Every improvement in HCSC, guided by AI, means a patient receives their treatment faster, a nurse has more time for care, and families face less uncertainty about healthcare availability.

> Healthcare's future is not just in the hands of doctors, but in the algorithms and data that empower them. —Ivan Kudrenko

References

1. Ivanov D, Dolgui A (2020) Viability of intertwined supply networks: extending the supply chain resilience angles towards survivability. A position paper motivated by COVID-19 outbreak. Int J Product Res 58(10):2904–2915. https://doi.org/10.1080/00207543.2020.1750727
2. Spieske A, Gebhardt M, Kopyto M, Birkel H (2022) Improving resilience of the healthcare supply chain in a pandemic: evidence from Europe during the COVID-19 crisis. J Purch Supply Manag 28(5):100748. https://doi.org/10.1016/j.pursup.2022.100748. Epub 31 Jan 2022. PMCID: PMC8801975
3. Tukamuhabwa B, Stevenson M, Busby J, Zorzini Bell M (2015) Supply chain resilience: definition, review, and theoretical foundations for further study. Int J Prod Res 53:1–32. https://doi.org/10.1080/00207543.2015.1037934

4. Mandal S (2017) The influence of organizational culture on healthcare supply chain resilience: moderating role of technology orientation. J Bus Ind Market 32:1021–1037. https://doi.org/10.1108/JBIM-08-2016-0187
5. Zepeda ED, Nyaga GN, Young GJ (2016) Supply chain risk management and hospital inventory: effects of system affiliation. J Oper Manag 44:30–47
6. Hohenstein N-O, Feisel E, Hartmann E, Giunipero L (2015) Research on the phenomenon of supply chain resilience: a systematic review and paths for further investigation. Int J Phys Distrib Logist Manag 45(1/2):90–117. https://doi.org/10.1108/IJPDLM-05-2013-0128
7. Iyengar K, Mabrouk A, Jain VK, Venkatesan A, Vaishya R (2020) Learning opportunities from COVID-19 and future effects on the health care system. Diabet Metab Syndr 14(5):943–946. https://doi.org/10.1016/j.dsx.2020.06.036. Epub 20 Jun 2020. PMID: 32599533; PMCID: PMC7305503
8. Jayaraman R, Salah K, King N (2019) Improving opportunities in healthcare supply chain processes via the Internet of things & blockchain technology. Int J Healthc Inf Syst Inf 14:49–65. https://doi.org/10.4018/IJHISI.2019040104
9. Finkenstadt D, Handfield R (2021) Tuning value chains for better signals in the post-COVID era: vaccine supply chain concerns. Int J Oper Product Manag. ahead-of-print. https://doi.org/10.1108/IJOPM-01-2021-0039
10. Koberg E, Longoni A (2019) A systematic review of sustainable supply chain management in global supply chains. J Clean Product 207:1084–1098. ISSN 0959-6526. https://doi.org/10.1016/j.jclepro.2018.10.033
11. Addy A (2023) Artificial intelligence in the supply chain management for vaccine distribution in the West African healthcare sector with a focus on Ghana. https://doi.org/10.13140/RG.2.2.21510.14408
12. Damoah I, Ayakwah A, Tingbani I (2021) Artificial intelligence (AI)-enhanced medical drones in the healthcare supply chain (HSC) for sustainability development: a case study. J Clean Product 328:129598. ISSN 0959-6526. https://doi.org/10.1016/j.jclepro.2021.129598
13. Kumar A, Mani V, Jain V, Gupta H, Venkatesh VG (2023) Managing healthcare supply chain through artificial intelligence (AI): a study of critical success factors. Comput Ind Eng 175:108815. ISSN 0360-8352. https://doi.org/10.1016/j.cie.2022.108815
14. Deveci M (2023) Effective use of artificial intelligence in healthcare supply chain resilience using fuzzy decision-making model. Soft Comput. https://doi.org/10.1007/s00500-023-08906-2
15. Guo W (2023) Exploring the value of AI technology in optimizing and implementing supply chain data for pharmaceutical companies. Innov Sci Technol 2(3):1–6. Retrieved from https://www.paradigmpress.org/ist/article/view/580

Ivan Kudrenko Graduated with a bachelor's degree in electrical engineering from Kuban State Technological University, Russia, and holds a master's degree in electrical engineering and business management from the University of Strathclyde, Glasgow, UK. He has recently earned his Master of Business Administration at the University of Michigan, with a concentration in operations and supply chain management. With over a decade of experience managing supply chain operations and continuous improvement projects in the manufacturing and aerospace industries, Ivan's research focuses on cutting-edge sustainable supply chain management practices and innovations in operations. His research interests include supply chain and operations management, blockchain and AI applications in logistics, and sustainability.

Role of Digital Twins, Generative AI, and Extended Reality in Cancer Care; CanConTech, a Human Factors Framework for Technology Connectedness

27

Safa Elkefi

Cancer is just a chapter in our lives and not the whole story.

— Allie Moreno

Abstract

The intersection of healthcare and technology has brought about a significant transformation in cancer care management. This shift is characterized by the integration of digital health innovations, which have the potential to significantly improve patient outcomes. In a recent paper, the CanConTech framework, a human factors approach that emphasizes the connectedness of emerging technologies in oncology, was introduced. The framework elucidates the pivotal roles of digital twins, generative AI, and extended reality (XR) and their synergistic potential to enhance patient care. Digital twins offer personalized simulations of patients' health responses, which enable precise treatment adaptations. Generative AI promises to revolutionize treatment planning and predictive diagnostics by analyzing extensive health data to unveil treatment responses and novel strategies. XR, encompassing virtual and augmented reality, delivers immersive experiences for both patients and healthcare professionals, facilitating advanced procedural training and patient education for informed decision-making. The CanConTech framework underscores the necessity of integrating these technologies to address the multifaceted challenges of cancer care. Telehealth and Electronic Health Records (EHR) are critical for ensuring continuous care and efficient data exchange, playing an indispensable

S. Elkefi (✉)
School of Nursing, Columbia University, New York, NY, USA
e-mail: se2649@columbia.edu

F. Jawab (ed.), *Hospital Supply Chain*, Integrated Science 27,
https://doi.org/10.1007/978-3-031-70292-1_27

role in patient monitoring and multidisciplinary collaboration. Wearables and mobile health (mHealth) apps extend the reach of patient management beyond clinical settings, promoting self-monitoring and adherence. Despite the transformative potential of these technologies, their implementation poses challenges, including Interoperability, data privacy, and ethical considerations. The discussion in the paper reviews these hurdles, highlighting the need for standardized protocols, ongoing professional development, and robust cybersecurity measures to ensure equitable access to these advancements. This comprehensive review and proposed framework aim to catalyze a coherent integration of digital tools in cancer care, striving for a healthcare system that is more effective, efficient, and patient-centered. The CanConTech framework lays the groundwork for a technology-infused future in oncology that prioritizes personalized care, aiming to improve outcomes and the quality of life for cancer patients.

Keywords

Technology • Ergonomics • Processes • Systems • Healthcare management • Artificial intelligence

1 Introduction

The field of cancer care presents challenges that cover various aspects like clinical, logistical, and emotional domains [1, 2]. This creates a set of obstacles for both patients undergoing treatment and healthcare providers trying to offer the best care possible [3]. The core challenge revolves around the diverse nature of cancer itself, which requires personalized treatment plans tailored to each patient's needs [3]. Developing and implementing these individualized plans can be overwhelming for experienced oncology professionals. Additionally, the field of oncology is dynamic, with breakthroughs and innovations that necessitate healthcare providers to stay updated and adapt to new treatment approaches.

For patients, the journey through cancer diagnosis and treatment is accompanied by emotional, physical, and financial burdens. Aggressive treatments, like chemotherapy and radiation, do not aim to fight the disease but also come with severe side effects that impact patients' quality of life and daily functioning. These physical challenges are intertwined with the toll that a cancer diagnosis takes on patients and their families, leading to uncertainty and distress that require comprehensive support. Furthermore, it is crucial to emphasize the significance of ensuring access to high-quality cancer care. Disparities based on geography and socioeconomic status often determine the level of care that individuals can receive, leaving those in underserved regions or with insurance coverage at a significant disadvantage. The exorbitant costs associated with cancer treatments exacerbate this divide, making these potentially lifesaving therapies unattainable for many. This financial barrier serves as a reminder of the inequalities within healthcare systems and underscores the pressing need for more equitable solutions. In addition, there is a need to allocate greater attention and resources towards meeting the emotional and psychological support required by cancer patients and their families. The journey through cancer is not a physical battle; it also represents an emotional ordeal that profoundly impacts every aspect of a patient's life and their loved ones. To navigate the complexities of diagnosis, treatment options, and contemplation of outcomes, a comprehensive support system encompassing both medical and psychological care is essential.

To effectively address these challenges in cancer care, a multidisciplinary approach that integrates the expertise of diverse healthcare professionals such as oncologists, nurses, social workers, and counselors is necessary. Through this effort, a holistic model of care can be established that caters to patients' physical well-being while also addressing their emotional needs and logistical considerations. In this scenario, technology plays a crucial role by acting as a valuable partner. It brings forth solutions that can improve the availability of healthcare treatments and offer support to both patients and their loved ones [4–6]. From services that bridge the gap in accessing care to digital platforms that provide psychological support and foster community connections, technology involvement in cancer care is becoming more and more essential. This highlights a path where innovation and collaboration work together to greatly reduce the burdens associated with cancer care. This technology can offer a more tailored approach to cancer care, where treatments can be optimized based on the patient's unique characteristics and requirements. On the other hand, extended reality technologies such as virtual reality and augmented reality can improve the training of surgeons and other healthcare professionals. They can provide a more immersive and engaging training experience, helping medical professionals develop the necessary skills and expertise to perform complex procedures with greater accuracy and precision. This, in turn, can lead to better patient outcomes and a higher level of care. Generative AI can also play a crucial role in cancer care. It can assist in the development of new and innovative cancer treatments by identifying patterns and relationships in large datasets. This technology can help researchers to discover new drug targets and develop more effective therapies. Moreover, generative AI can help reduce the time and costs of drug discovery, making it more accessible to a wider range of patients. By integrating these technologies into healthcare systems, we can take a comprehensive and personalized approach to cancer care. The proposed framework emphasizes the interdependence of these technologies and the importance of considering them as a whole rather than in isolation. This approach can lead to more effective and efficient cancer care, ultimately improving patient outcomes and quality of life. Although the adoption of these technologies may pose challenges, the potential benefits are significant, and the integration of digital twins, extended reality, and generative AI in cancer care should be further explored. The healthcare industry should continue to invest in research and development in these areas to realize the full potential of these technologies in cancer care. In this context, this chapter aims to provide a comprehensive literature review of how digital twins, extended reality, and generative AI can support cancer care workflows and processes. The review highlights the potential of digital twins in personalized medicine, where clinicians can simulate various scenarios and predict the effects of treatments on individual patients.

2 Role of Traditional Medical Informatics as Backbone to Cancer Care Development

Thanks to the advent of technology, the healthcare sector has witnessed a significant transformation in recent years. One of the areas that has benefited the most from these advancements is cancer care. While conventional technologies have been extensively studied and implemented, emerging technologies such as digital twins, extended reality, and generative AI have received limited attention in the literature. It is crucial to explore the integrative role of these advanced technologies with healthcare systems for maximum benefits. Medical informatics is becoming the backbone of cancer care. It, specifically, has the potential to improve the management of cancer care. For instance, it can help improve the quality of services and safety of procedures in addition to reducing costs and creating new paths of innovative care delivery processes in cancer care [5, 7]. Applications vary from tools for early diagnosis, ongoing monitoring, and treatment of patients [7, 8]. At its core, medical informatics involves the strategic collection, analysis, and application of data to optimize cancer care delivery, which allows it to act as a backbone of healthcare management. Digital health was known to enhance patient outcomes in cancer care by offering customized approaches to care and treatment [9]. Tailored approaches can lead to effective care strategies and improve survival rates [10]. Digital platforms facilitate collaboration among researchers, clinicians, and institutions by providing a means to share data and findings. This can help in accelerating the pace of cancer research and clinical practice [10]. The upcoming sections will detail the potential held by the different medical informatics in cancer care.

2.1 Electronic Health Records Improve Data Exchange Processes

One example of the benefits of electronic health records (EHR) is their ability to facilitate efficient data exchange and access. This ensures that critical health information is readily available to both professionals and patients, allowing for informed decision-making [11]. Additionally, EHR technology assists with better resource management, scheduling, and regulatory compliance in clinical settings, ultimately improving operational efficiency from an administrative perspective [6]. In fact, EHRs compile a detailed history of patient data, including information about treatment, diagnosis, medication records, and other types of information on cancer advancement. It then offers a comprehensive profiling of the patients, enabling oncologists to tailor their treatment strategies to the unique needs and specifications of the patients [12]. EHRs ensure that the oncologists' process is optimized while improving the outcomes for the patients [12]. In addition, cancer care requires coordination between the different specialists and therapists. By using this technology, we could allow seamless information sharing across multidisciplinary teams, ensuring all caregivers are informed about the patient's treatment plan, progress, and any changes in their condition [13]. This coordination reduces the complexity of cancer care delivery. Moreover, EHRs' importance could be seen in its role in monitoring quality indicators and outcomes across the cancer care continuum [13].

2.2 Telehealth Redesigns Traditional Clinical Visits

In addition to EHRs, telehealthcare has shown to be effective. The advancements in telehealth and telemedicine have greatly improved cancer care management, bringing benefits. One major advantage is the increased accessibility to oncology consultations in remote and underserved areas [14, 15]. This not only makes advice available to more people but also creates a more inclusive healthcare environment. Patient engagement and compliance have also significantly improved as telehealth offers convenience, making it easier for them to follow treatment plans and attend follow-up appointments, leading to health outcomes [16].

Financially, telehealth has helped ease the burden of cancer care expenses for patients and their families by reducing costs associated with travel and expenses [17]. This makes long-term treatment more sustainable [17]. Furthermore, the real-time monitoring capabilities of telehealth enable intervention, potentially reducing the need for emergency care or hospital admissions [18]. The ease of collaboration among teams through telehealth ensures that patient care is comprehensive, coordinated, and highly efficient—setting a gold standard for cancer treatment [19].

In times of health crises like COVID-19, telehealth has become extremely valuable in ensuring continuous cancer care and looking after the overall well-being of patients both physically and mentally [20]. Telehealth platforms have proven essential in providing access to health support and educational resources that go beyond physical health to address emotional and psychological needs. The ability to personalize treatment plans by analyzing data collected through telehealth exemplifies a shift towards a patient-centered approach in cancer care. Moreover, telehealth plays a role in reducing patients' exposure to infections acquired in hospitals, which is particularly important for the vulnerable cancer patient population. This highlights how telehealth not only maintains but also improves the quality of care within today's healthcare landscape. These advancements emphasize the impact of telehealth and telemedicine on managing cancer care, opening doors for a future where healthcare is accessible, personalized, and resilient against physical and geographical limitations.

2.3 Wearables and mHealth

Telehealth and EHRs have as important contributions as wearable devices in the realm of cancer care. Wearable devices and mobile health (mHealth) technologies are widely used in modern healthcare, providing real-time data on vital health metrics like heart rate, blood pressure, and glucose levels [6, 21]. These devices offer significant benefits to cancer patients and providers, enabling them to manage their cancer and other chronic conditions, post-diagnosis and post-treatment care, and preventive health measures [22]. Additionally, mHealth apps empower patients to take an active role in their cancer management by providing functionalities like medication reminders and mental health support [22]. These platforms facilitate easy communication between patients and healthcare providers through secure messaging, teleconsultations, and digital appointment scheduling [6, 21]. Furthermore, wearable devices equipped with features like fall detection and emergency alerts can be lifesaving for vulnerable individuals, ensuring timely medical attention in emergencies [23]. Integrating data from wearables and mHealth apps into EHRs can streamline clinical workflows, providing healthcare providers with a comprehensive view of a patient's health and leading to more efficient consultations and informed decision-making [21].

The different informatics tools act as pivotal enablers, transforming healthcare from a traditionally fragmented system into a more integrated, efficient, and patient-centric model. However, in the ever-evolving landscape of healthcare, the advent of cutting-edge technologies such as digital twins, extended reality (XR), and generative artificial intelligence (AI) marks a paradigm shift.

2.4 Challenges of Integrating the Different Technologies in Cancer Care

Integrating diverse technologies such as telehealth, digital twins, generative AI, and extended reality (XR) into cancer care presents several substantial challenges. Firstly, the Interoperability between these cutting-edge technologies and existing healthcare systems poses a significant barrier. Ensuring seamless communication and data exchange between different platforms and devices requires standardization of protocols and formats, which can be difficult to achieve given the rapidly evolving nature of digital technologies [24]. Additionally, the complexity of integrating these technologies necessitates a highly skilled workforce, implying that substantial investment in training and development is essential for healthcare professionals to effectively utilize these tools [25]. Data privacy and security concerns are heightened with the integration of technologies that handle sensitive patient information, necessitating robust cybersecurity measures to protect against breaches and unauthorized access [26]. Moreover, the high costs associated with implementing and maintaining these advanced technologies can be prohibitive, especially for healthcare institutions in low-resource settings, potentially exacerbating existing disparities in access to cancer care [27]. Lastly, regulatory challenges and the need for extensive validation to ensure the safety and efficacy of these integrated technologies before their widespread adoption in clinical settings can delay their implementation [28]. Cancer care is an incredibly complex field that requires a multifaceted approach to address the many challenges involved. These challenges include everything from early detection and accurate diagnosis to effective treatment and post-treatment care. In order to overcome these challenges and improve cancer care outcomes, it is crucial that policymakers, healthcare providers, and technology developers work together in a concerted effort to leverage the full potential of integrated digital technologies. By combining the latest advancements in medical technology with innovative approaches to healthcare delivery, we can help ensure that cancer patients receive the high-quality care they need and deserve. Whether it's through the development of new diagnostic tools or the implementation of cutting-edge treatment protocols, there are many ways that digital technologies can be used to improve cancer care outcomes. Ultimately, it will take a collaborative effort from all stakeholders to make these advancements a reality and help improve the lives of cancer patients around the world.

3 Potential Role of Futuristic Technology in Cancer Care Development

Technology such as digital twins, generative AI, and extended reality have started to show potential in the development of cancer care services.

3.1 Digital Twins

In the medical context, digital twins refer to virtual replicas of individual patients, processes, or systems created through the integration of various data sources, medical information, and real-time workflow data. Advancements in computational power, machine learning, and data analytics have facilitated their development.

In patient monitoring, digital twins enable real-time tracking of a patient's health parameters, providing physicians with valuable insights into their condition and allowing for early intervention [29]. For surgical planning, these digital replicas allow surgeons to rehearse procedures, minimizing risks and enhancing precision. Additionally, digital twins are utilized for treatment simulations, helping to tailor therapies and predict patient responses accurately [29].

Despite their promising potential, challenges such as data privacy, integration of diverse data sources, and the need for validation hinder widespread adoption. Nevertheless, the prospects for digital twins in medicine are bright, with the potential to revolutionize personalized healthcare, improve treatment outcomes, and drive advancements in medical research and education [29].

In cancer care, digital twins represent a significant leap forward in personalized medicine [30]. It creates a virtual replica of a patient's physical and biological characteristics created using data from medical imaging, genetic information, and patient history [30]. This innovative approach offers transformative potential, allowing oncologists to simulate and analyze cancer's behavior and progression in a controlled digital environment [30]. By predicting how a tumor might grow or respond to different treatments, healthcare providers can tailor therapy to the individual's specific cancer type and genetic makeup. Digital twins enable continuous monitoring and adjustments of treatment plans based on real-time data, leading to more responsive and adaptive cancer care [31]. This technology promises to enhance the precision and effectiveness of cancer treatments while opening avenues for research into new therapies, contributing significantly to the evolving landscape of cancer care [29, 31].

3.2 Extended Reality

The use of extended reality (XR) technologies in healthcare has revolutionized the way workflows and processes are optimized from a human factors perspective. XR encompasses augmented reality (AR), virtual reality (VR), and mixed reality (MR), providing a variety of applications in medical training, patient education, and therapeutic interventions. In oncology training, XR simulations enable practitioners to hone their skills in realistic scenarios, reducing the potential of errors during real procedures and enhancing the learning experience [32]. Cancer patients benefit from XR in education by interacting with 3D anatomical models, making complex medical information more accessible and empowering them to make informed decisions about their care [33]. Additionally, XR-based therapeutic interventions can provide immersive environments for pain management, rehabilitation, and mental health treatment [33]From a human factor standpoint, XR can significantly enhance cancer patient experience and medical outcomes by improving engagement, reducing anxiety, and enhancing medical information retention. As XR technologies continue to evolve, their integration into cancer care workflows offers the potential to enhance care quality, patient satisfaction, and overall cancer care delivery. However, it is crucial to consider issues of accessibility, usability, and user acceptance to ensure that XR applications are designed and implemented with the utmost consideration for human factors and user-centered design principles.

3.3 Generative AI (GenAI)

Generative AI, a cutting-edge subfield of artificial intelligence, is gaining attention for its potential to transform healthcare [34]. Utilizing tools like GPT-4 and DALL-E, generative AI generates fresh insights and data from existing information, providing significant benefits to healthcare workflows. For instance, it has the potential to support clinical operations.

Consider a hospital's corporate functions. Back-office work and administrative functions, such as finance and staffing, provide the foundations on which a hospital system runs. Nevertheless, they often operate in silos, relying on manual inputs across fragmented systems that may not allow for easy data sharing or synthesis. The potential benefits of Gen AI within hospital settings are vast [35]. By utilizing unstructured purchasing and accounts payable data, Gen-AI chatbots can assist with common IT and HR questions, ultimately enhancing employee experience and reducing administrative costs [36]. Clinical operations are also an area that could benefit from Gen AI's efficiencies [36]. Currently, healthcare providers and administrative staff are bogged down by numerous forms and other administrative tasks, which can contribute to employee burnout. However, with clinician oversight, Gen AI may be able to streamline discharge summaries, care coordination notes, and shift-hand-off notes, as well as generate real-time checklists, lab summaries, and clinical orders [36]. Additionally, Gen AI's language synthesis capabilities could improve EHR functionality by reducing manual inputs and human errors. Hospitals and physician groups are actively exploring Gen AI's capabilities, with some already implementing this technology through pilot programs.

In addition, it can enhance diagnostic precision by detecting patterns in medical images or patient data that are invisible to the human eye. Additionally, generative AI can facilitate personalized medicine by tailoring treatment plans to a patient's unique genetic profile. The integration of generative AI can enhance healthcare processes in multiple ways, such as automating administrative tasks to enhance operational efficiency and analyzing vast amounts of healthcare data to develop more effective treatment plans. For instance, studies have shown that it has the potential to contribute to enhancing electronic health records (EHRs) through automated conversation summarization, simplifying complex medical language into patient-friendly summaries, and providing personalized care recommendations using data from smartwatches and wearables [37].

However, the use of generative AI in healthcare requires careful consideration of ethical implications and potential risks. One key concern is safeguarding data privacy and security, as healthcare data is highly sensitive [34]. Additionally, there is a risk of AI-generated errors, which could lead to misdiagnosis or inappropriate treatment recommendations [34]. The issue of bias in AI algorithms is also significant, as it can result in unequal treatment recommendations for different demographic groups [34]. To address these concerns, it is essential to establish rigorous ethical guidelines and oversight mechanisms to ensure the responsible and effective use of generative AI in healthcare settings. By doing so, generative AI can serve as a potent tool in advancing healthcare, improving patient outcomes, and streamlining medical processes.

The use of Gen AI in cancer care is transforming the field by providing advanced diagnostic tools. This technology can identify patterns and anomalies that may be undetectable to the human eye, allowing for early detection and staging of cancer, which is critical for successful treatment. Moreover, Gen AI can simulate various scenarios to predict how different treatment regimens may impact a particular cancer type in an individual patient, enabling optimized and personalized treatment strategies. Additionally, Gen AI aids in patient monitoring by anticipating potential side effects and outcomes, enhancing the overall quality of cancer care. The implementation of Gen AI in oncology holds the promise of significant enhancements in patient outcomes and represents a more efficient, personalized approach to cancer treatment [38].

4 Integration of Technologies in Cancer Care Workflows

It is important to acknowledge that although these technologies have different roles, it is important to consider them interlinked for better outcomes and more connectedness between the different processes in cancer care. In this study, we suggest a framework that summarizes the different technologies' roles in order to emphasize their connections. This framework can help in understanding how technologies work for better design, implementation, and use (Fig. 1).

The integration of digital twins, extended reality (XR), and generative AI in cancer care represents a revolutionary convergence of technologies that has the potential to significantly transform patient care. This integration can enable the creation of highly personalized cancer treatment models, allowing healthcare professionals to visualize complex patient data and treatment scenarios in a more

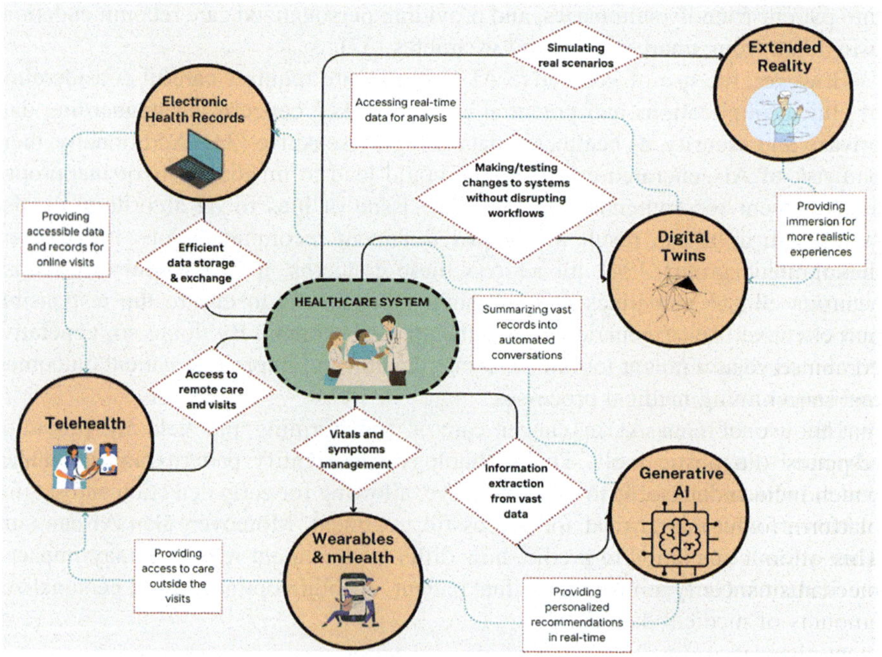

Fig. 1 CanConTech framework: Cancer and connected technologies framework

intuitive and immersive manner. Generative AI algorithms provide the capability to analyze vast amounts of medical data to predict treatment outcomes, simulate the effects of different therapies, and even generate novel treatment strategies. By leveraging these technologies, cancer care providers can better understand each patient's unique cancer profile and personalize treatments accordingly, resulting in increased efficacy of interventions.

Real-world examples of these integrated workflows include virtual tumor boards, where multidisciplinary teams use digital twins and XR to collaboratively plan and simulate cancer treatments. In surgical planning, surgeons use these technologies to rehearse complex procedures in a virtual environment, reducing risks and improving outcomes. The connectedness of different technologies in cancer care is crucial due to the inherently complex nature of the disease and the multifaceted approach required for effective treatment.

Integrating technologies such as genomics, artificial intelligence (AI), telemedicine, and digital health records enables a more comprehensive and cohesive understanding of each patient's unique cancer profile. This integration facilitates personalized medicine, where treatments are tailored to the individual characteristics of a patient's cancer. AI and machine learning algorithms can analyze vast datasets from various technologies to identify patterns and insights that might be missed in isolation, leading to more accurate diagnoses and predictions about disease progression. Telemedicine and digital records ensure continuous, real-time monitoring and seamless communication among healthcare providers, which is essential for timely decision-making and coordinated care. Moreover, the convergence of these technologies empowers patients with more information and control over their treatment journey, enhancing patient engagement and satisfaction.

Overall, the interconnectedness of technologies in cancer care is vital for advancing toward more effective, efficient, and patient-centered treatment paradigms. The integration of digital twins, XR, and generative AI represents an exciting opportunity to transform cancer care and improve patient outcomes.

The CanConTech framework, which stands for cancer and connected technologies framework, aims to combine digital tools in order to improve the quality and accuracy of cancer care. By understanding that each technology has its specific purpose while also being a part of a connected digital system, we can utilize their combined capabilities to create a more streamlined and effective approach to treating cancer. Within this framework, digital twins are replicas of physical entities that allow oncologists to simulate and analyze the progression of cancer and how it responds to treatments in a controlled digital environment. Extended reality (XR), which includes augmented and mixed reality technologies, provides an immersive platform for visualizing complex cellular structures and the effects of treatments. This offers clinicians a way to interact with patient data and understand disease mechanisms. Generative AI plays a role as an analytical engine sifting through vast amounts of medical data to predict how diseases might progress, customize treatment plans accordingly, and even develop innovative therapeutic strategies tailored specifically to an individual's genetic makeup.

When these technologies come together, they form a landscape that accurately reflects the complexity of providing cancer care. For example, virtual tumor boards utilize twins and XR technology so that multidisciplinary teams can collaborate in visualizing treatment plans and strategizing together. Surgeons can practice procedures in a virtual environment using XR technology. This allows them to anticipate challenges and improve their techniques before performing surgeries, which ultimately enhances precision and ensures safety.

The CanConTech framework highlights the nature of cancer treatment, necessitating a multifaceted approach. By combining genomics, AI, telemedicine, and electronic health records, this framework brings about changes that provide a comprehensive overview of a patient's cancer journey. It enables medicine by tailoring treatments not only to the specific type of cancer but also to each patient's unique biological characteristics.

AI and machine learning algorithms excel in analyzing the datasets generated by these technologies. They uncover patterns and insights that may be hidden when examining data in isolation. This leads to accurate diagnoses, reliable predictions about prognosis, and anticipation of potential treatment responses. Telemedicine offers remote access to healthcare services, which is especially important in the current pandemic situation. It allows doctors and patients to communicate in real time, leading to timely diagnoses, early intervention, and continuity of care.

In conclusion, the integration of digital twins, XR, and generative AI in cancer care represents a significant advancement in personalized medicine. The CanConTech framework provides a holistic approach to cancer care that leverages the capabilities of different technologies to improve outcomes for patients. By combining these technologies, we can create more effective, efficient, and patient-centered treatment paradigms that result in better care and improved quality of life for cancer patients.

5 Benefits and Limitations of the Framework

The **CanConTech** framework represents a modernization in cancer care, combining twins, generative AI, and extended reality (XR). It has the potential to greatly improve treatment accuracy and patient outcomes. One of its advantages is the ability to personalize healthcare on a scale. Digital twins create representations of patients' health, allowing for treatment effects in a controlled digital environment. This enables healthcare strategies that are predictive and adaptable. Additionally, generative AI analyzes health data to identify patterns and generate insights that assist in the development of tailored treatment plans. XR technologies, such as augmented reality, have proven valuable in education and patient therapy by providing immersive experiences that simplify complex medical information, reduce patient anxiety, and improve adherence to treatment plans.

However, there are challenges associated with implementing the **CanConTech** framework that should not be ignored. The primary challenge is the investment required for adopting cutting-edge technologies like this. Costs include infrastructure development, software acquisition, and staff training—expenses that may be too high for healthcare systems.

Emerging as concerns, data privacy and security become crucial due to the framework's reliance on collecting and analyzing amounts of personal health information. It is essential to have safeguards in place to prevent access and maintain patient confidentiality. Additionally, the complexity of these technologies poses maintenance challenges and necessitates updates to keep up with advancements in the field. This requires investment and technical expertise.

Another critical challenge is the widening of healthcare disparities. While advanced technologies offer benefits, they may not be accessible to patients in resource settings or those lacking digital literacy skills. As a result, we need to address this gap in healthcare equity.

Despite these obstacles, the **CanConTech** framework shows promise for transforming cancer care by integrating health technologies. By addressing these challenges through strategies and policies that focus on expanding access and ensuring ethical technology use, we can pave the way for personalized, efficient, and patient-centered cancer treatment in an era.

6 Conclusions

The field of cancer care has seen significant advancements in recent years, with the introduction of digital health technologies, such as digital twins, XR, and generative AI. The integration of these advanced technologies with existing digital health technologies has created a robust structure for personalized medicine that enables healthcare professionals to visualize, simulate, and predict treatment outcomes with greater accuracy. Virtual tumor boards and surgical planning are just a few examples of how these technologies are being practically applied to transform cancer care.

However, the integration of these technologies is not without its challenges. Obstacles such as data privacy, integration complexities, and the need for continual adaptation to technological advancements need to be addressed to ensure that the full potential of these technologies is realized. The **CanConTech** framework recognizes the importance of understanding and leveraging the interconnectedness of these technologies to enhance cancer care delivery.

As we progress in this field, the integration of digital health technologies is becoming increasingly important in the journey towards more personalized, accessible, and innovative cancer treatment strategies. With the right approach, the synergy of these technologies can propel a more effective, efficient, and patient-centric approach to cancer care. A quote to conclude with:

Cancer is complex the way it is. Technology is supposed to remove some of this complexity and not add more to it. In order to move forward in a coherent way, technology should be treated as a component of the management in cancer care settings.

— Safa Elkefi

References

1. Elkefi S, Asan O (2023) Perceived patient workload and its impact on outcomes during new cancer patient visits: analysis of a convenience sample. JMIR Hum Factors 10:e49490
2. Mao JJ et al (2022) Integrative oncology: addressing the global challenges of cancer prevention and treatment. CA: Cancer J Clin 72(2):144–164
3. Gavas S, Quazi S, Karpiński TM (2021) Nanoparticles for cancer therapy: current progress and challenges. Nanoscale Res Lett 16(1):173
4. Elkefi S, Asan O (2023) The health information technology preferences and perceptions of newly diagnosed patients with cancer. Int J Med Informatics 180:105275
5. ElKefi S, Asan O (2021) How technology impacts communication between cancer patients and their health care providers: a systematic literature review. Int J Med Informatics 149:104430
6. Elkefi S, Trapani D, Ryan S (2023) The role of digital health in supporting cancer patients' mental health and psychological well-being for a better quality of life: a systematic literature review. Int J Med Inf, 105065
7. Shekelle PG, Morton SC, Keeler EB (2006) Costs and benefits of health information technology. Evid Rep Technol Assess 132:1–71
8. Schoville RR, Titler MG (2015) Guiding healthcare technology implementation: a new integrated technology implementation model. CIN: Comput Inf Nurs 33(3):99–107
9. Howarth A et al (2018) The impact of digital health interventions on health-related outcomes in the workplace: a systematic review. Digital Health 4:2055207618770861
10. Albada A et al (2009) Tailored information about cancer risk and screening: a systematic review. Patient Educ Couns 77(2):155–171
11. Garcia SF et al (2019) Implementing electronic health record-integrated screening of patient-reported symptoms and supportive care needs in a comprehensive cancer center. Cancer 125(22):4059–4068
12. Stenehjem DD et al (2016) Evaluation of the relevance and access of EHR-based variables to support personalized medicine in breast cancer. Cogent Med 3(1):1234661
13. Asan O et al (2018) Oncologists' views regarding the role of electronic health records in care coordination. JCO Clin Cancer Inf 2:1–12
14. Elkefi S, Layeb S (2023) Telemedicine's future in the post-Covid-19 era, benefits, and challenges: a mixed-method cross-sectional study. Behav Inf Technol 42(15):2639–2653
15. Jiang CY et al (2021) Telehealth for cancer care in veterans: opportunities and challenges revealed by COVID. JCO Oncol Pract 17(1):22–29
16. Wu C et al (2018) Evaluation of the clinical outcomes of telehealth for managing diabetes: a PRISMA-compliant meta-analysis. Medicine 97(43)
17. Udsen FW, Hejlesen O, Ehlers LH (2014) A systematic review of the cost and cost-effectiveness of telehealth for patients suffering from chronic obstructive pulmonary disease. J Telemed Telecare 20(4):212–220
18. Gajarawala SN, Pelkowski JN (2021) Telehealth benefits and barriers. J Nurse Pract 17(2):218–221
19. Jarvis-Selinger S et al (2008) Clinical telehealth across the disciplines: lessons learned. Telemed e-Health 14(7):720–725
20. Jewett PI et al (2022) Telehealth in cancer care during COVID-19: disparities by age, race/ethnicity, and residential status. J Cancer Surviv 16(1):44–51

21. Elkefi S (2023) Access and usage of mobile health (mHealth) for communication, health monitoring, and decision-making among patients with multiple chronic diseases (comorbidities). IISE Trans Healthc Syst Eng, 1–14
22. Nasi G, Cucciniello M, Guerrazzi C (2015) The performance of mHealth in cancer supportive care: a research agenda. J Med Internet Res 17(2):e9
23. Fisch MJ, Chung AE, Accordino MK (2016) Using technology to improve cancer care: social media, wearables, and electronic health records. Am Soc Clin Oncol Educ Book 36:200–208
24. Skrocki M (2013) Standardization needs for effective interoperability
25. Sheikh A et al (2021) Health information technology and digital innovation for national learning health and care systems. The Lancet Digital Health 3(6):e383–e396
26. Deapen D (2006) Cancer surveillance and information: balancing public health with privacy and confidentiality concerns (United States). Cancer Causes Control 17:633–637
27. Goyen M, Debatin JF (2009) Healthcare costs for new technologies. Eur J Nucl Med Mol Imaging 36:139–143
28. Gabriel MH et al (2014) Progress and challenges: implementation and use of health information technology among critical-access hospitals. Health Aff 33(7):1262–1270
29. Elkefi S, Asan O (2022) Digital twins for managing health care systems: rapid literature review. J Med Internet Res 24(8):e37641
30. Batch KE et al (2022) Developing a cancer digital twin: supervised metastases detection from consecutive structured radiology reports. Front Artif Intell 5:826402
31. HamlAbadi KG et al (2021) Digital twins in cancer: state-of-the-art and open research. In: 2021 IEEE/ACM conference on connected health: applications, systems and engineering technologies (CHASE). IEEE
32. Koo H (2021) Training in lung cancer surgery through the metaverse, including extended reality, in the smart operating room of Seoul National University Bundang Hospital, Korea. J Educ Eval Health Professions 18
33. Sansoni M, Malighetti C, Riva G (2022) Psychological and educational interventions among cancer patients: a systematic review to analyze the role of immersive virtual reality for improving patients' well-being. In: International conference on extended reality. Springer
34. Zhang P, Kamel Boulos MN (2023) Generative AI in medicine and healthcare: promises, opportunities and challenges. Future Internet 15(9):286
35. Duffourc M, Gerke S (2023) Generative AI in health care and liability risks for physicians and safety concerns for patients. JAMA
36. Bhasker S et al (2023) Tackling healthcare's biggest burdens with generative AI. McKinsey & Company
37. Nova K (2023) Generative AI in healthcare: advancements in electronic health records, facilitating medical languages, and personalized patient care. J Adv Anal Healthc Manage 7(1):115–131
38. Uprety D, Zhu D, West H (2023) ChatGPT—a promising generative AI tool and its implications for cancer care. Cancer

Safa Elkefi obtained a Ph.D. in Engineering Management with research in Human factors from Stevens Institute of Technology in 2023 and a master's degree from the National Engineering School of Tunisia in 2019. He is now a project director at Columbia University and an Adjunct Professor at Stevens.

Leveraging the Role of Blockchain Technology in the Hospital Supply Chain: A Systematic Literature Review and Future Trends

28

Asmae El Jaouhari, Jabir Arif, Fouad Jawab, Ashutosh Samadhiya, and Anil Kumar

Abstract

Exploring the crucial role of Blockchain Technology (BCT) in Hospital Supply Chains (HSCs) remains one of the biggest challenges for researchers and practitioners, despite growing research interest in the technology. Based on various BCT-based HSC features and applications, more than 33 research papers were examined. In light of this, the research reported a thorough analysis of the BCT applications in HSC. By reviewing and evaluating the available studies, the authors of this paper aim to demonstrate the enormous potential and significance of BCT in HSCs. This study gives an overview of the incorporation of BCT in HSCs as well as a discussion of the issues associated with adoption, including interoperability, scalability, and high costs, and offers potential solutions. The study discovered that the applications of BCT for quality control, finance, and logistics have received the majority of research attention.

A. E. Jaouhari · J. Arif (✉) · F. Jawab
Laboratory of Technologies and Industrial Services, Higher School of Technology, Sidi Mohamed Ben Abdellah University, Fez, Morocco
e-mail: jabir.arif@usmba.ac.ma

A. E. Jaouhari
e-mail: asmae.eljaouhari@usmba.ac.ma

F. Jawab
e-mail: fouad.jawab@usmba.ac.ma

A. Samadhiya
Jindal Global Business School, OP Jindal Global University, Sonipat, India
e-mail: ashutosh.samadhiya@jgu.edu.in

A. Kumar
Guildhall School of Business and Law, London Metropolitan University, London, UK
e-mail: a.kumar@londonmet.ac.uk

F. Jawab (ed.), *Hospital Supply Chain*, Integrated Science 27,
https://doi.org/10.1007/978-3-031-70292-1_28

Keywords

Healthcare system • Quality control • Transparency • Traceability • PRISMA

1 Introduction

The healthcare sector is still under pressure from society to provide patients with safe, high-quality, and affordable care despite rising healthcare costs [21, 26–28, 30]. The need for effective use of healthcare resources is highlighted by the rising demand for healthcare services and the increasing healthcare costs [22, 29, 78]. More efficient use of healthcare assets is sparked by efficient supply chain management (SCM), which boosts operational effectiveness [13, 26–28, 30]. Healthcare costs are significantly reduced for businesses that focus on their supply chains [26–28, 30, 31, 45].

Hospital supply chains (HSCs) are networks of businesses with the goal of delivering supplies in the right quantity, at the right price, at the right place, and at the right moment [26–28, 30]. Hospital supply chains are typically more complex than those in other sectors when it comes to capacity planning and inventory management [23]. This is due to: (1) the lengthy lead times for drugs [19, 51] and uncertain lead times for medical supplies [26–28, 30], (2) hospitals typically carry a large quantity of expensive healthcare supplies like vaccines, drugs, instruments, medical devices, or other medical equipment [77], (3) multiple stakeholders, including medical experts and pharmacists, are involved in the decision-making process for inventory management, and these stakeholders frequently have competing interests and viewpoints regarding the inventory system as well as a lack of knowledge of SCM practices [26–28, 30], and (4) unpredictable patient demand, especially in emergency situations [18].

Although many have made assumptions about how BCT will affect HSCs, our knowledge of its potential is still limited. During the preliminary investigation for this article, ten prominent literature reviews on BCT-HSC interaction were located. Table 1 lists the details of these ten literature papers as well as the gaps that have been identified. The relationship between the concept of BCT and HSC is not discussed in any of the literature reviews listed in Table 1.

To fill this research gap, we conduct a literature review to mainly address the following research questions (RQs):

- *RQ1. What are the main HSC topics that are discussed in reviews of BCT in HSCs?*
- *RQ2. What are the current challenges and potential solutions with the integration of BCT in the HSC?*
- *RQ3. What future research directions have been identified in HSC reviews with regard to blockchain?*

Table 1 Main review studies on the BCT and HSC

S. No.	Reference	Article title	Journal	Main topic	Articles review	Gaps
1	Bamakan et al. [6]	"Towards blockchain-based hospital waste management systems; applications and future trends"	Journal of Cleaner Production	Investigating how BCT would meet the requirements of hospital waste management	129	The focus was not on BCT and hospital supply chain
2	Merlo et al. [52]	"On the exploitation of the blockchain technology in the healthcare sector: A systematic review"	Expert Systems with Applications	Identification of BCT applications in the healthcare sector	64	The only focus was identifying the research on *BCT in the healthcare sector*
3	Gurtu and Johny [33]	"Potential of blockchain technology in supply chain management: a literature review"	International Journal of Physical Distribution & Logistics Management	Exploring the role of BCT and its potential value in supply chain management	299	The study was much more general and concentrated on the role of BCT in SCM
4	Vanbrabant et al. [73]	"Improving hospital material supply chain performance by integrating decision problems: A literature review and future research directions"	Computers & Industrial Engineering	Integrating and optimizing decision making within the entire hospital supply chain	88	The only goal was to improve hospital supply chain decision-making

(continued)

Table 1 (continued)

S. No.	Reference	Article title	Journal	Main topic	Articles review	Gaps
5	Kumar Singh et al. [46]	"Blockchain applications for secured and resilient supply chains: A systematic literature review and future research agenda"	Computers & Industrial Engineering	Exploring the significance of BCT in developing a cyber-secure and resilient supply chain	122	The study focused on the role of BCT in supply chains and was much more comprehensive
6	Gad et al. [32]	"Emerging Trends in Blockchain Technology and Applications: A Review and Outlook"	Journal of King Saud University Computer and Information Sciences	Investigating and analyzing the current knowledge in BCT	8435	The article highlights the growing interest in BCT. However, it does not emphasize the part that BCT plays in hospital supply chain
7	Pandey et al. [60]	"Blockchain technology in food supply chains: Review and bibliometric analysis"	Technology in Society	Providing an overview of the application of BCT in food supply chains	150	The study looked at BCT in food supply chains. However, there is no discussion about hospital supply chains
8	Jadhav and Deshmukh [39]	"A review study of the blockchain-based healthcare supply chain"	Social Sciences & Humanities Open	Investigating how BCT is changing the way healthcare supply chains operate	61	The focus of the article was on the role of BCT in the healthcare supply chain and not the hospital supply chain

(continued)

Table 1 (continued)

S. No.	Reference	Article title	Journal	Main topic	Articles review	Gaps
9	Lim et al. [48]	"A literature review of blockchain technology applications in supply chains: A comprehensive analysis of themes, methodologies and industries"	Computers & Industrial Engineering	To fully explore research on BCT-based supply chains	106	The focus was not on BCT in hospital supply chains
10	Raj Kumar Reddy et al. [64]	"Developing a blockchain framework for the automotive supply chain: A systematic review"	Computers & Industrial Engineering	Investigating how to link supply chain visibility, information transparency with BCT for an efficient ASC	70	The only focus was identifying the research on *BCT in the automotive supply chain*

The remainder of the study is structured as follows. The research methodology for conducting the literature review is presented in Sect. 2. The literature is categorized in Sect. 3 using different criteria, and the papers that have been reviewed are classified thematically. Section 4 presents discussions, implications, and directions for future research. Finally, the conclusion is presented in Sect. 5.

2 Method

The primary goal of the research was to conduct a systematic literature review (SLR) of academic research papers in order to compile an unbiased overview of blockchain applications in HSC. Four stages are included in the SLR approach: (1) Planning the review; (2) Conducting the review; (3) Reporting the review findings; and (4) Descriptive analysis.

2.1 Planning the Review

First, we seek to categorize HSC topics addressed in terms of common metrics and requirements related to BCT perspectives (RQ1). The next step was to determine which aspects of BCT had been highlighted in the HSC context (RQ2). Finally, we intended to investigate the research avenues suggested for upcoming BCT and HSC-related works (RQ3).

For the purpose to identify, screen, and analyze the papers that were designated to be included in the sample, we followed the instructions in the Preferred Reporting Items for Systematic Reviews and Meta-Analyses (PRISMA) approach [47].

2.2 Conducting the Review

2.2.1 Material Collection

For this systematic review, we searched the articles using the Scopus database because it offers a wider variety of scholarly information and helped us develop a more thorough understanding of the research we wanted to conduct. Accordingly, we can rely on the research papers indexed in Scopus for academic purposes as they have been carefully selected for inclusion in the database [44, 75].

The study examined the abstracts of selected papers and found that not all of them were about BCT applications in HSC. The screening process then involved a manual review of each of these papers to determine whether they were appropriate for the topic, and papers that weren't were excluded. To verify the search result, relevant database titles and keywords were double-checked. Then, duplicate full-text articles were eliminated after being screened for relevance. A flowchart selected for search papers is shown in Fig. 1.

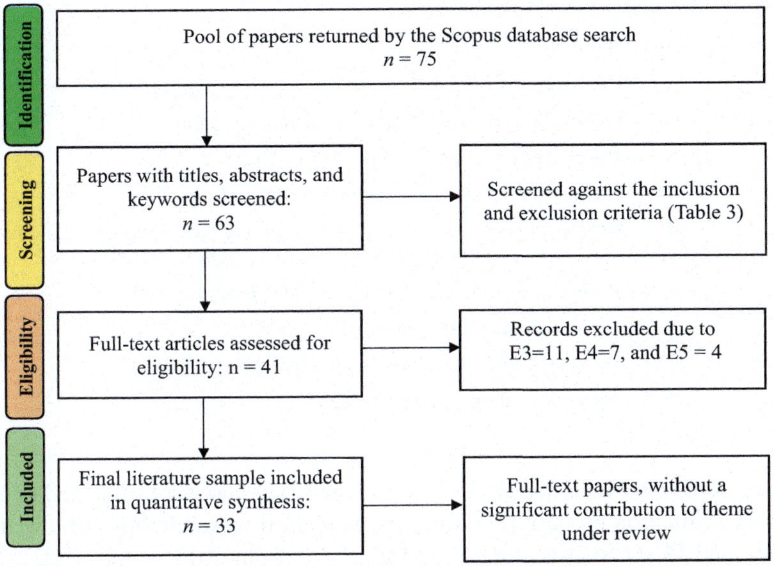

Fig. 1 Literature review publication selection process

2.2.2 Material Selection and Analysis

The inclusion criteria used during the process of selection were used to establish the initial pool of papers. Then, the exclusion criteria were used in the analysis phase. Table 3 lists the inclusion and exclusion criteria (Table 2).

Table 2 Search protocol

Information	Description
Search criteria	
Search database	• Scopus
Area	• Title, abstract, keywords
Language	• English
Article type	• Scholarly, academic, and peer-reviewed journals
Publication date	• From 2018 to July 2023
Keywords	• ["Blockchain" OR "block chain" OR "block-chain" OR "digital" AND "ledger" OR "shared" AND "ledger" OR "decentralized" AND "ledger" OR "smart" AND "contracts" OR "cryptocurrency" OR "distributed" AND "ledger" OR "Ethereum"] AND ["hospital supply chain*" OR "healthcare supply chain" OR "pharmaceutical supply chain" OR "drug traceability" OR "Health technology management" OR "Healthcare logistics" OR "Medical supply chain" OR "Hospital procurement" OR "hospital logistics"]

Table 3 Inclusion and exclusion guidelines

Criteria	Description
Inclusion (I)	I.1—The paper is a review or an article
	I.2—The article is published in a peer-reviewed journal
	I.3—The entire text has been written in English
	I.4—The publication date was between 2018 and July 2023
Exclusion (E)	E.1—Proceedings or conference papers, working papers, company/industry reports, editorials, market reports, and news reports
	E.2—Papers written in any language besides English
	E.3—Do not address HSC issues
	E.4—Do not explore blockchain-related issues
	E.5—Only focused on technical issues

Our sample only included articles and reviews (I1) that were subjected to a peer-reviewed evaluation process (I2). I3 requires that all research papers be written in English, and I4 specifies that the time frame was from 2018 to July 2023.

A total of two rounds of analysis were conducted. 33 research papers in total have been selected to make up the sample. Figure 1 displays the quantitative results for each step.

2.3 Result Reporting and Distribution

First, a descriptive analysis is provided to give a summary of the sample's characteristics. Following the steps outlined by [11], namely decontextualization, recontextualization, categorization, and compilation, content analysis is then carried out with a focus on HSC topics and BCT features.

2.4 Descriptive Analysis

In this section, we outlined the descriptive outcomes relating to the year of publications, tools, approaches, BCT applications, and content analysis.

In Fig. 2, the systematic review's analysis of the year-wise publication of research studies was presented.

Figure 3 displays the distribution of peer-reviewed papers based on BCT applications in HSCs. It claims that the majority of blockchain's applications are in the area of quality control. According to Figs. 4 and 5, as well as Appendix 2, the Ethereum platform, which uses smart contracts, is primarily used for applying BCT in HSCs (Table 4).

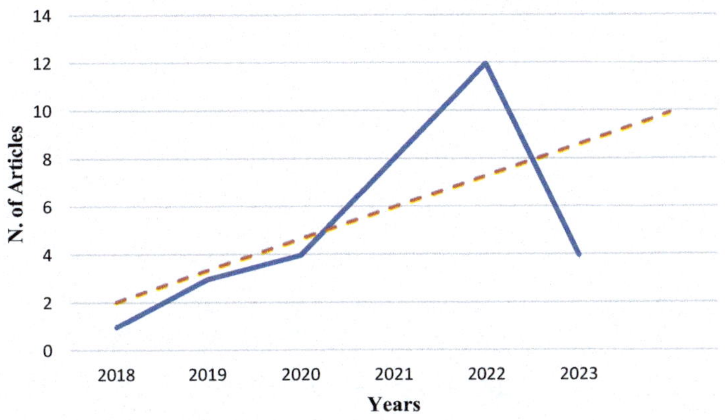

Fig. 2 Year-wise publication

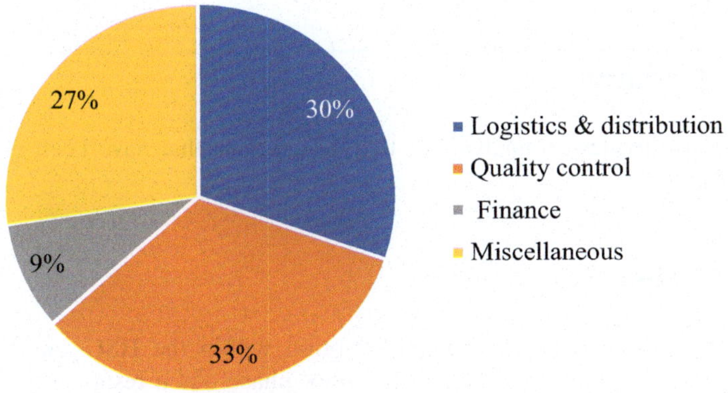

Fig. 3 Distribution of peer-reviewed papers based on the use of BCT in HSCs

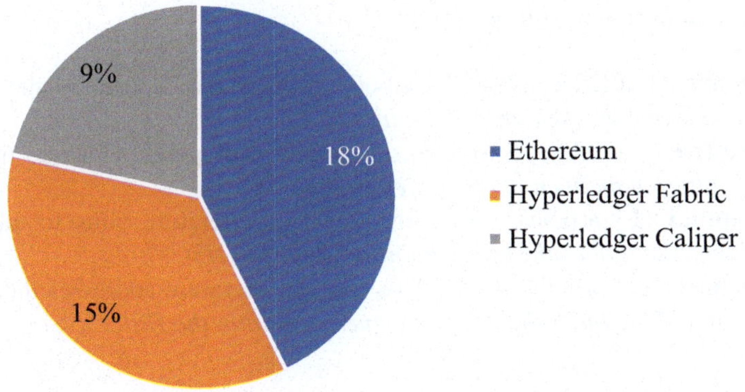

Fig. 4 Distribution of peer-reviewed papers based on the BCT platforms used

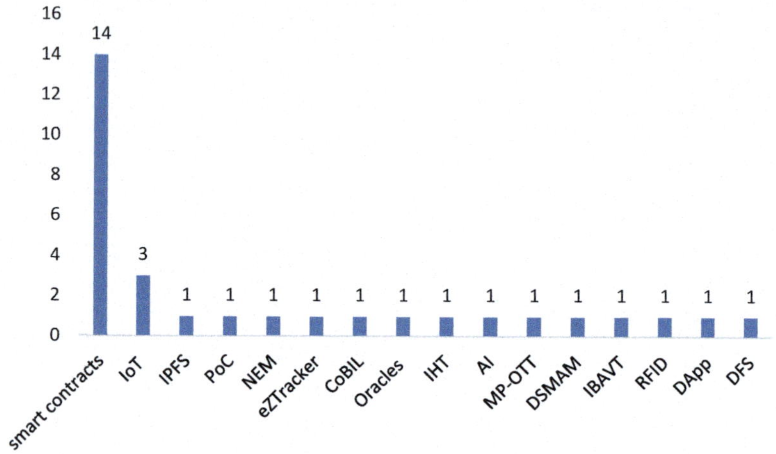

Fig. 5 Distribution of peer-reviewed papers based on the tools applied

3 Findings

This section provides an analysis of the publications that have been gathered on BCT in HSCs.

3.1 Taxonomy

There is no evidence of widespread adoption within the HSC, and most BCT deployments in practices are still in the pilot phase. As a result, it is difficult to determine whether the blockchain has helped or hurt current HSCs. We identified four key approaches to the blockchain in the body of HSC literature.

According to Fig. 6, we divided the studies into four categories: predictive, descriptive, conceptual, and prescriptive.

- **Predictive** (1 articles, 3%): This body of literature addresses the question, "*Where will the blockchain expand into HSCs?*".
- **Descriptive** (5 articles, 15%): Descriptive papers respond to the question: "*How has the blockchain been implemented in the HSC*?"
- **Conceptual** (13 articles, 39%): this body of literature aims to address the question: "*What does the blockchain mean for the HSC?*".
- **Prescriptive** (14 articles, 42%): This body of literature addresses the question: "*How should the blockchain be implemented within the HSC?*".

Table 4 Journal wise distribution of reviewed papers

S. No.	Journal name	No. of papers
1	IEEE Access	4
2	Applied Sciences (Switzerland)	2
3	Blockchain in Healthcare Today	2
4	International Journal of Healthcare Information Systems and Informatics	2
5	JMIR Medical Informatics	2
6	Sensors	2
7	Chimica Oggi/Chemistry Today	1
8	Computer Systems Science and Engineering	1
9	Computers and Industrial Engineering	1
10	Electronics (Switzerland)	1
11	Future Internet	1
12	IBIMA Business Review	1
13	ICT Express	1
14	IEEE Transactions on Emerging Topics in Computing	1
15	IET Networks	1
16	International Journal of Business Information Systems	1
17	International Journal of Scientific and Technology Research	1
18	International Journal of System Assurance Engineering and Management	1
19	JMIR Research Protocols	1
20	Journal of Cloud Computing	1
21	Multimedia Tools and Applications	1
22	Oncology (Switzerland)	1
23	Opsearch	1
24	Sustainability (Switzerland)	1

3.2 Application

Blockchain technology is one of the innovative technologies transforming HSCs by enhancing traceability and transparency and reducing reliance on intermediaries. Further, it enhances data management by decreasing information asymmetry [33, 64].

Emerging technologies like IoT, RFID, big data, Near Field Communication (NFC), robotics, and hyperspectral imaging are helping to develop a traceable HSC [42]. A tracking system for an HSC decreases the disparity in information and offers consumers accessibility to check for product counterfeiting [45].

Blockchain is primarily used in HSCs for quality control, finance, and distribution/logistics because these sectors need more visibility and traceability. As a

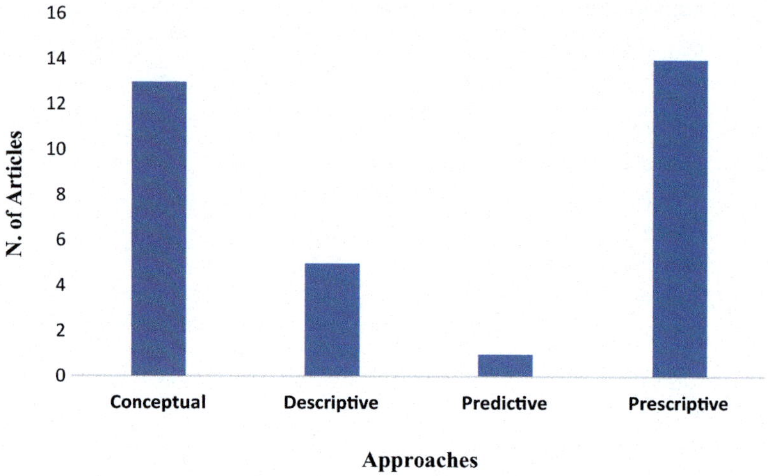

Fig. 6 Classification of peer-reviewed papers by approach

result, we divided this literature review into four categories (shown in Fig. 7) (i) Logistics and distribution, (ii) Quality control, (iii) Finance, and (iv) Miscellaneous. The papers that don't fit into the other three categories are included in the miscellaneous category.

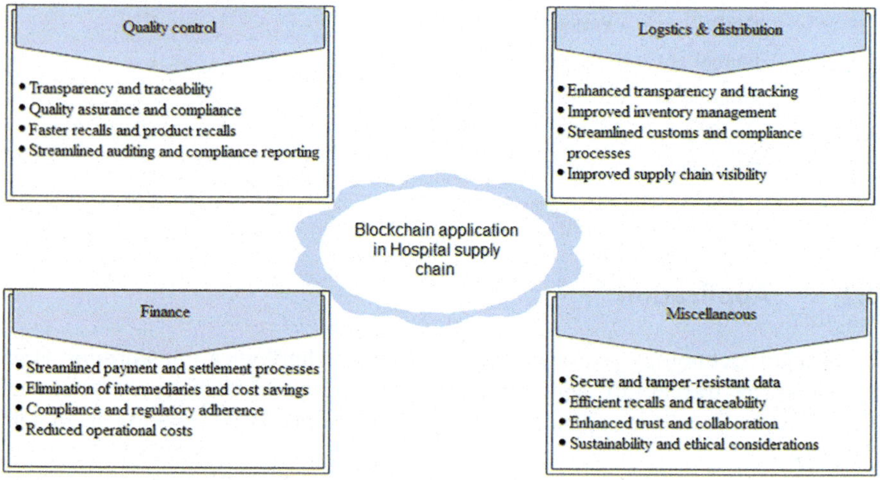

Fig. 7 Application of BCT in HSCs

3.2.1 Logistics and Distribution

In [7], the authors provided an Ethereum blockchain-based solution for a health care supply chain (HCSC) track-and-trace mechanism that applies data immutability and smart contracts to tackle conventional HCSC problems like inaccurate data, fraud, and lack of visibility.

Bapatla et al. [9] proposed a novel Distributed Ledger Technology (DLT)-based transparent supply chain for the pharmaceutical supply chain (PSC).

The authors of Sim et al. [68] used a case study of an industry-grade blockchain solution called eZTracker to investigate the business value that blockchain provides to the pharmaceutical supply chain with improved end-to-end traceability.

In [38], the authors outlined a pilot project between ARTiFACTs and the Distributed Pharmaceutical Analysis Laboratory (DPAL) that uses the blockchain to collect and handle key data created during the DPAL workflow, including a sample's advancement through the workflow, its physical location, lab reputability, and the provenance of metadata.

The procurement, forecasting, ordering, and distribution practices are still inadequate for providers. In this regard, Omar et al. [57] suggested a blockchain solution using decentralized storage and smart contracts to facilitate the Group Purchasing Organization (GPO) contract process and increase transparency.

The authors in [53] examined the concept of blockchain, its significant applications in the pharmaceutical industry, authentication of the drug supply chain, supply chain visibility to manufacturers, drug distribution, the drug serialization process, temperature excursion, and clinical trial management process.

In [70], the authors developed a blockchain-based pharma-surveillance system that will promote exchange of data along the official drug distribution network and test its functionality in a simulated network. With Swarm serving as the Distributed File System (DFS), a Distributed Application (DApp) powered by smart contracts has been created.

The summary of the above-discussed papers is provided in Appendix 2.

3.2.2 Quality Control

A Cooperative Blood Inventory Ledger (CoBIL) was proposed by the authors in [12], a blockchain-enabled system with smart contracts that is intended to reduce segmented operations, a shortage of detailed data sharing, and restricted real-time visibility.

The authors in [43] provided a case study on a blockchain-enabled medical supply chain that focuses on the recognition of non-functional requirements for blockchain-enabled systems, assisting software engineers with requirements elaboration and system design.

The study in [67] provided a conceptual framework for dealing with issues with advanced therapeutic medicinal products (ATMP) tracking and for resolving the problem of counterfeit medications.

A blockchain-based healthcare (medical supplies) solution has been proposed by the authors in [37], which ensures the accountability and commitment of all participants while preventing them from creating any unnecessary waste.

Blockchain applications in healthcare and public health were studied by [74]. The findings suggested that blockchain can advance the healthcare sector in five crucial areas: genomics, consent management, health insurance, and the supply chain for drugs and food.

The summary of the above-discussed papers is provided in Appendix 2.

3.2.3 Finance

Hammad et al. [35] proposed the BDA-SCV architecture, which uses the Hyperledger Fabric network to implement a version control healthcare system. The developer and authorizer ends are integrated into the dotnet web application.

The authors in [16] provided a hybrid blockchain for the healthcare supply chain employing the New Economy Movement (NEM) symbol blockchain to improve stakeholder experiences and foster trust in the healthcare ecosystem.

In [20], the authors recommended employing blockchain and smart contracts along with the information hiding technique to improve the privacy and security of data communication in critical systems such as smart healthcare supply chain communication networks.

The summary of the above-discussed papers is provided in Appendix 2.

3.2.4 Miscellaneous

The research papers on blockchain integrated with IoT mainly concentrated on supply chain, healthcare, and finance, according to the study [71].

In [25], the authors carried out a systematic literature review to provide an overview of how blockchain technology has been applied to resolve supply chain issues in healthcare, particularly for medical devices, drugs, and blood, organs, and tissues (BOTs). The results revealed a significant use of smart contracts ($n = 23$, 82%).

The authors in [14] performed a bibliometric analysis of the blockchain oracles research in the healthcare supply chain by highlighting the organizations and authors who are actively contributing to the oracle literature.

In [69], the authors conducted a survey to find out how blockchain technology assists healthcare supply chain networks in overcoming the primary barriers affecting the healthcare supply chain management system.

SARS-CoV2, a novel virus that emerged quickly and spread unchecked throughout the world after its outbreak in 2020, offers important research criteria to evaluate the weaknesses of our current health system. In this context, Baz et al. [10] investigated the use of blockchain technology and artificial intelligence to combat COVID-19 epidemic scenarios.

In [3], the authors proposed a communication healthcare system based on IOTA, and distributed ledger technology (DLT) is discussed with a systematic architecture for IoT devices and a future machine-to-machine (M2M) economy. Several use cases, such as sending data from the DHT-11 sensor to the IOTA tangle, are used to analyze the data exchange between IoT devices.

The Internet of Things (IoT) and blockchain are two cutting-edge technologies that can provide viable alternatives to issues with the healthcare supply chain processes, such as product recalls, tracking of product supply shortages, expiration, and counterfeit products. In this context, Jayaraman et al. [41] highlighted key challenges related to healthcare supply chains and illustrates how IoT-blockchain technologies can play a critical role in resolving these challenges either now or in the near future.

The summary of the above-discussed papers is provided in Appendix 2.

3.3 Challenges and Potential Solutions of Blockchain Adoption in the Hospital Supply Chain

In this section, the current challenges in this area are discussed, along with the potential solutions provided by researchers for BCT adoption in HSCs.

One of the emerging technologies is BCT, which can be incorporated into the HSC to address current issues and enhance performance [25, 39]. Many challenges arise when integrating blockchain into HSCs [52, 57]. Blockchain's effective implementation and sustainability in this field are hindered by a lack of indicators, tools, methods, and business models [61, 76]. A further roadblock to its implementation is the scarcity of blockchain developers and the lack of technical knowledge and expertise [69]. Different privacy policies regarding data sharing trigger current issues among the involved collaborators, disrupting the HSC collaboration [73].

4 Discussion

This section presents emerging literature trends and directions for future research based on the review's findings, then presents implications for theory and practices.

In this paper, we addressed three research questions. The RQ1 emphasized the primary HSC topics covered by reviews of the role of BCT in HSC. After doing extensive research, the authors found that blockchain is a well-known technology that has the potential to turn HSCs into a decentralized system that increases transparency and traceability while reducing the risk of fraud and information asymmetry.

The RQ2 emphasized the potential solutions offered by the researchers and the current challenges with incorporating BCT in HSCs. While BCT enables distributed and decentralized HSCs, its implementation is hindered by a number of factors, such as high cost, scalability, interoperability, high energy consumption, lack of understanding, data authenticity, sensitive data handling, privacy, and technological issues.

4.1 Primary Future Research Directions (RQ3)

According to the analyses conducted, some gaps were found, so we recommend the following research topics (RTs) as guidelines for upcoming research:

(1) Establishing standards to enable the most HSC participants to participate in BCT collaboration.
(2) Conducting a thorough examination of the factors that influence the adoption and implementation of BCT in HSCs processes, taking into account both limitations and solutions.
(3) An examination of the development of regulations and rules as well as their effects on the setup and operation of BCT in HSCs.
(4) An analysis of the effects that decentralized blockchain technology can have on governance structures, market dynamics, and the performance of modular, relational, hierarchy, and captive models of the HSC.
(5) Locating and outlining business models that can be implemented on a blockchain to take full advantage of its potential and leverage the performance of the HSC and its stakeholders.
(6) An analysis of BCT through the lens of particular theories, such as [56, 65], which relied on the resource-based view, or [15, 66], which relied on transaction cost theory
(7) Reviews that specifically address the integration of BCT with other technologies—such as artificial intelligence, big data, electronic data interchange (EDI), enterprise resource planning (ERP), and additive manufacturing— like the one provided by [2] that link IoT and blockchain.
(8) Investigation of the integration of either permissioned or public blockchains into HSC operations, or a structured assessment of both types of applications, as only [36, 55, 63] gave these configurations a scoping look.
(9) A thorough investigation focused on smart contracts, covering the standards adopted and the automated decision-making processes following their establishment in HSC contexts.
(10) The scheduling of the assets being currently digitalized, either separately or collectively using a multichain configuration (i.e., various blockchains connected).
(11) A schedule of the kinds of data and information that healthcare ecosystems are ready to put on the blockchain, as well as their frequency of updating, visibility, and goals.
(12) overviews of other industries, such as pharmaceuticals, healthcare, and drugs, taking into account applications and industry-specific traits.
(13) A risk analysis that includes possible aspects that can be reduced by various actors during the implementation and use of blockchain technology.
(14) A post-implementation analysis that includes lessons learned from both successes and failures will help to advance the discussion about the crucial success factors mentioned by [5, 34].

(15) Identification of solutions used to address issues like incompatibility of information, error correction, and interoperability without delving too deeply into computing-related issues.

4.2 Implications of the Study

In essence, the study delves into the critical role of BCT within HSC, an area that presents significant challenges to both researchers and practitioners despite growing interest. By reviewing over 33 research papers, the study offers a comprehensive analysis of BCT applications in HSCs, aiming to highlight its immense potential and importance. It discusses key features, applications, and research gaps within the field, emphasizing BCT's potential to enhance transparency, traceability, and trust among stakeholders. Additionally, the study addresses adoption challenges such as interoperability, scalability, and cost, while proposing potential solutions. Notably, BCT's applications in quality control, finance, and logistics have garnered significant attention, indicating its growing prominence in revolutionizing HSC operations.

5 Conclusion

The purpose of this study was to look into the role of BCT in HSCs using an SLR. 33 research papers from the Scopus international database were gathered for this purpose using specific keywords. To the best of our knowledge, this is the first study to investigate the use of BCT in HSCs, highlight the research-provided solutions for its effective implementation, and address the current challenges.

This paper offers three main categories for its contributions. First, a thorough and current analysis of the state of the art is provided, arguing that BCT is an appropriate technology for applications in quality control and logistics. Then, review analysis aids researchers in determining the contents to be investigated and preventing the development of duplicate reviews. Furthermore, the set of guidelines found in the sample serves as a useful starting point for directing the development of future research works.

After examining various aspects and potential applications of blockchain in HSCs, it is crucial to emphasize that this technology is primarily suggested as a solution for intra-organizational problems [6] and should not be wrongly viewed as "a solution seeking a problem" [45]. We also emphasize that business models can undergo radical and unforeseen changes [25], which can change the skill sets of employees and organizations [24]. Assessments should take these factors into account, and monitoring should continue both before and after implementation.

Finally, applying BCT to the field of HSCs seems to be a promising area with a wide range of potential theoretical and practical applications. In retrospect, we believe that the majority of the work done on the use of BCT in HSCs is conceptual

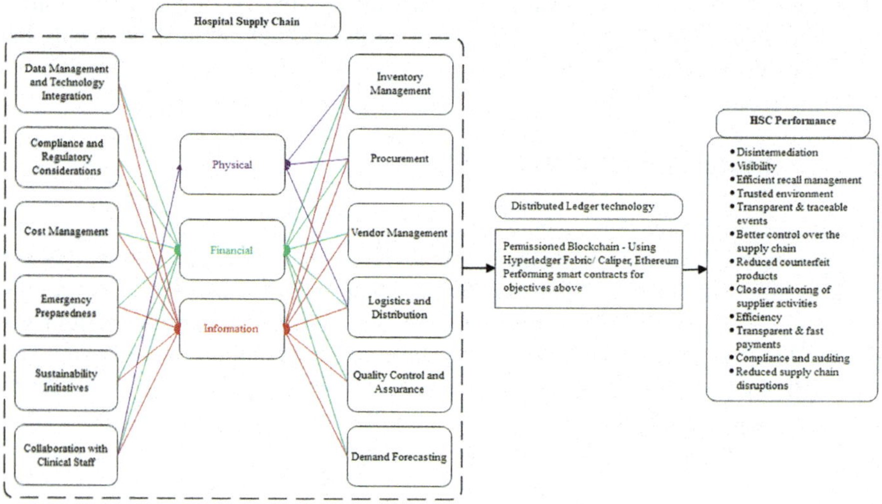

Fig. 8 Proposed BCT-based HSCs performance framework

in nature and needs the right infrastructure (including software and hardware facilities) to be implemented. According to numerous researchers, privacy, scalability, high cost, and interoperability are some of the primary challenges preventing the adoption of this technology. For researchers and practitioners who are interested in carrying out further studies in this field, the framework created in this study (see Fig. 8) will be instructive. Researchers can identify gaps in existing papers on the adoption of BCT in HSCs and conduct additional research using the information provided above.

Appendix 1: The Abbreviations Used Throughout the Paper

Abbreviation	Meaning
AI	Artificial Intelligence
ATMP	Advanced Therapeutic Medicinal Products
BCT	Blockchain Technology
BOTs	Blood, Organs, and Tissues
SC	Smart Contract
CoBIL	Cooperative Blood Inventory Ledger
DApp	Distributed Application
DFS	Distributed File System
DLT	Distributed Ledger Technology
DPAL	Distributed Pharmaceutical Analysis Laboratory

(continued)

(continued)

Abbreviation	Meaning
DPoS	Delegated Proof-Of-Stake
EDI	Electronic Data Interchange
ERP	Enterprise Resource Planning
FDA	Food and Drug Administration
GDP	Gross Domestic Product
GPO	Group Purchasing Organization
HCPs	Healthcare Practitioners
HCSC	Health Care Supply Chain
HSC	Hospital Supply Chain
IoT	Internet of Things
IPFS	Interplanetary File System
ISGX	Intel Software Guard Extensions
M2M	Machine-to-Machine
MP-OTT	Micro-Payment Enabled Over the Top
NEM	New Economy Movement
NFC	Near Field Communication
PBFT	Practical Byzantine Fault Tolerance
PoA	Proof of Authority
PoW	Proof-of-Work
PRISMA	Preferred Reporting Items for Systematic Reviews and Meta-Analyses
PSC	Pharmaceutical Supply Chain
RFID	Radio Frequency Identification
SCM	Supply Chain Management
SLR	Systematic Literature Review
WHO	World Health Organization

Appendix 2: Summary of Articles Identified Through Systematic Literature Review

S. No.	Research approaches	References	Applied areas	Purpose	Methods/tools used	Platform/algorithm
1	Prescriptive	Bandhu et al. [7]	Drug supply chain	To build a secure pharma supply chain application for blockchain 4.0	Case studies/smart contracts	Ethereum
2	Conceptual	Hammad et al. [37]	Healthcare supply chain	To manage the software version control	Simulation/Smart contracts	Proof of authority (PoA)
3	Descriptive	Bapatla et al. [9]	Pharmaceutical Supply Chain	To ensure counterfeit-free pharmaceutical supply chain	Distributed Ledger Technology, smart contract	–
4	Conceptual	Ucbas et al. [76]	Healthcare ecosystems	To evaluate scalability and performance	Internet of Things (IoT) and smart contract	Ethereum, Hyperledger Fabric, Hyperledger Caliper
5	Descriptive	Fiore et al. [27]	Healthcare supply chain	To summarize how blockchain technology has been used to address SC challenges in healthcare	Smart contracts	–

S. No.	Research approaches	References	Applied areas	Purpose	Methods/tools used	Platform/algorithm
6	Prescriptive	Mani et al. [54]	Medicine supply chain	To ensure transparency and data provenance	Interplanetary File System (IPFS) and smart contract	Hyperledger Caliper
7	Conceptual	Dubey et al. [18]	Healthcare supply chain	To engender trust, transparency, and immutable records	Proof of concept (PoC) and New Economy Movement (NEM)	–
8	Prescriptive	Sim et al. [73]	Pharma supply chain	To improve end-to-end traceability and resilience	EZTracker	Hyperledger Fabric
9	Descriptive	Bhandawat et al. [12]	Blood supply chain	To increase cooperation among all echelons of the blood supply chain	Smart-contract and the Cooperative Blood Inventory Ledger (CoBIL)	–
10	Conceptual	Caldarelli [14]	Healthcare supply chain	To investigate blockchain oracle research state of the art in healthcare supply chain	Oracles and smart contracts	–
11	Prescriptive	Khatter and DevanjaliRelan [46]	Medical supply chain	To identify the non-functional requirements for blockchain enabled systems	Case study	–

S. No.	Research approaches	References	Applied areas	Purpose	Methods/tools used	Platform/algorithm
12	Conceptual	Sharif [72]	Pharmaceutical supply chain	To make processes more efficient while increasing transparency and increasing data security	Systematic literature review	–
13	Prescriptive	EL Azzaoui et al. [22]	Medical supply chain	To hide sensitive information from being disclosed to malicious nodes	Information Hiding Techniques (IHT) and smart contract	–
14	Descriptive	Hawashin et al. [39]	Healthcare supply chain (medical supplies)	To ensure transparency, traceability, and security	Smart contracts	–
15	Prescriptive	Hayes et al. [40]	Pharmaceutical supply chain	To Monitor the quality of essential medicines	Case study	–
16	Descriptive	Sreerakhi et al. [74]	Healthcare supply chain	To effectively manage the healthcare supply chain	Survey	–
17	Conceptual	Elangovan et al. [26]	Healthcare supply chain	To recognize the accessibility and use of blockchain technology in the health care sector	Systematic literature review	–

S. No.	Research approaches	References	Applied areas	Purpose	Methods/tools used	Platform/algorithm
18	Prescriptive	Punathumkandi et al. [67]	Healthcare supply chain	To develop a sustainable a sustainable system	IoT, hyperledger frameworks	Ethereum
19	Predictive	Swathi and Venkatesan [63]	Healthcare supply chain	To improve scalability	–	Hyperledger fabric
20	Conceptual	Baz et al. [10]	Drug supply chain	To establish a health monitoring system	Distributed ledger and AI technology	–
21	Prescriptive	Akhtar et al. [3]	Healthcare supply chain	To ensure high scalability	Micro-payment enabled over the top" (MP-OTT), dual signature masked authenticated message (DSMAM) and index-based address value transaction (IBAVT)	Micro-payment enabled over the top" (MP-OTT)
22	Conceptual	Velmovitsky et al. [74]	Health care companies	To optimize processes, minimize inefficiencies, and increase trust	Systematic literature review	–
23	Prescriptive	Musamih et al. [59]	Drug supply chain	To ensure transparency, accountability, security, and data provenance	Smart contracts, privacy, security, and confidentiality analysis	Ethereum

S. No.	Research approaches	References	Applied areas	Purpose	Methods/tools used	Platform/algorithm
24	Prescriptive	Omar et al. [62]	Healthcare supply chain	To promote transparency, streamlines communication with stakeholders	Smart contracts	Ethereum
25	Conceptual	Kassab et al. [45]	Healthcare supply chain	To identify, extract, evaluate and synthesize the studies on the symbiosis of blockchain in healthcare	Systematic literature review	–
26	Conceptual	Agbo and Mahmoud [1]	Healthcare supply chain	To mitigate blockchain application challenges	Systematic literature review	–
27	Conceptual	Dubovitskaya et al. [19]	Pharmaceutical supply chain	To investigate the BCT potential in the pharmaceutical supply chain	Systematic literature review	–
28	Conceptual	Alharthi et al. [4]	Pharmaceutical supply chain	To explore the role of blockchain technology in the sustainability and effectiveness of the pharmaceutical supply chain	Systematic literature review	–

S. No.	Research approaches	References	Applied areas	Purpose	Methods/tools used	Platform/algorithm
29	Conceptual	Bao et al. [8]	Healthcare supply chain	To systematically discuss the application status of Intel software guard extensions (ISGX)	Systematic literature review	–
30	Prescriptive	Mohana and Ong [57]	Pharmaceutical supply chain	To enhance traceability and transparency	Radio frequency identification codes (RIFD)/survey	–
31	Prescriptive	Jamil et al. [42]	Drug supply chain	To handle secure drug supply cha n records	Smart contract	Hyperledger Caliper and Hyperledger Fabric
32	Predictive	Jayaraman et al. [43]	Healthcare supply chain	To track and trace products via a peer-to-peer distributed, secure, and shared ledger of the blockchain network	Internet of things (IoT)	–
33	Prescriptive	Sylim et al. [75]	Drug supply chain	To develop a pharmacosurveillance blockchain system and test its functions in a simulated network	Distributed Application (DApp), smart contracts, Distributed File System (DFS)	Ethereum, Hyperledger Fabric

References

1. Agbo CC, Mahmoud QH (2020) Blockchain in healthcare: opportunities, challenges, and possible solutions. Int J Healthc Inf Syst Inform IJHISI 15:82–97. https://doi.org/10.4018/IJHISI.2020070105
2. Aich S, Chakraborty S, Sain M, Lee H, Kim H-C (2019) A review on benefits of IoT integrated blockchain based supply chain management implementations across different sectors with case study. In: 2019 21st international conference on advanced communication technology (ICACT), pp 138–141. https://doi.org/10.23919/ICACT.2019.8701910
3. Akhtar MM, Rizvi DR, Ahad MA, Kanhere SS, Amjad M, Coviello G (2021) Efficient data communication using distributed ledger technology and IOTA-enabled internet of things for a future machine-to-machine economy. Sensors 21:4354. https://doi.org/10.3390/s21134354
4. Alharthi S, Cerotti PR, Maleki Far S (2020) An exploration of the role of blockchain in the sustainability and effectiveness of the pharmaceutical supply chain. J Supply Chain Cust Relatsh Manag. https://doi.org/10.5171/2020.562376
5. Bali S, Bali V, Mohanty RP, Gaur D (2022) Analysis of critical success factors for blockchain technology implementation in healthcare sector. Benchmarking Int J 30:1367–1399. https://doi.org/10.1108/BIJ-07-2021-0433
6. Bamakan SMH, Malekinejad P, Ziaeian M (2022) Towards blockchain-based hospital waste management systems; applications and future trends. J Clean Prod 349:131440. https://doi.org/10.1016/j.jclepro.2022.131440
7. Bandhu KC, Litoriya R, Lowanshi P, Jindal M, Chouhan L, Jain S (2023) Making drug supply chain secure traceable and efficient: a Blockchain and smart contract based implementation. Multimed. Tools Appl. 82:23541–23568. https://doi.org/10.1007/s11042-022-14238-4
8. Bao Z, Wang Q, Shi W, Wang L, Lei H, Chen B (2020) When Blockchain meets SGX: an overview, challenges, and open issues. IEEE Access 8:170404–170420. https://doi.org/10.1109/ACCESS.2020.3024254
9. Bapatla AK, Mohanty SP, Kougianos E, Puthal D, Bapatla A (2023) PharmaChain: a blockchain to ensure counterfeit-free pharmaceutical supply chain. IET Netw. 12:53–76. https://doi.org/10.1049/ntw2.12041
10. Baz M, Khatri S, Baz A, Alhakami H, Agrawal A, Khan R (2021) Blockchain and artificial intelligence applications to defeat COVID-19 pandemic. Comput Syst Sci Eng 40:691–702. https://doi.org/10.32604/csse.2022.019079
11. Bengtsson M (2016) How to plan and perform a qualitative study using content analysis. NursingPlus Open 2:8–14. https://doi.org/10.1016/j.npls.2016.01.001
12. Bhandawat R, Casucci S, Ramamurthy B, Walteros JL (2022) Cooperative Blood Inventory Ledger (CoBIL): a decentralized decision-making framework for improving blood product management. Comput Ind Eng 172:108571. https://doi.org/10.1016/j.cie.2022.108571
13. Bian W, Yang X, Li S, Yang X, Hua G (2021) Advantages of 3PLs as healthcare supply chain orchestrators. Comput Ind Eng 161:107628. https://doi.org/10.1016/j.cie.2021.107628
14. Caldarelli G (2022) Overview of blockchain oracle research. Future Internet 14:175. https://doi.org/10.3390/fi14060175
15. Chen W, Botchie D, Braganza A, Han H (2022) A transaction cost perspective on blockchain governance in global value chains. Strateg. Change 31:75–87. https://doi.org/10.1002/jsc.2487
16. Dubey S, Subramanian G, Shukla V, Dwivedi A, Puri K, Kamath SS (2022) Blockchain technology: a solution to address the challenges faced by the international travellers. Opsearch 59:1471–1488. https://doi.org/10.1007/s12597-022-00597-x
17. Dubovitskaya A, Novotny P, Xu Z, Wang F (2019) Applications of blockchain technology for data-sharing in oncology: results from a systematic literature review. Oncology 98:403–411. https://doi.org/10.1159/000504325
18. Dutta P, Nagurney A (2019) Multitiered blood supply chain network competition: linking blood service organizations, hospitals, and payers. Oper. Res. Health Care 23:100230. https://doi.org/10.1016/j.orhc.2019.100230

19. El Asri A, El Farouk II, Jawab F, Arif J, Moufad I (2022) The drug supply chain at the public hospital in Morocco: a literature review. In: 2022 14th international colloquium of logistics and supply chain management (LOGISTIQUA). IEEE, pp 1–5
20. EL Azzaoui A, Chen H, Kim SH, Pan Y, Park JH (2022) Blockchain-based distributed information hiding framework for data privacy preserving in medical supply chain systems. Sensors 22:1371. https://doi.org/10.3390/s22041371
21. El Farouk II, Jawab F (2020) Improving sustainability in public hospital through Medicines Supply chain management. In: 2020 IEEE 13th international colloquium of logistics and supply chain management (LOGISTIQUA). IEEE, pp 1–5
22. El Farouk II, Talbi A, Jawab F (2013) Development of a set of indicators to manage medicines supply chain in Moroccan public hospital, application of the SCOR model. Int. J. Bus. Dev 3(3):147–158
23. El Farouk II, Frichi Y, Jawab F (2020) An innovative approach to develop performance indicators for medicines supply chain in moroccan public hospitals. Int J Sci Technol Res 9:386–391
24. Elangovan D, Long CS, Bakrin FS, Tan CS, Goh KW, Yeoh SF, Loy MJ, Hussain Z, Lee KS, Idris AC, Ming LC (2022) The use of blockchain technology in the health care sector: systematic review. JMIR Med Inform 10:e17278. https://doi.org/10.2196/17278
25. Fiore M, Capodici A, Rucci P, Bianconi A, Longo G, Ricci M, Sanmarchi F, Golinelli D (2023) Blockchain for the healthcare supply chain: a systematic literature review. Appl Sci 13:686. https://doi.org/10.3390/app13020686
26. Frichi Y, Jawab F, Boutahari S (2020) Diagnosis of the main issues of extra-hospital medical patient transportation: Case of Morocco. In: 2020 IEEE 13th international colloquium of logistics and supply chain management (LOGISTIQUA). IEEE, pp 1–6
27. Frichi Y, Jawab F, Boutahari S (2020) Modeling the impact of hospital logistics on quality of care and patient satisfaction: results of a survey in three public healthcare facilities in Fez-Morocco. J Ind Eng Manage 13(2):296–320
28. Frichi Y, El Farouk II, Jawab F, Boutahari S (2020) Hospital logistics' effect on patient satisfaction. Int J Sci Technol Res 9(04):210–216
29. Frichi Y, Jawab F, Boutahari S (2019) SEM to analyze the interaction between hospital logistics and quality of care, a systematic review. In: 2019 international colloquium on logistics and supply chain management (LOGISTIQUA). IEEE, pp 1–5
30. Frichi Y, Kacem AB, Jawab F, Kamach O, Chafik S (2020) Improving interhospital medical patient transportation in morocco: a forecasting collaborative approach. In: Transportation, logistics, and supply chain management in home healthcare: emerging research and opportunities. IGI Global, pp. 136–162
31. Furstenau LB, Zani C, Terra SX, Sott MK, Choo K-KR, Saurin TA (2022) Resilience capabilities of healthcare supply chain and supportive digital technologies. Technol Soc 71:102095. https://doi.org/10.1016/j.techsoc.2022.102095
32. Gad AG, Mosa DT, Abualigah L, Abohany AA (2022) Emerging trends in blockchain technology and applications: a review and outlook. J King Saud Univ—Comput Inf Sci 34:6719–6742. https://doi.org/10.1016/j.jksuci.2022.03.007
33. Gurtu A, Johny J (2019) Potential of blockchain technology in supply chain management: a literature review. Int J Phys Distrib Logist Manag 49:881–900. https://doi.org/10.1108/IJPDLM-11-2018-0371
34. Haji M, Kerbache L, Sheriff KMM, Al-Ansari T (2021) Critical success factors and traceability technologies for establishing a safe pharmaceutical supply chain. Methods Protoc. 4:85. https://doi.org/10.3390/mps4040085
35. Hammad M, Iqbal J, ul Hassan CA, Hussain S, Ullah SS, Uddin M, Malik UA, Abdelhaq M, Alsaqour R (2023) Blockchain-based decentralized architecture for software version control. Appl Sci 13:3066. https://doi.org/10.3390/app13053066
36. Hasselgren A, Kralevska K, Gligoroski D, Pedersen SA, Faxvaag A (2020) Blockchain in healthcare and health sciences—a scoping review. Int J Med Inf 134:104040. https://doi.org/10.1016/j.ijmedinf.2019.104040

37. Hawashin D, Salah K, Jayaraman R, Yaqoob I, Musamih A (2022) A blockchain-based solution for mitigating overproduction and underconsumption of medical supplies. IEEE Access 10:71669–71682. https://doi.org/10.1109/ACCESS.2022.3188778
38. Hayes K, Meyers N, Sweet C, Ashenef A, Johann T, Lieberman M, Kochalko D (2022) Securing the chain of custody and integrity of data in a global north-south partnership to monitor the quality of essential medicines. Blockchain Healthc Today. https://doi.org/10.30953/bhty.v5.230
39. Jadhav JS, Deshmukh J (2022) A review study of the blockchain-based healthcare supply chain. Soc Sci Humanit Open 6:100328. https://doi.org/10.1016/j.ssaho.2022.100328
40. Jamil F, Hang L, Kim K, Kim D (2019) A Novel medical blockchain model for drug supply chain integrity management in a smart hospital. Electronics 8:505. https://doi.org/10.3390/electronics8050505
41. Jayaraman R, Salah K, King N (2019) Improving opportunities in healthcare supply chain processes via the internet of things and blockchain technology. Int. J. Healthc. Inf. Syst. Inform. IJHISI 14:49–65. https://doi.org/10.4018/IJHISI.2019040104
42. Kassab M, DeFranco J, Malas T, Laplante P, Destefanis G, Neto VVG (2021) Exploring research in blockchain for healthcare and a roadmap for the future. IEEE Trans Emerg Top Comput 9:1835–1852. https://doi.org/10.1109/TETC.2019.2936881
43. Khatter K, Relan D (2022) Non-functional requirements for blockchain enabled medical supply chain. Int J Syst Assur Eng Manag 13:1219–1231. https://doi.org/10.1007/s13198-021-01418-y
44. Kipper LM, Furstenau LB, Hoppe D, Frozza R, Iepsen S (2020) Scopus scientific mapping production in industry 4.0 (2011–2018): a bibliometric analysis. Int J Prod Res 58:1605–1627. https://doi.org/10.1080/00207543.2019.1671625
45. Kumar A, Naz F, Luthra S, Vashistha R, Kumar V, Garza-Reyes JA, Chhabra D (2023) Digging DEEP: futuristic building blocks of omni-channel healthcare supply chains resiliency using machine learning approach. J Bus Res 162:113903. https://doi.org/10.1016/j.jbusres.2023.113903
46. Kumar Singh R, Mishra R, Gupta S, Mukherjee AA (2023) Blockchain applications for secured and resilient supply chains: a systematic literature review and future research agenda. Comput Ind Eng 175:108854. https://doi.org/10.1016/j.cie.2022.108854
47. Liberati A, Altman DG, Tetzlaff J, Mulrow C, Gøtzsche PC, Ioannidis JPA, Clarke M, Devereaux PJ, Kleijnen J, Moher D (2009) The PRISMA statement for reporting systematic reviews and meta-analyses of studies that evaluate health care interventions: explanation and elaboration. J Clin Epidemiol 62:e1–e34. https://doi.org/10.1016/j.jclinepi.2009.06.006
48. Lim MK, Li Y, Wang C, Tseng M-L (2021) A literature review of blockchain technology applications in supply chains: a comprehensive analysis of themes, methodologies and industries. Comput Ind Eng 154:107133. https://doi.org/10.1016/j.cie.2021.107133
49. Lohmer J, Lasch R (2020) Blockchain in operations management and manufacturing: potential and barriers. Comput Ind Eng 149:106789. https://doi.org/10.1016/j.cie.2020.106789
50. Mani V, Prakash M, Lai WC (2022) Cloud-based blockchain technology to identify counterfeits. J. Cloud Comput. 11:67. https://doi.org/10.1186/s13677-022-00341-2
51. Martínez CS, Amery L, De Paoli G, Elofsson U, Fureby AM, Kwok S, López-Cabezas C, Rosenberger M, Schoenau C, Wahlgren M, Paulsson M (2023) Examination of the protein drug supply chain in a Swedish University Hospital: focus on handling risks and mitigation measures. J Pharm Sci. https://doi.org/10.1016/j.xphs.2023.05.003
52. Merlo V, Pio G, Giusto F, Bilancia M (2023) On the exploitation of the blockchain technology in the healthcare sector: a systematic review. Expert Syst Appl 213:118897. https://doi.org/10.1016/j.eswa.2022.118897
53. Mohana M, Ong G (2019) Implementation of pharmaceutical drug traceability using blockchain technology. INTI J
54. Musamih A, Jayaraman R, Salah K, Hasan HR, Yaqoob I, Al-Hammadi Y (2021) Blockchain-based solution for the administration of controlled medication. IEEE Access 9:145397–145414. https://doi.org/10.1109/ACCESS.2021.3121545

55. Nadir RM (2019) Comparative study of permissioned blockchain solutions for enterprises. In: 2019 international conference on innovative computing (ICIC), pp 1–6. https://doi.org/10.1109/ICIC48496.2019.8966735
56. Nandi ML, Nandi S, Moya H, Kaynak H (2020) Blockchain technology-enabled supply chain systems and supply chain performance: a resource-based view. Supply Chain Manag Int J 25:841–862. https://doi.org/10.1108/SCM-12-2019-0444
57. Omar IA, Jayaraman R, Debe MS, Salah K, Yaqoob I, Omar M (2021) Automating procurement contracts in the healthcare supply chain using blockchain smart contracts. IEEE Access 9:37397–37409. https://doi.org/10.1109/ACCESS.2021.3062471
58. Swathi P, Venkatesan M (2021) Scalability improvement and analysis of permissioned-blockchain. ICT Express 7:283–289. https://doi.org/10.1016/j.icte.2021.08.015
59. Pablo R-GJ, Roberto D-P, Victor S-U, Isabel G-R, Paul C, Elizabeth O-R (2022) Big data in the healthcare system: a synergy with artificial intelligence and blockchain technology. J Integr Bioinforma 19. https://doi.org/10.1515/jib-2020-0035
60. Pandey V, Pant M, Snasel V (2022) Blockchain technology in food supply chains: review and bibliometric analysis. Technol Soc 69:101954. https://doi.org/10.1016/j.techsoc.2022.101954
61. Pham HL, Tran TH, Nakashima Y (2018) A secure remote healthcare system for hospital using blockchain smart contract. In: 2018 IEEE globecom workshops (GC Wkshps), pp 1–6. https://doi.org/10.1109/GLOCOMW.2018.8644164
62. Punathumkandi S, Sundaram VM, Panneer P (2021) Interoperable permissioned-blockchain with sustainable performance. Sustainability 13:11132. https://doi.org/10.3390/su132011132
63. Putz B, Menges F, Pernul G (2019) A secure and auditable logging infrastructure based on a permissioned blockchain. Comput Secur 87:101602. https://doi.org/10.1016/j.cose.2019.101602
64. Raj Kumar Reddy K, Gunasekaran A, Kalpana P, Raja Sreedharan V, Arvind Kumar S (2021) Developing a blockchain framework for the automotive supply chain: a systematic review. Comput Ind Eng 157:107334. https://doi.org/10.1016/j.cie.2021.107334
65. Samadhiya A, Agrawal R, Kumar A, Garza-Reyes JA (2023) Blockchain technology and circular economy in the environment of total productive maintenance: a natural resource-based view perspective. J Manuf Technol Manag 34:293–314. https://doi.org/10.1108/JMTM-08-2022-0299
66. Schmidt CG, Wagner SM (2019) Blockchain and supply chain relations: a transaction cost theory perspective. J Purch Supply Manag 25:100552. https://doi.org/10.1016/j.pursup.2019.100552
67. Sharif R (2022) Around the block(chain)—applications in pharma. Chim Oggi Chem Today 40:64–65
68. Sim C, Zhang H, Chang ML (2022) Improving end-to-end traceability and pharma supply chain resilience with blockchain. Blockchain Healthc Today. https://doi.org/10.30953/bhty.v5.231
69. Sreerakhi V, Balagopal N, Mohan A (2022) Transforming supply chain network and logistics using blockchain—a survey. Int J Bus Inf Syst 39:193–218. https://doi.org/10.1504/IJBIS.2022.121430
70. Sylim P, Liu F, Marcelo A, Fontelo P (2018) Blockchain technology for detecting falsified and substandard drugs in distribution: pharmaceutical supply chain intervention. JMIR Res Protoc 7:e10163. https://doi.org/10.2196/10163
71. Ucbas Y, Eleyan A, Hammoudeh M, Alohaly M (2023) Performance and scalability analysis of ethereum and hyperledger fabric. IEEE Access 11:67156–67167. https://doi.org/10.1109/ACCESS.2023.3291618
72. Upadhyay A, Mukhuty S, Kumar V, Kazancoglu Y (2021) Blockchain technology and the circular economy: Implications for sustainability and social responsibility. J Clean Prod 293:126130. https://doi.org/10.1016/j.jclepro.2021.126130
73. Vanbrabant L, Verdonck L, Mertens S, Caris A (2023) Improving hospital material supply chain performance by integrating decision problems: a literature review and future research directions. Comput Ind Eng 180:109235. https://doi.org/10.1016/j.cie.2023.109235

74. Velmovitsky PE, Bublitz FM, Fadrique LX, Morita PP (2021) Blockchain applications in health care and public health: increased transparency. JMIR Med Inform 9:e20713. https://doi.org/10.2196/20713
75. Vieira E, Gomes J (2009) A comparison of Scopus and Web of Science for a typical university. Scientometrics 81:587–600. https://doi.org/10.1007/s11192-009-2178-0
76. Yazdinejad A, Srivastava G, Parizi RM, Dehghantanha A, Choo K-KR, Aledhari M (2020) Decentralized authentication of distributed patients in hospital networks using blockchain. IEEE J Biomed Health Inform 24:2146–2156. https://doi.org/10.1109/JBHI.2020.2969648
77. Zerka A, Jawab F, Frichi Y (2022) Mapping's process of the trajectory of pre-hospital transport by basic ambulance for road accidents' victims in TDABC. In: 2022 14th international colloquium of logistics and supply chain management (LOGISTIQUA). IEEE, pp 1–6
78. Zerka A, Jawab F (2022) Modelling the costs of pre-hospital transport service for victims of road accidents in TDABC. Arch Transp 61(1):89–101

Asmae El Jaouhari received a Ph.D. and Engineering degree in Industrial Engineering from the Sciences and Technologies Faculty and the National School of Applied Sciences Fez in 2023 and 2019, respectively, at Sidi Mohamed Ben Abdellah University, Morocco.in the laboratory of Technologies and Industrial Services. She began her career as a Project Leader within a multinational company operating in the automotive sector. Afterward, she worked as a visiting Professor at the Higher School of Technology, the European School of Management and International Business, and within MULTIHEXA Higher School.

Jabir Arif received the M.Sc., Engineering, Ph.D., HdR degrees in Industrial Engineering and Logistics from the National School of Applied Sciences Tangier, Faculty of Sciences and Technologies Fez, in 2008, 2010, 2016, and 2020 respectively. He is currently serving as an Associate Professor at Sidi Mohamed Ben Abdellah University, Morocco.

He began his career as a Production Planner within a multinational company operating in the automotive wiring harness. Afterward, he was appointed as State Engineer at the Ministry of Public Services and Modernization of Administration where he was in charge of the national major projects. Jabir Arif's main research area is Supply Chain Management & Logistics, Outsourcing of Logistic Activities, Risk Assessment, IoT, Artificial Intelligence, and Industrial engineering. Apart from teaching and research, he is acting as a reviewer in many ranked journals and conferences. He served as a Technical Committee member of several international conferences, tracks, and workshops.

Fouad Jawab Professor of Supply Chain at the Higher School of Technology of the Sidi Mohamed Ben Abdellah University of Fez, Morocco.

He has held several scientific and administrative responsibilities. He founded the International Conference on Logistics and Supply Chain Management (LOGISTIQUA), which he continues to develop with the support of several research teams in Morocco and abroad.

He is the author and co-author of more than 180 publications in national and international journals and proceedings. His research focuses on modeling, simulation and optimization of the supply chain, hospital supply chains and urban logistics. He is also an expert with several renowned organizations and a reviewer for prestigious journals.

Dr. Ashutosh Samadhiya is a distinguished academic figure in the field of Operations and Supply Chain Management, known for his significant contributions to research and education. Currently serving as an Assistant Professor at Jindal Global Business School, OP Jindal Global University, Sonipat, India, Dr. Samadhiya has amassed over eight years of experience in teaching, research, and innovation. His academic journey culminated in the attainment of a Ph.D. in Operations and Supply Chain Management from the esteemed Indian Institute of Technology Roorkee (IIT Roorkee), India. During his doctoral studies, Dr. Samadhiya showcased his innovative prowess by developing a groundbreaking handloom machine, a feat that earned him an Indian patent, granted by the Indian Government. Furthermore, he demonstrated his commitment to technological advancement by transferring the technology associated with the handloom machine. In recognition of his academic excellence and research acumen, Dr. Samadhiya was selected for the prestigious Newton-Bhabha Ph.D. placement program. This opportunity led him to collaborate with the Centre of Supply Chain at the University of Derby, UK, in 2021. Since then, he has maintained an honorary visiting researcher position at the University of Derby, fostering international collaborations and enriching his academic pursuits. In addition to his scholarly achievements, Dr. Samadhiya holds a design patent for an Artificial Intelligence Cash counting machine, showcasing his innovative spirit and commitment to technological innovation. Furthermore, he has made significant contributions to the academic community by serving as a reviewer and guest editor for esteemed journals, thereby enhancing the quality and rigor of scholarly publications. Overall, Dr. Ashutosh Samadhiya's career trajectory exemplifies a steadfast dedication to advancing knowledge, fostering innovation, and making meaningful contributions to the fields of Operations and Supply Chain Management, sustainability science, and beyond. Through his interdisciplinary approach and collaborative endeavors, he continues to shape the landscape of academia and inspire future generations of scholars and practitioners alike.

Dr. Anil Kumar is a Reader at Guildhall School of Business and Law, London Metropolitan University (LMU), London, U.K. For the last eleven years, he has been associated with teaching and research. Before joining LMU, he was Post-Doctoral Research Fellow in the area of Decision Sciences at the Centre for Supply Chain Improvement, University of Derby, United Kingdom (UK). He earned his Ph.D. in Management Science from ABV-Indian Institute of Information Technology and Management, Gwalior, India. He did his graduation in Mathematics (Hons) and MSc (Mathematics) from Kurukshetra University, India. He earned his Master of Business Administration (MBA) and qualified National Eligibility Test (NET), June 2011. He has contributed over 150+ research papers in international referred & national journals, and conferences at the international and national levels. He has sound analytical capabilities to handle commercial consultancy projects and to deliver business improvement projects. He has skills and expertise in Advance Statistics Models, Multivariate Analysis, Multi-Criteria Decision Making, Fuzzy Theory, Fuzzy Optimisation, Fuzzy Multi-Criteria Decision Making, Grey Theory and Analysis, Machine Learning, Application of Soft-Computing, Econometrics Models etc. His areas of research are sustainability science, green/sustainable supply chain management, customer retention, green purchasing behaviour, sustainable procurement, sustainable development, circular economy, Industry 4.0, performance measurement, human capital in supply chain and operations, decision modelling for sustainable business, and integration of operation area with other areas. He published many research articles in A*/A as per ABDC indexed and 3* as per ABS journals like Transportation Research Part E Logistics and Transportation Review, Journal of Business Research, International Journal of Production Research, Government Information Quarterly, Production Planning & Control, Technological Forecasting and Social Change, Business Strategy and the Environment, Journal of Cleaner Production etc.

Supporting Doctor-Patient Communication and the Therapeutic Alliance in Pediatric Care Through Extended Reality: A Systematic Review

29

Safa Elkefi and Noureddine Lourimi

The two areas that are changing... are information technology and medical technology. Those are the things that will make the world very different 20 years from now than it is today.

—Bill Gates

Abstract

This review investigates how extended reality (XR) can improve doctor-patient communication for children with medical complexity. The study used PRISMA guidelines to conduct a systematic review on the topic. It analyzed various databases using the systematic approach to shortlist the results into a list of 17 papers. We found that Virtual Reality can alleviate stress and anxiety in children and train healthcare professionals in effective communication. Augmented Reality interventions show promise in supporting emotional recognition and verbal abilities in pediatric patients, while mixed reality demonstrates potential for realistic interactions between caregivers and patients. Overall, the study

Supplementary Information The online version contains supplementary material available at https://doi.org/10.1007/978-3-031-70292-1_29.

S. Elkefi (✉)
School of Nursing, Columbia University, New York, USA
e-mail: Se2649@columbia.edu

S. Elkefi · N. Lourimi
Hphactors Lab, New York, USA
e-mail: Noureddine.lourimi@etudiant-enit.utm.tn

N. Lourimi
Industrial Engineering Department, National Engineering School of Tunis, Tunis, Tunisia

F. Jawab (ed.), *Hospital Supply Chain*, Integrated Science 27,
https://doi.org/10.1007/978-3-031-70292-1_29

highlights the versatility of XR technologies in enhancing communication and improving patient well-being.

Keywords

Children with medical complexity • Immersive technology • Virtual reality • Augmented reality • Mixed reality • Alliance

1 Introduction

Engaging patients in pediatric health services is challenging due to contextual factors related to families and hospitals [1]. Children and adolescents face unique physical, psychological, cognitive, and sensory challenges [2]. These challenges arise from their dependence on caregivers, emotional vulnerability, and limited understanding of medical processes. The complex procedures leave the child unable to comprehend the necessity of the various interventions, which can increase their anxiety and fear. Together with the uncertainty experienced regarding the next steps, this emotional pressure can hinder the child's cooperation with the suggested procedures [3]. Thus, many researchers emphasized the importance of building strong communication between healthcare providers and their patients (children, adolescents, and caregivers) to ensure flowing care and adherence to regimens [4].

Effective communication between patients and healthcare professionals in pediatric care was shown to be critically important in inducing positive health outcomes [5]. Delivering the right information to the child and his family can help accelerate their coping with different situations [5]. A study by Betsy et al. showed that using asthma children and their caregivers' inputs in the treatment plans can lead to better control over the children's medical adherence [4]. Successful communication between healthcare providers and patients' caregivers also improves satisfaction with care [6]. For example, in a study of youth with chronic conditions (e.g., asthma, diabetes mellitus, or sickle-cell disease) using videotapes of clinic visits, investigators found a significant association between clinic visit satisfaction (based on parent reports). They observed the friendliness of physicians toward parents [7]. Another similar study using a national survey of patients of youth with diabetes (SEARCH study) showed that 43% of parents reported that communication was a barrier to care, and 48% of parents reported that getting information (defined by having questions discussed/answered) was a barrier to care [8]. Thus, to improve health outcomes, it remains important to identify the factors impacting verbal and non-verbal communication and to use them in building better interaction strategies and strengthening therapeutic alliances in pediatric care [8].

Some communication strategies are built around using "affective interactions" involving emotion-based, motivational, and listening strategies [9]. Some other strategies focus on creating child-friendly environments where the languages spoken are built in a way that enhances the children's comprehension of their situations [10]. Carpenter et al. emphasized interpersonal communication skill implementation in inpatient consultations (e.g., inviting the child to answer questions directly and showing emotion and empathy to the child) [11]. At the same time, Feraco et al. suggested facilitating the teaching of feasible, low-variability communication skills through individual fellowship programs in a "train the trainer" approach [12]. Some communication issues come from the complexity of information-sharing channels suggested by doctors. The findings of a study by Coyne et al. suggest that professionals need to maintain an open mind about information-sharing strategies families may choose, remain sensitive to parents' and children's information requirements, and adopt a flexible approach to information provision [13]. Furthermore, some strategies resort to the use of health information technology (HIT) to empower the quality of communication [14].

By providing more advanced mechanisms for interaction with physicians, HIT can empower children and their families [15]. For example, telemedicine technologies are increasingly integrated into pediatric infectious disease programs with the aim of facilitating access to specialist care and reducing costs [16]. Most pediatric hospitals are adopting electronic information systems to manage personal health information and other data that affect children's health [17]. Using consumer informatics such as mobile-based communication tools (apps, chatbots, text messaging) to improve communication with doctors has also gained more popularity over the years [18]. Lately, more focus on immersive extended technologies in supporting pediatric care has been observed. Studies have extensively explored the potential of extended reality (XR) technologies in supporting pain, symptom, and emotion management among children with chronic diseases [19–21], in addition to treatment management and training of both children and their families [20, 22–28]. Although such technologies are still in the early stages of development, some studies showed that extended reality tools could support therapeutic alliances between doctors and patients [29, 30]. To our knowledge, this is the first review to investigate the potential of XR in supporting communication and therapeutic alliances between doctors and patients in pediatric care. This study reviews the literature to explore the extended reality applications used to support communication between patients with medical complexities and healthcare professionals. The findings of the study can help inform communication strategies and XR technologies' designers.

2 Methods

2.1 Search Strategy

This review study was conducted according to the PRISMA guidelines using a multi-method search strategy. PRISMA is the Preferred Reporting Item for Systematic Reviews and Meta-Analysis guidelines [31]. The following databases were searched for peer-reviewed papers within our scope: IEEExplore, ProQuest CENTRAL, PubMed, Scopus, Embase, Google Scholar, and Web of Science. The search was performed on Jun 13, 2023. The search strategy was built based on the PICOS framework. PICOS stands for Patient or problem, Intervention or exposure, Comparison or control, Outcome or measure, and Study designs [32, 33]. The PICOS framework is the most commonly used model for structuring clinical questions because it captures each key element required for a focused question [32, 33]. Our ***population*** is children (< 18 years old), doctors, and caregivers. Our Intervention is extended reality (XR), our ***comparison*** is based on the type of technology used (virtual reality (VR), augmented reality (AR), and mixed reality (MR)), our ***outcome*** is communication, and ***our study designs*** are clinical trials, cases controls, cross-sectional, case reports, and case series. The keywords selected were modified based on feedback received from content experts as well as the university librarian. The final list of keywords used is summarized in Appendix 1.

2.2 Inclusion and Exclusion Criteria

Included articles were based on the following eligibility criteria: (1) publications that are peer-reviewed, (2) described and reported findings from a study that conducted a formal evaluation of extended reality (VR, AR, MR), (3) the XR technology was implemented as a working prototype or fully functional solution in the users' environment, (4) written in English, and (5) focused on supporting the communication between children and their families with the healthcare professionals. Any publications that do not meet these criteria were excluded. Reviews and commentary articles were excluded, too. We did not include any article that reported communication outcomes that did not involve healthcare professionals and patients or their caregivers. For instance, articles covering social communication aspects were not relevant to our scope and were thus excluded.

2.3 Quality Assessment

To uphold the standards of reporting quality, a consensus among all authors was achieved for every step of the selection process. Additionally, we employed the Mixed Methods Appraisal Tool (MMAT) [34] to conduct a thorough quality assessment of the selected papers. The MMAT is designed to evaluate the quality of studies employing qualitative, quantitative, and mixed-methods approaches [34], with a focus on methodological criteria such as the nature of the study (randomized or non-randomized clinical trial) [34]. Each item was independently judged by reviewers, categorizing them as having a low risk of bias, high risk of bias, or unclear risk of bias. Studies meeting all criteria were considered to have a low likelihood of biases, receiving a quality grade of "A." If criteria were partially met, the probability of bias was moderate, resulting in a quality grade of "B." Studies failing to meet these criteria entirely were assigned a high probability of bias, leading to a quality grade of "C." Only articles with an overall quality level of A or B were included, while those with an overall quality level of C were excluded.

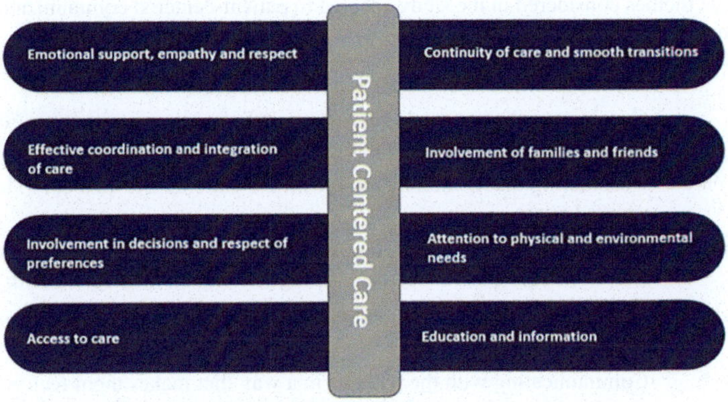

Fig. 1 Framework of the eight dimensions of patient-centered care [38, 39]

2.4 Studies Selection and Information Extraction

A first manual search using the keywords was conducted in each of the databases. We then merged all the results in an excel table and removed all duplicates. After that, a two-step filtering process was conducted based on the title and abstract first and then on the full paper reading to include the agreed-upon studies based on consensus. All authors conducted the filtering to minimize selection bias. A complementary manual search was conducted in the relevant informatics and pediatric journals mentioned in Appendix 2. In addition, to minimize the risk of missing relevant articles, the snowball method was used. The snowball method included checking references of relevant papers, serendipitously identifying references, alerts, and citation tracking as done in previous studies [35, 36].

Data from the included studies were extracted using Microsoft Excel 2016. The form included fields to be completed by a reviewer in the following order: title, year, country, objective, study design, sample size, patients' conditions, communication theme, verbal/non-verbal communication, type of Intervention, name of the technology, type of the technology, outcomes measured, important findings, and limitations of the study. To classify the themes of communication, we used the framework of the eight patient-centered care aspects developed by the Picker Institute and previously applied in pediatric care [37]. The eight dimensions are summarized in Fig. 1 [38].

The framework is employed to evaluate the standard of patient care and pinpoint areas for enhancement. Additionally, it is used to guide healthcare policy and practice to guarantee that patients get the best treatment available [40].

The themes considered are summarized and defined as in Table 1.

Table 1 The themes considered in the study adapted to patient-centered communication from the Picker framework [38]

Theme	Definition
Patients' preferences	Considering the patients' preferences, beliefs, interests, and requirements when deciding how to communicate with a person
Access to care	Considering that communication with the patients allows them to have better access to care
Continuity and transition	Considering ensuring continuous access to ongoing treatment and seamless transition between various care settings when communicating with patients
Family and friends	Engaging patient's friends and family when communicating with patients
Physical comfort	Communicating with the patients in a way that makes them feel as comfortable in the care settings as possible
Emotional support	Considering the patients' emotional well-being when communicating with patients
Coordination	Guaranteeing coordination and collaborating when communication with the patients
Information and education	Considering educating patients and delivering the needed information accurately when communicating with the patients

3 Results

3.1 Description of the Included Studies

After removing the duplicates, a total of 16,346 publications were thoroughly screened from among all the sources discovered, and 17 final papers were included in this review after full paper screening. The PRISMA flowchart in Fig. 2 provides a summary of the screening procedure.

A comprehensive analysis was conducted on a sample of 15 countries derived from the selected papers, with the objective of gaining insights into the geographic distribution of XR use in developed vs developing countries.

The geographic comparative analysis presents insights into the geographic distribution of the interventions. While certain developed countries showed a significant presence, other countries demonstrated a transitional status. The geographical distribution of the studies is shown in Fig. 3. Most of the included studies ($n = 14$, 82.4%) covered interventions in developed countries, and only ($n = 3$, 17.6%) of them took place in developing countries. The countries that covered interventions the most were the United States and the United Kingdom, accounting for 17.6% of the interventions each.

The findings are summarized in Tables 2 and 3 attached in the supplementary file. Table 2 summarizes information related to the study design and technology used, and Table 3 reports the communication-related findings.

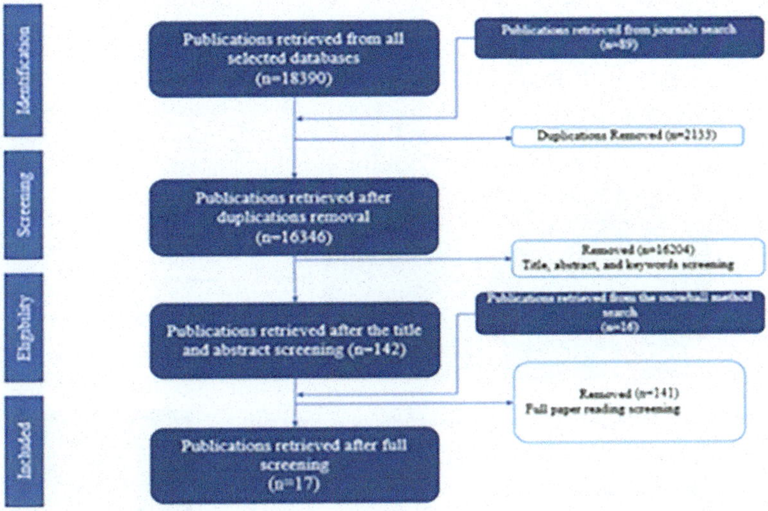

Fig. 2 PRISMA diagram flow of the articles' selection process

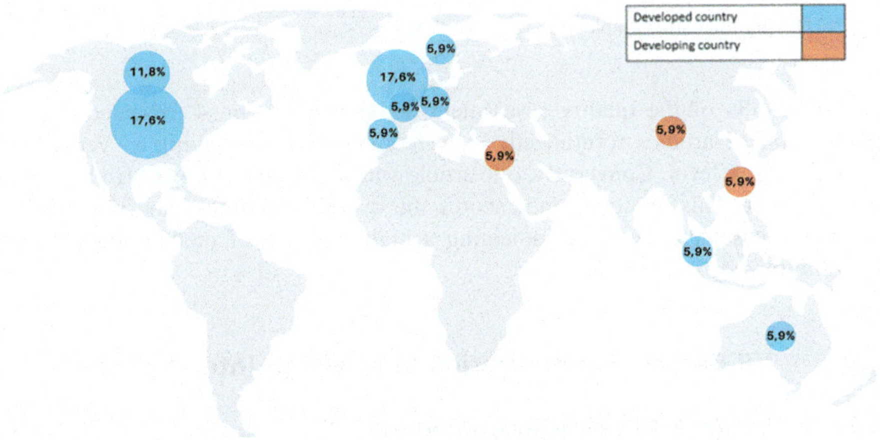

Fig. 3 Distribution of studies between developed and developing countries

3.2 Studies Design and Participants

The studies included various research designs and approaches, with experiments being the majority (n = 7). Some studies used mixed methods, combining experiments with surveys (n = 6) or interviews (n = 2). Participants had diverse health conditions, including neurodevelopmental (23.5%, n = 4) and mental health conditions (35.3%, n = 6), as well as other conditions (11.8%, n = 2) and undergoing surgical procedures (5.9%, n = 1). Risk of Bias and Quality Assessment.

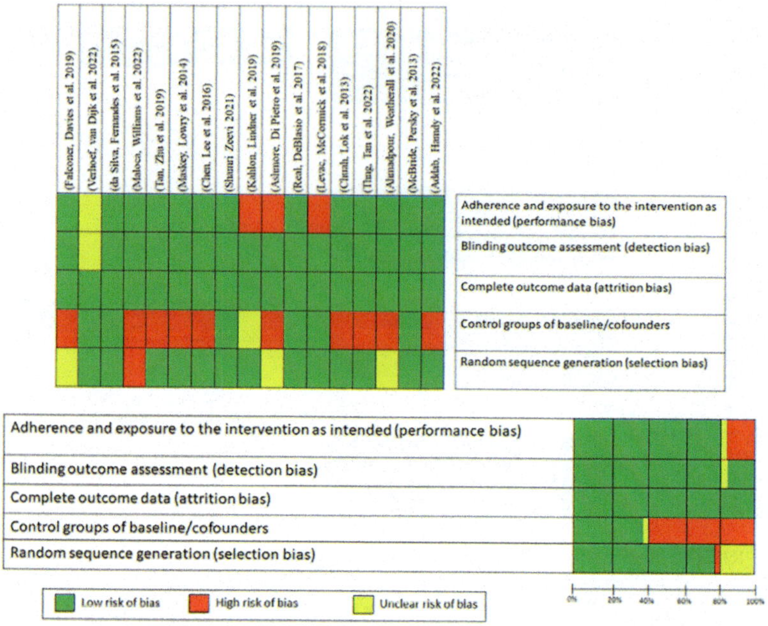

Fig. 4 Quality assessment table

The results of the quality assessment, as shown in Fig. 4, revealed that out of the total 17 articles scrutinized, 16 were categorized as having a "Very High" overall quality level. Conversely, one article was assessed to have a "High" overall quality level. This outcome underscores the overall robustness and reliability of most of the selected studies, indicating a high standard of methodological rigor and minimized risk of biases.

3.3 VR-Based Communication Supporting Interventions

3.3.1 Extended Reality Technologies

The technologies used in the studies included VR (n = 14), AR (n = 2), and MR (n = 1).

Virtual Reality-Based Interventions

VR was the most frequently employed technology in the interventions of the selected studies (n = 14). Head-mounted displays (HMDs), including commercially available tethered HMDs such as Oculus Rift, Oculus Quest, and HTC Vive [41–48], played a significant role in facilitating communication in various contexts.

First, a study conducted by Addab et al. [45] utilized VR as a distraction technique to alleviate pain and anxiety in children undergoing medical procedures, which promoted improved communication between nurses, physicians, and children, making them feel more at ease. Maloca et al. [41] found that VR was instrumental in ophthalmic medical communication for young children. Additionally, VR was employed to instruct medical residents on effective communication with caregivers to reduce influenza vaccine refusal for their children [43]. Another notable application of VR HMDs was communicating a child's inherited risk of obesity to mothers through an immersive restaurant buffet experience [44]. Furthermore, VR technology proved to be beneficial in art therapy for addressing communication difficulties in adolescents, providing a safe space for emotional expression and experiential exploration, thereby aiding therapists in navigating patients' emotions effectively [42]. Tan et al. [46] highlighted the use of VR to aid in the diagnosis and treatment of pediatric ADHD patients by integrating EEG caps and motion capture technology, complementing doctors' subjective assessments with nonverbal and verbal methods for medical communication. Lastly, in the context of low-cost HMDs, Kahlon et al. [48] conducted a Virtual Reality Exposure Therapy (VRET) session for adolescents with PSA, resulting in intensive interaction between the patient and therapist, significantly reducing social anxiety levels and increasing self-efficacy three months after exposure. Ashmore et al. [47] explored the use of low-cost HMDs to prepare pediatric patients for MRI tests, leading to improved patient understanding and better cooperation during medical procedures.

Furthermore, a study by Verhoef et al. [49] delved into the utilization of tablet-based VR technology to identify SIP profiles for children exhibiting aggressive behavior issues. This approach notably improved patient-doctor communication by tailoring cognitive-behavioral therapy to meet the individual needs of the children. In a similar vein, Falconer et al. [50] harnessed an interactive desktop avatar-based VR environment, specifically the ProReal VR program, to aid children with anxiety during face-to-face therapy. This novel approach allowed children to externalize their inner selves and facilitated a reevaluation of their thoughts, feelings, and experiences, thereby enhancing their ability to communicate effectively.

The Blue Room, a VRE, immerses users through the projection of audio-visual images onto 360-degree seamless screens [51]. This technology has proven highly effective in reducing specific phobias or fears in children with ASD when used in conjunction with CBT [51]. It offers a greater degree of control over stimuli compared to CBT alone. By maintaining the child's anxiety at a low level within the VRE, therapists can interact with the child when they are calm and attentive, thereby improving communication and therapeutic outcomes [51].

Expanding the horizons of VR, tools such as the Microsoft Kinect system have been employed for interactive gaming in children with cerebral palsy in tandem with a website. This combined approach significantly enhances communication between therapists and participating children and families [52]. This innovative strategy not only facilitates effective interaction but also fosters collaboration, solidifying its position as a potent therapeutic tool.

Added to that, the Teddy Bear Hospital VR platform [53] has emerged as a valuable tool in medical education. It enhances learning outcomes for medical students by increasing their empathy and improving their ability to communicate with children through interactive medical simulations.

Finally, a study by Ahmadpour et al. [54] investigated how VR apps can be designed to improve the periprocedural experiences of children and adolescents, particularly those with severe anxiety. The study suggested that one effective way to enhance patient-doctor communication and alleviate anxiety in pediatric patients is to integrate personalized communication strategies into VR apps designed for this purpose [54]. By tailoring communication methods to each child's individual preferences and understanding levels, healthcare providers can create a more comfortable and reassuring environment for young patients [54].

Augmented Reality-Based Interventions

Two studies used augmented reality for their interventions. The first one was conducted by Chen et al. [55]. The authors used the AR Video Modeling Storybook (ARVMS) to offer an interactive experience to children via a live direct or indirect view of a physical, real-world environment with elements augmented by computer-generated sensory input, e.g., sound, video, and graphics [55]. The technology mimics facial expressions and emotions, which could help pediatricians identify the child's emotions (anger, fear, disgust, happiness, sadness, and surprise) [55]. Thus, the ARVMS could help strengthen non-verbal communication by adapting the technology to the changing attentional focus of the child and supporting the mission of pediatricians [55].

Second, a study conducted by da Silva et al. [56] implemented Speech Therapy with Augmented Reality (STAR) for children with Autism Spectrum Disorder (ASD). STAR utilizes visual and aural sensory stimulation, incorporating rapid reinforcement while enriching the environment with virtual objects and audio to captivate and motivate children [56]. This approach serves to enhance their verbal abilities and creativity, primarily through the notable increase in initiated contact and communication by the children themselves [56]. Furthermore, the therapist can tailor activities and system behaviors to align with the unique needs and characteristics of each child [56].

Mixed Reality-Based Interventions

Despite its potential, only one study has utilized mixed reality for designing the Intervention. The technology leverages virtual humans, employing a set of high-fidelity, pre-programmed animations, and speeches [57]. This technology combines 3D display technology, head tracking, and fish-tank VR to create a mixed-reality environment in which virtual humans appear to coexist in the user's physical space, adapting their behavior and visual perspective according to the user's movements [57].

This immersive experience aims to foster realistic interactions and engagement with the virtual characters. Through its potential for interactivity, the authors introduced a mixed reality pediatric patient that provided health science students with a means to practice pediatric developmental exams. This has resulted in improved confidence levels when it comes to interacting with children, interviewing parents, and evaluating a child's development [57].

3.4 Communication Support Findings

The doctor-patient and doctor-caregiver communication methods used in the selected studies ranged between verbal and non-verbal communication. Most of the articles (n = 11) supported both verbal and nonverbal communication, while only one study supported nonverbal communication, and (n = 5) supported verbal communication. The themes of patient-centered communication were categorized as shown in Fig. 3. Most of the articles supported communication that respects patients' preferences (n = 8) and their emotional support (n = 6). As shown in Fig. 5, doctor-child communication through extended reality is experiencing more and more interest over the years.

3.4.1 Information and Education

When it comes to patient education and ensuring the accurate delivery of essential information during patient interactions, we find that this fundamental aspect of healthcare plays a pivotal role in fostering better understanding and collaboration between healthcare providers and their patients [58]. This is exemplified through the application of XR technologies to communicate crucial information to pediatric patients in the context of two specific studies, namely, studies [41] and [47]. These investigations focused on children facing challenges related to vision-threatening myopia and anxiety linked to MRI procedures. Both studies employed a blend of verbal and nonverbal communication methods to report their findings. Notably, both interventions adopted a training format that harnessed the capabilities of VR technology, seeking to enrich patient understanding and education

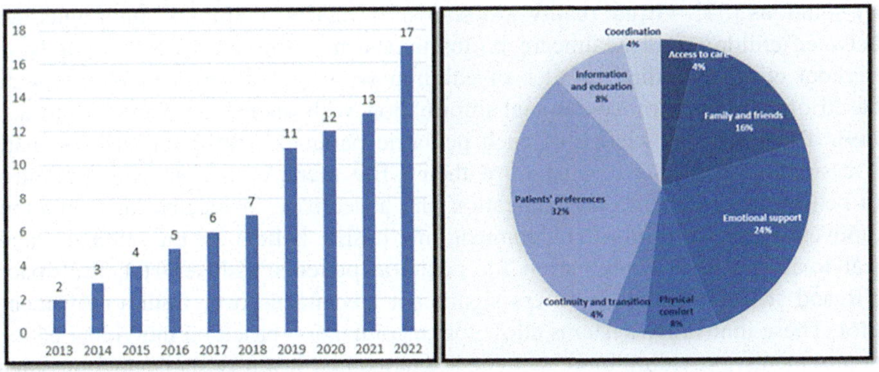

Fig. 5 Communication themes distribution and temporal distribution of the studies

about their condition. In one instance, pediatric patients facing vision-threatening myopia were introduced to a VR program called SpectoVR, which played a pivotal role in elucidating ophthalmological complications [41]. This innovative approach not only empowered patients with a deeper understanding of their condition but also facilitated more effective communication between healthcare professionals and pediatric patients. Specifically, the study found that a majority of participants (76%) agreed that the VR application enhanced their understanding of the topic, and half of participants (48%) agreed that the VR application would help with patient communication. Additionally, most participants disagreed that it was an unnecessary use of time (81%). Another compelling study involved the development of a VR experience geared towards alleviating anxiety in pediatric patients scheduled for magnetic resonance imaging (MRI) procedures [47]. The experience included panoramic 360-degree videos of the entire MRI journey, as it helped to educate and communicate with the child about the MRI process and reduce anxiety associated with the test, leading to better patient understanding and cooperation during the medical procedures.

3.4.2 Patients' Preferences

Children, especially the ones with medical complexity and special needs, require more attention and have different information needs. Considering their preferences, beliefs, interests, and requirements when deciding how to communicate with them is crucial for a seamless health integration [59]. Our study has shown that several XR applications were used to support communication between healthcare professionals and children by putting their preferences ahead of care [44, 46, 49, 52–54, 56, 57]. These studies supported children with different medical situations (e.g., ASD, anxiety, ADHD, aggressive behavior, cerebral palsy, etc.). Two of the studies reported outcomes related to nonverbal communication, one study reported using verbal communication, and 5 of them consisted of both verbal and nonverbal communication. The interventions were mainly in four formats: entertainment [49, 52], therapy sessions [49, 56], treatment [46], and training [44, 52, 54, 57] using augmented [56], virtual [44, 46, 49, 52, 54] and mixed reality solutions [57]. Virtual reality was shown to improve communication outcomes between children and healthcare professionals in 5 studies. In fact, a study by Verhoef et al. identified profiles of children with aggressive behavior problems based on how they process social information with an interactive VR approach [49]. The better knowledge of each pediatric patient's SIP characteristics made it easier for therapists to customize their CBD therapy session, which resulted in better doctor-patient communication and a decrease in reactive and proactive motives, anger-frustration temperament, and hostile beliefs. In the realm of medical treatment and rehabilitation for pediatric patients with ADHD, the use of VR and sensor technology offers significant advantages over traditional therapy [46]. These innovative systems allow for customization based on individual patient requirements, providing more suitable scenarios and lower costs through repeated use, which can offer supplementary insights to complement doctors' subjective assessments and guide subsequent treatment or nursing approaches. Another study involving children with cerebral palsy [52] explored the potential benefits of a clinic-based AVG component in addition to traditional therapy for children and youth with cerebral palsy. Therapists responded to any questions the child and family posed via emails sent and received through the website. Therefore, the study suggests that the use of a website can facilitate communication between therapists and participating children/families to customize their care. Moreover, the TBH offers a valuable platform for medical students to refine their communication and empathy skills with children, leveraging VR to immerse students in a child's perspective [53], which enhances medical student's ability, confidence, and comfort level in communicating with children and ability to empathize with their fears in the healthcare environment. Also, in a study focused on utilizing VR technology to assist children dealing with anxiety [54], the spotlight was on the importance of aligning patient-doctor communication with the preferences of pediatric patients. The study's qualitative data, derived from surveys, focus groups, and interviews, underscored the significance of tailoring communication methods to accommodate the distinct preferences and comprehension levels of each child. Added to that, AR was also shown to have the potential to enhance communication between healthcare professionals and pediatric patients by considering their preferences while communicating with them. For that, a study by da Silva et al. discussed the use of the use of augmented reality in communication treatments for children with ASD by comparing aspects of Augmented and Alternative Communication (AAC) and Applied Behavior Analysis (ABA) techniques [56]. Thus, therapists could define activities and system behaviors according to the needs and characteristics of each child. Lastly, a study introduces MR as a transformative strategy by employing virtual humans to replicate vulnerable populations like physically and intellectually disabled children [57]. This has led to an improvement in their confidence levels when it comes to interacting with children, interviewing parents, and evaluating a child's development to uplift the quality of care provided to these marginalized groups.

3.4.3 Physical Comfort

Effective communication with patients lies at the core of quality healthcare, with a primary focus on creating a supportive environment that not only ensures patients' voices are heard but also cultivates feelings of comfort and ease within healthcare settings [60]. Notably, the integration of XR technologies has emerged as a promising avenue in this endeavor, particularly when it comes to pediatric patients [51, 54]. This technological innovation has proven especially valuable for children dealing with anxiety and ASD. In the studies conducted, the outcomes were meticulously reported through various communication modalities. Some studies exclusively employed verbal communication, while others ingeniously combined both verbal and nonverbal channels to maximize patient understanding and engagement. It is noteworthy that the majority of these interventions followed a training-based approach [54], with one remarkable instance that incorporated a therapy session alongside training specifically tailored for the treatment of ASD [51]. In all the interventions examined, a consistent feature was their reliance on

VR technology. A specific study conducted by Maskey et al. [51] stands out in this regard. This study delved into the effectiveness of a combined treatment approach, employing CBT techniques alongside an immersive virtual reality environment. The primary objective was to assess the potential reduction or treatment of specific phobias or fears among young individuals diagnosed with ASD. In this study, a psychologist provided guidance through coaching sessions that involved relaxation and breathing exercises, helping participants manage anxiety and discomfort. They were gradually exposed to their fears, allowing them to become more comfortable and develop effective coping strategies, ultimately reducing the discomfort related to their specific phobias and fears.

Another study harnessed the power of VR technology for children with anxiety [54] and emphasized that enhancing patient-doctor communication and reducing anxiety in pediatric patients can be achieved by incorporating personalized communication strategies into VR apps. The outcome of the qualitative data from surveys, focus groups, and interviews suggests that customizing communication techniques to suit each child's unique preferences and comprehension levels helps healthcare providers establish a more comforting and reassuring atmosphere for young patients.

3.4.4 Emotional Support

Acknowledging and prioritizing patients' emotional well-being is a crucial element of effective healthcare communication. This entails understanding and addressing their emotional needs during interactions, which can ultimately lead to improved patient satisfaction and overall well-being [61]. Moreover, XR technologies play a vital role in enhancing this endeavor [42, 45, 48, 50, 53, 55], especially for children with ASD, anxiety, scheduled medical procedures, or various clinical conditions. The results were carefully documented using a range of communication methods. While three studies solely relied on verbal communication, the three others adeptly blended verbal and nonverbal approaches. The interventions ranged from entertainment [45, 50], therapy sessions [42, 48, 50], and training [53, 55] using VR [42, 45, 48, 50, 53] and AR [55] technologies.

VR has the potential to enhance communication between pediatric patients and their healthcare professionals by acknowledging and prioritizing their emotional well-being. In fact, one study utilized an avatar-based virtual reality therapy as a tool to facilitate communication and therapy with young individuals who struggle to express themselves during traditional talking therapy [50]. The use of avatars and virtual environments helps individuals externalize their inner worlds, leading to a reappraisal of thoughts, feelings, and experiences, ultimately supporting emotional well-being. Added to that, VR in adolescent art therapy for children with anxiety and social difficulties improves emotional communication by bridging the gap between reality and symbolism [42]. Therapists can maintain a healthy distance, allowing pediatric patients to explore emotions safely, benefiting those who find traditional art therapy challenging. As an outcome, it allows them to reduce anxiety levels and enhance self-confidence through a balanced social bond and self-body image. Affordable consumer VR equipment has demonstrated its effectiveness in providing valuable emotional support for adolescents struggling with PSA [48]. In a single-session approach, patients engage in open conversations with virtual characters while closely monitored by their therapist, who is physically present during the VR exposure therapy. This immersive interaction between the patient and therapist within the virtual environment has resulted in substantial reductions in social anxiety and notable increases in self-efficacy that persist for up to three months post-exposure. Another study harnessed the power of VR technology through a valuable platform known as TBH to enrich the communication and empathy skills of medical students when interacting with children, thereby creating a more comfortable environment [53]. TBH offers a unique perspective, allowing students to step into the shoes of a child and gain insights into their healthcare experiences. This includes understanding their distinct learning requirements and the varying degrees of anxiety they may feel toward medical settings. Such knowledge equips students with the essential tools needed to manage these situations effectively. Lastly, a study by Addab et al. [45]using VR as a distraction technique to reduce pain and anxiety in children undergoing medical procedures in a pediatric orthopedic setting provided valuable emotional support by fostering communication among healthcare stakeholders, such as nurses, physicians, and patients. Healthcare providers (HCPs) actively interacted with patients during the VR experience, offering reassurance and inviting feedback. This enhanced patient comfort and a sense of empowerment through communication with their HCPs. Even during medical procedures, HCPs regularly checked in with patients, providing explanations and guidance while patients remained immersed in the VR environment.

3.4.5 Access to Care

When healthcare providers prioritize clear and empathetic communication, patients not only feel heard and valued but are also better equipped to navigate the complex healthcare landscape, ultimately leading to better access to the care they need [61].

In this regard, a pioneering training VR curriculum designed for pediatric residents, as developed by Real et al. [43], set out to equip healthcare professionals with the verbal and nonverbal communication skills needed to effectively counsel hesitant caregivers who were reluctant to vaccinate their children against the flu. Remarkably, this immersive VR curriculum yielded a substantial decrease in influenza vaccine refusal rates among pediatric patients vulnerable to influenza. Those who participated in this immersive educational experience saw a notable reduction in post-curriculum refusal rates, with figures standing at 27.8% compared to the pre-curriculum rate of 37.1%. This success underscores the VR curriculum's efficacy in teaching critical communication skills, hinting at its transformative potential in reshaping physician–patient interactions and thereby contributing to improved access to comprehensive care.

3.4.6 Family and Friends

Incorporating a patient's friends and family into the communication process is a vital aspect of patient-centered care. By involving loved ones in discussions and decisions related to the patient's health, healthcare providers can create a more supportive and holistic healthcare environment [62]. Transitioning to the realm of XR technologies, we can explore how these innovative tools can play a pivotal role in ensuring that [43, 44, 51, 55] for various types of medical conditions, including ASD and kids at risk of obesity and influenza. Incorporating family or friends into the pediatric patient's treatment is achievable through training programs, a common intervention type in all of the studies [43, 44, 51]. Notably, only one study expanded beyond training, incorporating treatment and therapy sessions as additional interventions [51]. Among the studies conducted, two reported outcomes specifically related to verbal communication, while the remaining studies employed a mixed approach that combined both verbal and nonverbal communication methods using VR [43, 44, 51] and AR [55] technologies. Commencing with the crucial aspect of involving parents in CBT combined with VRE interventions for individuals with ASD [51] fosters a comprehensive understanding of how to support their child during the exposure steps effectively. This collaborative engagement empowers parents with the knowledge and communication skills necessary to engage with healthcare professionals more effectively, ultimately promoting a gradual and successful treatment process for individuals with ASD. In a study focusing on children at risk of influenza [43], an immersive VR curriculum was designed to equip pediatric residents with effective counseling skills. This approach aimed at engaging hesitant caregivers—family members—by providing residents the tools to address their concerns and increase vaccine acceptance. By equipping residents with these skills, the curriculum aimed to empower them to address caregivers' concerns and enhance vaccine acceptance among this demographic. Moreover, the impact of family communication is evident in research on childhood obesity risk [44]. Sharing personalized obesity risk information with mothers within a VR buffet restaurant influenced their feeding practices. Mothers who received high-risk messages demonstrated notable changes in their child's diet, reflecting the influence of family dynamics on health decisions. Another approach involves the use of AR technology in storybooks for autistic children, which allows parents and special education teachers to co-develop stories from the children's perspective [55]. This collaborative storytelling enhances therapists' understanding of the child's daily life experiences and emotions, leading to more effective interventions.

3.4.7 Continuity and Transition

Effective communication with patients involves ensuring uninterrupted access to ongoing treatment and facilitating seamless transitions between care settings. This approach promotes better patient outcomes and well-being [63]. Utilizing a VR-based approach for the treatment and diagnosis of children with ADHD [46], this innovative system generates objective physiological data, augmenting communication outcomes through both verbal and nonverbal channels. These insights serve as a valuable complement to doctors' subjective assessments, providing critical information to guide ongoing treatment and nursing. This approach ensures consistency of care as patients transition across various healthcare settings.

3.4.8 Coordination

Ensuring coordination and fostering collaboration in patient communication is paramount. By working together seamlessly, healthcare providers can deliver comprehensive and patient-centered care, resulting in better health outcomes and an improved overall healthcare experience for patients [64]. In a study conducted by Addab et al., the importance of coordination in improving patient experiences during pediatric orthopedic medical procedures was highlighted through the implementation of an entertaining VR intervention [45]. This Intervention allowed for effective verbal communication among various stakeholders, including physicians, nurses, and patients. As patients were immersed in the VR experience, healthcare providers were able to actively participate in their care, offering support and seeking feedback collaboratively. The coordinated approach resulted in enhanced patient comfort and a greater sense of control, allowing patients to continuously communicate with their healthcare providers throughout the procedure.

4 Discussion

This study is a systematic review that investigates the potential of using XR technologies in supporting communication between doctors and children with medical complexity. The 17 studies included provide valuable insights into the role of XR from multiple angles, with a majority of interventions taking place in developed countries (82.4%). The children subject to these studies had different medical complexities (ASD, mental health issues, etc.).

4.1 Extended Reality Abilities

The study reported that virtual reality (VR) technology was frequently employed to alleviate the stress and anxiety experienced by children during medical procedures. This effective use of VR technology improved communication among caregivers, children, and healthcare providers. The Blue Room Virtual Reality Environment (VRE) was found to effectively reduce phobias in children with Autism Spectrum Disorder (ASD) and enhance therapeutic communication. Furthermore, VR technology was utilized to train healthcare professionals in effective communication through an immersive experience. The Teddy Bear Hospital VR platform was also found to be useful in improving medical students' empathy and communication skills with children. The study findings suggest that VR technology can play a vital role in supporting communication with children with medical conditions (CMC). It should be considered as an intervention to help manage the risks associated with communication problems in this population. The study further highlights the potential of VR technology in preparing children for medical procedures and enhancing their preparedness, as validated in other settings [65]. Virtual Reality (VR) has the potential to enhance the effectiveness of medical procedures and therapies, thereby minimizing the requirement for repeated procedures or prolonged therapy sessions. This, in turn, can lead to cost savings for the healthcare system as a whole.

Augmented reality was also shown to support communication with the children. For instance, by offering an interactive experience that augments a real-world environment with computer-generated sensory inputs like sound, video, and graphics, AR mimics facial expressions and emotions, helping healthcare professionals identify emotions. Emotion recognition has been very challenging with this population [66]. It could also help support the verbal abilities and creativity of CMC, enhancing their abilities to convey their messages. AR can, thus, improve CMC's engagement in therapy by supporting their communication. This could facilitate healthcare professionals' jobs by improving the verbal and non-verbal communication flows with their patients. These findings can stimulate further research and development in the field of AR, leading to even more innovative and effective tools for child healthcare and therapy.

Although it is still limited in the number of technologies available, mixed reality has shown its potential through the MR technology that we included in this study, where communication was supported through an immersive experience where realistic interactions were supported to create a collaborative communication environment for caregivers, parents, patients, and healthcare providers. Future research is needed to investigate further the potential that such technologies can bring to the communication support realm.

4.2 Communication Support

The present review highlights the different ways in which XR-based communication with CMC is supported, which aligns with findings from previous studies in different settings [67]. The focus is given to both verbal and non-verbal communication support. XR has the potential to enhance communication and ensure its continuity and transition in care. It can create a tailored experience and ensure better communication outcomes, which could significantly enhance user experience and engagement in various settings, not limited to healthcare. The interdisciplinary nature of XR applications in healthcare highlights the potential for increased cross-disciplinary collaborations. The demand for more sophisticated XR applications will drive advancements in hardware and software, making these technologies more accessible and effective. Finally, the potential of XR to provide remote, immersive experiences can enhance global access to quality healthcare and education.

5 Conclusions

Our study highlighted the role of XR in supporting communication with CMC through different applications and approaches. The findings suggest that XR has the potential to enhance communication between patients and caregivers and CMC. It also suggests that XR needs further investigation to fully benefit from its potential. To sum up, we would like to say that:

> Extended reality will one day revolutionize the healthcare system. It will allow people to communicate without the extra effort communication needs now. And we are happy to contribute to that new realm.

Acknowledgements We would like to acknowledge the efforts put in by Rihem Berbere and Enas Aref for contributing to the early stages of data collection.

Appendix 1

Extended reality keywords:

("virtual reality" OR "augmented reality" OR "mixed reality" OR "immersive" OR VR OR AR OR XR)

AND

Population keywords:

(child OR pediatric OR children OR adolescent OR teenager OR caregiver)

AND

(therapist OR "health professional" OR physician OR doctor OR clinician OR "health practitioner" OR provider)

AND

Intervention keywords:

(Communication OR "doctor-patient relation" OR interaction OR relationship OR partnership OR agreement OR "therapeutic alliance" OR alliance)

Appendix 2

JAMA Pediatrics, Lancet Child and Adolescent Health, Journal of Child Psychology and Psychiatry and Allied Disciplines, Pediatrics, Child and Adolescent Psychiatry and Mental Health, Child Development Perspectives, JMIR Pediatrics and Parenting, JMIR Perioperative Medicine, Journal of Medical Internet

Research, JMIR Research Protocols, JMIR Mental Health, International Journal of Medical Informatics, Frontiers in Pediatrics, JMIR mHealth and uHealth, JMIR Formative Research, JMIR Medical Informatics, JMIR Public Health and Surveillance, JMIR Human Factors, JMIR Serious Games.

References

1. Flynn R, Walton S, Scott SD (2019) Engaging children and families in pediatric health research: a scoping review. Res Involvement Engage 5:1–8
2. Ghai S et al (2021) Needs and experiences of children and adolescents with pediatric multiple sclerosis and their caregivers: a systematic review. Children 8(6):445
3. Coyne I et al (2014) Children's participation in shared decision-making: children, adolescents, parents and healthcare professionals' perspectives and experiences. Eur J Oncol Nurs 18(3):273–280
4. Sleath B et al (2012) Communication during pediatric asthma visits and self-reported asthma medication adherence. Pediatrics 130(4):627–633
5. DiMatteo MR (2004) The role of effective communication with children and their families in fostering adherence to pediatric regimens. Patient Educ Couns 55(3):339–344
6. Nobile C, Drotar D (2003) Research on the quality of parent-provider communication in pediatric care: implications and recommendations. J Dev Behav Pediatr 24(4):279–290
7. Swedlund MP et al (2012) Effect of communication style and physician–family relationships on satisfaction with pediatric chronic disease care. Health Commun 27(5):498–505
8. Valenzuela JM et al (2014) Prevalence of and disparities in barriers to care experienced by youth with type 1 diabetes. J Pediatr 164(6):1369–1375.e1
9. Glenn TW et al (2021) Engagement and affective communication during pediatric nephrology clinic visits: associations with medication adherence. Patient Educ Couns 104(3):578–584
10. Donnelly M, Kilkelly U (2011) Child-friendly healthcare: delivering on the right to be heard. Med Law Rev 19(1):27–54
11. Carpenter DM et al (2013) The relationship between patient–provider communication and quality of life for children with asthma and their caregivers. J Asthma 50(7):791–798
12. Feraco AM et al (2016) Communication skills training in pediatric oncology: moving beyond role modeling. Pediatr Blood Cancer 63(6):966–972
13. Coyne I et al (2016) Information-sharing between healthcare professionals, parents and children with cancer: more than a matter of information exchange. Eur J Cancer Care 25(1):141–156
14. Seo W et al (2021) Learning from healthcare providers' strategies: designing technology to support effective child patient-provider communication. In: Proceedings of the 2021 CHI conference on human factors in computing systems
15. Diffin J et al (2019) The usefulness and acceptability of a personal health record to children and young people living with a complex health condition: a realist review of the literature. Child Care Health Dev 45(3):313–332
16. Pappalardo M et al (2021) Telemedicine in pediatric infectious diseases. Children 8(4):260
17. Krishna R (2017) The impact of health information technology on the doctor-patient relationship in child and adolescent psychiatry. Child and Adolesc Psychiatr Clin 26(1):67–75
18. Sharifi M et al (2013) Leveraging text messaging and mobile technology to support pediatric obesity-related behavior change: a qualitative study using parent focus groups and interviews. J Med Internet Res 15(12):e2780
19. Walther-Larsen S et al (2019) Immersive virtual reality for pediatric procedural pain: a randomized clinical trial. Hosp Pediatr 9(7):501–507
20. Won AS et al (2017) Immersive virtual reality for pediatric pain. Children 4(7):52

21. Eijlers R et al (2019) Meta-analysis: systematic review and meta-analysis of virtual reality in pediatrics: effects on pain and anxiety. Anesth Analg 129(5):1344
22. Dumoulin S et al (2019) A randomized controlled trial on the use of virtual reality for needle-related procedures in children and adolescents in the emergency department. Games Health J 8(4):285–293
23. Tas FQ et al (2022) Virtual reality in pediatrics, effects on pain and anxiety: A systematic review and meta-analysis update. Pediatr Anesthesia 32(12):1292–1304
24. Zhang M et al (2022) Virtual reality technology as an educational and intervention tool for children with autism spectrum disorder: current perspectives and future directions. Behav Sci (Basel) 12(5)
25. Pandrangi VC et al (2019) The application of virtual reality in patient education. Ann Vasc Surg 59:184–189
26. Badke CM et al (2022) Virtual reality in the pediatric intensive care unit: patient emotional and physiologic responses. Front Digit Health 4:867961
27. Goharinejad S et al (2022) The usefulness of virtual, augmented, and mixed reality technologies in the diagnosis and treatment of attention deficit hyperactivity disorder in children: an overview of relevant studies. BMC Psychiatry 22(1):4
28. Williams RM et al (2019) Augmented reality for rehabilitative therapy: patient experiences and practitioner perspectives. In: Proceedings of the human factors and ergonomics society annual meeting. Sage, Los Angeles, CA
29. Ong T et al (2021) Extended reality for enhanced telehealth during and beyond COVID-19: viewpoint. JMIR Serious Games 9(3):e26520
30. Lopez A et al (2019) Technology-based mental health treatment and the impact on the therapeutic alliance. Curr Psychiatry Rep 21(8):76
31. Levac D, Colquhoun H, O'Brien KK (2010) Scoping studies: advancing the methodology. Implement Sci 5(1):1–9
32. Huang X, Lin J, Demner-Fushman D (2006) Evaluation of PICO as a knowledge representation for clinical questions. In: AMIA annual symposium proceedings. American Medical Informatics Association
33. Barbosa RTdA et al (2018) Augmentative and alternative communication in children with Down's syndrome: a systematic review. BMC Pediatr 18:1–16
34. Hong QN et al (2018) Mixed methods appraisal tool (MMAT), version 2018, 1148552(10)
35. Perez-Bret E, Altisent R, Rocafort J (2016) Definition of compassion in healthcare: a systematic literature review. Int J Palliat Nurs 22(12):599–606
36. Debono DS et al (2013) Nurses' workarounds in acute healthcare settings: a scoping review. BMC Health Serv Res 13:1–16
37. Roué J-M et al (2017) Eight principles for patient-centred and family-centred care for newborns in the neonatal intensive care unit. Arch Dis Child Fetal Neonatal Ed 102(4):F364–F368
38. The Picker Institute (2018) Picker principles of person centred care
39. Kuipers SJ et al (2021) Easier said than done: Healthcare professionals' barriers to the provision of patient-centered primary care to patients with multimorbidity. Int J Environ Res Public Health 18(11):6057
40. Davis K, Schoenbaum SC, Audet A-M (2005) A 2020 vision of patient-centered primary care. J Gener Internal Med 20:953–957
41. Maloca PM et al (2022) Feasibility and tolerability of ophthalmic virtual reality as a medical communication tool in children and young people. Acta Opthalmol 100(2):e588–e597
42. Shamri Zeevi L (2021) Making art therapy virtual: integrating virtual reality into art therapy with adolescents. Front Psychol 12:584943
43. Real FJ et al (2017) A virtual reality curriculum for pediatric residents decreases rates of influenza vaccine refusal. Acad Pediatr 17(4):431–435
44. McBride CM et al (2013) Effects of providing personalized feedback of child's obesity risk on mothers' food choices using a virtual reality buffet. Int J Obes 37(10):1322–1327
45. Addab S et al (2022) The use of virtual reality during medical procedures in a pediatric orthopedic setting: a mixed-methods pilot feasibility study

46. Tan Y et al (2019) Virtual classroom: an ADHD assessment and diagnosis system based on virtual reality. In: 2019 IEEE international conference on industrial cyber physical systems (ICPS). IEEE
47. Ashmore J et al (2019) A free virtual reality experience to prepare pediatric patients for magnetic resonance imaging: cross-sectional questionnaire study. JMIR Pediatr Parent 2(1):e11684
48. Kahlon S et al (2019) Virtual reality exposure therapy for adolescents with fear of public speaking: a non-randomized feasibility and pilot study. Child Adolesc Psychiatr Mental Health 13(1):1–10
49. Verhoef RE et al (2022) Detecting social information processing profiles of boys with aggressive behavior problems: an interactive virtual reality approach. Dev Psychopathol, 1–13
50. Falconer CJ et al (2019) Innovations in practice: avatar-based virtual reality in CAMHS talking therapy: two exploratory case studies. Child Adolesc Ment Health 24(3):283–287
51. Maskey M et al (2014) Reducing specific phobia/fear in young people with autism spectrum disorders (ASDs) through a virtual reality environment intervention. PLoS One 9(7):e100374
52. Levac D et al (2018) Active video gaming for children with cerebral palsy: does a clinic-based virtual reality component offer an additive benefit? A pilot study. Phys Occup Therapy Pediatr 38(1):74–87
53. Thng JZH et al (2022) Combination of teddy bear hospital and virtual reality training increases empathy of medical students. Asia Pacific Scholar 7(3):33
54. Ahmadpour N et al (2020) Synthesizing multiple stakeholder perspectives on using virtual reality to improve the periprocedural experience in children and adolescents: survey study. J Med Internet Res 22(7):e19752
55. Chen C-H, Lee I-J, Lin L-Y (2016) Augmented reality-based video-modeling storybook of nonverbal facial cues for children with autism spectrum disorder to improve their perceptions and judgments of facial expressions and emotions. Comput Hum Behav 55:477–485
56. da Silva CA, Fernandes AR, Grohmann AP (2014) STAR: speech therapy with augmented reality for children with autism spectrum disorders. In: Enterprise information systems: 16th international conference, ICEIS 2014, Lisbon, Portugal, 27–30 April 2014, Revised selected papers 16. Springer
57. Chuah JH et al (2013) Applying mixed reality to simulate vulnerable populations for practicing clinical communication skills. IEEE Trans Vis Comput Graph 19(4):539–546
58. Paterick TE et al (2017) Improving health outcomes through patient education and partnerships with patients. Proc (Bayl Univ Med Cent) 30(1):112–113
59. Hinds PS et al (2005) End-of-life care preferences of pediatric patients with cancer. J Clin Oncol 23(36):9146–9154
60. Kwame A, Petrucka PM (2021) A literature-based study of patient-centered care and communication in nurse-patient interactions: barriers, facilitators, and the way forward. BMC Nurs 20(1):158
61. Moudatsou M et al (2020) The role of empathy in health and social care professionals. Healthcare (Basel) 8(1)
62. Goodridge D et al (2018) Structured approaches to promote patient and family engagement in treatment in acute care hospital settings: protocol for a systematic scoping review. Syst Rev 7(1):35
63. Cranwell K et al (2017) Improving care planning and coordination for service users with medical co-morbidity transitioning between tertiary medical and primary care services. J Psychiatr Ment Health Nurs 24(6):337–347
64. Morley L, Cashell A (2017) Collaboration in health care. J Med Imaging Radiation Sci 48(2):207–216
65. Chang S-L et al (2021) Virtual reality-based preprocedural education increases preparedness and satisfaction of patients about the catheter ablation of atrial fibrillation. J Chin Med Assoc 84(7):690–697
66. Assed MM et al (2020) Facial emotion recognition in maltreated children: a systematic review. J Child Fam Stud 29:1493–1509

67. Lee SAS (2019) Virtual speech-language therapy for individuals with communication disorders: current evidence, limitations, and benefits. Curr Dev Disord Rep 6:119–125

Safa Elkefi obtained a Ph.D. in Engineering Management with research in Human factors from Stevens Institute of Technology in 2023 and a master's degree from the National Engineering School of Tunisia in 2019. He is now a project director at Columbia University and an Adjunct Professor at Stevens.

Noureddine Lourimi is pursuing studies in industrial engineering with a specialization in data science at the National School of Engineers of Tunis (EN IT) alongside his studies in AI and signal processing at the University of the City of Paris and at ENIT. His research focuses on human–computer interaction and extended reality technologies.

30 Digital Transformation in Public Healthcare Organizations: A Case Study

Bilel Ben Arbia and Safa Bhar Layeb

Abstract

This work investigates the complex dynamics of digitally transforming complex public healthcare organizations. It focuses on the interaction between people, processes, and systems as it relates to the digital transformation of a procurement department in a Middle Eastern public healthcare institution. Based on more than fifty interviews with stakeholders—including end users and procurement staff—as well as an examination of corporate records and procurement procedures, the study emphasizes the negative consequences of introducing digital systems without first updating operational procedures and organizational frameworks. Significant differences between the new digital system and the current processes are found in the findings, which result in inefficiencies, a rise in mistakes, and a decline in staff morale. The study emphasizes the value of a comprehensive strategy for digital transformation that synchronizes people, technology, and processes. It also highlights the necessity of change management techniques and strategic integration. This case study contributes to change management theory by demonstrating the limitations of a technology-centric approach and highlights the necessity of considering the three pillars of transformation for successful digital initiatives.

Keywords

Health • Digitalization • Procurement • System • Middle East

B. B. Arbia
Tunis Business School, Tunis, Tunisia
e-mail: bbabilelbenarbia@gmail.com

S. B. Layeb (✉)
LR-OASIS, National Engineering School of Tunis, University of Tunis El Manar, Tunis, Tunisia
e-mail: safa.layeb@enit.utm.tn

F. Jawab (ed.), *Hospital Supply Chain*, Integrated Science 27,
https://doi.org/10.1007/978-3-031-70292-1_30

1 Introduction

In today's rapidly evolving technological landscape, the concept of digital transformation has emerged as a pivotal force that reshapes industries, organizations, and the very fabric of how business is conducted [15]. Digital transformation stands as a critical imperative in the modern business landscape, representing the fundamental rethinking of how organizations operate and deliver value in the digital age. As technology becomes increasingly integrated into all aspects of society, businesses must adapt to this new reality to remain competitive and relevant. The significance of digital transformation lies in its capacity to enhance operational efficiency, foster innovation, elevate customer experiences, and enable organizations to seize new opportunities in a rapidly evolving marketplace [4]. By embracing digital transformation, businesses not only optimize their processes and strategies but also position themselves to navigate the ever-changing technological landscape, ultimately securing their place at the forefront of their industries [3].

Within this context, the role of digital transformation is transforming not only technology but also the people, organization, and processes. Digital transformation is more than just the integration of technology; it represents a profound shift in how organizations operate, interact, and create value [12]. As companies embark on the journey of digital transformation, they are confronted with multifaceted challenges that extend beyond the realm of technology itself. One of the most critical dimensions of this transformation lies in the need to effectively address the human and organizational aspects that underpin success.

The transformation of individuals involves cultivating adaptability and continuous learning, enabling employees to navigate a technologically dynamic landscape [2]. Fostering a collaborative mind set for cross-functional cooperation and knowledge sharing is essential to maximize digitalization's advantages. Simultaneously, organizations must realign themselves with the digital era by shifting from traditional hierarchies to agile frameworks. This transition facilitates swift decision-making, streamlined communication, and the flexibility to respond to real-time market changes, departing from rigid annual planning.

Moreover, the most intricate aspect of digital transformation involves the reimagining of processes. Organizations must critically assess existing workflows, discard outdated practices, and design agile processes that leverage the capabilities of digital technologies [5]. This entails a holistic view of the end-user journey, where processes are optimized to deliver seamless experiences across both digital and physical touchpoints.

This study examines the complex dynamics involved in the digital transformation of the procurement department of a public health care organization in the Middle East. It sheds light on the critical interactions between people, processes, and systems during this transformative effort through the analysis of a real-world case study. It also highlights negative consequences associated with updating digital systems without simultaneous operational and organizational modernization. To ensure the success of such transformations, these findings underscore the importance of synchronizing the interaction between people, processes, and systems.

The studied case is structured based on over 50 interviews with key stakeholders, including procurement staff in multiple locations and end-users to know how satisfied they are with the transformation. These interviews provided insights into the perceptions, challenges, and expectations associated with digital transformation. Corporate documents are also collected to reinforce the case. Furthermore, the study involved mapping and analyzing the procurement processes before and after the transformation, allowing for a comprehensive understanding of how the organization adapted to align between the new digital system and the operational workflows. The analysis highlighted significant discrepancies between the newly implemented digital system and the existing operational processes. The lack of synchrony between technology, processes, and the workforce led to inefficiencies, increased errors, and a notable decline in employee morale. The study revealed that successful digital transformation requires more than technological adoption, it necessitates a strategic integration of people, processes, and systems to realize its potential benefits fully. The findings highlight the significance of change management strategies that encompass process realignment and employee engagement, and people organization redesign during digital transformations. The case study not only contributes to change management theory by providing empirical evidence of the limitations of a technology-centric approach but also emphasizes the necessity of embracing a holistic perspective that accounts for the intricate connections between technology, processes, and human factors.

The rest of the chapter is structured as follows. Section 2 reviews the background and the context of this work. Section 3 presents the case study. Section 4 discusses the results. The limitations and implications of the conducted work are presented in Sects. 5 and 6 respectively. Finally, Sect. 7 provides conclusions and avenues for future work.

2 Background

The operating model concept, which consists of people, processes, and systems, is essential for understanding the dynamics of an organization and the impact of changes. This framework, introduced by Levitt [9], analyzes the interaction between these three components and how alterations in one area can affect the others. Indeed, the operating model developed by Levitt [9] highlights the importance of considering people, processes, and systems as interconnected components of an organization. This perspective is crucial for successfully managing change, especially in digital transformation, where new technology integration must be accompanied by corresponding updates to processes and people [10]. Literature further shows that neglecting any of these components can lead to transformation failures, while a holistic approach that includes technological, organizational, and human factors is essential for success [6].

Figure 1 presented the operating model of Levitt [9] which proposes that the efficiency of an organization is reliant on the harmonization and integration of its people, processes, and systems. 'People' refers to the workforce and their

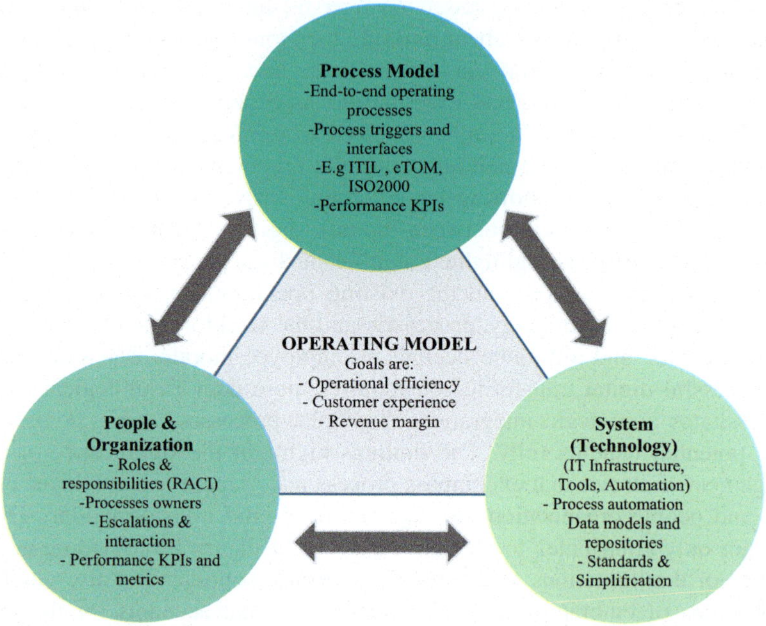

Fig. 1 Digital strategy framework: target operating model

skills, attitudes, and behaviors. 'Processes' are the methods and procedures used to carry out work, while 'Systems' denote the technological tools and infrastructure supporting the organization's activities.

During digital transformation, merely updating the system without simultaneously modifying processes and addressing the workforce's needs can lead to less-than-ideal results [11]. If the processes are not restructured to utilize the new technology or if the workforce is not properly trained to work with the updated system, the full potential benefits of the system may not be realized.

The necessity for a comprehensive approach to change is also supported by change management literature. Kotter [8] stresses the importance of a complete strategy that encompasses creating and communicating a vision for change and empowering employees to adopt the change. Moreover, the socio-technical systems theory, which looks at the interplay between people, technology, and organizational structures, emphasizes the need for a balanced approach to change due to the interdependence of these elements [13].

The failure to balance people, processes, and systems can result in unsuccessful transformation efforts. Besson and Rowe [1] note that mismatches between technology and organizational processes can lead to new systems being underutilized and resistance to change. Hammer [7] suggests that reengineering efforts often fail because they overlook the human aspect, resulting in employee dissatisfaction and a lack of buy-in.

Digital transformation involves more than technological upgrades; it requires a comprehensive shift in organizational culture, processes, and employee capabilities. Westerman et al. [15] point out that successful digital transformation entails rethinking business models, engaging with customers in new ways, and empowering employees with digital tools and skills. Vial [14] emphasizes that digital transformation is not just a technological challenge but also a strategic and organizational one, necessitating changes in leadership, culture, and capabilities.

In this line of research, this study highlights the importance of considering the three pillars of transformation to achieve successful outcomes in digital initiatives. The case study empirically demonstrates the limitations of a technology-focused approach and emphasizes the need for a comprehensive perspective that considers the complex interaction between technology, process, and human elements.

3 The Case Study

This study was conducted within a public health institution that governs more than 100 healthcare facilities in a country within the MENA region, where new IT systems were implemented to facilitate and optimize the procurement operation for hospitals associated with the public health institution. Figure 2 schematizes the structure of this Public healthcare organization.

Figure 2 shows that the public healthcare organization is structured on 5 levels:

Level 1: The Ministry of Health

The role of the ministry is governance over the delivery of health care. It formulates and implements health policies, regulates and ensures compliance with health standards, and plans and develops health infrastructure. It is also responsible for managing emergency preparedness and responses.

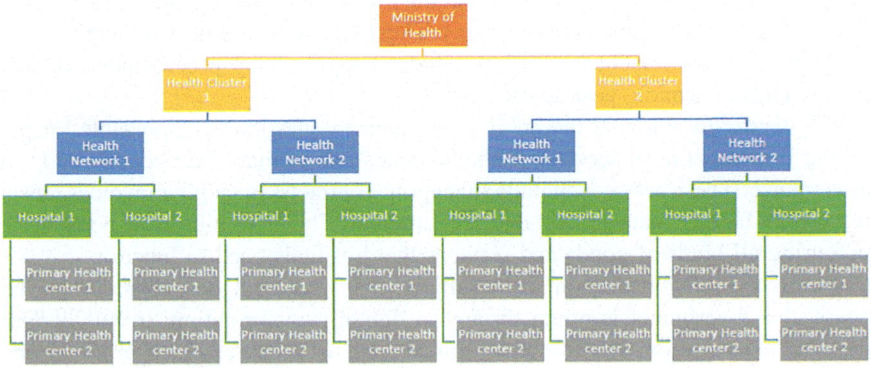

Fig. 2 Structure of the healthcare organization

Level 2: Health Clusters

Health clusters are designed to improve the efficiency and effectiveness of healthcare delivery by bringing together different healthcare providers under one administrative structure. This allows for better coordination of care, improved access to services, and increased efficiency in coordination between multiple hospitals and better use of resources. Health clusters govern the non-medical services in hospitals: Procurement, supply chain, facility management, etc.

They aim to Improve access to care, increased efficiency, enhanced collaboration, improved quality of care, while reducing costs. Health clusters don't directly provide medical services. They are limited to non-clinical services.

Level 3: Health Networks

Health networks were existing before the introduction of clusters. They are like clusters, but on a smaller scale. They are usually based in the largest hospital in the region. They provide facility management, supply chain, finance, and even procurement services to nearby hospitals. Their ultimate goal is coordinating between the different healthcare providers in their region to optimize the use of resources.

Level 4: Hospitals

Hospitals are the main healthcare providers. They do also have some non-medical aspects like procurement and facility management, but these functions are delivered under the governance of the health cluster. Hospitals also manage the non-clinical functions in Primary Health Centers attached to them.

Level 5: Primary Healthcare Centers

Primary Healthcare centers, also known as PHCs, provide only basic medical services. They work during day hours and have doctors who are available for simple checkups. All urgent or complex medical operations are provided uniquely by hospitals. PHCs are numerous and their purpose is making health services more accessible to neighborhoods without having to go to faraway hospitals. PHCs don't have any form of non-medical functions. These functions are fully managed by the hospitals they are attached to. This includes supply chain, procurement, finance, maintenance, cleaning, pest control, etc.

It's worthy to note that the public institution in question is responsible for providing the non-clinical services to the hospitals and primary care centers under its governance. These services include managing contracts, managing invoices, ensuring proper facility management and procurement. The institution is responsible for procuring all kinds of goods and services that hospitals need to function.

Being a public institution, it is subject to government decisions. In the last years, the government is going through a digital transformation. In this context, the health institution was forced to transfer all its procurement operations on 2 new systems introduced by the government. This was marketed as a huge digital transformation.

In this study, we will compare the mechanisms of the company on the three axes of the operating model. Toward this end, we have begun by collecting the data via document collection and interviews, then proceeded with an analysis of the data, and finally derived conclusions about the provided services before and after the transformation. It is worthy to note that for the data analysis, only qualitative data analysis methods are used; to analyze non-numerical data. Both content and narrative analysis were applied to analyze documents and interviews to map the processes in the studied case. Processes were assessed as well by analyzing the systems used in each step and the necessity of each step to identify the impact of implementing IT systems on the whole procurement operation and whether other changes are required to optimize procurement. The data analysis part of the case study will focus on analyzing the impact of the change in system on the operating model of the health cluster. Thus, the analysis will focus on processes, people, and systems.

3.1 Data Collection

Data collection for the case took around two months of work on the site of the health cluster. It was mainly through interviews and document collection. Indeed, the data collection for this study aims to understand how the procurement operations work in the health cluster, what systems are used, and how the organization is structured after the implementation of the digital transformation initiated by the government. This type of data is needed to assess the processes and the overall functioning of the procurement stream in the health cluster. The data collection was conducted in two phases: document collection and interviews.

Document collection

In the first phase, the following corporate documents of the procurement team were collected: They include their policies and procedures, organization chart, job descriptions, guides of the system used, forms and templates that are filled in different parts of the procurement process, and data about the number, qualifications, and positions of all employees. Table 1 details the purpose behind each collected document type.

Interviews

In the second phase, interviews were held with most of the stakeholders of procurement: Procurement Chief, Bids and contracts director, Direct Purchasing director, guarantees manager, tenders manager, contracts manager, some employees in the headquarters, procurement directors in the hospitals, some end users in hospitals. The discussions aimed to understand the structure of the procurement organization, and how procurement operations work. Table 2 reports Interviewed stakeholders and purpose of each interview.

Table 1 Details on the collected documents

Documents	Purpose
Policies and procedures	Understand the procurement processes
Organisation chart	Understand the structure of the procurement Team
Job descriptions	Understand what every employee has
Guides of systems used	Understand what systems are used and towards what purpose
Forms and templates (used in procurement operations)	Further understand the procurement process steps and the approvals needed to pass from one step to another
Employees information	Get to know the number of employees, their positions and geographical distribution, and their qualifications

Table 2 Details on the conducted interviews

Interview	Purpose
Procurement chief	Understand the role of procurement in the health cluster and get his point of view on potential issues
Bids and contracts director	Understand how the bids and contracts are managed
Direct Purchasing director	Understand what direct purchases are and how they are managed
Guarantees manager	Understand what guarantees are and how they are managed
Tenders manager	Understand how tenders are managed
Contracts manager	Understand how contracts are negotiated and managed
Employees in the headquarters	Understand what their role is in the procurement operation
Procurement directors in the hospitals	Get to know what their role is and what they are doing
End users in hospitals	Identify pain points and get to know how they perceive the digital transformation

3.2 Process: What Is the Process Adopted for Procurement?

Procurement is organized through 2 main routes: Direct Purchases (for items with value < 100 K SAR) and Tendering (for items > 100 K SAR). As the digital transformation has impacted the two processes in the exact same way, we will limit the case to the first process: Direct purchases. Table 3 details all steps, stakeholders and activities both before and after the transformation process.

Figure 3 illustrates a global visualization of this process. We can notice that the direct purchases process includes 8 stakeholders and 10 approval points. It usually takes 2 to 6 months to finish. The durations vary based on the good or service to

Table 3 Direct purchases process

Sub-process	#	Before the transformation		After the transformation	
		Activities	Responsible	Activities	Responsible
Direct purchase RFP (request for proposal) preparation and signature	1	Fill direct purchase request form + direct purchase order justification	End user	Fill direct purchase request form + direct purchase order justification	End user
	2	Approval of the purchase request form	Executive management in the facility	Approval of the purchase request form	Executive management in the facility
	3	Approval of the purchase request form	Technical department	Approval of the purchase request form	Technical Department
Initial budget reservation	4	Approval of the purchase request form	Procurement head	Create purchase requisition in the system	End user
	5	Initial budget reservation	Finance (budget)	Approval of the initial reservation request	Executive management in the facility
	6			Approval of the initial reservation request	Technical department
	7			Approval of the initial reservation request	Procurement head
	8			Approval of the initial reservation request	Finance (budget)
	9			Send the Purchase Request and all related documents to Procurement department	End user
Offers selection	10	Bid opening	Procurement team	Submit the application on the Finance ministry's IT system platform	Procurement team

(continued)

Table 3 (continued)

Sub-process	#	Before the transformation		After the transformation	
		Activities	Responsible	Activities	Responsible
	11	Receive offers after bid opening	Technical committee	Bid opening	Procurement team
	12	Choose the lowest price or provide justification	Technical committee	Receive offers after bid opening	Technical committee
	13			Choose the lowest price or provide justification	Technical committee
Final reservation	14	Final budget reservation request	Procurement team	Raise final reservation request in Health ministry's IT system	Procurement team
	15	Approval of the final reservation	Procurement head	Approval of the final reservation	Procurement head
	16	Approval of the final reservation	Finance (budget)	Approval of the final reservation	Finance (budget)
Contract finalization	17	Create a purchase order and send to authorized person for approval	Procurement team	Print and send purchase order to authorized person	Procurement team
	18	Approve purchase order	Procurement head	Approve purchase order	Procurement head
	19	Approve Purchase Order	Chief Financial Officer or Chief Executive Officer	Approve purchase order	Chief financial officer or chief executive officer
	20	Return paperwork to requesting entity for delivery	Procurement Team	Register transaction in the finance ministry's IT system	Procurement Team

(continued)

Table 3 (continued)

Sub-process	#	Before the transformation		After the transformation	
		Activities	Responsible	Activities	Responsible
	21			Obtain reference number	Procurement team
	22			Return paperwork to requesting entity for delivery	Procurement team
Contractor follow-up	23	Follow up on delivery	End user	Follow up on delivery	End user

be procured. However, based on the interviews, on average, the process is taking 2 weeks longer than before the transformation.

The introduction of a new IT system is supposed to streamline procurement processes and eliminate the time of reviewing that paperwork is complete before each approval and the time of collecting and transporting paper from one location to another to continue the transaction. However, what happened on the ground is that the procurement cycle is taking a longer time today because the same old processes are still being applied today with all the paperwork included. What makes the situation even worse is that 6 new steps of uploading documents and redoing approvals on the system are added to direct purchases process to comply with the requirements of the new finance ministry's IT system.

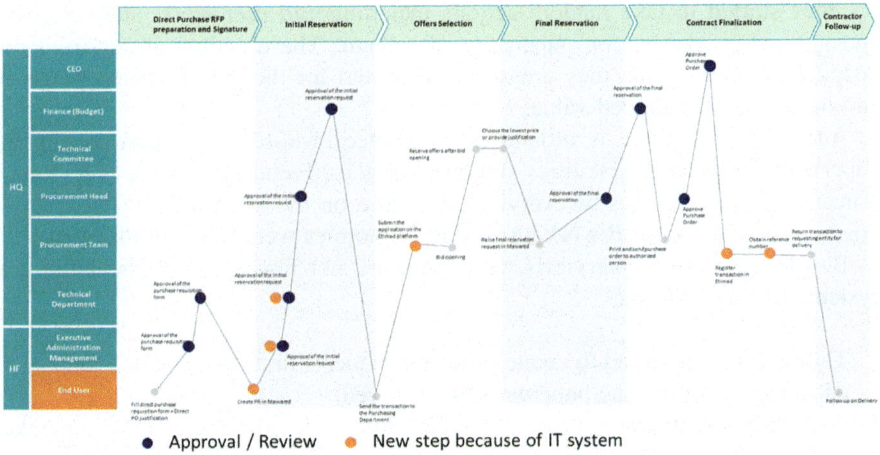

Fig. 3 Process: direct purchases

We conclude that the current result of applying an IT system under the title "Digital Transformation" is clearly making procurement less efficient. The only added value of the new systems in their current application are having all transactions archived and visible to both the ministry of finance and ministry of health in real time. But, in terms of lead times, the institution was better off before the implementation of the new IT systems.

3.3 People: What Are the Roles of Procurement Employees?

The health institution has around 70 procurement employees distributed between its main headquarters and the healthcare facilities associated with it. Table 4 compares their roles before and after the digital transformation.

Table 4 shows that the implementation of the new IT systems caused a big change in the roles and responsibilities of procurement employees, mainly employees in facilities. In finance ministry's IT system, all approvals are required to be on the system, even paper requests are required to be scanned and uploaded on the system. The vision is to minimize paperwork and to have all transactions centralized on the same system. As a result, lead times would be optimized by removing all double work and double approvals.

However, as the governance was poor, process did not officially change, and physical copies of all transactions are still needed to be archived, employees in facilities were in a situation where they only authority they have on the system is to view purchase requests initiated by end users on the system and take no action, but their work are still required to take some actions by their higher management. So, they started to take random actions including end user work, and reviewing and approving requests on paper, out of system. These actions differ from one hospital to another, but, they are all not essential for the procurement operations and have almost no added value.

Added to that, there is around 20 employees whose job is transporting the paperwork between the facilities and headquarters. Technically, there is no longer a need for their services as everything became on the system. But, due to poor governance, they are still working and no economies were made in this area.

Besides, based on interviews, end users are not happy either about the new systems for two reasons:

- They are now required to create purchase requests first on paper and then again on the system once the paperwork is approved.
- The whole procurement process is taking longer than before and the items they are requesting to buy are taking longer to be purchased and delivered.

Table 4 Roles and responsibilities before/after the digital transformation

	Before the transformation	After the transformation
Roles of employees in the facilities	• Review purchase requests • Approve purchase requests • Fill the needed paperwork • Send the papers physically to HQ • Call employees at HQ to ask about progress and update the end user about progress • Plan and control the purchases of the hospital internally • Get the approval of hospital coo to proceed with the purchase • Communicate with Finance department in the hospital to manage payments • Do all procurement work independently when amounts are small (< 30 K SAR)	• Fill the needed paperwork • Send the papers physically to headquarters • Call employees at Headquarters to ask about progress and update the end user about progress • Review purchase requests
Roles of employees in the headquarters	• Process tenders and direct purchases • Communicate with vendors • Do technical and financial evaluations • Manage dispute resolution with vendors • Manage financial guarantees • Prepare procurement plan • Communicate with finance team to manage payment • Develop procurement strategies • Create agreements with vendors	• Process tenders and direct purchases • Approve Purchase requests • Process tenders and direct purchases (including purchases under 30 K SAR) • Communicate with vendors • Do technical and financial evaluations • Manage dispute resolution with vendors • Manage financial guarantees • Prepare procurement plan • Communicate with finance team to manage payment • Develop procurement strategies • Create agreements with vendors

3.4 System: What Systems Are Used to Deliver Procurement Services in This Institution?

Before the transformation, only 1 IT system was used in the context of procurement. It was introduced by the ministry of health more than 10 years ago and it is used to scan, send, and archive official paperwork. All procurement related transactions are managed using paperwork.

After the transformation, the health institution is using 3 IT systems in its procurement operations:

- The first system is the already existing one used to scan, send, and archive official paperwork.
- The second is introduced by the ministry of health in the context of this transformation. It is used to manage the procurement requests and approvals. Example: end users need to raise a purchase request on this system and related approvals should be managed on this system.
- The third system is introduced by the ministry of Finance in the context of this transformation. It is used to manage the budget, reserve budget for transactions, and manage payments vendor payments.

The ministry of health and the ministry of finance have forced the health institution to adopt their new systems and make a fast transition. The request was to have all the steps of the procurement process on the systems. Figure 4 shows the consequences because the organization was not ready.

Figure 4 illustrates that 13% of the steps in the direct purchasing process are fully out of IT systems and 60% of steps in the direct purchasing process are duplicated. Done out of system and then uploaded to system.

Both IT systems are capable of accommodating all the procurement steps. But, this didn't result in a smooth transition from full paperwork to full automation. What happened is that some steps are done fully out of system, some other ones are done in duplication, first on paper and then again on the system. This is very

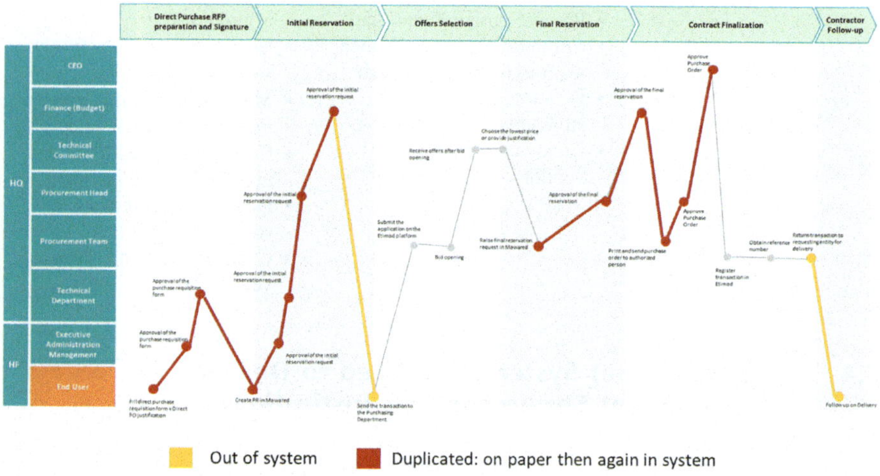

Fig. 4 Systems used in direct purchasing process

clear for example in the first steps of direct purchases: we have one request and then 2 approvals on paper and then the same request and the same two approvals on the system.

We can conclude that having the perfect system didn't automatically result in a perfect digital transformation. In this case, the system caused a parallel process: The procurement process goes as is, and each step has to be reported on the system after it is finished on paper, which is not the purpose of having this IT system.

4 Discussion

In the scope of the country's digital transformation, the public health institution subject of this case was forced to switch to new IT systems developed by the government in very short time lapse. This institution was not ready for the huge transformation and the yielding results were as follows:

- Procurement processes did not change to adapt to the transformation. What happened is having the paper process as is, plus uploading the files and redoing the approvals on the system. Having two processes running in parallel resulted in a lower efficiency and longer process times.
- The procurement organization did not change to adapt for the transformation. Positions such as "administrative communication" who deliver the paperwork from hospitals to the headquarters of this institution, and procurement employees in the hospitals whose job is to manage the paperwork and make sure that all purchase requests papers are complete are no longer needed, but they are still in their roles after 4 years of the transformation. They are still doing their old tasks even though they are no longer necessary for the procurement process. This results in having lost efficiency and higher payrolls that could have been dedicated to more strategic roles.
- The new systems are not fully implemented. Multiple functionalities that are new such as data analysis, reporting, or strategic sourcing modules are available in the system but not used because in the old procurement processes they were not existing. In parallel, some reports are still being done manually using excel. The procurement team did not receive trainings on how to use advanced modules in the systems. Thus, they are still using some ad-hoc third-party systems or excels filled manually to prepare reports, track performances, etc. while these functions are already available for less effort and better quality in the new IT systems.

This study sheds light on the negative impacts of changing a system within an organization without simultaneously updating its processes and addressing the needs of its people, underscoring the importance of a holistic digital transformation that encompasses people, processes, and the operational model. However, its generalizability is limited by its focus on one single organization whose exact identity is not revealed for confidentiality. The unique characteristics of each organization, such as size, industry, location, and culture, can significantly influence the outcomes of system changes. Additionally, the case study's specific context may not capture the complexities of system changes in other organizations, which may employ different change management strategies and have varying levels of technology adoption and process maturity. The study's timeframe may also not provide a comprehensive understanding of the long-term effects of the system change. Thus, it is crucial to note that digital transformations that solely focus on system transformation without considering people and processes have often failed. This can result in some organizations reverting to paper-based operations in order to regain efficiency.

5 Limitations

While the findings of this study provide valuable insights into the negative impacts of changing a system within an organization without simultaneously updating its processes and addressing the needs of its people and as a result proves that a digital transformation should include the transformation of people organization and the transformation of the processes to cover the whole operational model and have a positive impact on the organization, it is important to acknowledge certain limitations that could impact the generalizability of the results.

The primary limitation lies in the scope of the study, which focused solely on one organization which is the health cluster in Saudi Arabia. As such, the findings may not be fully representative of the diverse range of organizational structures, cultures, and industries that exist across the business landscape. Each organization is unique, and factors such as organization size, industry type, geographical location, and organizational culture can significantly influence the outcomes of a system change. Therefore, while the negative impacts observed in this study provide valuable insights, caution should be exercised when attempting to generalize these results to all organizations.

Furthermore, the case study's context and the specific circumstances of the organization studied may not fully capture the complexities that arise during system changes in other organizations. Different organizations may employ various change management strategies, training programs, and communication approaches that could mitigate some of the negative impacts observed in this study. Additionally, variations in the level of technology adoption, employee engagement, and process maturity across different organizations can influence the extent to which system changes impact operations and morale.

It is also important to note that the timeframe within which the study was conducted might not allow for a comprehensive understanding of the long-term effects of the system change. The immediate negative impacts observed in the aftermath of the change may evolve over time as the organization adapts and refines its processes and employee training strategies.

6 Implications

The case study examining the negative impacts of changing a system within an organization without concurrently updating its processes and people has significant implications for both theoretical understanding and practical application in the realm of organizational change management. Additionally, it suggests avenues for future research that could further enhance our understanding of this complex interplay.

The findings of this case study contribute to the existing body of knowledge on change management theory by highlighting the crucial interdependence of people, processes, and systems during periods of transformation. The case underscores the limitations of a technology-centric approach, emphasizing the need to consider the broader organizational ecosystem. This underscores the significance of a holistic approach that accounts for the alignment and synchronization of these three key pillars. The study's findings challenge traditional linear models of change and underscore the importance of incorporating organizational culture, employee engagement, and process adaptation into change management theories. This case provides empirical evidence that supports a more integrated and multidimensional perspective on organizational change.

For practitioners and organizational leaders, this case study underscores the imperative of comprehensive change management strategies during system upgrades. The study underscores the necessity of aligning processes with technology, providing adequate training to employees, and fostering a culture of openness and engagement. The findings emphasize that the success of system changes hinges on clear communication, proper training, and a nuanced understanding of the potential impacts on the workforce. By adopting a holistic change management approach that includes process reengineering, employee involvement, and effective communication, organizations can minimize disruptions, mitigate resistance, and foster a smoother transition to new technologies.

Finally, this case study opens avenues for future research that can delve deeper into the intricate dynamics of system changes and their implications for organizations. Potential research directions include:

- Comparative Analysis: Conducting comparative studies across multiple organizations and industries to identify commonalities and differences in the impacts of system changes, thereby enriching our understanding of the nuances associated with different contexts.
- Long-Term Effects: Examining the long-term effects of system changes on organizational performance, culture, and employee satisfaction, taking into account the adjustments and adaptations that occur over time.
- Change Management Strategies: Investigating the effectiveness of various change management strategies in mitigating negative impacts during system changes, particularly focusing on best practices that integrate people, processes, and systems.

- Human-Centric Technology Integration: Exploring innovative methods for integrating new technology into organizational ecosystems that prioritize employee readiness, engagement, and learning, ultimately enhancing technology adoption.
- Cultural Considerations: Analyzing the influence of organizational culture on the success of system changes, and identifying strategies to ensure that cultural values align with technological advancements.

By delving into these areas, future research can provide more comprehensive insights, inform evidence-based practices, and contribute to the development of a more holistic understanding of organizational change management in the face of evolving technologies and processes.

7 Conclusion

This work explores the complex dynamics involved in transforming healthcare organization. The case study conducted within the MENA region highlights the critical interplay between individuals, processes, and systems during this transformative process. Precisely, the studied case is about the implementation of a new IT system for procurement in a health public institution in the MENA region. The new system was forced by the ministry of Health and the ministry of Finance in a short period of time. Thus, this institution didn't change any of its processes or people organization to adapt to the new system and this had negative impacts on all the aspects of the organization. The data presented in this case is real data collected from on multiple company documents including policies, procedures, Job descriptions, HR data, and system user guides. Interviews were also conducted with all procurement employees in this institution and in the health care facilities to understand how they conduct their work before and after the digital transformation and with end users to know about their satisfaction of the provided services before and after the transformation.

The case study demonstrates the detrimental consequences of changing a system within an organization without considering the intricate interplay between people, processes, and systems. Neglecting to update processes and provide appropriate training to the workforce during a system change can lead to disruptions in operations, employee resistance, and decreased morale. These factors can, in turn, result in inaccuracies, inefficiencies, and end-user dissatisfaction, ultimately impacting the organization's reputation. The case underscores the importance of a holistic approach to change management, where all three pillars of the operating model are harmoniously updated and aligned to ensure a smooth transition and sustainable success. This illustrates clearly that an impactful digital transformation can never be limited to a transformation of systems, but should also include a transformation of people and processes to align with the new system.

The conducted study highlights the importance of a holistic approach in organizational change management, emphasizing the interdependence of people, processes, and systems as three important pillars and success factors of a digital transformation. It challenges traditional linear models and advocates for integrating organizational culture, employee engagement, and process adaptation into change theories. For practitioners, it underscores the need for comprehensive strategies that align processes with technology, provide proper training, and foster open communication for successful system upgrades. The study also opens avenues for future research avenues, such as comparative analysis, long-term effects, effectiveness of change management strategies, human-centric technology integration, and cultural considerations, to deepen our understanding of system changes and their organizational implications.

Acknowledgements The authors extend their sincere gratitude to Mr. Helmi Ismail, a digital health expert with extensive experience spanning various sectors including healthcare and telecommunications, for his invaluable insights.

References

1. Besson P, Rowe F (2012) Strategizing information systems-enabled organizational transformation: A transdisciplinary review and new directions. J Strat Inf Syst 21(2):103–124
2. Boneva M (2018) Challenges related to the digital transformation of business companies. In: Innovation management, entrepreneurship and sustainability (IMES 2018). Vysoká škola ekonomická v Praze, pp 101–114
3. da Silva JB, Espinal M, Garcia-Saiso S, Fitzgerald J, Marti M, Bascolo E, Haddad AE, D'Agostino M (2024) A digital transformation for primary health care. Bull World Health Organ 102(1):2
4. Demirkan H, Spohrer JC, Welser JJ (2016) Digital innovation and strategic transformation. It Professional 18(6):14–18
5. Favoretto C, Mendes GHDS, Filho MG, Gouvea de Oliveira M, Ganga GMD (2022) Digital transformation of business model in manufacturing companies: challenges and research agenda. J Bus Ind Mark 37(4):748–767
6. Gillani F, Chatha KA, Jajja SS, Cao D, Ma X (2024) Unpacking digital transformation: identifying key enablers, transition stages and digital archetypes. Technol Forecast Soc Chang 203:123335
7. Hammer M (1990) Reengineering work: don't automate, obliterate. Harv Bus Rev 68(4):104–112
8. Kotter JP (1996) Leading change. Harvard Business School Press
9. Levitt T (1965) Exploit the product life cycle. Harv Bus Rev 43(6):81–94
10. Onesi-Ozigagun O, Ololade YJ, Eyo-Udo NL, Ogundipe DO (2024) Leading digital transformation in non-digital sectors: a strategic review. Int J Manage Entrepreneur Res 6(4):1157–1175
11. Rogers DL (2016) The digital transformation playbook: rethink your business for the digital age. Columbia University Press
12. Schwertner K (2017) Digital transformation of business. Trakia J Sci 15(1):388–393
13. Trist EL, Bamforth KW (1951) Some social and psychological consequences of the longwall method of coal-getting. Human Relations 4(1):3–38
14. Vial G (2019) Understanding digital transformation: a review and a research agenda. J Strateg Inf Syst 28(2):118–144
15. Westerman G, Bonnet D, McAfee A (2014) Leading digital: turning technology into business transformation. Harvard Business Review Press

Bilel Ben Arbia is currently a senior management consultant working on transformation projects in multiple industries in Saudi Arabia. Bilel holds a research Master's degree in Business Analytics. He is an active member of the scientific research community at Tunis Business School. He presented his past work on digital transformation in the International Conference on Optimization and Data Science in Industrial Engineering that took place in Turkey in 2023. His consulting and research interests include operational excellence, strategy and performance management, and the impact of technology on the business landscape.

Safa Bhar Layeb is currently a professor of industrial engineering and an active member of the OASIS Laboratory at the National Engineering School of Tunis, Tunisia. Safa holds a Polytechnic Engineering degree, a Master's degree in Mathematical Engineering, a Ph.D. in Applied Mathematics, and a university habilitation (HDR) in Industrial Engineering. She is the founding chair of the African Working Group in Health Systems and a member of the Executive Committee of the African Federation of Operations Research Societies (AFROS). She has served as guest editor and reviewer for over twenty international journals. She is an active member of the editorial, organizing, and scientific committees of several international conferences. She has supervised over thirty Master and Ph.D. theses in collaboration with several international institutes. Her teaching and research interests include Operations research, optimization, and data science approaches and their applications in healthcare organizations, industrial engineering, logistics, and supply chain management.

Author Index

A

Aissaoui, Najla, 267
Alexandra, Claudia, 75, 117
Alvina, Grace, 75, 117
Arbia, Bilel Ben, 643
Arif, Jabir, 313, 587

B

Beaulieu, Martin, 3, 99, 185, 511
Bélanger, Valérie, 511
Benghabrit, Asmaa, 245, 485
Bentahar, Omar, 3
Benzidia, Smail, 3
Bouhaddou, Imane, 245, 485

C

Chabchoub, Habib, 395
Chtioui, Ahmed, 245, 485
Cousineau, Martin, 511

D

Dasaklis, Thomas K., 533
de Souza Gomes dos Santos, Ana Carla, 205

E

El Asri, Amine, 461
Elkefi, Safa, 359, 571, 619
El Mhamedi, Abderrahman, 337, 439

F

Frichi, Youness, 413

G

Guezzen, Amine Hakim, 47

H

Hachemi, Khalid, 439
Hadinata, Valencia, 75, 117

I

Ibn El Farouk, Imane, 285, 461

J

Jaouhari, Asmae El, 587
Jawab, Fouad, 285, 379, 413, 461, 587
Jedliński, Mariusz, 161
Jlassi, Jihene, 337, 395

K

Kaabar, Mohamed Yassine, 267
Kudrenko, Ivan, 553
Kumar, Anil, 587

L

Layeb, Safa Bhar, 267, 643
Lisec, Andrej, 313
Lourimi, Noureddine, 619

M

Majidi, Fatima Zahra, 285
Marujo, Lino G., 205
Mejri, Imen, 267

F. Jawab (ed.), *Hospital Supply Chain*, Integrated Science 27,
https://doi.org/10.1007/978-3-031-70292-1

N
Nascimento do, Ingrid Teixeira, 205

O
Ouhoud, Amina, 47

P
Pedroso, Carolina Belotti, 99, 185
Putro, Gerry Dwi, 75, 117

R
Rahiel, Naima, 439
Rebolledo, Claudia, 185
Rekik, Ines, 337, 395
Rexana, Fritzie A., 75, 117
Rodrigues, Leonardo Mangia, 205
Roy, Jacques, 99

S
Sabra, Roa, 359
Samadhiya, Ashutosh, 587
Senna, Pedro, 205
Setiawan, Felicia, 75, 117
Shahin, Reza, 511
Silva da, Maria Eduarda Alves, 205

T
Talib, Mohamed Syazwan Ab, 141
Torres, Fernanda Pinto, 205
Triqui, Lamia, 23, 225
Tsoulfas, Giannis T., 533

V
Vos, Frederik G. S., 99

W
Wahab, Siti Norida, 141
Werghi, Khadija, 337

Z
Zerka, Abdelaziz, 379

Subject Index

A

Ambulance, 413–419, 421, 422, 424, 425, 427, 430, 431
Analysis, Analytics, 205, 207, 209, 210, 212, 214, 217–219, 267–270, 272, 273, 275–278, 341, 387, 391, 553, 555–558, 560–563, 565, 567–569
Analytical Hierarchy Process (AHP), 285, 287, 293–295, 298, 337, 341, 342, 346, 347, 355
Artificial intelligence, 553, 557, 576, 578, 581
Augmented reality, 619, 622, 628, 631, 636

B

Barriers, 76, 82, 85, 87–90, 94, 100–104, 109–111
Blockchain, 587, 589–594, 596, 597, 599–603
Blood, 225–234, 236–241

C

Cancer, 359–366, 371–375, 571–583
Care, 24–27, 29–33, 36, 37, 101, 105, 106, 109, 111, 339–342, 344, 350, 351, 355, 359–367, 370–375, 485–488, 492, 494–497, 500, 501, 503, 505–507, 571–583, 620, 621, 623, 630, 631, 633–636, 644, 647, 648, 660
Case, 99, 100, 104, 105, 109–112, 338, 340, 342, 351, 354, 461, 470, 471, 473, 490, 498, 500, 506, 643–645, 647, 649, 650, 657–660
Challenges, 76–80, 82–90, 92–95, 185–187, 189, 195, 196
Children, 619–622, 626–636
Countries, 76–80, 83, 85, 86, 88, 90–95, 117–120, 122, 123, 125, 127, 129, 133–137
COVID-19, 485–487, 489–491, 493, 494, 496–499, 503, 505–507, 511–515, 517–519, 521, 522, 524, 527
Crisis, 485–487, 490, 491, 493–497, 499–502, 506, 507
Criteria, 186, 188–191, 194, 196, 198, 199

D

Design, 31, 48–53, 61–64, 66, 72
Digital, Digital twins, 571, 573, 574, 576–578, 581–583, 643–650, 654, 655, 657, 658, 660, 661
Discrete-event, 417, 419, 429
Donor, Donation, 205–210, 212–216, 218, 219, 225, 227, 228, 230–234, 238, 239
Drug, 285, 286, 291, 297, 298, 301, 302, 304–308, 464, 465, 473–477, 479–481

E

Emergency, 117–125, 127–137, 414, 417, 419, 425, 427
Equity, 413–418, 421–431
Ergonomics, 359–361, 364–367, 369–375
Extended reality, 571, 573, 574, 576–578, 580–582, 619, 621, 622, 626, 629, 635, 637

F

Forecasting, 102, 106–110

F. Jawab (ed.), *Hospital Supply Chain*, Integrated Science 27,
https://doi.org/10.1007/978-3-031-70292-1

Framework, 245, 247, 250, 251, 254, 257, 261, 262, 359, 364, 366–369, 371–375, 571–573, 580–583
Future, 533, 535, 541, 543, 555, 556, 561, 562, 567–569, 588, 589, 597, 600, 601, 603

H

Halal, 141–156
Health, 3, 4, 8–16, 18, 23–26, 29–31, 33, 34, 36, 37, 103, 105, 107, 112, 141, 148, 149, 155, 190, 313, 316, 319, 322–324, 327, 328, 343, 360–362, 364, 367, 370, 372, 382, 384, 386, 391, 396, 399–401, 403, 440, 441, 445, 446, 452, 455, 456, 462, 465, 480, 512–519, 522, 523, 527, 528, 534, 539, 544, 557, 563–566, 568, 571, 574–579, 581–583, 593, 600, 644, 647–650, 652, 654–658, 660, 661
Healthcare, 3–8, 10, 12, 13, 16, 18, 19, 23–26, 29, 31–37, 49–51, 62, 64, 66, 69, 72, 99–111, 141, 144–149, 151–156, 185–188, 190, 195–200, 313, 314, 316, 338–344, 346, 349, 350, 355, 359–375, 395, 398–402, 439–443, 445, 446, 448–451, 453–456, 462–465, 474, 476, 480, 511–519, 521–524, 527, 533–546, 553–569, 571–583, 588–590, 593, 597, 599–602, 643, 647, 648, 654, 660, 661
Hospital, 47–51, 53, 56, 62–69, 72, 245, 247, 248, 250, 252, 254, 256, 257, 259, 261, 262, 267–272, 280, 285–287, 290, 291, 294–298, 301, 306–308, 313, 316, 379–388, 390–392, 395–399, 402–404, 407, 439–441, 443–457, 461–468, 470, 473–478, 480, 481, 485–502, 505–507, 587–591, 593, 601
Human, 360, 366, 367, 571, 578, 579

I

Immersive technology, 620
Implementation, 26, 33, 37, 100, 102, 104, 110, 111
Industry, Industry 4.0, 313, 319, 533, 534, 540, 542–546
Inequities, 413, 417–419, 424, 425, 431
Inventory, 102, 106, 108, 110, 267–274, 276–280, 514–516, 518, 519, 525–527, 553, 555–561, 563, 565, 566, 569

L

Lean, 267, 277–279
Logistics, 3–7, 9–18, 20, 99–106, 108, 110, 111, 162–164, 169, 170, 172, 174–176, 178, 179, 313, 315–319, 321, 322, 324, 326, 331, 379–384, 386–388, 391, 395, 398, 404, 410, 554, 559, 560, 563, 565, 566

M

Management, 99, 101, 102, 104–106, 108–111, 141, 143–147, 149, 152, 153, 157, 205–209, 211–213, 216, 218, 219, 245–248, 250–252, 254–262, 267–277, 279, 280, 553, 555–560, 562, 564–567, 569, 571, 572, 574–576, 578, 584
Medical, 117–124, 126, 127, 129, 131, 133–137, 245–251, 255–260, 267–270, 272, 277, 278, 414, 427, 533–539, 542–546, 619–621, 626–628, 630–636
Medicines, 285, 286, 294, 295, 297, 308, 461, 464, 465, 473, 474, 478, 480
Model, 337, 339–342, 345, 347–351, 354, 355, 415–417, 419–426, 428–430, 461, 462, 465–473, 475, 476, 478, 481

N

Network, 226, 232–234, 238, 240, 241

O

Optimise, 29, 30, 143, 144, 271, 279, 398, 400, 401
Organ, 205–215, 217–219

P

Pandemic, 511–519, 521, 527, 528
Patient, 47, 49–51, 62, 64, 66, 69, 313, 316, 338–344, 346, 348, 350, 351, 355, 359, 360, 362, 363, 365, 367, 368, 370–373, 375, 380–386, 388–392,

395–398, 400–403, 405, 410, 619, 622, 623, 627–635
Pediatric, 619–621, 623, 627–635
Pharmaceutical, 161–167, 169–179
Procurement, 185–190, 195–199, 643–645, 647–657, 660
Public, 268, 270, 272, 285, 286, 290, 291, 295, 306, 308, 461–463, 465, 473, 481, 643, 644, 647, 648, 657, 660
Purchasing, 185–190, 195–199, 285–298, 302, 305–308, 516, 517

Q
Quality, 102, 108–110, 267–272, 279, 280, 587, 588, 594, 597, 599, 603

R
Radiology, 379, 381, 383, 385
Resilience, 439, 441–457, 485, 498, 511–516, 523, 527, 528, 533–535, 539, 540, 545
Risk, 205–209, 212–217, 219

S
Satisfaction, 338–342, 345, 346, 348, 350, 351, 355, 396–399, 403
Sourcing, 285–289, 294, 295, 313, 326, 329, 330
Strategic, 25, 26, 29, 33, 37, 118, 120, 123, 128, 129, 131, 135, 136, 189, 196, 199, 285–293, 295–297, 300–308, 513, 514, 516, 527
Supplier, 186–190, 194–199
Supply chain, 99–101, 103, 104, 106–109, 111, 117–137, 141, 143–147, 149–157, 162, 164, 169, 170, 172, 173, 176, 179, 205–209, 211–219, 225–228, 230, 231, 233, 241, 245, 247, 248, 252, 259, 313, 315, 316, 318, 319, 322–324, 326, 329, 439, 448, 456, 461–471, 473, 477–481, 485–487, 490, 491, 494, 495, 498, 506, 507, 511–519, 521, 523, 525, 527, 528, 533–546, 553–569, 587–591, 593, 599–601
Sustainability, 533, 534, 543, 544

T
Technology, 535, 536, 539–546, 571–574, 577–579, 581–584, 587, 589–591, 593, 597, 599–604, 620–624, 626–636
Therapeutic, 620, 621, 627, 635
Transfusion, 226, 227, 229–231, 233, 241
Transport, 379, 385, 386, 391

V
Virtual reality, 619, 622, 626, 627, 630, 632, 635, 636

W
Warehousing, 553, 555, 559, 560, 569
Waste, 245–250, 252, 254–258, 260, 261

SPRINGER NATURE

GPSR Compliance

The European Union's (EU) General Product Safety Regulation (GPSR) is a set of rules that requires consumer products to be safe and our obligations to ensure this.

If you have any concerns about our products, you can contact us on ProductSafety@springernature.com

In case Publisher is established outside the EU, the EU authorized representative is:

Springer Nature Customer Service Center GmbH
Europaplatz 3
69115 Heidelberg, Germany

The manufacturer's authorised representative in the EU is Springer Nature Customer Service Centre GmbH, Europaplatz 3, 69115 Heidelberg, Germany. If you have any concerns regarding our products, please contact ProductSafety@springernature.com

Printed and bound by CPI Group (UK) Ltd, Croydon, CR0 4YY
30/09/2026
02225593-0017